SMALL-BOAT
SEAMANSHIP
MANUAL

SMALL-BOAT
SEAMANSHIP
M A N U A L

Edited by Richard N. Aarons

International Marine / McGraw-Hill

Camden, Maine • New York • Chicago • San Francisco • Lisbon • London • Madrid
Mexico City • Milan • New Delhi • San Juan • Seoul • Singapore • Sydney • Toronto

Dedication

This book is dedicated to the men and women of the United States Coast Guard and the Coast Guard Auxiliary who practice the skills and techniques herein every day to preserve life at sea.

Semper Paratus—Always Ready

The McGraw·Hill Companies

10 9 8 7 6 5 4 3   QPD QPD 0 9 8

Copyright © 2002, 2006 International Marine

The Library of Congress has cataloged the cloth edition as follows:
United States. Coast Guard.
Small-boat seamanship manual / US Coast Guard.
     p.   cm.
Includes index.
 ISBN 0-07-138800-1 (hardcover)
 1. Boats and boating—Handbooks, manuals, etc. 2.
Seamanship—Handbooks, manuals, etc. I. Title.
 GV777.6 .U65 2002
 797.1—dc21   2002006390
Paperback ISBN 0-07-146882-X

Questions regarding the content of this book should be addressed to
International Marine/McGraw-Hill
     P.O. Box 220
     Camden, ME 04843
     www.internationalmarine.com

Questions regarding the ordering of this book should be addressed to
The McGraw-Hill Companies
     Customer Service Department
     P.O. Box 547
     Blacklick, OH 43004
     Retail customers: 1-800-262-4729
     Bookstores: 1-800-722-4726

All photos and line art courtesy the United States Coast Guard.

Contents

EDITOR'S INTRODUCTION

Welcome to the recreational boater's version of the "Coasties' Bible." This unique book, *Small-Boat Seamanship,* is proudly based on the *U.S. Coast Guard Boatcrew Seamanship Manual*, the how-to text and manual used daily by all Coast Guard mariners—career, reservist, and Auxiliary.

Small-Boat Seamanship enables you to look over the shoulders of the world's most proficient small-boat handlers and adapt their best practices to your own kit of boating skills. How do Coast Guard coxswains and crew deal with heavy seas, foul weather, search-and-rescue planning, towing, coastal navigation, risk assessment and reduction, close-quarters boat handling, and dozens of other on-the-water challenges? It's all here. And it is presented in a structured format that facilitates a front-to-back read or a hurried consultation when the going gets rough.

Small-Boat Seamanship discusses topics rarely found in other recreational boating texts—issues such as small-boat stability and handling theory, maritime firefighting techniques, first aid for marine mishaps, mechanical and electrical system troubleshooting, and procedures for donning float coats and dry suits. The book also includes important discussions of crew coordination on small boats, a critical safety element missing from most small-boat handling courses and texts. Spend time with this manual and you will become a better boater and a better leader, and you'll certainly be better prepared to work with the Coast Guard should you ever need their assistance with a tow or a helicopter pickup. If you have your sights set on a Coast Guard captain's license (OUPV or Master), *Small-Boat Seamanship* is an excellent place to start. Its no-frills delivery of essential deck and bridge know-how is unmatched, and why not learn it straight from the administrator of the exams?

Today's Coast Guard is an amalgamation of five federal agencies—the Revenue Cutter Service, the Lighthouse Service, the Steamboat Inspection Service, the Bureau of Navigation, and the Lifesaving Service—the oldest of which dates back to 1789. The Coast Guard's *Boatcrew Seamanship Manual* has thus evolved through more than 200 years from notes, checklists, and station SOPs into the sophisticated manual upon which *Small-Boat Seamanship* is based. I first encountered the Coastie boat-crew manual in 1990, when I began to work toward my "crew" qualification in the Coast Guard Auxiliary. I used later editions as I worked through my "coxswain" qualifications and then put the manual to work as I helped other Auxiliary volunteers learn on-the-water skills. Recently, the manual was my guide as I studied for the deck knowledge exams for an OUPV and the 50-ton Coast Guard Master's License. It has become my on-the-water bible, and I suspect you will find it just as valuable.

It is good to understand as you explore these Coast Guard techniques that the work of the Coasties often places them in situations no sane recreational boater will intentionally seek out. Running a boat in a breaking surf comes to mind, as does crossing a bar in adverse winds and seas. But, while you certainly will avoid such places and situations if you can, happenstance may put you there someday, and knowing how expertly trained boat crews deal with these challenges might then save your boat—or your life.

You might wonder what is meant by "small boat." The Coast Guard's smaller boats range from their 52-foot motor lifeboats (MLB) down to their bright orange, outboard-powered rigid-hull inflatables. The workhorse station boat is the 41-foot utility boat (UTB), a tough platform designed to operate under moderate weather and sea conditions where speed and maneuverability are critical. Of course, "moderate" in the Coast Guard lexicon carries significant latitude. You've probably seen videos of 41-footers rolling through 360 degrees as helmsmen train in the Columbia River bars. Even the coxswains and crews on Coast Guard cutters—which range from 65 feet to just under 400 feet LOA—study this manual regularly. So no matter what your boat, the information between these covers pertains to you.

The Coast Guard's boats are called "facilities" and are all similarly appointed and outfitted. On the other hand, Coast Guard Auxiliarists employ a limitless variety of civilian (specially equipped) boats in their safety patrols and search and rescue missions. Therefore, the Coast Guard authors of the original seamanship manual attempted to keep discussions as generic as possible. In editing this edition, I have attempted to do the same, so most of the tips, techniques, recommendations, cautions, and procedures in *Small-Boat Seamanship* are applicable to the operation of most vessels used by recreational boaters, and, for that matter, by professional skippers.

I have made only minor style and organization changes to tailor the Coast Guard manual to the needs of recreational boaters. After all, the Coast Guard uses its *Boatcrew Seamanship Manual* to help raw recruits—young men and women with little or no boating experience—evolve quickly into superb boat handlers.

The *Small-Boat Seamanship Manual*'s emphasis on crew coordination, risk analysis, and situational awareness will help you become a safer, more thoughtful, and proficient boater. It will provide you with a basic understanding of on-water leadership. It will show you how to perform like a "professional" mariner even when you are in command of the smallest of boats.

Part of the joy of recreational boating—a large part, I think—is found in mastering the skills of the seaman and learning the lure of the sea. *Small-Boat Seamanship* is a wonderful aid in doing both.

Richard N. Aarons
Ridgefield, CT

DISCLAIMER

The *Small-Boat Seamanship Manual* is based on the *U.S. Coast Guard Boatcrew Seamanship Manual* but is not an official Coast Guard publication. The Coast Guard would also like you to know that:

- There may be updates to the *U.S. Coast Guard Boatcrew Seamanship Manual* that are not included in the *Small-Boat Seamanship Manual*.

- Some of the procedures described in this book are designed for use only by trained professionals.

- The U.S. Coast Guard takes no responsibility for any adverse consequences that may arise from use of this book.

- The *U.S. Coast Guard Boatcrew Seamanship Manual* is intended for internal use only and is not intended to create any duty or obligation of the USCG.

Safe boating!

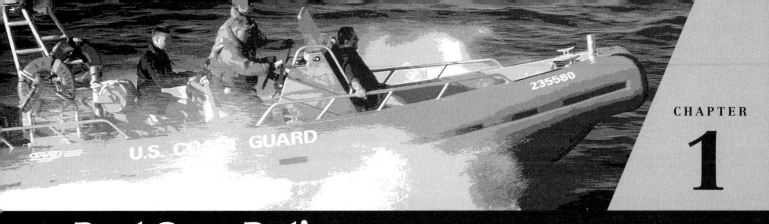

Boat Crew Duties and Responsibilities

Editor's Note: The smallest vessels operated by the regular Coast Guard and the Coast Guard Auxiliary have a crew of only two people—a coxswain and a crewman. Nevertheless, this crew of two uses the same team coordination skills as those employed by the dozens of crewmembers on a seagoing cutter. The crew watchstanding procedures and techniques discussed in this chapter will work on any vessel with any number of crew so long as good communication is maintained. All but the smallest boats can benefit from a thoughtful distribution of responsibilities among all those on board. Note that the Coasties make extensive use of checklists every time they get underway. That's not a bad idea for recreational boaters too. (Are you sure you can find the first-aid kit? And, how about flares—can you find them? What's the expiration date?) You can use the Coast Guard discussion here to design your own checks.

In this chapter

SECTION A

Overview

Introduction

Coast Guard and Auxiliary boat crews perform duties requiring both skill and knowledge. This chapter discusses general crew duties and related watchstanding procedures for the successful completion of Coast Guard missions. General duties for crew members are outlined in this chapter. Assignments and procedures for specific tasks, such as towing or retrieving people from the water, are found in other chapters.

NOTE

More specific information for Auxiliary boat crews may be found in COMDTINST M16798.3 (series) *Auxiliary Operations Policy Manual.*

The Boat Crew

Overview

A.1. INTRODUCTION

There are three basic boat crew positions on Coast Guard boats:

- Coxswain
- Engineer (the Auxiliary program does not have a boat engineer position)
- Crew member

A.2. DETERMINING CREW SIZE

There are several factors in determining crew size:

- Boat type
- Operational need
- Minimum crew size prescribed by higher authority

A.3. MINIMUM CREW SIZE

Commandant sets minimum crew sizes for standard boats. For example, the 47-foot motor life boat (MLB) carries a minimum crew of four—a coxswain, an engineer, and two crew members. Area and District Commanders set minimum crew sizes for non-standard boats assigned to their units. Coast Guard boats and Auxiliary boats may carry two to six people as crew. Often the crew of a non-standard boat, Auxiliary boat, or cutter's boat comprises only a coxswain and a crew member.

A.4. QUALIFICATION AND CERTIFICATION

Boat crew members, engineers, and coxswains are qualified and certified in accordance with the *Boat Crew Training Manual*, COMDTINST M16114.9 (series). Qualification as a boat crew member is a prerequisite to qualification as boat engineer, coxswain, and surfman. Coast Guard Auxiliarists may qualify and certify for crew member and engineer in the same way. Auxiliarists are not permitted to be certified as coxswain on Coast Guard boats. Auxiliarists qualifications for crewing Auxiliary boats are covered in the *Auxiliary Boat Crew Training and Qualification Guide–Crewman and Coxswain*, COMDTINST M16798.28 (series).

A.5. THE AUXILIARY

An Auxiliarist on official orders may perform many Coast Guard duties, including boat crew member and boat engineer, but is not a military member of the Coast Guard. Although trained and qualified to an equivalent level, the Auxiliary member may not be assigned any authority or responsibility specifically reserved by regulation for military or law enforcement personnel.

AUXILIARY CREW MEMBERS Since the coxswain of an Auxiliary boat is responsible for assigning (and often selecting) their crew members to duty, the controlling Coast Guard unit may not know the identity of all crew members. Therefore, the names of all crew members (including crew trainees) must be passed to the controlling unit by land line or other method immediately before the facility's departure to be sure an accurate accounting is on record.

For further guidance, refer to *Auxiliary Operations Manual*, COMDTINST M16798.3 (series) and directives issued by the District Director of Auxiliary.

Boat Crew Duties

Overview

Introduction

The Coast Guard and Auxiliary boat crew training programs are based on the concept that sailors must be trained at sea. This manual, and specifically this chapter, is designed to provide an outline of the **duties** typically performed by various members of boat crews and the skills and knowledge required to perform tasks assigned. For people seeking to be members of a boat crew, it is fundamental that they understand these duties and the importance of crew members working together as a team.

In this section

Topic	See Page(s)
Trainee	2–3
Crew Member	3
Boat Engineer	3
Coxswain	4
Surfman	4–5

Trainee

B.1. GENERAL

A trainee can be either a Coast Guard Active Duty member, an Auxiliarist (referred to as Candidate), or a Reservist who qualifies as a boat crew member. The trainee rides on board *only* to observe actual operational missions, not as a member of the crew counted towards minimum crew requirements.

B.2. PERFORMANCE, SKILL, AND KNOWLEDGE REQUIREMENTS

The duties of a trainee are to learn and safely perform the practical tasks prescribed for crew members. These duties are in the qualification manuals and are performed under the supervision of a qualified crew member assigned to the boat.

Crew Member

B.3. GENERAL

Crew members safely perform their duties under the supervision of a coxswain. They stand:

- helm,
- lookout,
- towing watches, and
- anchor watch.

They also:

- rig towing and mooring lines,
- act as the surface swimmer,
- administer first aid, and
- operate damage control equipment.

This position provides valuable training for future duties and responsibilities.

NOTE

Refer to the Coast Guard Addendum to the *National SAR Manual,* COMDTINST M16130.2 (series) for policy on swimmers. The Auxiliary does not have surface swimmers.

B.4. PERFORMANCE, SKILL, AND KNOWLEDGE REQUIREMENTS

To be effective, boat crew members must execute orders quickly and must have the following knowledge and performance skills:

- Marlinespike seamanship and line handling
- Basic navigation (including radar) and boat handling
- Survival, safety, and damage control equipment
- Emergency and casualty control
- Watchstanding and communications
- First aid
- Preventive maintenance procedures for the boat in port

RISK MANAGEMENT A keen knowledge of the boat's characteristics and limitations, the outfit equipment, and the stowage will be invaluable in times of crisis. Frequent drills practicing the procedures for different emergency circumstances will teach crew members how to react correctly to each situation. All crew members must continuously think about emergency situations and answer the hypothetical question, "What should I do if . . . ?" so that an appropriate response can be initiated immediately when the question becomes, "What do I do now?"

KNOWING THE OPERATING AREA Boat crew members must have knowledge of their local Operating Area (OPAREA), also called Area of Responsibility (AOR).

Boat Engineer

B.5. GENERAL

Boat engineers are responsible for propulsion and auxiliary machinery while underway. They also have other responsibilities:

- Boat crew member duties
- Preventive and corrective maintenance performed on the boat in port

---

NOTE

There is no engineer position in the Auxiliary program.

B.6. PERFORMANCE, SKILL, AND KNOWLEDGE REQUIREMENTS

The skill and knowledge requirements for boat engineers are as extensive as those for coxswains. They must be able to take quick and proper action when faced with any boat engineering casualty. In addition to basic crew member skills, the following required knowledge and performance skills are necessary:

- Demonstrate complete knowledge of general engineering specifications and functional performance characteristics.
- Perform pre-start, light off, and securing functions for propulsion machinery.
- Monitor, detect, and respond to machinery and electrical system casualties or failures.
- Operate auxiliary machinery and systems, e.g., pumps, eductors, tillers, etc.
- Use on board damage control equipment to minimize damage from fire, grounding, or collision.

Coxswain

B.7. GENERAL

Coast Guard boats underway must have a **coxswain** on board who is certified by the unit commander to operate that particular type of boat. The district director of Auxiliary certifies Auxiliary coxswains to operate an Auxiliary boat. Coxswains are in charge of the boat and crew. The coxswain's duty is unique. The coxswain's range and degree of responsibility are comparable to that of a cutter's deck watch officer. The Coast Guard places great trust in the coxswain's ability to provide effective boat crew leadership, coordination, and risk management skills. (For more information on risk management, see Chapter 4—Team Coordination and Risk Management.)

B.8. RESPONSIBILITY AND AUTHORITY

The extent of the coxswain's responsibility and authority are specified in *Coast Guard Regulations*, COMDTINST M5000.3 (series). Coxswains shall be responsible, in order of priority, for the following:

- Safety and conduct of passengers and crew
- Safe operation and navigation of the boat
- Completion of the sortie(s) or mission(s)

Coxswains will respond to the following:

- Hazards to life or property
- Violations of law or regulations, except for Auxiliarists
- Discrepancies in aids to navigation

B.9. PERFORMANCE, SKILL, AND KNOWLEDGE REQUIREMENTS

The knowledge requirements and performance skills for coxswains are extensive. Coxswains must apply good judgment, intelligence, and initiative. They must make decisions with the safety of their crew and boat in mind. In addition to basic crew member skills, a coxswain requires these additional knowledge and performance skills:

- Demonstrate leadership that effectively coordinates, directs, and guides the performance of the boat crew during watches and tasks (e.g., towing, fog navigation, and man overboard).
- Demonstrate correct application of regulations, policy, and guidance delineated by the unit commander or higher authority to the

circumstances at hand (e.g., safe navigation, safe speed, law enforcement, and rendering assistance).

- Know the boat's limitations:

  maximum sea conditions boat can operate in,

  maximum wind conditions boat can operate in, and

  maximum size of boat that can be towed by your boat.

- Navigate and pilot a boat.
- Know the local operations area with minimal reference to charts and publications.
- Demonstrate boat handling skills to safely and prudently control the movement of a boat while underway.
- Understand the principles of risk management and incorporate them into the decision making process. These principles include detection, identification, evaluation, and mitigation or control of risk as part of making decisions (e.g., slow to safe speed in restricted visibility, cast off a tow because the assisted vessel is losing stability).

Surfman

B.10. GENERAL

The **Surfman** is considered an advanced coxswain qualification. A Surfman is a highly motivated, experienced boat handler capable of operating a Motor Lifeboat (MLB) or Surf Rescue Boat (SRB) in surf. The Surfman also leads, motivates and trains boat crews to operate in these extreme types of conditions.

NOTE

There is no Surfman boat crew position in the Auxiliary program.

B.11. PERFORMANCE, SKILL, AND KNOWLEDGE REQUIREMENTS

A surfman must be previously qualified and certified as an MLB Coxswain. There are several knowledge and performance skills required in addition to basic Coxswain skills:

- Thorough understanding of ocean currents, weather, and hydrodynamics. How they pertain to the local bar/inlet conditions.

- Boat handling skills and procedures while operating in surf.
- Boat crew safety and emergency procedures.

B.12. ADDITIONAL RESPONSIBILITIES

A Surfman is expected to have additional responsibilities at an MLB station that include:

- Boat crew management in high risk, high stress situations.
- Monitoring all levels of training. They must train and pass their skills and experience on to new coxswains.
- Making important risk assessment decisions during heavy weather and surf.
- Overseeing readiness of equipment and personnel.
- Standing watch during heavy weather and surf conditions.

SECTION C

Watchstanding Responsibilities

Overview

Introduction

Under the direction of the coxswain, crew members are assigned various watches which are described in this section.

In this section

Lookout Watch

C.1. REQUIREMENT

The *Navigation Rules, International-Inland*, COMDTINST M16672.2 (series) states that "Every vessel shall at all times maintain a proper lookout by sight and hearing as well as by all available means appropriate in the prevailing circumstances and conditions so as to make a full appraisal of the situation and of the risk of collision."

C.2. ASSIGN AND STATION

Coxswains must assign and station **lookouts** properly in order to comply with the requirement noted above. Lookouts must report to the coxswain everything seen, smelled, or heard while the boat is underway that may endanger the boat or may indicate a situation to investigate (e.g., distress, law enforcement, or pollution). Some examples are:

- Ships
- Land
- Obstructions
- Lights
- Buoys
- Beacons
- Discolored water
- Reefs
- Fog signals
- Anything that could affect safe navigation

NOTE

Although not specifically assigned the duty of lookout, the entire crew must perform lookout duties unless directed otherwise.

NOTE

It is most important for the coxswain to consider the experience level and abilities of individual crew members when making assignments. In the past, the inappropriate assignment of crew duties has contributed to mishaps resulting in fatalities.

C.3. GUIDELINES

Use the following guidelines to stand a proper **lookout watch**:

- Remain alert and give full attention to your assigned duty.
- Remain at your station until relieved.
- Do not distract yourself or others with excessive conversation. (However, *some* conversation among crew members may be beneficial in reducing fatigue and maintaining alertness.)

- Speak loudly and distinctly when making a report.

- If you cannot positively identify the object sighted, smelled or heard, report what you think at that moment.

- Repeat your report until it is acknowledged by the coxswain.

- When conditions impair your ability to see, smell, or hear, report the condition so the coxswain can take corrective action.

- Report everything you see including floating material, even if you have to report it several times.

- Make certain you understand your duties. If you do not understand your duties, ask for more information.

C.4. LOOKOUT POSITIONING

Lookouts must be posted by the coxswain so they have the best possible chance of seeing and hearing an approaching vessel or searching for an object in the water. The coxswain should use the following steps when **positioning lookouts**:

1. Choose a boat speed that enables lookouts to effectively and safely perform their duties.

2. Position lookouts so they can effectively and safely perform their duties under the operating conditions, e.g., restricted visibility, boat speed, sea state, weather.

3. During periods of rain, sleet, and snow or when taking spray over the bow, select lookout positions that minimize impairment of vision.

4. During a search, post two lookouts when able. Lookouts should be positioned on each side of the vessel so that each can scan a sector from dead ahead to directly aft.

5. Select a stable location that will not place the lookouts in danger of being blown or swept overboard.

C.5. OBJECT IDENTIFICATION

Lookouts must report what they see, smell, or hear with as much detail as possible. **Object type** is immediately important (vessel, buoy, breaking waves), but additional details may help the coxswain in decision making. The following are some obvious characteristics of objects:

- Color
- Shape
- Size

At night, lookouts must identify the color of all lights. This is the specific reason why all boat crew members must have normal color vision.

C.6. RELATIVE BEARING

Lookouts make reports using **relative bearings only**. This means that the bearings are measured with reference to the vessel's heading, or to the fore and aft line of the boat's keel. These bearings run clockwise from zero degrees (000°) or dead ahead, through one-eight-zero degrees (180°) or dead astern, around to three-six-zero degrees (360°) or dead ahead again.

The following steps are important in reporting relative bearings:

1. Study the diagram on major reference points of relative bearings. Picture in your mind the complete circle of relative bearings around your boat in 10 degree increments (see Figure 1-1).

2. Bearings are always reported in three digits and distinctly spoken digit by digit. To ensure one number is not mistaken for another, the following pronunciation is required.

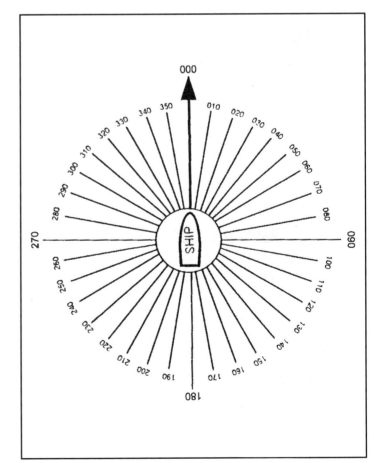

Figure 1-1 Relative Bearings

Numeral	Spoken as	Numeral	Spoken as
0	ZERO	5	FI-YIV
1	WUN	6	SIX
2	TOO	7	SEVEN
3	THUH-REE	8	ATE
4	FO-WER	9	NINER

3. The following are examples of how to report bearings:

Bearing	Reported as
000°	ZERO ZERO ZERO
010°	ZERO WUN ZERO
045°	ZERO FO-WER FI-YIV
090°	ZERO NINER ZERO
135°	WUN THUH-REE FI-YIV
180°	WUN ATE ZERO
225°	TOO TOO FI-YIV
260°	TOO SIX ZERO
270°	TOO SEVEN ZERO
315°	THUH-REE ONE FI-YIV

C.7. POSITION ANGLE

Objects in the sky are located by their relative bearing and **position angle**. The position angle of an aircraft is its height in degrees above the horizon as seen from the boat. The horizon is 0° and directly overhead is 90°. The position angle can never be more than 90°. Position angles are reported in one or two digits and the word "Position Angle" is always spoken before the numerals (see Figure 1-2).

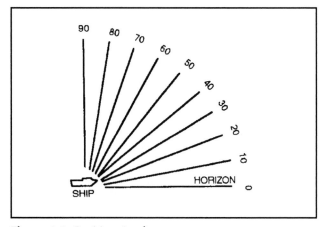

Figure 1-2 Position Angles

C.8. DISTANCE

Report **distances** in yards. Knowing the distance to the horizon, land, or other reference point, will help estimate distance. By dividing the distance from you to your reference point, you can estimate the distance to another object. Ranges in yards are reported digit by digit, except when reporting yards in hundreds or thousands which are spoken as listed below.

Number of Yards	Spoken as
50	FI-YIV ZERO
500	FI-YIV HUNDRED
5,000	FI-YIV THOUSAND

C.9. MAKING REPORTS

When making reports, the lookout names or describes the object sighted, the direction (in relative degrees) and the range to the object (in yards). Give reports in the following format:

- Object name or description
- Bearing
- Range

For example:
Discolored water on a bearing of 340° relative to the bow of the boat and at a distance of 2,000 yards.
REPORTED AS: "Discolored water Bearing THUH-REE FO-WER ZERO, Range TOO THOUSAND".

An aircraft bearing 280° relative to the bow of the ship, 30° above the horizon, and at a distance of 9,000 yards.
REPORTED AS: "Aircraft TOO ATE ZERO, Position Angle THUH-REE ZERO, Range NINER THOUSAND".

C.10. SCANNING

The lookout's method of eye search is called **scanning**. Scanning is a step-by-step method of visually searching for objects. Good scanning techniques will ensure that objects are not missed. Scanning also reduces eye fatigue. Development of a systematic scanning technique is important. There are two common scanning methods:

- Left to right and back again
- Top to bottom and bottom to top

In either case, move your eyes in increments. This creates overlaps in your field of vision and fewer objects will be missed.

1. When looking for an object, scan the sky, sea, and horizon slowly and regularly. Scan from left to right and back again or from top to bottom and bottom to top.

2. When scanning, do not look directly at the horizon; look above it. Move your head from side to side and keep your eyes fixed. This will give any stationary objects in your field of vision the appearance of moving and make them easier to see.

   One technique is to scan in small steps of about 10 degrees and have them slightly overlap as you move across your field of view.

3. Fatigue, boredom, and environmental conditions affect scanning. For example, after prolonged scanning, with little or no contrast, your eyes develop a tendency to focus short of where you think you are looking. To prevent this, periodically focus on a close object such as whitecaps or the bow of the boat.

NOTE

For more details on scanning, refer to the Search Operations Chapter of the *National Search and Rescue Manual*, COMDTINST M16120.5 (series).

NIGHT SCANNING When binoculars are used for night scanning, hold them straight forward and shift your line of sight in a circular path around the inside of the binocular field. When you think you see an object, look all around it, not at it. The chances are it will appear in dim outline. Using binoculars at night on a stable platform increases your range of vision significantly; however, objects will not appear in clear detail.

FOG SCANNING Fog lookouts scan slowly and rely on their ears. The best position for a fog lookout is where sight and hearing are not interfered with by radios, conversation, or other distractions. Usually at the bow is best, if conditions allow.

Night Lookout Watch

C.11. GENERAL

Although the duties for day and **night lookout** watches are the same, safety and caution during night watches are especially important. Your eyes respond much more slowly at night and pick up moving objects more readily than fixed objects. It takes about 30 minutes for your eyes to become accustomed to the limited light available at night.

C.12. GUIDELINES

The guidelines for lookout watches also apply for night lookout watches.

NOTE

Night vision is based on your eyes receiving and interpreting a different type of light than exists during daylight.

C.13. DARK ADAPTATION

Dark adaptation is the improvement of vision in dim light. It is very difficult to see colors at night. Most objects are seen in various shades of gray. Although dark adaptation requires at least 30 minutes, a bright light will destroy night vision in a fraction of a second. In this brief period, the eyes readjust themselves to daylight conditions and the process of dark adaptation must begin all over again.

NOTE

Avoid looking at bright lights during nighttime operations. When a light must be used, use a red light.

C.14. SCANNING

Scan the sky, sea, and horizon slowly and regularly when looking for an object. Scan from left to right and back again or from top to bottom and from bottom to top.

Helm Watch

C.15. GENERAL

The **helm watch** or helmsman is responsible for the following:

- Safely steering the boat
- Maintaining a course
- Carrying out all helm commands given by the coxswain

The helm watch can be carried out by the coxswain or by any designated crew member. Every crewman should learn to steer and control the boat. They must learn to use both the primary steering system and, when appropriate, the emergency steering system, to ensure safe operations of the boat under normal and abnormal conditions.

C.16. GUIDELINES

When a boat uses a helmsman, there are several guidelines for the helm watch:

- Check with the coxswain for any special instructions and for the course you will steer.
- Repeat all commands given by the coxswain.
- Execute all commands given by the coxswain.
- Maintain a given course within 5°.
- Remain at the helm until properly relieved.
- Execute maneuvers only when expressly ordered, however, minor changes in heading to avoid debris, which could damage propeller or rudders, are essential.
- Operate the emergency tiller (if equipped) during loss of steering.
- Properly inform relief of all pertinent information.

Towing Watch

C.17. GENERAL

A towing watch is normally performed aft on the boat. The primary duty of the towing watch is to keep the towline and the boat being towed under constant observation. (For more information on towing procedures, see Chapter 17—Towing.)

C.18. GUIDELINES

The guidelines for standing this watch are as follows:

- Observe how the tow is riding, e.g., in step, listing, or veering.
- Report any unusual conditions to the coxswain.
- Ensure chafing gear is riding in place.
- Adjust the scope of the towline upon command of the coxswain.
- Report any equipment failure or problems observed to the coxswain immediately.
- Keep deck space area clear of unnecessary gear and people.
- Stay clear of the immediate area around the towline due to possible line snap back.
- Know when and how to do an emergency breakaway.

C.19. OBSERVED DANGER

The towing watch must be aware of and report any signs of danger. Many of the signs of danger include:

- Yawing—disabled boat veers from one side to the other which may cause one or both boats to capsize.
- List increasing on towed boat.
- In step—the proper distance between the towed boat and the towing boat to maintain control and prevent breaking the tow line.
- Towed boat taking on water.
- Deck hardware failure due to stress, no backing plates, etc.
- Towline about to part due to stress, chafing, or other damage.
- Towed boat overtaking your boat due to sudden reduction in speed.
- Positioning of towed boat's crew.

C.20. MAINTAINING WATCH

Maintain a tow watch until the disabled boat is moored or until relieved. When relieved, make sure that all important information is passed to the relief (i.e., problems with chafing gear, towed boat yaws, etc.).

Anchor Watch

C.21. GENERAL

When the boat is anchored, an **anchor watch** is set. The person on watch must ensure that the anchor line does not chafe and that the anchor does not drag. The individual on watch also looks for other vessels in the area. Even when the boat is anchored, there is the possibility that it can be hit by another boat.

C.22. GUIDELINES

Use the following guidelines when standing anchor watch:

- Check the strain on the anchor line frequently.
- Check that the anchor line is not chafing.
- Confirm the position of the boat at least every 15 minutes, or at shorter intervals as directed by the coxswain.
- Report bearing or range (distance) changes to the coxswain immediately.
- Report approaching vessels to the coxswain immediately.
- Report major changes in wind velocity or direction.

- Check for current or tidal changes.
- Report any unusual conditions.

C.23. CHECK FOR CHAFING

Once the anchor is set, apply **chafing** gear to the anchor line. It is the job of the anchor watch to ensure chafing gear stays in place and the anchor line does not chafe through.

C.24. CHECK FOR DRAGGING

There are two methods to determine if your anchor is **dragging**.

- Check for tension on the anchor line
- Check the boat's position

If the anchor is dragging over the bottom, you can sometimes feel vibration in the line. Periodically check your position by taking a navigational fix. *Always use both methods.*

C.25. CHECK YOUR POSITION

It is important to routinely **check your position** to ensure you are not drifting or dragging anchor:

- Take compass bearings to three separate objects spread at least 45° apart. Any bearing changes may indicate that you are beginning to drift.

- On a boat equipped with radar, determine the distance (range) to three points of land on your radar screen. Any change in the ranges may indicate anchor drag.

- On a Loran or GPS equipped boat, mark your position with your equipment. Periodically check your LAT/LONG readout. Any change would show your position is changing.

- Make a note of each time you check your bearings or ranges. Also note your position and the depth of water regularly. A small note pad is acceptable for this purpose. If the water depth or position changes, the anchor may be dragging.

As the wind or water current changes direction, your boat will swing about its anchor. This is a **swing circle** centered around the position of the anchor, with a radius equal to the boat's length plus the horizontal component of the length of anchor line in use; simply stated, **horizontal component + boat length = radius of swing circle at its greatest length**. (The horizontal component decreases as the water depth increases.) Ensure your swing circle is clear of other vessels and underwater obstructions. When checking your position, it should fall inside the swing circle.

Pre-Underway Checklist

1. Brief all crew members on the mission, preferably before getting underway, or as soon as possible afterwards. The briefing should be complete. State:

   a. Purpose of mission

   b. Special circumstances

   c. Working radio frequency for the mission

   d. Plan of action upon arrival at destination

   e. Speed and course to be steered to destination

   f. Weather and sea conditions

2. Ensure that all doors and hatches are secured (watertight integrity).

NOTE

In an enclosed pilot house, at least one door or window to the weather decks should normally be opened to facilitate hearing sound signals from approaching vessels and aids to navigation.

---

3. Ensure that all loose gear is safely tied down or stowed.

4. Ensure that all gear necessary to perform the mission is on board. This includes any supplemental equipment not normally on the boat but needed for the specific mission.

5. Ensure crew members wear personal protective equipment required for the environment (e.g., PFDs, helmets, anti-exposure coveralls, or dry suits with PFDs). Commandant policy requires PFDs to be worn at all times when underway. On Coast Guard boats, the crew is also required to wear the boat crew signal kit at all times.

6. The boat engineer must check the boat's mechanical and electrical systems and make reports to the coxswain concerning the status and readiness of all the following:

   a. Fuel levels

   b. Oil levels for engines and marine (reduction) gears

   c. Cooling water level

   d. Hydraulic steering oil

   e. Engine/marine (reduction) gear psi/temperature gauges

   f. Electrical systems energized

g. Navigational lights (e.g., night, reduced visibility)

h. Open sea suction

i. Shore-power tie disconnected

j. Overboard discharge

7. Test the boat's electronic equipment and report the status to the coxswain:

a. Radios

b. Depth sounder

c. Radar

d. All navigational systems

e. Chart and compass light

8. Test the engine controls, both FORWARD and REVERSE. Note the reaction time in each direction.

9. Cast off all lines, stow the lines, and bring on board any fenders.

10. Notify the unit of the time underway and number of crew members on board. Also report any personnel or boat discrepancies at this time.

Normal Cruising Checklist (Coxswain)

1. Always KEEP ALERT and position lookouts appropriately for current conditions.

NOTE

Lookouts are required by the International Regulations for Preventing Collisions at Sea (COLREGS). Under all circumstances, keep alert for other vessels, aids to navigation, and hazards including: breakers, rocks, piping, "dead heads," and fishing nets.

---

2. When proceeding normally with good visibility and your boat is NOT engaged in an active search, keep your crew in a protected location. Designate crew members to act as a lookouts.

3. Always know the whereabouts of your crew.

4. Observe aids to navigation for all of the following:

a. Position

b. Condition

c. Operation

5. Conduct drills and training frequently, including all of the following:

a. Boat handling

b. Anchoring

c. Navigation Rules (Inland & International)

d. Navigation

e. Man overboard

f. Emergency steering

g. Search patterns

h. Firefighting on board

i. Helicopter operations (if helicopter is available)

6. Frequently observe the depth finder and compare the water depth reported to that shown on the chart for your location.

7. Always be on the alert for vessels or people that may be in distress.

8. Make OPs (operations and position) reports to the parent unit as required by local directives and procedures.

9. When you are operating in any conditions where your visibility is reduced for any reason, **EXTRA PRECAUTIONS MUST BE TAKEN**:

a. Position lookouts appropriately and explain their duties.

b. Keep alert for all vessels and sound signals.

c. Watch for aids to navigation which do not have audible sound devices.

d. Lay out charts with the main course, time, and speed plotted on them.

e. Begin plotting navigational fixes, record times, and positions regularly.

f. Sound appropriate signals.

g. Display appropriate navigational lights.

h. Maintain a speed that will enable you to take proper action to avoid a collision and stop within a distance appropriate to the prevailing circumstances and conditions (that is, do not go too fast).

NOTE

The aft lookout should be alert for overtaking vessels and for signals missed by the forward lookout.

Auxiliary Pre-Underway Checklist

Overview

Prior to getting underway conduct a pre-underway check-off of your boat. Check for proper condition, operation, and stowage of required equipment. Routine mechanical, electrical, and engine checks must also be done. Ensure all crew members are aware of emergency procedures, and the location and use of emergency equipment. Inform the Operational Commander of the number of persons onboard and their names prior to getting underway. Prepare a pre-underway check-off sheet for your specific boat. Below is a sample pre-underway checklist.

Date:

Facility Name:

Facility Number:

1. Verified appropriate Coast Guard patrol orders have been issued.

2. Located and checked the proper condition, operation, and stowage of the following equipment:

   a. Personal flotation devices (PFDs)

   b. Fire extinguishers

   c. Visual distress signals

   d. Anchors and anchor lines

   e. Dewatering device

   f. Watch or clock

   g. Boarding ladder (or other means of boarding)

   h. Kicker skiff hook (if required)

   i. Binoculars

   j. Blanket

   k. Fenders

   l. Towline

   m. Bridle

   n. Heaving lines

   o. Mooring lines

   p. Searchlight

   q. Spare navigation light bulbs

   r. Boat hook

   s. Navigation lights

   t. Lead line or sounding pole

   u. Charts, navigation plotting instruments

   v. Tools and spare parts

   w. First aid kit

   x. Sound producing device

   y. Current Rules of the Road publication on board, if applicable.

3. Completed the required mechanical, electrical, and engine checks listed below.

   a. Oil level (if applicable)

   b. Water level (if applicable)

   c. Reduction gear oil level (if applicable)

   d. Fuel system, especially fuel shut-off valves

   e. Ventilation system (if applicable)

4. Conducted crew briefing:

   a. Purpose of mission

   b. Any special circumstances concerning the mission

   c. Working radio frequency to be used for the mission

   d. Expected weather and sea conditions

   e. Crew members in proper uniform and proper equipment

   f. Inform Operational Commander of the number and names of persons onboard

   g. Confirm the mission is within the facility's operational standard.

5. Secured all openings.

6. Secured boat for sea (no loose gear).

7. Displayed proper flags and signboards.

8. Opened sea suction.

9. Ventilated the engine compartment before starting engine/s.

10. Started the engine/s.

    a. Energized the electrical and electronic systems (bilge pump, etc.)

    b. Engine/marine gear pressures and temperatures satisfactory (if equipped)

11. Disconnected shore-power line.

12. Tested the following electronic equipment (if equipped).

    a. VHF-FM radio

    b. Loud hailer

    c. Depth finder

    d. Loran-C

    e. Radar

    f. GPS

13. Tested engine controls in forward and reverse with lines still attached to the dock; noted the reaction times for both directions.

Patrols

Editor's Note: *While you may never participate formally in a Coast Guard patrol, this chapter will show you what the Coasties are up to during routine safety patrols or when staking out the corners of a regatta. Remember that ANY boater can and should notify the Coast Guard when he or she discovers pollution, floating hazards, problems with aids to navigation (ATONs), and distressed vessels that cannot communicate for themselves. NOAA also asks recreational boaters to notify the cartography agencies with appropriate chart updates. Of course, if your organization is sponsoring an on-water event in navigable waters, the Coast Guard will assist you with the appropriate permissions and provide a Regatta Patrol when safety dictates.*

In this chapter

Overview

Introduction

Shore units will get their boats underway to conduct a variety of patrols. The intent of this chapter is to discuss types of boat patrol and their respective procedures. Patrols may have different titles for the same type of task or one general title to cover many tasks. Examples include safety, familiarization, training, harbor, and regatta patrols. In all cases, the crew is underway at the direction of the operational commander. The patrol may be in response to a known problem or meant as a method of prevention or early detection.

SECTION A

Safety Patrols

Overview

Introduction

Safety patrols directly support the Coast Guard's maritime safety responsibilities. For the Auxiliary, the safety patrol supports the search and rescue (SAR) mission specifically to locate and help persons and boats in distress. While a routine safety patrol is being conducted, it is common practice to perform other missions, such as checking aids to navigation (ATON) or pollution levels. Auxiliary safety patrols work for a Coast Guard operational commander.

In this section

Benefits of Safety Patrols

A.1. GENERAL

Safety patrols provide important benefits for the boat crew, Coast Guard, and the public. These benefits include:

- Practice for the crew and familiarization with their area of responsibility (AOR).
- Public seeing the Coast Guard in action.
- Public awareness that distress assistance is available.
- Increased opportunity for the boating public to obtain boating safety information, sea condition reports, or navigation hazard notices.
- Information for the federal, state, and local agencies responsible for updating navigation aids and charts.
- Detection of unreported events, including SAR and pollution.

NOTE

Patrols scheduled before sundown, or on receipt of a severe storm warning are to help boaters to get to a secure harbor. This is considered "Preventive SAR".

Auxiliary Safety Patrol Boat Duties

A.2. GENERAL

A boat on patrol should always be ready to answer distress or assistance calls expediently, even when ordered to stand by at a pier. To help boaters, many boat crews carry additional equipment, perhaps an extra battery and a good array of tools onboard. The district commander may require boats to carry equipment to meet the unique needs of the district.

A.3. COXSWAIN'S RESPONSIBILITY

Coxswains should know and follow the local guidance and modifications to the primary directives for Coast Guard policy and procedures. This information comes from the Coast Guard group commander, Director of Auxiliary, or order-issuing authority in response to the local needs or changing conditions. Before getting underway, the coxswain should:

- Know the patrol area and review factors such as tidal action, weather patterns, fishing areas, and navigational aids.
- Verify that fuel tanks are full and all equipment is checked and operating properly.
- Ensure that the required crew is aboard in the correct uniform and properly certified.
- Verify that at least one other crew member is qualified to command the boat in case the coxswain needs to seek relief.
- Ensure all crew members are physically capable of performing mission.
- Provide a thorough briefing on the boat, its equipment, and its operation. Specifically address possible hazards, risk awareness and situation awareness.
- Once satisfied, go to the assigned patrol sector and notify the operational commander of your arrival or departure, the number and names of persons on board, and verify that conditions are within the facility's operational standards.

A.4. REPORTING RESPONSIBILITY

Proper reports keep boaters and the Coast Guard informed about boat patrols and local boating conditions. Whether it is a routine position report, a sea condition report, or a log entry, all reports should be accurate.

OPERATIONAL STATUS REPORTS While underway, maintain communications with the your unit if you're operating within radio range. Report your boat's location and operational status (operations and position reports) to the cognizant authority at regular intervals—normally, every 30 to 60 minutes.

PATROL LOGS Keep a log of significant patrol activities. The narrative of each event should be a brief but accurate description of situations, procedures, actions, and activities. The log will help back up reports sent to the Coast Guard and answer any inquiries.

SEA CONDITION REPORTS Report sea conditions to the public by arranging a broadcast program with a local radio station. The patrol boat's report will normally be taped so that it can be replayed several times during the day. This provides reports of wind and wave conditions in simple terms to the boating public. Remember that only actual conditions are described; weather forecasting is to be left to professional meteorologists.

NOTE

Ensure that arrangements with the radio station to broadcast sea condition reports do not imply any endorsement by the Coast Guard or Auxiliary of any products or services.

A.5. PATROLLING

Make a preliminary sweep of the area to establish familiarity with the prevailing conditions, potential trouble areas, and to announce to local boaters that your crew is on patrol. Keep your speed down while patrolling to enable the crew to keep a sharp lookout in all directions, and to conserve fuel.

A.6. CONTINUING PATROL DURING HEAVY WEATHER

The patrol boat should not be the first to leave an area when adverse conditions develop. While a coxswain should never jeopardize the boat crew, during heavy weather it is important that a patrol continue as long as possible. In case of a sudden storm, many pleasure boats will probably be in need of some type of assistance.

A.7. ASSISTANCE

While on patrol, boat crews will encounter many types of assistance situations. Always approach them with caution, considering the different policies and procedures concerning assistance, including:

- Coast Guard Addendum to the National SAR Manual,
- Maritime SAR Assistance Policy,
- general salvage policy,
- risk assessment processes,
- proper operations to help the boat, and
- other concerns, such as the need for additional boats to help.

NOTE

Do not hesitate to call for additional help as necessary when providing assistance.

A.8. ASSISTING OTHER PATROLS

When a safety patrol boat in an adjoining area is assigned an assistance mission, boats in the surrounding areas should move to the line between the two sectors. This allows them to answer a call in either of the sectors. Precise direction should be obtained from the operational commander.

A.9. PERMISSION TO SECURE

When it is time to end the patrol, notify the appropriate Coast Guard unit and request permission to secure. A final sweep normally will be made through the patrol area before securing.

NOTE

A patrol boat that is damaged or has a crew member injured while on official patrol must contact the Coast Guard operational commander as soon as possible, and follow the prescribed procedures for the situation.

Regatta Patrols and Marine Parades

Overview

Introduction

A regatta or marine parade is an organized water event of limited duration that is conducted according to a prearranged schedule. Regattas involve both participant and spectator boats in activities such as racing, water skiing, demonstrations, and similar grouped or classed marine skills and equipment. The safety of the participant boats is the responsibility of the sponsoring organization, unless they ask for Coast Guard assistance. The safety of the spectator boats is a Coast Guard responsibility, but should be verified with the event sponsors. The sponsor of the marine event is responsible for applying for approval of the event. The application must be submitted to the proper Coast Guard or civil authority at least 30 days prior to the event. For new or major marine events the application should be submitted well in advance (90–120 days).

In this section

Patrolling Regattas

B.1. GENERAL

Regattas usually take place over a closed course where patrol sectors are established alongside and at each end of the course. The primary functions of a regatta patrol are to control the spectator boats and transient craft for their protection, and to ensure safety hazards do not enter into the event area.

NOTE

The primary responsibility to protect participants from the hazards of the event, including other participants, rests with the sponsoring organization.

B.2. PATROL COMMANDER SELECTION

The district commander, Captain of the Port (COTP), or Coast Guard group commander will designate the Patrol Commander (PATCOM) for a regatta or marine event. The PATCOM is normally a Coast Guard commissioned officer, Warrant officer, or an appropriate Auxiliarist.

NOTE

Written instructions will describe the authority of the Auxiliarist to act as PATCOM. These instructions include: Patrol requirements; Prebrief to all participants—duties and responsibilities; Establish communication frequencies and networks; and instructions for completing after patrol reports. The Auxiliary must coordinate and cooperate with any law enforcement agency that might be on scene.

B.3. DESIGNATING AN AUXILIARY BOAT COMMANDER

When a regatta or marine event is under the control of a Coast Guard PATCOM and the Auxiliary is also assisting, an Auxiliary boat commander (AUXCOM) will be designated. AUXCOM will work closely with the PATCOM to coordinate the Auxiliary boats and personnel, act as liaison in preparing, conducting, and securing the event. (AUXCOM is also that person's radio call sign during the event.)

B.4. ESTABLISHING SECTORS

The length, size and shape of the course depend upon the type of regatta. To maintain operational control, regatta event courses are usually divided into sectors. (See Figure 2-1.) All sectors should be as small as is reasonable to allow patrols to regulate traffic and keep obstructions or boats from the course. Small sectors may limit mobility. Large sectors are too difficult for patrol boats to cover it effectively, and spectator boats might get too close to the course before a patrol boat can issue a warning. Patrol boats should move only within their assigned sectors. The following steps should help the PATCOM to establish and assign sectors.

1. Divide large patrol areas into at least five sectors, one to three sectors along each outer side, and at least two at each end.
2. Operate all boats from the same charts.
3. Mark the charts with the patrol sectors.
4. Assign each patrol boat to a patrol sector.
5. Ensure that each boat reports its location and movements.
6. Establish more sectors as needed (e.g., change in course size or more spectator boats than expected).

B.5. THE GRID SYSTEM

The grid system is an effective method of organizing patrol area operations. When using the grid system, transparent grid overlays are essential. All grids must be identical in size and identification (Figure 2-1). The benefits of using grids are:

- PATCOM and the patrol boat captains can read grid coordinates exactly.
- Coxswains can request assistance, by giving a location, using the grid on the chart.
- PATCOM can also assign additional patrol boats to the position.
- Location of a distress can be easily shown.

Patrol Boat Assignments

B.6. GENERAL

After completing all pre-race activities, the PATCOM dispatches the boats to their patrol positions.

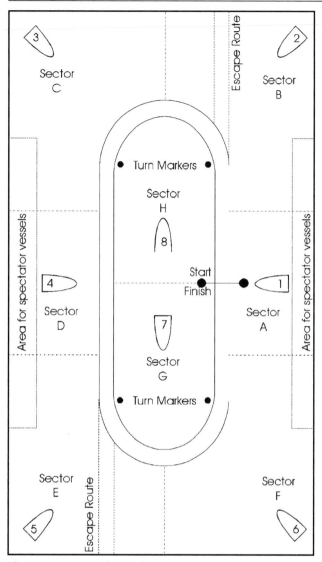

Figure 2-1 Typical Patrol Assignments and Sectors

En route and within its sector, each patrol boat should examine the course for objects or debris that could affect participant, spectator, or patrol boat safety. This is especially important in events involving high-speed racing craft. Items such as a partially submerged soft drink container can cause a disaster if struck by a race boat at high speeds.

B.7. USING PATROL BOATS AS MARKER OR SCREEN BOATS

Patrol boats on regatta patrol may be used two ways, either as marker boats or screen boats.

MARKER BOATS Position marker boats at designated places, either stationary or mobile, to mark limits of restricted areas. The event sponsor must provide marker boats to locate turning points for the regatta participants.

SCREEN BOATS Use screen vessels as either moving or stationary screens. These boats maneuver in formation around the perimeter of the race course to be between the participants and the spectators. A stationary screen boat acts in the same manner as the marker boat.

NOTE

Wakes could create hazards to boats in events. Patrol and spectator boats' speed must be kept to a minimum. In an emergency, patrol boats can increase their speed.

B.8. BOAT ENSIGN DISPLAY

Boats on regatta patrol must display the proper identification signs, and all crew members must be in proper uniform. If an active duty Coast Guard PATCOM rides on an Auxiliary boat, remove the Auxiliary ensign temporarily, and display the Coast Guard ensign along with the special Coast Guard patrol signs.

B.9. PATROL BOAT

Each patrol boat has the responsibility to maintain a sharp lookout. Patrol observers should not become so engrossed in a racing event that they ignore the movement of the participants and the spectators within their sector.

B.10. CLOSING A SECTION

Under certain conditions it is necessary for the Coast Guard to close a section of the course or the area in which the event is being held. It is a responsibility of the patrol boats to constantly be present in these areas. If there are not enough patrol boats, use floats or log booms. Warn spectators so they will not strike these objects.

B.11. SPECTATOR BOAT ANCHORING

Ensure that all spectator boats anchor only in designated areas. All boats must anchor so that they do not swing into restricted zones. It is necessary to be alert for weather changes, a wind shift, or a current condition that might cause anchored boats to swing into the restricted zones.

B.12. SPECTATOR BOATS

Spectator boat areas should be patrolled to ensure all boats are safely clear of the course or safety zone. Advise each spectator boat that is not in a proper position to move to a safe position. Be courteous. In case of failure to comply with a request, report all facts regarding the circumstances to the PATCOM for action.

NOTE

The Auxiliary does not have any law enforcement authority. Use the words "please" and "thank you," and convey all messages in a courteous tone of voice.

B.13. CASUALTY ASSISTANCE

Patrol boats must advise the PATCOM of all problems in case the event needs to be stopped or the course closed temporarily. No patrol boat will leave its sector unless ordered to do so by the PATCOM. Take action only on direction from the PATCOM. This is to maintain order and efficiency of the operation. The table below summarizes possible emergency situations and the initial actions to take.

B.14. SECURING A REGATTA PATROL

Do not secure a regatta patrol operation until the course area is clear. The PATCOM will designate one patrol boat or more, if required, to make a final sweep of the area. Use the sweep to see that the

Possible Emergency Situations	
If . . .	**Then . . .**
you observe a casualty	advise the PATCOM of all details, who will direct the proper patrol boat to the scene. If a participant boat is the casualty, the event's sponsor may be the only boat to respond.
an accident occurs within your patrol boat's sector	assist immediately. If no arrangement has been made with the event sponsors, "stand by, observe" but defer all action to the (sponsor) committee boats designated for that purpose.
a boat is assigned to help outside its sector	it must report to the PATCOM upon completion of the assistance.
there is an emergency	rescue the people first before any attempt is made to salvage a boat. The protection of lives and personal safety are more important than the saving of property.

course is in the condition it was before the regatta. Any debris or markers that have not been picked up should be reported to the PATCOM, who will relay this information to the sponsoring organization with responsibility for policing the area.

Patrolling the Various Regattas

B.15. GENERAL

Knowing the sponsor rules, the boats involved and patrol responsibilities will ensure the safety of your crew, participant boats and spectators. The table opposite introduces the responsibilities of the sponsor and patrol boats during powerboat, sailing, rowing, and the other various regattas.

SPONSOR ORGANIZATION RESPONSIBILITY Any type of regatta is usually sponsored by an organization. Powerboats may have a corporate sponsor; sailboats are sponsored by yachting clubs or associations; and rowing regattas are usually sanctioned by a prep school or collegiate organization. The sponsors have rules that the participants of a race must follow. At times, the sponsors provide especially trained crews to assist during emergencies.

PATROL BOAT RESPONSIBILITY Only assist a participant or spectator boat if agreed upon or requested by the sponsor and approved by the Patrol Commander. Know the sponsor's rules. Be aware of the construction, use, and particulars of the boats used in the regatta. During an emergency with either the participant or spectator boats, an abrupt action by an inexperienced boat crew may cause a participant's disqualification.

NOTE

PATCOM should keep close liaison with regatta sponsor officials before, during, and after the regatta event.

Marine Parades

B.16. GENERAL

The term "marine parade" denotes a boat or a group of boats participating in a parade. Depending upon the nature of the event, a patrol boat will maintain the grouping or allow it to vary. The event is usually moving, and does not ordinarily retrace its path, although the parade may end at its starting point.

Regattas	Powerboat	Sailing	Rowing (crew racing)
Course Layout	Large rectangle or long oval course involving the escape valve idea, diagonally opposite at each end, enabling race boats to leave the course. (Figure 2-1).	Nearly all courses are triangular, allowing for use of the basic sailing positions. Course must be laid out to conform with the prevailing wind direction. (Figure 2-2).	The races are held on a straight course with marker craft on either side and a moving screen behind to prevent spectator boats from interfering.
Operation Sectors	Use boats as moving or stationary screens along sides of the course. Maintain a line, behind which spectator boats stay. The ends of the course require moving screens if it is longer than it is wide, to keep spectators from entering the course.	Course type and maneuvering calls for a combination of marker, stationary boats, and moving screen boats to stop passing boats from entering the course. Moving screen patrols move with the regatta. (Figure 2-3).	Use stationary positions and do not leave these positions unless assistance is required. (Figure 2-4).
Participant Boat Particulars	Fragile construction. Sensitive to wakes.	Possibility of capsizing. Identifying capsized boats difficult because of lack of noise and sailboats closely grouped.	The craft are very light, have a very low freeboard and require quiet water.
Handling Participant Boat Emergencies	Emergencies on the course should be left to the sponsor rescue craft, unless asked.	Ask the skipper if assistance is wanted, then allow him to direct the operation.	Check with event sponsors, but assume it is okay to assist participants, who usually do not wear life preservers.
Spectator Boats	Sponsors and patrols share responsibility for the safety of spectator boats. Keep spectator boat wakes small.	Sponsors and patrols share responsibility for the safety of spectator boats. Tactfully attempt to keep spectator boats from entering the course or going between the sailboats. This happens when a spectator or transient boat is unaware of an ongoing race, or they presume they may proceed following navigation rules.	Sponsors and patrols share responsibility for the safety of spectator boats. Ensure that all spectator boats are in place well before the start of the race so that wake-driven wave action will subside. Prevent spectator boats from entering the course.
Other Responsibilities	Move about looking out for debris that may endanger participant or spectator boats.	Be alert to course legs being moved or rotated, and advise patrol boats.	Keep wakes down.
In Addition	Special communication problems may arise when operating near loud engines, and may require traffic control signs, headphones, etc.	Racing sailboats take advantage of wind conditions and are tacking back and forth along the course. Try not to place patrol boats in the infield, they could be in the way. Instead, set patrol boats downwind and astern of the participating boats. Discuss assisting, sailboat righting, and towing at the pre-race briefing.	Patrol boats should minimize the use of hailing equipment whenever the rowers are nearby to eliminate interference with their cadence. Other types of rowing regattas feature dories, lifeboats, whaleboats, canoes, and even bathtubs. Patrol these regattas in the same manner as crew races.

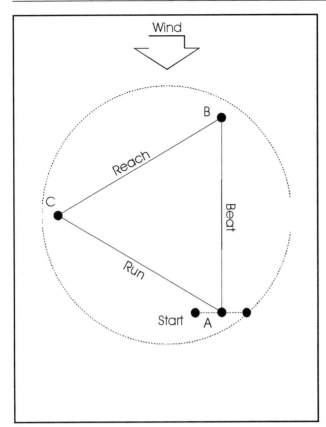

Figure 2-2 Typical Sailboat Regatta Course

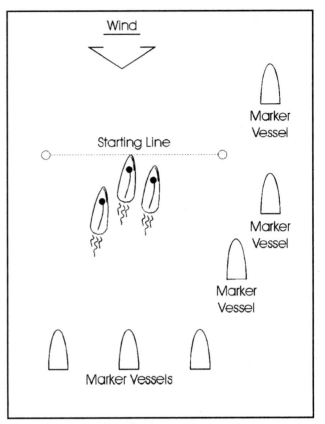

Figure 2-3 Typical Sailboat Regatta Patrol

Over ninety Coast Guard Auxiliary boats were on patrol during the OPSAIL 2000 parade of tall ships in New York Harbor.

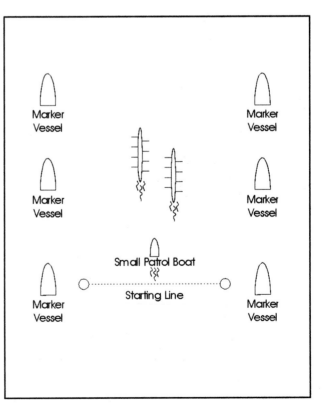

Figure 2-4 Typical Rowing Regatta Patrol

A patrol commander (PATCOM) will normally be assigned. PATCOM and patrol boat duties typically include:

- Selecting a vantage point for the PATCOM with maximum visibility of the event; usually a moving facility.

- Maintaining communications between the PATCOM and the marine parade marshal or committee.

- Maintaining parade configuration per established routes and times.

- Assigning patrol boats to:

  Stationary sectors along the parade course containing spectator boats that are to remain within a prescribed limit.

  Move sectors of patrol boats ahead, behind, and alongside the participating boats.

  Sectors between the welcomed boat and the moving welcoming fleet, for such events.

  Prevent transient boats from disrupting the parade.

  Render assistance to life threatening situations and endangered property.

SECTION C

Aids to Navigation Patrols

C.1. GENERAL

Coast Guard Regulations state that coxswains shall make every effort to observe and report any aid to navigation (ATON) that is out of order or off station. (The boat crew assists by keeping a sharp eye out for discrepancies.) This is usually done underway while on routine operations. However, Coast Guard resources may be directed to get underway specifically to check for ATON discrepancies. In addition to patrolling, local boat resources may be used to assist the ATON units that maintain and service these aids.

C.2. REPORTING ATON DISCREPANCIES

Report any aids that are damaged, off station, or otherwise not serving their intended purpose (i.e., not watching properly) to the Coast Guard unit that you are patrolling for. Clearly identify the aid, its location, and the discrepancy. The chart, Light List, or Local Notice to Mariners should be used to verify the correct ATON information.

The Auxiliary has established procedures for their reporting of ATON discrepancies. The following criteria are used to select the method of reporting a discrepancy:

Reporting a Discrepancy		
Criticality	**Report by**	**Criteria**
Critical	Radio	Failure to report by the most expeditious means may result in loss of life and/or damage to a boat. *Examples:* • Aid iced and light is obscured. • Light signal failure. • Light signal showing improper characteristic. • Sinking or submerged buoy. • Aid off station/adrift/ missing. • Radiobeacon off the air (improper characteristic).
Urgent	Telephone	Failure to report will result in no danger of loss of life or boat damage. However, the discrepancy may contribute to the stranding of a boat. *Examples:* • Missing daymarks. • Sound signal failure. • Radiobeacon timing sequence incorrect.
Routine	U.S. Mail	Failure to report will result in a very low likelihood of a grounding or stranding, but corrective maintenance is necessary. *Examples:* • Signal obscured (by foliage or other objects). • Faded daymark. • Leaning structure. • Bird's nest. • Improper day markings. • Retroreflective material missing or inadequate. • Numbers missing.

SECTION D

Chart Updating Patrols

D.1. AGREEMENT WITH NOAA

The Auxiliary has a formal agreement with the National Ocean Service (NOAA-NOS), an agency under the Department of Commerce. The agreement provides for liaison and cooperation to provide accurate and up-to-date chart information to the boating public.

The agreement between NOAA-NOS and the Auxiliary authorizes and encourages the scheduling of safety patrols to verify the accuracy of published navigation charts. These patrols, called Chart Updating Patrols, are not restricted solely to areas covered by NOAA-NOS charts. Other federal and state agencies also publish charts or maps used by the boater. Chart updating patrols on local, state, and federal waters covered by these charts are also authorized.

D.2. DISCREPANCIES

Any discrepancies found should be reported on the appropriate chart updating form.

Members of the Auxiliary need not be performing on a scheduled patrol to notice and report discrepancies. Alert coxswains should always compare chart information with the actual conditions and report differences. Chart updating patrols should always be alert to the actions and activities of other boaters and be ready to render assistance.

SECTION E

Disaster Patrols

E.1. GENERAL

District or unit Standard Operating Procedures (SOP) typically provide for patrolling in the event of a natural or manmade disaster. This type of patrol, sometimes called a Disaster Patrol, deals with emergencies either imminent, in progress, or the result of events such as hurricanes, storms, waterfront explosions, fires, or floods.

E.2. ROLE OF BOAT CREW

Boat crew may be used to transmit warnings to waterfront and isolated areas. They can also transport supplies and personnel, evacuate stricken areas, and coordinate boat traffic. This includes acting as guides to safe moorings, securing small craft, or any other tasks necessary to speed preparations for, or relief from, emergency conditions.

E.3. ROLE OF COAST GUARD

The Coast Guard is typically part of any local emergency management plan. In this role, Coast Guard boats may be called upon to assist in evacuations of the civilian population. As seen in many disasters, there often are people who do not want to evacuate ahead of time. The Coast Guard has federal law enforcement powers (the Auxiliary does not), but the local officials are the proper people to handle these civil situations and to provide guidance. However, politely explaining the situation may convince a reluctant person to take the right action.

SECTION F

Port Security and Maritime Pollution

F.1. GENERAL

Port security and maritime pollution issues both fall under the Coast Guard Directorate of Marine Safety and Maritime Environmental Protection. Typically, the Captain of the Port (COTP) is the field unit responsible to implement these programs. The COTP may have the resources or may have to call upon local Coast Guard facilities to provide boats. Port security is concerned about waterside security measures, typically within a security zone. Maritime pollution patrols focus on detecting, reporting, and monitoring of oil spills and hazardous material discharges into U.S. navigable waters.

F.2. SECURITY ZONE PATROL

There is no federal, state, or local military service or civilian agency with the waterside resources, expertise, and lawful maritime authority comparable to that of the Coast Guard. The COTP has developed tactics and countermeasures to deal with waterborne threats. Assets likely to be at risk include:

- ship
- pier or port complex
- waterfront facility
- people

OPERATIONS The COTP will provide specialized equipment and training, if needed. A command center should be established with direct control by the COTP over all Coast Guard deployed resources. Most security zone enforcement requires simple patrolling or "policing" of the zone boundaries. This is usually done by one or two boats patrolling the perimeter. The security zone may be established around a fixed site such as a pier, or it may be a moving security zone for a vessel underway. The moving security zone usually requires at least two boats.

NOTE

No security operation is routine. Keep alert and aware of your surroundings at all times.

F.3. POLLUTION PATROL

There are usually two types of pollution patrol: a patrol to detect or prevent spills, and a patrol in response to a spill. The boat may be given specific areas to visually inspect or given general direction to cruise along the waterfront and shoreline to look for any discharges.

DETECTION OR PREVENTION The local operational commander will have a boat patrol to detect any unreported spills or discharges. Early detection this way may keep the incident from growing into a major spill. Also, the source of the spill may be identified—this may stop someone from intentionally discharging pollution AND also identify the person or company who will pay the costs for cleanup.

RESPONSE TO A SPILL Response to a pollution incident will often involve boats in some type of patrol duty, such as monitoring the situation. The person coordinating the response to the incident, the On-Scene Commander (OSC), will have an incident command structure to provide tasking and guidance for boat operations.

CHAPTER

3

Crew Efficiency Factors

Editor's Note: *Boating can be a relaxing, joyful pastime. But boating can also become a fatiguing, stressful ordeal when the seas build or machines fail or the weather turns. Certainly, being relatively fit physically can help in any of these situations, and it's interesting to see how the Coasties measure fitness. But even the most fit boaters can run afoul of fatigue, motion sickness, lethal fumes, hyperthermia, hypothermia, or any of the other hazards discussed here. Notice that the Coast Guard places great emphasis on the "buddy system"—that is, watching each other for signs of fatigue or physical distress. The techniques offered here to deal with those problems will work on your boat too.*

In this chapter

Overview

Introduction

This chapter specifies the physical fitness standards that all crew members are required to meet. It also describes some of the hazards and unique discomforts boat crews cope with when operating boats in the marine environment. The combination of many factors such as extreme hot or cold weather, fatigue, and seasickness are all factors that can impair crew performance. Understanding these factors will help crew members remain at the highest possible level of efficiency while underway.

NOTE

Specific treatment procedures for the conditions described in this chapter are covered in Chapter 5—First Aid.

SECTION A

Physical Fitness Standards

A.1. GENERAL

All Coast Guard crew members are required to meet the following standards of physical fitness. Physical fitness standards are required to ensure crew members have sufficient strength, flexibility, and endurance to safely perform duties during normal and adverse conditions. Knowing these standards will ensure that personnel are able to accurately gauge their level of fitness and make improvements where necessary.

NOTE

Auxiliary Physical Standards are found in COMDTINST M16798.3 (series) for being a crew member on an Auxiliary facility.

A.2. ARM AND SHOULDER STRENGTH

The requirements to meet for arm and shoulder strength are to perform as many correct push-ups as possible in one minute. Refer to Figure 3-1 for the required fitness standards.

ONE MINUTE PUSH-UPS Perform as many correct push-ups as possible in one minute.

1. Start with hands shoulder-width apart.
2. Males will be on hands and toes only, females will place knees on the deck and position hands slightly forward of shoulders.
3. In the up position, the elbows must be fully extended.
4. For a proper push-up to be completed, lower the body until the chest is within one fist distance of the deck, and then return to the up position.

NOTE

The back must be kept straight the entire time.

A.3. ABDOMINAL AND TRUNK STRENGTH

The requirements to meet for abdominal and trunk strength are to perform as many correct sit-ups as possible in one minute. Refer to Figure 3-1 for the required fitness standards.

ONE MINUTE SIT-UPS Perform as many correct sit-ups as possible in one minute.

1. Lie on back, bend knees, place heels flat on the floor about 18 inches away from buttocks, and keep fingers loosely on side of the head. Hands may not come off of side of head for sit-up to count.
2. In the up position, elbows will touch the knees, and then return so that both shoulder blades are touching the deck.
3. The buttocks should never leave the deck.

NOTE

Feet may be anchored.

NOTE

Any resting should be done in the up position.

A.4. FLEXIBILITY

To meet the flexibility standard you must be able to reach to at least a specified measured distance.

SIT AND REACH Place a yardstick on top of a box with the 15-inch mark even with the edge of the box.

1. Warm up and stretch sufficiently.
2. Remove shoes and sit with feet flat against the box.

Figure 3-1 *Physical Fitness Standards*

Males	Push-ups	Sit-ups	Sit and Reach	1.5 Mile Run	12 Minute Swim*
under 30	29	38	16.5"	12:51	500 yds.
30 to 39	24	35	15.5"	13:36	450 yds.
40 to 49	18	29	14.25"	14:29	400 yds.
50 to 59	15	25	12.5"	15:26	350 yds.
60+	13	22	11.5"	16:43	300 yds.
Females	**Push-ups**	**Sit-ups**	**Sit and Reach**	**1.5 Mile Run**	**12 Minute Swim***
under 30	23	32	19.25"	15:26	400 yds.
30 to 39	19	25	18.25"	15:57	350 yds.
40 to 49	13	20	17.25"	16:58	300 yds.
50 to 59	11	16	16.25"	17:55	250 yds.
60+	9	15	16.25"	18:44	200 yds.

*Note: 12 minute swim test chart is based on Dr. Kenneth Cooper's research.

3. Feet must be no more than eight (8) inches apart.

4. Place the hands exactly together, one on top of the other, with the fingers extended.

5. Keep the knees extended and the hands together.

6. Lean forward without lunging and reach as far down the yardstick as possible.

7. Record the reach to the nearest ½ inch.

8. Three trials are allowed to pass the minimum standard.

NOTE

The 15-inch mark is between the individual's feet with the end of the yardstick, 0 inches through 15 inches, extending forward towards the subject's knees.

A.5. ENDURANCE

The requirement to meet the endurance standard is to run/walk 1.5 miles or perform a 12-minute swim. Refer to Figure 3-1 for the required fitness standards.

1.5 MILE RUN/WALK For the endurance qualification, an individual will be required to run/walk 1.5 miles or perform a 12-minute swim within the indicated time.

1. Refrain from smoking or eating for two (2) hours prior to this test.

2. Warm up and stretch sufficiently.

3. Run or walk 1.5 miles in the required amount of time for the appropriate age bracket.

4. If possible, receive pacing assistance, either by having a trained pacer run alongside or by calling out lap times during the test.

5. Be forewarned not to start out too fast and not to run to complete exhaustion during the test.

6. At the end of the test, walk for an additional five (5) minutes to aid in recovery.

12-MINUTE SWIM The 12-minute swim is an alternative method to fulfill the endurance qualification.

1. Warm up and stretch sufficiently.

2. Swim the required distance for the appropriate age bracket in 12 minutes.

3. Use whichever stroke desired and rest as necessary.

A.6. ANNUAL ASSESSMENT

Annual assessment should be performed by unit Wellness Representative (WR), unit Fitness Leader (FL), or independent support command Wellness Coordinator (WC) who has been trained to perform the same fitness assessments. These personnel not only perform the annual test, but also create unit or individual fitness routines to maintain or increase physical fitness.

Crew Fatigue

B.1. GENERAL

The crew's physiological well-being plays an important role in the safe and successful accomplishment of each Coast Guard mission. As a boat crew member you will assist people during the worst conditions. At times you may feel like you have reached the limits of your physical and mental endurance.

B.2. FATIGUE

Mental and physical fatigue are among the greatest dangers during rough weather operations. Fatigue dramatically reduces the powers of observation, concentration, and judgment. This, in turn, reduces the ability to exert the effort necessary, and increases the probability that unnecessary chances will be taken and prescribed safety precautions will be disregarded. The following are examples of situations that may cause fatigue:

- Operating in extreme hot or cold weather conditions
- Eye strain from hours of looking through seaspray blurred windshields
- The effort of holding on and maintaining balance
- Stress
- Exposure to noise
- Exposure to the sun
- Poor physical conditioning
- Lack of sleep
- Boredom

In these situations, do not be tempted to take chances, such as towing too fast or crossing a bar under dangerous conditions. Always keep the safety of the crew and other passengers as the foremost concern.

B.3. CREW RESPONSIBILITY

The crew's safety and welfare are the coxswain's primary responsibility. Coxswains must be constantly aware of stress signs evident in their crews, and learn to recognize fatigue and take corrective action. Crew members must watch each other's condition to prevent excessive fatigue from taking its toll. Note the ability of each member to respond to normal conversation and to complete routine tasks.

B.4. SYMPTOMS

The primary symptoms of fatigue are:

- Inability to focus or concentrate/narrowed attention span
- Mental confusion or judgment error
- Decreased coordination of motor skills and sensory ability (hearing, seeing)
- Increased irritability
- Decreased performance
- Decreased concern for safety

Any one of these symptoms can cause mistakes in judgment or cause you to take shortcuts that could threaten the safety of the mission and crew. It is important to ward off the effects of fatigue before it gets too great. Fatigue can lead to faulty decisions and a "don't care" attitude.

B.5. PREVENTION

Coxswains must be aware of the dangers that exist when crew members push themselves beyond reasonable limits of performance. They should help eliminate mistakes caused by fatigue. Coxswains must not hesitate to call for assistance when fatigue begins to impair the efficiency of their crew.

Some preventive measures are:

- Adequate crew rest
- Dress appropriate for weather
- Rotate crew duties
- Provide food and refreshments suitable for conditions
- Observe other crew members for signs of fatigue

ENVIRONMENTAL CONDITIONS Despite the normal operating climate in a particular area, all crew members must dress (or have clothing available) for unexpected weather. Keeping warm in cold weather and cool in hot weather helps prevent fatigue. Some other environmental conditions that also promote fatigue are:

- Motion sickness
- Glare from the sun
- Wind and rough sea conditions
- Rain or snow
- Vibration (boat engine)

NOTE

Information on Boat Crew Fatigue Standards may be found in COMDTINST 16130.2 (series), *CG Addendum to National SAR Manual.*

SECTION C

Motion Sickness

C.1. CAUSES OF MOTION SICKNESS

Motion sickness (seasickness) occurs when there is an imbalance between visual images and the portion of the middle ear which senses motion. Mental and physical stress, as well as the rolling or pitching motion of a boat, contribute to motion sickness. Reading chart work, or other tasks that require close attention, will aggravate motion sickness.

C.2. SYMPTOMS

The motion of the boat, especially when the boat's heading produces a wallowing or rolling motion, can cause the typical symptoms of nausea and vomiting. The primary symptoms of seasickness are:

- Nausea and vomiting
- Increased salivation
- Unusual paleness
- Sweating
- Drowsiness
- Overall weakness
- Stomach discomfort

C.3. PREVENTION/ MEDICATION

Motion sickness can often be prevented or made less severe with different kinds of antimotion sickness medication, including the use of Scopolamine patches. Crew members who are especially susceptible to motion discomfort should take medication when weather and sea conditions are such that motion sickness is likely to occur.

Crew members susceptible to motion discomfort should take antimotion sickness medication throughout their watch since they never know when they will be dispatched on a mission. This medication taken just before getting underway may not have its maximum effect during the mission.

> ## CAUTION!
> Some antimotion sickness medications may cause drowsiness. Consult a medical professional to determine if other alternatives are available.

Besides taking medication, there are other things that can be done to help prevent seasickness.

- Stay out of confined spaces
- Stay above deck in the fresh air
- Avoid concentrating on the movement of the boat by looking out over the water toward the horizon or shoreline
- Avoid smoking

C.4. RESTRICTIONS

COMDTINST M6710.15 (series), *Antimotion Sickness Medications* restricts medication use. Specifically, it must not be given under the following circumstances:

- Without medical supervision
- Within 12 hours of alcohol consumption
- To pregnant crew members

Do not take antimotion sickness medication if any of these restrictions apply to you.

SECTION D

Lethal Fumes

CO Poisoning

D.1. INTRODUCTION

Every year, people are at risk of injury or death from exposure to lethal fumes. Carbon monoxide (CO) is a colorless and odorless gas. It is the most common lethal gas encountered during boat operations.

D.2. CONDITIONS WHERE CO MAY BE PRESENT

The following conditions are associated with CO poisoning:

- Fuel-burning devices
- Enclosed areas
- Underway
- Fires

FUEL-BURNING DEVICES Operating any fuel-burning devices such as gasoline or diesel engines, CG-P1 and CG-P5 pumps, propane or alcohol stoves, acetylene torches and kerosene heaters, produces CO fumes.

ENCLOSED AREAS Personnel can be quickly affected by CO fumes in areas such as closed cockpits or unventilated spaces below decks.

- Sleeping in a closed cabin while using certain types of catalytic and/or flame producing heaters.
- Working alone in an engine compartment with the engines operating.
- A defective exhaust system can allow fumes to accumulate in a confined space on board a vessel.

NOTE

If you find yourself in a compartment which may be affected by lethal fumes, breathable air may be found near the deck. Crouch or crawl on the deck to reach an exit.

UNDERWAY The boat does not need to be stationary for a problem with CO fumes to occur. For example, a following wind can circulate exhaust gases throughout the cockpit of a slow-moving boat.

The construction of some cockpits or cabins can cause the eddies from a wind current to draw fumes back aboard.

FIRES Breathing the by-products of a fire is another source of dangerous fumes exposure. Even a recently extinguished fire is still dangerous. Fires can also create other highly lethal fumes such as cyanide gases. This happens when different types of plastics, upholstery, cushions, or electronics insulation burn.

D.3. SYMPTOMS

Symptoms of lethal fume poisoning can include one or more of the following:

- Throbbing temples
- Dizziness
- Ears ringing
- Watering and itching eyes
- Headache
- Cherry-pink skin color

D.4. PREVENTION

- Always ensure adequate circulation of fresh air throughout the vessel.
- Try to minimize the effect of exhaust fumes on the vessel. This may be as simple as making a minor course change or increasing speed, or opening a window or cracking open a door, etc.

D.5. RESPONSE TO VICTIMS

The first senses affected by poison gases are those that control a person's judgment and decision-making ability. Once a person is affected by dangerous fumes, they may not be able to help themselves.

If carbon monoxide or any other type of poisoning is suspected, get the victim to fresh air and get medical help immediately.

Noise

E.1. NOISE AS A FATIGUE FACTOR

Any continual noise at the same pitch can distract, lull, or aggravate to the point where it adversely affects temperament and the ability to perform properly. Moreover, loud noise can cause hearing loss and contribute to excessive fatigue. Coxswains should be aware of the effect noise may be having on the crew.

NOISE MANAGEMENT These are a few measures to help manage noise:

- Make minor changes to engine speed
- Adjust radio controls so they produce a minimum amount of static
- Use ear protection whenever noise levels exceed 85 decibels (see Figure 3-2 for decibel scale).

Guidelines for preserving hearing are contained in COMDTINST M5100.47 (series), *Safety and Environmental Health Manual* and COMDTINST M6000.1 (series), *Medical Manual.*

NOTE

Ear protection is required when working in, or making rounds in, an enclosed engineering space.

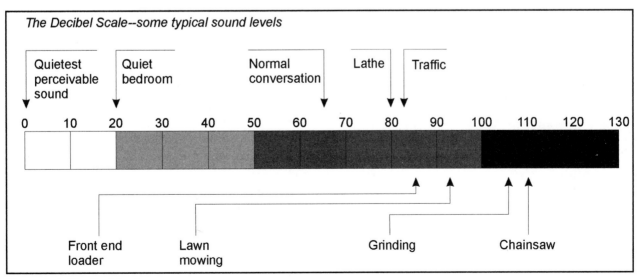

Figure 3-2 Decibel Scale

Drugs and Alcohol

F.1. GENERAL

Alcohol and drug use cause slower reaction time, lack of coordination, slurred speech, drowsiness, or an overconfident attitude. Hangovers also cause irritability, drowsiness, seasickness, and a lack of concentration. Crew members who knowingly get underway for a Coast Guard mission while under the influence are violating Coast Guard policy and put themselves and others at risk.

F.2. PRESCRIPTION DRUGS

Prescription drugs have the ability to adversely affect or incapacitate crew members. Certain medications can be as incapacitating as alcohol. In addition, many medications, if taken with alcohol, accentuate the action of both. Always notify the command if you are taking prescription drugs which may affect your performance or prevent you from performing your duties.

F.3. ALCOHOL

Alcohol is a well-recognized central nervous system depressant. It is one of the most frequently used and abused drugs in our society. Even small amounts of alcohol in the blood can seriously impair judgment, reflexes, muscular control and also reduce the restorative effects of sleep. The level of alcohol in the body varies with the frequency and amount of alcohol intake, the length of time following cessation of drinking, and an individual's body weight. A zero alcohol level is essential for boat crew personnel to meet the rigorous demands of boat operations. Detectable blood alcohol levels or symptomatic hangovers are causes for restricting boat crew personnel from operations. Although some personnel may completely metabolize all alcohol well within eight or twelve hours, this time span allows an adequate margin of safety before resuming operations.

F.4. TOBACCO

The nicotine contained in tobacco is a quick-acting poison. Excessive smoking causes depression of the nervous system and impairment of vision. The carbon monoxide resulting from the combustion of tobacco is absorbed by the bloodstream in preference to oxygen, resulting in a lowering of altitude tolerance. Tobacco smoke also irritates the respiratory system.

F.5. CAFFEINE

The drug caffeine, contained in coffee, tea, and many soft drinks, can produce an adverse effect on the body. The amount of caffeine contained in just two cups of coffee appreciably affects the rates of blood flow and respiration. In small amounts, coffee can be considered a nervous system stimulant. Excessive amounts may produce nervousness, inability to concentrate, headaches, and dizziness. Individuals accustomed to daily intake of caffeine may develop headaches and experience a loss of sharpness if daily intake is stopped or significantly curtailed. Caffeine withdrawal syndrome may impact flight safety.

Cold Related Factors

Overview

Introduction

The purpose of this section is to briefly describe the precautions to take while operating in cold weather. Cold rain, snow, ice storms, and high winds can develop with very little warning in some parts of the country. Preparation before encountering these conditions and understanding the effects of cold on personnel safety is vital.

In this section

Title	See Page(s)
Effects of Cold Weather	30–31
Hypothermia	31–32
Frostbite	32
Layering Clothing	32–33

Effects of Cold Weather

G.1. GENERAL

Operating in a cold climate presents the challenge of keeping warm enough to tolerate the weather and yet effective enough to carry out the mission. As the temperature drops or you become wet and tired, more insulation is required to keep the body from losing its heat.

G.2. WIND

Wind affects body temperature. Those parts of the body exposed directly to the wind will lose heat quickly, a condition commonly referred to as "wind chill." On bare skin, wind will significantly reduce skin temperature, through evaporation, to below the actual air temperature.

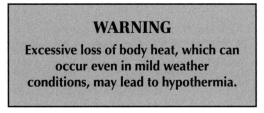

> **WARNING**
>
> Excessive loss of body heat, which can occur even in mild weather conditions, may lead to hypothermia.

G.3. CREW FATIGUE

The combination of rough seas, cold temperatures and wet conditions can quickly cause the crew to become less effective. Crew fatigue will occur more quickly when these conditions are present. Many accidents occur when cold-induced fatigue sets in because the mind loses attentiveness and physical coordination diminishes. Even a crew that is moderately cold and damp will exhibit a decrease in reaction time which is also a symptom to the onset of hypothermia.

Hypothermia

G.4. HYPOTHERMIA

Hypothermia is the loss of internal body temperature. Normal internal body temperature is 98.6°F (39°C) and is automatically regulated by our bodies to remain very close to this temperature at all times. A minor deviation either up or down interferes with the bodily processes. Being too cold will adversely affect the body. Even a minor loss of internal body temperature may cause incapacitation.

OBSERVABLE SIGNS Signs that a person may be suffering from hypothermia include:

- Pale appearance
- Skin cold to the touch
- Pupils are dilated and will not adjust properly when exposed to light
- Poor coordination
- Slurred speech/appears to be intoxicated
- Incoherent thinking
- Unconsciousness
- Muscle rigidity
- Weak pulse
- Very slow and labored breathing
- Irregular heart beat

Expect a hypothermic person to tremble and shiver; however, these symptoms may not always be present. When a person stops shivering, their hypothermia may have advanced beyond the initial stages.

> **WARNING**
>
> Prolonged exposure to the wind may lead to hypothermia and/or frostbite.

> **WARNING**
>
> Never give hypothermia victims anything by mouth, especially alcohol.

PREVENTION Cold and hypothermia affect crew safety and mission performance, and prevention must be a top priority. Coast Guard policy calls for hypothermia protective clothing to be worn when the water temperature is below 60°F (15.5°C).

The Commanding Officer or Officer in Charge may waive the requirement for wearing a hypothermia protective device on a case-by-case basis if the degree of risk to hypothermia is minimal, such as in nonhazardous daylight operations in calm water. However, proper personal protective equipment must be carried onboard.

Antiexposure coveralls are designed to be worn over the uniform in the same manner as standard coveralls. For added protection, wear polypropylene thermal underwear next to the skin to act as a moisture wicking layer.

NOTE

Treatment for hypothermia is covered in Chapter 5—First Aid.

NOTE

Units shall carry hypothermia protective devices on board under waiver conditions (except for ship's boats operating within sight of the ship). Coxswains shall make sure crew members don a hypothermia protective device when waiver conditions no longer apply (for example, when they encounter or anticipate heavy weather or hazardous operating conditions).

Auxiliary boat crews must gain approval and direction from their operations commander for waivers.

Frostbite

G.5. FROSTBITE

Frostbite is the development of ice crystals within body tissues. Frostbite is most likely to develop in air temperatures less than 20°F (–6.6°C). These are factors contributing to frostbite development:

- Cold stressors, such as wind, air temperature, or exposure to water
- Any restriction of blood flow
- Lack of appropriate protection
- Skin exposure

SYMPTOMS A frostbite victim will complain of painful cold and numbness in the affected area. Waxy white or yellow white, hard, cold, and insensitive areas will develop. As the area begins to thaw, it will be extremely painful and swelling (reddish-purple) or blisters may appear. Areas prone to frostbite include all extremities where the blood has traveled farthest from the heart, such as the hands, feet, face, and ear lobes. A patient suffering from frostbite should also be treated for hypothermia.

PREVENTION Cold weather clothing and equipment is essential in preventing cold related injuries and fatigue. Such items include thermal boots, woolen socks, watch caps, gloves, and thermal undergarments (polypropylene) fleece or pile. During cold conditions, coxswains should discuss the possibilities of frostbite with the crew before getting underway.

> ### CAUTION!
> **Any person who has had frostbite previously is at an increased risk for cold exposure injury in that same area of the body.**

Layering Clothing

G.6. FIRST LAYER—WICKING

Staying dry is an essential factor to maintaining body temperature. Clothing worn next to the skin must carry or "wick" moisture away from the body. Cotton clothes pose particular problems. They absorb and retain moisture, which will rob body heat through evaporation. Wool has good insulating properties even when wet, but it is less than ideal because it stays wet. Modern synthetic wicking fibers such as polypropylene, Thermax™, or Capilene™. do not retain moisture. They will actually draw moisture from the skin and transport it to an absorbent outer layer. This gear works well by itself or it can be combined with a second layer for extreme cold.

G.7. SECOND LAYER—INSULATION

The insulating effect of a fabric is related to how much air it can trap. This is why a loose-knit or fuzzy material is better than one that is tightly knit. It is also why two thin layers of a given material are better than one thick one. The second layer traps air, which retains body heat, while absorbing excess moisture from the first layer. Wool or cotton thermals are an acceptable second layer if worn over a wicking layer, but a number of synthetic fleece or pile garments do a much better job. An example of this is the fleece coverall.

G.8. THIRD LAYER—MOISTURE BARRIER

The outer layer should stop wind and water, so the inner layers can work as designed. Choices include the anti-exposure coverall, dry suit, or "rain gear." The dry suits and rain gear have no insulating properties and will require extra insulation for cold weather. Also, as most dry suits do not "breathe," an absorbent second layer is needed so that perspiration has a place to go.

NOTE

Dry suits require a PFD. They have no inherent buoyancy.

G.9. EXTREMITIES

Most heat loss occurs through the extremities, especially the head. It is particularly important to cover these areas well. It is still important to layer properly, but thinner, or else use all-in-one materials to reduce bulk. For the head, a wool cap may work, but a heavy wicking hood or cap worn alone or under a wool cap will keep you drier and warmer. A rain hat/hood/sou'wester should be considered for wet weather. Gloves should be waterproof, and a wicking liner glove will work better than wool. High top rubber boots are the only option for wet weather. A wicking liner sock under a wool, cotton, or fleece outer sock will provide the best warmth. Insoles should be non-absorbent. A perforated foam insole also works well.

NOTE

For additional information on Hypothermia, read COMDTPUB P3131.6 (series), *A Pocket Guide to Cold Water Survival.*

SECTION H

Sun and Heat Related Factors

Overview

Introduction

Crew members must be aware of the dangers of too much exposure to the sun and take preventative measures to guard against a decrease in performance. Performance can easily be affected by the heat and vibration of the boat which can increase fatigue. This section discusses the various sun and heat related factors that crew members may encounter during their activities.

In this section

Sun Burns

H.1. GENERAL

Continuous exposure to the sun can cause sunburn and other complications such as heat stroke, dehydration, etc. Unprotected exposed skin will suffer from premature aging and an increased chance of skin cancer.

SYMPTOMS Sunburn appears as an area of redness, swelling, or blistering of the skin. Other effects of overexposure to the sun are fever, gastrointestinal symptoms, malaise, and pigment changes in the skin.

PREVENTION If exposed to the sun for prolonged periods of time, take precautions. Stay in the shade when possible. However, just getting out of direct sunlight is not always enough since sun can be just as harmful when reflected off a bright surface, such as sand or water. Use sun screen lotion with a sun protection factor (SPF) of 15 or higher. Wear protective clothing, such as a hat with a brim and sunglasses with UV protection for eyes.

NOTE

For additional information on heat related injuries, refer to COMDTPUB P6200.12 (series), *Preventive Heat Casualties.*

TREATMENT Most sunburns do not appear fully until after the victim has been exposed to the sun for several hours. Treatment consists of applying cool wet towels to the affected area. Cooling the skin temperature is very important. Keep the skin moist but be wary of what product is applied. Many lotions contain perfumes, alcohol, or wax which will only aggravate the burn. Several types of first aid sprays give fast but short-lived relief.

Dehydration

H.2. FLUID LOSS AND HYDRATION

An adequate fluid intake is essential to remain healthy while underway. Fluids are lost from the body in several ways. The most obvious loss is through the kidneys. The less obvious loss of body fluid occurs through perspiration from the skin and respiration through the lungs. As a result, an average, healthy adult requires two or three liters of fluid a day to replace these losses. Extremely warm weather significantly increases the loss of fluids. Try to stay away from liquids such as tea, alcohol, coffee, and soft drinks. These liquids speed up fluid loss.

One vital element of body fluids that must be maintained are electrolytes. The balance of electrolytes between intake and loss is important and must be maintained. Recent medical studies have identified that normal dietary practices will maintain an adequate electrolyte level.

> **CAUTION!**
>
> **Do not use salt tablets unless prescribed by a physician. The use of salt tablets does not improve well-being despite the amount of perspiration or salt/electrolyte loss.**

SYMPTOMS Healthy adults must satisfy their water and electrolyte requirements. When water and electrolytes are not replaced, the body experiences dehydration. Drinking alcohol and caffeine increases dehydration. At first there is thirst and general discomfort, followed by an inclination to slow physical movement, and a loss of appetite. As more water is lost, an individual becomes sleepy and experiences a rise in body temperature. By the time the body loses 5% of body weight in fluids, the individual begins to feel nauseated. When 6 to 10% of body fluids are lost, symptoms increase in this order:

- Dry mouth
- Dizziness
- Headache
- Difficulty in breathing
- Tingling in the arms and legs
- Skin color turns bluish
- Indistinct speech
- Inability to walk
- Cramping legs and stomach

PREVENTION Drinking fresh clean water is the best and easiest method to replace fluid loss and prevent dehydration. Almost all fluids are suitable including fruit juices, soups, and water. Drinks that do not contain sodium (salt) are recommended. Drink plenty of fluids throughout the day, especially in warm, dry climates.

If you know you will be away from a source of water for a long period of time, bring an ample supply of water with you.

TREATMENT The signs of dehydration can be subtle. Be particularly watchful of other crew members under extreme conditions of sun and heat. The crew should be encouraged to drink fluids throughout the mission. Rotating crews between sun exposure tasks and shaded tasks will help prevent dehydration. If a crew member becomes dehydrated, remove the person immediately from further exposure to heat and/or sun. Get prompt medical attention. Mild cases will become serious if activity continues in the setting where the illness first occurred.

> **WARNING**
>
> **Never force fluid by mouth to a person who is unconscious or semiconscious.**

Heat Rash (Prickly Heat)

H.3. GENERAL

Heat rash is prevalent among those living and working in warm, humid climates or in hot spaces ashore or aboard boats. It may occur in cool weather if a person overdresses.

SYMPTOMS Heat rash is caused by:

- breakdown of the body's ability to perspire, and
- decreased evaporative cooling of the skin.

Heat rash interferes with sleep, resulting in decreased efficiency and increased cumulative fatigue, making the individual susceptible to more serious heat disorders. Heat rash also accelerates the onset of heat stroke. Symptoms are:

- Pink or red minute lesions
- Skin irritation (prickling)
- Frequent, severe itching.

PREVENTION Coxswains and crew members must be aware of negative effects brought on by heat rash, and be alert for symptoms when operating in a hot environment. Rotating crews between heat-related tasks and those jobs in a cooler environment will help prevent heat rash from occurring.

TREATMENT If heat rash occurs, remove a crew member from further exposure to excessive heat immediately. Take positive action to prevent the onset of more serious disorders. Apply cool, wet towels to the affected areas.

Heat Cramps

H.4. GENERAL

Heat cramps are painful contractions caused by excessive salt and water depletion. Heat cramps may occur as an isolated occurrence with normal body temperature or during heat exhaustion. Recently stressed muscles are prone to heat cramps, particularly those muscles in the extremities and abdomen.

SYMPTOMS The victims legs will be drawn up and excessive sweating will occur. The victim may grimace and cry out in pain.

PREVENTION Follow the guidelines discussed previously for other heat related illnesses.

TREATMENT Treat heat cramps by placing the victim in a cool place. Encourage the victim to lie down in a comfortable position. Offer cool drinks to replace fluid loss. Solutions containing electrolytes, like a sports drink, are also useful, however, do not allow the ingestion of excessive salt. Do not treat cramped muscles with heat packs or massage. Get prompt medical assistance for severe or persistent conditions.

Heat Exhaustion

H.5. GENERAL

Heat exhaustion is more complex than heat cramps. The cause of heat exhaustion is a loss of too much water through perspiration.

SYMPTOMS When suffering from heat exhaustion, a person collapses and sweats profusely. The victim has pale skin, a pounding heart, nausea, headache, and acts restless.

PREVENTION Follow the guidelines discussed previously for other heat related illnesses.

TREATMENT Immediately provide first aid treatment followed by rapid removal (in a litter, if possible) of the patient to a location that can provide proper medical care.

Heat Stroke

H.6. GENERAL

Heat stroke is a major medical emergency and results from the complete breakdown of the body's sweating and heat regulatory mechanisms. Heat stroke or "sun stroke" is caused by operating in bright sun or working in a hot environment, such as an engine compartment. The onset of heat stroke is very rapid.

SYMPTOMS The major symptoms of heat stroke are:

- Skin is red, hot, and dry to the touch (cessation of sweating); characteristic body temperature above 105°F (40.5°C)
- Headache
- Weak and rapid pulse
- Confusion, violence, lack of coordination, delirium, and/or unconsciousness
- Brain damage will occur if immediate medical treatment is not given

PREVENTION Guard against heat stroke (in most cases) by using the procedures for preventing other heat related illnesses described earlier in this chapter.

TREATMENT Heat stroke is the most serious of all heat disorders and is an immediate threat to life. No matter which type of operation or assigned mission you are conducting, ALL INCIDENTS OF HEAT STROKE MUST BE CONSIDERED AS MEDICAL EMERGENCIES. There is a high mortality rate associated with heat stroke. Remember, heat exhaustion is the result of overloaded heat balance mechanisms that are still functioning. Heat stroke strikes the victim when the thermo-regulatory mechanisms are not functioning, and the main avenue of heat loss, evaporation of sweat, is blocked. Treat the patient immediately or death may occur.

Susceptibility to Heat Problems

H.7. GENERAL

Personnel who are not accustomed to strenuous physical activity in hot and humid environments are particularly susceptible to heat injuries. Excess body weight contributes to this susceptibility.

H.8. CLOTHING AND EQUIPMENT

Impermeable clothing does not "breathe" and thus greatly increases an individual's susceptibility to heat-related illnesses. Clothing acts as a barrier that prevents evaporative cooling. Many synthetic fabrics reduce the absorption and dispersal of sweat needed to achieve optimum heat loss by evaporation.

Clothing and equipment should be worn so that there is free circulation of air between the uniform and the body surface. Wearing shirt collars, shirt cuffs, and trouser bottoms open will aid in ventilation. However, this practice may not be permissible in those areas where loose fitting or open style clothing would present a safety hazard (e.g., around machinery with moving parts).

In full sunlight or a high radiant heat source (e.g., machinery spaces), keeping the body covered with permeable clothing reduces the radiant heat load upon the body. When not working in these areas, removal of the outer layer of clothing will help reduce body temperature. Impermeable clothing must be avoided. When using impermeable clothing, take precautions to avoid the rapid buildup of body heat. Heat illnesses may be manifested in minutes if impermeable clothing is worn.

H.9. FEVER

Febrile illnesses (fever) increases the chance of rapid heat buildup within the body. The presence of fever before heat stress exposure reduces the allowable exposure times.

H.10. FATIGUE

Cumulative fatigue may develop slowly. Failure to recognize this slow development increases an individual's susceptibility to heat related problems.

H.11. PRIOR HEAT ILLNESSES

Prior heat illnesses lead to heat illnesses of greater severity with each incidence. There are several preventive measures:

- Water
- Salt

WATER The body needs water only in quantities sufficient to prevent dehydration and electrolyte imbalances that result from losses in sweat, urine, etc. Under conditions of profuse sweating, each person will require one pint (0.5 liters) or more of fluid intake per hour. Take water in small quantities at frequent intervals, such as every 20 or 30 minutes.

SALT The average diet provides from 15–20 grams of salt daily. This amount of salt is adequate for the prevention of most heat related illnesses.

Team Coordination and Risk Management

Editor's Note: *We all say we want to operate our boats safely, but have you ever thought about what that really means? The Coast Guard has, and it teaches the subject to its coxswains and boat crew members under the general topic heading of "Team Coordination and Risk Management." The central concept in team coordination is simple—get everybody on board paying attention (situational awareness) and communicating (team coordination). The central theme in risk management is just as straightforward—identify all the hazards, eliminate those you can, and figure out how to compensate for those you can't eliminate. Of course, the risk assessment must be reworked continually as the situation changes. The principles discussed here can be applied aboard any boat.*

Overview

Introduction

This chapter addresses human error and risk decision-making. Both greatly affect the safety of boat operations. Human error has been and continues to be a significant cause of boat mishaps. Ineffective risk decisions often place boats and crews at greater risk than necessary. Technical knowledge and skill alone cannot prevent mishaps. Operational safety also requires teamwork that minimizes, recognizes, and corrects human errors and a systematic process to continuously assess and manage safety risks.

Prudent seamen have exhibited and human factors researchers have described seven critical skills that reduce the potential for human error–induced mishaps. Within these skills are important processes that serve to control safety risks and improve team performance. These critical skills are collectively titled "Team Coordination." The processes are risk management, crew briefing, and crew debrief.

This chapter mandates the use of team coordination, risk management, crew briefing, and crew debrief as part of standard boat operations. It describes the skills, performance standards for each, coxswain responsibilities and training requirements. It also describes the risk management, crew briefing and crew debrief processes. **To promote these skills and processes, performance in team coordination shall be assessed as part of crew debriefs, Ready For Operations inspections, and Standardization Team visits.**

In this chapter

SECTION A

Team Coordination

Overview

Introduction

A team is a collection of people that uses the technical abilities of its members to achieve a common mission. This chapter discusses how team coordination can:

- control human error,
- manage safety risks,
- and provide directions for continuous improvement in team performance.

In this section

Team Relationship

A.1. THE LARGER TEAM

The boat consisting of the coxswain and crew is a team. But it also is a part of a larger team. Boats seldom perform missions without interacting with other people. Members of this larger team are:

- the mission coordinator (the officer-in-charge or duty officer),
- other assigned Coast Guard assets (aircraft, boats, and cutters),
- other government, commercial and private parties (federal, state, and local officials),
- commercial salvagers, and Good Samaritans, as well as
- the "customer."

In this case, the customer is the person or vessel that is the focus of the mission. The mission is the reason for getting the boat underway.

A.2. COXSWAIN

The coxswain wears two hats as:

1. the person-in-charge of the boat team, and

2. a member of the larger team.

Because the majority of boat missions have inherent safety risks, effective coordination of the boat team and the larger team is a cornerstone for mishap prevention.

Team Coordination and Risk Management

A.3. GENERAL

Team coordination is like having a set of tools that if properly used can:

- control human error,
- manage safety risks, and
- provide direction for continuous improvement in team performance.

Proper use requires team members—the coxswain and boat crew—to use all seven team coordination skills all the time. The skills are the good habits of exemplary leaders. They have been tested within complex missions, under ever changing conditions, and when crew stress and safety risks were high. Like the navigational rules of the road, when team coordination and risk management is properly used, an adequate safety margin for mission operations can be maintained.

A.4. SEVEN TEAM SKILLS

The seven team coordination skills are:

LEADERSHIP: Directing and guiding the activities on the boat, stimulating the crew to work together as a team, and providing feedback to the crew regarding their performance.

MISSION ANALYSIS: Making plans, managing risks, organizing and briefing the crew, assigning tasks, and monitoring mission effectiveness, including debriefing the crew.

ADAPTABILITY AND FLEXIBILITY: Altering a course of action to meet changing demands, managing stress, workload and fatigue to maintain an optimal performance level, and working effectively with others.

SITUATION AWARENESS: Knowing at all times what is happening to:

- the boat,
- the coxswain and crew, and
- the mission.

DECISION-MAKING: Applying logical and sound judgment based on the available information.

COMMUNICATION: Clearly and accurately sending and acknowledging information, instructions and commands, as well as providing useful feedback.

ASSERTIVENESS: Actively participating in problem-solving, by stating and maintaining a position until convinced by the facts that your position is wrong.

Speaking up and/or taking action when appropriate.

Team Coordination Standards

Overview

Introduction

Team Coordination Standards identify expected behaviors among:

- the mission coordinator,
- coxswain, and
- crew

necessary to affect safe mission performance. These standards represent the expected performance in all missions.

Coxswain responsibilities

Coxswain responsibilities represent the minimum required actions of a coxswain to achieve team coordination and risk management.

These standards and responsibilities shall be evaluated as part of crew debriefs, Ready For Operations (RFO) inspections and Standardization Team visits.

In this section

Leadership Standard

B.1. STANDARDS OF LEADERSHIP

The standards of leadership are:

- The boat crew members respect each other. The climate is an open one, in which crew members are free to talk and ask questions about the mission.
- Regardless of assigned duties, the individual with the most information about the situation-at-hand is allowed to participate in mission decisions.
- When disagreements arise, the coxswain and crew directly confront the issues over which the disagreements began.
- The primary focus is on solutions to problems. The solutions are generally seen as reasonable. Problem resolution ends on a positive note with very little grumbling among the coxswain and crew.

B.2. COXSWAIN RESPONSIBILITIES

The coxswain shall:

- Be in charge and give clear and understandable direction to the boat crew.
- Monitor crew safety and progress. If unable to monitor safety, the coxswain shall designate a safety observer.
- Balance and monitor crew workload and manage crew stress.
- Remain approachable and open to ideas and suggestions.
- Update the crew on significant mission changes.
- Provide to the crew timely, constructive feedback on performance.
- Provide to the mission coordinator timely updates on boat status.

Mission Analysis Standard

B.3. MISSION ANALYSIS PROCEDURE

The following steps are involved in mission analysis.

1. The mission coordinator, coxswain, and crew know the mission objective.
2. The mission coordinator and coxswain discuss a plan for the mission.
3. Potential problems are briefly discussed.
4. Time is taken to:
   - assess risks,
   - eliminate unnecessary ones, and
   - reduce unacceptable risks.
5. The crew is briefed on the plan and may provide suggestions.

6. Mission tasks are assigned to specific individuals.

7. Contingency planning is done by the mission coordinator and coxswain.

8. As additional information becomes available, the plan is updated.

9. Some discussion takes place to clarify actions in the event of unexpected problems.

10. The coxswain reviews crew actions and conducts a debrief of the mission.

11. Strengths and weaknesses are identified; remedial actions are assigned to improve future performance.

B.4. COXSWAIN RESPONSIBILITIES

The coxswain shall:

- Discuss mission objectives and hazards with the mission coordinator as part of planning before getting underway. Understand level of risk that the mission has and how much risk the coxswain is authorized to take.

- Take no unnecessary risks and have contingencies to deal with unacceptable risks.

- Brief the crew on mission objectives and the plan. Permit open discussion to ensure that tasks are understood and crew ideas are considered.

- Update plans based on changes in the situation and/or mission objectives.

- Debrief the crew on mission performance; identify areas for improvement.

Adaptability and Flexibility Standard

B.5. ADAPTABILITY AND FLEXIBILITY STANDARD

The following describe the standards for adaptability and flexibility necessary for mission analysis.

- Most distractions are avoided. The crew polices each other for fixation; takes positive action to regain situation awareness.

- The coxswain can decide what information and activities are mission essential. Most nonessential information is set aside.

- Crew tasks are prioritized to ensure safe performance. The boat crew is aware of each others' workload. When a crew member appears overloaded, the workload is redistributed.

- The mission coordinator and coxswain are alert to possible crew fatigue, complacency, or high stress

B.6. COXSWAIN RESPONSIBILITIES

The coxswain shall:

- Remain aware of own stress and own hazardous thought patterns. Take positive action to counter subconscious tendencies to react to the excitement of the moment or arbitrarily discard information that conflicts with own perceptions.

- Implement cross checks of coxswain and crew actions to combat the effects of fatigue for night missions or those that extend time awake beyond 18 hours.

- Remain alert to the effects of complacency and high stress on the crew. Take positive action to manage crew stress.

- Remain alert to work overload within the crew and redistribute work as necessary.

- Notify the mission coordinator if the physiological condition of the crew becomes a safety concern.

Situation Awareness Standard

B.7. SITUATION AWARENESS PROCEDURE

1. The coxswain provides the mission coordinator and the crew with mission status (e.g., current operations and/or perceived location).

2. Changes to situation awareness are verbalized.

3. The crew or mission coordinator recognizes that a risk decision or action must be made and offers suggestions or information to the coxswain. The mission coordinator serves as a check of the coxswain's risk decisions.

4. If the mission coordinator perceives the boat or crew is taking unacceptable risks, positive action is taken to control the situation (e.g., stopping or slowing boat activities and/or providing additional assets).

5. The boat crew checks each other's task performance for errors. Anyone who makes a mistake is informed and makes needed corrections.

6. The coxswain maintains an effective lookout.

B.8. COXSWAIN RESPONSIBILITIES

The coxswain shall:

- Not get underway without an understanding of the mission objective, the known risks, and a plan of action.

- Ensure that the crew understands the mission plan, assigned tasks.

- Remain alert to mistakes in planning and crew errors. Likewise empower the crew to double check coxswain decisions and actions.

- Remain vigilant to changes in the situation. Remain alert to conflicting or ambiguous information that may indicate that the perceived situation is different than the actual one.

- Periodically update the mission coordinator and the crew as to the perceived situation.

Decision-Making Standard

B.9. GENERAL

The following points reflect the standards of decision-making:

- Coxswain decisions reflect a willingness to use available information from all sources.

- Most decisions are timely, but may be affected by stress.

- Most decisions are appropriate for the situation; however the crew may overlook options or discount risk.

- The boat crew does not exhibit hazardous thought patterns (e.g., anti-authority, invincibility, impulsiveness, machismo, or resignation).

- Before the coxswain decides and implements a change in objective, the situation may worsen; however, mission accomplishment is not affected and no loss occurs.

B.10. COXSWAIN RESPONSIBILITIES

The coxswain shall:

- Assess current situation and available information to determine ability to meet mission objectives.

- Make use of available time to develop contingencies or alternative courses of actions.

- Consciously weigh the risks versus the gain. Implement the best contingency or action to address the situation.

- Monitor the situation to ensure that the decision produced the desired outcome.

Communication Standard

B.11. GENERAL

The following items reflect the standards of communication for a boat crew team.

- The boat crew and mission coordinator communicate about the mission as required. Standard terminology is used.

- Receivers acknowledge messages. Receivers ask questions when they do not understand.

- Senders usually pursue confirmation when no response is forthcoming and the message is important.

- When changes to crew tasks occur, all hands are aware. The coxswain states risk decisions to the mission coordinator and crew and as time permits informs the crew of the reasons and any adjustments they have to make.

- The mission coordinator and crew acknowledges their awareness of the risk decisions. Anyone may ask mission-related questions to clarify information.

B.12. COXSWAIN RESPONSIBILITIES

The coxswain shall:

- Use standard terminology in giving commands to the crew and in conducting external communications.

- Ensure that information and orders conveyed to the crew are acknowledged by the intended receiver.

- Communicate intentions associated with risks to the mission coordinator and the crew.

Assertiveness Standard

B.13. GENERAL

The following standards reflect the assertiveness necessary for each member of the boat crew team.

- The mission coordinator, coxswain and/or crew occasionally raise questions about the plan or actions when they are either in doubt, or when they believe the boat is standing into danger. Most of these questions are relevant to risk decision-making.

- The coxswain alerts the crew or mission co-ordinator when input is needed to make risk decisions.
- The crew or mission coordinator responds to the coxswain's request with pertinent, brief, and timely information. Everyone remains open to questions about the mission.
- Suggestions are listened to without criticism.
- Requests for task assistance are made when overloaded.

B.14. COXSWAIN RESPONSIBILITIES

The coxswain shall:

- Speak up when an error or poor judgment is perceived.
- Notify the mission coordinator when the coxswain perceives either: the level of risk has changed; the mission is beyond the capabilities of the boat; or the crew has become overloaded or overly fatigued.
- Encourage input and feedback from the crew.
- Treat questions and concerns of the crew with respect.

SECTION C

Risk Management Process

Overview

Introduction

Risk management shall be performed during the planning and execution of missions. Risk management is an element of the mission analysis skill and is a process to identify and control unacceptable safety risks. Every mission event—getting underway, transit, on scene operations, mooring—has some level of risk and not all the risks are known. Every event requires that risks are kept within controls (safeguards) that have been designed to handle them.

Examples of these controls include the proper use of installed communications and navigation systems and proper execution of operating procedures. Effective risk management is highly dependent upon technical knowledge and experience.

In this section

Four Rules of Risk Management

C.1. GENERAL

To use the risk management process correctly the team must follow these four rules.

C.2. RULE #1

Integrate risk management into mission planning and execution.

- Risk management is an iterative and continuous process.
- Risk management is most effective when it is proactive. Whenever new information on risks is received, the ability to control those risks must be reviewed. The coxswain and crew must remain vigilant and think safety until the boat is secured and the mission is over.

C.3. RULE #2

Accept no unnecessary risks.

- Accepting unnecessary risk does not contribute to the safe accomplishment of a mission. You are accepting unnecessary risk when you operate beyond the known capabilities of the crew and/or boat without considering other alternatives.
- Unnecessary risks often are taken when decision makers rationalize that the boat is the only alternative or that urgency is more important than safety.
- Unnecessary risk taking constitutes gambling with lives, government, and private property.

C.4. RULE #3

Make risk decisions at the appropriate level. Many times mishaps occur because the level of risk is not perceived by an individual.

- Understanding risk is highly dependent upon technical knowledge and expertise; therefore, risk decisions must be made by clear-thinking, technically competent people with an understanding of the situation.

- The mission coordinator and coxswain should work as a team in making risk decisions.

C.5. RULE #4

Accept risks if benefits outweigh costs. Identifying and eliminating unnecessary risk, leaves risk that is either acceptable or unacceptable for mission accomplishment.

- Who owns the mission owns the risk.

- In some cases mission directives outline what is acceptable (like sustaining personnel injury and equipment damage to save lives). However in high stress situations, the line between acceptable and unacceptable may become fuzzy.

- Again, clear-thinking, technically competent people with an understanding of the situation must be involved in the risk decision.

- Again, the mission coordinator and coxswain should work as a team in making risk vs. gain decisions

Risk Management Process, Step 1

C.6. GENERAL

Continuous risk management during the course of boat operations requires cycling through the following seven steps.

C.7. STEP 1

Defining the mission objective and tasks.

Risk Management Process, Step 2

C.8. STEP 2: IDENTIFYING HAZARDS

Identify possible hazards to the boat and the crew. Hazards include anything that can go wrong with equipment, in the environment, or with the team.

- Equipment: Is the equipment functioning properly and can it be expected to function properly throughout the mission?

- Environment: How will the weather, sea conditions, proximity to shoals, vessel traffic, and available light affect the mission?

- People: Is the team properly trained and capable of handling the demands of the mission? Are crew members fatigued, complacent, or suffering from physical or mental stress?

RISK CATEGORIES Hazards must be discussed within the crew and between the coxswain and mission coordinator to ensure that few hazards are missed. Use these risk categories to facilitate discussion:

PLANNING: Was there adequate time and information to develop a good plan? As the planning time increases and more information becomes available, the risk is reduced. As mission complexity increases, the time for planning should also increase.

EVENT COMPLEXITY: The mission is made up of a chain of events. How complex are these events? Do they require significant know-how to perform? Many routine events are complex. As the event requires more know-how and attention to perform correctly, the possibility that something could go wrong increases. Event complexity can be greatly increased by darkness, which in turn increases risk.

ASSET SELECTION: Is the boat and this coxswain and crew best suited to perform this mission? Is the ready boat the right boat? The capability and readiness condition of the boat along with the qualifications, experience, and physiological condition (health and alertness) of the coxswain and crew must be compared to the event complexity and environmental conditions.

COMMUNICATIONS AND SUPERVISION: External communications and supervision—Will the boat be able to maintain good communications with the mission coordinator and other on scene units? Will the mission coordinator be able to provide real-time oversight of boat activities as a double check for safety? The less capable the communications, the higher the possibility that relevant information will not reach decision makers. Risk control may be less effective; double checks will be more difficult.

Communications within the boat—Can the crew hear orders over the ambient noise? Are they assertively communicating through accurate, bold and concise statements?

Supervision of the boat crew—Even if the boat crew is qualified to perform tasks, supervision by the coxswain can act as a control to further minimize risk. The higher the safety risk, the more the coxswain needs to be focused on observing and checking. When coxswains are actively involved in doing tasks, they can be easily distracted and should not be considered effective safety observers in moderate to high risk conditions.

ENVIRONMENTAL CONDITIONS: Are the current and forecasted conditions, in transit and on scene, within the capability of the boat and the crew? As the environment changes, risk controls need to be updated.

Risk Management Process, Step 3

C.9. STEP 3: ASSESSING THE RISKS

Risk is a function of the severity, probability and exposure.

- Severity describes the potential loss. Should something go wrong, what would be the injury to personnel or damage to equipment.

- Probability is the likelihood that the consequences described above will happen.

- Exposure is the amount of time, people or equipment exposed to the hazard.

RISK CATEGORIES Each risk category must be examined in terms of severity, probability and exposure to arrive at a subjective rating of risk. Again it is useful to discuss individual perceptions of risk among the crew and between the coxswain and mission coordinator

HIGH RISK: Risks cannot be managed with constant control.

Loss in terms of personnel injury or equipment damage is expected.

The boat and/or crew is operating beyond their capability.

Whether this risk is acceptable or not is dependent upon the mission objective.

High risk must be communicated to the mission coordinator.

An example is entering the surf zone with a utility boat.

MEDIUM RISK: Risks are manageable with constant control.

Loss is not expected if the situation remains stable, the crew adheres to all standard operating procedures, and boat systems respond as designed.

The boat and/or crew are operating at their capability.

LOW RISK: Risks are manageable with control as required.

Loss is not expected because the mission has established margins of safety in place and the objective will be modified if the margins are reduced.

The boat and/or crew are operating within their capability.

An example is transit of a familiar area at a safe speed during the day in good visibility with a full, qualified crew aboard.

Risk Management Process, Steps 4, 5, 6, & 7

C.10. STEP 4: IDENTIFYING THE OPTIONS

Unnecessary risk has to be eliminated. What changes can be made to reduce risks to an acceptable level without changing the mission objective? This can be done by examining:

- changes to the planned op tempo (e.g., slowing),

- command and control (e.g., more guidance and/or supervision),

- mission tasks (e.g., simplifying),

- timing of tasks (e.g., sequential as opposed to concurrent or daytime as opposed to nighttime),

- boat requirements (e.g., more capable) or crew qualifications (e.g., more experienced),

- number of assigned boats (e.g., standby) and/or crew (e.g., additional members),

- required equipment and/or protective equipment.

If the discussion of options is limited to those that can be provided by the boat, few are available. This step needs to evaluate the options the larger team can recommend to reduce risk. The larger team may have additional resources. The larger team may be able to spread out the risk among responders or transfer the risk to more capable assets.

C.11. STEP 5: EVALUATING THE RISK VERSUS GAIN

Did the mission coordinator validate that the risk assumed by the coxswain is worth the mission objective? If risks seem unacceptable, can the mission objective be modified to reduce risk to an acceptable level?

C.12. STEP 6: EXECUTING THE RISK DECISION

This decision implements the best option given the risks and gains. In executing the decision, the crew is made aware of what the expected outcome should be.

C.13. STEP 7: MONITOR THE SITUATION

Did the action achieve the desired outcome? Are the risks within the mission changing? If so, repeat the steps to manage those risks.

Informal Crew Briefing and Debriefing

Overview

Introduction

Informal crew briefings are required before the boat gets underway. Briefings for the coxswain and the crew helps create a shared mental picture of what is expected to happen and sets rules for the mission.

Informal crew debriefs should be performed after most missions. The debrief is the best opportunity to evaluate performance and recognize individual and team accomplishment. **When correctly performed, the debrief can serve as a valuable tool for continuous improvement.** It can show the way from just 'doing things right' to knowing how to do 'right things right.'

In this section

Informal Crew Briefing

D.1. GENERAL

The informal crew briefing shall be comprised of the following topics:

D.2. INCLUDE THE MISSION OBJECTIVE

Include the mission objective, known information and risks regarding the mission, and the planned course of action.

D.3. SPECIFY DUTIES AND RESPONSIBILITIES

Be specific in assigning duties and responsibilities. Mission coordinator expectations should be understood by the coxswain and conveyed to the crew. Don't let the crew have to second guess what is needed to be done, or in special situations, how it should be done.

D.4. ESTABLISH POSITIVE CLIMATE FOR TEAMWORK

Establish a positive climate for teamwork. The crew is encouraged to double check each other, point out errors, speak up when they have relevant information, and ask questions when they do not understand.

D.5. DISCUSS IMPROVEMENT GOALS

Restate the goal for improving one or two weak areas in crew coordination. This goal was generated from a previous crew debrief. Try to be as specific as possible in describing what is considered an improvement.

Informal Crew Debrief

D.6. GENERAL

The informal crew debrief shall cover the following topics.

D.7. RECAP MAJOR EVENTS

Recap major events of the mission (e.g., preparations, transit, on-scene operations).

D.8. DETERMINE LEVEL OF PERFORMANCE

Determine level of performance within key events. Key events include the crew brief, critical navigation segments of the transit, bar crossings, approaches to vessels, personnel transfers and other hazardous parts of the assigned mission.

D.9. WHAT AFFECTED THE OUTCOME OF EVENTS?

Have the coxswain and crew, and when possible the command, discuss what human behavior or risk decisions affected the outcome in these events. This discussion is for professional growth and learning. Discuss what behavior/decisions exceeded the Boat

Crew Coordination Standards, and what behavior/decisions failed to meet Boat Crew Coordination Standards.

D.10. HAS GOAL BEEN MET?

Determine if the goal to improve one or two weak coordination areas had been met.

D.11. SET NEW GOALS

Set, change, or affirm a specific goal for improving one or two weak areas in crew coordination. Goals are set or changed with the knowledge and guidance of the command.

First Aid

Editor's Note: Boaters should know basic first aid—no exceptions. The very nature of boating means some time will pass between an injury or the onset of illness and the availability of professional help. You can find competent first aid instruction right in your own community through the Red Cross or your local emergency response organizations. The discussions in this chapter deal with the most likely health emergencies encountered on the water—hypothermia and heat sickness, lacerations and bone breaks, sea creature bites and stings, exhaustion, cardiovascular problems, and similar events. You'll notice that Coast Guard crews are trained to identify and treat shock as a part of routine first aid for any injury for illness. Also, Coasties are trained to treat, communicate, and transport— a good plan for any boater managing a first aid emergency. A well-equipped medical kit is a must on any boat. So too are a working VHF radio, a cell phone, and barrier protection for dealing with bodily fluids—injured and sick people leak, and exposure to blood-borne and airborne pathogens can be avoided by use of rubber gloves and eye protection available from any pharmacy at minimal cost.

Overview

Introduction

This chapter provides basic first aid and transporting information for injuries encountered in the marine environment. First aid is doing what must be done before expert help is available. It may include:

- Being immediate, and temporary
- Saving life
- Preventing further injury or unfavorable progression
- Preserving vitality and resistance to infection
- Delivering the victim if necessary

In this chapter

SECTION A

Crew Members' Roles

Overview

Introduction

Knowledge and skill in first aid are essential for boat crew members. A well-trained crew that responds effectively and professionally to an emergency situation may be the difference between life and death or between temporary injury and permanent disability of the victim.

In this section

Crew Responsibilities

A.1. GENERAL

The Coast Guard authorizes crew members to render first aid, consistent with their training, in their role as emergency assistants regardless of their first aid qualifications. A unit commander should always be advised of emergency medical situations. In addition, crew members must contact the Station or Group watchstander and request immediate medical assistance for serious injury cases so that appropriate medical resources can be contacted. The Station or Group will activate an established Emergency Medical Services (EMS) system such as 911, or local fire/rescue squad. Crew members providing first aid must do the following:

- Evaluate the scene.
- Consider—are rescuers trained and equipped to safely render assistance.
- Protect themselves from injury or infection.
- Keep calm.
- Act quickly.
- Call station or group as appropriate to activate EMS if necessary.

A.2. SCENE ASSESSMENT

When responding, make a quick survey of the scene. Do not enter an unsafe scene until fully prepared and protected against hazards such as exposed electrical wires, toxic vapors, fire, blood, or body fluids. Remember, if you become injured during a rescue attempt you will be unable to help anyone else and will complicate an already difficult situation.

INITIAL PATIENT ASSESSMENT Stop and assess the overall condition of the victim. Determine whether assisting the patient with the resources at hand is possible or if additional help is required. When more definitive care is required for more serious injury cases, seek assistance immediately. Call for help and activate the local EMS system. The following information is important to gather during an initial assessment:

- Number of patients
- General condition of patient(s)
- Mechanism [type] of injury
- Patient(s) level of consciousness
- Monitoring for causes or symptoms of shock:

  Mechanisms consistent with a serious injury such as a gun shot wound, fall from a great height, major burn, crushing accident, etc.

If the patient's state-of-health has been compromised, for example, prolonged exposure to the elements, dehydration, malnourishment, etc.

NOTE

In this section, serious injury cases are considered those that need attention from a medical professional. A serious case also may be one in which a crew decides the injury is beyond its medical capabilities.

A.3. PROTECTIVE DEVICES

Human blood may contain blood-borne pathogens such as Hepatitis B virus or HIV, which cause Hepatitis B and AIDS, respectively. Crew members should take all reasonable precautions to prevent direct contact with human blood by wearing personal protective equipment (PPE) such as clean disposable gloves or more complete equipment depending on the degree of contamination before making contact with the patient. If available, wear masks and eye protection in any instance of known or suspected respiratory infection (i.e., TB). Dispose of blood-soaked gloves and other material with great care. Contact a medical clinic or emergency room for disposal advice. Coast Guard units should maintain information on medical waste disposal.

> **WARNING**
>
> Unprotected crew members who come in direct contact with human blood should immediately report each incident to their operational command servicing medical facility and follow professional medical advice. Refer to COMDTINST M6220.8, *Prevention of Blood Borne Pathogen Transmission*, for more information.

Handling and Transporting of the Injured

A.4. GENERAL

Transporting injured persons aboard boats to medical treatment facilities is a serious problem regularly encountered by boat crew members. In many situations, it is difficult, if not impossible, for medical help to reach victims. Therefore, the boat crew must possess a basic knowledge of how to transport injured persons safely and quickly to a location where appropriate medical treatment is available.

A.5. COXSWAIN DUTY

The sooner a victim arrives at a place where medical attention is available, the better. It is the responsibility of the coxswain and crew to safely transport the victim as rapidly as possible, while preventing further injury, shock, or unnecessary pain.

A.6. MOVING A PATIENT

Moving a patient is precise work and any carelessness is unacceptable. It requires close teamwork and great care. Even procedures that may seem simple and obvious, such as placing a patient on a stretcher, demand training, coordination, and skill.

These are important rules to remember when transporting an injured person:

- Notify station so that appropriate medical resources can be activated.

- If possible, avoid moving the patient until that person is examined and all injuries are protected by properly applied splints, dressing, etc.

- If head or neck injury is suspected, immobilize prior to movement.

- Seek assistance before moving a patient.

- For conscious patients, always explain the move procedure in advance.

- Patient movements should be careful, deliberate, and the minimum required.

- Almost all patients are transported lying down.

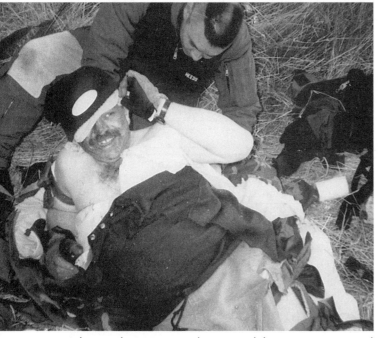

Adequately preparing the injured for transport is vital for preventing further injury.

Treatment for Shock

Overview

Introduction

Shock can be effectively reduced or eliminated if proper steps are taken. It is important that crew members understand how to identify and treat shock. Shock may accompany injury and can reduce a victim's ability to deal with and survive serious injuries. Shock by itself, even when no injuries are involved, can be very serious and life threatening. **Crew members must be aware of the events and symptoms that cause shock.**

In this section

Topic	See Page(s)
Shock Syndromes	49–51
Anaphylactic Shock	51

Shock

B.1. GENERAL

Shock is a depressed physiological or mental state. Shock Syndrome—the set of symptoms that occur together—can change throughout treating an injury and is unique for every casualty. Signs and symptoms of shock may develop rapidly or be delayed for several hours after the triggering event. The symptoms usually precede the signs. Several types of shock exist; therefore, recognizing and treating shock immediately is important. Some symptoms do not appear in every casualty, nor are they equally noticeable.

NOTE

Shock can occur at anytime during administration of first aid and should be assessed first and monitored throughout treatment.

B.2. CAUSES

Some events that typically cause shock are:

- Trauma (bleeding, blunt trauma—e.g., a fall, being struck by a blunt object, etc.—fractures, and burns)

- Allergic reactions

- Hypothermia
- Drugs
- Toxins
- Heart attack
- Illnesses such as diabetes
- Emotional reactions

B.3. SYMPTOMS AND SIGNS

Symptoms include:

- Restlessness
- Faintness
- Thirst
- Nausea
- Weakness
- Anxiousness
- Fright
- Dizziness

Signs include:

- Pulse—weak and rapid
- Breathing—shallow, rapid, and irregular
- Skin—cold, clammy (sweating)
- Pupils—dilated
- State of consciousness—alert (may be deceiving) to unconscious

B.4. ASSESSMENT

Strong signs and symptoms of shock can be identified by observing the victim's skin color, pulse rate, respiration rate and level of consciousness. The table below describes the signs of shock.

B.5. TREATMENT

To properly treat shock once it has been identified, boat crew members must administer initial treatment, followed by executing steps to ensure the effects of shock are kept at a minimum.

INITIAL TREATMENT Initial treatment for shock includes limiting the patient's activity and remaining alert for the signs and symptoms of shock. Have the patient lie down if possible. If the patient is unconscious activate EMS response and institute resuscitation procedures.

If CPR is not necessary, then identify other injuries, lie the victim down, keep the victim warm if the victim is not already overheated.

CONTINUING TREATMENT Additional procedures must be followed and completed to control the effects of shock upon the victim:

- Check for "medic alert" or other information tags
- Obtain history for medical problems (heart disease, diabetes, allergies, medications)

Assessing Shock		
Area	**Normal**	**Signs**
Skin Color	Adult skin is normally dry, not excessively pale or wet to the touch, and the observed mental condition is normally calm.	A person in shock may have pale looking skin that is cold and clammy to the touch.
Eyes		Pupils appear to be dilated.
Pulse	Normal pulse for an adult is regular, strong, and between 60–100 beats per minute.	A shock patient will appear restless, and has a pulse that feels weak and is more rapid than normal, usually greater than 100 beats per minute.
Respiration	Normal adult respiration is between 16–24 breaths per minute.	A strong indicator of respiratory distress would be less than 16 breaths per minute, rapid and irregular, or greater than 24 breaths per minute. Immediate assistance is required in these instances to avoid respiratory arrest.
Consciousness	Any time a patient's level of consciousness is other than fully alert, it is a serious indication to seek medical assistance immediately.	A person's level of alertness can appear anywhere from fully alert to unconscious.

- Notify station or group to obtain help and transport as advised
- Provide specific treatment if advised and trained to do so
- Position—flat on back, elevate the lower extremities about 8 to 10 inches, if no head injury or trouble breathing and being careful of any other injuries (see Figure 5-1)
- Cardiopulmonary resuscitation (CPR) if indicated and trained to provide
- Warm with blankets (if hot, do not warm)
- Moisten lips, do not allow patient to eat or drink
- Never give alcohol
- Handle gently

Anaphylactic Shock

B.6. GENERAL

Anaphylactic shock is a rapid, extreme allergic reaction. People who are subject to this type of shock should carry medical identification at all times. Sensitivity reactions can occur within seconds of contact and can result in death within minutes of contact. It is imperative that personnel are able to recognize the signs and symptoms of anaphylactic shock in order to relay the gravity of the situation to qualified medical personnel.

B.7. CAUSES

Anaphylactic shock can be caused by eating fish or shellfish, ingesting particular types of berries or oral drugs such as penicillin. Reactions also can be caused by insect stings (yellow jackets, hornets, wasps, etc.), injected drugs, exercise, cold, and inhaled substances such as pollen or dust.

B.8. SYMPTOMS AND SIGNS

Symptoms of anaphylactic shock include:

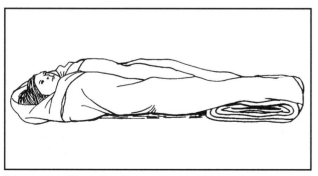

Figure 5-1 Elevating Lower Extremities

- Skin: itching; hives (raised rash); flushing (redness)
- Swelling of lips; tongue; feet; throat; hands
- Respiratory tract: wheezing; shortness of breath; coughing
- Gastrointestinal: nausea and vomiting; abdominal cramps; diarrhea
- Headache
- Sense of impending doom
- Loss of consciousness

Onset of symptoms may be rapid, within seconds, or delayed (up to two hours).

The signs for anaphylaxis are the same as those of shock.

B.9. TREATMENT

Anaphylactic shock requires medication to counteract the allergic reaction to the substance. If the victim carries an epinephrine kit, you may assist them in administration, if trained. Treat the victim for shock and, if necessary, proceed to administer CPR.

- do not minimize an allergic reaction
- death can occur within minutes
- always keep station apprised of the situation so that appropriate medical resources can be activated: medical attention should be obtained regardless of patient's response
- record all that is observed or performed
- reactions with similar symptoms include hyperventilation; alcohol intoxication; hypothermia; low blood sugar; anxiety attack

Resuscitation Methods and Emergencies

Overview

Introduction

When a person stops breathing, seconds count. Death can occur within four to six minutes after respiratory failure. It is imperative to start resuscitation immediately. Boat crew members are required to attend training every six months to learn and maintain effective resuscitation methods and skills. Auxiliary crew members, although not required, are encouraged to maintain their skills through training by qualified, certified instructors and maintain their record of certification.

Events that may cause people to stop breathing include:

- Near-drowning
- Suffocation
- Electrocution
- Poison gas
- Heart attack
- Drug overdose
- Choking

In this section

Resuscitation Procedures

C.1. GENERAL

Resuscitation is a general term that covers all measures taken to restore life or consciousness to an individual. Measures taken to restore life include artificial respiration, cardiac compression, and cardiopulmonary resuscitation (CPR).

C.2. ARTIFICIAL RESPIRATION

Artificial respiration, starting normal respiratory function, includes rescue breathing maneuvers such as mouth-to-mouth, mouth-to-nose, and mouth-to-stoma. A stoma is the opening in the lower neck through which individuals breathe when they have had their voice box removed.

C.3. CARDIAC COMPRESSION

Cardiac compression is a method used to restore normal blood flow to the brain.

C.4. CPR

Cardiopulmonary resuscitation (CPR) uses both artificial respiration and cardiac compression to revive a victim with respiratory failure. Once started, it must be continued until properly relieved. The resuscitation procedures are outlined in the following list.

1. **Establish unresponsiveness:** attempt to rouse the victim by shaking and shouting (initial eval-

uation entails determination of patient's responsiveness). Activate EMS prior to starting any further evaluation or treatment.

Look: to see if the chest rises and falls

Listen: for air exhalation through nose and mouth

- Clear the victim's airway if there are no signs of exhalation and listen again for air exchange.

Feel: for the victim's pulse and air flow from nose or mouth

- If there is no pulse or respiration, call for help immediately. Attempt two breaths of CPR, and, if there is no response, perform the 1-man CPR procedure prescribed by the American Heart Association or American Red Cross for Basic Life Support.

2. **Treat for shock.**

3. **Perform CPR:** if the victim's heart stops or respiratory failure reoccurs after initial resuscitation, reinstitute CPR.

4. **Obstructed Airway Procedures:** should be performed if the victim begins choking.

- Attempt to clear the object first by chest thrusts (infants, obese, or pregnant persons) and back blows (infants) or by abdominal thrusts.

- Next, attempt back blows.

- If the object is still not cleared, reposition the patient's airway and sweep his or her throat. Do not probe blindly as this may force the object deeper into the throat.

- Continue with back blows or abdominal thrusts until the airway is clear or until medical assistance arrives.

Heart Attack

C.5. GENERAL

A **heart attack** is always considered a medical emergency since the victim is in significant danger of going into cardiopulmonary arrest and dying. Contact medical assistance immediately.

C.6. SYMPTOMS

There are many symptoms of a heart attack, some of which may not be noticed or recognized by a victim. Though heart attacks can occur without displaying all of these symptoms, the following are all symptoms of a heart attack:

- Severe, crushing type of pain under the breastbone, arms, neck, and jaw
- Profuse sweating
- Shortness of breath
- Extreme anxiety
- Nausea and vomiting
- Bluish discoloration of lips, fingernails, and skin

C.7. TREATMENT

The following is the treatment for a heart attack:

- Keep a victim quiet and at rest. Administer oxygen via face mask.
- Place a victim in the position of most comfort. Sometimes the victim may want to sit up, especially if the person is short of breath.
- Seek immediate medical assistance, activate local EMS system.
- Determine if a victim is on any type of medication for a heart condition such as nitroglycerin. If so, determine if the victim has taken the medication as prescribed.
- Reassure the patient that assistance is on the way or that transport to a hospital is imminent.
- Transport as quickly, but as safely, as possible.

Stroke

C.8. GENERAL

A **stroke** is any bleeding or clotting affecting the blood vessels of the brain. Strokes can be mild or extremely serious and care must be taken to treat and transport stroke victims so that additional injury does not occur. Seek medical attention immediately.

C.9. SYMPTOMS

The symptoms of a major stroke are unconsciousness and shock, analysis of any part of the body or visual disturbances. However, if brain damage is slight, the only symptoms may be:

- visual disturbances,
- dizziness,
- headache,
- facial droop,
- difficulty in speaking, or
- muscular difficulty involving a body part.

Signs and symptoms may be temporary or come and go.

C.10. TREATMENT

Activate EMS. Obtain medical assistance immediately. Treat as for shock. If the victim has difficulty breathing, help the person maintain an open airway and give mouth to mouth resuscitation, if needed.

Scuba Incidents

C.11. COAST GUARD ACTION

The Coast Guard has no statutory responsibility for providing recompression treatment equipment or for managing decompression sickness cases in SAR cases involving self contained underwater breathing apparatus (SCUBA) diving accidents. However, individuals may request Coast Guard assistance in locating appropriate treatment facilities and for transport to such facilities. The Coast Guard shall limit assistance to arranging or providing transportation for victims and advising interested parties of the location for the nearest recompression facility. The Coast Guard boat crew should treat for shock (do not elevate the legs), while arranging for evacuations.

C.12. TYPES OF SCUBA INCIDENTS

Scuba diving accidents include all types of body injuries and near-drowning. Commonly, a scuba diving accident occurs due to an existing medical problem. There are two special problems usually seen in scuba diving accidents:

- Air emboli
- The "bends"

AIR EMBOLI, or air bubbles in a diver's blood, are most often found in divers who hold their breath during ascent. This typically happens following an equipment failure, or some other underwater emergency. Divers can develop an air embolism in very shallow waters. The onset of symptoms is often rapid and a victim's senses may become distorted. Victims may have convulsions and can quickly lose consciousness.

THE "BENDS" is decompression sickness, which may occur as the result of coming up too quickly from a deep, prolonged dive. Rapid ascent defeats the body's ability to filter escaping gases through the lungs resulting in nitrogen gas bubbles in the blood stream. The onset of the "bends" is usually slow for scuba divers, taking from one to 48 hours to appear. Divers increase the risk of decompression sickness if they fly within 12 hours after a dive. The symptoms and signs of decompression sickness include deep pain to the muscles and joints, choking, coughing, labored breathing, chest pains, and blotches on the skin (mottling).

NOTE

Immediately transport or evacuate all patients with possible air emboli or decompression sickness to the nearest medical facility.

ASSOCIATED MEDICAL PROBLEMS Major medical problems associated with the escape of air into the chest cavity or tissues may occur in asthmatics who participate in scuba activities. The symptoms may be acute shortness of breath and the signs may be similar to shock. Immediate advance medical attention is required. Activate EMS and transport as quickly as possible. Treat for shock.

C.13. TREATING SCUBA INCIDENTS

Position a patient for optimum breathing comfort, which for a conscious patient is usually sitting up:

- Treat for shock
- Do not let a patient lie flat or elevate legs
- Get dive profile

C.14. EQUIPMENT AVAILABILITY

Each District Rescue Coordination Center (RCC) and Group Operations Center (OPCEN) has information on all recompression chambers located within its area of operations. In addition, Diver's Alert Network (DAN) can be contacted by telephone for further assistance at (919) 684-8111. The RCC or OPCEN will need the following medical information to arrange the correct response for a scuba incident:

- Depth of a victim's diving activities
- Number of dives that day
- Victim's overall medical condition including current level of consciousness
- First occurrence of victim's symptoms (i.e., during ascent, immediately after reaching the surface, etc.)
- Problems which may have occurred during the dive, such as a panic ascent, loss of air at depth, or equipment failure

Treatment for Wounds, Fractures, and Burns

Overview

Introduction

In emergency situations, boat crew members must be able to temporarily treat severe hemorrhaging wounds, broken bones, and burn victims. As the first on the scene, boat crew members must try to keep a victim calm, immobile, and alive until professional medical assistance can be provided.

In this section

Topic	See Page(s)
Bandages	54–55
Bleeding	55–58
Fractures (Broken Bones)	58–62
Burns	62–63

Bandages

D.1. GENERAL

This section provides basic information about first aid bandages and splints. Preferably, use sterile bandage material in standard first aid or EMT kits. Otherwise, any large piece of clean cloth can be used as a bandage, binder, or sling.

D.2. TYPES OF BANDAGES

A bandage is a strip of woven material that holds a wound, dressing, or splint in place, helping to immobilize, support, and protect an injured part of the body.

Various types of bandages come in first aid kits. They are designed to be adaptable to many different situations. For example, some are for covering large areas but may be used as slings and others are useful as a thick pad for applying pressure over a wound to control hemorrhaging. The following list describes the different types of bandages and their uses.

BINDER: A binder of muslin is used for injuries to the chest or abdomen. Use a large towel or part of a sheet as a substitute for a binder. Hold the binder in place with pins, multiple ties, or other bandages—

e.g., cravat bandages. Do not apply a binder so tightly that it interferes with breathing.

GAUZE BANDAGES: Gauze is useful as a bandage for almost any part of the body. Most common uses of gauze bandages are as circular bandages and spiral bandages.

BAND-AIDS: Band-Aids or substitutes are useful for small wounds that are clean.

TRIANGULAR BANDAGES: Triangular bandages are useful as an emergency cover for an entire scalp, hand, foot, or other large area. Also, use these bandages as a sling for a fracture or other injury to an arm or hand. A triangular bandage can be rolled into a cravat bandage (a long, narrow strip). It is also useful as a figure eight bandage, tie for a splint, constricting band, or tourniquet. A folded cravat bandage can serve as an emergency dressing for control of bleeding, or over another dressing, to provide protection and pressure.

NOTE

If bandages are not available, other emergency bandages can be handkerchiefs, linen, belts, ties, etc. Hold a substitute bandage in place with adhesive, plastic, or masking tape, safety pins, etc.

D.3. BANDAGE APPLICATION

There are two general principles for bandage application:

- A bandage should be snug, but not so tight as to interfere with circulation either at the time of application or later if swelling occurs.
- A bandage is useless if tied too loosely.

CIRCULATION Prevent interfering with circulation by:

- Leaving the person's fingertips or toes exposed when applying a splint or bandage to arms or legs.
- Loosening bandages immediately if a victim complains of numbness or a tingling sensation.
- Watching for swelling, color changes, and cold or cool tips of fingers or toes.

Bleeding

D.4. GENERAL

Hemorrhage, or bleeding, is the escape of blood from arteries, veins, or even capillaries because of a break in their walls.

D.5. TYPES OF BLEEDING

There are several different types of bleeding. Boat crew members must learn to recognize the basic types in order to know how to stop the hemorrhaging as quickly as possible. Types of bleeding include:

- Arterial
- Venous
- Capillary

ARTERIAL BLEEDING Blood that is coming from an artery is bright red and gushes forth in jets or spurts that are synchronized with the victim's pulse.

VENOUS BLEEDING Blood coming from a vein is dark red and comes in a steady flow.

CAPILLARY BLEEDING Blood coming from damaged capillaries (smaller veins) is bright red in color and oozes from the wound.

D.6. RISK ASSESSMENT AND MANAGEMENT FOR PREVENTION OF BLOOD-BORNE PATHOGENS

Evaluate the risk of acquiring a blood-borne pathogen such as Hepatitis B or HIV. Risk may be managed by the use of appropriate personal protective equipment. Use at least latex or vinyl gloves. More extensive equipment may be required depending on the situation. If not trained or equipped to handle the situation, notify the group or station so that appropriately trained and equipped personnel can be mobilized. Do not become involved if not adequately protected.

UNIVERSAL MEDICAL PRECAUTION In those instances where crew members may be exposed to human tissues (e.g., blood, seepage from burns, saliva, urine or feces), members should take appropriate precautions to prevent contamination by using protective gloves and goggles. Additional precautionary measures include the wearing of masks and protective gowns or aprons. Under all circumstances, thorough washing of hands and any contaminated area should be done with soap and water. Thoroughly wash hands with soap and water, even if gloves have been used.

D.7. CONTROL OF BLEEDING

Control of a severe hemorrhage is always urgent. With only 10 pints of blood in the human body, arterial bleeding can cause death in a short time.

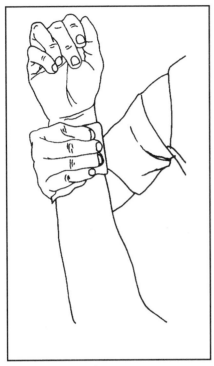

Figure 5-2 Applying Direct Pressure

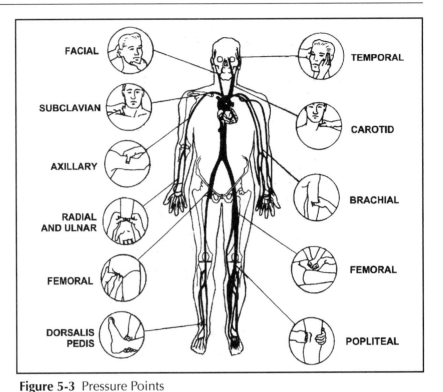

Figure 5-3 Pressure Points

DIRECT PRESSURE The best method to control hemorrhaging is applying direct pressure to the wound. To apply direct pressure, place the palm of a gloved hand over the wound. Use sterile disposable gloves and never apply an ungloved hand onto an exposed wound. To reduce the flow of bleeding, raise the injury so that it is at a level higher than the heart. Do this only if a change in position will not cause additional harm to a victim (see Figure 5-2). If immediately available, or if direct pressure does not control the bleeding, try using a thick pad of cloth held between the gloved hand and the wound.

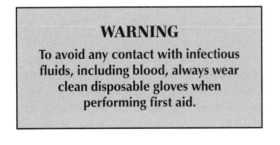

WARNING

To avoid any contact with infectious fluids, including blood, always wear clean disposable gloves when performing first aid.

PRESSURE POINTS If bleeding persists after applying direct pressure or if there is severe arterial bleeding, digital pressure can be applied at pressure points. Pressure points are areas in the body where a major artery flows over a bony prominence. There are 26 pressure points in the human body, 13 on each side, situated along the main arteries (refer to Figure 5-3):

- Temporal
- Facial
- Carotid
- Subclavian
- Axillary
- Brachial
- Radial and Ulnar
- Femoral
- Popliteal
- Doralis pedis

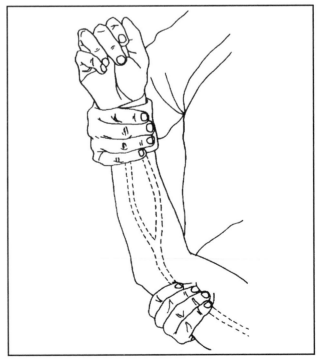

Figure 5-4 Brachial Artery

Always be extremely careful when applying indirect pressure (pressure points) as it may cause damage to the limb due to inadequate blood flow. Do not substitute indirect pressure for direct pressure, use both simultaneously. Refer to the table below for location of pressure points and related areas, and the procedure to apply pressure to each area.

D.8. TREATMENT

Refer to the following list for procedures for treating hemorrhages.

BANDAGE APPLICATION: Apply a sterile, if available, or clean piece of gauze or cloth to the wound. Do not remove this dressing if it becomes blood soaked. Reinforce the dressing with a second or third bandage on top of the original one. Elevating the extremity after applying direct pressure should control most bleeding.

PRESSURE BANDAGE: A pressure bandage can replace direct hand pressure on most parts of the body. Apply the pressure bandage by placing the center of the bandage or strip of cloth directly over

Pressure Points

Pressure Point	Location	Procedure
Temporal	Scalp or head	Use this pressure point for no longer than 30 seconds as it may cut off blood to the brain.
Facial	This point is located in the "ridge" along the lower edge of the bony structure of the jaw.	Use only for a minute or two to help slow blood flow from a cut on the face.
Carotid	Begin at the trachea at the midline of the neck	Slide your fingers to the sight of the bleeding and feel for the pulsations of the carotid artery. Place fingers over the artery and thumb behind the neck. Apply pressure by squeezing fingers toward the thumb. Never apply pressure to both sides of the neck at the same time. Apply pressure for only a few seconds as this procedure cuts off blood circulation to the brain.
Subclavian	Deep behind the collar bone in the "sink" of the shoulder	Push thumb through the thick layer of muscle at the top of the shoulder and press the artery against the collarbone.
Axillary	Under the upper arm	Press the artery just under the upper arm against the bone from underneath.
Brachial	Groove on the inside of the arm and elbow; two locations, near the elbow joint.	Apply pressure to the point, grasp the victim's arm with the thumb on the outside of the arm and fingers on the inside. Press fingers towards the thumb. See Figure 5-4.
Radial and Ulnar	Radial point located on forearm close to the wrist on the thumb side of the hand; ulnar point located on little finger side of the hand	Apply pressure to both points to control bleeding of the hand. Use the radial point to control bleeding of the wrist.
Femoral	Front center part of the crease in the groin area, pelvic basin; two locations	Used to control severe bleeding on the lower extremity and leg amputation. Place heel of the hand directly on the point and apply a small amount of pressure to the artery across the pelvic basin.
Popliteal	Back of the knee	Apply pressure to the point to control bleeding from a leg wound.
Dorsalis Pedis	Top of foot	Apply pressure to control bleeding from the foot and toes.

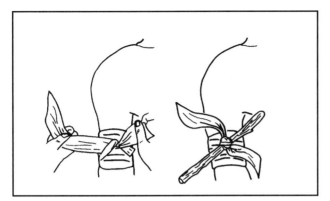

Figure 5-5 Pressure Bandage

the pad. Hold the pad in place by circling the bandage ends around the body part and tie it off with a knot directly over the pad (see Figure 5-5).

ELEVATING INJURED AREA: If direct pressure does not control the bleeding, then elevate the injured area, but only if no bone injury is involved.

PRESSURE POINTS: Apply pressure by placing the heel of the gloved hand directly over the spot. Lean forward with the arm straight to apply direct and constant pressure.

TOURNIQUET: If severe bleeding cannot be controlled after trying all other means and the victim is in danger of bleeding to death, use a tourniquet. Remember that a tourniquet is useful only on arms and legs. A tourniquet is a constricting band placed around an extremity, then tightened until bleeding from an artery has stopped. When a tourniquet is required, use the tourniquets available in a standard Coast Guard first aid kit. Otherwise, use any wide gauge material such as a webbed belt strap with a buckle.

Apply a tourniquet as outlined in the following steps.

APPLYING TOURNIQUETS Refer to the following list when applying a tourniquet.

1. Place the tourniquet two to three inches above the wound, but not touching the wound edges. If the wound is in a joint area or just below a joint, place the tourniquet directly above the joint.

2. Wrap the tourniquet band tightly around the limb twice and secure it in place.

3. Attach a note to the victim giving the location of the tourniquet and the time that it was applied. Always leave the tourniquet exposed to view. If it is not possible to attach a note, write the letter "T" on the patient's forehead with a grease pen,

lipstick, or other suitable marker, and show the time it was applied.

4. After making the decision, and applying a tourniquet, DO NOT LOOSEN IT. This requirement may be modified, but only under the following circumstances. As soon as the tourniquet is applied, if the injured person does not otherwise require treatment for other life threatening conditions (e.g., shock or hypothermia), the wound site should be cleaned to facilitate evaluation of the bleeding site. Once the source of the bleeding has been identified, the crew man can now initiate primary control of the bleeding by direct pressure or packing with pressure, followed by the release of the tourniquet. The process of bleeding control (i.e., direct pressure, pressure points) can be repeated as necessary.

5. Continue to treat for shock and obtain medical attention IMMEDIATELY.

> ## WARNING
> **Tourniquets can be extremely dangerous! Tourniquets should only be used when a victim is in danger of bleeding to death! A tourniquet should only be tight enough to stop the bleeding! Never hide a tourniquet with a splint or bandage.**

Fractures (Broken Bones)

D.9. GENERAL

Broken bones are frequently encountered by boat crews in the course of many rescue situations. It is important to develop the ability to identify fractures immediately and treat them properly. Failure to do so can seriously complicate a fracture as well as cause other injuries.

D.10. TYPES OF FRACTURES

A fracture is a broken or cracked bone. For performing first aid, boat crew members should be aware that there are two types of fractures:

- **Compound (open) Fracture:** The bone has broken and an open wound is present. The bone may protrude from the wound, leaving little doubt that there is a fracture.

- **Simple (closed) Fracture:** No open wound is present, but the bone may be broken or cracked. Take care when handling a closed fracture as careless treatment may cause an open fracture, lacerate a blood vessel, or cause more injury.

D.11. SYMPTOMS

Indications that a fracture has occurred may include:

- Pain, swelling, and discoloration at the injury site
- Misalignment (deformity) and/or disability of the injured part
- Victim's information (may have heard a "crack" or "snap")

D.12. HANDLING A FRACTURE

Treat every suspected fracture as if it were a fracture until it is proven otherwise. Handle as follows:

LIMIT MOVEMENT Do not attempt to straighten broken limbs. Eliminate all unnecessary handling of the injured part. Be gentle and use great care when handling any broken limb.

IMMOBILIZE Protect and immobilize all injured areas. Check for the possibility of more than one fracture. Do not be deceived by the absence of deformity and/or disability. (In many fracture cases, the victim may still have some ability to use the limb). Keep the broken bone ends and the joints immobilized above and below the injury.

CHECK PULSE Check pulse in the area of the fracture before and after splint application.

SPLINT Use a splint to immobilize the fracture. Selecting exactly the proper splint is less important than achieving immobilization. Whenever possible, splint a fractured arm to the patient's chest and a fractured leg to the other (unbroken) leg. Apply splints before moving the victim, while avoiding manipulating the injured areas. Apply the splint snugly, but do not cut off circulation. Splints should be well padded. Leave tips of fingers and toes exposed and check them often for circulation adequacy.

SHOCK Treat the injured person for shock. (Refer to Section B of this chapter.) Be alert for the development of shock during treatment. Shock may develop as a result of the fracture, pain from the treatment or other injuries not evident on initial assessment.

D.13. TREATMENT OF SPECIFIC BONES

In the human body there are 206 bones. Several of these bones, if broken or injured, require very specific treatment based on the sensitive nature of their functions or their proximity to delicate organs or arteries.

SPINE Any actual or suspected damage to the spine requires definitive care and careful management. Permanent disability, paralysis, or death can result from a spine injury.

- Treat all suspected spinal injuries by maintaining alignment and immobilizing the spine as quickly and completely as possible.
- Seek further medical assistance immediately.
- Move a patient only as a last resort.
- Keep a patient flat and do not move the person's head.
- When transporting a patient, immobilize on a rigid stretcher and carry the patient face up.
- Do not splint neck and spine fractures unless properly trained.

SKULL The primary aim is to prevent further injury to the head, so do not spend time figuring out whether there is a fracture or penetration to the skull.

- Do not let a patient move or try to move the person any more than absolutely necessary.
- Do not let a patient with a head injury become cold and do not give the person anything to drink or any pain medication.
- Control bleeding by the use of absorbent dressings without applying direct pressure.
- Seek immediate medical assistance.

EXTREMITIES When encountering actual or suspected fractures to any of a victim's extremities, these are the general steps that must be followed:

1. Check for a pulse and sensation of touch in fingers or toes before and after a splint has been applied. If either of these is absent, it increases the likelihood of permanent damage. Make certain a splint is not applied over a bony prominence or tied too tightly. Loosen if necessary to reestablish feeling and pulse.

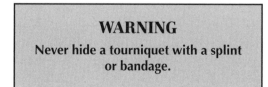

WARNING
Never hide a tourniquet with a splint or bandage.

2. If possible, splint the injured part in proper alignment. If this is not possible, splint to immobilize the limb in the position found.

3. If bone ends protrude from the skin, cover the exposed bone with a sterile dressing and handle with great care when splinting.

FOREARM Place two well padded splints, top and bottom, from elbow to wrist. Bandage in place. Hold the forearm across the chest with a sling (see Figure 5-6).

UPPER ARM For fracture near the shoulder, put a towel or pad in the armpit, bandage the arm to the body, and support the forearm in a sling. For fracture of the middle upper arm, use one splint on the outside of the arm, shoulder to elbow. Fasten the arm to the body and support the forearm in a sling. For a fracture near the elbow, do not move the arm at all. Splint it as it is found (see Figure 5-7).

THIGH Due to the large artery and muscle mass, this is often a major injury and a traction splint may be required. Seek immediate medical assistance. This treatment management requires an EMT or person with more detailed training.

If an EMT or other qualified person is unavailable:

1. Use two splints, an outside one from armpit to foot and an inside one from crotch to foot.

2. Fasten the splints around the ankle, over the knee, below the hip, around the pelvis, and below the armpit.

3. Tie both legs together. Do not move a patient until this has been done (see Figure 5-8).

This injury is often associated with major trauma and bleeding may occur if the thigh bone severs the adjacent femoral artery. Closely monitor a patient for signs of shock and do not manipulate the leg.

LOWER LEG Use three splints, one on each side and one underneath. Always pad these splints well, especially under the knee and at the ankle bones. Also, use a pillow under the leg with the edges brought around in front and pinned; then add two side splints (Figure 5-9).

COLLARBONE Use the following procedures to immobilize the collarbone:

1. On the injured side, place the forearm across the chest, palm turned in, thumb up, with hand four inches above the elbow.

2. Support the arm in this position with a sling.

3. Fasten the arm to the body with several turns of bandages around the body and over the hand to keep the arm close against the body (Figure 5-10).

RIB A broken rib can be very painful and very dangerous because of the opportunity for a broken rib to puncture a lung. A patient coughing up frothy bright red blood may have a punctured lung. Seek assistance immediately and activate EMS.

If the crew member believes that a rib is broken, but the victim indicates that there is no pain, then do not do anything to try to ease pain (see Figure 5-11).

Administer oxygen with patient at rest in a sitting position. This eases the effort required to breathe. Patients with known or suspected fractured ribs should be given a high priority for transport to a medical facility.

NOSE Stop the bleeding. If conscious, have the patient sit with his or her head tilted backward. DO NOT tip head back if victim feels nauseated. A patient should breathe through mouth. A cold compress or an ice bag over the nose eases pain, reduces swelling, and usually stops the bleeding. Place unconscious victim on his or her side to keep airway open.

JAW If an injury to the jaw area interferes with a victim's breathing:

1. Pull the lower jaw and tongue forward and keep them forward.

2. Apply a four-tailed bandage under the jaw, with two ends tied on top of the front of the head.

3. Tie the other two tails on top of the head, and at the back, so the bandage pulls the jaw up and to the rear.

A bandage must support and immobilize the jaw, but not press on the throat. Place an unconscious victim on his or her side. Have a conscious victim sit up.

PELVIS Treat a patient with a pelvis injury for shock, but do not move unless absolutely necessary. When moving a patient, handle the person the same as a victim with a fractured spine.

- Bandage the legs together at the ankles and knees and place a pillow at each hip and secure them.

> **WARNING**
> Never "log-roll" a victim with a pelvic fracture.

Figure 5-6 Broken Forearm

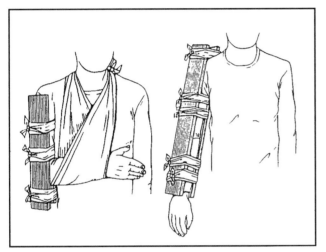

Figure 5-7 Broken Upper Arm

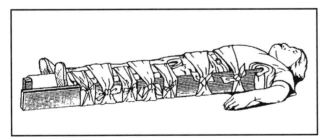

Figure 5-8 Broken Thigh

Figure 5-9 Broken Lower Leg

Figure 5-10 Broken Collarbone

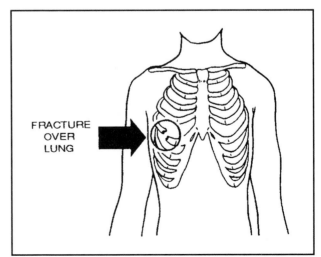

FRACTURE
OVER
LUNG

Figure 5-11 Broken Rib

- Fasten the patient securely to the stretcher.

This injury is often associated with major trauma and frequently involves bleeding that is undetectable. Closely monitor a patient with a pelvic fracture for signs of shock which may be caused by heavy internal bleeding.

Burns

D.14. GENERAL

Burns are classified by depth or degree of skin damage. The following are the three general classifications of burns:

- First degree
- Second degree
- Third degree

D.15. CAUSES OF BURNS

Causes of burns include:

- Thermal
- Chemical
- Sunburn
- Electric shock, and
- Radiation

NOTE

Burns, regardless of the cause, may cause a person to go into shock.

D.16. BURN CLASSIFICATION

Burns can range from minor irritations to life threatening and disabling. Proper first aid, administered quickly, can minimize damage resulting from burns and can make the difference between life and death in serious situations. For these reasons, it is very important that boat crew members be able to quickly determine the type and seriousness of burns in order to treat them quickly and properly. In general, the size of the burn is more important than the degree of the burn.

FIRST DEGREE First degree burns are the mildest form of burns. These burns involve only the outer layer of skin and produce redness, increased warmth, tenderness, and mild pain.

SECOND DEGREE Second degree burns extend through the outer layers of the skin. These burns involve the inner layers of the skin, but not enough to prevent rapid regeneration. They produce blis-ters and are characterized by severe pain, redness, and warmth.

THIRD DEGREE Third degree burns are those that penetrate the full thickness of the skin, destroying both the outer and inner layers. Severe pain, characteristic of second degree burns, may be absent because nerve endings have been destroyed. Color may range from white and lifeless to black (charred). Healing occurs only after many months, and results in scarring of the skin tissue. Skin grafts are generally required to achieve full healing.

NOTE

Burns of the respiratory tract are very serious and may be diagnosed by singed eyelashes, hoarseness, sore throat, or coughing of blood.

D.17. BURN FIRST AID

In order to determine roughly what percentage of a victim's body surface area has suffered some type of damage (burns, etc.), use the following estimates for adult patients:

CHEST	=	18%
BACK	=	18%
EACH ARM	=	9%
EACH LEG	=	18%
HEAD	=	9%
GENITALS	=	1%

General first aid procedures for all burns include the following:

- Eliminate the source of the burn. Extinguish and remove smoldering clothing. Do not remove charred clothing that may be sticking to the burn.
- For burns resulting from electrical shock—ensure the patient is no longer receiving electrical shock.
- Treat to prevent or reduce shock.
- Try to prevent infection.
- Do not apply any type of ointment on burns.

In addition to these general steps, the following are first aid procedures for burns that apply specifically to particular classes of burns.

FIRST DEGREE Minor burns: immerse in cool water until pain is relieved. Flush chemical burns for at least 20 minutes. Cover with clean or sterile airtight wrap. Plastic food wrap applied over a clean or sterile dressing can be used to reduce air exposure.

SECOND DEGREE Use the same treatment as for first degree burns. Do not break open any blisters. Cover with a dry, sterile, non adhesive dressing.

THIRD DEGREE For third degree, or deep, second degree burns:

- Cover the burn to reduce exposure to air.
- Cool the burn.
- Do not remove clothing unless smoldering.
- Treat for shock even if not apparent.
- Always obtain medical care.
- Monitor the patient's airway.
- Assess vital signs every five minutes.
- Give nothing to eat or drink.
- Do not place ice on the burn.
- Do not apply ointments to the burn.
- Burns of the respiratory tract are always a medical emergency.

D.18. CHEMICAL BURNS

Chemical burns of the skin or eyes produce the same type of burn as flash fires, flames, steam, or hot liquids.

FIRST AID First aid for this type of burn is to wash the chemical away completely and as quickly as possible using large quantities of water. Continue flushing the burn for at least 20 minutes.

When the burn involves an eye, flush the eye with water for five minutes. Then, cover both eyes with a clean, dry, protective dressing and seek medical attention as quickly as possible. Give first aid for shock.

If the chemical is a powder, brush off as much as possible before flushing with water.

SECTION E

Environmental Injuries

Overview

Introduction

Environmental injuries occur when an individual suffers from over-exposure to extreme environmental elements or when taking poor precautions for activity in environmental elements. In severe cases, environmental injuries can cause permanent tissue damage or loss of life. These types of injuries include emergencies caused by heat or cold such as heat stroke or hypothermia.

Additionally, these injuries are not only limited to environmental conditions but include other environmental factors such as injuries inflicted by non-human predators of the habitat. In the marine habitat, environmental injuries include those inflicted by aquatic life.

In this section

Topic	See Page(s)
Emergencies Caused by Heat	63–64
Emergencies Caused by Cold	64–65
Hypothermia	65–68
Near-Drowning	68
Fish Bites and Stings	68

Emergencies Caused by Heat

E.1. HEAT

Excessive heat or prolonged exposure to heat can cause at least three types of emergencies:

- Heat Cramps
- Heat Exhaustion
- Heat Stroke

E.2. HEAT CRAMPS

Heat cramps are painful contractions of various skeletal muscles. They are caused by depletion of salts from body fluids, normally due to excessive sweating.

SYMPTOMS Heat cramps affect the muscles of the extremities and of the abdominal wall. Pain may be severe. Body temperature may be normal or elevated.

TREATMENT The treatment for heat cramps is drinking cool fluids to afford both relief and continued protection. "Sports" drinks may speed up recovery. Do not re-expose to heat for at least 12 hours.

NOTE

The use of hot packs on cramped muscles will only make the situation worse. DO NOT administer salt tablets for heat cramps!

E.3. HEAT EXHAUSTION

Heat exhaustion results from too much fluid loss by perspiration. Even the most physically fit person can fall victim to heat exhaustion while working in a hot environment. With proper treatment heat exhaustion is seldom fatal.

SYMPTOMS The signs and symptoms of heat exhaustion are similar to those of shock. An individual who collapses in the heat and continues to perspire freely almost surely has heat exhaustion. The presence of sweating usually rules out heat stroke.

TREATMENT To treat a person with heat exhaustion:

- Remove the patient from the hot environment to a cool location.
- Place a patient on his or her back, with legs elevated.
- Cool a patient but DO NOT chill.
- If the victim is conscious, administer cool sips of water or sports drink.
- Treat for shock.
- If equipped and trained, administer oxygen.

With general supportive treatment, a victim of heat exhaustion will usually recover consciousness promptly, although the person may not feel well for some time. Do not re-expose to heat for at least 24 hours.

E.4. HEAT STROKE

Heat stroke is a serious medical emergency. The most important sign of heat stroke is an extreme elevation of body temperature, indicating failure of the body's sweating mechanism. Heat stroke calls for immediate measures to reduce body temperatures in order to prevent brain damage and/or death.

SYMPTOMS The symptoms of heat stroke are:

- headache,
- dizziness,
- irritability, and
- vision disturbances.

A person will suddenly become unconscious, have hot, dry skin, and contracted pupils. A heat-stroke victim will also have a full pulse, strong and bounding, may have convulsions, and a body temperature that ranges from 105° to 109°F.

TREATMENT To treat a person with heat stroke:

- Seek help and activate the local EMS.
- Place the patient in the shade or a cool place. Assess breathing and circulation, loosen clothing, and lay the victim down with the head and shoulders slightly elevated.
- Begin the movement of air by fanning with a shirt, electric fan or other means.
- Reduce the body temperature as rapidly as possible to prevent brain damage. Total immersion in an ice water bath is probably the most efficient method. If this is not possible, decrease the patient's body temperature by pouring cool or cold water over the body, rubbing the body with ice and placing pieces of ice in the armpits, or covering the patient with sheets soaked in ice water.
- DO NOT give anything by mouth.
- Treat for shock.

NOTE

Carry out these procedures while seeking additional medical assistance.

Emergencies Caused by Cold

E.5. COLD INJURIES

The type and severity of cold injuries depends on the temperature and amount of exposure an individual has endured. Refer to the table opposite for a description of various cold injury causes and symptoms.

E.6. TREATMENT

When treating cold injuries:

DOs	DON'Ts
• Take care when removing clothing or gear so as not to injure the numbed skin. Remove only if blankets or dry clothing are available.	• DO NOT place anything constricting on the affected area.
• Cover the area with a dry dressing and warm with a blanket.	• DO NOT give the victim alcohol or tobacco.
• Exercise care to prevent infection if open sores are present.	• DO NOT massage or rub the affected parts.
• Under the supervision of a medical professional, rapidly warm a frostbitten body part in a controlled temperature water bath (105° to 110°F).	• DO NOT break blisters.
	• DO NOT thaw an affected part if the transport time is short or if there is a possibility that the

DOs	DON'Ts
Attempt this only where there is a certainty of the water temperature.	body part may re-freeze after warming.
• Transport the patient to an appropriate medical facility as soon as possible.	• DO NOT give alcohol.
• Monitor for shock.	

Hypothermia

E.7. GENERAL

Hypothermia is a lowering of a person's core temperature. It occurs when a person suffers a loss of body heat. General body hypothermia is the leading cause of death among survivors of shipwrecks, and other disasters at sea. If not recognized and treated promptly, hypothermia can rapidly turn survivors into fatalities. Survivors in critical hypothermia conditions may suffer a fatal loss of body temperature from physical exertion, or as a result of any delay in taking immediate and positive measures to restore body heat. Struggling survivors, trying to aid in their own rescue, may drive their body temperature down to the point where unconsciousness and/or death results. Survivors removed from the water and left untreated may suffer further critical loss in body temperature, bringing on death after rescue. Note that survivors in "warm" water can also suffer from hypothermia if exposed for long enough periods of time. Also, cold air temperatures can bring on hypothermia if adequate protective clothing is not worn.

NOTE

Never treat cold injuries lightly! Tissue loss and nerve damage are caused by these injuries.

Cold Injuries

Injury	Cause	Symptoms
Chilblains	Repeated exposure for several hours at a time to temperatures between 32° and 60°F, generally associated with high humidity.	Signs and symptoms include: redness and swelling, itching dermatitis, tingling, and deep aches in later stages.
Immersion Foot	Exposure to cold water 50°F and below for 12 hours or more, or exposure to water of approximately 70°F for several days.	Signs and symptoms include: swelling of the legs and feet, cyanosis (a bluish discoloration, especially of the skin due to a lack of properly oxygenated blood), numbness, tingling, itching, blisters, intense burning pain, and neuromuscular changes.
Trench Foot	Exposure to cold between 32° and 50°F, damp weather for periods ranging from several hours to 14 days. The average length of exposure to produce symptoms is three days. The body part affected blanches, tingles, then becomes numb.	Signs and symptoms include: swelling of the legs and feet, cyanosis, blisters, intense burning pain, and neuromuscular changes.
Frostbite	Generally, brief exposure to extreme cold –20°F and below, or exposure to approximately 0°F weather for several hours will cause frostbite.	Signs and symptoms include: first burning and stinging then numbness, ice crystals in the skin that cause white or gray waxy color, skin moves over bony prominences, edema (excessive accumulation of fluids within portions of the body), blisters, pain, loss of motion, and gangrene and loss of tissue in later stages.
Freezing	Caused by exposure of skin to temperatures of –20°F and below. May happen rapidly to exposed toes and fingers with other extremities involved as exposure is prolonged.	Signs and symptoms include: ice crystals in entire thickness of the body part, including bone, which is indicated by pallid, yellow waxy color, skin will not move over bony prominences. After thawing, edema, large blisters, intense pain, loss of motion; and gangrene and loss of the body part in later stages.

E.8. SURVIVABILITY

Survival times in water vary considerably. Survival depends on the type of clothing worn, the amount of physical exertion, blood alcohol levels and other factors. Some survivors, when taken aboard during a search and rescue case, may appear to be under the influence of drugs or alcohol. A person moderately hypothermic will manifest symptoms of an intoxicated person.

E.9. SYMPTOMS AND SIGNS

When a victim may be suffering from hypothermia, there are symptoms that are visible and some that must be measured to establish a diagnosis. These include:

- low body temperature
- low blood pressure
- slow, weak pulse
- unconsciousness
- general appearance
- cold skin
- may simulate or accompany shock

Signs may include:

- skin is cold
- shivering
- clouded mental capacity (may seem disoriented)
- slow and labored breathing
- pulse weak and slow, may be irregular or absent
- dilated pupils
- speech slurred (may seem intoxicated)

BODY TEMPERATURE Body temperature is the most useful yardstick for identifying hypothermia. Hypothermia victims will have a rectal temperature below normal (normal is 98°F–99°F). Only rectal temperatures are of value, since it is the body's core temperature that determines the severity of hypothermia. Neither oral or auxiliary temperatures, nor the temperatures of the extremities, reflect core temperature. DO NOT attempt to take rectal temperatures in the field. Treat the patient as visible signs and symptoms suggest.

NOTE

The leading cause of death in cold water maritime accidents is hypothermia.

Temperature	Visible Signs and Symptoms
99°–96°F	Intense uncontrollable shivering; impaired ability to perform complex tasks.
95°–91°F	Violent shivering; difficulty speaking; sluggish movements; amnesia begins.
90°–86°F	Shivering is replaced by muscular rigidity; muscle coordination impaired; erratic movements.
85°–81°F	Irrational; stupor; lost contact with surroundings; pulse and respiration slow.
80°–78°F	No response to words; reflexes stop working; heartbeat is erratic; victim loses consciousness.
Below 78°F	Failure of heart and lungs; internal bleeding; death.

BLOOD PRESSURE Hypothermia victims may have a lower than normal **blood pressure** (normal is about 120/80).

VISIBLE SYMPTOMS These are outwardly visible symptoms that can help to identify hypothermia victims:

- Slow, weak, and often irregular, **pulse**.
- **Level of consciousness** becomes clouded as their body temperature approaches 90°F and they generally lose consciousness at 85°F.
- **Pale in appearance**, with **constricted pupils, and slow and labored respiration**. **Violent shivering** or **muscular rigidity** may be present. Victims may appear to be intoxicated.

Begin treatment if a victim's **skin feels cold** to the touch.

E.10. RESCUE PRECAUTIONS

When it is suspected a survivor has critical hypothermia, make rescue attempts that avoid rough handling and minimize the amount of exertion by a victim. This can be accomplished by sending a surface swimmer into the water to assist the survivor into the rescue craft. Take care to handle a victim gently. Excessive movement may cause heart beat irregularities which can be fatal. During the rescue and afterwards, keep a patient calm and quiet. DO NOT allow a person to perform any physical activity other than what is absolutely necessary. Exertion can use up large amounts of body heat which would otherwise be available to raise the survivor's internal body temperature.

E.11. BASIC TREATMENT

Treatment for hypothermia will depend on both the condition of a survivor and the facilities available for treating the victim. Survivors who are rational and capable of recounting their experiences (even if shivering dramatically) will generally require only that all wet clothes be removed and dry clothes or blankets and a warm environment be provided for resting.

E.12. ADVANCED TREATMENT

In more serious cases, where victims are semiconscious or near death, contact a medical facility as soon as possible for detailed instructions for proper care and handling. While awaiting medical instructions, immediately administer first aid to survivors using these steps:

1. After recovering a victim from the cold, avoid rough handling of the victim as this can cause further harm. Check for the presence of breathing and heartbeat. If the victim is not breathing and has no heart beat, begin CPR immediately. If the victim is breathing, and has a pulse, gently transfer the person to a warm environment. Be sure to check the person's breathing and heart beat frequently. Always remain prepared to immediately begin CPR if breathing and heart beat stop. Activate EMS. Do not minimize, always obtain medical help.

2. Lay an unconscious or semiconscious victim face up with the head slightly lower than the rest of the body. If vomiting occurs, turn the patient's head to one side. Observe respiration closely and remove any secretions from a victim's nose and mouth.

3. Remove a victim's clothes with minimum movement of the body. Cut the clothes away with scissors or a knife if necessary. If a patient cannot be removed to a compartment to be warmed with blankets, dry clothing, or other warming methods, then DO NOT remove wet clothing. Under these circumstances, the wet clothing is better than no clothing.

4. Give nothing orally. Giving alcohol as a treatment for hypothermia victims is not recommended because it further restricts circulation.

5. Insulate a victim from further heat loss by wrapping the person in a blanket. DO NOT attempt to aggressively rewarm an unconscious or semiconscious victim, as rapid warming can cause dangerous complications. DO NOT rub frozen body areas. A victim will be very sensitive to rough handling. The primary objective after a person has been removed from the water is to prevent the person from getting colder.

6. If properly trained and equipped, administer warm, humidified oxygen by face mask. The oxygen will not only assist victims if they are having difficulty breathing or have a low respiratory rate, it will also provide rewarming of the internal body core.

7. When there will be a delay getting a victim to a hospital, begin gentle rewarming techniques. Rewarming techniques include:

    Wrapping the victim in a blanket. Under the blanket, apply heating pads or hot water bottles (if available) to the victim's head, neck and groin.

    Applying your body warmth by direct body-to-body contact with a victim. A blanket should be wrapped around you and the victim to preserve the heat.

8. Treat for shock. Be alert to the ABC's of shock treatment.

CAUTION!
Semiconscious or unconscious persons should not be given anything to eat or drink.

WARNING
Hypothermia patients are very prone to burns. Hot packs, heating pads, and hot water bottles may cause third degree burns and must be administered with extreme care.

---

9. Evacuate a victim to a medical facility soon after or during emergency treatment. A medical phone patch can be set up through the Coast Guard station if needed. A helicopter with an EMT can be sent to provide help and to evacuate a victim.

Near-Drowning

E.13. GENERAL

Victims who inhale water or who are found floating face-down in the water may be suffering from **near-drowning**. Medical researchers have only recently discovered the phenomenon of the "mammalian diving reflex." In this condition, a person immersed in water (particularly a child), even under ice, could still be alive. Even after extended periods of time, the body delivers a tiny trickle of oxygen to the brain. A victim also exhibits an almost complete constriction of all peripheral blood vessels. Their respiration and circulation almost stop. Properly administered CPR may successfully revive a near-drowning victim without serious complications, even after being underwater for an hour or longer.

E.14. TREATMENT

To treat a person in a near-drowning situation:

- Evaluate ABC's
- Identify any other injuries
- Activate EMS
- Initiate CPR if indicated and trained
- Treat for shock
- Inform station of status of victim
- Transport as soon as possible
- Remove wet clothing
- Treat for hypothermia as appropriate
- Constantly monitor the victim's airway
- Reevaluate victims vital signs every 5 minutes
- Document:
  length of submersion
  water temperature
  fresh or salt water
  drug or alcohol use
  any treatment rendered

Fish Bites and Stings

E.15. GENERAL

Fish bites and stings are another common problem encountered by boat crews during rescues. They can range from innocuous to deadly and boat crew members must be constantly alert to identify bites and stings as quickly as possible.

E.16. TYPES OF BITES AND STINGS

Victims may suffer many different types of bites and stings. The types encountered will depend in a large part on the area of operations and the sea life that exists there. It is important that to become familiar with the most common types of bites and stings that are encountered and the proper treatments for them.

E.17. EFFECTS AND TREATMENT

The table at right describes the effects and proper treatment for various fish bites/stings encountered.

Miscellaneous Emergencies

Overview

Introduction

Boat crew member will face a variety of emergencies that will require performing first aid. This section discusses miscellaneous emergencies that boat crew members will encounter aboard their own vessel or when dealing with marine casualties.

In this section

Topic	See Page(s)
Carbon Monoxide Poisoning	68–69
Poisoning by Mouth	69–70
Eye Injuries	70

Carbon Monoxide Poisoning

F.1. GENERAL

Carbon monoxide (CO) is a colorless, odorless toxic gas that is the product of incomplete combustion. Motor vehicles, heater and appliances that use carbon based fuels are the main sources of this poison.

F.2. SIGNS AND SYMPTOMS

Can include headache, dizziness, fatigue, weakness, drowsiness, nausea, vomiting, loss of consciousness, skin pallor, shortness of breath on exertion, palpitation, confusion, irritability and irrational behavior.

F.3. TREATMENT

Removal the victim from the carbon monoxide–containing atmosphere. Treat for shock. Administer oxygen as available and trained to do so. Start CPR as appropriate.

Poisoning by Mouth

F.4. GENERAL

When poisoning occurs, it is vital that proper first aid be given immediately.

F.5. SEEKING ADVICE

The product container will often include specific treatment instructions. If not, seek medical assistance immediately. The boat crew should contact its unit, provide information about substance taken and an estimate of the quantity taken and have the unit immediately contact the local poison control center. Take the container and any samples of vomit with a victim when transporting to a medical facility.

F.6. MEDICAL ASSISTANCE NOT AVAILABLE

If medical advice is not immediately available and the patient is conscious, determine if the poison is a strong acid, alkali or petroleum product. If any

Treating Fish Bites and Stings

Bite/Sting	Effects	Treatment
Shark and Barracuda Bites	Shark and barracuda bites generally result in loss of large amounts of tissue. Prompt and vigorous action to control hemorrhage and shock are required to save a victim's life.	Control bleeding with pressure dressings, if possible. If not, use pressure points or tourniquets. Seek medical help immediately.
Fish Stings	Fish sting symptoms include: • burning, • stinging, • redness, • swelling, • rash, • blisters, • abdominal cramps, • numbness, • dizziness, • and shock.	Individuals extremely sensitive to fish stings may rapidly go into shock and require immediate evacuation to save their life.
Portuguese Man-of-War and Jellyfish	Jellyfish sting symptoms include burning, stinging, redness, and jelly-like matter from tentacles stuck on the body	For Portuguese Man-of-War and jellyfish stings, remove all tentacles immediately and wash the surface of the skin with alcohol. Apply calamine lotion, meat tenderizer, or ammonia water to neutralize the effects of the toxin contained in the tentacles.
Stingray Injuries	Stingray injuries typically have a small open wound with swelling.	• Immediately irrigate the wound from a stingray with cold salt water. Most of the toxins will wash out and the cold water will reduce the pain. • Immerse the wounded area in hot water for 30 to 60 minutes. Keep the water as hot as a patient can tolerate without injury. • Apply hot compresses to wounds in areas not lending themselves to complete immersion. • Apply a sterile dressing after the soak.

of these have been ingested, do not attempt to induce vomiting by applying pressure to the back of a victim's tongue. Do not induce vomiting if patient is not fully conscious.

> ### CAUTION!
> **Determine if the victim shows signs of a sensitivity reaction to the substance. This will indicate a victim in anaphylactic shock. In this case, treat the victim accordingly (Refer to Section B, "Treatment for Shock.")**

F.7. TREATMENT

Closely observe the ABC's for shock treatment during transport.

Eye Injuries

F.8. GENERAL

Eye injuries are potentially serious, and may be permanent, unless handled promptly and properly. Eyes should be moist. Any dressing applied to eyes should also be moist to prevent excessive drying.

Eye movement is conjugal, that is if one eye moves, the other also moves in the same manner. When dealing with a penetrating injury to an eye, or a foreign object in an eye, the objective is to limit eye movement. Because of conjugal movement, this is best accomplished by covering both eyes. In most cases, a patient with an eye injury is transported sitting up.

F.9. BLINDNESS

Patients who have experienced a blinding injury become totally dependent upon their rescuer. Never leave these patients alone. Keep in constant contact and talk with them continuously to reduce anxiety.

F.10. TYPES OF EYE INJURIES

There are many injuries that may occur to a victim's eyes. Any eye injury is normally the cause of great anxiety for a victim, many times causing more concern than more serious injuries to other parts of the body. As a boat crew member, keep this thought in mind while rescuing or treating victims.

F.11. SYMPTOMS AND TREATMENTS

The following table describes the symptoms and appropriate treatments for the various eye injuries.

Eye Injuries		
Eye Injury	**Symptom**	**Treatment**
Blunt Eye Trauma	Blows to a victim's head and eye area may result in a fracture to the orbit (the bony socket encircling the eye), entrapping vessels and nerves to the eye.	Managing such injuries requires covering both eyes with a moist dressing. This is important since movement by an uninjured eye is mimicked by the injured eye. Refer the patient to medical care for follow up. Since this injury may involve a head injury, closely observe the patient for signs of further damage.
Penetrating Objects and Foreign Bodies	Common objects include fish hooks, wood splinters, or pieces of glass.	Any object that has penetrated the eye must NOT be removed as first aid treatment. Cover both eyes with a moist dressing, and support the object if it protrudes to prevent movement. A protective cup for the eye can be made from a plastic or Styrofoam cup taped over the eye, with a moist dressing inside. Immediately refer this patient for further medical care.
Caustics, Acids, or Burns	Symptoms may include remains of the substance itself, pain, swelling, discoloration of the skin, peeling of skin, and blisters.	Immediately flush both eyes with large quantities of gently flowing water. Each eye should be flushed with water for a minimum of 10–15 minutes away from the unaffected eye. Never use a neutralizing agent for flushing, use only plain tap water. A moist dressing may be helpful. After flushing, refer the patient for further care.

Survival Equipment and Pyrotechnics

Editor's Note: *Your boat is equipped with personal flotation devices (PFDs or "life preservers"), signaling devices, and other survival equipment, but this gear is useless unless it is available for immediate use and in good working condition. Of course, you and your crew must know how to use these things competently and without hesitation. Are your PFDs available for immediate use, or are they floating around in the bilge under a pile of fishing gear and old dock lines? Are your pyrotechnic signals in date? Do you know how to use them? You won't be able to read the how-to label on the side of a smoke signal if your bifocals are lost as you abandon ship. Can you recognize the twenty or so visual signals used by mariners in trouble? Do you know how to get out of a capsized cruiser? This chapter deals with those topics and more—it's vitally important stuff because it addresses the fundamental survival skills needed by all who go out on the water.*

Overview

Introduction

The danger of falling overboard, capsizing or sinking is always present. Few people can stay alive for long periods of time in the water without some type of survival equipment. Fear, fatigue, and exposure are the enemies of water survival. The desire to live, think clearly, and to use proficiently all available equipment make the difference between life and death. The boat coxswain has overall responsibility for the safety of the boat and crew—that all required safety equipment is on board,

readily accessible, in working condition, and that its use and operation is understood by all. However, each boat crew member has a personal responsibility to stay alert and knowledgeable in these matters. This chapter addresses the characteristics and use of survival gear and signaling devices, including pyrotechnics.

NOTE

For specific policies, guidance, and technical information concerning configuration, application, stowage, and maintenance of survival equipment discussed in this chapter, refer to the *Coast Guard Rescue and Survival Systems Manual*, COMDTINST M10470.10 (series).

In this chapter

Personal Flotation Device (PFD)

Overview

Introduction

The term **"personal flotation device" (PFD)** is a general name for the various types of devices designed to keep you afloat in water. PFDs include life preservers, vests, cushions, rings, and other throwable items. They are available in five different types: Type I, II, III, IV and V. Each type of PFD provides a certain amount of flotation.

Regardless of the type, all PFDs must be Coast Guard approved, meaning they must comply with Coast Guard specifications and regulations relating to performance, construction, and materials. A usable PFD is one that is labeled Coast Guard approved, in good serviceable condition, and of appropriate size for the intended user. Each boat crew member must wear a usable PFD and signal kit.

NOTE

A wearable PFD can save your life, but only if you wear it.

In this section

Type I PFD

A.1. GENERAL

The **Type I PFD**, or "offshore life jacket," is a one-piece, reversible PFD intended primarily for use by survivors, passengers on towed vessels, or prisoners aboard vessels. A Type I PFD provides an unconscious person the greatest chance of survival in the water. The Type I PFD is the only wearable

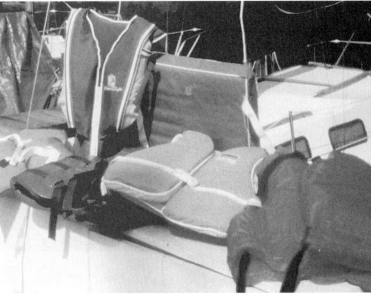

Life jackets come in many varieties, all designed to ensure a safe boating experience.

device required to be reversible. It comes in two sizes, an adult size (90 pounds and over), which provides at least 20 pounds of buoyancy, and a child size (less than 90 pounds), which provides at least 11 pounds of buoyancy, and must be international orange in color.

A.2. ADVANTAGES

Type I PFD is effective for all waters, especially open, rough, or remote waters where rescue may be delayed. It is designed to turn most unconscious wearers in the water from a face-down position to a vertical or slightly backward position, allowing the wearer to maintain that position and providing **at least 20 pounds** of buoyancy. This buoyancy will allow you to relax and save energy while in the water, thus extending your survival time.

A.3. DISADVANTAGES

There are three major disadvantages to this type of PFD:

- Bulky and it restricts movement.
- Its buoyancy restricts the underwater swimming ability you may need to escape from a capsized boat or to avoid burning oil or other hazards on the surface of the water.
- Minimal protection against hypothermia.

NOTE

This type of PFD is *not* recommended for use by boat crews because it restricts mobility.

A.4. DONNING

Before entering the water, don and adjust a Type I PFD using the following steps:

1. Grasp the PFD at the lower part of head opening and pull outward to expand opening.

2. Slip your head through opening.

3. Pass the body strap around your back and fasten at the front of the PFD, then adjust the strap for a snug fit.

> ### WARNING
> For safety, always tuck all loose straps into your pockets, shirt, or belt. Adjust straps on injured people *before* they are lowered into the water.

A.5. ENTERING THE WATER

Use the following procedures to enter the water.

NOTE

Follow these steps before entering the water wearing any type of PFD or combination of cold weather protective device (e.g., dry suit) and PFD.

---

1. Ensure all straps on the PFD are securely fastened, tightened to a snug fit, and tucked in to prevent them from snagging.

2. Stand on the boat's gunwale, on the windward side, at a point closest to the water.

3. Fold your arms across your chest and grip the

Three-year-old twins Nora (left) and Addie (right) Pollard sport their life vests during the Coast Guard's National Safe-Boating Week kickoff in Washington, D.C.

PFD with your fingers. This will prevent the PFD from riding-up and striking your chin or neck.

4. Keep your body erect and legs held together and crossed when entering the water. It is better to gently slip in, if possible, rather than jumping.

5. If you must jump into water with chemicals, oil, or burning oil on the surface, place one hand over your mouth with the palm under your chin and split fingers tightly squeezing your nostrils shut. Place your other hand on the PFD collar to keep it in place.

Type II PFD

A.6. GENERAL

The **Type II PFD**, also known as a "near-shore buoyant vest," is a wearable device that will turn some unconscious wearers to a face-up position in the water. It comes in different colors and in three categories:

- adult (more than 90 pounds), which provides at least 15.5 pounds of buoyancy;

- child, medium (50 to 90 pounds), which provides at least 11 pounds of buoyancy; and

- infant (available in two sizes, less than 50 pounds and less than 30 pounds), which provides at least seven pounds of buoyancy.

A.7. ADVANTAGES

The Type II is usually more comfortable to wear than the Type I. It is usually the preferred PFD if there is a chance of a quick rescue, such as when other boats or people are nearby.

A.8. DISADVANTAGES

The turning characteristic of the Type II is not as strong as it is with a Type I because of a lesser amount of flotation material, and therefore, under similar conditions, the Type II PFD will not be as effective in turning a person to a face-up position.

A.9. DONNING

Before entering the water, don and adjust a Type II PFD using the following steps:

1. Grasp the PFD at the lower part of head opening and pull outward to expand opening.

2. Slip your head through opening.

3. Pass the body strap around your back and fasten at the front of the PFD, then adjust the strap for a snug fit.

4. Secure the chest tie with a bow knot for a snug fit.

A.10. ENTERING THE WATER

To enter the water while wearing a Type II PFD, follow the instructions in Section A.5. above.

Type III PFD

A.11. GENERAL

The **Type III PFD**, also known as a "flotation aid," is routinely worn aboard boats when freedom of movement is required, the risk of falling over the side is minimal, and the water temperature is greater than 15°C/60°F. It is **not designed** to turn an unconscious wearer to a face-up position; the design is such that conscious wearers can place themselves in a vertical or slightly backward position. It has a minimum of **15.5 pounds** of buoyancy and comes in many sizes and colors. Figure 6-1 shows the Type III PFD vest that boat crews are authorized to wear. Most approved flotation coats ("float coats") are also Type III PFDs.

A.12. ADVANTAGES

Type III PFD offers boat crew members greater comfort and freedom of movement. It is designed so **wearers can place themselves** in a face-up position in the water. The Type III PFD allows greater wearing comfort and is particularly useful when water skiing, sailing, hunting from a boat, or other water activities.

A.13. DISADVANTAGES

There are some disadvantages in the Type III PFD:

- Flotation characteristics are marginal and not suitable for wear in heavy seas
- Tendency to ride-up on the wearer in the water
- Wearer may have to tilt head back to avoid a face-down position in the water
- While the Type III has the same amount of buoyancy material as the Type II PFD, the distribution of the flotation material in a Type III reduces or eliminates the turning ability.

> **WARNING**
>
> The Type III PFD will not provide an adequate level of buoyancy when worn with a full complement of law enforcement gear. If unable to remain afloat, jettison easily accessible equipment.

Figure 6-1 Type III PFD Vest

A.14. DONNING

Before entering the water, don and adjust a Type III PFD using the following steps:

1. Place your arms through the openings in the vest.
2. Close zipper, if provided. Close front slide fasteners.
3. Adjust waist straps for a snug fit.

Type IV PFD

A.15. GENERAL

The Type IV PFD is a Coast Guard approved device that is thrown to a person in the water and is grasped by the user until rescued. The most common Type IV devices are buoyant cushions and ring buoys. Buoyant cushions come in many different colors. Ring buoys must be white or orange in color. One of the disadvantages of the Type IV PFD is that it is not worn, although some can be secured to the body once reached in the water.

Type V PFD

A.16. GENERAL

Type V PFDs are also known as "Special Use Devices." They are intended for specific activities and may be carried instead of another PFD **only if used according to the approval condition on the label**. For example, a Type V PFD designed for use during commercial white-water rafting will only be acceptable during commercial rafting; it is not acceptable for other activities unless specified on the label. Examples of Type V PFDs are: the Coast Guard work vest with unicellular foam pads, sailboard PFDs with harness, "thermal protective" PFDs (deck suits/exposure suits), and hybrid inflatable PFDs.

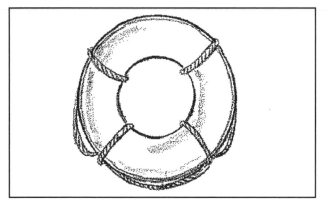

Figure 6-2 Life Ring

A.17. HYPOTHERMIA PROTECTION

Some Type V devices provide significant hypothermia protection. Refer to Section C for more information on the antiexposure coverall.

PFD Storage and Care

A.18. STORAGE

Stowing PFDs in moist, damp lockers will increase the deterioration rate of the fabric due to mildew despite the mildew inhibitor provided by the manufacturer. Heat, moisture, and sunlight also will increase the deterioration rates of various parts of PFDs. So, store PFDs in a cool, dry place out of direct sunlight. A "dry" area is considered any suitable area where water will not condense on PFDs. All PFDs should be kept away from oil, paint, and greasy substances. Remember, more important than their storage condition is that they are readily accessible. The Coast Guard does not consider any PFD "readily accessible" if it is kept in its original wrapper. Persons under stress may be unable to get them out promptly. Also, the wrapper can trap moisture leading to mildew and rot.

A.19. CARE

If a PFD requires cleaning, wash it in fresh, warm water with a mild detergent. Then rinse the PFD in clean, fresh water.

PFD Survival Equipment

A.20. GENERAL

PFD survival equipment is attached to a PFD to provide a means of signaling a position from the surface of the water using sight and sound signals.

A.21. STANDARD OUTFITTING

All PFDs in service shall be outfitted with two accessories:

- Whistle secured to the PFD with a lanyard.
- Distress signal light (battery operated strobe light OR the Personnel Marker Light (PML) chemical light) secured to the PFD.

The requirement for a whistle and a distress signal light may be waived if the PFD is worn in conjunction with the Boat Crew Signal Kit.

NOTE

Auxiliary PFD survival equipment requirements are in the *Auxiliary Operations Policy Manual*, COMDTINST M16798.3 (series).

A.22. PERSONNEL MARKER LIGHT (PML)

A PML is a device that uses either battery or chemical action to provide light for the wearer to be seen during darkness. The yellow-green light of a PML is visible for a distance of approximately one mile on a clear night and lasts as long as eight hours. It is the only chemical light approved for use as a distress signal light on a PFD. A certified PML complies with regulation 46 CFR 161.012 (Coast Guard approved). Large marine supply houses carry Coast Guard approved PMLs. They are specifically designed to be attached to a PFD without damaging or interfering with the PFD's performance. The PML's hard plastic sleeve protects the glass ampoules inside the tube from

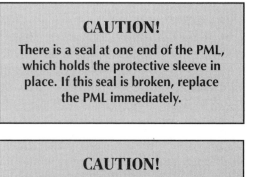

CAUTION!

There is a seal at one end of the PML, which holds the protective sleeve in place. If this seal is broken, replace the PML immediately.

CAUTION!

The PML replaces only the distress signal light that is required to be attached to all PFDs in service. It does not replace the distress signal light (SDU-5/E or CG-1 strobe) that boat crew members are required to carry in their boat crew signal kit.

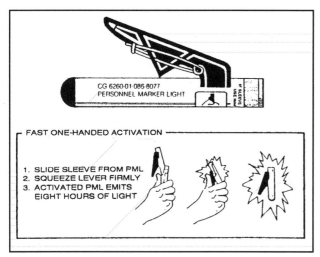

Figure 6-3 Personnel Marker Light (PML)

breakage or deterioration from the effects of light. There are three steps needed to activate the PML:

1. Squeeze the handle to break the glass vials of activating chemical compounds suspended inside the tube.

2. Remove the black sleeve.

3. Squeeze the handle again if the PML does not light.

The intensity of the PML light in cold weather (below 0°C/32°F) is reduced. In colder temperatures, the light will last longer, but will not have the same brilliance as in warmer conditions. Units that consistently operate in temperatures below 0°C/32°F shall use distress signal lights in place of PMLs.

NOTE

Most batteries or chemicals have a useful shelf life of about two years. Therefore, check PMLs for the expiration date (located somewhere on the device) to find out when replacement is in order.

NOTE

The time period a chemical light provides effective illumination depends upon its age and the temperature. A recently purchased light stick used in 21–27°C/70–80°F temperatures (ideal conditions) will provide 8 to 12 hours of light. As the device gets older, its effective operating period will decrease.

A.23. RETROREFLECTIVE MATERIAL

The Coast Guard attaches retroreflective material on all PFDs for increased visibility in the dark. All Auxiliarists are required to use retroreflective material on their PFDs. It is a very simple, but effective, addition to the safety effort. Use a Coast Guard approved reflective material. Instructions for applying this are usually found on the retroreflective material packaging.

Standard Navy Preserver

A.24. GENERAL CHARACTERISTICS

The Standard Navy Preserver, although not Coast Guard approved, is a common PFD used by the naval services. This preserver is one of the best devices for keeping a person afloat; however, it requires significant training to don this device quickly and properly because of its complex straps and fastenings. Consequently, the Standard Navy Preserver is not Coast Guard approved for civilian use. Any Auxiliarist who plans to go aboard a Coast Guard boat or cutter as crew (or passenger) should request instructions in the donning of this PFD.

SECTION B

Hypothermia Protective Clothing

Overview

Introduction

Accidentally falling into cold water has two potentially lethal consequences: drowning or hypothermia. Previously, we discussed the protection provided by PFDs against drowning. The Coast Guard requires active duty Coast Guard and Auxiliary crews to wear hypothermia protective clothing in heavy weather or hazardous operating conditions (water temperature below 15°C/60°F). The operational commander may waive this requirement, but only on a case-by-case basis.

Hypothermia protective clothing is designed to permit you to function in cold weather and water conditions. The Coast Guard uses primary types:

- Antiexposure Coverall
- Dry Suit
- Wet Suit (surface swimmers only)
- Survival (Exposure) Suit

The survival (exposure) suit—extremely bulky and awkward to work in—will not be discussed since it is limited to use for crews operating in cold water when abandoning ship.

A local Coast Guard unit or district may purchase the Coast Guard's antiexposure coverall, survival, and wet suits and lend them to the Auxiliary. The descriptive information below is for those who wish to purchase their own suits.

NOTE

A special type float coat, with a Type V-approval label, meets the same flotation requirements as the antiexposure coverall, but provides only partial covering and less thermal protection.

NOTE

Hypothermia protective clothing shall be worn by boat crew members when the water temperature is below 15°C/60°F.

In this section

Requirements

B.1. GENERAL

The unit commander may waive the requirement for hypothermia protective clothing for boat crew members on a case by case basis **when the degree of risk to exposure and hypothermia is minimal** (e.g., non-hazardous daylight operations in calm water). When a waiver is granted, hypothermia protective clothing must be carried on the boat. **Coxswains shall require boat crew members to don proper hypothermia protective clothing during heavy weather or hazardous operations (e.g., recovery of a person from the water or helicopter operations).** Unit commanders are responsible for the enforcement of this policy for Auxiliary facilities under their operational control. If an Auxiliary facility is granted a waiver, it is not required to carry protective clothing aboard.

NOTE

Timely rescue is a high priority when victims are in the water. When the boat has prior knowledge of a victim in the water, the surface swimmer, if available, will don a dry or wet suit and swimmer's safety harness before entering the water. Coxswains of boats operating in water temperatures that dictate the use of a dry or wet suit shall ensure that the surface swimmer is correctly outfitted.

B.2. PROPER CLOTHING

The best way to avoid cold related injuries is to wear proper clothing. When choosing clothing

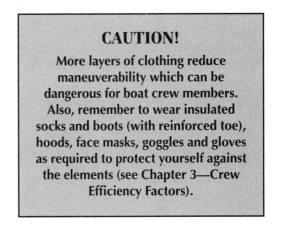

CAUTION!

More layers of clothing reduce maneuverability which can be dangerous for boat crew members. Also, remember to wear insulated socks and boots (with reinforced toe), hoods, face masks, goggles and gloves as required to protect yourself against the elements (see Chapter 3—Crew Efficiency Factors).

combinations, the best advice is to layer clothing. As the work effort changes or when an article of clothing becomes damp, the number of layers can be adjusted for comfort.

B.3. MAINTAINING BODY HEAT

Wet clothing robs the body of heat by breaking down the thermal protection of insulated clothing. It is extremely important to replace wet clothing as soon as possible to prevent cold related injuries, particularly if the person is idle after a period of heavy perspiring. Many cold weather medical problems involve wet hands and feet. These areas should receive special care.

B.4. WEARING A PFD

Boat crew members shall wear PFDs at all times when they wear dry suits. Crew members should not wear PFDs over antiexposure coveralls. (A wet suit is not authorized for use by boat crew members—it may be worn by a surface swimmer.)

B.5. DISTRESS SIGNAL DEVICES

Boat crew members shall wear the contents of the boat crew signal kit (discussed later in this chapter) tethered to the hypothermia protective device when worn. Surface swimmers wearing a dry suit or a wet suit may carry a distress signal light and a signal whistle in lieu of the contents of the boat crew signal kit. Wearing a PML is recommended for boat crew members and the surface swimmer.

Antiexposure Coverall

B.6. GENERAL

Antiexposure coveralls are Type V PFD. The antiexposure coverall is the standard garment for cold weather operations with closed cockpit boats (see Figure 6-4). It provides good durability and out-of-water protection from the elements but limited protection from hypothermia in the water.

B.7. CHARACTERISTICS

Antiexposure coveralls are constructed with a fabric cover and a closed cell foam lining. These suits provide a full range of movement and come in a variety of sizes. They provide adequate mobility and protection from limited exposure to outside elements such as wind and spray. The flotation characteristics of the coverall are similar to those of the Type III PFD. The approved coveralls feature an orally inflated pillow for a better flotation angle for extended periods of exposure.

> ### CAUTION!
> When wearing this type of suit, it is important to tighten all closures and adjustments before entering the water. A loose-fitting suit may allow too much water in and greatly reduce the thermal effectiveness of the suit leading to hypothermia.

B.8. USE

Antiexposure coveralls provide hypothermia protection when the wearer is **only periodically exposed** to conditions which cause hypothermia. When more than periodic exposure is anticipated, even on boats with closed cockpits, a dry suit should be worn.

> ### WARNING
> Wearing a Type I or III PFD over an antiexposure coverall may be dangerous in certain situations. The additional buoyancy may restrict the wearer's ability to swim out from under a capsized boat. In extreme situations, where buoyancy is a limitation instead of an advantage, you may need to remove your PFD.

B.9. DONNING

Antiexposure coveralls are designed to be worn over your uniform in the same manner as standard coveralls. For added protection, wear polypropylene thermal underwear as a moisture wicking layer next to the skin. Also use insulated socks and boots (with reinforced toe), hoods, face masks, goggles and gloves to protect against the elements.

B.10. ENTERING THE WATER

Before entering the water with antiexposure coveralls, follow these steps:

1. Ensure the zipper is completely closed.

2. Tighten straps at the neck, waist, thigh, and ankle to reduce transfer of cold water inside the suit. This increases the degree of hypothermia protection.

3. Orally inflate the pillow behind the collar. This will provide support for your head.

Dry Suit

B.11. GENERAL

The **dry suit** shall be worn when operating open cockpit boats when the water temperature is below 10°C/50°F and the air temperature is below 7°C/45°F. It provides protection in areas where exposure to wind, spray, cold water, and hypothermia is likely (see Figure 6-5). The dry suit, with proper undergarments, provides the best protection for crew members in adverse weather and cold water immersion.

B.12. CHARACTERISTICS

Dry suits are constructed of a trilaminate, breathable fabric. They have watertight seals at the neck, wrist, and ankles to keep the wearer dry and are designed so that one common size will fit most adults.

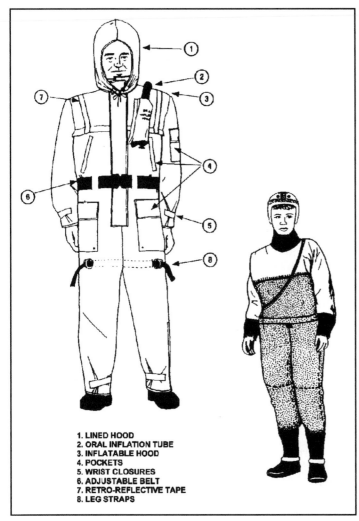

1. LINED HOOD
2. ORAL INFLATION TUBE
3. INFLATABLE HOOD
4. POCKETS
5. WRIST CLOSURES
6. ADJUSTABLE BELT
7. RETRO-REFLECTIVE TAPE
8. LEG STRAPS

Figure 6-4 (left) Antiexposure Coverall
Figure 6-5 (right) Dry Suit

WARNING

Dry suits provide no inherent buoyancy. A PFD must be worn over a dry suit at all times while underway.

WARNING

Dry suits alone provide inadequate insulation or hypothermic protection. Wear thermal underwear layered underneath the dry suit. Fully close the zipper prior to entering the water. Consult the *Coast Guard Rescue and Survival Systems Manual,* COMDTINST M10470.10 (series) for a complete list of undergarments.

In cold weather, a dry suit—as well as gloves and a balaclava—provides protection when operating open cockpit boats.

B.13. USE

When worn with a PFD and proper undergarments, a dry suit offers mobility and superior protection against the effects of wind, spray and cold water immersion.

B.14. DONNING

Don a dry suit as described in the *Coast Guard Rescue and Survival Systems Manual,* COMDTINST M10470.10 (series). Multifilament polypropylene thermal underwear must be worn under the suit for proper protection against cold. By layering underwear, crew members achieve maximum protection from hypothermia under most conditions. A wearer may don this suit quickly and easily over regular clothing. Consequently, this suit is more bulky and loose fitting than a diver's wet suit. PFDs must also be worn because a dry suit has no inherent buoyancy. **A dry suit is not a PFD.** Surface swimmers wearing a dry suit may carry a distress signal light and a signal whistle tethered to the garment in lieu of the boat crew signal kit.

B.15. ENTERING THE WATER

Before entering the water, follow these three steps.

1. Slip on a wet suit hood.
2. Close all zippers and tighten all wrist and ankle straps.
3. Put on gloves.

Wet Suit

B.16. GENERAL

The wet suit may be worn by surface swimmers in the water. The wet suit is not authorized for use by boat crew members. It provides protection from exposure to cold water, but will not keep you dry. A dry suit or antiexposure coverall provides more out-of-water protection (see Figure 6-6).

B.17. CHARACTERISTICS

The standard wet suit is fabricated of ³⁄₁₆" neoprene foam, an elastic material with high-flotation characteristics. The surface swimmer's wet suit ensemble consists of a custom fitted two piece farmer-john style wet suit, a custom fitted one piece shorty wet suit, hood, gloves and boots. Refer to the *Coast Guard Rescue and Survival Systems Manual*, COMDTINST M10470.10 (series) for procurement and inspection.

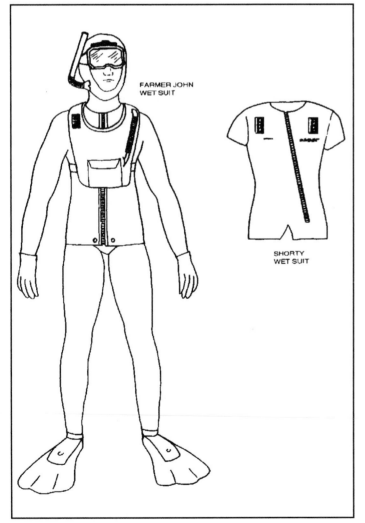

Figure 6-6 Wet Suit (typically neoprene)

B.18. USE

Units should issue wet suits to personnel designated as surface swimmers. Wet suits should be individually fitted. For added comfort and warmth, the suit may be worn over polypropylene cold weather underwear. Units shall issue custom-fitted wet suits as non-returnable items.

NOTE

Wet suits are not authorized for crew members operating boats. Surface swimmers may wear either a dry suit or a wet suit when in the water, depending on water temperature.

B.19. DONNING

When properly worn and with all fasteners closed, a wet suit should fit almost skin-tight. Surface swimmers wearing a wet suit may carry a distress signal light and a signal whistle tethered to the garment in lieu of the boat crew signal kit.

B.20. ENTERING THE WATER

To enter the water while wearing a wet suit, follow the instructions in Section A.5. above for PFDs.

SECTION C

Headgear

C.1. THERMAL PROTECTION

The Navy standard wool watch cap is worn for thermal protection. However, under extreme weather conditions it offers little protection to the face and neck. When operating in a cold environment, the polypropylene or fleece balaclava should be worn in conjunction with the wool watch cap or protective helmet.

C.2. PROTECTIVE HELMET

The wearing of helmets on boats under hazardous conditions, such as heavy weather and helicopter operations, is mandatory for Coast Guard crews and strongly recommended for Auxiliarists. A lightweight kayaker-type helmet is the best.

NOTE

The use of helmets by RHIB crews is recommended for all operations.

Boat Crew Signal Kit

Introduction

The equipment in a **Boat Crew Signal Kit** provides crew members a means to signal their position on the surface of the water, day or night. The Boat Crew Signal Kit shall be carried in the pockets and tethered to the PFD, mesh survival vest, or hypothermia protective device. The kit does not interfere with wearing a PFD or hypothermia protective clothing. Auxiliary survival equipment requirements are in the *Auxiliary Operations Policy Manual*, COMDTINST M16798.3 (series).

In this section

Contents

D.1. CONTENTS

Boat Crew Signal Kits contain the equipment listed here, with their use, characteristics, and operation described later in this section.

1 Emergency Signaling Mirror

1 Signal Whistle

1 Marine Smoke and Illumination Signal

1 Illumination Signal Kit

1 Distress Signal Light

NOTE

The PML is not an authorized substitute for the Distress Signal Light.

NOTE

A boat coxswain is responsible for ensuring that each boat crew member wears a PFD, vest, or hypothermia protective device containing all required items.

CAUTION!

To prevent losing signal kit equipment overboard while being handled, each item shall be tethered to the vest with a lanyard.

Emergency Signaling Mirror

D.2. GENERAL

The **emergency signaling mirror** is a pocket-sized mirror with a sighting hole in the center and a lanyard attached (see Figure 6-7). However, any common mirror is useful as an emergency signaling device.

D.3. USE

The mirror is used to attract the attention of passing aircraft, boats, or ground rescue teams by reflecting light at them.

D.4. CHARACTERISTICS

Light reflected in this manner can be seen at a great distance from the point of origin. Practice is the key to effective use of a signal mirror.

D.5. OPERATION

Instructions for using the mirror are printed on its back. The following steps describe how to properly use this accessory.

1. Face a point about halfway between the sun and an object you wish to signal.

2. Reflect sunlight from the mirror onto a nearby surface such as the raft, your hand, etc.

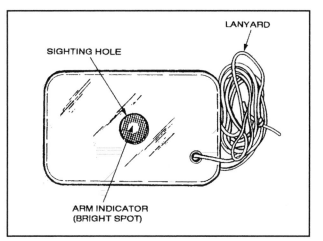

Figure 6-7 Emergency Signaling Mirror, MK-3

3. Slowly bring the mirror up to eye-level and look through the sighting hole. You will see a bright light spot, this is the aim indicator.

4. Hold the mirror near your eye and slowly turn and manipulate it so the bright light spot is on target.

Signal Whistle

D.6. GENERAL

The **whistle** is a small, hand-held device that produces a loud sound when you blow into it (see Figure 6-8). The standard whistle is constructed of plastic and resembles a police officer's whistle.

D.7. USE

The sound produced by a whistle will attract the attention of rescuers and guide them to your location. During periods of restricted visibility, fog, and darkness, the sound it produces may be heard by rescuers before they sight your distress signal light.

D.8. CHARACTERISTICS

Depending on weather conditions, a whistle's audible sound may be heard up to 1,000 meters/ 1,100 yards. Wind has the effect of carrying the sound downwind.

D.9. OPERATION

Place the reed part of a whistle between your lips and blow. If the whistle does not produce a distinct whistle-like tone, quickly turn the whistle over and blow the water out the bail air relief hole and try again.

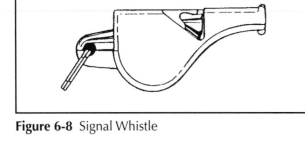

Figure 6-8 Signal Whistle

Smoke and Illumination Signal, MK-124 MOD 0

D.10. GENERAL

The MK-124 MOD 0 is a pyrotechnic smoke and illumination signal used day or night as a distress signal at sea or on land (see Figure 6-9). One end produces orange smoke as the day signal and the other end produces a red flare as the night signal. Because of its weight, about eight ounces, and size, it may be carried in a PFD, vest, antiexposure coverall, or life raft.

NOTE

Auxiliary crew members may use commercially available Coast Guard approved survival equipment while operating an Auxiliary facility. See COMDTINST M16798.3 series for specific requirements.

D.11. USE

These signals are used to attract vessels, aircraft, and ground rescue teams in daylight or nighttime. The signal may be used to indicate wind direction for helicopter hoists. It is labeled with the following operating instructions:

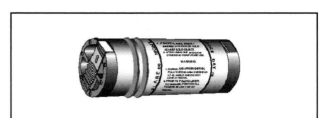

Figure 6-9 Smoke and Illumination Signal, MK-124 MOD 0

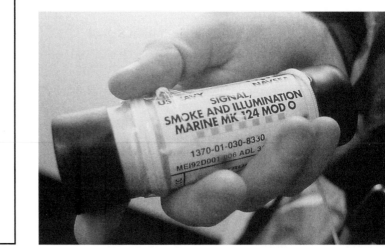

Smoke and Illumination Signal, MK-124 MOD 0

- Do not dispose of the signal until both ends have been used.

- **Only when signals misfire** should you dispose of them over the side. Misfires are a safety hazard if kept on board a vessel.

- When **both ends** of the signal have been discharged, properly dispose of it. In an actual distress situation, toss spent signals over the side.

> **WARNING**
>
> Under no circumstances shall personnel ignite both ends at one time.

D.12. CHARACTERISTICS

As mentioned above, both ends of the device produce a signal and each end burns for about 20 seconds. The night end produces a RED FLARE (similar to a road flare) and the day end produces ORANGE SMOKE.

D.13. OPERATION

The device has two raised bands around its circumference on its night end (flare). These beads positively identify the night end by sense of touch. Also, a label on the case identifies the day (smoke) and night (flare) ends and provides instructions for use.

After choosing which end to use, follow the operating instructions:

1. Remove the black rubber protective cap from the end to be ignited.

2. Slide the plastic lever in the direction of the arrow until fully extended.

3. Hold the signal downwind and overhead at a 45° angle from the horizon over the side of the raft or away from dry debris to prevent burns from hot drippings.

4. Using your thumb, pull down on the extended tab to ignite signal. See Figure 6-10.

5. If the smoke signal end flames up, briefly immerse it in water or hold it against a solid object.

6. After using one end, douse in water to cool it, or if on land place it on the ground to cool. Save the signal to use the other end when needed.

All life rafts must be equipped with flares.

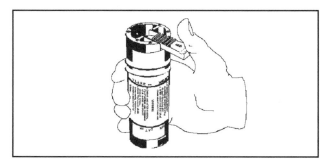

Figure 6-10 Operating the MK-124 MOD 0 Signal Flare

> **WARNING**
>
> Prior to pulling lever downward, position all fingers below top of signal.

> **WARNING**
>
> Do not direct either end of a signal toward another person.

> **WARNING**
>
> After ignition, the outer case may overheat and burn the hand. Dropping the signal on land will not decrease its effectiveness.

Illumination Signal Kit, MK-79 MOD 0

D.14. GENERAL

The Illumination Signal Kit, MK-79 is a pyrotechnic that contains seven screw-in cartridge flares and one pencil type projector. The projector in this kit is used to aim and fire a signal cartridge (see Figure 6-11).

D.15. USE

The Illumination Signal Kit, MK-79 is used to attract vessels, aircraft, and ground rescue teams.

D.16. CHARACTERISTICS

These signals produce a red star display at an altitude of 250–650 feet for a minimum time of 4.5 seconds. Their luminous intensity is about 12,000 candle power.

D.17. OPERATION

The following are steps for operating the MK-79.

1. Remove the bandolier and projector from the plastic envelope.

2. Cock the firing pin of the projector by moving the trigger screw to the bottom of the vertical slot and slipping it to the right so that it catches at the top of the angular (safety) slot.

3. Bend protective plastic tab away from signal in bandolier to allow attachment to projector.

4. Mate a signal flare with the projector and rotate clockwise until signal is seated.

5. Hold projector overhead with arm fully extended. The projector should be pointed at a slight angle away from the body.

6. While firmly gripping the projector, fire the signal by slipping the trigger screw to the left out of the safety slot and into the firing slot.

7. If the signal fails to fire, try again twice by depressing the trigger screw to the bottom of the firing slot with the thumb and releasing it quickly. If it still fails to fire, wait 30 seconds before unscrewing, to eliminate possibility of hang fire.

8. Unscrew the spent signal case or signal that has failed to fire. Discard by throwing overboard.

9. To fire another signal, repeat the steps above.

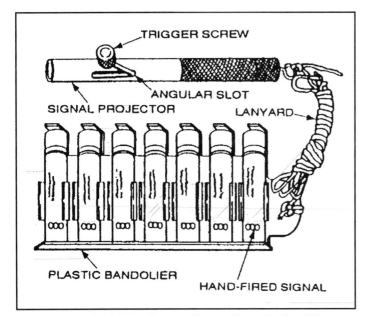

Figure 6-11 Illumination Signal Kit, MK-79 MOD 0

This action should be one continuous movement so that your thumb does not interfere with the upward motion of the trigger screw when it is brought into the firing slot. The trigger screw must "snap" upward.

WARNING

Do not aim at aircraft or other objects.

Distress Signal Light

D.18. GENERAL

The **Distress Signal Light** is a lightweight, compact, battery-operated strobe light that emits a high intensity visual distress signal (see Figure 6-12). The strobe light model that is currently in use is the battery operated SDU-5/E or CG-1 Strobe Light. Some lights are also Coast Guard approved as PMLs.

D.19. USE

This light is used to attract the attention of aircraft, ships, or ground parties. It is sold on the market as a rescue/anti-collision light. Crew members carry the distress signal light in a pocket, or attach it to a line or belt. Keep it tethered to a garment that you are wearing.

D.20. CHARACTERISTICS

The SDU-5/E and the CG-1 distress signal lights emit approximately 50 flashes per minute. At the peak of each flash, the luminous intensity is 100,000 candlepower. Under continuous operation it will flash for nine hours, or 18 hours when operated intermittently. On a clear night, the Distress Signal Light has a minimum visual range of five miles. However, the range of visibility will be determined by the height of eye of the observer. For an observer low on a boat, the range will most likely be much less than the advertised five miles.

D.21. OPERATION

The following are the steps to operate the Distress Signal Light.

1. Turn ON. Push the switch in until a click is heard, then release. Light should begin flashing within seconds.

2. Turn OFF. Push the switch in until click is heard, then release. The light should stop flashing.

3. If you test this light and it fails to perform within operational limits, replace the battery. If it still does not operate properly, remove it from service.

SECTION E

Personnel Survival Kit

E.1. GENERAL

As part of the boat outfit list, the Coast Guard requires a personnel survival kit to help the crew survive in hazardous situations, such as when a boat capsizes or sinks, or someone is lost overboard. The kit should be in a watertight bag that is readily available in an emergency. It includes the boat crew signal kit (discussed earlier) and the following individual survival items:

- Survival Knife
- Boat Crew Signal Kit
- Visual Distress Signals

These components may also be carried or worn by the crew members. Auxiliarists may build a kit with regular marine store merchandise

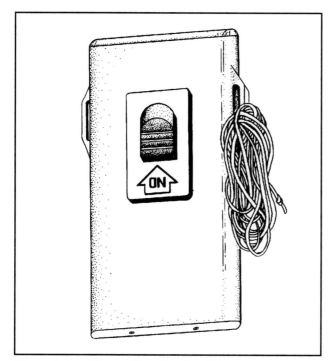

Figure 6-12 Distress Signal Light, CG-1

E.2. SURVIVAL KNIFE

The survival knife is the basic tool used to free yourself from entangling lines. It is also used to cut material blocking a path in escaping a capsized or sinking boat. The selection of a knife is critical; your life may depend upon it. Folding knives (which may be issued by the unit to each crew member) are convenient to carry, but may be impossible to open with gloves or with loss of dexterity due to a cold environment. Folding knives may also lack the blade strength required in an emergency. A knife designed for water use such as a diver's knife is the best choice for a survival knife. It should be double edged, corrosion resistant, and checked periodically for sharpness (Figure 6-13).

E.3. BOAT CREW SIGNAL KIT

The boat crew signal kit was discussed earlier in this chapter. Individual items were listed along with their use, characteristics, and operation.

E.4. VISUAL DISTRESS SIGNALS

Visual distress signals include pyrotechnics and other visual signals that may be displayed by any vessel. Pyrotechnics are discussed in a following section, and distress signals in general are discussed in Chapter 11—Communications. Unit commanders will outfit boats with the required visual distress signaling devices. All Auxiliary boats must carry visual distress signaling devices that meet facility requirements.

SECTION F

Pyrotechnics

F.1. GENERAL

If the boat becomes disabled during a mission, its crew must have some means of signaling aircraft or vessels for assistance. Signaling devices include **pyrotechnics**. The Smoke and Illumination Signal, Marine MK-124, MOD 0 and the MK 79, MOD 0 Signal Kit were discussed earlier in this chapter under the boat crew signal kit. Additional information is provided below. Visual distress signals in general are discussed in Chapter 11—Communications.

F.2. REQUIREMENTS

Stowage and handling of pyrotechnics is done in accordance with *the Coast Guard Ordnance Man-*

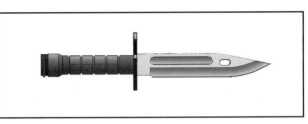

Figure 6-13 Survival Knife

ual, COMDTINST M8000.2 (series) and the Navy publication NAVSEA SW050-AB-MMA-010. Coast Guard unit commanders will outfit their boats with the required pyrotechnics. All Auxiliary boats must carry visual distress signals that meet facility requirements. The pyrotechnic devices carried as part of their personnel survival kit should be small enough to be carried comfortably and be well protected from the elements. The following are Coast Guard approved visual distress signal devices typically used by the Auxiliary.

CFR No. Marked on Device	Device Description	Quantity
160.021	Hand-held red flare distress signals, day and night	3
160.022	Floating orange smoke distress signals, day only	3
160.024	Pistol-projected parachute red flare distress signals, day and night	3
160.037	Hand-held orange smoke distress signals, day only	3
160.057	Floating orange smoke distress signals, day only	3
160.066	Distress signal for boats, red aerial pyrotechnic flare, day and night	3

NOTE

Pyrotechnic devices should not be used until a rescue craft is actually in sight.

F.3. PARACHUTE ILLUMINATION SIGNAL, MK-127A1

The Parachute Illumination Signal, MK-127A1 is a nighttime illumination signaling device. When fired, it climbs to an altitude of 650 to 700 feet before igniting. Upon ignition, it produces a parachute-suspended white star flare that burns for about 36 seconds with 125,000 candlepower. The signal descends at a rate of 10 to 15 feet per second (see Figure 6-14).

FIRING INSTRUCTIONS The procedures for firing the parachute illumination signal are described below.

1. Do not remove a signal from its sealed container until just before use.

2. Remove a signal from the container in accordance with instructions printed on the container.

3. In all handling, avoid striking the signal primer.

4. Do not use signals that are dented, cracked, or otherwise damaged.

5. Hold the signal in your left hand with the RED band of the signal FACING UP. Align your left thumb and forefinger along the red band.

6. Withdraw the firing cap from the lower end of the signal.

7. Point the ejection end of the signal (the end opposite the red knurled band) away from the body and away from other people, equipment, and materials. Slowly push the cap onto the primer (red band) end until the cap meets the edge of the knurled band. DO NOT PERMIT THE CAP TO GO BEYOND THE RED BAND.

8. Hold the signal FIRMLY at arm's length with the left hand, with the ejection end facing straight up. The signal should be held in a vertical position (90° elevation) when firing.

9. Strike the firing cap bottom sharply with the palm of the right hand, keeping the left arm rigid and pointing straight up.

10. If a signal misfires while on land, place it in a secure position to prevent people from being hurt should the signal fire. The signal must not be approached for at least 30 minutes. If a misfire occurs while underway, toss it overboard.

CAUTION!

Exercise due care to prevent the expended rocket body from falling on people, water craft, and structures.

FIRING ANGLES Firing a signal at angles other than a vertical position may be necessary under the following circumstances:

- To compensate for high wind velocities
- To place the signal display in a better position to be seen by searching aircraft

---

WARNING

If a signal is fired at an angle less than 90° elevation (directly overhead), the altitude reached is reduced and the altitude of candle burnout is lessened. If the firing angle is 60° or less, the candle will, in almost all cases, still be burning when it strikes the surface.

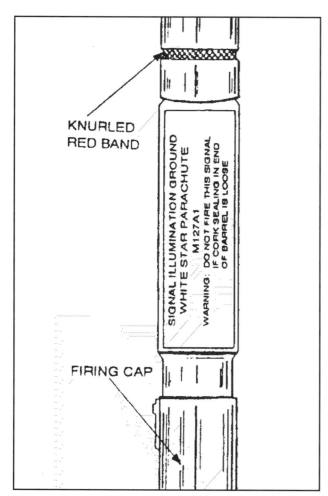

Figure 6-14 Parachute Illumination Signal, MK-127A1

SECTION G

Rescue and Survival Raft

G.1. GENERAL

The six person rescue and survival raft is a multipurpose raft designed for crew survival or rescue and assistance to persons in distress. It is usually carried on Coast Guard boats greater than 30 feet long. The discussion here applies to a Coast Guard procured raft but the general procedures apply to almost any commercially available raft. The Auxiliary may use commercially available Coast Guard approved life rafts which may typically be less complete but still serve the same purpose. The instructions for use and maintenance of any life raft should always be reviewed.

G.2. AUTOMATIC INFLATION AND DEPLOYMENT

When properly stowed, this life raft is designed to automatically float free from its storage rack and

Larger vessels need to provide enough life rafts to fit all passengers. This canister contains a life raft large enough to hold six adults.

inflate in the event of capsizing or sinking. As the raft container is released and drifts away, the inflation cable attached to the raft-end of the 50-foot painter line is pulled tight. When this occurs, the CO_2 cylinder will automatically discharge and inflate the life raft. The painter line will remain attached to the rack by a weak link which requires 500 pounds of force to separate. Separation will also occur by heaving around on the painter line or by the stress exerted on it from the raft's buoyancy if the boat sinks to a depth greater than 50 feet.

G.3. MANUAL DEPLOYMENT

To manually deploy the rescue and survival raft (see Figure 6-15), do the following:

1. Remove the raft container from its storage rack and remove the stainless steel bands from the raft box.

2. Place the raft container in the water on the leeward side of the boat.

3. Completely pull the 50-foot painter line from the raft container. This will inflate the raft.

4. If practical, pull the raft alongside the boat and board the raft directly from the boat.

5. If time permits, take extra survival equipment and supplies aboard the raft. Such equipment may include illumination signals, portable radios, food, water, first aid supplies, and fishing gear.

6. Untie the canopy and pull it over the support tube. Then re-tie it in the closed position.

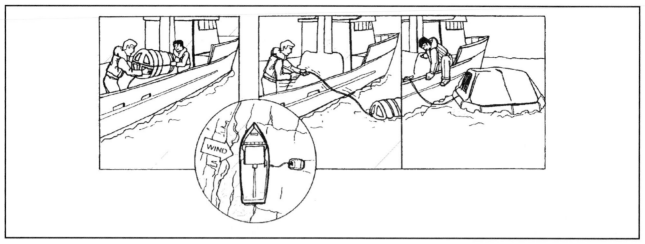

Figure 6-15 Manual Deployment of Survival Raft

G.4. BOARDING A RAFT

Try to remain in the general area of the boat. If the boat does not sink immediately, leave the operating painter line attached to the raft storage rack on the boat. If the boat sinks rapidly, cut the painter line before it breaks (at the weak link) under the strain caused when the boat goes under.

G.5. TASKS ON BOARD A RAFT

Upon boarding a raft, complete the following tasks as soon as possible:

1. Account for everyone and search for survivors.

2. If more than one raft is deployed, tie them together.

3. Check the physical condition of all people aboard. Give first aid as necessary. If weather permits, wash any oil or gasoline from your clothing and body. These substances will not only burn your skin, but also pose a fire hazard. Additionally, they may be transferred from your skin to the raft, deteriorating the rubber surfaces.

4. Salvage any floating equipment which may be useful. Inventory, stow, and secure all survival items.

5. To provide stability in moderate to heavy sea, life rafts on Coast Guard boats automatically deploy a sea anchor upon inflation.

6. Check the raft for proper inflation and points of possible chafing (areas where equipment may wear a hole in the buoyancy tubes).

7. Bail out any water that may have entered the raft.

8. Inflate the floor immediately.

9. In cold water, put on hypothermia protective clothing, if available. Rig the entrance cover, close when necessary.

10. If other people are with you, huddle together for warmth.

CAUTION!

Be careful not to snag the raft with your shoes or with sharp objects.

G.6. CONDUCT IN A RAFT

The safety and survival of everyone in a raft depends on clear thinking and common sense. To protect those aboard and increase survival time, take the following steps:

1. Maintain a positive attitude.

2. Inventory *all* equipment. Ration water and food. Assign lookout and other necessary duties to crew members.

3. DO NOT rely on memory. KEEP A WRITTEN LOG. Record the time of entry into the water, names and physical condition of survivors, ration schedule, winds, weather, direction of swells, times of sunrise and sunset and other navigation data.

G.7. USING A RAFT TO RESCUE OTHERS

When it is impossible or too dangerous to maneuver close to a distressed vessel, the life raft may be used to ferry survivors to your boat. It may also be used to recover people from the water if you cannot get a boat close enough to them. Use the following procedures when deploying a life raft during a rescue attempt (see Figure 6-16).

1. Remove the raft container from its storage rack.

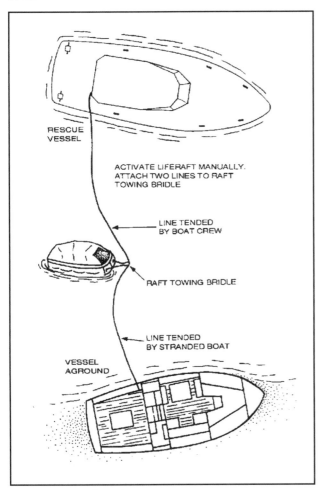

Figure 6-16 Life Raft as Rescue Ferry

2. Do not manually or automatically inflate the life raft as you remove the tape sealing the life raft case (half shells) together.

3. Roll the life raft out of the case and place it in the water on the leeward side of the boat.

4. Pull the 50-foot painter line from the raft container, manually inflate the raft, and hold it alongside your boat.

5. Attach two lines, each of a length longer than the maximum distance between your boat and the people in distress.

6. Use one line to tend the life raft from your boat during the evolution (NEVER LET GO OF THIS LINE).

7. Pass the other line to the people in distress with a heaving line or let the current float it down to them.

8. Tell the persons being assisted to haul the life raft to their position.

9. Once the life raft is alongside, direct the persons to board the life raft, one person at a time.

10. If the number of people being assisted is more than the carrying capacity of the raft, direct the people remaining to tend the line attached to the life raft from their location; haul back the maximum number of survivors and repeat the procedure.

11. After recovering all people, deflate the raft and bring it aboard the rescue boat. The raft may have taken on water during the rescue evolution. De-ballast the raft before bringing it aboard. Use the handles located on the ballast bags and slowly lift one side of the raft until all the water has run out.

12. Once the raft is aboard, do not repack the raft. Wash the raft and have it repacked at a certified packing station before returning it to service.

WARNING

Although the raft is ballasted and very stable in most sea states, it may capsize in large breaking waves. For this reason, consider other methods for rescue of people in breaking surf or seas (e.g., helicopter rescue).

WARNING

Ensure each person is wearing a PFD. Do not permit more people to enter the raft than is allowed by the raft's specifications.

SECTION H

Emergency Procedures in the Event of Capsizing

H.1. GENERAL

The key to surviving a capsize is to prevent it from happening. If it can not be avoided, then the crew must recognize when it could happen and be prepared. Chapter 9—Stability, Chapter 10—Boat Handling, and the Heavy Weather Addendum all discuss situations and conditions where capsizing could result. These chapters also present warning signs and measures to take to minimize risk. The coxswain must continually assess the conditions to ensure the safety of the boat crew and of those in distress; however, all crew members have the responsibility to keep the coxswain advised if the situation changes.

H.2. PREVENTION

A boat is less likely to capsize in deep, open water. The chances of capsizing are greatest while operating in or near the surf or breaking seas. The force needed to capsize is most likely to come from heavy seas directly astern (following seas), or large breakers striking abeam. Stay at sea until conditions change. The safest point for most boats to take heavy seas is nearly bow-on. Do not operate or tow in conditions beyond the capability of the boat or crew. In such conditions, advise the operational commander so that the proper resource (e.g., MLB, SRB, cutter, or helicopter) can respond. Conditions present in many capsizings included:

- Surf or breaking seas
- Shallow water depth (less than 20 feet)
- Going against a strong tidal current and with steep following seas
- Escorting or towing another boat through an inlet
- Restricted visibility due to darkness, rain, or fog
- Stability reduced by low fuel in the tank, excessive amounts of water in bilges, icing of topsides, or too many people on board

H.3. PRECAUTIONS

If the hull is intact after capsizing, it will not sink for some time, even in rough seas. The crew will have time to escape if panic is avoided. Precautions ahead of time include:

- Learn the boat's interior. Initially the crew will be disoriented due to being upside down and with a lack of lighting.
- Stow all loose gear and have all equipment and doors operating properly for ease in escaping.
- Know the location and use of all survival equipment. Check it regularly to be sure that it is adequate, in good repair, and that all signaling devices work.
- Be ready to grab a sturdy support to prevent being thrown about.

H.4. ESCAPE PROCEDURES

If trapped in or under the boat, seek out an air pocket near the top (inverted bottom). Gather the crew together in the air pocket. Take time to have everyone settle down and focus on planning a safe escape. Discuss the escape route and objects of reference along the route. Look down; light may be visible and escape immediate.

- Make every effort to escape. The boat may sink or the air will eventually escape through hull fittings, cracks, or holes, or become unfit to breathe (fuel vapors, bilge waste, or lack of oxygen due to survivors breathing).
- Before attempting to escape, check for needed survival equipment, especially flotation and signaling devices.
- PFDs may have to be removed temporarily for people to fit through spaces or to go underwater to reach an exit. If necessary, tie a line to the PFD and pull it out after exiting.
- Avoid the stern if the engines are still running.
- If caught in an open cockpit area, swim down below the gunwales and surface alongside the boat.

ESCAPE FROM AN ENCLOSED COMPARTMENT
Escape from an enclosed compartment will require additional planning. Advice includes:

- All exits are upside down when the boat capsizes. Locate an exit route and reference points from the compartment to open water.
- PFDs may have to be removed temporarily for people to fit through spaces or to go underwater to reach an exit. If necessary, tie a line to the PFD and pull it out after exiting.
- Swim underwater through the exit and out from the boat. If a line is available, the best swimmer should exit first through a cabin door or window, carrying the line. If no line is available, have the best swimmer go first, followed by a poorer swimmer and lastly a good swimmer. (If the poorer swimmers are left alone inside, they are likely to panic and not escape.) The first swimmer, when free, should tap on the hull to signal success in getting out to the others.
- Cold water decreases the length of time anyone can hold their breath underwater. Immersion in cold water may also give a sensation of tightness in the chest. Experiment inside the compartment before attempting to escape. This will decrease the possibility of panic during the escape attempt.

ALONGSIDE A CAPSIZED BOAT Survivors from a capsized boat should attempt to stay with the boat or other visible floating debris.

- Get onboard a life raft if available.
- If a life raft is not available, climb onto the boat, if possible. Otherwise, hold onto the largest floating object available.
- Generally, everyone should stay with the boat and not swim for shore. Distances to the beach can be deceiving and strenuous activities such as swimming in cold water can hasten the onset of hypothermia.

Survivors should consider tying themselves to the boat if there is a rapid means of untying or cutting free, in case the boat shifts or sinks. Most people are likely to become tired or develop hypothermia.

REMAINING INSIDE A CAPSIZED BOAT If someone cannot exit the capsized boat:

- Remain calm and stay within an air pocket.
- Trap the air in the compartments (e.g., close any hull valves that can be located).
- When hearing rescuers, attempt to communicate to them by shouting or tapping on the hull.
- Conserve oxygen by remaining calm and minimizing physical activity. If possible, get out of the water to reduce hypothermia.
- Remember that rescuers should arrive soon.

In the event of a capsize where no life raft is available, climb onto the boat or the largest piece of floating debris. Get as much of your body out of the water as possible to avoid hypothermia.

Marlinespike Seamanship

Overview

Introduction

Editor's Note: There is nothing exclusive to the Coast Guard about the marlinespike seamanship discussed here. All mariners must be proficient with basic knots, bends, and splices, and the presentation here focuses on those most useful in day-to-day on-water operations. You will also find an important discussion on the breaking strengths and working loads of lines—an important safety consideration.

Marlinespike seamanship is the art of handling and working with all kinds of rope and lines. Discussion here includes knotting, splicing and creation of fancy decorative work. There is no better measure of a sailor's worth than his or her skill in marlinespike seamanship. You will need much practice to gain proficiency in these skills, but you will be more than amply rewarded for the effort. Knowledge of line handling terminology will assure clear, unambiguous communication among crew members. To be less than proficient in marlinespike seamanship can be costly. Often the safety of life and property depends on the crew's knowledge of these techniques.

This chapter contains information on the types of rope used by mariners—their characteristics, use and care. You will find definitions, safety practices, and line handling commands, as well as directions for tying knots and making splices commonly used on Coast Guard boats and Auxiliary facilities. You will find technical information for determining which line, hooks and shackles are safe and appropriate for various tasks.

In this chapter

Types and Characteristics of Line

Overview

Introduction

The uses for a particular line will depend heavily upon the type and characteristics of the line. This section includes information regarding the different types of line used in boat handling.

In this section

Line Characteristics

A.1. GENERAL LINE CONSTRUCTION

Lines are made of natural or synthetic fibers twisted into yarns. The yarns are grouped together in such a way to form strands. Finally, the strands are twisted, plaited, or braided, in various patterns, to form line.

A.2. COAST GUARD LINE

Line used on Coast Guard boats is classified in two different ways: material used, and construction of the line.

MATERIAL USED Lines are categorized as natural fiber or synthetic fiber. Refer to Figure 7-1 on pages 96–97 for fiber line characteristics. The characteristics of the natural and synthetic fiber lines will be explained further in this section.

CONSTRUCTION Strands are twisted to either the right or the left. This twisting is the "lay" of the line. Line may have either a left lay or a right lay depending upon how the strands are twisted together. Line is usually constructed as plain laid, plaited and double braided lines. Figure 7-2 illustrates fiber rope components and construction. The type of construction will depend upon the intended use of the line.

PLAIN LAID: Made of three strands, right or left-laid. Most common is right-hand laid.

CABLE LAID: Made of three, right-hand, plain-laid lines laid together to the left to make a larger cable.

PLAITED LINE: Made of eight strands, four right-twisted and four left-twisted. Strands are paired and worked like a four strand braid.

BRAIDED LINE: Usually made from three strands (sometimes four) braided together. The more common braided lines are hollow-braided, stuffer-braided, solid-braided, and double braided.

DOUBLE BRAIDED LINE: Two hollow-braided ropes, one inside the other. The core is made of large single yarns in a slack braid. The cover is also made of large single yarns but in a tight braid that compresses and holds the core. This line is manufactured only from synthetics, and about 50% of the strength is in the core.

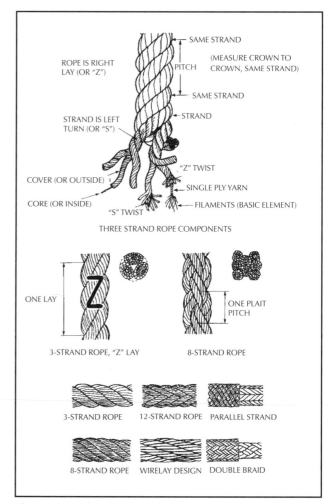

Figure 7-2 Fiber Rope Components and Construction

Natural Fiber Line

A.3. COMPOSITION

Natural fiber line is made from organic material, specifically, plant fiber. The list below describes the various natural fiber lines.

MANILA: Made from fibers of the abaca plant and is the strongest and most expensive of the natural fibers.

SISAL: Made from the agave plant and is next in strength to manila, being rated at 80% of manila's strength.

HEMP: Made from the fiber of the stalk of the hemp plant, is now rarely used.

COTTON: Made from natural fibers of the cotton plant, may be three-stranded, right-lay or of braided construction used for fancy work and lashings.

A.4. USES OF NATURAL FIBER LINE

We use natural fiber lines, usually manila, hemp or sisal, for tying off fenders, securing chafing gear, and other small stuff (i.e., line 1¾ in. in circumference and smaller).

Braided line is most commonly used for signal halyard, heaving lines, and lead lines.

Plain laid line may be used for towlines, mooring lines, anchoring, securing loose gear, fender lines, and fancy work.

A.5. LIMITATIONS

Natural fiber line has a lower breaking strength than synthetic fiber line of an equal size, and unlike synthetic line, natural fiber line does not recover after being stretched (elasticity). In the Coast Guard, we do not use it for load bearing purposes on boats. Another limitation of natural fiber line is the likelihood of rotting if stowed wet.

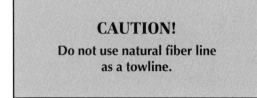

CAUTION!

Do not use natural fiber line as a towline.

A.6. CONSTRUCTION

A close look at a natural fiber line will reveal that the strands are twisted together. They will have either a right or left lay.

A.7. PLAIN LAID LINES

Plain laid line is the most common type of natural fiber line used in the Coast Guard. In plain laid three strands are twisted together to the right in an alternating pattern. Because of the number of strands, this line is sometimes called "three strand" line. The yarns making up the strands are laid in the opposite direction of the strands. These are twisted together in the opposite direction to make the line. The direction of the twist determines the lay of the line. In the case of plain laid lines, the yarns are twisted to the right. They are then twisted together to the left to make the strands. The strands are twisted together to the right to make the line (see figure 7-2).

Synthetic Line

A.8. COMPOSITION

Synthetic line is made of inorganic (man-made) materials. The characteristics of synthetic line are considerably different from natural fiber line. The differences will vary depending on the type of material from which the line is made. The following list identifies the various types of synthetic fiber line used.

NYLON: A synthetic fiber of great strength, elasticity, and resistance to weather. It comes in twisted, braided, and plaited construction, and can be used for almost any purpose where its slippery surface and elasticity is not a disadvantage.

DACRON: A synthetic fiber of about 80% if the strength of nylon but will only stretch 10% of its original length.

POLYETHYLENE AND POLYPROPYLENE: A synthetic fiber of about half the strength of nylon, 25% lighter than nylon making it easier to handle, and floats in water.

A.9. COMMONLY USED TYPES

The most common types of synthetic line used on Coast Guard boats are nylon and polypropylene. Because of its superior strength and elasticity, nylon is used where the line must bear a load.

A.10. DOUBLE BRAIDED NYLON LINE

Double braided nylon line is the only line used for towlines on Coast Guard boats. However, Auxiliary facilities use towlines of various types and sizes. When double braided line is made, the yarns are woven together much like the individual yarns

Figure 7-1 *Characteristics of Natural and Synthetic Fiber Line*

Characteristics	Manila	Sisal	Cotton
Strength:			
Wall strength compared to dry strength	Up to 120%	Up to 120%	Up to 120%
Shock load absorption ability	Poor	Poor	Poor
Weight:			
Specific gravity	1.38	1.38	1.54
Able to float	No	No	No
Elongation:			
Percent at break	10–12%	10–12%	5–12%
Creep (extension under sustained load)	Very Low	Very Low	
Effects of Moisture:			
Water absorption of individual fibers	Up to 100%	Up to 100%	Up to 100%
Resistance to rot, mildew, and deterioration due to marine organisms	Poor	Very Poor	Very Poor
Degradation:			
Resistance to U.V. in sunlight	Good	Good	Good
Resistance to aging for properly stored rope	Good	Good	Good
Rope Abrasion Resistance:			
Surface	Good	Fair	Poor
Internal	Good	Good	Good
Thermal Properties:			
High temperature working limit	300°F	300°F	300°F
Low temperature working limit	–100°F	–100°F	–100°F
Melts at			Chars 300°F
Chemical Resistance:			
Effects of Acid	Will disintegrate in hot diluted and cold concentrated acids	Same as Manila	Same as Manila
Effect of alkalis	Poor Resistance will lose strength where exposed	Same as Manila	May swell but will not be damaged
Effect of organic solvents	Fair resistance for fiber, but hydrocarbons will remove protective lubricants on rope	Good Resistance	Poor Resistance

Figure 7-1 *Characteristics of Natural and Synthetic Fiber Line (cont.)*

Characteristics	Nylon	Polyester	Polypropylene	Polyethylene
Strength:				
Wall strength compared to dry strength	85–90%[1]	100%[1]	100%	105%
Shock load absorption ability	Excellent	Very Good	Very Good	Fair
Weight:				
Specific gravity	1.14	1.38	0.91	0.95
Able to float	No	No	Yes	Yes
Elongation:				
Percent at break	15–28%	12–15%	18–22%	20–24%
Creep (extension under sustained load)	Moderate	Low	High	High
Effects of Moisture:				
Water absorption of individual fibers	2.0-6.0%	<1.0%	None	None
Resistance to rot, mildew, and deterioration due to marine organisms	Excellent	Excellent	Excellent	Excellent
Degradation:				
Resistance to U.V. in sunlight	Good	Excellent	Fair[2]	Fair[2]
Resistance to aging for properly stored rope	Excellent	Excellent	Excellent	Excellent
Rope Abrasion Resistance:				
Surface	Very Good[3]	Very Good[1]	Good	Fair
Internal	Very Good[3]	Excellent[1]	Good	Good
Thermal Properties:				
High temperature working limit	250°F	275°F	200°F	150°F
Low temperature working limit	–70°F	–70°F	–20°F	–100°F
Melts at	490–500°F	490–500°F	330°F	285°F
Chemical Resistance:				
Effects of Acid	Decompose by strong mineral acids; resistant to weak acids	Resistant to most mineral acids; disintegrate by 95% sulfuric acid	Very Resistant	Very Resistant
Effect of alkalis	Little or none	No effect cold; slowly disintegrate by strong alkalis at the boil	Very Resistant	Very Resistant
Effect of organic solvents	Resistant. Soluble in some phenolic compounds and in 90% formic acid	Generally unaffected; soluble in some phenolic compounds	Soluble in chlorinated hydrocarbons at 160°F	Same as polypropylene

[1]Grades with special overfinishes are available to enhance wet strength and abrasion properties.
[2]For non-UV stabilized product, consult manufacturer.
[3]Dry condition. Under wet condition: Good.

in a piece of cloth are woven. The actual line consists of two hollow braid lines, an inner core and an outer cover. The core is woven into a slack, limp braid from large single yarns. The cover is woven from even larger yarns into a tight braid to cover and compress the core.

ELONGATION AND ELASTICITY Double braided nylon has two other characteristics which increase its strength. These are elongation and elasticity. Elongation refers to the stretch of the line and elasticity refers to the ability of the line to recover from elongation. Synthetic line will stretch farther and recover better than natural line. Because of this, synthetic line can absorb the intermittent forces and surges resulting from waves or seas much better than natural fiber line.

LIMITATIONS While its superior strength makes double braided nylon line the preferred choice for load bearing there are disadvantages. Because it will stretch further (elongate) and still recover (elasticity), the snap back potential if the line parts is greater than with natural fiber line. Also, if nylon line is doubled and placed under excessive strain, there is a danger that the deck fittings might fail. If that happens, the line will snap back like a rubber band, bringing the deck fitting with it. Additionally, damage to the engine or deck fittings could occur if the bollard pull is exceeded.

DEFINITION Bollard pull is the point where the static pulling force becomes such that any increase in engine load could lead to damage to the engine or the towing bitt.

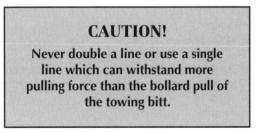

CAUTION!
Never double a line or use a single line which can withstand more pulling force than the bollard pull of the towing bitt.

A.11. PLAIN LAID POLYPROPYLENE LINE

Orange colored polypropylene line is used on Coast Guard boats for life rings, and kapok heaving lines. The advantage to this line is high visibility and floatation.

LIMITATIONS The main disadvantage of polypropylene line is its lack of strength compared to nylon

line of equal size. Its loose, coarse weave makes it easy to splice but susceptible to chafing. Aggravating this is polypropylene's characteristic of deteriorating rapidly when exposed to continuous sunlight. It can in fact, lose up to 40% of its strength over three months of exposure. For this reason the line is best kept covered when not in use, and inspected and replaced on a regular basis.

A.12. SLIPPAGE

Synthetic line slips much easier than natural line. Because of this, it will slip through deck fittings and not hold knots as well. Be careful when bending synthetic line to an object or to another line to ensure the knot will not slip out. One way to help prevent this is to leave a longer tail on the running or bitter end than you would with natural fiber line.

A.13. CONSIDERATIONS

When using synthetic lines consider the following:

- Synthetic line will slip more easily than natural fiber line. You must use caution when paying it or surging it from deck fittings.
- Beware of slippage when bending synthetic line together or securing it.
- Never stand in any position exposing yourself to the dangers of snap back if the line parts.
- Do not double up the line during a towing operation.
- Keep working surfaces of bitts free of paint and rust.
- Do not stand in the bight of a line or directly in line with its direction of pull.

CAUTION!
To minimize the hazard of being pulled into a deck fitting when a line suddenly surges ensure all crew members stand as far as possible from the equipment. Work the lines with your hands a safe distance from the fittings. This is particularly important during towing operations.

A.14. CUTTING

The use of a hot knife is the preferred method for cutting nylon and polypropylene line. Using a hot knife eliminates the need for burning the ends.

Commercial electric knives, used by sailmakers, are available. Some soldering irons can be fit with blades for cutting line. The most accessible method for most people is to heat an old knife or scraper using a propane torch.

When cutting the line, let the heat do the job. Do not force the blade or saw through the line The best method is to work from the outside in. First, an incision is made around the circumference of the line. Then cut through the center.

NOTE

Remember, when a piece of rope is cut, it will fray. Always finish the end of the line whether before or immediately after cutting the line.

Inspection, Handling, Maintenance, and Stowage of Line

Overview

Introduction

Boat crewmen must know how to inspect, handle, maintain, and stow line. This section provides the necessary information regarding basic inspection, maintenance, and stowage of line.

In this section

Topic	See Page(s)
Inspection	99–100
Uncoiling and Unreeling	100–101
Maintenance	101–2
Stowing Lines	102–3

Inspection

B.1. GENERAL

A periodic inspection of all lines used should be made, paying special attention to the following items:

- Aging
- Fiber wear
- Fiber damage
- Chafing
- Kinks
- Cockles
- Cutting
- Overloading or shock loading
- Rust
- Eye splices

AGING Aging affects natural fibers more severely than synthetic. Cellulose, the main component in natural fibers will deteriorate with age, getting more brittle and turning yellow or brownish. When bent over bitts or cleats, the fibers easily rupture and break. During bending, line strength may decrease up to five times. To check for aging, open the lay of the line and note the color of the interior fibers. In an old line they will be gray or dark brown. Aging is not a significant problem for nylon line, though it will color with age. As stated before though, polypropylene line does deteriorate rapidly when exposed to sunlight.

CAUTION!
Synthetic double braided line should not be taken apart for internal inspection.

FIBER WEAR When natural fiber line is under strain, the friction of the fibers, yarns and strands against each other, causes internal wear. You can check for internal wear when you check for aging. Upon opening the lay of the line, look for the presence of a white powdery substance. This residue comprises small particles of line worn off by friction.

FIBER DAMAGE Damage to internal natural fibers occurs when a line under a strain exceeds 75% of its breaking strength. Although this load is not enough to part the line, it is enough to cause some of the internal fibers to break. Check for internal fiber damage when you check for aging and internal wear. Internal broken fibers indicate that the line has been damaged. With synthetic line some of the individual synthetic fibers of the line may break if overloaded. These will be visible on the outer surface of the line.

CHAFING Chafing is wear that affects the outer surface of a line, caused by the friction of the line rubbing against a rough surface. To check for chafing, visually inspect the outer surface of the line for frayed threads and broken or flattened strands.

With synthetic line, chafing can also cause hardening and fusing of the outer layer.

KINKS A kink (Figure 7-3) is a twist or curl caused when the line doubles back on itself. Never place a line with a kink in it under strain. The tension will put a permanent distortion in the line. Remove all kinks before using a line.

COCKLES A cockle (or hockle) is actually a kink in an inner yarn that forces the yarns to the surface. Cockles can be corrected by stretching the line and twisting the free end to restore the original lay. A cockle can reduce line strength by as much as a third.

> *NOTE*
>
> Braided line will not kink or hockle.

CUTTING A line damaged by cutting will usually show brooming and yarn end protrusion. This can weaken the line and probably cause line failure under strain.

OVERLOADING OR SHOCK-LOADING Signs that a line was overloaded are stretch out and hardness. Line stretched to the point where it will not come back has a decreased diameter. To determine this place the line under slight tension and measure the circumference of a reduced area and of a normal area. If the circumference is reduced by five percent or more, replace the line.

Another indication of synthetic line overloading, is hardness to the touch. You will notice this hardness if you gently squeeze the line. Don't use overloaded line.

A line under strain is dangerous. If it parts, it will do so with a lot of energy, depending on the size and type of line, and how much strain it is under when it parts. As a general rule, when a line is under stress, always keep an eye on it. If you stand in line with the strain you might be seriously injured if the line parts and snaps back at you.

RUST Rust stains, extending into the cross section of natural fiber and nylon fiber yarns can lower line strength as much as 40%.

EYE SPLICES (DOUBLE BRAIDED NYLON LINE) Prior to each use inspect all eye splices in your towline and side lines (mooring lines). Pay particular attention to the female section ensuring there are not "flat spots" where the crossover is buried at the base of the eye. Also inspect the entire eye for chafing and cuts. (See Appendix 7-D for illustrations.)

Uncoiling and Unreeling

B.2. GENERAL

Proper use and care will significantly extend the lifetime of the lines used. Everyone should be responsible for protecting lines from damage. Along with good inspections some of the ways to accomplish this are proper breakout, stowage, and care.

> *NOTE*
>
> Never permanently cover natural fiber line with anything that will prevent the evaporation of moisture.

B.3. UNCOILING NATURAL FIBER LAID LINE

To uncoil natural fiber laid line:

1. Look inside the center tunnel of the coil to locate the end of the line.

2. Position the coil so the inside line end is at the bottom of the center tunnel.

3. Start uncoiling the line by drawing the INSIDE END UP THROUGH THE TOP OF THE TUNNEL. (See Figure 7-4).

Do not pull on any kinks that develop, as they will develop into permanent strand cockles. If kinks develop, lay the line out straight and remove them before use.

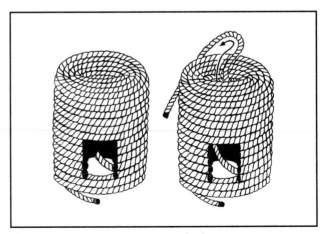

Figure 7-4 Opening a New Coil of Line

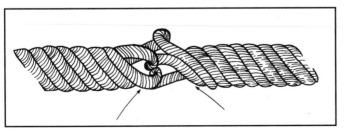

Figure 7-3 Line with a Kink

B.4. UNREELING SYNTHETIC FIBER LINE

The recommended method for unreeling synthetic fiber lines is to:

- Insert a pipe through the center and hang the reel off the deck.
- Draw the line from the lower reel surface.

DO NOT "throw" twisted fiber lines off the reel as it will cause tangles and kinks. It is recommended that three-strand synthetic lines be faked down on deck and allowed to relax for twenty four hours. Lengths less than 50 feet will relax in one hour when laid out straight. Fake down double braided line in figure-eight patterns. (See Figure 7-5.)

Maintenance

B.5. BASIC LINE MAINTENANCE

While there is not anything that can be done to restore bad line, there are precautions to take to lengthen its lifetime. The following are some of the things that can be done to extend the life of lines.

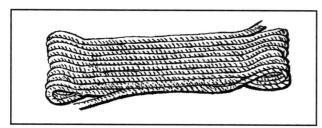

Figure 7-5 Line Faked Down

Proper maintenance can extend the life of any line.

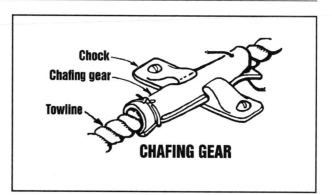

Figure 7-6 Chafing Gear

KEEP LINES CLEAN Keep lines free from grit or dirt. Gritty material can work down into the fibers while a line is relaxed. Under tension the movement of the grit will act as an abrasive and will cause serious damage to the fibers.

USE CHAFING GEAR Chafing gear is made of old hoses, leather, or heavy canvas. It is used to protect short pieces of line where they run over taff rails, chocks, or other surfaces (see Figure 7-6).

KEEP DECK FITTINGS CLEAN AND SMOOTH Bitts, cleats, and chock surfaces should be kept smooth to reduce line abrasion.

WATCH FOR FROZEN WATER Do not let water freeze on lines. Ice is abrasive and can cut fibers.

CRUSHING OR PINCHING LINES Do not walk on, place loads on, drag loads over, or in other ways crush or pinch a line.

SHARP BENDS Bending under a load causes internal abrasion between the strands of the line. If a line has to go around something, use a fair lead. A fair lead is any hole, bull's-eye, lizard, suitably placed roller, sheave, etc., serving to guide or *lead* a rope in a desired direction. If a fair lead is not used, remember that the bigger the bend, the less the abrasive effect.

B.6. CARE OF NATURAL FIBER LINE

The practices that should be avoided or observed in the maintenance of natural fiber line are listed in the table on page 102.

B.7. CARE OF SYNTHETIC FIBER LINE

Most of the practices in the maintenance of natural fiber line are the same for synthetic fiber line.

Dos	Don'ts
• Dry line before stowing it.	• Stow wet or damp line in an unventilated compartment or cover it so that it cannot dry. Mildew will form and weaken the fibers.
• Protect line from weather when possible.	
• Use chafing gear (canvas, short lengths of old fire hose, etc.) where line runs over sharp edges or rough surfaces.	• Subject the line to intense heat or unnecessarily allow it to lie in the hot sun. The lubricant will dry out, thus shortening the useful life of the line.
• Slack off taut lines when it rains. Wet lines shrink and if the line is taut, the resulting strain may be enough to break some of the fibers	• Subject a line to loads exceeding its safe working load. Individual fibers will break, reducing the strength.
• Reverse turns on winches periodically to keep out the kinks.	• Allow line to bear on sharp edges or run over rough surfaces.
	• Try to tie knots or hitches in new places as much as possible so as not to wear out the line.
• Lay right-laid lines clockwise on reels or capstans and left-laid lines counterclockwise until they are broken in.	• Scrub line. The lubricant will be washed away, and caustics in strong soap may harm the fibers.
• Inspect lines for fiber damage and other wear conditions before each use.	• Try to lubricate line. The lubricant you add may do more harm than good.
• Occasionally end-for-ending (swap one end for the other) to help reduce excessive wear at certain points.	• Put a strain on a line with a kink in it.
	• Let wear become localized in one spot.
	• Unbalance line by continued use on winch in same direction.

However, the differences are as follows:

- Nylon is not subject to mildew, and it may and should be scrubbed if it becomes slippery because of oil or grease. Spots may be removed by cleaning with light oils such as kerosene or diesel oil, or with liquid soap and water.
- Synthetic line stretches when put under a load. Allow plenty of time for the line to recover to its original length before coiling on a drum or reel.

Stowing Lines

B.8. GENERAL

To prevent the deteriorating effects of sunlight, chemicals, paints soaps, and linseed or cotton seed oils, store lines to prevent contact with harmful items or conditions.

B.9. NATURAL FIBER LINES

Natural fiber lines can be damaged by contact with just about anything. They are especially susceptible to the rotting and mildewing effects of moisture. After use, allow natural fiber line to dry thoroughly and stow it in a cool, dark, well ventilated space.

B.10. SYNTHETIC FIBER LINES

Synthetic fiber lines are not as susceptible to the effects of moisture as natural fiber lines. They are, though, affected by all of the other conditions and materials that will hurt line. Keep the boat's towline and other synthetic lines covered or stored in a dark area when not in use.

Synthetic line should not be constantly coiled in the same direction as doing this tends to tighten the twist. Three-strand synthetic line is often coiled clockwise to reduce a natural tendency to tighten up. It can be coiled in figure eights to avoid kinks when paying out. (See Figure 7-7.)

Whereas synthetic line stretches when put under a load, allow plenty of time for the line to recover to its original length before coiling on a drum or reel.

NOTE

Stow lines in designated space when not in use.

B.11. TOWLINE

See Chapter 17—Towing, for procedures to stow towlines.

Figure 7-7 Figure Eight Coils

Figure 7-8 Flemishing a Line

B.12. COILING

The most common method of stowing the extra line on deck or on the dock after making fast to a cleat is to coil it.

B.13. FLEMISHING A LINE

Flemishing a line consists of coiling a line clockwise against the deck. It is used for appearance (e.g.: inspections, seaman-like appearance). (See Figure 7-8.)

Breaking Strength and Safe Working Load

Overview

Introduction

This section provides the necessary information to determine the breaking strength and safe working load of a line.

In this section

Breaking Strength and Safe Working Load of a Line

C.1. GENERAL

A line stretches as it takes on a load. It will continue to do so as tension increases until it reaches its breaking point. Then it will part and snap back. There have been many injuries and deaths caused by lines snapping when working under tension. Safe line handling is a combination of knowledge and skill. The ability to determine the breaking strength (BS) and safe working load (SWL) of a line is an important factor in safe line handling.

C.2. BREAKING STRENGTH (BS)

The BS of a line is measured in the number of pounds of stress a line can take before it parts. It is a part of the technical information provided to a purchaser. The number comes from stress tests conducted by the manufacturer of the line and is an average of all the lines tested. This means, it is not necessarily accurate for any specific line. You must apply a safety factor to determine the SWL of a line.

C.3. SAFE WORKING LOAD (SWL)

Line should be selected with its intended usage, or working load, in mind. A common seamanship practice says that the SWL of a line should be not more than one-fifth of its breaking strength, or that the BS should be five times the weight of the object attached to the rope. This five-to-one safety factor allows for sudden strains, shock loading, and normal deterioration as the line ages.

VARIOUS TYPES OF LINE Figure 7-9 provides the breaking strengths and safe working loads in pounds for various types of line used on Coast Guard boats. In the table, each size of line is classified as "good," "average" or "poor."

The SWL and BS of the lines below were figured mathematically based on the circumference of each line. Line procured through government supply sources is measured in circumference. Commercially procured line, however, is measured in diameter. The formula for converting circumference to diameter and vice versa is contained in Appendix A. For simplicity, both the diameter and the circumference of the most commonly used Coast Guard lines are provided below.

NOTE

The only type of synthetic line authorized by the Coast Guard for towing is double braided nylon. The other lines listed in the table are for comparison purposes.

THREE-STRAND NYLON LINE The Auxiliary may use three-strand nylon line for towing. Typical line size and average breaking strength are summarized below. The safe working load condition and specific values can be calculated as shown in Appendix A.

Breaking Strength and Safe Working Load for Shackles and Hooks

C.4. GENERAL

Given a choice between the hardware breaking or the line parting, it is usually safer for the line to part.

Figure 7-9 *Minimum Breaking Strengths and Safe Working Loads for Natural and Synthetic Lines*

Size Diam.	Size Cir.	Manila BS lbs.	SWL by Line Condition Good	Average	Poor	Nylon (Double Braided) BS lbs.	SWL by Line Condition Good	Average	Poor
5/8	2	3,600	720	360	240	9,000	3,000	2,250	1,500
11/16	2 1/2	5,625	1,123	562	375	14,062	4,687	3,515	2,343
7/8	2 3/4	6,804	1,360	680	454	17,010	5,670	4,242	2,835
1	3	8,100	1,620	810	540	20,250	6,750	5,062	3,375

Size Diam.	Size Cir.	Polypropylene/Polyethylene BS lbs.	SWL by Line Condition Good	Average	Poor	Polyester (Dacron) BS lbs.	SWL by Line Condition Good	Average	Poor
5/8	2	5,040	1,008	840	630	7,200	2,400	1,800	1,200
11/16	2 1/2	7,875	1,575	1,312	840	11,250	3,750	2,812	1,875
7/8	2 3/4	9,525	1,905	1,588	1,190	13,608	4,536	3,402	2,268
1	3	11,340	2,268	1,890	1,417	16,200	5,400	4,050	2,700

Size Diam.	Size Cir.	Three-strand Nylon BS lbs.	SWL by Line Condition Good	Average	Poor
5/8	2	10,300	3,433	2,575	1,717
7/8	2 3/4	19,600	6,533	4,900	3,267
1	3	25,000	8,333	6,250	4,167

The BS of shackles is six times greater than their SWL. Figure 7-10 shows the sizes of shackles and hooks. The relationship is based on the SWL of hooks, shackles, and towlines. It is consistent with the general rule that you never use a shackle or hook with a SWL less than the SWL of the line being used.

C.5. DETERMINING SAFETY

To determine whether any of the shackles or hooks listed below are safe with a particular line, extract the SWL of the shackle or hook from the table. Next extract the SWL for the line. Finally, compare the two. The SWL of the shackle or hook should be equal to or greater than the SWL of the line.

Appendix A contains the formulas for computing the BS and SWL of line, hooks and shackles. The figures derived by using these formulas are only estimates of actual strengths for guidance purposes. Best judgment and experience must be applied when using these formulas.

Considerations and Limitations

C.6. GENERAL

Even though you may correctly determine the SWL of lines, shackles and hooks, there are many variables affecting the equipment. In actual use it is not always possible to operate within the SWL. Sometimes you can't match appropriate hardware with particular lines.

C.7. KEEP ALERT

It is necessary for you to keep a constant eye on a line under stress. The unpredictable, unforeseen and often dangerous forces in the marine environment will catch you by surprise unless you are always on guard. By using good judgment you can usually make timely adjustments to correct for these adverse forces.

C.8. STAY WITHIN LIMITS

Try to keep the tension on line and equipment well within their SWL. It is difficult to tell when the SWL is reached or surpassed. A sudden surging (pulling) of a towline may cause the tension on the line and hardware to approach their breaking points. This is when the danger of parting becomes a safety hazard.

C.9. UNKNOWN BS AND SWL

The moment you connect your towline to a distressed vessel's deck fittings, your entire towing sys-

Figure 7-10 Recommended Shackles and Hooks to be Used With Coast Guard Authorized Towline

Size Inches	BS lbs.	SWL lbs.	Size Length	BS lbs.	SWL lbs.
3/8	12,000	3,000	55/8	12,000	3,000
1/2	24,000	6,000	615/16	24,000	6,000
5/8	39,000	9,750	815/32	39,000	9,000

tem assumes an unknown BS and SWL factor. You often cannot get a reliable estimate of BS and SWL even when you can attach the proper equipment to the disabled craft. Because this is the weak link in towing, you must keep the towline and the boat in tow under constant observation.

C.10. MEASURE PERCENTAGE OF ELONGATION

The device used to measure the percentage of elongation is called a Tattletale Cord or a Strain Gauge. A tattletale cord is a bight of heavy cord or light small stuff which is cut to a specific length depending on the type of synthetic line it is used with. The ends of the tattletale cord are secured at a specified distance apart on the line, again, depending on the type of synthetic line. As the line elongates under strain, the tattletale cord stretches with it. When the cord is drawn taut the line has reached the percent of critical strength for various synthetic lines, the length of tattletale cord used to measure this elongation and the distance the ends of the cord must be tied apart when secured on the line.

Dimensions for tattletale cords can be summarized as follows:

Type of Synthetic Line	Length of Tattle- tale in Inches	Distance Cord in Inches Stretch	Critical in Percent
Nylon (3 strand)	40	30	40
Nylon (double braided)	48	40	20
Nylon (plaited)	40	30	40
Polyester (3 strand)	34	34	20
Polypropylene (3 strand)	36	30	20

NOTE

Navy studies have shown that tattletales will give warning for a line that has been shock loaded. Their use and position of placement on towlines is optional.

Knots and Splices

Overview

Introduction

This section details the procedures regarding the art of knots and splices.

In this section

Estimating the Length of a Line

D.1. PROCEDURE

Estimating a length of a line can be a useful skill. One method of doing so is as follows:

1. Hold the end of a length of line in one hand.

2. Reach across with your other hand and pull the line through the first hand, fully extending both arms from the shoulder.

The length of line from one hand to the other, across your chest, will be roughly six feet (one fathom). Actually, this distance will be closer to your height, but this measure is close enough for a rough and quick estimate of line needed.

If more line is needed, repeat the process keeping the first hand in place on the line as a marker until you have measured off the length of line required. For example, if you need 36' of line, you would repeat the procedure six times.

Breaking Strength

D.2. KNOTS AND SPLICES

Knots are used for pulling, holding, lifting, and lowering. When using line for these purposes it is often necessary to join two or more lines together. Knots and bends are used for temporary joining, and splices provide a permanent joining. In either

Figure 7-11 *Percent of Line Breaking Strength Loss*

Knots or Splice Remaining	Percent of Line Breaking Strength Lost	Percent of Line Breaking Strength Remaining
Square	46	54
Bowline	37	63
Two Bowlines (Eye in Eye)	43	57
Becket Bend	41	59
Double Becket Bend	41	59
Round Turn	30–35	65–70
Timber Hitch	30–35	65–70
Clove Hitch	40	60
Eye Splice	5–10	90–95
Short Splice	15	85

case, the BS of the joined line is normally less than the BS of the separated lines.

The weakest point in a line is the knot or splice. They can reduce the BS of a line as much as 50 to 60 percent. A splice, however, is stronger than a knot. Figure 7-11 lists each of the commonly used knots and splices. It provides their percent of line BS lost and percent of line BS remaining.

Basic Knots

D.3. GENERAL

Knots are the intertwining of the parts of one or more lines to secure the lines to themselves, each other (bends), or other objects (hitches). Because knots decrease the strength of the line, they should always be treated as temporary. If you need something permanent, use a splice or seizing.

D.4. DEFINITIONS

In making knots and splices you must know the names for the parts of a line and the basic turns employed. Refer to Figures 7-12 and 7-13 for an example of the following knots.

BITTER END: The running end or the free end of a line. It is the end of the line that is worked with.

STANDING PART: The long unused or belayed end. The remaining part of the line including the end that is not worked.

OVERHAND LOOP: A loop made in a line by crossing the bitter end over the standing part.

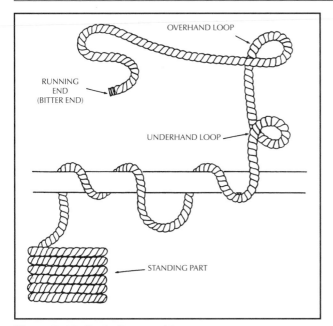

Figure 7-12 Basic Parts and Loops

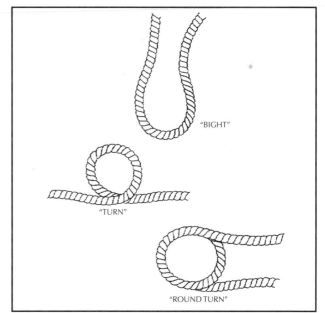

Figure 7-13 Bight and Turns

UNDERHAND LOOP: A loop made in the line by crossing the bitter end under the standing part.

BIGHT: A half loop formed by turning the line back on itself.

TURN: A single wind or bight of a rope, laid around a belaying-pin, post, bollard, or the like.

ROUND TURN: A complete turn or encircling of a line about an object, as opposed to a single turn.

D.5. ANATOMY OF A KNOT

Good knots are easy to tie, easy to untie, and hold well. A good knot should not untie itself. A knot used to secure lines together is a bend. A knot used to secure a line to an object, such as a ring or eye, is a hitch. The knots listed below are those most commonly used in boat operations. Learn to tie them well, for the time may come when the skill to do so could decide the outcome of a mission.

BOWLINE The bowline is a versatile knot. Use it anytime you need a temporary eye in the end of a line. It also works for tying two lines securely together, though there are better knots for this. An advantage of bowlines is that they do not slip or jam easily. Refer to Figure 7-14 (page 108) as you follow these steps:

1. Make an overhand loop in the line the size of the eye desired.
2. Pass the bitter end up through the eye.

3. Bring the bitter end around the standing part and back down through the eye.

4. Pull the knot tight by holding the bitter end and the loop with one hand and pulling on the standing part with the other.

HALF HITCHES Hitches are used for temporarily securing a line to objects such as a ring or eye. One of their advantages is their ease in untying. The half hitch is the smallest and simplest hitch. Tie it only to objects having a right hand pull. Since a single half hitch may slip easily, use care in cases where it will encounter extreme stress. Refer to Figure 7-15 (page 108) as you follow these steps:

1. Pass the line around the object.
2. Bring the working end "a" around the standing part and back under itself.

TWO HALF HITCHES To reinforce or strengthen a single half hitch, tie more. Two half hitches make a more reliable knot than a single half hitch. Use them to make the ends of a line fast around its own standing part. A round turn or two, secured with a couple of half hitches, is a quick way to secure a line to a pole or spar. Two half hitches are needed to secure a line at an angle where it might slide vertically or horizontally. Refer to Figure 7-16 (page 108).

1. Take a turn around the object.
2. Bring the bitter end (running end) under and over the standing part and back under itself.
3. Continue by passing bitter end under and over the standing part and back under itself.

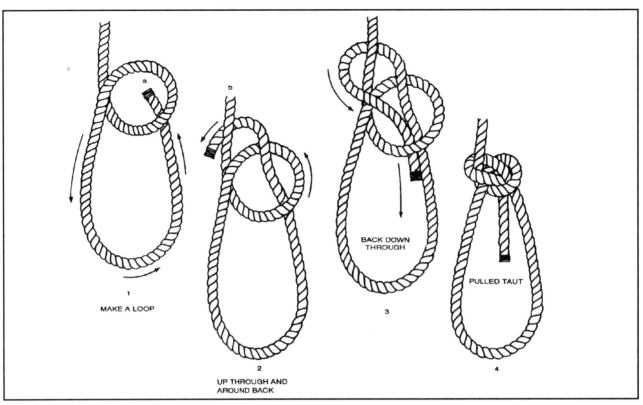

Figure 7-14 Bowline

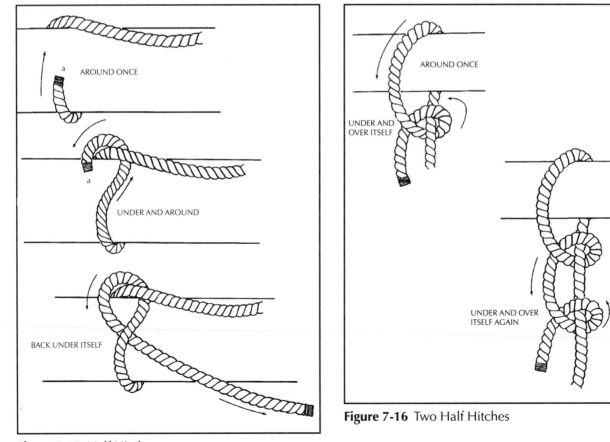

Figure 7-15 Half Hitch

Figure 7-16 Two Half Hitches

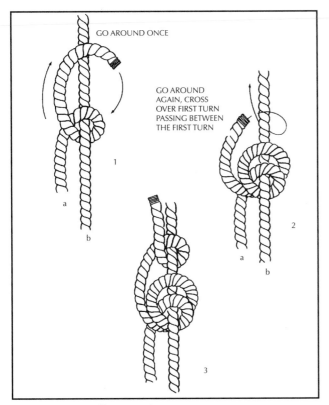

Figure 7-17 Rolling Hitch

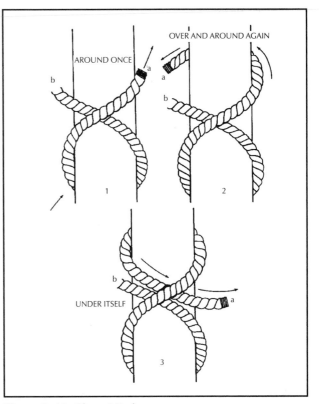

Figure 7-18 Clove Hitch

ROLLING HITCH (STOPPER) A rolling hitch is used to attach one line to another, where the second line is under a strain and cannot be bent. Refer to Figure 7-17 as you follow the steps below left.

1. With the bitter end "a" make a turn over and under the second line "b" and pass the link over itself.

2. Pass "a" over and under "b" again bringing "a" through the space between the two lines on the first turn.

3. Pull taut and make another turn with the bitter end "a" taking it over, then under, then back over itself.

4. Pull taut and tie a half hitch.

CLOVE HITCH A clove hitch is preferred for securing a heaving line to a towline. It is the best all-around knot for securing a line to a ring or spar. Correctly tied, a clove hitch will not jam or loosen. However, if it is not tied tight enough it may work itself out. Reinforce it with a half hitch. Refer to Figure 7-18 as you follow the steps below.

1. Pass the bitter end "a" around the object so the first turn crosses the standing part.

2. Bring the bitter end "a" around again and pass it through itself.

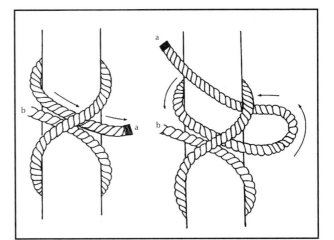

Figure 7-19 Slip Clove Hitch

3. Pull taut.

4. Reinforce by tying a half hitch.

SLIP CLOVE HITCH Use a slip clove hitch in lieu of a clove. Tie it in the same manner as the clove hitch but finish it with a bight to allow for quick release. (See Figure 7-19.) It is sometimes used for stowing lines and fenders. It should not be used when working with the line.

TIMBER HITCH Timber hitches are used to secure a line to logs, spars, planks or other rough-surfaced material. Do not use it on pipes or other metal objects. Refer to Figure 7-20 as you follow the steps below.

1. Tie a half hitch.

2. Continue taking the bitter end "a" over and under the standing part.

3. Pull the standing part taut.

4. You may add two half hitches for extra holding (See Figure 7-21.) Unless you can slip the half hitch over the end of the object, tie it before making the timber hitch.

SINGLE BECKET BEND (SHEET BEND) Lines can be lengthened by bending one to another using a becket bend. It is the best knot for connecting a line to an eye splice in another line. It can be readily taken apart even after being under a load. Single becket bends are used to join line of the same size or nearly the same size. It is intended to be temporary. Refer to Figure 7-22 as you follow the steps below.

1. Form a bight in one of the lines to be joined together, line "a."

2. Pass the bitter end of the second line "b" up through the bight formed by the first line "a."

3. Wrap the end of line "b" around the bight in "a."

4. Pass the end of "b" under its own standing part.

5. Pull taut.

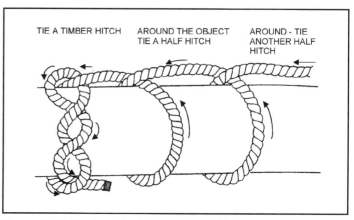

Figure 7-21 Timber Hitch with Two Half Hitches

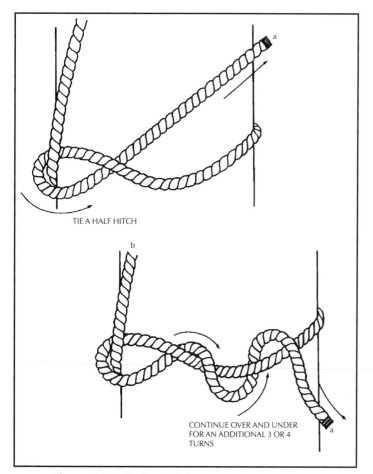

Figure 7-20 Timber Hitch

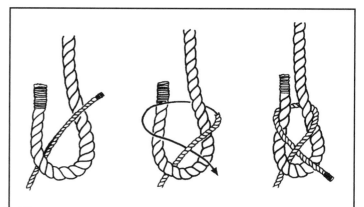

Figure 7-22 Single Becket/Sheet Bend

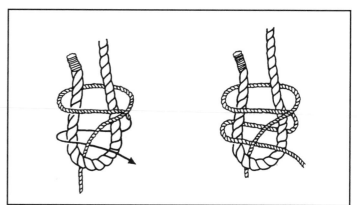

Figure 7-23 Double Becket/Sheet Bend

DOUBLE BECKET BEND (DOUBLE SHEET BEND) The double becket bend works for joining lines of unequal size. It is tied in the same manner as the single becket bend except for the following variation in step 4 above: Pass line "b" around and under its standing part twice. (See Figure 7-23.)

REEF KNOT (SQUARE KNOT) Called a square knot by Boy Scouts, the reef knot is one of the most commonly used knots in marlinespike seamanship. However, reef knots are rarely used on small boats because they jam badly under strain. Also, reef knots do not effectively hold lines of different sizes or materials. Reef knots are best used to finish se-

curing laces (canvas cover, awning, sail to a gaff, etc.), temporary whippings, and other small stuff. Refer to Figure 7-24 while tying this knot.

1. Tie a single overhand knot.

2. Tie a second overhand knot on top so it mirrors (right and left reversed) the first one. The ends should come out together.

3. Draw tight.

THE MONKEY'S FIST Because some lines, such as towlines, are too heavy and awkward to throw any distance, a heaving line, with a monkey's fist tied on one end, is used. On Coast Guard boats, heaving lines are normally 75 to 100 feet of cotton line with a weighted core. Refer to Figure 7-25 while tying this knot.

1. Lay a bight of the line across the fingers of the left hand, about three and one-half feet from the end, holding the standing part with the left thumb.

2. With your fingers separated, take three turns around them.

3. Next take three turns around the first three and at right angles to them.

4. Take the knot off your fingers and take an additional three turns around the second three and inside the first three.

5. Take additional care at this step. Place the core weight into the knot and tighten it down carefully.

6. After tightening, there should be about 18 inches of line left on the bitter end. This can be brought up and seized alongside to the standing part.

FIGURE EIGHT (STOPPER) A figure eight knot is an overhand knot with an extra twist. It will prevent the end of a line from feeding through a block or fairlead when heavy loads are involved. It is also easier to untie and does not jam as hard as the over hand knot. (See Figure 7-26.)

Figure 7-24 Reef Knot (Square Knot)

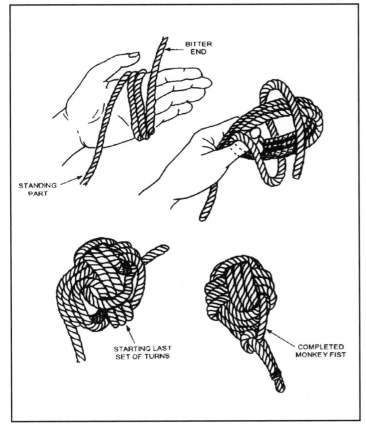

Figure 7-25 Monkey's Fist

Figure 7-26 Figure Eight Knot

SHEEPSHANK This hitch is used for temporarily shortening a piece of line. It consists of two bights of line, side-by-side, with a half hitch at either end. (See Figure 7-27.)

FISHERMAN'S OR ANCHOR BEND This bend is used to secure a line to a ring in an anchor or mooring buoy. It can also be tied around a spar. (See Figure 7-28.)

1. Pass the bitter end through the ring and around twice creating two loops spiraling downward

2. Wrap the bitter end up around the standing end and pass back through the loops at the top.

3. Tie a half hitch.

4. Pull taut.

CROWN KNOT A crown knot may be used to prevent an unwhipped line from unlaying. (See Figure 7-29.)

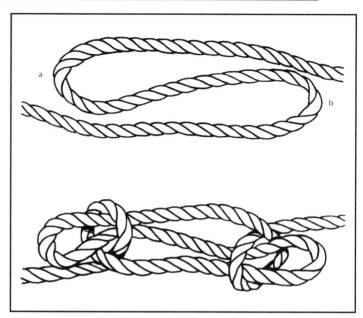

Figure 7-27 Sheepshank

Figure 7-28 Fisherman's or Anchor Bend

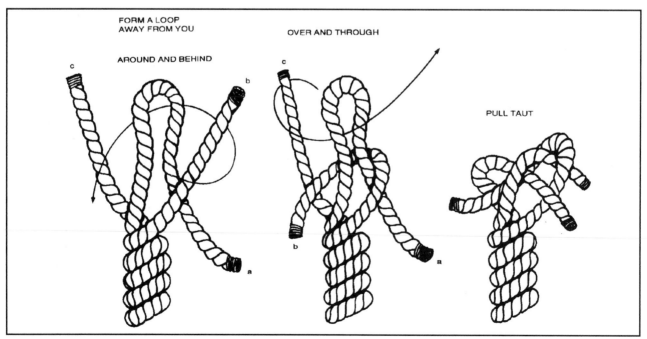

Figure 7-29 Crown Knot

1. Unlay the strands of the line about 12".

2. Separate the strands and hold them up with the middle strand facing you.

3. Bend the middle strand "a" away from you and form a loop.

4. Bring the right strand "b" around behind the loop, placing it between strand "c."

5. Bring strand "c" over strand "b" and through the loop formed by strand "a."

6. Pull taut by heaving on each of the three strands.

7. Lay the back splice by tucking each strand back up the line. The splicing is done as if making an eye splice.

Splices

D.6. GENERAL

Splices make a more permanent joining of two lines or two parts of a line. It is done by unlaying the strands or parts of the line(s) to be spliced and then putting the strands or parts back together to form a new union. The type of splice used depends on the type of joint and the type of line. On Coast Guard boats the most common splices are eye splices at the working end of the towline, side lines, and

mooring lines. Because double splices in braided nylon is the accepted line for towlines, eye splices in double braid will be shown. For those people who use three-strand nylon for mooring lines, three-strand eye splices will be illustrated. Additionally, directions for three strand back slices are given. They are a handy way for finishing off the ends of the lines on fenders and three strand heaving lines.

EYE SPLICE IN THREE STRAND PLAID LAID LINE The eye splice makes a permanent loop (the eye) in the end of a line. Refer to Figure 7-30 as you follow the steps below.

1. Unlay the strands of the line about 12".

2. Make a bight the size of the eye required.

3. Hold the strands up so the middle strand is facing you.

4. Tuck the middle strand "a."

5. Cross strand "b" over the strand just tucked and then under the strand just below it.

6. Turn the entire eye splice over and tuck strand "c."

7. Pull all strands tight.

8. Pass each strand over the adjacent strand and under the next strand until there are three tucks in each strand (synthetic line requires an additional tuck).

NOTE

Always tuck the middle strand first and keep the right-hand strand of the side of the line that is facing toward you. All tucks are made from outboard toward you.

BACK SPLICE IN THREE STRAND PLAIN LAID LINE Use a back splice to finish off the end of a line. On Coast Guard boats it can be used on the ends of fender lines. Start with unlaying the strands at the end. Then bend them back on the line, and then interweave them back through the strands of the standing part. The procedure for making a back splice is as follows (see Figure 7-31):

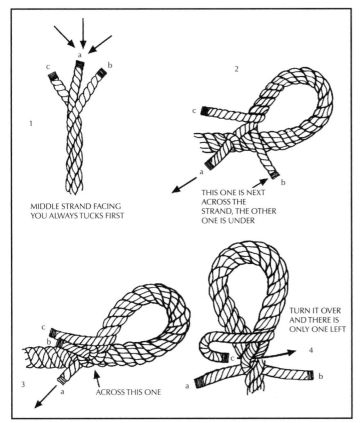

Figure 7-30 Three Stranded Eye Splice

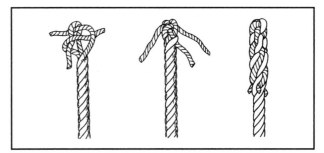

Figure 7-31 Back Splice (Three Strand)

1. Begin the back splice by tying a crown knot. Each strand goes under and out from its neighbor in the direction of the lay.

2. Pass each strand under itself, just beneath the crown knot. Do not pull these first tucks too tight.

3. Proceed with three more rounds of tucks—over one, under one, as in an eye splice.

4. If preferred, it can finished by trimming the ends of the strands.

SHORT SPLICE A short splice is used to permanently connect two ends of a line. It is important to note that a short splice is never used in a line that must pass over a pulley or sheeve. The procedure for making a short splice is as follows (see Figure 7-32):

1. Unlay the strands of the lines to be spliced, about 12".

2. Bring the ends together by alternating strands.

3. Slide the two ends together, that is—butt them and temporarily seize them with sail twine or tape.

4. Tuck each strand over and under three times, the same way as in eye splicing. (Synthetic line requires an additional tuck.)

5. Remove the seizing.

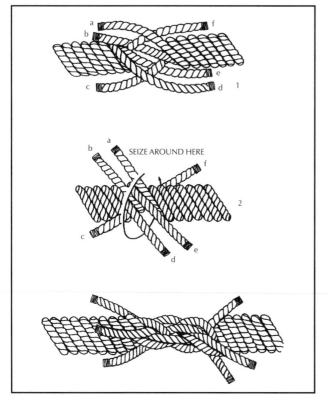

Figure 7-32 Short Splice

If desired, taper the short splice in the same manner as the eye splice.

EYE SPLICE IN DOUBLE BRAID LINE Splicing double braid entails pulling the core out of the cover and then putting the line back together to make the splice. The basic principle for putting it back together is:

1. The cover goes into the core.

2. Then the core goes back into the cover.

Splicing double braid requires the use of a special fid, or similar tool. The most common type is a bullet-nosed, hollow, tubular device. Use it with a proper sized line. This type of fid requires a "pusher" which resembles a long, blunt-pointed ice pick. For instructions on splicing double braided nylon, see Appendix 7-D.

Whipping

D.7. GENERAL

The end of a cut line will unravel and fray if not secured with a whipping or back-spliced. Whippings may be permanent or temporary.

D.8. TEMPORARY WHIPPING

Sometimes called the common whipping, temporary whippings make temporary repairs and secure strands of lines while splicing. They are not very durable and easily unravel if snagged. They are normally done using sail twine, although almost any small stuff will do. The procedures below instruct how to make temporary whipping.

1. Cut a piece of sail twine or small stuff, in length about ten times the circumference of the line being seized.

2. Lay the sail twine or small stuff alongside the line to be whipped (see Figure 7-33.)

3. Form an overhand loop in the sail twine or small stuff such that the loop extends about ½" beyond the end.

4. Holding end "a," make a series of turns over the loop toward the bitter end of the line. Make enough so the length of the turns are about equal to the diameter of the line.

5. Slip end "a" through the loop "c."

6. Secure by pulling loop end from sight by pulling on "b."

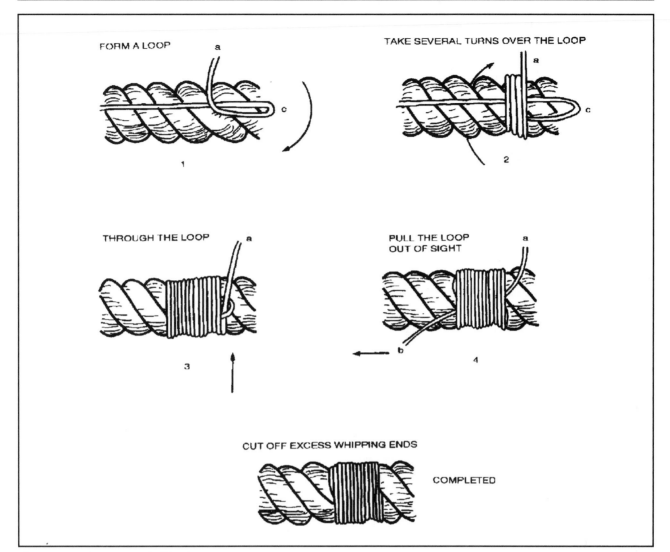

FORM A LOOP

1

TAKE SEVERAL TURNS OVER THE LOOP

2

THROUGH THE LOOP

3

PULL THE LOOP OUT OF SIGHT

4

CUT OFF EXCESS WHIPPING ENDS

COMPLETED

Figure 7-33 Temporary Whipping

7. Cut off excess whipping ends or secure them by tying them together with a reef or square knot.

D.9. PERMANENT WHIPPING

Permanent whippings are made to last. To make one, take several wraps around the line using shot line or waxed nylon. Then sew the ends of the whipping line across the whipping and through the line. (See Figure 7-34.)

1. Cut enough of the whipping line to allow for 15 to 20 wraps, with at least a foot of line left over.

2. Secure the whipping line by sewing it through the line. If you want, you can add strength by sewing through more than once.

3. Wind the whipping line around the line 15 to 20 times, working toward the end of the line. Make sure the body of the whipping covers the secured end of the whipping line.

4. Secure the whipping by sewing through the line. Then bring the line across the whipping and sewing it through the line. Do this three or more times, depending on the size of the line.

5. Finish the whipping by sewing through the line a couple more times and cutting the whipping line off close. A pull on the line will pull the end of the whipping line inside, hiding it from view.

Mousing Hooks and Shackles

D.10. HOOKS

A hook is moused to keep slings and straps from slipping out or off the hooks. This is accomplished by either mechanical means or by seizing the hook, using seizing wire or small stuff, from opposite sides. (See Figure 7-35.)

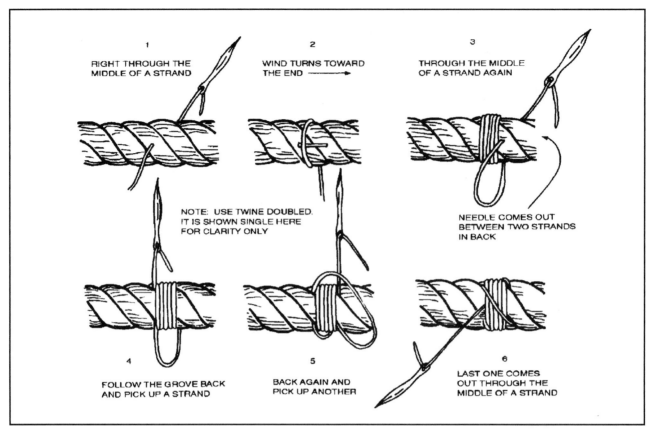

Figure 7-34 Permanent Whipping

D.11. SHACKLES

Shackles are moused to prevent the pin from backing out. This is usually done on screw-pin shackles. Mousing is accomplished by taking several turns, using seizing wire or small stuff, through the pin eye and around the shackle itself in such a way so the pin cannot turn.

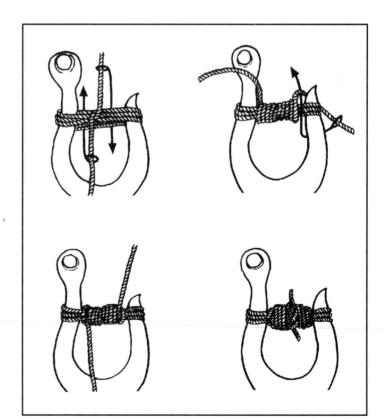

Figure 7-35 Mousing a Hook

Deck Fittings and Line Handling

Overview

Introduction

This section explains the procedures for securing lines to the various types of deck fittings.

In this section

Topic	See Page(s)
Deck Fittings	117
Line Handling	117–19

Deck Fittings

E.1. GENERAL

Deck fittings are attachments or securing points for lines. They permit easy handling and reduce wear and friction on lines.

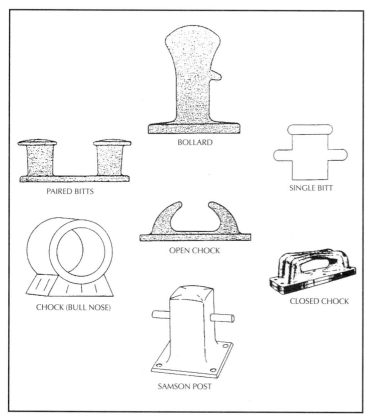

Figure 7-36 Types of Deck Fittings

E.2. TYPES OF FITTINGS

There are three basic types of deck fittings: Bitts, cleats, and chocks. Several types of deck fittings are shown in Figure 7-36.

Line Handling

E.3. GENERAL

Most Coast Guard standard boats have a towing bitt and a bow bitt. You find cleats on the decks next to the gunwales on each side of a boat used with bitts and cleats to help prevent chafing of the line. The chock provides a smooth surface for the line to run over or through. Because of the difference in the structural design of nonstandard boats, the strength of their deck fittings will vary widely.

E.4. USING PROPER SIZED LINE

The size of the deck hardware depends on the size of line to be used for mooring docking and towing. Cleats are sized by length, and the rule of thumb is the line should be $\frac{1}{16}$" in diameter for each inch of cleat ($\frac{3}{8}$" line = 6" cleat, $\frac{1}{2}$" line = 8" cleat).

NOTE

On Auxiliary operational facilities (as a rule of thumb) no tow should be attempted with smaller than $\frac{3}{8}$" line; therefore, the smallest size cleat on a facility should be 6".

E.5. BACK-UP PLATES

All deck hardware that is used for towing should have back-up plates to distribute the load over a wide area (see Figure 7-37). The back-up plate can be made of pressure treated hardwood or exterior grade plywood, at least twice as thick as the largest bolt diameter. Use bolts, not screws. A flat washer and a lock washer must be used with the bolt. The

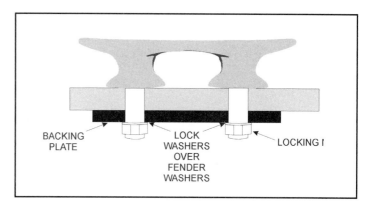

Figure 7-37 Back-Up Plate

flat washer is three times the bolt diameter. If metal is used, the thickness should be at least the same as the bold diameter. The use of soft aluminum is not recommended. Bedding compound should be used in all installations.

E.6. SECURING A LINE TO A BITT

The procedures below describe how to secure a line to a bitt:

1. Make a complete turn around the near horn (see Figure 7-38).

2. Make several figure eights around both horns. (Size of line and cleats may restrict the number of turns. Minimum of 3 turns is the standard).

3. Finish off with a round turn.

NOTE

Avoid the use of half hitches, weather hitches, and lock hitches on standard boats.

E.7. SECURING A LINE TO A SAMSON POST

A Samson post is a vertical timber or king post on the forward deck of a boat. It is used as a bow cleat or bitt.

1. Make a complete turn around the base of the Samson post (see Figure 7-39).

2. Form several figure eights around the horns of the Samson post. (Standard is 3 turns.)

E.8. SECURING A LINE TO A STANDARD CLEAT

The procedures below describe how to secure a line to a standard cleat (see Figure 7-40).

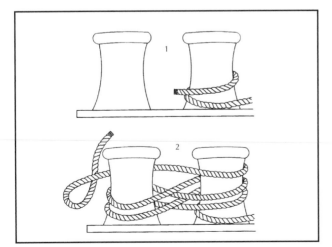

Figure 7-38 Securing a Line to a Bitt

1. Make a complete turn around the cleat.

2. Lead the line over the top of the cleat and around the horn to form a figure eight.

3. If possible, make two more figure eights.

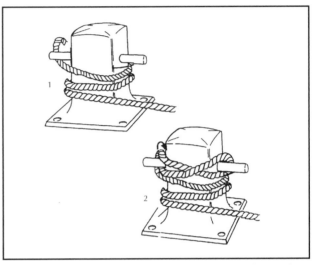

Figure 7-39 Securing a Line to a Samson Post (figure does not show extra figure eights)

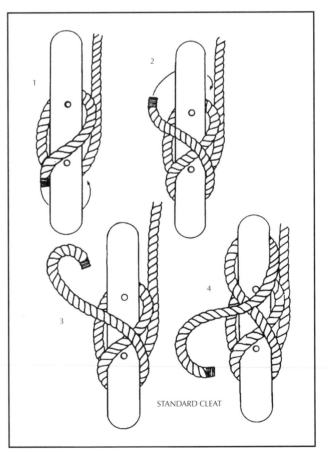

STANDARD CLEAT

Figure 7-40 Securing a Line to a Standard Cleat (figure does not show the extra figure eights)

E.9. SECURING A LINE TO A MOORING CLEAT

The procedures below describe how to secure a line to a mooring cleat (see Figure 7-41).

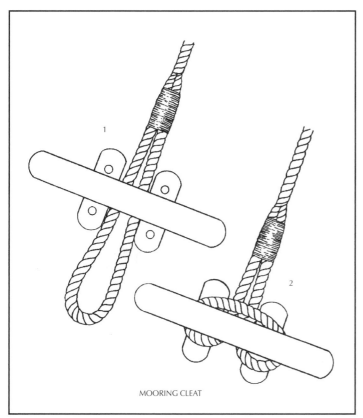

Figure 7-41 Securing a Line to a Mooring Cleat

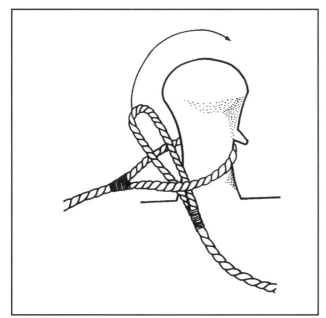

Figure 7-42 Dipping the Eye

1. Feed the eye of the line through the opening.
2. Loop the line back over both horns and pull the line taut.

E.10. DIPPING THE EYE

When two lines with eye splices are placed on a bollard, it may not be possible to remove the bottom line until the top line is removed. By dipping the eye, both lines can be placed for easy removal (see Figure 7-42).

1. Place the eye of one mooring line over the bollard.
2. Take the eye of the second line up through the eye of the first line.
3. Place the eye of the second line over the bollard.

E.11. SECURING A TOWLINE

The towline is a potential danger to anyone near it. Towlines should be made up so slack can be paid out at any time or so the line can be slipped (cast off) in an emergency. Procedures for securing the towlines on standard Coast Guard boats may be found in their respective operator manuals. Additional information on the use of towlines is in Chapter 17.

APPENDIX 7-A

Estimating the Breaking Strength and Safe Working Load of Lines

General

The following paragraphs provide a detailed explanation of how to estimate the breaking strengths of particular types of lines. It also explains how to use this number to figure the safe working load. Each type of line has a different breaking strength, and a different safe working load.

BREAKING STRENGTH OF NATURAL LINE

The estimated breaking strength (BS) of a piece of manila line can be found by squaring the circumference (C) of the line and then multiplying that number by 900 pounds. The formula for this is:

$$BS = C2 \times 900 \text{ pounds.}$$

Example:

Suppose the circumference of a piece of manila line is three inches. The breaking strength of that line can be determined as follows:

$$BS = C2 \times 900 \text{ pounds}$$
$$C2 = 3 \times 3 = 9$$
$$BS = 9 \times 900 \text{ pounds}$$
$$BS = 8{,}100 \text{ pounds}$$

BREAKING STRENGTH OF SYNTHETIC LINE

Use the same basic formula to estimate the breaking strength of synthetic lines by the addition of one more step. Because synthetic lines are stronger than manila line, the number of pounds representing their breaking strengths is multiplied by their comparison factors (CF).

COMPARISON FACTORS

Comparison factors are based on the strength of a synthetic line in comparison to natural manila line. The comparison factors given in Table A-1 reveal that synthetic line is stronger than manila line.

Table A-1 Comparison Factors (CF) for Synthetic Line	
Line Name	**CF to Manila Line**
Polypropylene	1.4
Polyethylene	1.4
Polyester (Dacron)	2.0
Nylon	2.5

ESTIMATING BS OF SYNTHETIC LINE

The formula for estimating the breaking strength of synthetic line is

$$BS = C2 \times 900 \times CF.$$
$$BS = C2 \times 900 \times CF$$
$$C2 = 3 \times 3 = 9$$
$$BS = 9 \times 900 \text{ pounds} \times CF$$
$$BS = 8{,}100 \text{ pounds} \times CF$$

CF = 2.0 for polyester (Dacron) line (taken from Table A-1)

$$BS = 8{,}100 \text{ pounds} \times 2$$
$$BS = 16{,}200 \text{ pounds}$$

SAFE WORKING LOAD OF NATURAL AND SYNTHETIC LINE

Breaking strength is the tension, measured in pounds, a line can absorb before it breaks. To be on the safe side you do not want to stress a line anywhere near its breaking point. The safe working load (SWL) of the line is considerably less than its breaking strength.

As a line wears, stretches or is spliced, its breaking strength decreases. Quite naturally, this also causes a decrease in the safe working load of the line. By making a quick inspection of a piece of line and determining whether it is in good, average or poor condition you can calculate an estimate of the safe working load of a line. Once the condition of the line is determined enter Table A-2 and apply the safety factor (SF) into its breaking strength using the formula:

$$SWL = BS/SF.$$

Table A-2 Safety Factors for Natural and Synthetic Lines			
Condition	**Manila**	**Nylon & Polyester**	**Polypropylene Polyethylene**
Good	5	3	5
Average	10	4	6
Poor	15	6	8

SWL OF MANILA LINE

Figure the safe working load of a three-inch manila line, in average condition, with a breaking strength of 8,100 lbs.

Determine the condition of the line and extract the appropriate safety factor from Table A-2. In this case

$$SF = 10.$$
$$SWL = BS/SF$$
$$SWL = 8{,}100 \text{ lbs.} \div 10$$
$$SWL = 810 \text{ lbs.}$$

SWL OF POLYESTER LINE

Figure the safe working load of a two-inch polyester (Dacron) line in poor condition:

$$BS = C2 \times 900 \text{ pounds} \times CF$$
$$C2 = 2 \times 2 = 4$$
$$BS = 4 \times 900 \times CF$$
$$BS = 3{,}600 \times CF$$
$$CF = 2 \text{ (Table A-1)}$$
$$BS = 3{,}600 \times 2$$
$$BS = 7{,}200 \text{ pounds}$$

DETERMINING THE CONDITION OF LINE

Determine condition of line and extract the appropriate safety factor from Table A-2:

$$SF = 6$$
$$SWL = BS/SF$$
$$SWL = 7200 \div 6$$
$$SWL = 1,200 \text{ pounds}$$

DETERMINING THE DIAMETER OF A LINE

The following formulas will help when determining the diameter of a line using two methods:

- Converting diameter to circumference
- Converting circumference to diameter

CONVERT DIAMETER TO CIRCUMFERENCE

Some sources of supply measure line by diameter. Sailors measure and refer to line by circumference. The formula to convert diameter to circumference is

$$C = D \times 3.1416.$$

Convert a diameter of ½ inch into circumference:

$$C = \tfrac{1}{2}" \times 3.1416$$
$$C = 1.5708"$$
$$C = 1\tfrac{1}{2}" \text{ (rounded off)}$$

CONVERT CIRCUMFERENCE TO DIAMETER

For converting circumference to diameter, you just turn the formula over; use

$$D = C/3.1416.$$

Convert a circumference of 3" into a diameter.

$$D = 3"/3.1416$$
$$D = 0.955"$$
$$D = 1" \text{ (rounded off)}$$

Estimating the Safe Working Load of Shackles

General

There is no formula to determine the breaking strength of shackles. Use the manufacturer's specifications. Bear in mind that damaged, bent or severely rusted shackles are unusable.

DETERMINING THE SWL

To determine the SWL of a shackle first measure the diameter (D) of the shackle at the point on the shackle shown in Figure 1-28. Technically, this is referred to as the Wire Diameter. The SWL of a shackle, in tons, is calculated by using the formula

$$SWL = 3 \times D2.$$

Use 3 tons as a constant and apply it to all usable shackles.

Calculate the SWL of a shackle with a 2 inch wire diameter as follows:

$$SWL = 3 \text{ tons} \times D2$$
$$D2 = 2 \times 2 = 4$$
$$SWL = 3 \text{ tons} \times 4$$
$$SWL = 12 \text{ tons}$$

Estimating the Safe Working Load of Hooks

General

The breaking strength of hooks can be found in the manufacturer's specifications or by using the formula below. Damaged, bent, or severely rusted hooks are unusable. The condition of a hook is either usable or unusable.

DETERMINING THE SWL

To determine the SWL of a hook measure the diameter (D).

Use "⅔" of a ton as a constant factor and apply it to all usable hooks by using the formula

$$SWL = ⅔ \text{ ton} \times D2.$$

Calculate the safe working load of a hook with a 2 inch diameter as follows:

$$SWL = ⅔ \text{ ton} \times D2$$
$$D2 = 2 \times 2 = 4 \text{ or } ⁴/₁$$
$$SWL = ⅔ \text{ ton} \times ⁴/₁$$
$$SWL = ⁸/₃ \text{ or } ²²/₃ \text{ ton}$$
$$SWL = 2.66 \text{ tons}$$

Eye Splice in Double Braid Line

The following series of steps (which is under copyright by Samson Ocean Systems, Inc.) is reprinted here by permission. It shows the specific steps needed to accomplish the splice for Samson double braided line. Other manufacturers of double braided line provide splicing instructions. Request specific information for splicing from the appropriate manufacturer.

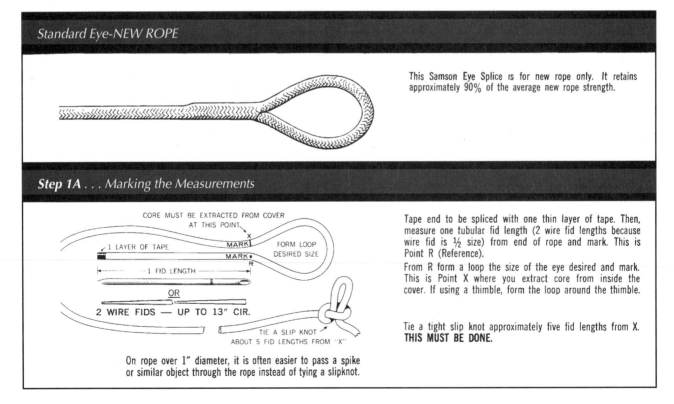

Standard Eye-NEW ROPE

This Samson Eye Splice is for new rope only. It retains approximately 90% of the average new rope strength.

Step 1A . . . Marking the Measurements

CORE MUST BE EXTRACTED FROM COVER AT THIS POINT
1 LAYER OF TAPE
MARK
FORM LOOP DESIRED SIZE
MARK
1 FID LENGTH
OR
2 WIRE FIDS — UP TO 13" CIR.
TIE A SLIP KNOT ABOUT 5 FID LENGTHS FROM "X"

On rope over 1" diameter, it is often easier to pass a spike or similar object through the rope instead of tying a slipknot.

Tape end to be spliced with one thin layer of tape. Then, measure one tubular fid length (2 wire fid lengths because wire fid is ½ size) from end of rope and mark. This is Point R (Reference).

From R form a loop the size of the eye desired and mark. This is Point X where you extract core from inside the cover. If using a thimble, form the loop around the thimble.

Tie a tight slip knot approximately five fid lengths from X. **THIS MUST BE DONE.**

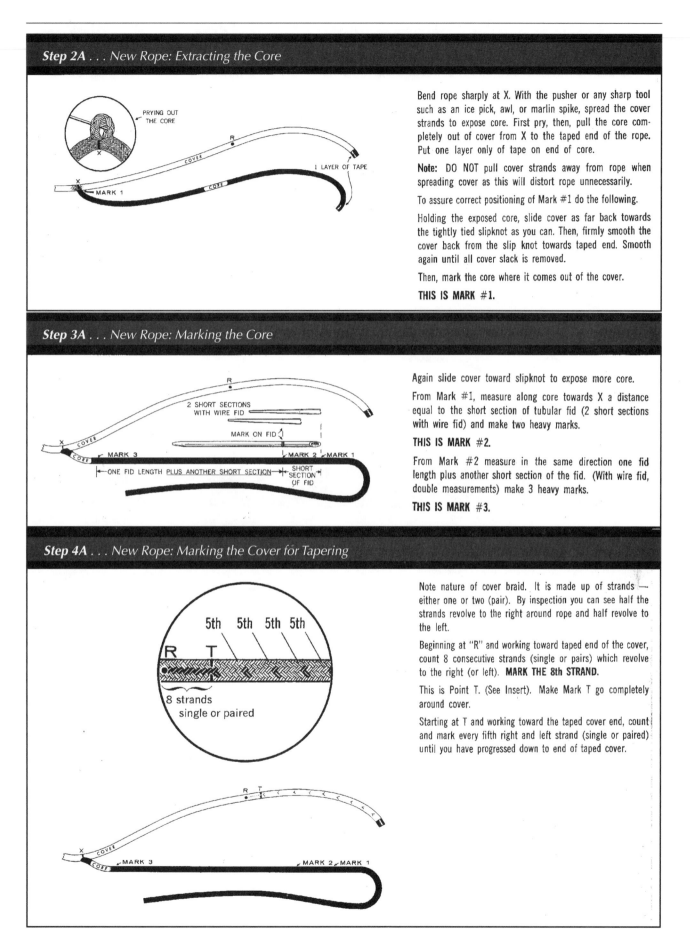

Step 2A . . . New Rope: Extracting the Core

PRYING OUT THE CORE

COVER

CORE

MARK 1

R

1 LAYER OF TAPE

Bend rope sharply at X. With the pusher or any sharp tool such as an ice pick, awl, or marlin spike, spread the cover strands to expose core. First pry, then, pull the core completely out of cover from X to the taped end of the rope. Put one layer only of tape on end of core.

Note: DO NOT pull cover strands away from rope when spreading cover as this will distort rope unnecessarily.

To assure correct positioning of Mark #1 do the following.

Holding the exposed core, slide cover as far back towards the tightly tied slipknot as you can. Then, firmly smooth the cover back from the slip knot towards taped end. Smooth again until all cover slack is removed.

Then, mark the core where it comes out of the cover.

THIS IS MARK #1.

Step 3A . . . New Rope: Marking the Core

R

2 SHORT SECTIONS WITH WIRE FID

MARK ON FID

COVER

CORE

MARK 3

MARK 2   MARK 1

ONE FID LENGTH PLUS ANOTHER SHORT SECTION   SHORT SECTION OF FID

Again slide cover toward slipknot to expose more core.

From Mark #1, measure along core towards X a distance equal to the short section of tubular fid (2 short sections with wire fid) and make two heavy marks.

THIS IS MARK #2.

From Mark #2 measure in the same direction one fid length plus another short section of the fid. (With wire fid, double measurements) make 3 heavy marks.

THIS IS MARK #3.

Step 4A . . . New Rope: Marking the Cover for Tapering

5th   5th   5th   5th

R   T

8 strands
single or paired

X

COVER

CORE

MARK 3

R   T

MARK 2   MARK 1

Note nature of cover braid. It is made up of strands — either one or two (pair). By inspection you can see half the strands revolve to the right around rope and half revolve to the left.

Beginning at "R" and working toward taped end of the cover, count 8 consecutive strands (single or pairs) which revolve to the right (or left). **MARK THE 8th STRAND.**

This is Point T. (See Insert). Make Mark T go completely around cover.

Starting at T and working toward the taped cover end, count and mark every fifth right and left strand (single or paired) until you have progressed down to end of taped cover.

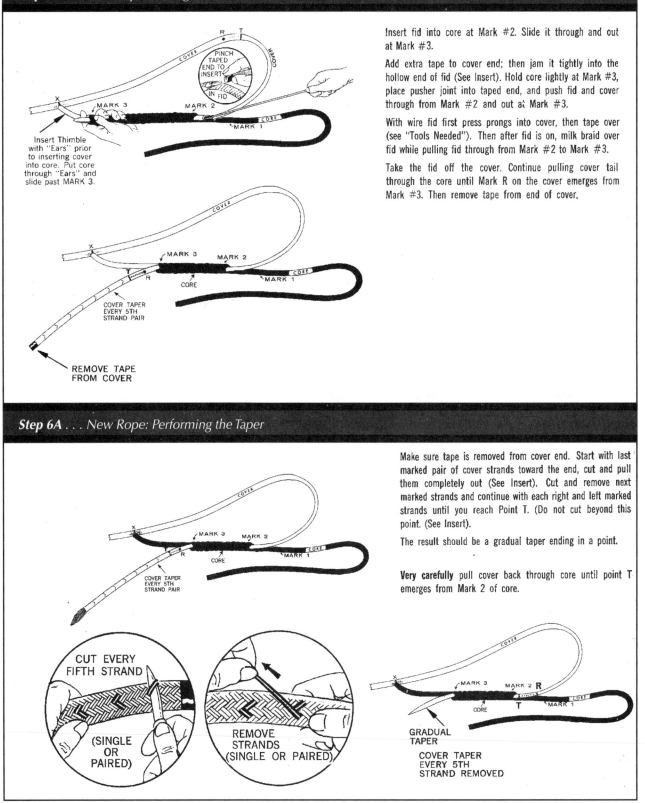

Insert fid into core at Mark #2. Slide it through and out at Mark #3.

Add extra tape to cover end; then jam it tightly into the hollow end of fid (See Insert). Hold core lightly at Mark #3, place pusher joint into taped end, and push fid and cover through from Mark #2 and out at Mark #3.

With wire fid first press prongs into cover, then tape over (see "Tools Needed"). Then after fid is on, milk braid over fid while pulling fid through from Mark #2 to Mark #3.

Take the fid off the cover. Continue pulling cover tail through the core until Mark R on the cover emerges from Mark #3. Then remove tape from end of cover.

Make sure tape is removed from cover end. Start with last marked pair of cover strands toward the end, cut and pull them completely out (See Insert). Cut and remove next marked strands and continue with each right and left marked strands until you reach Point T. (Do not cut beyond this point. (See Insert).

The result should be a gradual taper ending in a point.

Very carefully pull cover back through core until point T emerges from Mark 2 of core.

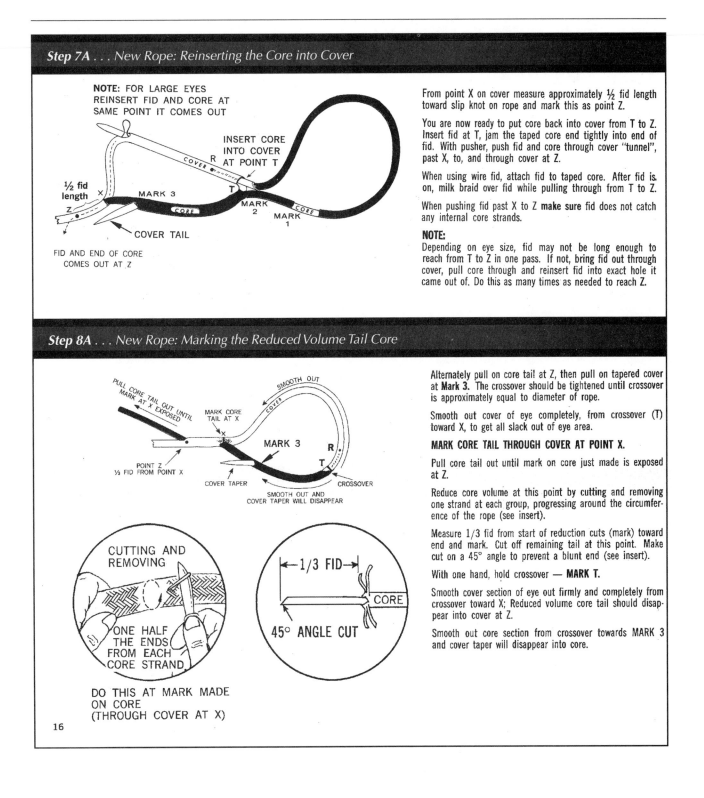

NOTE: FOR LARGE EYES REINSERT FID AND CORE AT SAME POINT IT COMES OUT

INSERT CORE INTO COVER AT POINT T

COVER R

½ fid length

MARK 3

X

Z

CORE

MARK 2

MARK 1

CORE

T

COVER TAIL

FID AND END OF CORE COMES OUT AT Z

From point X on cover measure approximately ½ fid length toward slip knot on rope and mark this as point Z.

You are now ready to put core back into cover from T to Z. Insert fid at T, jam the taped core end tightly into end of fid. With pusher, push fid and core through cover "tunnel", past X, to, and through cover at Z.

When using wire fid, attach fid to taped core. After fid is. on, milk braid over fid while pulling through from T to Z.

When pushing fid past X to Z **make sure** fid does not catch any internal core strands.

NOTE:
Depending on eye size, fid may not be long enough to reach from T to Z in one pass. If not, bring fid out through cover, pull core through and reinsert fid into exact hole it came out of. Do this as many times as needed to reach Z.

PULL CORE TAIL OUT UNTIL MARK AT X EXPOSED

SMOOTH OUT

COVER

MARK CORE TAIL AT X

X

MARK 3

R

T

POINT Z ⅓ FID FROM POINT X

COVER TAPER

CROSSOVER

SMOOTH OUT AND COVER TAPER WILL DISAPPEAR

CUTTING AND REMOVING

ONE HALF THE ENDS FROM EACH CORE STRAND

DO THIS AT MARK MADE ON CORE (THROUGH COVER AT X)

1/3 FID

CORE

45° ANGLE CUT

Alternately pull on core tail at Z, then pull on tapered cover at **Mark 3**. The crossover should be tightened until crossover is approximately equal to diameter of rope.

Smooth out cover of eye completely, from crossover (T) toward X, to get all slack out of eye area.

MARK CORE TAIL THROUGH COVER AT POINT X.

Pull core tail out until mark on core just made is exposed at Z.

Reduce core volume at this point by cutting and removing one strand at each group, progressing around the circumference of the rope (see insert).

Measure 1/3 fid from start of reduction cuts (mark) toward end and mark. Cut off remaining tail at this point. Make cut on a 45° angle to prevent a blunt end (see insert).

With one hand, hold crossover — **MARK T.**

Smooth cover section of eye out firmly and completely from crossover toward X; Reduced volume core tail should disappear into cover at Z.

Smooth out core section from crossover towards MARK 3 and cover taper will disappear into core.

16

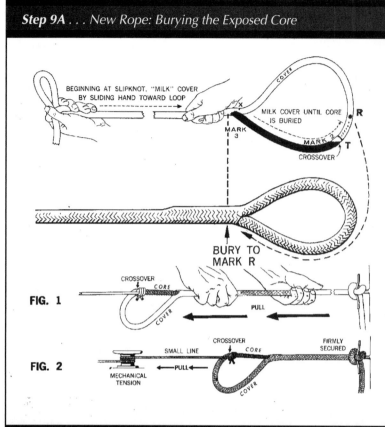

BEGINNING AT SLIPKNOT, "MILK" COVER BY SLIDING HAND TOWARD LOOP

MILK COVER UNTIL CORE IS BURIED

MARK 3

MARK 2

CROSSOVER

R

T

BURY TO MARK R

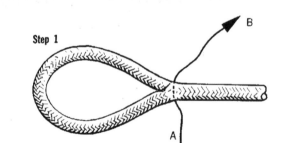

FIG. 1

CROSSOVER

CORE

COVER

PULL

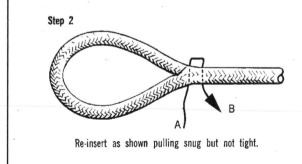

FIG. 2

SMALL LINE

CROSSOVER

CORE

FIRMLY SECURED

COVER

MECHANICAL TENSION

PULL

Hold rope at slipknot and with other hand milk cover toward splice, gently at first, then more firmly. Cover will slide over Mark #3, Mark #2, the crossover, and T and R. (It may be necessary to occasionally smooth out eye during milking to prevent reduced volume tail catching in throat of splice).

If bunching occurs at cross-over preventing full burying, smooth cover from T to X. Grasp crossover at T with one hand and then firmly smooth cover slack (female side of eye) with other hand towards throat (X). Repeat as necessary until bunching disappears.

Continue milking until all cover slack between knot and throat of eye has been removed.

TIP:
Before burying the cover over the crossover:

A. Anchor loop of slip-knot by tying it to stationary object before starting to bury. You can then use both hands and weight of body to more easily bury cover over core and crossover. (See Fig. 1 & 2).

B. Holding the crossover tightly milk all the excess cover from R to X.

Flex and loosen the rope at the crossover point during the final burying process. Hammering cover at point X will help loosen strands.

With larger ropes it is helpful to securely anchor slip-knot, attach a small line to the braided core at the crossover and mechanically apply tension with either a block and tackle, capstan, come-a-long, or power winch. Tension will reduce diameter of core and crossover for easier burying. (See Fig. 2).

Step 1

B

A

Pass stitching through spliced area near throat of eye as shown.

Step 2

B

A

Re-insert as shown pulling snug but not tight.

Stitch locking is advantageous on splices to prevent no-load opening due to mishandling.

Material Required — About one (1) fid length of Nylon or Polyester Whipping Twine approximately the same size of the strands in the size rope you are stitch locking. The same strands cut from the rope you are stitch locking may also be used.

Step 3

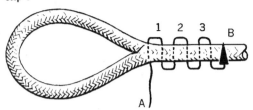

Continue to re-insert as shown until you have at least three (3) complete stitches.

Step 4

After completing Step #3, rotate spliced part of rope 90° and re-insert end "A" into splice area in the same fashion as in steps #1, #2, and #3. The splice will now be stitched on two planes perpendicular to each other. Make sure you do not pull stitching too tight.

Configuration of cross section after completing Step #4.

Step 5

After stitching at least three (3) complete stitches as in step #3, extract two ends A & B together through the same opening in the braid. Tie them together with a square knot and re-insert back into braid between cover and core.

End-for-End Double Braid

The Samson Standard End-for-End Splice can be performed on new and used rope. This is an all-purpose splice technique designed for people who generally splice used rope as frequently as new rope. It retains up to 85% of average new rope strength and in used rope up to 85% of the remaining used rope strength.

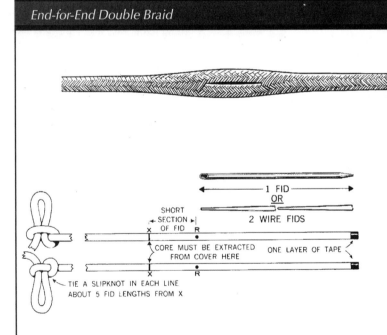

Tape the end of each rope with one thin layer of tape. Lay two ropes to be spliced side by side and measure one tubular fid length (2 wire fid lengths because wire fid is ½ size) from end of each rope and make a mark. This is Point R (Reference).

From R measure one short fid section length as scribed on the fid; then, mark again. This is Point X where you should extract core from inside cover. Be sure both ropes are identically marked.

Tie a tight slipknot approximately 5 fid lengths from X.

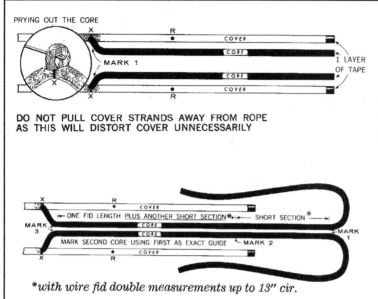

PRYING OUT THE CORE

MARK 1

1 LAYER OF TAPE

DO NOT PULL COVER STRANDS AWAY FROM ROPE AS THIS WILL DISTORT COVER UNNECESSARILY

Bend rope sharply at X. With the pusher or any sharp tool such as an ice pick, awl, or marlin spike, spread cover strands to expose core. First pry; then, pull core completely out of cover from X to the end of rope. Put one layer only of tape on end of core.

To assure correct positioning of Mark #1 do the following. Holding the exposed core, slide cover as far back towards the tightly tied slip knot as you can. Then, firmly smooth cover back from the slip knot towards taped end. Smooth again until all cover slack is removed. Then, mark core where it comes out of cover. This is Mark #1. Do this to both ropes.

MARK 3

ONE FID LENGTH PLUS ANOTHER SHORT SECTION ✽   SHORT SECTION ✽

MARK SECOND CORE USING FIRST AS EXACT GUIDE   MARK 2

MARK 1

✽with wire fid double measurements up to 13" cir.

Hold one core at Mark #1 and slide cover back to expose more core.

From Mark #1, measure along core towards X a distance equal to the short section of fid ✽and make two heavy marks. This is Mark #2.

From Mark #2, measure in the same direction **one fid length plus another short section** ✽and make three heavy marks. This is Mark #3.

Mark second core by laying it alongside the first and using it as an exact guide.

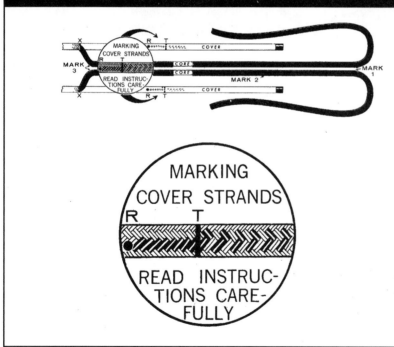

MARKING COVER STRANDS

READ INSTRUC- TIONS CARE- FULLY

MARK 3

MARK 2

MARK 1

MARKING
COVER STRANDS
R   T
READ INSTRUC-
TIONS CARE-
FULLY

Note nature of the cover braid. It is made up of strands. By inspection you can see that half the strands revolve to the right around the rope and half revolve to the left.

Beginning at R and working toward the taped end of cover, count 8 consecutive pairs of cover strands which revolve to the right (or left). Mark the 8th pair. This is Point T (See Insert). Make Mark T go completely around cover.

Starting at T and working toward taped cover end **count** and **mark every second right pair** of strands for a total of 6. Again, starting at T, count and mark every second left pair of strands for a total of 6. (See Insert).

Make both ropes identical.

Step 5 . . . Performing the Taper

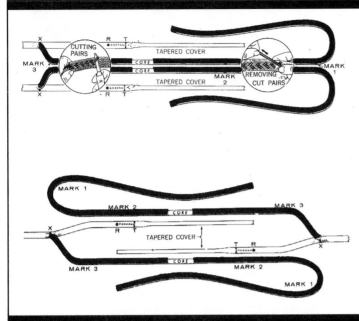

First remove tape from cover end. Starting with last marked pair of cover strands toward the end, cut and pull them completely out (See Insert). Cut and remove next marked strands and continue with each right and left marked strands until you reach Point T. **Do not cut beyond this point.** (See Insert)

Retape tapered end.

Cut and remove marked strands on the other marked cover, again stopping at T. Retape tapered end.

Reposition ropes for splicing according to diagram. Note how cover of one rope has been paired off with core of the opposite line. **Avoid twisting.**

Step 7 . . . Putting the Cover Inside Core

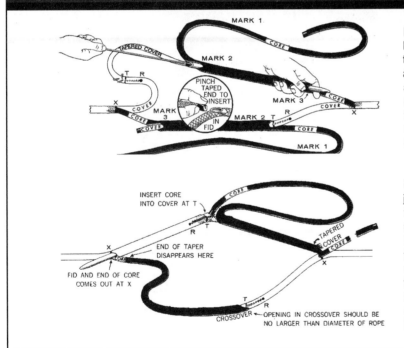

Insert fid into one core at Mark #2 and bring it out at Mark #3. Add extra tape to tapered cover end then jam it tightly into hollow end of fid (see insert). Hold core lightly at Mark #3, place pusher point into taped end pushing fid and with cover in it from Mark #2 out at Mark #3. When using wire fid, attach fid to cover. Then pull fid through from Mark #2 to Mark #3. Pull cover tail through core until Mark T on cover meets Mark #2 on core. Insert other cover into core in same manner.

Now put core back into cover from T to X. Insert fid at T, jam taped core tightly into end of fid. With pusher, push fid and core through cover bringing out at Point X. When using wire fid attach fid to taped core. Then pull fid and braid through from T to X. Do this to both cores. Remove tape from end of cover. Bring crossover up tight by pulling on core tail and on tapered covered tail. Hold crossover tightly smoothing out all excess braid away from crossover in each direction. Trim end of Tapered cover on an angle to eliminate blunt end. Tapered cover tail will disappear at Mark #3. Cut core tail off close to Point X at an angle.

CHAPTER

8

Boat Characteristics

Editor's Note: *Among the best operating guidelines Coast Guard coxswains can offer is the admonition to know your boat—all about your boat. Understand its limitations and capabilities. Know its construction, its layout, and its carrying capacity. Know how its systems work, especially the power plants and electrics. Obtain the appropriate manuals and keep them on board. Develop checklists for complex procedures, and know how to deal with common mechanical problems. The information in this chapter provides great tips in all these areas.*

Overview

Introduction

Knowledge of your boat's equipment and characteristics is essential to safe operations. All crew members must be able to locate any piece of gear quickly (even in darkness) and know how to operate all equipment efficiently and effectively. Therefore, crew members must be intimately familiar with the boat's layout. Also, each boat has specific operational characteristics and limitations with which the crew must be familiar. This information is available in the boat's standard manuals. For non-standard boats, the owner/operator manual will provide most the information. Some of the more important operating characteristics and limitations are:

- maximum speed
- economical cruising speed
- maximum range at various speeds
- maximum endurance of boat at cruising speed
- minimum required crew

- maximum number of people that can be safely carried
- maximum load capacity

This section covers the basics you must know to operate your boat. For additional definitions, see the Glossary.

In this chapter

SECTION A

Boat Nomenclature and Terminology

A.1. GENERAL

As with any profession or skill, there are special terms that mariners use. Many of these terms have fascinating histories. Fellow mariners will expect you to be familiar with these terms and use them in your routine conversation.

A.2. DEFINITIONS

The following are common terms used for location, position and direction aboard a boat. Figure

8-1 provides a diagram of a boat with the more common terms noted.

BOW The front end of a boat is the bow. When *you* move toward the bow, you are going **forward**; when the *boat* moves forward, it is going **ahead**. When you face the bow, the front right side is the **starboard bow**, and the front left side is the **port bow**.

AMIDSHIPS The central or middle area of a boat is amidships. The right center side is the **starboard beam** and the left center side is the **port beam**.

STERN The rear of a boat is the stern. When *you* move toward the stern, you are going **aft**. When the *boat* moves backwards, it is going **astern**. If you are standing at the stern looking forward, you call the right rear section the **starboard quarter** and the left rear section the **port quarter**.

STARBOARD The entire right side of a boat, from bow to stern is called the starboard side.

PORT The entire left side of a boat from bow to stern is called the port side.

FORE AND AFT A line, or anything else, running parallel to the centerline of a boat.

ATHWARTSHIPS A line or anything else running from side to side.

OUTBOARD From the centerline of the boat toward either port or starboard side.

INBOARD From either side toward the centerline. However, there is a variation in the use of outboard and inboard when a boat is tied up alongside something (e.g., pier or another vessel). The side tied up is inboard; the side away is outboard.

GOING TOPSIDE Moving from a lower deck to a weather deck or upper deck.

GOING BELOW Moving from an upper deck to a lower deck.

GOING ALOFT Going up into the boat's rigging.

WEATHER DECK Deck exposed to the elements (weather).

LIFELINES Lifelines or railings, erected around the edge of weather decks, are all technically called lifelines although they may have different proper names.

WINDWARD In the direction from which the wind is blowing; toward the wind.

LEEWARD Opposite point from which the wind is blowing; away from the wind. Pronounced "loo-urd".

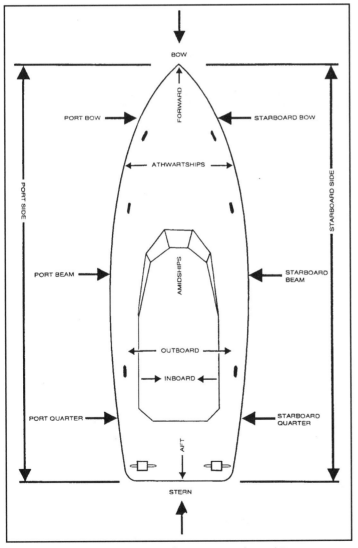

Figure 8-1 Position and Direction Aboard Boats

Boat Construction

Overview

Introduction

The boat construction terms discussed in this section include terms that the boat crew will use on a daily basis in normal conversations and in operational situations. Proper understanding of these terms and concepts is important for clear, unambiguous communication.

In this section ·

Hull Types

B.1. GENERAL

The hull is the main body of a boat. It consists of a structural framework and a skin or shell plating. The hull may be constructed of many different materials, most commonly metal or fiberglass. A metal skin is usually welded to the structural framework, although sometimes skins are riveted to the framework. A vessel could be monohull or multihull (catamarans and trimarans). The three hull forms based on vessel speed are:

- Displacement hull
- Planing hull
- Semidisplacement hull

B.2. FACTORS INFLUENCING HULL SHAPES

Many factors influence hull shapes and affect the boat's **buoyancy** (its ability to float) and **stability** (its ability to remain upright). Factors that influence hull shapes are discussed as follows:

FLARE: Flare is the outward turn of the hull as the sides of the hull come up from the waterline. As the boat is launched into the water, the flare increases the boat's displacement and creates a positive buoyant force to float the boat.

TUMBLEHOME: Tumblehome is the reverse of flare and is the shape of the hull as it moves outboard going from the gunwale to the waterline. This feature is most noticeable on the transoms of older classic cruisers.

CAMBER: A deck usually curves athwartships, making it higher at the centerline than at the gunwales. This curvature, called camber, allows water to flow off the deck.

SHEER: Sheer is the curvature of the main deck from the stem to the stern. Pronounced sheer with the bow of the boat higher than the main deck at amidship provides added buoyancy at the bow. Reserve buoyancy is the additional flotation provided by flare and sheer.

CHINE: The turn of the boat's hull below the waterline is called the **chine**. It is "soft" if it is rounded and "hard" if it is squared off. Chine affects the boat's speed and turning characteristics.

TRANSOM: The **transom** at the stern of the boat is either wide, flat, or curved. The shape of the stern affects the speed, hull resistance, and performance of the boat.

WATERLINE LENGTH: The boat's **length on waterline** (LWL) is the distance from the bow to the stern, measured at the waterline when the boat is stationary. Note that this length changes as the boat rides high or low in the water. Another way of measuring the length of the boat is the length of the craft from its stem to its stern in a straight line. This is termed **length over all** (LOA) and does not change according to the way the boat sits in the water.

BEAM AND BREADTH: **Beam** and **breadth** are measures of a boat's width. Beam is the measurement of the widest part of the hull. Breadth is the measurement of a frame from its port inside edge to its starboard inside edge.

Molded beam is the distance between outside surfaces of the shell plating of the hull at its widest point.

Extreme breadth is the distance between outside edges of the frames at the widest point of the hull.

DRAFT: **Draft** is the depth of the boat from the actual waterline to the bottom of its keel.

DRAFT APPENDAGE: **Draft appendage** is the depth of the boat from the actual waterline to the bottom of its keel or other permanent projection (e.g., propeller, rudder, skeg, etc.), if such a projection is deeper than the keel. The draft is also the depth of water necessary to float the boat. The draft varies according to how the boat lies in the water.

TRIM: **Trim** is a relative term that refers to the way the boat sets in the water and describes generally its stability and buoyancy. A **change in trim** may be defined as the change in the difference between drafts forward and aft. A boat is **trimmed** by the bow when the draft forward increases and the draft is greater than the stern draft. A boat is trimmed by the stern if it is down by the stern.

B.3. DISPLACEMENT HULL

A displacement hull boat pushes away (displaces) water allowing the hull to settle down into the water. Underway, the hull pushes out this water, creating waves. (See Figure 8-2.) The water separates at the bow and closes at the stern. Tremendous forces work against a displacement hull as the power pushing it and the boat's speed both increase. At maximum displacement speed, there are distinct **bow** and **stern** waves. The length of these waves depends upon the boat's length and speed. (The longer the boat the longer the wave length.) As speed increases, the bow and the stern ride lower in the water, and the water level alongside (amidships) becomes lower than that of the surrounding water.

These effects are caused by the increase in the velocity of the water flowing under the boat and its interaction with the bow and stern waves. As the boat travels along, it rides in a depression created by its own passage. The displacement hull vessel's maximum speed is determined by the vessel's waterline length. Heavy displacement hulls cannot exceed a speed of 1.34 times the square root of their waterline length without requiring excessive power. This speed is known as **critical** speed. When towing a vessel, you must be careful not to tow beyond that vessel's critical speed. For details on towing displacement hulls, see Chapter 17—Towing.

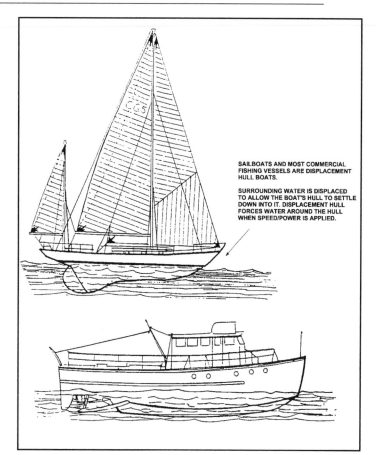

SAILBOATS AND MOST COMMERCIAL FISHING VESSELS ARE DISPLACEMENT HULL BOATS.

SURROUNDING WATER IS DISPLACED TO ALLOW THE BOAT'S HULL TO SETTLE DOWN INTO IT. DISPLACEMENT HULL FORCES WATER AROUND THE HULL WHEN SPEED/POWER IS APPLIED.

Figure 8-2 Displacement Hulls

WARNING When towing a vessel, be careful not to tow beyond the vessel's design speed.

B.4. PLANING HULL

At rest the planing hull and the displacement hull both displace the water around them. The planing hull reacts nearly the same as a displacement hull when it gets underway initially—it takes considerable power to produce a small increase in speed. But at a certain point, external forces acting on the shape lift the hull is onto the surface of the water. (See Figure 8-3.) The planing hull skims along the surface of the water whereas the displacement hull always forces water around it. Riding on top of the water is called planing. Once "on top," the power/speed ratio is considerably altered—very small in-

creases in power (thrust) result in a large increases in speed. You must apply power gradually when going from the displacement mode to the planing mode or from the planing mode to the displacement mode. When you decrease the power gradually, the hull makes an even, steady transition, like slowly moving your hand from above the water's surface, through it, and into the liquid below. However, if power is rapidly decreased the transition will be a rough one, for the hull will slap the surface of the water like the slap resulting by hitting a liquid surface with your hand.

Additionally, the rapid "re-entry" into the displacement mode from above the surface, through the surface, and back into the water causes rapid deceleration as the forces in the water exert pressure against the hull. The effect is like rapidly braking an automobile.

B.5. SEMIDISPLACEMENT HULL

The semidisplacement hull is a combination of characteristics of the displacement hull and the planing hull. Many Coast Guard boats are this type (e.g., 44 ft. MLB). This means that up to a certain power

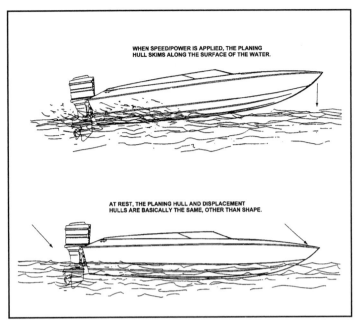

WHEN SPEED/POWER IS APPLIED, THE PLANING HULL SKIMS ALONG THE SURFACE OF THE WATER.

AT REST, THE PLANING HULL AND DISPLACEMENT HULLS ARE BASICALLY THE SAME, OTHER THAN SHAPE.

Figure 8-3 Planing Hulls

level and speed (power/speed ratio), the hull remains in the displacement mode. Beyond this point, the hull is raised to a partial plane. Essentially, the semidisplacement hull, like the displacement hull, always remains in the water; it never gets "on top." When in the displacement mode, the power/ speed ratio is similar to the power/speed ratio described above for the displacement hull. When in the semi-planing mode, the hull is affected by a combination of displacement mode and planing mode forces. Thus, while a small power increase will increase speed, the amount of acceleration will not be as great as the same power increase would produce for a planing hull.

Keel

B.6. GENERAL

The keel is literally the backbone of the boat. It runs fore and aft along the center bottom of the boat.

B.7. KEEL PARTS

The following are all integral parts of the keel.

FRAMES **Frames** are attached to the keel and extend athwartships (from side to side). The skin of the boat is attached to the frames. The keel and the frames strengthen the hull to resist external forces and distribute the boat's weight.

STEM The **stem** is an extension of the forward end of the keel. Although there are a number of common stem shapes, all are normally slanted forward (raked) at an upward angle to reduce water friction.

STERNPOST The **sternpost** is a vertical extension of the aft end of the keel.

B.8. KEEL TYPES

There are many types of keels. However, in metal boats, there are two types of particular interest: the bar keel and the flat plate keel.

BAR KEEL The bar keel is popular because its **stiffeners** (vertical or upright members which increase strength) protect the boat's hull plating if the boat grounds on a hard bottom. It also reduces rolling in much the same way as the more modern bilge keel does. The bilge keel is a fin or stabilizer fastened horizontally to the turn of the bilge. A disadvantage of the bar keel is that it extends below the hull and increases the boat's draft.

FLAT OR FLAT PLATE KEEL The flat keel consists of an "I" beam fastened to the flat plate or it may be built-up from a "rider plate"—a metal plate reinforcing the upper or inner surface of the keel, a vertical keel, and a flat keel. The flat keel, with its vertical keel and rider plate, is built within the boat's hull.

Principal Boat Parts

B.9. BOW

The shape of a boat's bow—its profile, form, and construction—determine hull resistance as the boat advances through the water. Hull resistance develops from surface friction and from the wave the hull makes as it moves through the water. Wave making resistance depends on the boat's speed.

The bow of a boat must be designed with enough buoyancy so it lifts with the waves and does not cut through them. The bow flare provides this buoyancy.

Boats intended for operation in rough seas and heavy weather have "full" bows. The bow increases the buoyancy of the forward part of a boat and deflects water and spray. When a boat is heading into a wave, the bow will initially start to cut into the wave. It may be immersed momentarily if the seas are rough. As the bow flare cuts into the wave it causes the water to fall away from a boat's stern, causing the center of buoyancy to move forward from the center of gravity. The bow lifts with the wave and the wave passes under the boat, shifting the center of buoyancy aft. This action causes the bow to drop back down and the vessel achieves a level attitude.

B.10. STERN

The shape of the stern affects the speed, resistance, and performance of the boat. It also affects the way water flows to the propellers.

The design of the stern is critical to operation in following seas where the stern is the first part of a boat to meet the waves. If following waves lift the stern too high, the bow may be buried in the sea. The force of the wave will push the stern causing it to pivot around toward the bow. If this is not controlled, the may pitch pole or broach.

ROUNDED TYPE STERN The rounded, cruiser type stern presents less flat surface area for a following sea to push upon (see Figure 8-4).

CRUISER TYPE STERN The cruiser type stern tends to split the waves of a following sea allowing them to pass forward along each side of the boat. Thus the wave has minimum impact on the attitude of the vessel and provides additional buoyancy for the stern. Always steer into any sideways movement of the stern. For example, when the stern slips to starboard, turn to starboard. It is particularly important that these corrections be made quickly and accurately in short, choppy following seas. Transom sterns provide a larger surface area for the seas to push upon and should not be exposed to heavy following seas or surf conditions (see Figure 8-5).

B.11. RUDDER

The rudder controls the direction of the boat and may vary widely in size, design, and method of construction. The shape of the stern, the number of propellers, and the characteristics of the boat determine the type of rudder a boat has. Rudder types are shown in Figure 8-6:

- Balanced—blade about half forward and half aft of the rudder post

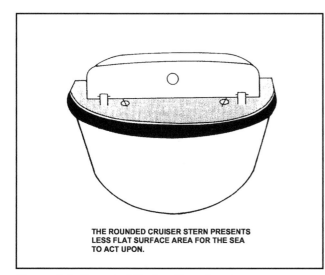

Figure 8-4 Rounded Cruiser Type Stern

- Semi-balanced—more than half of the blade aft of the rudder post
- Unbalanced—blade entirely aft of the rudder post

B.12. PROPELLER

Most boats are driven by one or more screw propellers which move in spirals somewhat like the threads on a screw. That is why the propeller is commonly referred to as a screw. The most common propellers are built with three and four blades. The propeller on a single-screw boat typically turns in a clockwise direction (looking from aft forward) as the boat moves forward. Such screws are referred to as "right-handed." On twin screw boats, the screws turn in opposite directions, rotating outward from the centerline of the boat. The port screw is "left-handed" and turns counter-clockwise. The starboard screw is "right-handed" and turns clockwise.

PROPELLER PARTS A propeller consists of blades and a hub. The section of the blade near the hub is called the **root** and its outer edge is called the **tip** (see Figure 8-7).

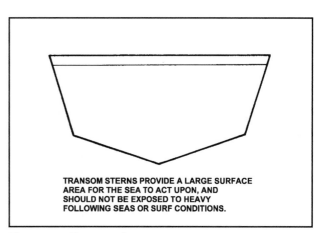

Figure 8-5 Transom Stern

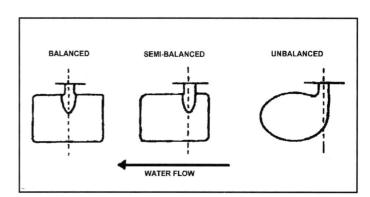

Figure 8-6 Rudder Types

PROPELLER EDGE The edge of the blade that strikes the water first is the **leading edge**; the opposite edge is the **following edge**. The diameter of the screw, the circle made by its tips and its circumference, is called the **tip circle**. Each blade has a degree of twist from root to tip called **pitch** (see Figure 8-7).

PITCH Pitch is the distance a propeller advances in one revolution with no slip (see Figure 8-7). Generally, less pitch in the same diameter propeller makes it easier for the engine to reach its preferred maximum RPM; thus, like putting a car in first gear, more power (and sometimes more speed) is available. Similarly, like third gear in a car more pitch may give more speed, but lower RPMs gives less power. Optimum performance is obtained when pitch is matched to the optimum design speed (RPM) of the engine.

B.13. FRAMES

As previously stated, it is the framing that gives the hull its strength. Frames are of two types:

TRANSVERSE FRAMES Watertight bulkheads or web frames are located at certain points in the hull to increase the strength of the hull. Just as the keel is the backbone of the hull, transverse frames and are often referred to as ribs. Transverse frames extend athwartships and are perpendicular (vertical or upright) to the keel and are spaced at specified distances. (See Figure 8-8.) They vary in size from the bow to the stern giving the boat hull its distinct shape. Traditionally, ribs are numbered from the bow to the stern to help you quickly identify a particular location in the interior and, in the event of damage to the hull, to isolate the area of damage.

LONGITUDINAL FRAMES Longitudinal frames provide hull strength along the length of the hull (fore and aft). (See Figure 8-9.) They run parallel to the keel and at right angles to the transverse frames. In addition to strengthening the hull, the

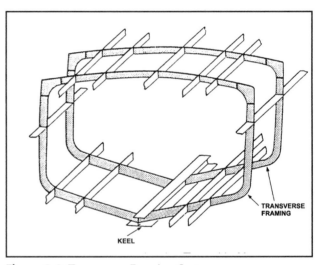

Figure 8-8 Transverse Framing System

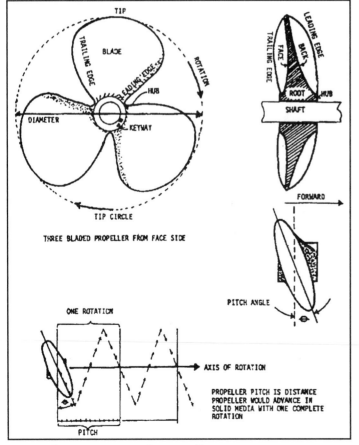

Figure 8-7 Parts of a Propeller

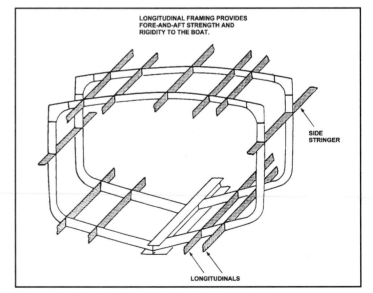

Figure 8-9 Longitudinal Framing System

top longitudinal frames provide a skeletal structure over which deck plating is laid.

B.14. DECKS

A deck is a seagoing floor and provides strength to the hull by reinforcing the transverse frames and deck beams. The top deck of a boat is called the weather deck because it is exposed to the elements and is watertight. In general, decks have a slight downward slope from the bow. The slope makes any water taken aboard run aft. A deck also has a rounded, athwartship curve called **camber**. The two low points of this curve are on the port and starboard sides of the boat where the weather deck meets the hull. Water that runs aft down the sheer line is forced to the port or starboard side of the boat by the camber. When the water reaches one of the sides, it flows overboard through holes, or **scuppers**, in the side railings.

Hatches and Doors

B.15. HATCHES

If decks are seagoing floors, then hatches are seagoing doors. In order for a **bulkhead** (a seagoing wall) with a hatch in it to be watertight, the hatch must be watertight. A weather deck hatch is made watertight by sealing it into a raised framework called a **coaming**. Hatches operate with quick-act-

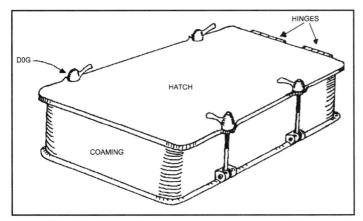

Figure 8-10 Watertight Hatch

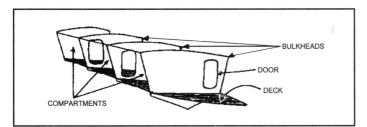

Figure 8-11 Watertight Compartment

ing devices such as wheels or handles or they may be secured with individual dogs (see Figure 8-10).

B.16. SCUTTLES

Scuttles are small openings. A "scuttle cover," fitted with a gasket and dogs, is used to secure the scuttle. A tool called a "T-handle wrench" is used to tighten down the scuttle cover dogs.

B.17. DOORS

Watertight doors are designed to resist as much pressure as the bulkheads through which they provide access. Some doors have dogs that must be individually closed and opened; others, called "quick-acting watertight doors" have handwheels or a handle, which operate all dogs at once.

B.18. GASKETS

Rubber gaskets form tight seals on most watertight closure devices. These gaskets, mounted on the covering surface of the closure device (e.g., door, hatch, scuttle cover), are pressed into a groove around the covering. The gaskets are sealed tight by pressing against a fixed position "knife edge."

B.19. KNIFE EDGES

Watertight closures must have clean, bright, unpainted, smooth knife edges for the gaskets to press against. A well-fitted watertight closure device with new gaskets will still leak if knife edges are not properly maintained.

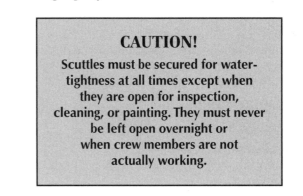

CAUTION!

Scuttles must be secured for watertightness at all times except when they are open for inspection, cleaning, or painting. They must never be left open overnight or when crew members are not actually working.

B.20. INTERIOR

The interior of a boat is compartmentalized into bulkheads, decks, and hatches. The hatches are "doors" through the bulkheads. When the hatches are closed, the space between them becomes watertight and is called a **watertight compartment** (see Figure 8-11). These watertight compartments are extremely important. Without them the boat has no **watertight integrity** and a hole anywhere in the hull will cause it to sink. By dividing the hull into several watertight compartments, the watertight integrity of the boat is significantly increased. One or more of these compartments may flood without causing the boat to sink. A boat could be made unsinkable if its hull could be divided into enough watertight compartments. Unfortunately, excessive compartmentation would interfere with the engineering spaces and restrict your movement in the interior spaces.

Boat Measurements

B.21. GENERAL

There are specific terms for the length and width of a boat and also specific methods for determining these measurements. The more common boat measurements are discussed below.

B.22. OVERALL LENGTH

The overall length of a boat is technically called the length overall (LOA) and is the distance from the foremost to the aftermost points on the boat's hull.

B.23. WATERLINE LENGTH

The waterline length of a boat is technically called the length on waterline (LWL). It is the distance between fore and aft where the surface of the water touches the hull when a boat is normally loaded.

B.24. BEAM AND BREADTH

Beam and breadth are measures of a boat's width. **Beam** refers to the distance from the outside hull plating on one side of the boat to the outside hull plating on the other side. **Extreme breadth** refers to the distance between the outside edge of a frame on one side of the boat to the outside edge of the same numbered frame on the opposite side.

Displacement

B.25. GENERAL

Displacement is the weight of a boat and is measured in long tons (2,240 lbs) or pounds.

B.26. GROSS TONS

The the total cubic capacity of a boat expressed in tons of 100 cubic feet

B.27. NET TONS

The carrying capacity of a boat expressed in tons of 100 cubic feet. It is calculated by measuring the cubic content of the cargo and passenger spaces.

B.28. DEADWEIGHT TONS

Deadweight is the difference between the **light**

displacement and the **maximum loaded displacement** of a boat and is expressed in long tons or pounds.

LIGHT DISPLACEMENT Light displacement is the weight of the boat excluding fuel, water, outfit, cargo, crew, and passengers.

LOADED DISPLACEMENT Loaded displacement is the weight of the boat including fuel, water, outfit, cargo, crew, and passengers.

SECTION C

Watertight Integrity

Overview

Introduction

Watertight integrity describes a compartment or fitting that is designed to prevent the passage of water into it. An important concern in boat operations is to ensure the watertight integrity of the vessel. A boat may sustain heavy damage and remain afloat if watertight integrity is maintained. Doors, hatches, and scuttle covers must be securely dogged while the boat is underway and while it is moored and unattended by crew members.

In this section

Topic	See Page(s)
Closing and Opening Watertight Doors and Hatches	138–39
Entering a Closed Compartment After Damage	139

Closing and Opening Watertight Doors and Hatches

C.1. GENERAL

Watertight doors and hatches will retain their efficiency longer and require less maintenance if they are properly closed and opened as described below.

C.2. CLOSING

The procedure for closing a watertight door is as follows:

1. Begin by tightening a dog that is opposite the hinges.

2. Place just enough pressure on the dog to keep the door shut.

3. Tighten up the other dogs evenly to obtain uniform pressure all around the closing device.

For quick-acting watertight doors, simply turn the wheels or handles in the correct direction (clockwise).

C.3. OPENING

If the dogs on watertight doors and hatches open individually, open the dog nearest the hinge first. This keeps the closing device from springing and makes loosening the other dogs easier.

For quick-acting watertight doors, turn the wheels or handles in the correct direction (counterclockwise).

Entering a Closed Compartment After Damage

C.4. GENERAL

Do not open watertight doors, hatches, and scuttle covers on a damaged boat until you determine the following:

- flooding did not occur or, if flooded,
- further flooding will not occur if you open the closure.

NOTE

Suspect flooding if air escapes when you release the dogs on a door or hatch.

> **CAUTION!**
> Extreme caution is always necessary when opening compartments below the waterline near hull damage.

SECTION D

General Boat Equipment

Overview

D.1. INTRODUCTION

All boats should carry basic equipment for the routine procedures, such as tying up and anchoring.

Equipment also is needed to conduct specific operations, such as search and rescue, towing, and pollution response. Crew members must be familiar with the use of the equipment carried on board and where it is located. A complete listing of required equipment is contained in the **Boat Outfit List**. Each type of boat has its own outfit list. You will find outfit lists for all standard Coast Guard boats in their boat type manuals. For Coast Guard utility boats (UTBs) and motor lifeboats (MLBs), they are also in the *Motor Lifeboat (MLB) & Utility Boat (UTB) Standardization Program Manual*, COMDTINST M16114.24 (series). Each Auxiliary vessel should have a boat outfit of the types of items listed below.

D.2. GENERAL BOAT EQUIPMENT LIST

The general equipment found on Coast Guard boats and a brief statement of the purpose of each item is provided below.

ANCHORS: For anchoring in calm, moderate, and heavy weather.

ANCHOR LINES: Provides scope to prevent the anchor from dragging. Enables retrieval of the anchor. Serves as an additional towline if necessary.

CHAFING CHAIN: Assists in preventing chafing of the anchor line on the bottom.

SCREW PIN SHACKLE: Attaches chafing chain to shank of anchor.

SWIVEL: Allows anchor line to spin freely.

THIMBLE: Prevents chafing of anchor line at connection point with associated hardware

TOWLINE: Used for towing astern

ALONGSIDE LINES: Used for alongside towing, joining to kicker hooks, passing a pump, etc.

HEAVING LINES (75' TO 100'): Used for passing a towline when a close approach is not possible

GRAPNEL HOOK WITH 100' OF LINE: Used for recovering objects from the water.

WOOD BOAT HOOK: For reaching dockside lines, fending boat from boat, and recovering objects from water.

KICKER HOOK: Attaches to trailer eyebolt on small boats for towing, weighing anchor, or disabled boats, etc.

SHACKLES: For weighing a disabled boat's anchor, attaching towing bridles to towlines, attaching towlines to trailer eyebolt, etc.

LEAD LINE (SOUNDING POLE): Used in determining water depth and bottom type.

FIRST AID KIT: For emergency treatment of injuries suffered by crew members or survivors.

PERSONNEL SURVIVAL KITS: Used by crew members in the event of a capsizing or person overboard.

HEAVY WEATHER CREW SAFETY BELT: For personnel safety during heavy weather or surf operations. Secures a crew member to the boat.

PFDs, EACH WITH A DISTRESS SIGNAL LIGHT, A WHISTLE, AND RETROREFLECTIVE TAPE: Provides personal flotation support. Keeps the head of an unconscious or injured person out of the water. Worn by crew members and given to survivors who are brought on board. Also worn by survivors who remain on their own boat when it is in tow.

RING BUOY, 30" DIAMETER: Used during person overboard emergencies.

SECTION E

Troubleshooting Basic Mechanical Problems

Overview

Introduction

Troubleshooting mechanical problems is typically the responsibility of the boat engineer, if one is assigned. However, not all Coast Guard boats or Auxiliary facilities deploy with a dedicated boat engineer. Boats without engineers should be able to provide basic help for themselves and those vessels that they are trying to assist. Often, a simple mechanical fix can avoid a long tow or other loss of use of a Coast Guard boat. The primary source for a boat's maintenance and repair requirements should be the operator manuals that come with the boat.

NOTE

In all casualties keep the station/unit command advised of the problem and updates of changing status. If in restricted water, consider anchoring.

In this section

Troubleshooting Diesel Engines

E.1. GENERAL

Inboard diesel engines commonly used for boat prolpulsion. They are very reliable when properly maintained. Typical problems, their possible causes, and potential solutions are outlined below.

PROBLEM

1. Engine will not turn over when starter button is pushed.

Cause: Main power switch off.
Solution: Turn main power switch on.

Cause: Battery cable loose or corroded.
Solution: Tighten, clean, or replace cable, terminals.

Cause: Starter motor cable loose or corroded.
Solution: Tighten, clean, or replace cable.

Cause: Batteries are low or dead.
Solution: Charge or replace batteries.

Cause: Engine seized hydraulic lock (fuel or water in cylinders).
Solution: Remove injectors, bar engine over by hand after (to relieve pressure & prevent internal damage).

Cause: Misalignment of controls, neutral safety switch.
Solution: Make appropriate adjustment, realign controls.

Cause: Non-operation or chattering solenoid switch.

Solution: Replace, repair cable. Replace solenoid. Check battery voltage.

PROBLEM

2. Irregular engine operation. (Engine runs unevenly or stalls.)

Cause: Strainers & fuel filter clogged.
Solution: Clean, replace, or purge air (bleed).

Cause: Lines & fitting leaking.
Solution: Check fuel lines & fittings for leaks, tighten, or replace.

Cause: Insufficient fuel/aeration of fuel.
Solution: Sound tanks—shift suction, refuel if necessary.

Cause: Binding fuel control linkages.
Solution: Inspect and adjust.

Cause: Insufficient intake of air.
Solution: Inspect intake for obstructions from air silencer. Check emergency air shutdown for possible restriction.

PROBLEM

3. Engine overspeeds or overruns.

Cause: Loose or jammed linkage.
Solution: Tighten or free linkage.

Cause: If engine RPMs increase, an internal engine malfunction has occurred. A stuck injector, a clutch that slipped into neutral, a lost prop, a ruptured lube oil seal could be the cause. Most engines overspeed after someone has performed maintenance. For this reason, it is most important that the operator assess what is occurring promptly. Regardless, when the engine overspeeds follow the procedure in the next column.
Solution: If an engine appears to be operating normally at cruising speed but fails to slow down as the throttle is being returned to neutral, do not place the throttle in neutral until a determination is made that the engine is in fact out of control (i.e., check for throttle linkage that became detached). By keeping the engine in gear it will prevent it from being destroyed. Secure the engine by following the steps below:

If overspeed continues pull engine stops (kill switch). If engine RPMs still overspeed, shut off fuel supply. If problem continues stuff rags against air silencer. As a last resort, shoot CO_2 into the air intake.

PROBLEM

4. Engine oil pressure high.

Cause: Incorrect grade of oil.
Solution: Monitor and if pressure becomes too high, secure engine.

Cause: Oil filters dirty.
Solution: Change oil filters.

Cause: Cold engine not up to operating temperature.
Solution: Warm up engine.

Cause: Relief valve stuck.
Solution: Adjust, remove, or clean.

Cause: External oil leaks.
Solution: Tighten connections if possible. Add oil monitor and secure engine if necessary.

Cause: Internal oil leaks.
Solution: Secure engine.

Cause: Worn or damaged engine parts.
Solution: Monitor, add oil, and secure engine if excessive consumption continues.

PROBLEM

5. Engine surges.

Cause: Air in fuel system.
Solution: Secure engine. Bleed air out of fuel system.

Cause: Clogged fuel strainers/filters.
Solution: Switch/change fuel filters.

Cause: Aeration of fuel (from heavy weather).
Solution: Shift to lower fuel function.

Cause: Governor instability.
Solution: Adjust the buffer screw (G.M.) Check free movement of fly weights.

Cause: Loose throttle linkage.
Solution: Tighten linkage.

PROBLEM

6. Marine (reduction) gear fails to engage.

Cause: Loss of gear oil.

Solution: Add gear oil. Check and correct leaks.

Cause: Strainer/filter clogged.
Solution: Clean strainer, change filter.

Cause: Loose, broken maladjusted linkage.
Solution: Inspect and correct, as necessary.

PROBLEM

7. **Unusual noise in reduction gear.**

Cause: Loss of gear oil.
Solution: Secure engine, check gear oil. Refill and resume operation for trail.

Cause: Worn out reduction gear.
Solution: Secure engine.

Cause: Misalignment of gear.
Solution: Secure engine.

PROBLEM

8. **Loss of gear oil pressure to reduction gear.**

Cause: Loss of gear oil.
Solution: Inspect all high pressure lines for leaks and repair. If unable to repair, secure engine.

PROBLEM

9. **Temperature of engine coolant higher than normal.**

Cause: Thermostat faulty, expansion tank cap faulty, leaky hoses, etc.
Solution: Inspect all lines for leaks and repair.

PROBLEM

10. **Engine smokes**
a. **Black or gray smoke**

Cause: Incompletely burned fuel.
Solution: High exhaust back pressure or a restricted air inlet causes insufficient air for combustion and will result in incompletely burned fuel. High exhaust back pressure is caused by faulty exhaust piping or muffler obstruction and is measured at the exhaust manifold outlet with a manometer, a meter gauge which measures differential pressure. Replace faulty parts. Restricted air inlet to the engine cylinders is caused by clogged cylinder liner ports, air cleaner or blower air inlet screen. Clean these items. Check the emergency stop to make sure that it is completely open and readjust if necessary.

Cause: Excessive fuel or irregular fuel distribution.
Solution: Check for improperly timed injectors and improperly positioned injector rack control levers. Time the fuel injectors and perform the appropriate governor tune up.

Replace faulty injectors if this condition continues. Avoid lugging the engine as this will cause incomplete combustion.

Cause: Improper grade of fuel.
Solution: Check for use of an improper grade of fuel.

b. **Blue smoke.**

Cause: Lubricating oil being burned (blow by valves/seals).
Solution: Check for internal lubricating oil leaks.

Conduct compression test.

Check valve and rings.

Cause: Bad oil seals in the turbocharger.
Solution: Return to mooring.

c. **White smoke.**

Cause: Misfiring cylinders.
Solution: Check for faulty injectors and replace as necessary.

Cause: Cold engine.
Solution: Allow engine to warm under a light load.

Cause: Water in the fuel.
Solution: Drain off strainers/filters. Strip fuel tanks.

Troubleshooting Gasoline Inboard Engines (Except Outboards)

E.2. **INDICATORS**

Normal operation indicators are:

a. Ease of starting.

b. Engine reaches specified RPMs at full throttle.

c. Correct shift and reverse RPMs.

d. Smooth idle.

e. Correct operating temperatures.

f. Adequate cooling water discharge and kill switch.

g. Smooth acceleration from idle to full RPMs.

E.3. BASIC TROUBLESHOOTING

An initial quick check of the following may reveal a simple fix for a problem that does not appear simple at first:

a. A visual inspection for obvious damage.

b. A rough compression check can be accomplished by removing a spark plug and placing a finger over the opening and cranking the engine.

c. Check the spark plugs for fouling.

d. Check ignition system for spark.

e. Check linkages for adjustments.

f. Check neutral/start switch.

g. Check gear case and lubricants in the engine.

E.4. REPAIRS ADVICE

The manufacturer's technical manual should be consulted for all adjustments and specifications. Use the following examples as a guide but always follow the specific engine's technical manual.

- Engine stops suddenly after a period of operation: Inspect for obvious damage of engine components such as loose wires, leaking fuel lines, leaking of coolant, excessive heat. Check ignition system for broken or loose wiring, distributor cap, points, or coil. Check for clogged fuel filters, quality/quantity of fuel.

- Engine stops suddenly with no spark to spark plugs: Inspect for obvious damage, check the ignition system for broken or loose wiring, distributor cap, points, or coil.

- Engine stops, restarts when cool and stops again when hot: Have the ignition coil and condenser checked out; they may be breaking down when hot.

- Engine stops after a period of rough uneven operation: Inspect for obvious damage. Check the ignition system for broken or loose wiring, distributor cap, points, or coil. Check the battery, ignition timing, and the fuel filter.

- Engine runs by spurts, and stops with the fuel filter clean: Check the fuel tank and fuel lines. Check the ignition system for obvious damage. Check ignition timing and points. Check the fuel pump for proper operation.

- Engine runs by spurts, stops and water is present in the fuel filter: Clean fuel filter. Check the fuel tank for presence of water and drain if necessary. If the carburetor is filled with water. It must also be drained. Take ap-

propriate action safety precautions to avoid fire explosion.

- Engine misses, gallops, spits, backfires and has a loss of power: Inspect for obvious damage. Carburetor may be dirty. Check ignition system for broken or loose wiring, distributor cap, rotor points and coil. Check fuel filter and fuel lines. Check for plugged vent.

- Engine starts hard, especially in cold weather: Battery voltage may be low. Check ignition timing and points. Check ignition system for obvious damage. Exhaust valves may be burned. May have to change to a lighter engine oil.

- Engine pops and pings in exhaust pipe at all speeds: Exhaust valves may be burned, worn piston rings or worn valve guides. Time for engine overhaul. Timing may be off. Too low octane fuel.

- Starter turns engine but engine will not start: Check fuel level. Inspect for obvious damage to ignition system, broken or loose wiring, distributor cap, rotor points, or coil. Check ignition timing and points. Check fuel pump.

WARNING
Beware of fuel vapors before starting engine.

Casualties Common to Both Diesel and Gasoline Engines

E.5. GENERAL

Diesel and gasoline engines employ different operating schemes; however their failure modes and the solutions for them are often similar.

PROBLEM

1. Starter whines. Engine doesn't crank over, doesn't engage. Starter relay may chatter.

Cause: Defective starter. Bendix is not engaged. Defective starter relay.
Solution: Call for assistance. Replace or repair starter or relay. Check bendix on return to dock.

Cause: Low battery voltage.

Solution: Check battery cables for loose connection (or corrosion) to starter. Charge or replace battery.

PROBLEM

2. Engine fails to start with starter turning over.

Cause: Fuel stop closed.
Solution: Open it.

Cause: Fuel shutoff valve closed.
Solution: Open it.

Cause: Clogged air cleaner.
Solution: Remove and clean air cleaner.

Cause: Fuel supply exhausted.
Solution: Refill fuel tanks, bleed and prime system.

Cause: Clogged strainer.
Solution: Shift strainer and clean, bleed off.

Cause: Fuel filters clogged.
Solution: Shift and replace elements, bleed air off.

Cause: Clogged/crimped restricted fuel line.
Solution: Replace or repair fuel line.

Cause: Inoperable fuel pump.
Solution: Replace.

Cause: Emergency air shut off blower tripped.
Solution: Reset.

Cause: Clogged air intake.
Solution: Remove, clean, or replace.

Cause: Low battery voltage causes slow cranking.
Solution: Charge battery or replace.

Cause: Cold engine.
Solution: Check hot start.

PROBLEM

3. Engine temperature high.

Cause: Closed or partially closed sea suction valve.
Solution: Check raw water overboard discharge; if little or none, check sea suction valve. Open it.

Cause: Dirty plugged raw water strainer. (Especially in shallow water.)
Solution: Replace strainer.

Cause: Broken raw water hose.
Solution: Secure engine, replace hose.

Cause: Broken or loose raw water pump drive belt.
Solution: Secure engine, replace or tighten belt.

Cause: Faulty raw water pump.
Solution: Call for assistance.

Cause: Clogged heat exchanger.
Solution: Inspect heat exchanger.

Cause: No/low water in expansion tank (fresh water system).
Solution: Handle the same as for a car radiator—open with caution releasing pressure before removing cap. With engine running add fresh water.

Cause: Broken fresh water hose.
Solution: Secure engine, replace, add fresh water.

Cause: Broken belts/drive fresh water system.
Solution: Treat same as raw water system.

Cause: Faulty water pump, fresh water system.
Solution: Call for assistance.

Cause: Thermostat stuck, fresh water system.
Solution: Secure engine, remove thermostat, add fresh water.

Cause: Water in lube oil.
Solution: Check lube oil for "milky" color. If found, secure engine.

Cause: Blown head gasket.
Solution: Secure engine, lock shaft, return to mooring.

Cause: Engine overload (towing too big a vessel or towing too fast).
Solution: Reduce engine speed.

Cause: Ice clogged sea strainers (especially during operation in slush ice).
Solution: Shift sea strainer, open deicing valve.

Cause: Air bound sea chest.
Solution: Open/clear sea chest vent valve.

Cause: Rubber impeller on raw water pump is inoperable.
Solution: Renew.

PROBLEM

4. Engine lube oil pressure fails.

Cause: Lube oil level low.
Solution: If above red line, check oil, add if needed. If below red line, secure engine.

Cause: External oil leak.
Solution: Tighten fittings if possible. If not, secure engine.

Cause: Lube oil dilution.
Solution: Secure engine if beyond 5% fuel dilution.

Cause: Lube oil gauge defective.
Solution: Take load off engine, if applicable, check to confirm if gauge appears to operate normally.

Cause: Mechanical damage to engine.
Solution: Secure engine.

PROBLEM

5. No oil pressure.

Cause: Lube oil pump failure.
Solution: Secure engine. Repeat all procedures for problem #4 above.

Cause: Defective gauge.
Solution: Verify that failure is only in gauge. Otherwise secure engine.

PROBLEM

6. Loss of electrical power.

Cause: Short circuit/loose connections causing tripped circuit breaker or blown fuse.
Solution: Check for shorts/grounds. Reset circuit breakers, replace fuses as necessary.

Cause: Corroded wiring connections
Solution: Clean or replace cables/wires.

Cause: Overloaded circuit.
Solution: Secure all unnecessary circuits, reset circuit breakers, replace fuses.

Cause: Dead battery
Solution: Charge or replace battery.

PROBLEM

7. Alternator indicator light on.

Cause: Loose/broken belt.
Solution: Replace/tighten belt.

Cause: Loose terminal connections.
Solution: Inspect and tighten as necessary.

Cause: Defective alternator or regulator.
Solution: Replace defective item.

REGARDLESS OF CAUSE, FOLLOW PROCEDURES BELOW.

Cause: Packing too tight.
Solution: Reduce speed, but do not secure engine or shaft.

Cause: Bent shaft.
Solution: Reduce speed, check hull for damage or leaks.

Cause: Valve to stern closed/restriction in the line.
Solution: Loosen packing nuts by turning the two nuts securing spacer plate.

When the housing is cool, tighten the two nuts on the space plate until a discharge of about 10 drops of water per minute is obtained.

In cases where nuts will not back, use raw water from a bucket, wet rag and place on shaft packing housing.

Maintain watch on water flow (step #3) and adjust discharge as needed.

Check coolness by placing the back of your hand on the packing gland housing.

PROBLEM

8. Shaft vibration (REGARDLESS OF CAUSE FOLLOW THE PROCEDURE BELOW).

Cause: Damaged or fouled propeller.
Solution: Place throttles in neutral if possible.

Cause: Bent shaft.

Solution: Reduce speed, check hull for damage or leaks.

Cause: Cutlass bearing worn.
Solution: Check for line fouled in the propeller or shaft.

Cause: Engine or shaft out of alignment.
Solution: Slowly increase speed on engine. On twin propeller boats, do one engine at a time to figure out which shaft is vibrating.

If vibration continues even at low speeds, secure the engine or engines involved.

If engines are secured, lock the shafts.

PROBLEM

9. Engine room fire (FOR ALL FIRES FOLLOW THE PROCEDURE BELOW).
a. Petroleum based.

Cause: Oil and grease in bilges.
Solution: Secure engines, turn off fuel at the tank if possible.

Cause: Fuel or lube oil spill.
Solution: Call for assistance at earliest opportunity.

Cause: Improper containers of flammable liquids.
Solution: Secure electrical power to and from engine room.

Cause: Improper venting of engine room before starting engine.
Solution: Use any available portable fire extinguisher (Purple K, CO_2, etc.)

Seal compartment.

b. Electrical fires.
Solution: Turn off electricity if possible. Select the proper extinguished agent and employ.

PROBLEM

10. Engine stops suddenly and will not turn through a full revolution.
Solution: Check for an obstruction within the cylinder such as water or a broken, bent or shut valve.

PROBLEM

11. Engine stops firing hot and won't turn over when cool.
Solution: The engine seized for one reason or another and must be overhauled.

PROBLEM

12. Engine stops with a loud clatter.
Solution: Inspect for obvious damage. Damage may be to internal parts such as valve, valve spring, bearings, piston rings, etc. Overhaul of the engine is required.

PROBLEM

13. Engine oil level rises, oil looks and feels gummy.
Solution: There may be coolant leaking into the engine oil. Check for internal leakage. Repair the engine before continuing operation.

PROBLEM

14. Engine oil rises or feels thin.
Solution: Fuel is leaking into the crankcase. Check fuel pump. After problem has been corrected change oil and filters.

PROBLEM

15. Hot water in bilges.
Solution: Inspect the exhaust piping muffler, and/or cooling water level. It is probably leaking into the bilges. Check all hoses.

PROBLEM

16. Engine runs with a thumping or knocking noise.
Solution: Inspect for obvious damage to internal parts of the engine. They may be damaged. Disassemble the engine and repair or overhaul.

NOTE

For all high temperature situations the immediate action is to place the throttle in neutral then look for the probable cause.

When an overheated engine must be secured, turn the engine over periodically to keep it from seizing.

Troubleshooting the Outboard

E.6. GENERAL

Outboard motors are very common on recreational boats and many Coast Guard boats. The operator manual provides the best guidance. Working over the transom of the boat poses a hazard to the operator and for loss of parts and tools.

PROBLEM

1. Engine won't start.

Possible cause/correction:

- Fuel tank empty.
- Fuel tank vent closed.
- Fuel line improperly connected or damaged; check both ends.
- Engine not primed.
- Engine flooded, look for fuel overflow.
- Clogged fuel filter or line.
- Spark plug wires reversed.
- Loose battery connections.
- Cracked or fouled spark plug.
- Fuel pump not primed.

PROBLEM

2. Starter motor won't work (electric starter).

Possible cause/correction:

- Gear shift not in neutral.
- Defective starter switch (sometimes gets wet and corrodes if motor is mounted too low).

PROBLEM

3. Loss of power.

Possible cause/correction:

- Too much oil in fuel mix.
- Fuel/air mix too lean (backfires).
- Fuel hose kinked.
- Slight blockage in fuel line or fuel filter.
- Weeds or some other matter on propeller.
- Water has condensed in fuel.
- Spark plug fouled.
- Magneto or distributor points fouled.

PROBLEM

4. Engine misfires.

Possible cause/correction:

- Spark plug damaged.
- Spark plug loose.
- Faulty coil or condenser.
- Spark plug incorrect.
- Spark plug dirty.
- Choke needs adjusting.
- Improper oil and fuel mixture.
- Dirty carburetor filter.
- Partially clogged water intake.
- Distributor cap cracked.

Routine maintenance helps ensure trouble-free engine operation.

PROBLEM

5. Overheating.

Possible cause/correction:

- Mud or grease on cooling system intakes.

- Too little oil.

- Water pump is worn or impeller (rubber) is broken or sips.

- Defective water pump.

PROBLEM

6. Blue smoke.

Possible cause/correction:

- Spark plugs are fouled, means too much oil.

PROBLEM

7. Engine surges.

Possible cause/correction:

- Outboard not properly mounted—propeller rides out of the water.

- Carburetor needs adjustments.

PROBLEM

8. Poor performance on boat.

Possible cause/correction:

- Wrong propeller.

- Engine improperly tilted compared with transom. Engine should be vertical when boat is underway.

- Bent propeller—usually accompanied by high level of vibration.

- Improper load distribution in boat.

- Heavy marine growth on boat bottom.

- Cavitation.

Steering Casualty

E.7. GENERAL

A steering casualty may have a simple solution or require outside assistance. It may also test your boat handling skills if the boat has two propellers. General advice is provided below.

PROBLEM

1. Broken or jammed cable.

Possible cause/correction:

- Rig emergency steering as applicable. Advise operational commander.

PROBLEM

2. Broken hydraulic line, or hydraulic systems malfunction.

Possible cause/correction:

- Inspect hoses for leaks, check fluid level, add if necessary.

- Replace hose if spare is on board.

- Rig emergency steering as applicable.

- Notify controlling unit.

- Steer with engines if twin propeller.

- Try to center rudder amidships.

- Anchor, if necessary.

PROBLEM

3. "Frozen," damaged or blocked rudder, outdrive or outboard

Possible cause/correction:

- Attempt to free, if possible.

- Center rudder, if possible, and block in place.

Basic Engine Maintenance for Auxiliary Facilities

E.8. MAINTENANCE LOGS

A very important maintenance procedure is to maintain a hull and engine maintenance log. Ideally, the log should be in two parts. One part would include a series of alphabetically arranged entries: battery, filters, oil, zincs, etc. (This makes it easy, for example, to look up "S" for spark plugs or "P" for points.) The other should contain several pages available for chronologically entering haul-outs and major maintenance work. To structure the log properly, the engine manufacturer's maintenance manual is needed. Also, a good practice is to buy a large ring binder and put in it every instruction or technical manual for electronics, instruments, heads, stoves, etc. that comes with the boat.

E.9. BASIC MAINTENANCE ACTIONS

There is not enough space in this chapter to write a maintenance manual for each type of Auxiliary boat. The primary source for a boat's maintenance requirements should be the appropriate engine maintenance manual. However, any Auxiliarist can accomplish the following engine maintenance actions:

a. Change engine oil, oil filters, and fuel filters.

b. Select, gap, and properly torque to specifications, new spark plugs.

c. Check and change, if necessary, heat exchanger zincs (if equipped). In some areas this should be done monthly.

d. Drain and replace hydraulic drive fluids.

e. Replace and adjust engine fan belts.

f. Adjust and tighten stuffing box fittings, steering cable or hydraulics, stuffing boxes, and hull fittings.

g. Replace defective engine hoses.

h. Clean the air cleaner and flame arrester.

i. Check and charge batteries.

j. Lube and maintain salt-water intakes/sea cocks.

NOTE

Keep the tools aboard needed to affect these repairs. With the right spares aboard and the hand tools to install them, you can avoid becoming a SAR case.

E.10. ADVANCED MAINTENANCE ACTIONS

The more experienced power boater can change ignition points, adjust timing, align engine coupling faces, etc.

E.11. INBOARD BOATS KEPT IN SALT WATER

A selection of wire brushes, spray cans of primer, engine touch up paint, and a small 5 x 7-inch mirror should be kept on board. About twice a month, get in the bilges and really inspect the engines (mounts, etc.,) for rust and corrosion. Remove corrosion with a wire brush and spray the area with touch up paint. (There is no reason for engines to be lumps of rust.) Also, inspect the powerplant for leaking hoses, gaskets, loose wires, etc. Many engine problems relate to electrical problems, including loss of electrical ground and oxidation of leads or connectors. Inspect these areas regularly. The 5 x 7-inch mirror is used to inspect the blind side of the engine.

E.12. BUYING ENGINE PARTS

A note about buying engine parts—spark plugs, hoses, belts, ignition wires, and points can be purchased at auto supply stores. However, alternators, distributors, and carburetors used on boats *must* have marine safety features, screens, etc. Any attempt to replace them with auto components creates a risk of fire and explosion.

NOTE

Do not use auto parts on your boat.

Stability

Editor's Note: The matter of stability is too important to be left to engineers and naval architects. Skippers must understand how any number of processes can destabilize a boat—improper loading, icing, free-surface liquids, flooding, and topside modifications have all led recreational boaters to grief. Instability must be avoided and, of course, recognized when it does occur. Instability can be especially hazardous when you are attempting to help a boat in distress. Good Samaritans have been lost when they've boarded an unstable boat only to have it capsize under them. People on unstable boats under tow have been lost in similar circumstances. In one case a Connecticut commercial fishing crew was lost within sight of their dock when they lifted their iced-up outrigger booms, thus raising the boat's center of gravity above its metacenter. Don't worry—both center of gravity and metacenter are explained in this chapter. The more you understand about instability, the less likely you are to get into trouble because of it.

Overview

Introduction

This chapter discusses stability—the ability of a vessel to return to an upright position after being heeled over. Many forces influence the stability of a vessel in the water and each type of has vessel unique stability characteristics. Coxswains must be aware of how internal forces (those caused by the boat's design and loading) and external forces (those caused by nature) affect the boat. With practice and experience, coxswains can learn to anticipate how a vessel being piloted and how a vessel being assisted will react to various internal and external forces.

The ability to recognize unstable vessel conditions is vitally important to safety for the crew of the assisting boat and the persons aboard the craft in distress.

In this chapter

SECTION A

Safety and Risk Management Control

A.1. GENERAL

Safety of both the boat crew and persons in distress is of paramount importance during any emergency evolution. Mishaps resulting in death or injury have occurred while Coast Guard boat crews attempted to assist vessels in distress. Accident investigation reports reveal that injury or property damage often result from lapses in common sense and safety awareness during the pressing urgency of an emergency. If in the process of trying to assist another mariner you are injured or your vessel is damaged, you become part of the problem instead of the solution to it. Chapter 4 of this manual provides general discussion of risk management.

A.2. SAFETY ASSESSMENT AND MANAGEMENT GUIDELINES

Emergency situations can cause people to panic or act before thinking despite the best of training and preparation. Therefore, boat crews must work together as a team to minimize potential or immediate jeopardy for both civilian and rescue crew casualties. **Never** enter an emergency situation without first assessing the risk involved for the boat crew members and civilian victims **(Risk Assessment)**, always be aware of the dynamics of the emergency situation **(Situational Awareness)**, and always implement a control plan to fit the unique emergency presented **(Stability Risk Management Plan)**.

RISK ASSESSMENT AND MANAGEMENT Risk assessment starts with understanding why mishaps occur. Responsibility for identifying and managing risk lies with every member of the boat crew. Realistic training based on standard techniques, critical analysis, and debriefing missions will help every person in a boat crew to contribute to developing and implementing a **Risk Management Plan**. A Risk Management Plan identifies and controls risk according to a set of preconceived parameters.

- Make the best attempt to account for all persons.
- Attempt to have all lines, rigging, etc. removed from the water around the vessel to avoid fouling the screws.
- Have all required equipment ready and test run pumps.

Refer to Chapter 4 of this manual for a more complete discussion of areas where failure typically contributes significantly to serious mishaps.

SITUATIONAL AWARENESS **Situational awareness** is the accurate perception of the factors and conditions affecting the boat crew at a given time during any evolution. More simply stated, situational awareness is knowing what is going on around you at all times while continuing to perform the task assigned to you.

Anytime you identify an indication that situational awareness is about to be lost, you must make a decision whether to continue with the rescue attempt. Everyone in the crew owns some responsibility for making these important decisions. The decision takes the form of **action/reaction** and **communication**. The person in charge of the boat makes the final decision but the boat crew has the responsibility to recognize dangerous situations and bring them to the attention of the coxswain.

NOTE

Crews who have a high level of SITUATIONAL AWARENESS perform in a safe manner.

STABILITY RISK MANAGEMENT PLAN The entire crew must constantly watch for any loss of stability in their own vessel and that of the distressed craft. Do not assume that the coxswain has been able to observe all of the warning signs. Advise the coxswain of any warning signs he/she may have overlooked. Use these elements below in your Stability Risk Management Plan.

- Observe the roll of your own boat and, observe the roll of a distressed vessel as you approaching it initially and while it is under tow.
- Be aware of external forces—wind, waves and the effect of water depth.
- Be aware of loading—the amount of weight and its placement on all vessels involved. Rearrange loading if necessary.
- Attempt to keep your equipment aboard your vessel when dewatering the vessel.
- Attempt to tow the distressed vessel **only** after any loss of stability has been corrected.
- Adjust course, speed, or both as necessary to decrease rolling or listing.
- Avoid sharp turns or turns at high speed when loss of stability is possible.
- Maintain communication between the coxswain and crew.
- Keep the operational commander or parent unit informed of the situation through regular and frequent reports.

> ### WARNING
> When a vessel is visibly unstable (i.e., listing, trimmed to the bow/stern or when downflooding occurs) never make your vessel fast to or tow the distressed vessel. A flooded vessel may appear stable when it in fact is not. Compare the distressed boat's reaction to sea conditions with your own boat's movements

Understanding Stability

Overview

Introduction

When a vessel is heeled over in reaction to some external influence, other than damage to the vessel, it tends to either return to an upright position or to continue to heel over and capsize. The tendency of a vessel to remain upright is its **stability**. The greater the tendency to remain upright, and the stronger the force required to heel the vessel over in any direction, the more stability the vessel achieves. The stability of a vessel in the water is very important to the safety of all members of a boat crew. Being able to anticipate how your vessel and the vessel you are assisting will react in any given set of circumstances is dependent on your knowledge of stability. Weight and buoyancy are the two primary forces that affect the stability of a floating vessel. Weight is the force that pushes a vessel down into the water. Buoyancy is the force that pushes up from the water to keep the vessel afloat. The interaction of these two forces determines the vessel's stability.

Many factors affect the stability of vessels at sea. In this photo sailors await rescue from a capsized trimaran. Multihulls—unlike monohulls—are usually not able to right themselves.

Center of Gravity

B.1. CENTER OF GRAVITY

The center of gravity is the point at which the weight of the boat acts vertically downwards. Thus, the boat acts as though all of its weight is concentrated at the center of gravity. Generally, the lower the center of gravity, the more stable the vessel.

CHANGES IN THE CENTER OF GRAVITY The center of gravity of a boat is fixed for stability and does not shift unless weight is added, subtracted or shifted. When weight is added—for example when a vessel takes on water—the center of gravity moves toward the added weight. When the weight is removed, the center of gravity moves in the opposite direction.

If a vessel has been damaged so that water is flowing in and out of a hole below the waterline, known as free communication with the sea, the result is a loss of buoyancy which generally means a significant reduction in stability.

Buoyancy

B.2. BUOYANCY

Buoyancy is the upward force of water displaced by the hull. The force of buoyancy keeps the boat afloat; however, buoyancy may be overcome and the boat sunk if too much weight is added.

CENTER OF BUOYANCY The center of buoyancy is the center of gravity of displaced water. This is the point on which all upward/vertical force is considered to act. It lies in the center of the underwater form of the hull (see Figure 9-1).

Equilibrium

B.3. EQUILIBRIUM

When a boat is at rest, the center of buoyancy acting upwards/vertically is below the center of gravity acting downwards. A boat is considered to be in equilibrium. Equilibrium is affected by movement of the center of gravity or center of buoyancy or by some outside forces, such as wind and waves (see Figure 9-1).

ROLLING When a boat rolls, the force of the center of gravity will move in the same direction as the roll. The downward force of gravity is offset by the upward force of buoyancy and causes the boat to heel.

HEELING In heeling, the underwater volume of the boat changes shape causing the center of buoyancy to move.

The center of buoyancy will move towards the part of the hull that is more deeply immersed. When this happens the center of buoyancy will no longer be aligned vertically with the center of gravity. The intersection of the vertical line thru the center of buoyancy and the vertical centerline of the boat is called the metacenter. When the metacentric height—the distance between center of gravity and metacenter—is positive, the forces of buoyancy and gravity will act to bring the boat back to an upright position. In this case, the center of buoyancy is outboard of the center of gravity and the boat is considered to be stable. If the center of buoyancy is inboard of the center of gravity—that is the metacentric height is negative—the forces of buoyancy and gravity will tend to roll the boat further towards capsize (see Figure 9-2).

LISTING If the center of gravity is not on the centerline of the boat, the boat will heel until equilibrium is reached with the center of buoyancy and center of gravity in alignment. This condition is referred to as **list**.

NOTE

Heeling is a temporary leaning, listing is a permanent leaning, and both are different from rolling which is a periodic side-to-side motion.

Types of Stability

B.4. TYPES OF STABILITY

A boat has two principle types of stability:

- Longitudinal
- Transverse

A boat is usually much longer than it is wide. Therefore, the longitudinal plane (fore and aft) is more stable than its transverse plane (beam).

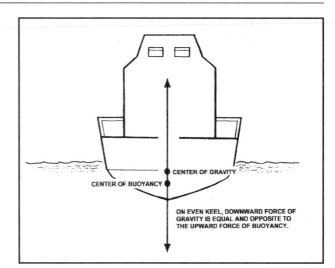

Figure 9-1 Stability In Equilibrium

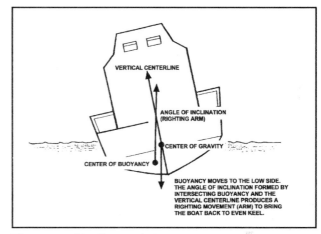

Figure 9-2 Heeling

LONGITUDINAL (FORE AND AFT) STABILITY
Longitudinal (fore and aft) stability tends to balance the boat, preventing it from pitching end-over-end (pitch poling). Vessels are designed with enough longitudinal stability to avoid damage under normal circumstances. However, differences in vessel design create boats with different longitudinal stability characteristics. Some vessels can suffer excessive pitching and offer a very wet and uncomfortable ride in rough sea and weather conditions. Such an uncomfortable ride often affects the endurance and capability of people on vessels you are assisting.

TRANSVERSE (ATHWARTSHIPS) STABILITY
Transverse (athwartships) stability tends to keep the boat from rolling over (capsizing). Additional weight above the boat's center of gravity increases the distance between the center of gravity and the center of buoyancy. As a result, stability is decreased. Removal of weight from below the boat's center of gravity also

decreases stability. If the loaded center of gravity is raised high enough, the boat will become unstable.

Moment and Forces

B.5. MOMENT AND FORCES

The force that causes a vessel to return to an even keel, or upright position is called the vessel's **moment**. Both static and dynamic forces can reduce stability and moment. Moments, and the internal and external forces that act to increase or decrease the righting moment, are important factors in determining the stability of a vessel at any given point in time.

RIGHTING MOMENT AND CAPSIZING A **righting moment** is the force causing a vessel to react against a roll and return to an even keel. Generally, the broader a boat's beam, the more stable that boat will be and the less likely it is to capsize. For any given condition of loading, the center of gravity is at a fixed position. As a boat heels, the center of buoyancy moves to the lower side of the boat forming an angle of inclination. Larger heeling angles result in corresponding movement of the center of buoyancy. This outboard movment of the center of buoyancy generates a greater righting moment, up to a maximum angle of inclination.

Too much weight added to the side of a vessel that is heeled over already can overcome the forces supporting stability and cause the vessel to capsize. (See Figure 9-3.)

A boat may also capsize when aground because the volume of water beneath the vessel decreases and the vessel loses balance. As the amount of water supporting the vessel is reduced, the buoyancy force being provided by that water is lost. At the same time, the upward force acting at the point of grounding further destabilizes the vessel by tipping the unsupported hull to one side.

STATIC AND DYNAMIC FORCES Unless acted upon by some external force, a boat that is properly designed and loaded remains on an even keel. The two principle forces that affect stability are **static** and **dynamic** forces.

1. Static forces are caused by placement of weight within the hull. Adding weight on one side of a boat's centerline or above its center of gravity usually reduces stability. Flooding or grounding a boat makes it susceptible to static forces which may adversely affect stability.

2. Dynamic forces are caused by actions outside the hull such as wind and waves. Strong gusts of wind or heavy seas, especially in shallow water, may build up forces that tend to capsize a boat.

It is essential that boat crew members understand these forces.

- Watch the time required for a complete roll from side to side. The time should remain about the same regardless of the severity of the angle or roll.

- If the time increases significantly or the boat hesitates at the end of a roll, the boat is approaching or past the position of maximum righting effect. Take immediate steps to decrease the roll by changing course or speed or both.

B.6. VESSEL DESIGN

General vessel design features that influence stability include:

- Size and shape of the hull
- Draft of the boat (the distance from the surface of the water to the keel)
- Trim (the angle from horizontal at which a vessel rides)
- Displacement
- Freeboard
- Superstructure size, shape, and weight
- Non-watertight openings

Many of these features are discussed in Chapter 8—Boat Characteristics.

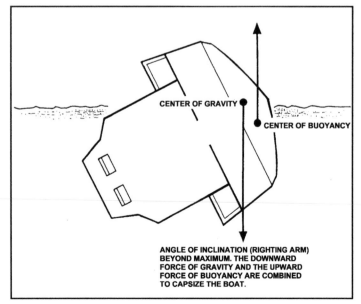

CENTER OF GRAVITY

CENTER OF BUOYANCY

ANGLE OF INCLINATION (RIGHTING ARM) BEYOND MAXIMUM. THE DOWNWARD FORCE OF GRAVITY AND THE UPWARD FORCE OF BUOYANCY ARE COMBINED TO CAPSIZE THE BOAT.

Figure 9-3 Righting Moment and Capsizing

Losing Stability

Overview

Introduction

A vessel may be displaced from its upright position by certain internal and external influences such as:

- Waves
- Wind
- Turning forces when the rudder is put over
- Shifting of weights on board
- Addition or removal of weights
- Loss of buoyancy (damage)

These influences exert heeling moments on a vessel causing it to list (permanent) or heel (temporary). A stable boat does not capsize when subjected to normal heeling moments due to the boat's tendency to right itself (righting moment).

In this section

Stability After Damage

C.1. GENERAL

When assisting a damaged vessel consider that any change in stability may result in the loss of the vessel. The added weight of assisting personnel or equipment may cause the vessel to lose its righting moment, lose stability, and capsize. This consequence, and the danger involved, must be considered when determining risk to avoid harm to the crew and further damage or loss of a vessel.

Free Surface Effect

C.2. GENERAL

Compartments in a vessel may contain liquids as a matter of design or as a result of damage. If a compartment is only partly filled, the liquid can flow from side to side as the vessel rolls or pitches. The surface of the liquid tends to remain parallel to the waterline. Liquid that only partly fills a compartment is said to have **free surface** and water in such a compartment is called **loose water**. When loose water shifts from side to side or forward and aft due to turning, speed changes, or wave action, the vessel does not want to right itself. This causes a loss of stability. This can cause the vessel to capsize or sink. A cargo of fish free to move about inside a compartment will have the same effect, a condition commonly found on fishing vessels (see Figures 9-4 and 9-5).

NOTE

Note that the area of free surface is very important, and in particular its width. If the free surface area doubles in width, its adverse effect on stability will change by a factor of four.

C.3. CORRECTIVE ACTIONS

Corrective actions include:

- Minimize the number of partially filled tanks (fuel, water, or cargo); ballast with sea water as necessary.
- Maintain fish wells completely empty or filled at all times.
- Prevent cargo such as fish from rolling back and forth on the deck.

Free Communication with the Sea

C.4. GENERAL

Damage to the hull of a vessel can create free communication with the sea, the movement of sea water into and out of the vessel.

C.5. CORRECTIVE ACTIONS

Corrective actions include:

- Patch the hull opening.
- Place weight on the high side to decrease the list toward the damaged side.
- Remove weight above the center of gravity on the damaged side.

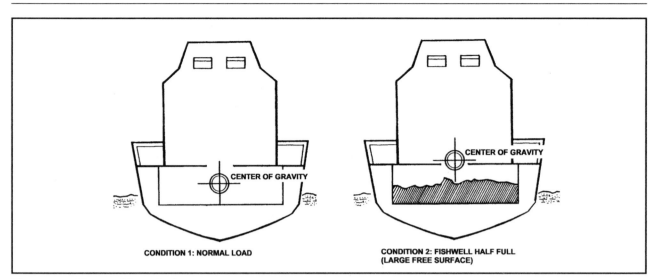

Figure 9-4 Effects of Free Surface

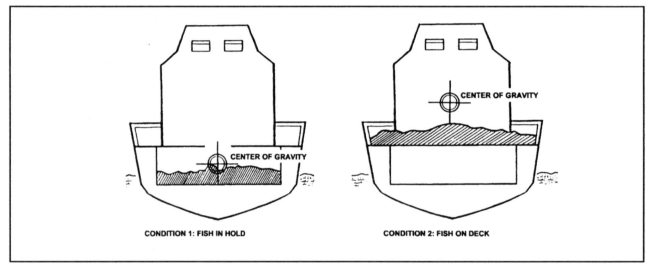

Figure 9-5 Effects of Load Weight

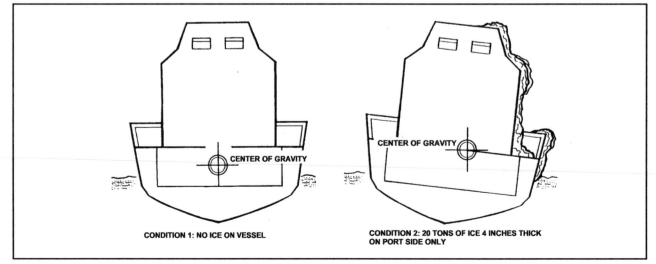

Figure 9-6 Effects of Icing

Effects of Icing

C.6. GENERAL

Icing can increase the displacement of a boat by adding weight above the center of gravity and causing it to rise. This can cause a vessel to heel over and greatly reduce stability. Sea swells, sharp turns, or quick changes in speed can capsize a vessel that has accumulated ice on its topside surfaces. (See Figure 9-6.)

C.7. CORRECTIVE ACTIONS

Corrective actions include:

- Change course, speed or both to reduce freezing spray and rolling.
- Physically remove the ice.

Effects of Downflooding

C.8. GENERAL

Downflooding is the entry of water into the hull resulting in progressive flooding and loss of stability. Vessels are designed with sufficient stability and proper righting moments as long as they are not overloaded. These design features cannot compensate for the carelessness of a boat crew who fails to maintain the watertight integrity of a vessel and allow it to needlessly take on water. (See Figure 9-7.)

C.9. CORRECTIVE ACTIONS

Corrective actions include:

- Keep all watertight fittings and openings secured when a vessel is underway.
- Pump out the water.

Effects of Water on Deck

C.10. GENERAL

Water on deck can cause stability problems by:

- Increasing displacement (increasing draft and decreasing stability and trim).
- Contributing to free surface effect.
- Amplifying the rolling motion of the vessel which may result in capsizing.

Heavy icing on a harbor tug.

C.11. CORRECTIVE ACTIONS

Corrective actions include:

- Decrease trim, increase freeboard.

- Change course, speed or both.
- Ensure drain openings are unobstructed (see Figure 9-8).

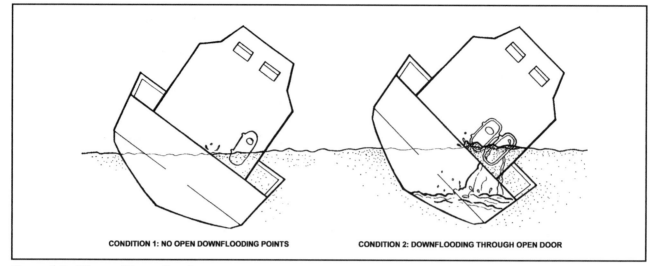

Figure 9-7 Effects of Downflooding

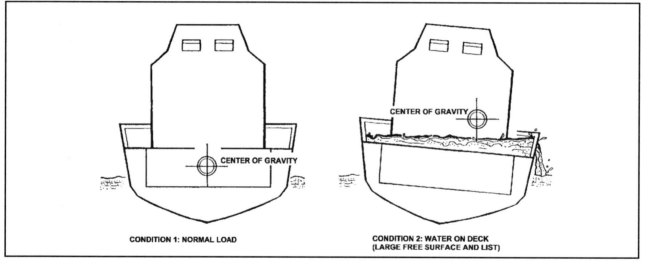

Figure 9-8 Effects of Water on Deck

Boat Handling

Editor's Note: There is no better way to gain proficiency in safe boat handling than to get out on the water and do it. Handling a boat safely and effectively in ever changing sea and wind conditions requires experience developed through thoughtful practice. On the other hand, doing a bit of homework early on can reduce some of the hazard (and cost) of learning this material the hard way. In this chapter, Coast Guard instructors introduce their personnel to boat handling with an emphasis on dealing with the often difficult operating environment faced by the crews of rescue boats—maneuvering close to other boats and objects and dealing with rough sea conditions. Of course, this chapter also looks at the basics and provides solid operational theory for any boater.

Overview

Introduction

This chapter covers handling vessels under power. Vessels under sail and personal watercraft are not addressed. Topics include:

- Internal and external forces that act upon a vessel,

- General maneuvering and boat handling techniques, and

- Task-oriented boat handling evolutions and procedures.

Handling a boat competently requires an understanding of many variables and complex dynamics. Although you can develop boat handling skills only through hands-on experience, the principles and practices described in this chapter will provide a foundation for your on-water practice.

The Best Coxswains

Though good coxswains are familiar with the characteristics of their boats and how they operate, the best coxswains are knowledgeable in the operation of all types of small craft, including sailboats and personal watercraft. They know how varying weather and sea conditions affect the operation of not just their vessel, but are also keenly aware of the limitations that the weather and sea impose on other vessels. They have a thorough knowledge of navigation, piloting and characteristics of their operating area. Above all, the best coxswains understand how to mesh the capabilities of their vessels to weather and sea conditions to conduct the safest possible boat operations.

In this chapter

Forces

Overview

Introduction

Various forces act on a vessel's hull, causing it to move in a particular direction or to change direction. These forces include environmental forces, propulsion, and steering.

In this section

Environmental Forces

A.1. GENERAL

Environmental forces that affect the horizontal motion of a vessel are wind, seas and current. Remember you have no control over them. Take the time to observe how the wind, seas and current, alone and together, affect your vessel. Determine how these forces cause your vessel to drift—at what speed and angle. You must use environmental forces to best advantage and use propulsion and steering to overcome environmental forces when necessary. Usually, a good mix of using and overcoming environmental forces results in smooth, safe boat handling.

A.2. WINDS

The wind acts on the hull topsides, superstructure, and even the crew on smaller boats. The amount of surface upon which the wind acts is called sail area. The vessel will make "leeway" (drift downwind) at a speed proportional to the wind velocity and the amount of sail area. The "aspect" or angle the vessel takes due to the wind will depend on where the sail area is centered compared to the underwater hull's center of lateral resistance. A vessel with a high cabin near the bow and low freeboard aft (Figure 10-1) will tend to ride stern to the wind. If a vessel's draft is shallower

Figure 10-1 High Cabin Near Bow, Low Freeboard Aft

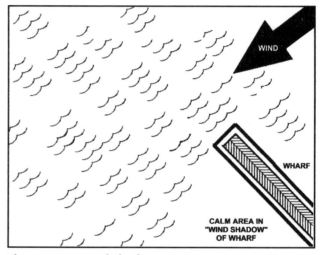

Figure 10-2 Wind Shadow

forward than aft, the wind will affect the bow more than the stern. A sudden gust of wind from abeam when mooring a vessel like this can quickly set the bow down on a pier.

CLOSE QUARTERS SITUATIONS Knowledge of how the wind affects a vessel is very important in all close quarters situations, such as docking, recovery of an object in the water, or maneuvering close aboard another vessel. If maneuvering from a downwind or leeward side of a vessel or pier, look for any wind shadow the vessel or pier makes by blocking the wind (Figure 10-2). Account for the change in wind by planning maneuvers with this wind shadow in mind.

A.3. SEAS

Seas are a product of the wind acting on the surface of the water. Seas affect boat handling in various ways depending on their height and direction and on the vessel's characteristics. Vessels that readily react to wave motion, particularly pitching, will often expose part of the underwater hull to the wind. In situations such as this, the bow or stern may tend to "fall off" the wind when cresting a wave, because less underwater hull is available to prevent this downwind movement.

Relatively large seas have the effect of making a temporary wind shadow for smaller vessels. In the trough between two crests, the wind may be substantially less than the wind at the wave crest. Very small vessels may need to make corrective maneuvers in the trough before approaching the next crest.

A.4. CURRENT

Current will act on a vessel's underwater hull. Although wind will cause a vessel to make leeway through the water, current will cause drift over the ground. A one-knot current may affect a vessel to the same degree as 30 knots of wind. Strong current will easily move a vessel upwind.

Learn to look for the signs of current flow so you are prepared when current affects your vessel. Be particularly aware of instances where current sheer is present. A large, stationary object such as a breakwater or jetty will cause major changes in the amount and direction of current (Figure 10-3). Note the amount of current around floating piers or those with open pile supports. Use caution when maneuvering in close quarters to buoys and anchored vessels. Observe the effect of current by looking for current wake or flow patterns around buoys or piers. Watch how currents affect other vessels.

A.5. COMBINED ENVIRONMENTAL FORCES

Environmental conditions can range from perfectly calm and with no current to a howling gale at spring tides. Even if you don't operate at either extreme, you will experience some amount of environmental forces whenever you are underway.

KNOW THE VESSEL'S RESPONSE Know how your vessel responds to combinations of wind and current and determine which one has the greatest effect on your vessel. It may be that current has more effect on your vessel up to a given wind speed, but above that wind speed, your boat may sail like a kite. Know what will happen if you encounter a sudden gust of wind. Will your boat veer immediately, or will it take a sustained wind to start it turning?

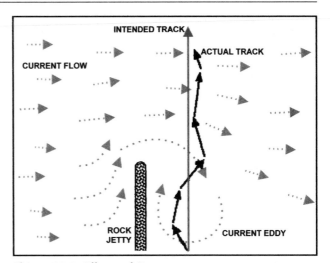

Figure 10-3 Effects of Current

Wave patterns will be steeper and closer together when current runs against the wind. Be particularly cautious whenever current or wind is funneled against the other. Tide rips, breaking bars, or gorge conditions frequently generate these conditions and and may present a challenge to the most proficient coxswain.

Making leeway while drifting downstream (down current) requires a change in approach to prevent overshooting your landing.

NOTE

Stay constantly aware of conditions, how they may be changing, and how they affect your vessel.

Forces Acting on a Vessel

A.6. GENERAL

Before learning how to overcome these forces, you must learn how they act on a vessel.

A.7. ASSUMPTIONS

For this discussion of propulsion, we make the following assumptions:

- If a vessel has a single-shaft motor or drive unit, it is mounted on the vessel's centerline.

- When applying thrust to go forward, the propeller turns clockwise (the top to the right or a "right-handed" propeller), viewed from astern, and turns counterclockwise viewed from astern when making thrust to go astern.

- If twin propulsion is used, the propeller to starboard operates as above (right-hand turning), while the port unit turns counterclockwise when making thrust to go forward when viewed from astern (left-hand turning). See Figure 10-4.

- Be aware that some propeller drive units rotate in only one direction, and changing the propeller blade angle of attack controls ahead or astern thrust (controllable pitch propeller).

A.8. PROPULSION AND STEERING

The key to powered vessel movement is the effective transfer of energy from the source of the power (an internal combustion engine) to the water through a mechanism that converts the engine's power into thrust. This thrust moves the boat. There must also be an element of directional control, both fore and aft, and from side to side.

Propulsion and steering are considered together here for two reasons. Applying thrust has no use if you can't control the vessel's direction, and often the device providing the propulsion also provides the steering.

There are three common methods to transfer power and provide directional control:

- Rotating shaft and propeller with separate rudder,
- A movable (steerable) combination as an outboard motor or stern drive, or
- By an engine-driven pump mechanism with directional control, called a waterjet.

All three arrangements have advantages and disadvantages from the standpoint of mechanical efficiency, maintainability, and vessel control. Selecting one type of propulsion over another is a matter of vessel design and use parameters, operating area limitations, life cycle cost and personal preference. There is no single "best choice" for all applications. Regardless of which type propulsion system your boat employs, you must be familiar with how each operates and how the differences in operation affect vessel movement.

NOTE

Almost every marine propulsion and steering arrangement is designed to operate more efficiently and effectively when going ahead than when going astern. Also, every vessel rotates in a transverse direction about a vertical axis on its pivot point (Figure 10-5). The fore and aft location of the pivot point varies from boat to boat, but typically is located immediately forward of amidships when the boat is at rest. The effective position of the pivot point moves either forward or aft as the hull moves ahead or astern respectively.

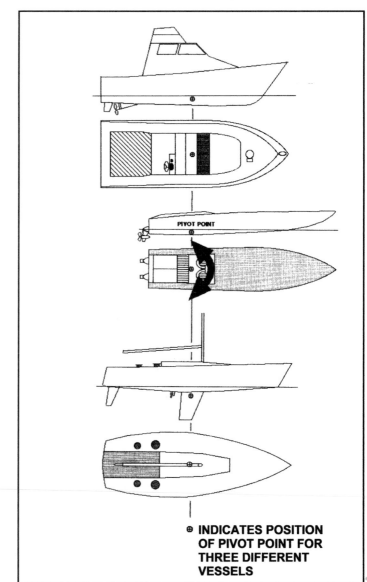

⊕ **INDICATES POSITION OF PIVOT POINT FOR THREE DIFFERENT VESSELS**

Figure 10-5 Pivot Point

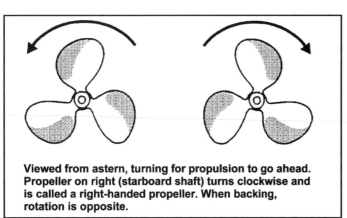

Viewed from astern, turning for propulsion to go ahead. Propeller on right (starboard shaft) turns clockwise and is called a right-handed propeller. When backing, rotation is opposite.

Figure 10-4 Propellers

Shaft, Propeller, and Rudder

A.9. SHAFT

In small craft installations, the propeller shaft usually penetrates the bottom of the hull at an angle to the vessel's designed waterline and true horizontal. The practical reason for this design is that the engine or marine gear must be inside the hull while the diameter of the propeller must be outside and beneath the hull. Additionally, there must be a space between the propeller blade arc of rotation and the bottom of the hull. For single-screw vessels, the shaft is generally aligned to the centerline of the vessel. However, in some installations, a slight offset (approximately one degree) is used to compensate for shaft torque. The rudder is usually mounted directly astern of the propeller.

For twin-screw vessels, we will consider only the case in which both shafts are parallel to the vessel's centerline (or nearly so), the rudders are mounted astern of the propellers, and the rudders turn on vertical rudder posts.

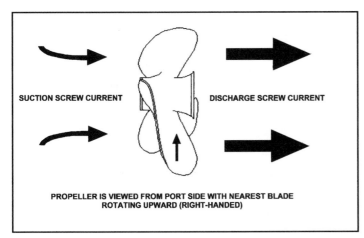

Figure 10-6 Screw Current

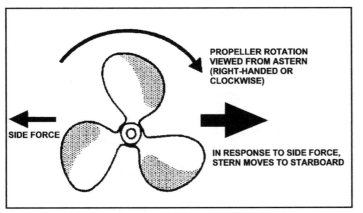

Figure 10-7 Side Force

A.10. PROPELLER ACTION

When rotating to move in a forward direction, a propeller draws its supply of water from every direction forward of and around the blades. Each blade's shape and pitch develop a low pressure area on the forward face of the blade and a high pressure area on the after face of the blade, forcing water thrusting stream toward the stern. This thrust, or dynamic pressure, along the propeller's rotation axis is transmitted through the shaft, moving the boat ahead as the propeller tries to move into the area of lower pressure.

SCREW CURRENT Regardless of whether the propeller is turning to go ahead or astern, the water flow pattern into the propeller's arc of rotation is called **suction screw current**, and the thrust flow pattern out of the propeller is called **discharge screw current** (Figure 10-6). The discharge screw current will always be stronger and more concentrated than the suction screw current.

SIDE FORCE In addition to the thrust along the shaft axis, another effect of propeller rotation is **side force**. Explanations for side force include:

- Propeller reaction to interference from the vessel hull as the hull drags a layer of water along with it (the propeller encounters boundary layer "frictional wake"),

- Effect of discharge screw current on the rudder,

- Transference of energy by the propeller blade at the top of its arc to the water surface (prop wash) or to the hull (noise),

- Due to the angle of the propeller shaft, the effective pitch angle is different for ascending and descending propeller blades, resulting in an unequal blade thrust. (The descending blade has a higher effective pitch angle and causes more thrust.) This net effect is sometimes referred to as sideways blade pressure.

NOTE

The important facts to know: for a right-handed screw turning ahead, the stern will tend to move to starboard (Figure 10-7), and for a right-handed screw when backing, the stern will tend to move to port. For a left-handed screw (normally the port shaft on a twin-screw boat), the action is the opposite.

An easy way to remember how side force will push the stern is to think of the propeller as a wheel on the ground. As the wheel rolls clockwise, it moves to the right. As a propeller turns clockwise when viewed from astern, the stern moves to starboard.

CAVITATION Cavitation usually occurs when the propeller rotates at very high speed and a partial vacuum forms air bubbles at the tips of the propeller blades. Cavitation can also occur when trying to get a stopped propeller to spin at maximum speed, rapidly going from ahead to astern (or vice-versa), or by operating in aerated water where bubbles are dragged into the propeller flow.

Cavitation occurs more readily when trying to back, as the suction screw current draws water from behind the transom, and air at the waterline mixes with the water and is drawn into the propeller. Cavitation frequently occurs when backing with outboard motors. In this case, through-hub exhaust gas bubbles are also drawn forward into the propeller blade arc.

NOTE

A small degree of cavitation is normal. For our purposes, we will use the term to cover the situation in which effective thrust is lost and the propeller just spins and makes bubbles. Cavitation can diminish propeller efficiency to this point. Once cavitation occurs, the quickest way to regain thrust is to reduce propeller speed (RPM) and, as cavitation bubbles subside, gradually increase RPM. Propeller cavitation can occur on vessels of any size.

A.11. RUDDER ACTION

You normally use the rudder to change the vessel's heading when a a vessel is moving through the water (even without propulsion). As a hull moves forward and the rudder is held steady amidships, pressure on either side of the rudder is relatively equal and the vessel will usually maintain a straight track. When you turn the rudder to port or starboard, pressure decreases on one side of the rudder and increases on the other. This force causes the vessel's stern to move to one side or the other. As the stern moves in one direction, the bow moves in the other because a vessel rotates about its pivot point. (Figures 10-8a and 10-8b.)

The speed of the water flowing past the rudder greatly enhances the rudder's force. The thrust or screw discharge current from a propeller operating ahead increases the water flow speed past the rudder. When you turn the rudder to a side, about one-half of the propeller thrust is directed to that side adding a major component of force to move the stern (Figures 10-8c and 10-8d).

When operating astern, the rudder is in the screw suction current. The rudder, therefore, cannot direct any of the propeller thrust. Because the screw suction current is neither as strong nor as concentrated as the screw discharge current, water flow past the rudder does not increase as much. The combined effects of screw current and rudder force when operating astern are not nearly as effective as when operating ahead.

As rudder force is determined by water flow along it, a rudder loses some of its effectiveness if the propeller cavitates and aerated water flows along the rudder.

Outboard Motors and Stern Drives

A.12. GENERAL

Outboard motors and stern drives will be considered together as both include a pivoting gear case and propeller drive unit (called a lower unit on an outboard). The difference between these drive

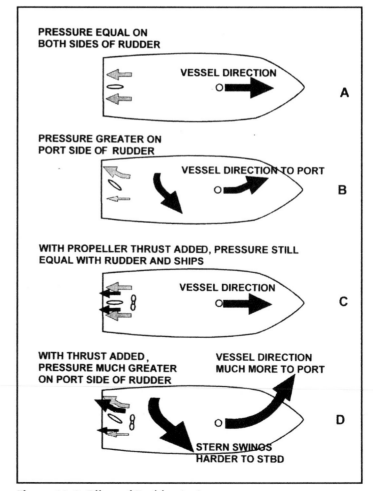

Figure 10-8 Effect of Rudder Action

arrangements and the traditional shaft/propeller/ rudder arrangement is that the screw currents and thrust produced by an outboard or stern drive can be developed at an angle to the vessel centerline. Also, the point where thrust and steering are developed is usually aft of the vessel hull.

The lower unit contains drive gears, a spline connection, and on many set-ups, through-the-propeller hub exhaust. Many lower unit gear housings are over six inches in diameter. When the stern drive is powered by an inboard engine attached through the transom to the drive unit (outdrive), they propulsion system is called an "inboard/outdrive" or "I/O." When the powerhead (engine) is mounted directly above the lower unit, the propulsion system is termed an "outboard engine" or simply "outboard." Both outboards and I/O stern drives can usually direct thrust up to 35 to 40 degrees off the vessel centerline. Also, both types generally allow the coxswain some amount of trim control. Trim control adjusts the angle of the propeller axis relative to the horizontal or surface of the water.

The major difference in operation between the I/O and outboard is that the outboard motor, operating with a vertical crankshaft and driveshaft, devel-

ops some degree of rotational torque that can cause "pull" in the steering, usually when accelerating or in a sharp turn to starboard. This condition, called "torque lock," can make it difficult to stop a turning action. The easiest way to overcome torque lock is to reduce RPM before attempting to counter-steer.

A.13. THRUST AND DIRECTIONAL CONTROL

Outboards and stern drives are equipped with small steering vanes or skegs below their propellers. The housing above the gear case (below the waterline) is generally foil shaped. Though these features help directional control, particularly at speed, the larger amount of steering force from an outboard or stern drive is based upon the ability to direct the screw discharge current thrust at an angle to the vessel's centerline (Figure 10-9). This directed thrust provides extremely effective directional control when powering ahead. When making way with no propeller RPM, the lower unit and skeg are not as effective as a rudder would be in providing directional control.

NOTE

The propeller forces discussed above in Section A.8. (screw current and side force) also apply to the propellers on outboards or outdrives. However, because you can direct these drives, you can counter side force. The steering vane/skeg angle is usually adjustable, also assisting in countering side force.

A.14. PROPELLER SIDE FORCE

When backing, you can direct outboard/outdrive thrust to move the stern to port or starboard. When backing with the unit hard over to port, propeller side force introduces an element of forward motion (Figure 10-10), but can be countered through less helm. When backing to starboard, the side force tends to cause an element of astern motion and also tries to offset the initial starboard movement. Many lower units are fitted with a small vertical vane, slightly offset from centerline, directly above and astern of the propeller. This vane also acts to counter side force, particularly at higher speeds.

A.15. VERTICAL THRUST

Outboards and stern drives usually allow a level of vertical thrust control. Trim systems control the angle of attack between the propeller's axis of rotation and both the vessel waterline and the surface of the water. Vertical thrust control, especially applied

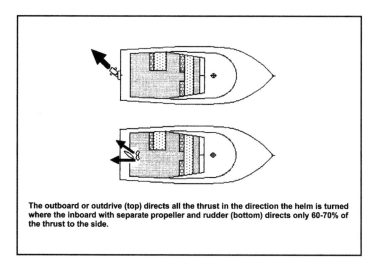

The outboard or outdrive (top) directs all the thrust in the direction the helm is turned where the inboard with separate propeller and rudder (bottom) directs only 60-70% of the thrust to the side.

Figure 10-9 Lower Unit/Outdrive Directed Thrust

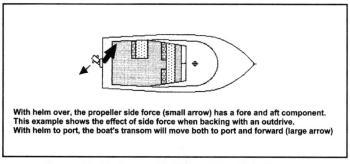

With helm over, the propeller side force (small arrow) has a fore and aft component. This example shows the effect of side force when backing with an outdrive. With helm to port, the boat's transom will move both to port and forward (large arrow)

Figure 10-10 Lower Unit/Outdrive Side Force

aft of the transom, changes the attitude of the vessel hull relative to the water (Figure 10-11). Use small amounts of trim to offset for extreme loading conditions or to adjust how the vessel goes through chop.

In addition to trim, a vertical component of thrust develops in another situation. Depending on the type of hull, if a vessel is forced into an extremely tight turn with power applied, thrust is directed sideways while the vessel heels, actually trying to force the transom up out of the water, causing a turn to tighten even more.

> ### WARNING
>
> **In lightweight or highly buoyant outboard powered boats, use of full power in tight turns can cause loss of control or ejection of crew or coxswain. The helmsman should always attach the engine kill switch lanyard to themselves if one is available.**

A.16. CAVITATION

As noted earlier, cavitation frequently occurs when backing with outboard motors. As through-hub exhaust gas bubbles are drawn forward into the propeller blade arc, the aerated water increases the possibility of cavitation. Though outboards and stern-drives are fitted with anti-cavitation plates above the propeller, always take care to limit cavitation, particularly when backing or maneuvering using large amounts of throttle.

Waterjets

A.17. GENERAL

A waterjet is an engine-driven impeller mounted in a housing. The impeller draws water in and forces it out through a nozzle. The suction (inlet) side of the waterjet is forward of the nozzle, usually mounted at the deepest draft near the after sections of the hull. The discharge nozzle is mounted low in the hull, exiting through the transom. The cross-sectional area of the inlet is much larger than that of the nozzle. The volume of water entering the inlet is the same as being discharged through the nozzle, so the water flow is much stronger at the nozzle than at the intake. This pump-drive system is strictly a directed-thrust drive arrangement. A waterjet normally has no appendages, nor does it extend below the bottom of the vessel hull, allowing for operation in very shallow water.

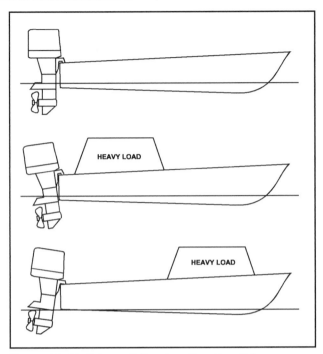

Figure 10-11 Trim to Offset Loading Condition

A.18. THRUST AND DIRECTIONAL CONTROL

Vessel control is through the nozzle-directed thrust. To attain forward motion, the thrust is directed astern. For turning, the nozzle pivots (as a stern drive) to provide a transverse thrust component that moves the stern. For astern motion, a bucket-like deflector drops down behind the nozzle and directs the thrust forward. Some waterjet applications include trim control as with a stern drive or outboard. With this, thrust can be directed slightly upward or downward to offset vessel loading or improve ride.

From time to time, you might see a waterjet with a small steering vane, but in most cases the only vessel control is by the nozzle-directed thrust. A waterjet will not turn from its heading if power is suddenly reduced to neutral even if the helm is put hard over. Of the three drive arrangements discussed, the waterjet alone has no directional control when there is no power.

A.19. NO SIDE FORCE

Since the waterjet impeller is fully enclosed in the pump-drive housing, no propeller side force is generated. The only way to move the stern to port or starboard is by using the directed thrust.

A.20. CAVITATION

Waterjet impeller blades revolve at an extremely high speed. They can tolerate much more cavitation without significant thrust loss than can traditional propellers. In fact, a telltale indicator of waterjet propulsion is a pronounced aerated-water discharge frequently seen as a rooster tail astern of such craft.

Because impeller rotation does not change with thrust direction, frequent shifting from ahead to astern motion does not induce cavitation. However, as the thrust to make astern motion reaches the waterjet inlet, the aerated water is drawn into the jet, causing some reduction of effective thrust. As with all types of propulsion, slowing the impeller until clear of the aerated water reduces cavitation effects.

Basic Maneuvering

Overview

Introduction

To learn basic handling and maneuvering characteristics of a vessel, a trainee must first observe a skilled coxswain. Also, one must first learn to operate the vessel in relatively open water, away from fixed piers and moored vessels or the critical gaze of onlookers.

In this section

Learning the Controls

B.1. GENERAL

When you step up to the controls of any vessel for the first time, immediately familiarize yourself with any physical constraints or limitations of the helm and engine controls. Ideally, controls should be designed and mounted to allow a wide range of operators of different arm length and hand size, though this is not always so.

B.2. OBSTRUCTIONS/HAZARDS

Determine if anything obstructs hand or arm movement for helm and throttle control. Check for a firm grasp of the wheel through 360 degrees, anything that prevents use of the spokes, awkward position of throttle/gear selector, layout that prevents use of heavy gloves, inaccessible engine shut-down handles, an easily fouled outboard kill-switch lanyard or other common-sense items. Learn what they are before you snag a sleeve while maneuvering in close quarters or bang a knee or elbow in choppy seas.

NOTE

Check control operation while moored with engines secured. Some larger vessels require engine operation to operate controls such as engine assisted hydraulic steering. If so, check throttle controls with engines secured.

B.3. DETERMINE THE HELM LIMITS

The following are some guidelines for determining the helm limits.

1. Determine the amount of helm from full right rudder to full left rudder.

2. Check for any binding, play, or slop in the helm and rudder control and at what angle it occurs.

3. Ensure that the helm indicates rudder amidships.

4. Ensure that a rudder angle indicator accurately matches rudder position and matches a centered helm.

B.4. CHECK ENGINE CONTROL ACTION

Examine the following when checking engine control action.

1. Is throttle separate from shifting/direction mechanism?

2. Any detent, notch or stops that separate neutral, ahead and astern.

3. Force required to shift from neutral to ahead or astern.

4. Binding or excessive looseness at any stage of the throttle control.

5. Is "neutral" easily found without looking at the control handle?

6. Do the controls stay put or do they tend to slide back?

7. Does the kill-switch lanyard allow adequate but not excessive range of motion?

8. Does an engine shut down handle work properly?

9. Is idle speed adjusted properly?

> **WARNING**
>
> Smooth, positive operation of helm and engine controls is absolutely necessary for safe boat operation. Don't accept improper control configuration, mismatched equipment, or improper maintenance as a reason for poorly operating controls. Poor control operation causes unsafe boat operations.

B.5. RECHECKING CONTROLS

After checking all controls while moored with engines secured, recheck their operation with engines running while securely moored. It may not be safe to apply full ahead to astern throttle, but note any time lag between throttle shift and propulsion, from neutral to ahead, neutral to astern, ahead to astern, and astern to ahead.

> **CAUTION!**
>
> When going from ahead position to astern position, and when going from astern position to ahead position, pause briefly at the neutral position.

When training, an experienced individual should get the vessel underway and into open water before turning control over to anyone not familiar with the particular boat's operation. Once in open water, turn control over to the new coxswain and have them recheck helm and engine control operation at clutch speed.

NOTE

Perform these steps as part of every getting-underway check.

Before operating any vessel, familiarize yourself with all its engine controls.

Moving Forward in a Straight Line

B.6. GENERAL

When moving forward in a straight line, advance throttle gradually and firmly. If the vessel is single-screw, outboard, or outdrive, propeller side force will tend to move the stern slightly to starboard (Figure 10-12). Offset the side force with slight starboard helm. If twin-engine, advance throttles together. The vessel should not yaw in either direction if power is applied evenly. Adjust engine RPM so both engines turn at the same speed. Some vessels have a separate indicator to show if engine speeds match, but be sure to compare tachometer readings too.

NOTE

Don't ram throttles forward when starting up. As the engines try to transfer the excessive power, the stern will squat, raising the bow and decreasing visibility (Figure 10-13), and propellers or impellers may cavitate.

B.7. USE HELM TO CONTROL DIRECTION

Use small amounts of helm to offset any propeller side force or the effects of winds and seas. Always note compass course and correct frequently to

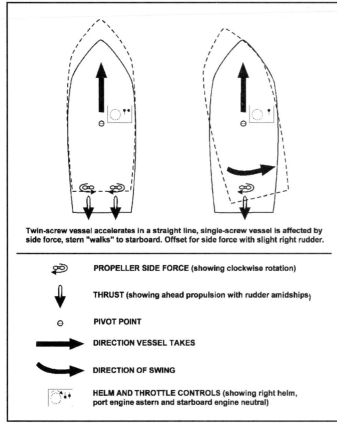

Twin-screw vessel accelerates in a straight line, single-screw vessel is affected by side force, stern "walks" to starboard. Offset for side force with slight right rudder.

🐚	**PROPELLER SIDE FORCE** (showing clockwise rotation)
⬇	**THRUST** (showing ahead propulsion with rudder amidships)
⊖	**PIVOT POINT**
➡	**DIRECTION VESSEL TAKES**
➥	**DIRECTION OF SWING**
⬚	**HELM AND THROTTLE CONTROLS** (showing right helm, port engine astern and starboard engine neutral)

Figure 10-12 Accelerated Ahead

stay on course. Develop a practiced eye and steer on a geographic point or range. Try to steer for a point between buoys. Apply small, early helm corrections to stay on course, rather than large corrections after drifting well off course. Don't oversteer, leaving a snake-like path. At low speeds, helm correction will be more frequent than at higher speeds.

B.8. GET ON PLANE

For planing or semidisplacement hulls, the boat will gradually gain speed until planing. If fitted with trim control (including trim tabs on inboard boats), slight, bow-down trim may lessen the amount of time needed to get on plane or "on step."

B.9. DETERMINE APPROPRIATE SPEED

Don't ram the throttle to the stop and leave it there.

LEAVE A MARGIN OF POWER Always leave a margin of power available for emergencies. Determine the best speed for your vessel. Many vessels will not exceed or will only marginally exceed a given speed, regardless of the power applied. At some point, the only effect of applying additional

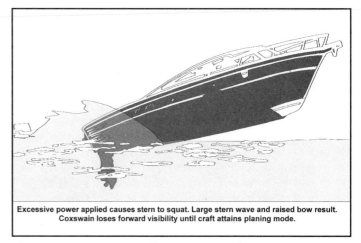

Excessive power applied causes stern to squat. Large stern wave and raised bow result. Coxswain loses forward visibility until craft attains planing mode.

Figure 10-13 Pronounced Squat on Acceleration

throttle is increased fuel consumption with no speed increase. A good normal operating limit for semidisplacement vessels is usually 90 percent maximum power, allowing the remaining 10 percent for emergency use or to get out of a tight spot.

MAINTAIN SAFE SPEED FOR ABILITY OR CONDITIONS A boat at high speed has a large amount of force. With an untrained operator, this force can be dangerous. Consider different factors to determine safe speed.

- *High seas*. **Slow down as winds and seas increase:** the boat will handle more easily. Pounding or becoming airborne fatigues the hull and could injure the crew or cause them chronic skeletal problems. If it takes tremendous effort just to hang on, the crew will be spent and not able to perform their jobs. Minimize taking spray and water on deck.

- *Traffic density*. **Don't use high speed in high traffic density areas.** A safe speed allows you to respond to developing situations and minimize risk of collision, not only with the nearest approaching vessel, but with others around it.

- *Visibility*. **If you can't see where you're going, slow down.** Fog, rain, and snow are obvious limits to visibility, but there are others. Geographic features and obstructions (river bends, piers, bridges and causeways), along with heavy vessel traffic, can limit the view of "the big picture." Darkness or steering directly into the sun lessens ability to see objects or judge distances. Prevent spray on the windscreen (particularly salt spray or freezing spray) as much as possible and clean it regularly. Spray build-up on the windscreen is particularly hazardous in darkness or in glare.

Maintaining a safe speed at all times is critical to safe boating.

- *Shoal waters.* In extremely shallow water, the bottom has an effect on the movement of the vessel. **Slow down in shallow waters.** In extremely shallow water, the vessel's stern tends to "squat" and actually moves closer to the bottom.

NOTE

Find the most comfortable, secure location for the entire crew. For many vessels, this means in the immediate vicinity of the helm.

> **WARNING**
>
> Being "on plane" will not let you cross a shoal that would ground your vessel in the displacement mode. At high planing speed, the stern will squat as it gets in shallow water, possibly grounding at a very damaging speed.

B.10. BANK CUSHION AND BANK SUCTION

In extremely narrow channels, a vessel moving through the water will cause the "wedge" of water between the bow and the nearer bank to build up higher than on the other side. This bow cushion or bank cushion tends to push the bow away from the edge of the channel.

As the stern moves along, screw suction and water is needed to "fill-in" where the boat was creating stern or bank suction. This causes the stern to move towards the bank. The combined effect of momentary bank cushion and bank suction may cause

a sudden sheer toward the opposite bank. Bank cushion and bank suction are strongest when the bank of a channel is steep. They are weakest when the edge of the channel shoals gradually and extends in a large shallow area. When possible, stay exactly in the center of an extremely narrow channel to avoid these forces (Figure 10-14). Slower speed also reduces the amount of cushion and suction. Offset for continuous cushion and suction effects by some rudder offset towards the closer bank.

If a strong, sudden sheer occurs, counteract it with full rudder towards the bank and increasing speed. Remember, on a single-screw vessel, propeller side force will cause the stern to move to starboard.

> **CAUTION!**
>
> Don't overcompensate for bank cushion and bank suction. Too much helm in the direction of the bank could cause the bow to veer into the bank. Then, a subsequent large helm movement to turn the bow away from the bank may cause the stern to swing into the bank.

B.11. BOW CUSHION AND STERN SUCTION

When meeting another vessel close aboard, bow cushion and stern suction occur between the vessels much the same as bank cushion and suction. Use helm corrections to compensate. As both vessels move through the water, the combined effect is greater than what a single vessel encounters from bank interaction. Use caution so the bow does not veer too far from the intended track and the stern swings into the path of the other vessel.

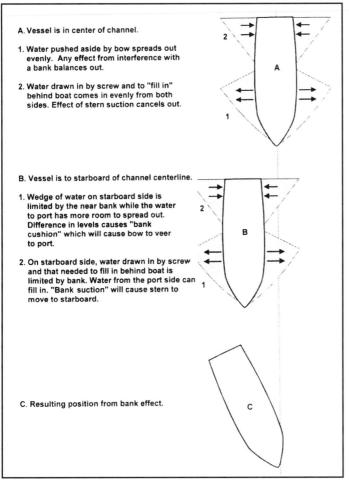

A. Vessel is in center of channel.

1. Water pushed aside by bow spreads out evenly. Any effect from interference with a bank balances out.

2. Water drawn in by screw and to "fill in" behind boat comes in evenly from both sides. Effect of stern suction cancels out.

B. Vessel is to starboard of channel centerline.

1. Wedge of water on starboard side is limited by the near bank while the water to port has more room to spread out. Difference in levels causes "bank cushion" which will cause bow to veer to port.

2. On starboard side, water drawn in by screw and that needed to fill in behind boat is limited by bank. Water from the port side can fill in. "Bank suction" will cause stern to move to starboard.

C. Resulting position from bank effect.

Figure 10-14 Bow Cushion and Stern Suction

Assume a port-to-port meeting situation. Before vessels are bow-to-bow, use a small amount of right rudder to ensure the bows clear. The bow cushion will increase separation. As the vessels near bow-to-beam, use left rudder to keep away from the right-hand bank and to stay parallel to the channel. When the vessels are bow-to-quarter, the bow cushion will be offset by the stern suction, and bank cushion may need to be offset by some right rudder. Finally, as the vessels are quarter-to-quarter, stern suction will predominate, and will require left rudder to keep the sterns apart.

NOTE

The following bow cushion and stern suction considerations apply when meeting another vessel in a narrow channel and when operating near a bank.

- The deeper the vessel's draft, the greater the cushion and suction effect, particularly if draft approaches water depth.

- The closer to a bank or another vessel, the greater the cushion and suction.

- In very narrow waterways, slow down to decrease cushion and suction effects, but not to the point that you lose adequate steerage.

When you meet another vessel in a narrow channel, balance the bow cushion and stern suction effects caused by the other vessel with the bank cushion and suction effects due to the channel.

B.12. WATCH YOUR WAKE

As a vessel proceeds, a combination of bow and stern waves move outward at an angle to the vessel track. The wake height and speed depend on vessel speed and hull type. Some of the largest wakes are caused by relatively large, semidisplacement hulls, proceeding at cruising speed. Some lighter craft actually generate less wake at top speed in the planing mode than they do at a slower speed. Displacement craft make the largest wake at hull speed. Determine how to make your vessel leave the least wake; it may require slowing appreciably.

All vessels are responsible for their wake and any injury or damage it causes. Only an unaware coxswain trails a large wake through a mooring area or shallows, tossing vessels and straining moorings. "Get-home-itis" and a false sense of urgency are two reasons coxswains forget to watch their wake. A large, unnecessary wake, particularly in enclosed waters or near other, smaller vessels, ruins a professional image.

CAUTION!

Whenever you maneuver, keep the crew informed, especially if rapidly accelerating, turning or slowing. A quick warning shout can prevent injury.

Turning the Boat with the Helm

B.13. GENERAL

To move in a straight line, small, frequent, momentary helm inputs adjust the position of the stern and bow to head in the desired direction. To change the vessel heading, use larger, more sustained helm movement.

Keep your wake small in crowded waterways. You are legally responsible for damage caused by your wake.

B.14. BE AWARE OF THE PIVOT POINT

You change the direction of the bow by moving the stern in the opposite direction. As the stern swings a certain angle, the bow swings the same angle. Depending on the fore and aft position of the pivot point, the stern could swing through a larger distance than the bow, at the same angle. When a hull moves forward through the water, the effective pivot point moves forward. The higher the forward speed, the farther forward the pivot point moves.

B.15. NOTE HOW PROPULSION TYPE AFFECTS TURNING

Outboards, stern drives and waterjets use propulsion thrust for directional control and can make a much tighter turns (using helm alone) that similar hulls outfitted with shaft, propeller and rudder. Boats equipped with extended outboard mounting brackets have a pivot point further aft than similar hulled vessels with other propulsion systems. Indeed, some brackets move the thrust three to four feet aft of the hull. The distance the stern will kick away from the direction of the turn depends on the amount of directed thrust and the distance it is located aft of the pivot point. The stern of a boat equipped with directed thrust propulsion will typically skid outward making the bow describe a very tight arc compared with a similar hull equipped with shaft, propeller and rudder, systems. (Figure 10-15).

B.16. LEARN THE VESSEL'S TURNING CHARACTERISTICS

If you proceed on a steady heading and then put the helm over to one side or the other, the boat begins to turn. Up to the time the boat turns through 90 degrees, the boat has continued to advance in the original direction. By the time the boat has turned through 90 degrees, it is well off to the side of the original track. This distance is called *transfer*. As the boat continues through 180 degrees, its path has defined its *tactical diameter*. For a particular vessel, these values vary for speed and rudder angle (Figure 10-16).

Develop a working knowledge of your vessel's turning characteristics. This will allow you to decide whether to attempt a particular maneuver in a the available space solely with the helm or whether other maneuvering is needed. Learn when to ease the helm to avoid oversteering a course change.

B.17. NOTE LOSS OF SPEED THROUGH THE WATER

Some planing hulls and most semidisplacement craft will slow appreciably when turning at high speeds. As the boat heels into a turn, the hull provides less buoyancy to keep the vessel on plane. Also, as the aft part of the hull skids across the water while in a heel, the hull presents a flat shape in the original direction of movement and pushes water outward. The bottom becomes a braking

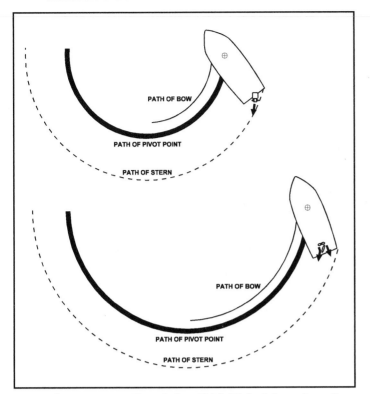

Figure 10-15 Pivot Point, Skid, Kick, Inboard vs. Outboard

surface. For light-displacement vessels, a full helm at high speed maneuver minimizes advance.

> **WARNING**
>
> With light-displacement, high-powered craft, applying maximum helm at high speed will stop a boat's progress in the original direction of movement quite quickly. Though such a turning action is effective to avoid contact with an immediate hazard, the violent motion could eject unsuspecting crewmembers. Don't use this technique except as an emergency maneuver, and especially don't use this maneuver to demonstrate the boat's capability to non-crew.

B.18. MAKE COURSE CHANGES AND TURNS IN CHANNELS

Bank suction, bank cushion (see B.10. above) and currents will all affect a boat navigating a sharp bend in a narrow channel. Where natural waterways have bends or turns, the water is always deepest and the current is always strongest on the

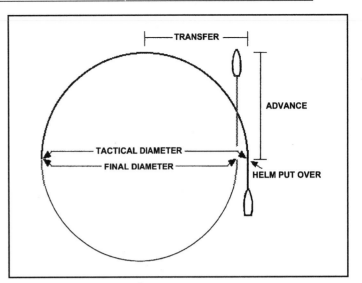

Figure 10-16 Turning Characteristics

outside of the bend. This is true for 15-degree jogs in a tidal estuary and for the "S" shaped meanders on the Mississippi River. This is so because flowing water has momentum and resists having its direction changed. As flowing water strikes the outside of the bank, it erodes the earth and carries the particles with it. The particles fall out farther downstream in areas of less current (the inside of a turn or bend) and cause shoaling. In some turns or bends, there may be circular currents or eddies in either the deep outside of the bend or the shallow inside. Back currents also occur at times near eddies on the inside of a bend. When eddies or back currents occur, those near the shallows are much weaker than those at the outside of the bend.

Because bank cushion and suction are strongest when the bank of a channel is steep and weakest when the edge of the channel shoals gradually, bank effect is stronger on the outside of bends or turns. Be aware of the mix of current and bank effect and use these forces to your advantage.

COUNTER A HEAD CURRENT THROUGH A BEND Minimize the effect of a head current by steering along the inside quarter of the channel. Make sure you avoid shoals. If the bow gets into the area of greater current, it may begin to sheer towards the outside of the bend. Counter it by moving the helm towards the inside of the bend and by getting the stern directly down-current from the bow. Gradually work back to the inside quarter of the channel.

- If you start from the outside of the bend, you will encounter the full force of the current. Bank cushion should keep the bow from the outside edge, but the stern is limited in its movement by bank suction. Initial helm towards the inside of the turn may allow the current to cause the bow to sheer rapidly away from the outside. If this should happen, use power and helm immediately to keep the bow pointed upstream. Use gradual helm with constant power to get out of the main force of the current and work across to the inside quarter of the channel.

NAVIGATE WITH A FOLLOWING CURRENT Approach the turn on a course just to the outside of the middle of the channel. This will avoid the strongest currents at the outside edge while still getting a reasonable push. As you turn, the strongest current will accentuate the swing of the stern quarter to the outside of the channel. Because of this, and because the following current tends to carry the boat toward the outside, begin the turn early in the bend.

- If you stay too far to the outside of the bend, timing the turn is difficult. Turn too early and stern suction on the quarter in the strongest current may cause an extreme veer to the inside of the turn. Any bow cushion will accentuate the sheer. Turn too late and the stern suction and the quartering current could cause grounding.

- If you try to hug the inside of the turn, both current and bank effect will be lessened. Use a small amount of rudder toward the inside bank to enter the turn. As the channel begins to bend, use less rudder while the boat starts to move from the inside bank. Use caution as the current under the quarter affects the stern, giving in an increase in sheer towards the inside bank. Slack water or an eddy down current on the inside will increase this sheer while bow cushion may not be enough to prevent grounding.

Stopping the Boat

B.19. GENERAL

If you pull back the throttle to neutral, the vessel will begin to lose forward motion. For a heavy-displacement vessel, once propulsion is stopped, the vessel will continue to move forward for some distance. The vessel carries its momentum without propulsion. For a semidisplacement hull or planing hull, as you retard throttle and reduce power, the boat quickly comes off plane. As the vessel reverts to displacement mode, the resistance of the hull going through the water instead of on top of the water slows the boat. The vessel still carries some

way, but at only a fraction of the original speed. Experiment with your vessel and see how rapidly the boat slows after going from cruising speed to neutral throttle. Know the amount of head reach your vessel carries from different speeds. It is very important when maneuvering.

B.20. USE ASTERN PROPULSION TO STOP THE VESSEL

Slowing the vessel's forward movement won't always do; a complete and quick stop to dead in the water may be required. Accomplish a quick stop by applying astern propulsion while the vessel continues to make forward way. First, slow the vessel as much as possible by retarding throttle. After the vessel begins to lose way, apply astern propulsion firmly and forcefully. Power must be higher than that available at clutch speed to prevent engine stall. On a single-screw vessel, the stern will want to swing to port. After all way is off, throttle to neutral.

At low forward speeds, astern propulsion is frequently used to maneuver, both to check forward way and to gain sternway.

With a waterjet, reverse thrust is immediate. No marine gear or drive unit changes shaft and propeller rotation. The clamshell or bucket shaped deflector plate drops down and redirects thrust forward. As with other drives, use enough astern engine power to overcome potential engine stall.

Though many vessels are tested and capable of immediately going from full speed ahead to full reverse throttle, this crash stop technique is extremely harsh on the drive train and may cause engine stall. Though much of the power goes to propeller cavitation, this technique can be effective in an emergency.

WARNING

The crash stop is an *emergency* maneuver. It may damage the drive train and stall the engine(s). In most cases, with high levels of crew professionalism, skill and situational awareness, it is not necessary.

B.21. USE FULL HELM TO STOP FORWARD WAY

As noted above, with light-displacement, high-powered craft, maximum helm at high speed will quickly stop a boat's progress in the original direction of movement. To fully stop, throttle down to neutral after entering the skid. If done properly, no astern propulsion is required.

With a jet drive, no directional control will be available without thrust. The boat must be in a skid before you reduce power. If you reduce thrust before attempting to turn, the boat will slow on the original heading.

WARNING

As with the crash stop, a full-helm, high-speed stop is an emergency maneuver. The violent motion could eject crewmembers. Don't use this maneuver in choppy waters as a chine could "trip" and cause the vessel to snap-roll and flip or capsize.

Backing the Vessel

B.22. GENERAL

Control while making sternway is essential. Because vessels are designed to go forward, many vessels don't easily back in a straight line. Due to higher freeboard and superstructure forward (increased sail area), many vessels back into the wind. Knowledge of how environmental forces affect your boat is critical when backing.

Besides watching where the stern goes, keep track of the bow. The stern will move in one direction about the pivot point, and the bow about the other. As a vessel develops sternway, the effective pivot point moves aft and the bow may swing through a greater distance. Keep firm control of the helm to prevent the rudder or drive from swinging to a hard-over angle.

CAUTION!

Don't back in a way that allows water to ship over the transom. Be careful with boats with very low freeboard aft. Outboard powered vessels, with low cut-outs for motor mounting and large amount of weight aft are susceptible to shipping water while backing, particularly in a chop. Stability is jeopardized if shipped water does not drain immediately.

CAUTION!

Most inboard engines exhaust through the transom. Outboard motors exhaust astern. Backing could subject the crew and cabin spaces to a large amount of exhaust fumes. Limit exposure to exhaust fumes as much as possible. During training sessions, frequently change vessel aspect to the wind to clear fumes. After backing, ventilate interior spaces.

B.23. SCREW AND RUDDER

While backing, the rudders are in the weaker, less concentrated screw suction current, and most steering control comes from flow across the rudder due to sternway.

SINGLE-ENGINE VESSELS Propeller side force presents a major obstacle to backing in the direction you want. The rudder does not have much effect until sternway is made, and even then, many boats will back into the wind despite your best efforts. You should know at what wind speed the boat will back into the wind without backing to port.

- Before starting to back, apply right full rudder to get any advantage available.

- A quick burst of power astern will cause the stern to swing to port, but use it to get the boat moving.

- Once moving, reduce power somewhat to reduce propeller side force and steer with the rudder. As sternway increases, less rudder will be needed to maintain a straight track astern.

- If more sternway is needed to improve steerage, increase power gradually; a strong burst astern will quickly swing the stern to port.

- If stern swing to port cannot be controlled by the rudder alone, use a burst of power ahead for propeller side force to swing the stern to starboard. Don't apply so much power as to stop sternway or to set up a screw discharge current that would cause the stern to swing farther to port. (As the vessel backs, it uses sternway water flow across the rudder to steer.)

- If this fails, use a larger burst of power ahead, with helm to port. Sternway will probably stop, but propeller side force and discharge current across the shifted rudder will move the stern to starboard. Now try backing again.

TWIN-ENGINE VESSELS Back both engines evenly to offset propeller side force. Use asymmetric power (one engine at higher RPM than the other) to help steer the stern. Asymmetric power will also give unequal propeller side force that will help steer.

- Apply astern power evenly, keeping rudders amidships.

- If the stern tends to one side, first try to control direction with slight helm adjustment. If not effective, either increase backing power on the side toward the direction of veer or decrease power on the opposite side.

B.24. STERN DRIVES AND OUTBOARDS

Use the directed thrust to pull the stern to one side or the other. As the power is applied aft of the transom, use care to keep the bow from falling off course due to winds. Avoid cavitation. It can develop quickly when backing with a lower unit. Propeller side force is present, but is offset through helm. A lower unit that is not providing thrust is not efficient when trying to steer while backing. It is better to keep steady, slow RPMs than to vary between high power and neutral.

SINGLE-OUTBOARD/OUTDRIVE

- Offset propeller side force with right rudder.

- Apply astern power gradually, but be careful not to cause propeller cavitation.

TWIN-OUTBOARD/OUTDRIVE If astern power is matched, propeller side forces will cancel. As with twin inboards, first try to offset any stern swing with helm before using asymmetric power.

If less thrust than that provided by both drives at clutch speed is needed, use one motor or engine. This will keep speed low but will keep thrust available for steering, rather than shifting one or both engines from reverse to neutral. If using one unit, compensate with helm for propeller side force and the increased, off-centered drag caused by the other lower unit.

B.25. WATERJETS

There is no propeller side force and thrust is directed. Going from forward to reverse thrust has no marine gear or drive train to slow things. Thrust is simply redirected with the "bucket." Unless thrust is applied and being directed, there is no directional control at all.

Avoid bursts of power astern when backing. Bursts of power when making astern thrust will aerate excessively the waterjet intake flow ahead of the transom.

Using Asymmetric or Opposed Propulsion (Twin Screw Theory)

B.26. GENERAL

Asymmetric propulsion while backing was covered above. The techniques presented here are additional methods of maneuvering that capitalize on twin-engine vessel capability to differ the amount or direction of thrust produced by the two engines. Any asymmetry in thrust affects the boat's heading. The amount of heading adjustment can vary from asymmetry needed to hold a course at cruising speed to large differences used to maneuver a boat 360 degrees around its pivot point by using opposing propulsion (splitting throttles). Liken the concept of using asymmetric thrust or opposed propulsion to "twisting" the boat. (Remember, the fundamentals and forces discussed earlier—pivot point, propeller side force and turning characteristics—still come into play and affect vessel response.) Because the drives on a twin screw vessel are offset from the vessel centerline, they can apply a turning moment to the hull. Twin outboard motors on a bracket apply this twist aft of the hull (and well aft of the hull pivot point), while twin inboards apply most of this twist to the hull at the first thrust-bearing member of the drive train (usually the reduction gear or V-drive, much closer to the pivot point). With inboards, propeller side force is transferred through strut and stern tube to the hull.

Up to a point, the greater the difference in RPM, the greater the effect on the change in heading. Above that point, specific for each boat, type of propulsion, sea conditions and operating speed, cavitation or aeration will occur, and propulsion efficiency will decrease, at least on one drive.

NOTE

As with all boat handling techniques, learn the use of asymmetric thrust first in calm weather, in open water and at low speeds.

B.27. HOLD A COURSE

Depending on a vessel's topside profile, wind may cause the bow to fall off to leeward. Though the helmsman can compensate for this by holding constant pressure to the steering system to hold desired course, a less taxing technique is to adjust the throttles so the leeward engine turns at higher speed than the windward engine. Fine-tune the difference in RPM until helm pressure is relieved.

Changing Vessel Heading Using Asymmetric or Opposed Propulsion (Twin Screw Theory)

B.28. GENERAL

Using asymmetric thrust techniques causes a faster change in heading by increasing both skid and kick, reducing advance and transfer and (if the heading change is held long enough) the overall tactical diameter.

B.29. ROTATE ABOUT THE PIVOT POINT

This is a low-speed maneuver. It is important because you will face situations in which you need to change the boat's heading (to the weather or another vessel) or to move the bow or stern in a limited area. Oppose the engines to turn in an extremely tight space. Perform this maneuver first at clutch speed in calm conditions to see how the vessel reacts and what type of arcs the bow and stern describe. With no way on, there is no initial advance and transfer, so depending on the boat, this maneuver might yield a tactical diameter of zero if you change heading 360 degrees (rotating the vessel in its own length).

Consider the forces involved. Vessels with propellers will develop side force from both drives during this maneuver. The rudder (where equipped) can use screw discharge current from the ahead engine to help pivot the stern. Because boats operate more efficiently ahead, some headway may develop.

HELM OVER HARD TO PORT Put the helm over hard to port:

- Perform the same procedures as with helm amidships. When stopping and reversing direction of swing, shift the helm to starboard.

- In addition to the observations made with helm amidships, note whether the sizes of the arcs were smaller (due to directed thrust by lower unit or rudder).

HELM AMIDSHIPS With helm amidships:

1. At dead in the water and throttles in neutral, simultaneously clutch ahead with starboard engine, and clutch astern with port engine (keep both engine RPMs the same, though in opposite direction).

2. Note the arcs described by bow and stern as the vessel swings through 360 degrees to determine vessel pivot point.

3. If vessel moved forward (along its centerline) during the rotation, slightly increase astern RPM to compensate.

4. Now, simultaneously shift throttles so port is clutch ahead and starboard is clutch astern; note how long it takes to stop and reverse direction of swing.

5. Again, check bow and stern arcs as vessel swings through 360 degrees, then stop the swing.

DEVELOPING SKILLS With the basic skill in hand, practice controlling the amount of swing. Use the compass and gradually limit the degree of rotation down to 30 degrees each side of the original heading. Next, increase amount of throttle applied. Note the effect on vessel movement especially as to the rate of swing.

Develop your boat handling knowledge and skills to know the degree of throttle splitting or asymmetric thrust for best effect in any situation. Maneuvering near the face of a breaking wave may require opposing engines at one-third or more their available RPM, while maneuvering near the pier might only require a short, small burst on one engine to bring the bow through the wind.

CAUTION!

All crew members must pay close attention to throttle changes and vessel movements. Firmly hold on to the vessel during these maneuvers.

NOTE

Experiment with your vessel.

- Though rudder use should help increase the rate of swing, the increase in turn rate might not be worth the workload increase (stop-to-stop helm use). Due to rudder swing rate, full helm use may not be as effective as leaving the helm centered.

- At some level of power for each vessel and drive train arrangement, cavitation will occur with split throttles. Know at what throttle settings cavitation occurs. More power will not increase turning ability and might cause temporary loss of maneuverability until cavitation subsides. In critical situations, loss of effective power could leave a vessel vulnerable.

B.30. REDUCE TACTICAL DIAMETER AT SPEED

An emergency maneuver at cruising speed may require a turn with reduced tactical diameter.

TURN AND DRAG ONE PROPELLER An effective technique for a twin-propeller boat is to have one propeller act as a brake. This creates drag on the side with that propeller and reduces the turning diameter.

1. Put helm hard over.
2. Bring throttle on the engine in the direction of the turn to "clutch-ahead."

NOTE
Don't put throttle to neutral position. In neutral, the propeller will "free-wheel" and rotate without any resistance. By staying at clutch ahead, the marine gear and engine will keep the propeller from spinning at a rate that corresponds to the vessel's speed through the water, "braking" the vessel.

TURN AND SPLIT THROTTLES This practice also is more effective with shaft, propeller and rudder arrangement than with directed thrust drives. One propeller will still be providing forward thrust while the other will be backing. As with opposing thrust in low speed maneuvering, propeller side force is multiplied. Cavitation will be pronounced on the backing screw, but the vessel's forward motion keeps advancing this screw into relatively undisturbed (or not-aerated) water.

1. Put helm hard over.
2. Bring throttle on the engine in the direction of the turn firmly to and through neutral, then

---

WARNING

As with the crash stop, this maneuver is extremely hard on the engine and drive train. The backing engine's power must be higher than that available at clutch speed to prevent engine stall.

---

past, the clutch-astern position, and gradually increase astern RPM.

NOTE
Fully develop your boat handling skills and key them to the particular craft you operate. For instance, the Destroyer Turn described above (turn and split throttles) was developed for twin-screw ships operating in the open ocean. Though it has been carried into boat operations as a standard procedure for man-overboard recovery, a highly maneuverable, planing-hulled boat might be much more effective in recovery by doing a crash stop then pivoting, while staying within immediate range (and sight) of the person in the water.

Performing Single-Screw Compound Maneuvering (Single Screw Theory)

B.31. GENERAL

Apply basic maneuvering techniques in combination with a single propeller at low speed to further boat handling skills. Learn these maneuvers as best possible in calm, no-current situations before learning to overcome environmental forces.

A single-screw vessel never has the ability to use asymmetric or opposed propulsion, and its coxswain must develop boat handling skills with this in mind. The operator of a twin-engine vessel could easily become limited to use of one drive due to engine failure or fouling a screw, and must also become a proficient, single-screw boat handler.

For the discussion here, we will use the case of a single-engine propeller vessel with right-hand turning screw. When maneuvering a twin-engine vessel on one drive, the coxswain must account for the propeller rotation and side force for the particular drive used (normally starboard: right-hand turning, port: left-hand turning), and the offset of the drive from centerline.

B.32. BACK AND FILL

The back and fill technique, also known as casting, provides a method to turn a vessel in little more than its own length. At some point, anyone who operates a single-screw vessel will need to rely on these concepts when they operate a boat, particularly in close-quarters maneuvering. To back and fill, rely on the tendency of a vessel to back to port, and then use the rudder to direct thrust when powering ahead. Decide the radius of the circle where you want to stay (at most, 25 to 35 percent larger than the vessel's overall length), and the intended change in direction (usually no more than 180 degrees) before starting. For initial training, turn through at least 360 degrees.

From dead-in-the-water:

1. Put helm at right full and momentarily throttle ahead, being careful not to make much headway. (Rudder directs screw discharge current thrust to starboard, more than offsetting propeller side force and moves stern to port.)

2. Before gaining much headway quickly throttle astern and shift helm to left full. (With throttle astern, side force much stronger than screw suction, rudder to port takes advantage of any sternway.)

3. Once sternway begins, simultaneously shift helm to full right and throttle ahead as in step 1.

4. Repeat steps until vessel has come to desired heading, then put helm amidships and apply appropriate propulsion.

NOTE

- A firm grasp of your vessel's maneuvering characteristics is necessary to know whether you will need to back and fill rather than just maneuver at full rudder.
- The number of back-and-fill steps used will depend on size of your turning area and the desired change in heading. The smaller the area, the more backing and filling required.
- Winds will play a factor in casting. If your vessel bow is easily blown off course, your vessel probably has a tendency to back into the wind. Set up your maneuver (including direction of turn) to take advantage of this in getting the bow to change direction. Strong winds will offset both propeller side force and any rudder effect.
- A quick helm hand is a prerequisite for casting with an outboard or stern drive. To get full advantage of the lower unit's directed thrust, fully shift the helm before applying propulsion. With helm at left full, the propeller side force when backing will have an element that tries to move the stern "forward" around the pivot point.

Maneuvering Near Other Objects

Overview

Introduction

This section discusses the application of basic maneuvering principles to control your vessel with respect to other objects. Later parts will cover mooring, unmooring, and coming alongside other vessels or objects.

In this section

Topic	See Page(s)
Keeping Station	179–81
Maneuvering	181

Keeping Station

C.1. GENERAL

Learn to manage the effects of environmental forces by keeping station on an object. Keeping station means you maintain your distance, position and aspect to or from an object. If your boat is equipped with twin propulsion, you should develop the skills necessary to keep station at any aspect to any object in most conditions. Though many single-drive boats are less maneuverable then twins, you will be able to station-keep with effectively with practice. It is important that you practice station-keeping in various levels of wind, seas and current.

This section includes considerations for establishing a maneuvering zone, maneuvering on different types of objects and using different techniques to keep station.

NOTE

All coxswains of twin-drive vessels must train frequently for single drive operation. This includes station-keeping.

C.2. DETERMINE A MANEUVERING ZONE

Each operational situation requires a safe maneuvering zone. The vessel must be maneuvered to an optimal position near the target object so an evolution can be conducted safely and effectively, i.e., equipment transfer, object recovery, surveillance, etc.

Before you keep station, get the "big picture:"

1. Evaluate environmental conditions and how they affect the situation.

2. Determine if obstructions on the object or in and above the water limit your safe maneuvering zone.

3. Account for them and keep the environmental forces in mind

4. Avoid vessel outriggers or hull protrusions, loose pier camels or broken pilings, ice guards, shoals, rocks or other submerged obstructions, low overhead cables or bridge spans.

5. Define the maneuvering zone by distance, position and aspect. Put limits on each element and maneuver to stay within those limits.

CAUTION!

When station-keeping, always have a safe escape route to get clear of the object or any hazard. As you keep station, ensure the escape route stays clear. This may require changing position to establish a new escape route.

DISTANCE Keep station close enough to complete a mission or evolution, yet far enough to prevent collision or allision. Minimum distance to the object will probably vary around the object or along its length. Environmental conditions and boat maneuverability are major factors in determining distance.

1. *Use a practiced eye* and ranging techniques to keep distance.

2. *Use identifiable keys* such as a boat length. Unless well practiced, each crewmember will probably differ in how they view 25 feet or 25 yards.

3. *Use knowledge of your own vessel.* If your boat has a twelve-foot beam at the transom, for example, transpose that measurement to the gap between your boat and an object.

4. If the coxswain station does not allow a clear view of the object, *use points on your vessel* (windscreen brackets, antennae, or fittings) to set up range-keeping clues.

5. *Position:* The angle from the object to your vessel (or the reciprocal) is termed "position." To keep station on another vessel, particularly one that is disabled and adrift, use the angle your vessel makes relative to the other vessel's center-

line. When keeping station on a moored or fixed object, use a geographic or compass bearing.

6. *Aspect:* The relative "face" your vessel shows to the other object—for example, bow-to, stern-to, beam-to etc. You may need to keep the object at a certain aspect to pass equipment such as a pump or towline or to maintain surveillance.

C.3. DIFFERENCES IN OBJECTS

Differences in objects determine the maneuvering situation. Become fully capable of station keeping in a variety of situations altering both type of target object and the environmental conditions.

KEEP STATION ON A FREE-DRIFTING OBJECT
Object type and size ranges from small items to other vessels. Free-drifting objects will present a different drift rate from that of your vessel. Develop station-keeping techniques by first matching your drift rate to the object, then overcoming the difference.

Have another vessel maintain a steady course at low speed. Pace your vessel to the other vessel and then maneuver around it. Pacing your movement to the other vessel is critical before safely going alongside.

NO LEEWAY: Practice with a floating (but ballasted) item that does not drift with the wind. A weighted mannequin with PFD or weighted duffel bag with a float in one end will work. The object's drift will be limited to the surface current, while your vessel will respond to currents and winds. This type of object simulates a person-in-the-water.

LEEWAY: Wind-drift is the main consideration here. Practice with paired fenders, a partially filled 6-gallon bucket or a small skiff. Though wind will have a measurable effect on object drift, current will play little role. As above, your vessel will be subject to both wind and current.

OTHER VESSEL: Become proficient at station-keeping on a variety of vessel types including one like your own. Different vessels react differently to environmental forces. Learn how other vessels drift compared to your own. See how other vessels lie to the wind, then maneuver your vessel to an optimal position for observation, coming alongside or passing a tow rig.

KEEP STATION ON AN ANCHORED OBJECT
Anchoring limits much of the object's movement due to wind and current, but the object will often surge and swing. Your vessel will react freely to the

wind and current. The object will ride with its moored end into the strongest environmental force affecting it, while the combination of forces on your vessel may cause it to take a different aspect.

Practicing station keeping on an anchored object helps you learn where you can or cannot maneuver. Upstream of a buoy, strong current could easily carry you down on it. On the other hand, the only safe approach to a disabled vessel, anchored off a lee shore, may be from dead-to-weather.

BUOY OR FLOAT: In general, attempt to approach a moored buoy or float from down-current or downwind, bow to the object. If servicing a floating aid to navigation, the approach may require centering your stern on the buoy. To train, keep station at various distances and angles to an object. Pick something totally surrounded by safe water. Next, maneuver up-current or upwind.

A VESSEL: Surveillance, personnel or equipment transfer, or fire fighting may require station-keeping on an anchored vessel. Develop skills to keep station at all distances and angles. Different sizes and types of vessels will ride their anchors differently. Deep draft or a large underbody will make a vessel ride with the current, while high freeboard and superstructure may make the vessel tend downwind. Evaluate the combination of forces as you keep station.

Note vessel interaction. If you are close aboard and upwind, a small, light vessel may ride the anchor differently than if you weren't there. A larger vessel may affect the forces on you by making a lee. Watch a vessel's motions while it "rides" anchor. Some vessels don't "steady out," but veer back and forth. Observe and plan accordingly.

FIXED OBJECT: Keep station on a pier, seawall, or breakwater. View this as a step before mooring. Also, you may need these skills to transfer someone to a fixed aid to navigation or to remove a person stranded on rocks. Station keeping on fixed objects requires you deal with forces that affect your boat, but not the object. Often, the fixed object affects the environmental forces by funneling, blocking, or changing direction of the current or wind.

Maneuvering

C.4. GENERAL

Station-keeping will usually require frequent to near-continuous applications of power and helm to stay in the safe maneuvering zone. As you keep station and try to stay within the maneuvering zone

limits, you will find that adjusting for one of the parameters (distance, position, aspect), will almost always involve a change to one or both of the other two. While using power and helm to compensate for and to overcome wind and current, use the wind and current to your best advantage.

C.5. STEM THE FORCES

To stem the forces means to keep the current or wind directly on the bow or stern and hold position by setting boat speed to equally oppose the speed of drift.

C.6. CRAB THE BOAT SIDEWAYS

To do this, use the environmental forces to move the boat at a right angle to the forces. Put the bow at a shallow angle (20 to 30 degrees) to the prevailing force and use ahead propulsion and helm to prevent your boat from being set backward. Maintain the shallow angle to the prevailing environmental force.

C.7. OPEN AND CLOSE

Make your vessel "open" and "close" the distance on the object at various angles, both to leeward and to weather. You need only to compensate for the fore and aft drift rate and to maintain a steady heading when the target object is on the bow or stern directly up-drift or down-drift from you. The more difficult scenario is opening or closing distance abeam.

1. Use a combination of control and environmental forces: side force, ahead and astern thrust, rudder force, leeway, current drift.

2. Remember to account for pivot point when moving the bow or the stern.

3. Use reasonable limits and stay within them.

Maneuvering to or from a Dock

Overview

Introduction

The most challenging and probably most frequent maneuvering you will encounter is that associated with getting in and out of slips, dock areas, piers, boat basins or marinas.

In this section

General Considerations

D.1. GENERAL

When maneuvering to or from a dock, keep the following points in mind. Brief the crew on procedures to be used.

D.2. COMPENSATE FOR WIND OR CURRENT

Check the conditions before maneuvering. Always try to take advantage of wind and current when docking or mooring. To maintain best control, approach against the wind and current and moor on the leeward side of a mooring when possible. Chances are that when you get underway, conditions will not be the same as they were when you moored.

D.3. RIG AND LEAD MOORING LINES AND FENDERS EARLY

Rig and lead mooring lines and fenders well before the approach. Get the noise and confusion over with long before the coxswain must concentrate and maneuver to the dock.

Though common practice is to leave mooring lines attached to the home pier, always have a spare mooring line and a moveable fender on the boat and at the ready while approaching any dock, including the home pier.

D.4. CONTROL, NOT SPEED

Emphasize control, not speed, when docking. Keep just enough headway or sternway to counteract the winds and currents and allow steerage while making progress to the dock. Keep an eye on the amount of stern or bow swing. With a high foredeck, the wind can get the bow swinging much easier than it is to stop. In higher winds, a greater amount of maneuvering speed may be needed to lessen the time exposed to the winds and currents, but be careful not to overdo it.

D.5. USE CLEAR LINE HANDLING COMMANDS

Line handling is extremely important when docking. Give specific line-handling instructions in a loud, clear voice. Ensure instructions are understood, particularly by any helpful individuals near the dock. Less-than-good line handling always ruins the docking at the end of a perfect approach. Ideally, try to have the boat stopped, alongside the pier before putting lines over.

Basic Maneuvers

D.6. GENERAL

Often, the presence of other craft or obstructions will complicate the clearing of a berth, or any simple maneuver. Wind and/or current can also become a factor. Before maneuvering, evaluate the options in order to take full advantage of the prevailing conditions.

This part has three examples of mooring and unmooring.

D.7. CLEAR A SLIP

This example assumes that there is no wind or current and the vessel is a single-screw. See Figure 10-17.

1. Set rudder amidships.

2. Apply slight right rudder to offset propeller side force (A).

3. Use ahead throttle and move ahead slowly (B).

4. As the boat gains headway, apply additional helm to turn (C). Remember that the rudder causes the stern to swing in the opposite direction of the bow. Before starting a turn, make sure the stern will clear the pier.

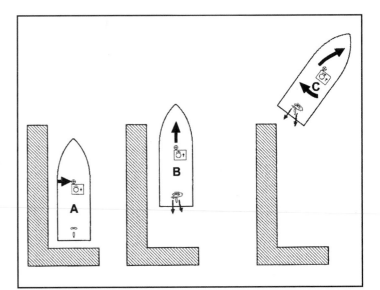

Figure 10-17 Clear a Slip (no wind or current, single screw)

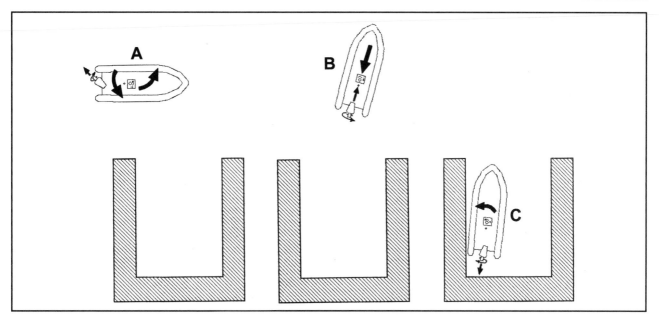

Figure 10-18 Back Into a Slip (no wind or current, single outboard/stern drive)

D.8. BACK INTO A SLIP

This exercise assumes there is no wind or current and the vessel is a single-screw, outboard or I/O. See Figure 10-18.

1. Approach at low speed, perpendicular to slip, approximately one-half to one boat-length away.

2. As the amidship section is even with the nearest edge of the slip, apply hard left rudder and "bump" throttle ahead to swing the stern to starboard.

3. As bow swings to port, go to neutral throttle and aim lower unit at the back corner of the slip. Immediately apply astern throttle to stop headway and acquire sternway. Side force will stop swing.

4. Steer lower unit towards slip, just aft of desired final position, offsetting for side force as necessary, using astern clutch speed and neutral to keep speed down.

5. When almost alongside, apply slight left rudder and "bump" throttle ahead, then go to neutral.

D.9. CLEAR A PIER

This exercise assumes the vessel is a twin-screw, has its port side to windward side of pier, and that there are vessels moored ahead and astern.

1. Go ahead on starboard screw, with rudder amidship, hold bow spring line (a).

2. Put starboard in neutral, back on port, right rudder, take in spring line (b).

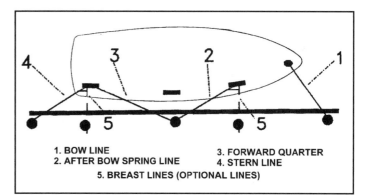

Figure 10-19 Mooring Lines

1. BOW LINE
2. AFTER BOW SPRING LINE
3. FORWARD QUARTER
4. STERN LINE
5. BREAST LINES (OPTIONAL LINES)

3. As stern clears vessel behind, back on starboard.

4. Get bow away from pier by going ahead on port, while watching stern swing (c).

5. Stop stern swing, if necessary by neutral on starboard.

6. If far enough off pier to clear vessel ahead, go ahead on both engines and steer away from pier.

MOORING LINES Use mooring lines to help maneuver. (See Figure 10-19.) The bow, #1, and stern, #4, lines are simple to deploy and are usually sufficient, if they are of adequate size. Use finders at strategic points along the hull to prevent chafing against the dock or float.

SPRING LINES Use the spring lines to prevent the fore and aft movement, or the surge of a boat alongside the dock.

Use just the after bow spring, or bow spring, #2, (leads aft to the dock from the bow) to "spring out" or move the stern away from the dock. The stern will move away with the rudder turned full toward the dock and the engines ahead. With the rudder turned full away from the dock, the stern will move toward the dock or "spring in."

Use only the foreword quarter spring, or stern spring, #3, (leads forward to the dock from the quarter) to "spring out" or move the bow away from the dock. By backing down on a boat's engines with just the forward quarter spring (stern spring) attached to the dock, the bow will move away from the dock (see Figure 10-20).

RIG LINES Use the rig lines under stress for slipping, particularly when no shore side line handlers are available. Both bitter ends should be aboard the boat with the bight around the shore side attachment point. Then the spring line may be let go, or cast off, releasing one end and hauling in the other. Tend a spring line carefully so that it does not foul the rudder or screw or get caught on the dock. When maneuvering, always watch a line tied to a bitt or cleat, never leave it unattended.

Rules of Thumb

D.10. RESPONSIBILITY

The coxswain is always responsible for the boat regardless of the existing environmental conditions and situations. Care must be exercised before assigning newly qualified coxswains to missions in extreme weather conditions.

D.11. SLOW SPEEDS

When maneuvering at slow speeds alongside, use full left (or right) rudders. On twin-screw boats, with the rudders left amidships, use the screws at clutch (idle) speed to maneuver.

D.12. ALONGSIDE

When maneuvering alongside, speed should be kept to a minimum. Apply power in short bursts (with rudder at left or right for single screw boats) to get changes in heading; but keep the bursts short enough so you don't increase your speed.

D.13. PORT SIDE

Port side moorings are the easiest for single-screw boats with "right-hand" props.

D.14. BACKING AND FILLING

Slow speed maneuvers to starboard are best for single-screw boats with "right-hand" props in restricted areas. Do this by:

- Alternately going ahead with the rudder at left full and astern with the rudder at right full.

- When going ahead, give a quick burst to direct water past the rudder for as long as possible to get maximum twist with minimum headway.

- When going astern, gradually increase power for as long as the bow continues to go to starboard, or as room permits.

D.15. PRECISE CONTROL

When requiring precise control, keep the boat's heading into the predominate wind or current, or as close as possible. When maneuvering the boat so that the set from the wind or current is on the starboard or port bow, the boat may "crab" (move sideways) in the opposite direction.

D.16. WIND AND CURRENT

Wind and current are among the most important forces to consider in maneuvering. The operator should use them to advantage, if possible, rather than attempting to fight the elements.

D.17. SPRING LINES

Spring lines are very useful when mooring with an off dock set; or when unmooring with an on-dock set. Use the spring lines to spring either the bow or stern in or out (see Figures 10-21 and 10-22).

D.18. THRUSTING AWAY FROM ANOTHER BOAT

To thrust away from another boat, a camel, or a ship, use the prop wash or "screw knuckle." Just apply full power astern in a short burst then return to neutral. The prop wash will move forward between the boat and the surface alongside, pushing the boat away

D.19. FENDERS

Never attempt to fend a boat off a pier, float, etc., by hand or foot—always use a fender. Always keep the proper sized fenders handy.

D.20. MOORING/OFF-DOCK WIND

When mooring with an off-dock wind, the approach should be made at a sharp angle—45° or more.

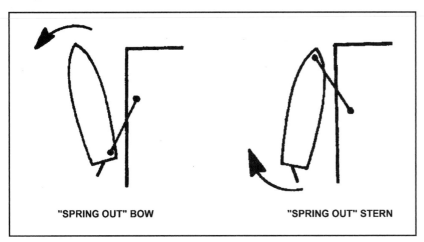

"SPRING OUT" BOW   "SPRING OUT" STERN

Figure 10-20 Basic Spring Line Maneuvers

Figure 10-21 Going Ahead With Left Rudder Use of Spring Line

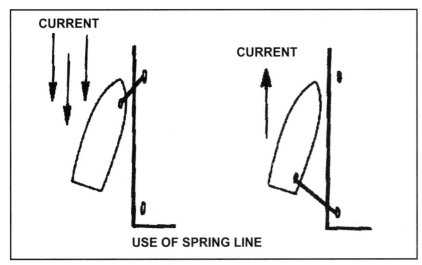

CURRENT   CURRENT

USE OF SPRING LINE

Figure 10-22 Making Use of Current

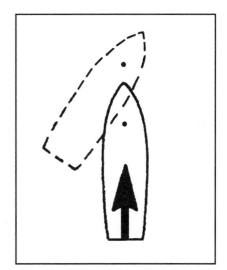

Figure 10-23 Pivot Point

D.21. MOORING/ON-DOCK WIND

When mooring with an on-dock wind, approach parallel with the intended berth and rig the fender in appropriate positions. Ensure that the boat has no fore and aft movement when contacting the dock.

D.22. TYING DOWN

Except for using the forward quarter spring, #3, never tie down the stern of a boat while maneuvering beside a dock, this restricts maneuverability.

D.23. PIVOT POINT

The pivot point of a boat is approximately one-third of the way aft of the bow when the boat is underway at standard speed. This point moves forward as speed is increased and aft as speed is decreased (see Figure 10-23).

D.24. PROTECTING THE STERN

Keep the stern away from danger. If your propellers and rudder become damaged, you are crippled. If the stern is free to maneuver, you can work your boat out of trouble.

D.25. CONTROL OF THE BOAT

The greatest amount of control over the boat is gained by maneuvering into the prevailing face of the wind or sea. Boats turn more slowly into the wind and sea than away from them. A single-screw boat will generally back into the wind when the boat has more "sail" area forward of the boat's pivot point than aft.

D.26. THE WAKE

You are responsible for the boat's wake.

D.27. INFORMING THE CREW

The coxswain must keep the crew informed. Never assume the crew knows everything that you are thinking.

D.28. SEA CONDITIONS

The most experienced coxswains know what sea conditions they can operate in and in what conditions they cannot.

D.29. FORETHOUGHT

Think ahead. Don't take chances.

SECTION E

Maneuvering Alongside Another Vessel

Overview

Introduction

Many missions will require going alongside in contact with another vessel. Activity can vary from a RIB going alongside a large merchant vessel to a large twin-screw boat going alongside a small canoe. Comparative vessel size, mission requirements and prevailing conditions all dictate maneuvering practices. For many recreational and commercial mariners, your arrival and maneuvering alongside their vessel is often the first "up close and personal" look they get of the Coast Guard.

In this section

Determining Approach

E.1. GENERAL

When you determine your approach, consider prevailing weather and currents, location, vessel sizes, traffic density. Discuss your intentions with the other vessel's master.

NOTE

If going alongside a disabled vessel or one that is underway but dead-in-the-water, compare rela-

tive drift rates. When approaching a larger vessel with a low drift rate, approach from leeward. If approaching a smaller vessel, determine if your vessel makes a wind shadow that will slow the other vessel's drift. In this case an approach from windward may be better and the smaller vessel will then be protected from winds and waves by your vessel. See Chapter 17—Towing, for more information.

> **CAUTION!**
>
> **Don't approach from leeward if it will put your vessel and crew in jeopardy, whether from shoal water or obstructions farther to leeward or from smoke or hazardous fumes.**

E.2. COURSE AND SPEED

If prudent, have the vessel maintain a course and speed to make your approach as smooth as possible for both vessels.

ALTERING COURSE Most large vessels will not be able to alter course significantly in a limited area to provide ideal alongside conditions. If it is not practical for the large vessel to change course, have it reduce speed so the effects of bow and stern waves are reduced.

SMALL VESSELS Small vessels don't ride well when not making way in any kind of winds or seas. Unless the weather is perfectly calm, have a small vessel maintain a course and speed that makes for safe, comfortable navigation while allowing mission completion. Ensure speed is slow enough for safely coming alongside, but enough for both vessels to maintain steerageway when alongside one another.

STABILITY Many sailing vessels are much more stable while under sail than when powering or

> **CAUTION!**
>
> **Make sure the other vessel does not begin to change course while you are approaching or coming alongside. If this happens, break off and start the approach over once the other vessel is on a steady course.**

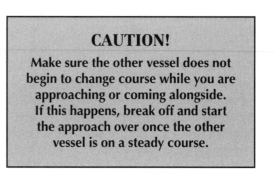

drifting. Consider coming alongside while the other vessel is under sail. Be sure that spars, standing or running rigging or control lines don't foul either vessel. Discuss the situation with the other vessel's master.

E.3. APPROACH FROM LEEWARD AND ASTERN

A large vessel will create a wind shadow and block most of the seas. Take advantage of this as in mooring to the leeward side of a pier. Though a small vessel will probably not block the elements to any degree, approach from leeward to control rate of closure and limit any effect your vessel would have on the small vessel drift.

NOTE

If an approach from leeward is not possible (due to lack of sea room or other conditions such as smoke or hazardous vapors), use caution to prevent being pinned up against the side of another vessel. A bow-in approach might provide the most maneuverability.

E.4. LINE AND FENDERS

Rig lines and fenders as needed. Remember that the more fenders you use, the better.

Going Alongside

E.5. INTRODUCTION

After completing your approach preparations, go alongside. Determine where you want to make contact on both vessels.

WARNING

Pick a contact point well clear of a larger vessel's propeller (including in the area of suction screw current), rudder, and quarter wave. Forces from these could cause loss of control.

E.6. BEGIN TO CLOSE

Conditions permitting, match your speed to the other vessel, and then start closing in from the side.

ANGLE Close at a 15 to 30 degree angle to the other vessel's heading. This should provide a comfortable rate of lateral closure at no more than one-half the forward speed.

NOTE

If your initial heading was parallel to the other vessel, you will have to increase speed slightly when you start to close at an angle.

USE A SEA PAINTER In some instances, a sea painter may be used in coming alongside a larger vessel underway. The sea painter is a line used to sheer a boat clear of a ship's side, when underway or at anchor, to hold a boat in position under shipboard hoisting davits and occasionally to hold the boat alongside a ship in order to embark or disembark personnel. It leads from the larger vessel's deck, well forward of where the boat will come alongside.

Follow these steps when securing a sea painter to the boat.

1. Use a position well forward, yet aft of the bow on the side of the boat that will be alongside the larger vessel.

2. Lead it outboard of handrails, stanchions, and fittings. It makes a pivoting point on the "inboard" bow of the boat.

3. Never secure the sea painter to the boat's stem nor to the side of the boat away from the ship. If secured to the "outboard" side of the boat, capsizing could result.

As both the boat and ship have headway, the pressure of water on the boat's bow will cause it to sheer away from the ship. Use this force by a touch of the helm to control sheer, in or out or, by catching the current on one side of the bow or the other. Riding a sea painter helps maintain position and control of the boat.

Follow these steps if using a sea painter.

1. Come along side of the vessel, matching its course and speed. When close aboard the larger vessel, and forward of the desired contact point ask the ship to pass the sea painter.

2. Receive it and secure it to an inboard cleat just aft of the bow.

3. The sea painter is usually passed by use of a heaving line. Quickly haul in the heaving line and adjust the boat's heading and speed to control slack in the sea painter so that these lines do not get into the boat's propeller.

4. Reduce your speed slowly and drift back on the painter (ride the painter).

5. Use helm to hold the boat at the desired position alongside or at some distance off the ship.

6. If set toward the ship, apply rudder to sheer the bow out. If too far away, apply rudder to sheer the bow in. The forward strain on the painter will pull the boat and provide steeringway.

NOTE

When sheering in or out apply rudder slowly and be prepared to counteract the tendency of the boat to close or open quickly.

NOTE

If approaching a vessel anchored in a strong current, the sea painter provides a means to lay alongside. Procedures are the same as if the vessel is making way. Approach from leeward against the current.

MAKE AND HOLD CONTACT Make contact with the forward sections of your boat (about halfway between the bow and amidships. Use helm and power (if not on a sea painter) to hold your bow in to the other vessel, at the same forward speed. Don't use so much helm or power that you cause the other vessel to change course.

CONDUCT THE MISSION When alongside, do what has to be done. Minimize time alongside. If necessary, "make-up" to the other vessel rather than relying on helm and power to maintain contact.

CLEARING Clear the side. Avoid getting set toward the side or stern of the vessel.

1. Sheer the stern in with helm to get the bow out.

2. Apply gradual power to gain slight relative speed.

NOTE

If on a sea painter, its strain sheers the boat clear.

NOTE

If on a sea painter, use enough speed to get slack in the line, then cast off once clear. Ensure the sea painter is hauled back aboard the larger vessel immediately to keep from getting it caught in your screws. Avoid it with your vessel.

If operating a twin-screw boat, go ahead slowly on the inboard engine. This also helps keeps the boat clear of the ship's side.

CAUTION!

Never back down when clearing alongside parallel to another vessel that is making way.

SECTION F

Maneuvering in Rough Weather

Overview

Introduction

At some time, every boat and crew will encounter wind or sea conditions that challenge safe, successful boat operation. Due to size and design differences, extreme weather for one vessel is not necessarily challenging for another. Also, crew training, experience, and skill more often than not make the difference between safety and danger, regardless of the vessel.

Size, stability, and power are vessel characteristics that enhance safety and allow some forgiveness in large waves and high winds or due to the occasional lapse in skill or judgment. On the other hand, light weight, speed, and agility give the crew a means to avoid or to outrun conditions, but offer little protection or forgiveness for the slightest miscalculation.

Learn to operate your vessel through the full range of conditions you can expect. Begin in light winds and small waves and work up to varied conditions that build your knowledge and confidence.

WARNING

Don't exceed any vessel operating limits as specified in Standard Boat Operator's Handbooks or through district-use guidelines for other vessels.

In this section

Using Caution

F.1. GENERAL

Use caution at all times. Never underestimate the power of winds and waves and what they can do to your vessel or crew. The following concepts will increase the level of safety at which you operate.

F.2. KNOW YOUR VESSEL

Be familiar with your vessel's operating characteristics and limitations to safely and confidently handle conditions that approach those limits.

LEARN YOUR VESSEL'S MOTIONS AND PECULIARITIES Operate your vessel frequently and develop a working knowledge of its response to waves and winds. Excessive boat motion is very fatiguing and can cause motion sickness.

Even the largest vessels have difficulty maneuvering in rough weather. Here a 551-foot container ship struggles to keep its cargo aboard.

- Learn the motions your boat makes in response to the seas. Find out if your vessel has any distinctive tendencies, for instance, attaining a dangerous heel while cresting a wave in high winds, burying the bow in all but the longest swells, or "lightness" to the stern in quartering conditions.

- Learn and develop techniques to minimize vessel motion in all conditions. A small tweak of the throttle or a smooth helm-hand can make the ride much smoother and less fatiguing.

- On smaller vessels, keep crew weight centered around the helm position. This is usually near the boat's center of gravity. It will make the ride more comfortable for the crew and will allow the hull to ride as designed, with more stability, than if weight is in the ends or at the extreme beam.

These are some common boat motions:

PITCH: The up and down motion of the bow (and stern). In small waves at high speeds, pitch can be very small and barely noticed. As seas increase, the bow might rise up when it meets a wave, and fully clear the water. As it comes back down, it immerses to a point on the hull above the designed waterline, sometimes with a heavy slam. Pitch is usually associated with crossing head seas. Reduce pitch by slowing or by taking head seas at more of an angle.

ROLL: The side to side motion as each side goes up and down. This is associated with beam seas. A round-bottomed vessel will roll even in near-calm conditions. Reduce roll by setting a course that does not have the seas directly on the beam.

HEAVE: The vertical motion the entire boat makes. Though frequently hidden by combined pitch and roll, it is felt as a boat encounters large waves or a heavy swell.

KNOW YOUR VESSEL'S LIMITS Know what wind speed puts the boat "in irons" with loss of maneuverability. Learn how to heave to and ride out the worst winds or seas.

ENSURE PROPER OPERATION Don't use a vessel in rough weather when it is not operationally ready. A small discrepancy can lead to serious consequences. Properly stow all required gear and remove everything else. Rough weather will dislodge things.

ONLY USE THE RIGHT VESSEL When conditions exceed a particular vessel's limits, use a more capable vessel. If one is not available, tell higher authority. Don't use the wrong tool for a job. Always apply risk assessment.

F.3. KNOW YOUR AREA

Learn to handle your vessel in the types of winds and seas found in your specific area. Learn their interaction with local geography and hydrography.

OBSERVE ALL AREAS BEFOREHAND Learn your area's tide rips, bars, gorges, coastal currents and local waters before you must maneuver there in rough weather.

1. Find out where wind funnels between headlands or in a river constriction.

2. Get the "big picture," if possible. Spend time in a watch tower or on an overlook, map the patterns of waves, where and when they break.

3. Follow the tracks of severe storms or squall lines. Learn how local geography affects their motion, winds or intensity.

4. Pay attention to forecasts, then frequently compare them to actual conditions in your area.

5. Know location of points, capes, bars, hazards to navigation, i.e., piers, wrecks, submerged piles, etc.

OBSERVE BEFORE YOU ACT Evaluate on-scene conditions before committing to a maneuver.

1. Time the series of waves, note relative lulls between the large ones, any places where the waves don't curl and break with intensity, or where they seem to peak and break continuously.

2. Note if an approaching thunderstorm has a wall cloud or if a "downburst" is visible.

3. Determine the best way to lessen the effect of a sudden, extreme gust of wind.

F.4. KNOW YOURSELF AND YOUR CREW

You and your crew have limitations. Know what they are. Be aware of the human factors and clues associated with risk management. False bravado or over-confidence in rough weather will not compensate for inexperience or fear. The following are common sense guidelines to follow:

- **When in doubt, don't.** Experience helps hone good judgment in risk assessment.

- **Understand your responsibility.** Rough weather is not a game or a sport. Use your head.

- **Know when to end an evolution.** This is particularly true in training. Damage or injury during training removes resources and people from operational availability.

- **Perform as a team.** While the coxswain concentrates on the detailed maneuvering, the crew must act as an additional eyes and ears.

Negotiating Head Seas

F.5. GENERAL

Use your vessel's inherent capabilities. Bow flare provides additional buoyancy to help lift the bow, but you must meet larger seas much slower than you would smaller ones. A slower speed of approach gives the bow time to rise and meet the waves.

NOTE

The following parts on maneuvering are general in nature. Remember that each specific boat type will perform differently.

NOTE

Keep in mind that aerated, broken, sloughing, or "white" water will not provide as much buoyancy as "green" water. Also, propulsion and helm response will be sluggish. Aerated water favors cavitation.

F.6. MANEUVER CONSTANTLY

Look and drive for the path of least resistance. The best way to get through waves is to avoid as many as possible. Anticipate patterns and take advantage of them.

BREAKING WAVES Pick your way around breaking waves. Take advantage of any lulls between the higher series of waves. Look for gaps or windows in the breaking waves, but watch them to see if they close out before you approach. Don't try to steer a perfectly straight course, steer the smoothest course.

CRESTS Avoid the highest crests. Stay away from waves that begin to peak in a triangular fashion. A "square" wave leaves no room to maneuver, and the trough behind is much deeper than others.

F.7. WORKING OVER WAVES

Work your way over each wave individually. Vary speed and angle of approach to account for differences in each wave.

1. Slow down, approach at an angle. Too much speed could "launch" a boat as it leaves a crest and result in a severe drop. Approach at a 10–25 degree angle to the wave rather than straight into it. Cross the crest at this angle to stay in the water and keep the propellers and rudders working.

2. Stay ready to maneuver. You may have to straighten out quickly or to "fall off" to avoid a forming break.

3. Continually adjust boat speed. Increase speed to keep the screw and rudder or drive in the water and working, but then immediately reduce it to minimize wave impact.

4. Don't drive the bow into the wave.

NOTE

If you must go through a breaking wave, keep headway. Just as the breaking sea hits the bow, increase power to lift the bow so the sea will not spill on deck, then immediately reduce power.

NOTE

If the sea is about to break directly ahead and plunge onto the bow, back down squarely and quickly to avoid the plunging water. The boat will settle as the aerated froth passes, and propulsion and steering will lose some effectiveness until the white water passes.

CAUTION!
Don't use so much power to cause cavitation when backing away from a wave. If you cavitate, you will lose all thrust and maneuverability.

WARNING
If your vessel is a single-screw, don't attempt this if you were originally going to take the wave on the port bow. Backing down will throw the stern to port and the vessel could end up beam-to the crashing wave.

F.8. MANAGE YOUR POWER

Keep one hand constantly on the throttle control(s).

HEAVIER VESSELS Use the following procedures when managing the power of heavier vessels.

1. Use only enough power to get the bow sections safely over or through the crest.

2. Let momentum carry, and cut back power to let the boat slide down the back side of the swell. When the stern is high, gravity pulls the boat downward and the engines may race somewhat, but stay in gear. Don't decrease RPMs to the point where the engines need time to "spool up" to regain enough power to deal with the next wave.

3. Increase speed in the trough to counteract the reversed water flow and maintain directional control as the next wave approaches.

4. Slow down again and approach the next wave.

LIGHTER CRAFT (INCLUDING RIBs) Use the following procedures when managing the power of light craft.

1. Use enough power to get the entire boat safely over or through the crest. Lighter craft will not carry momentum so constant application of power is necessary.

2. Keep a slight, bow-up angle at all times.

3. Once through the crest, a slight, bow-up angle, will let the after sections provide a good contact surface if the boat clears the water. A bow up attitude will help to approach the next wave.

4. Increase speed in the trough to counteract the reversed water flow and maintain directional control as the next wave approaches.

5. Slow down again and approach the next wave.

F.9. STAY IN THE WATER

Don't "fly through" the crest. Avoid this at all costs.

- If airborne coming through a wave with a large vessel, you threaten your crew with serious injury and could damage the vessel when it lands.

- With lighter craft, ensure the after sections stay in contact with the water, but don't let the bow sections get too high. If the bow sections get too high while going through a crest, the apparent wind or the break can carry the bow over backward. On the other hand, if forward way is lost with the stern at the crest, the bow might fall downward requiring you to redevelop speed and bow-up attitude before the next wave approaches.

F.10. HOLD ON BUT STAY FLEXED

Keep a firm grasp on controls or hand holds, but don't rigidly brace yourself. Staying rigid and tense will quickly sap your strength. If standing, keep your knees flexed.

Running Before a Sea

F.11. GENERAL

A following sea does not present the high relative closure rate of head seas, but keeping vessel control and stability is probably more challenging.

Operation in a following sea, especially a breaking sea, involves the risk of having the stern lifted up and forced forward by the onrushing swell or breaker. Surfing down the face of a wave is extremely dangerous and nearly impossible to control. Quite often, surfing will force the boat to "broach" and capsize or to "pitchpole" end over end. Through proper boat handling, a skilled coxswain may be able to keep a vessel ahead of breaking seas while maintaining control of both direction and speed. Only specially designed vessels like motor life boats have balanced buoyancy and sea keeping abilities to handle extremely rough weather, including large, breaking, following seas. Vessels such as this also have the ability to quickly right after capsize.

F.12. USE EXTREME CAUTION

Be very careful when running in a large following sea. Some boats slip down the back of seas and heel strongly. In large stern seas, the rudder may get sluggish. Depending on the vessel, make your down-swell heading anywhere from directly downswell to a 15 degree angle to the swells.

NOTE

A great deal of skill is needed to maintain a heading in large, quartering seas (30–45 degrees off the stern), especially in restricted waters. In addition to the action from astern, the forces from abeam will set up a rolling action that causes large changes in the vessel's underwater hull shape (on anything except a round-bottomed, displacement hull). This causes asymmetric forces that increase steering difficulty and could set up "chine-riding," loss of effective helm, and a pronounced veer to the side as the vessel begins to surf along the face of the wave. Even in open water, quartering seas present a challenge.

F.13. RIDE THE BACKS OF THE SWELLS

In waves with a wide regular pattern, ride the back of the swell. Never ride on the front of a wave. On most vessels, wider and flatter after hull sections are more buoyant than the bow. On the front of a wave, the boat may begin to surf, pushed along by the wave. As the bow nears the wave trough, it will tend to "dig in" while stern continues to be pushed. This sets up either a broadside "broach" or an end-for-end "pitchpole" as the breaking crest acts on the boat.

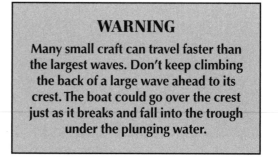

CAUTION!

Don't let a wave break over the transom and poop the boat. Be extremely careful in small craft with outboard motors, the relatively low transom-well offers little protection from even a small, breaking wave. A wave that breaks over the transom could fill the cockpit with water and swamp the boat. Without self-bailing, this leaves you vulnerable to capsize by the next wave.

WHERE TO LOOK Keep an eye both ahead and astern. If you totally concentrate on the wave ahead, you let your guard down on waves from astern. Since larger waves travel faster than smaller ones, one much larger than the one you are on may move up quickly from astern and catch you unaware.

SPEED Adjust your speed to stay on the back of the swell. Pay extremely close attention to the way the crest ahead of you breaks. If you keep gaining on the crest ahead, slow down.

WARNING

Many small craft can travel faster than the largest waves. Don't keep climbing the back of a large wave ahead to its crest. The boat could go over the crest just as it breaks and fall into the trough under the plunging water.

F.14. KEEP RESERVE POWER

Large seas run at over 20 knots. If the boat is being pulled back towards a following sea, open the throttle. If the boat is still pulled back, watch for "mushy" helm response and engine racing. If either happens, reduce throttle, then apply full throttle to try to kick out of the wave.

F.15. SLOW, BACK OR COME ABOUT

If running with the seas and a wave is gaining astern, don't let it break on the transom.

1. Slow Down: with a well-found vessel, you may be able to slow just enough so the crest passes by before it breaks. This will cause some loss of positive steering and propulsion control as the crest passes because the water in the crest will be moving forward faster than the boat.

2. Back Down: you may need to back and gain sternway to steer before the crest reaches the screws and rudder, particularly if the wave breaks and aerated water will slough past.

3. Come About: the safest point for most vessels to take a breaking sea is nearly bow-on. Always stay aware of the time and distance between crests. If time and distance allow, come about and present the bow to the sea with headway.

> **WARNING**
>
> Coming about in large seas can be dangerous. It puts the boat beam-to the seas. Don't try this unless well trained and experienced. Any close, steep swells will test all your skills. Sluggish rudder, sail area, and irregular waves may cause the stern to slew off and result in a broach.

> **CAUTION!**
>
> If you must come about before a wave, use judicious helm and throttle. Too much throttle, especially when splitting throttles, could easily result in cavitation and leave no positive control in the face of the oncoming sea.

Traversing Beam Seas

F.16. GENERAL

In large beam seas, the wave action will cause the boat to roll. The rolling will cause asymmetric hydrodynamic forces and will affect steering. Do your best to keep drive and rudder immersed.

F.17. BREAKING WAVES

Minimize the number of breaking waves you encounter. If traversing near a surf zone, go farther out into deeper water.

F.18. USE YOUR LOCAL KNOWLEDGE

Avoid areas that break when no other areas do. Offset your transit from areas of shifting bars.

NOTE

If you must operate in the surf zone, complete wave avoidance is not possible. The coxswain must be totally involved in operating the boat while the crew carries out the details of the mission (search, recovery, etc.).

F.19. KEEP A WEATHER EYE TO THE WAVES

As with head seas and following seas, the boat will be pulled towards the next, oncoming wave while in the trough, and set down-swell by the crest.

1. Look for a lull in the series to cross seas. If necessary, slow to allow a large series of waves to cross ahead.

2. Use caution to avoid a forming break. Watch how the waves break. Plan to cross an oncoming wave well before it begins to break. Don't get caught racing a break to cross at a particular point. Use procedures for negotiating head seas to cross oncoming waves. As with head seas, cross them at the lowest part.

3. Never get caught broadside to a breaking sea. A breaking swell taken on the beam can easily capsize the most well-found vessel.

4. Don't get trapped. If the boat gets into closer and closer seas, look for an out. If shallow water or a current against the seas is on one side, work your way in the other direction.

Transiting Harbor Entrances, Inlets, or River Entrances

F.20. GENERAL

Transiting harbor entrances, inlets, or river entrances in rough weather. You will encounter times when you must either leave or enter port in challenging conditions. Though certain locations have extreme conditions much more often than others, learn how rough weather affects the various harbors and entrances throughout your local area. Methods covered above for maneuvering in head, following, and beam seas still apply, but the entrance areas add additional consideration.

F.21. **KNOW THE ENTRANCE**

Though mentioned above, local knowledge is key. Know as much as possible before transiting an entrance in rough weather.

1. Watch where waves break. Know how far out into the channel, whether near jetties, or shoals or directly across the entrance the waves break.

2. Pay close attention to how the entrance affects wave patterns. A jettied entrance may reflect waves back across an entrance where they combine with the original waves.

3. Some entrances have an outer bar that breaks, along with additional breaks farther in. Others are susceptible to a large, heaving motion that creates a heavy surge as it hits rocks or structures.

4. Know where the channel is. If shoaling has occurred, room to maneuver may be significantly lessened.

5. Know the actual depths of the water. Account for any difference between actual and charted depth due to water stage, height of tide, recent rainfall, or atmospheric pressure effects.

F.22. **TRANSIT WHEN CURRENT OPPOSES THE SEAS**

This presents the most challenging situation near an entrance. In opposition to the seas, a current has the effect of shortening the wavelength, without reducing the wave height. This makes waves much more unstable and much closer together.

1. When going into the seas, the current behind will push the boat into them, at a relatively higher speed.

2. Reduce the effect (which will also give more time to react between waves) by slowing, but because the current is behind, keep enough headway to ensure effective steering.

3. Don't let the current push the boat into a large cresting wave, combined waves peaking together. In an entrance, maneuvering room is often limited. The only safe water may be where you have just been. Stay ready to back down and avoid a breaking crest.

4. In following seas and a head current, the situation can be critical. The waves will overtake at a higher rate. They become unstable more quickly, and will break more often. The current reduces the boat's progress over the ground, subjecting you to more waves.

5. As with all following seas, stay on the back of the wave ahead of you. Because the waves become unstable and break more quickly, use extra caution not to go over the crest ahead. Concentrate both on the crest ahead and the waves behind.

6. Keep a hand on the throttle and adjust power continuously. In many entrances, there is not enough room to come about and take a breaking wave bow-on. Anticipate. If a wave looks ready to break, the only out may be to back down before it gets to you.

7. Stay extremely aware of any wave combinations and avoid spots ahead where they tend to peak. If they peak ahead in the same place, chances are they will peak there when you are closer. However, don't let a slightly different wave or wave combination catch you by surprise.

8. The crew must keep an eye on the situation and pass information freely.

F.23. **TRANSIT WHEN CURRENT AND SEAS COINCIDE**

Here, a current has the effect of lengthening the waves. Longer waves are more stable, with the crests farther apart, but caution is still needed.

1. When going into the seas and current, progress over the ground will be less, so you will spend more time in the entrance. Increasing boat speed may be warranted.

2. Don't increase boat speed so that negotiating waves becomes hazardous. The waves are just as high, so if you increased overall speed, reduce speed to negotiate each crest individually.

3. With following seas and a tail current, speed over the ground will be increased. Because the waves are farther apart, the task of riding the back of the wave ahead should be easier. Because the current is behind, additional forward way will be required to maintain steering control.

4. As with all following seas, stay on the back of the wave ahead of you. Don't be lulled into a false sense of security. With higher speed over the ground and less maneuverability due to the following current, there is not as much time to avoid a situation ahead.

5. Keep a hand on the throttle and adjust power continuously.

6. Because you will spend less time in the entrance, look for spots ahead to avoid. Maneuver early as the current will carry the boat.

7. The crew must keep an eye on the situation and pass information freely.

Coping with High Winds

F.24. GENERAL

Though preceding discussions dealt with encountering severe wave action, high winds don't always accompany large swells. Also, there will be instances when extreme winds occur without sufficient duration to make large waves. Much of the time, though, high winds and building seas will coincide

F.25. CRAB THROUGH STEADY WINDS

Depending on the vessel's sail area, you may need to apply steady helm or asymmetric propulsion to hold a course in high winds. Learn to "read" the water for stronger gusts. The amount of chop on the surface will increase in gusts, and extremely powerful gusts may even blow the tops off waves. Anticipate the effect of a gust before it hits your vessel.

1. In large waves, the wave crest will block much of the wind when the boat is in the trough. Plan to offset its full force at the crest. The force of the wind may accentuate a breaking crest, and require you steer into the wind as you near the crest in head seas. Depending on the vessel, winds may force the bow off to one side as you cross the crest.

2. For light vessels, the force of the wind at the wave crest could easily get under the bow sections (or sponson on a RIB), lift the bow to an unsafe angle, or force it sideways. Though a light vessel must keep some speed to get over or through the crest of a large wave, don't use so much speed that most of the bottom is exposed to a high wind as you clear the crest. Be particularly cautious in gusty conditions and stay ready for a sudden large gust when clearing a wave.

3. With twin-engine craft, be ready to use asymmetric propulsion to get the bow into or through the wind. As with all other maneuvers, early and steady application of power is much more effective than a "catch-up" burst of power.

4. Vessels with large sail area and superstructures will develop an almost constant list during high

winds. In a gust, sudden heel, at times becoming extreme, may develop. This could cause handling difficulties at the crest of high waves. If your vessel exhibits theses tendencies, exercise extreme caution when cresting waves. You must learn to safely balance available power and steering against the effects of winds and waves.

NOTE

Boats that show extreme motion and minimal control in high winds and seas, regardless of size and power are not well suited for missions in these conditions. If caught in marginal conditions, safety of your own vessel and crew must be the only concern. Other, more capable resources must conduct the mission.

F.26. AVOIDING SEVERE WEATHER

Avoid thunderstorms, downbursts, squalls and waterspouts. Many areas regularly get severe weather with localized winds in excess of fifty knots. As these conditions often arise at peak times in the recreational boating season, chances are that you may find yourself underway in them. Since numerous cells can occur in one thunderstorm, you may be faced with maneuvering among many, different storms. Keep an eye on what is approaching.

NOTE

If faced with a severe storm while on the water, reduce as much sail area as possible. Lower bimini tops, dodgers, outriggers, antennas, flags and ensigns. This significantly improves vessel stability and response to high winds. Also, stow all loose gear, close hatches and doors, and stay low.

GUSTS Try to avoid the highest gusts. Some storm cells have their own gust fronts that precede them. Look for what appears to be a layer of steam on the water. A fifty-knot gust front will actually turn the surface of the water into spray, with the highest gusts mixing with the relative heat of the water to lift the spray vertically.

NOTE

If sea-room permits, move away from (perpendicular to) the direction of the gust.

DRIFTING STERN-TO THE WINDS Consider drifting stern-to the winds. At the speed these gusts move, they often don't have time to develop much of a sea. If so, you may be able to lie safely, stern-to the wind, engines in neutral. This way, you will not have to fight the overpowering force to keep the bow directly into the wind.

GETTING BETWEEN A STORM AND SHORE
Don't get between a severe storm and a near, lee shore. Work your way across a gust front, before it arrives, as best possible to safe haven or open water.

> ## CAUTION!
> **Laying stern-to is not safe if an approaching storm has enough open water (fetch) to develop and build seas. A strong thunderstorm needs as few as five miles of open water to build a three- to four-foot chop. In combination with fifty-knot winds, this chop can easily swamp small vessels.**

Heaving-To

F.27. GENERAL

Heave-to when necessary. If unable to reach safe haven in extreme weather, heaving-to might be the only option to ride out conditions. Basically, heaving to is putting the bow into the wind or seas, and holding it there with helm and throttle. For vessels with a large sail area or superstructure, this might not be possible, as every wave or gust of wind may cause the vessel to "fall-off" the wind and lie beam-to or stern-to.

F.28. MANEUVERING

Maneuver only to keep a bow-on aspect to the weather. Heave-to only because you cannot safely make progress in a desired direction.

> ## WARNING
> **Only heave-to when there is adequate sea room to leeward. Drift will be downwind and down sea.**

1. Offset for the strongest force. Wind and seas might not be from exactly the same direction.
2. Try to keep seas between 10 and 25 degrees off the bow as if negotiating head seas and note the compass heading. You will still negotiate the seas, but not make any progress. If the wind allows holding this angle, it will give the best ride. Determine a mix of helm and throttle to hold the heading, try not to use full rudder or throttle as it leaves no reserve for an emergency maneuver.

3. If the winds are gusty and have frequent shifts, they can easily force the bow off the desired heading. Listen for signs of an approaching gust and start to counteract its effect before it actually strikes the boat.

4. If seas are not the strongest force, keep the bow directly into the wind.

F.29. SEA ANCHOR

Use a sea anchor if necessary. If unable to hold a heading, use a drogue as a sea anchor, made fast to the bow, to hold it into the weather. Use as much scope as available up to 300 feet. Let the rode pay out and see whether the vessel motions settle down. The bow may continue to "sail" back and forth. Counteract this by using some ahead power and helm to hold the bow at a constant compass angle.

Maneuvering in Rivers

Overview

Introduction

This section discusses the techniques and hazards of maneuvering in narrow rivers.

In this section

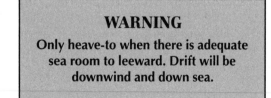

Operating in a Narrow Channel

G.1. BANK CUSHION

Bank cushion effect refers to a boat being pushed away from the nearest river bank, and it occurs only when operating in close proximity to the bank. As the boat moves ahead in the river, the water between the bow and the near river bank builds up on the side of the boat, causing the bow to move away from the bank. The bank cushion effect is especially prevalent if the draft of the boat is nearly equal to the depth of the water, or in narrow channels with steep banks.

G.2. BANK SUCTION

Bank suction effect refers to the stern of a boat being pulled toward the bank. As the boat moves ahead while near the river bank, the unbalanced pressure of water on the aft quarter lowers the water level between the boat and the bank. This forces the stern to move toward the bank. Bank suction effect occurs most notably with a twin-screw boats.

G.3. COMBINED EFFECT

The combined effect of bank cushion and bank suction may cause a boat to take a sudden sheer toward the opposite bank (see Figure 10-24).

SINGLE-SCREW BOATS A single-screw boat going at a very slow speed with its starboard side near the right bank may lose control if sheer occurs. To bring the boat under control, increase speed and add a small amount of right rudder.

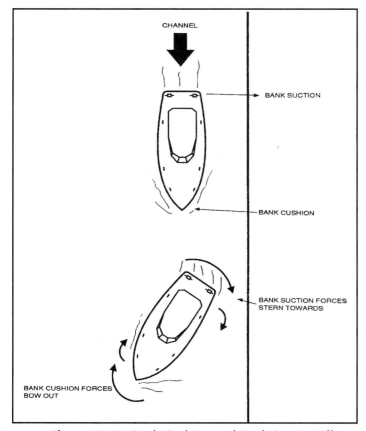

Figure 10-24 Bank Cushion and Bank Suction Effects: Narrow Straight Channel

TWIN-SCREW BOATS A twin-screw boat under the conditions described above usually can be recovered from this sheer by increasing speed on the port engine, and adding right rudder.

G.4. CURRENT

Current is the horizontal flow or movement of water in a river. Maximum current occurs during runoff and/or high water and the greatest velocity is in the area of the channel. Restricted or narrow channels tend to have a venturi effect, in that rushing water squeezes into a passage and accelerates. Current in a bend will tend to flow away from the inside point (to the outside), creating eddies, counter currents, and slack water immediately past the point. These actions build shoals at the point or inside a bend. The prudent operator will be alert to the changing current within a waterway.

G.5. EXTREMELY NARROW CHANNELS

In extremely narrow channels where bank cushion and bank suction are expected, proceed at a very slow speed. Keep near the middle of the channel and pass other boats closer than normal. In a meeting situation in a narrow channel, reduce headway but not enough to lose steerage. On approaching the boat, apply a small amount of right rudder to head slightly toward the bank; shortly after passing the other boat, reverse the rudder and straighten up. A little right rudder may be needed to hold course against the bank cushion effect. Because of wash from passing boats, use extreme caution.

Turning in a Bend

G.6. GENERAL

Bank suction, bank cushion, currents and wind are factors that affect a boat's turn in a sharp bend in a narrow channel. Bank cushion and bank suction are strongest when the bank of a channel is steep. They are weakest when the edge of a channel shoals gradually and extends into a large area. Bank suction and bank cushion increase with the boat's speed. Channel currents are usually strongest in the bend with eddies or counter-currents and shoaling on the lee side of the point. Speed of the current is greater in deeper water than in shallow water.

G.7. FOLLOWING CURRENT

In a following current, the boat makes good speed with little help from the engines. When making a sharp turn with a following current, it is possible to make the following maneuvers:

- Hug the Point
- Stay in the Bend
- Proceed on the Bend Side, Middle of the Channel

An experienced operator can accomplish any of the three; however, the third choice, called the "Bend Side, Middle of the Channel," is the safest and therefore the preferred choice.

HUG THE POINT The operator carries a small amount of rudder toward the near bank to steer a straight course. As the channel begins to bend and the boat moves from the bank, less rudder will be necessary. This condition is a signal that it is time to begin the turn. However, slack water or eddies may be around the bend, making it difficult to prevent a sheer toward the near bank, especially in shallow water. The current under the quarter may affect the stern, and result in an increase in sheer (see Figure 10-25).

STAY IN THE BEND This maneuver is a turn in the bend away from the point and it takes precise timing. If done too late, the boat may ground on the bank in the bend. If done too soon, there is extreme danger that a strong and sudden sheer will occur.

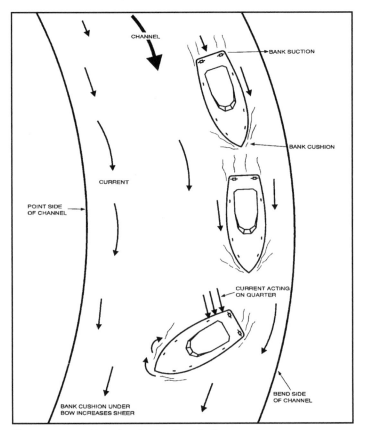

Figure 10-26 Keeping in the Bend: Current Astern

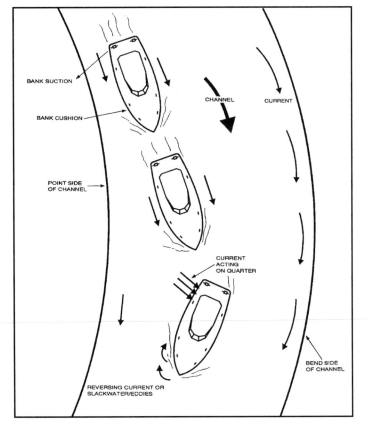

Figure 10-25 Nudging the Point: Current Astern

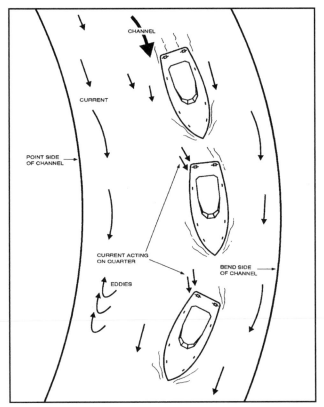

Figure 10-27 Approaching Slightly on the Bend Side of the Channel: Current Astern

The bank suction on one quarter combines with the current on the other quarter to give the boat the sheer. Also, the bank cushion under the bow will increase the sheer (see Figure 10-26).

BEND SIDE, MIDDLE OF THE CHANNEL This is the safest method when the current is following. Approach the turn steering a course toward the bend side of the middle of the channel. By doing this, the boat avoids eddies under the point and the increase in currents in the bend. The operator can also use the force of the current against the quarter to help in the turn. A following current will force a boat toward the bend side; consequently, commence the turn early in the bend. When head currents tend to force the boat toward the point side, wait and commence the turn later (see Figure 10-27).

SECTION H

Anchoring

Overview

Introduction

Anchoring must be performed correctly in order to be effective. This section discusses the techniques necessary to properly anchor a boat.

In this section

General Information

H.1. BASIC ELEMENTS

The basic elements of proper anchoring technique include:

- availability of proper equipment
- knowledge to use that equipment
- ability to select good anchoring areas

H.2. TERMS AND DEFINITIONS

The Anchoring System is all the gear used in conjunction with the anchor. The table below defines several of the terms used to describe the different parts of most modern types of anchors.

ANCHOR: A device designed to engage the bottom of a waterway and through its resistance to drag maintain a vessel within a given radius.

ANCHOR CHOCKS: Fittings on the deck of a vessel used to stow an anchor when it is not in use.

BOW CHOCKS: Fittings, usually on the rail of a vessel near its stem, having jaws that serve as fairleads for anchor rodes and other lines.

GROUND TACKLE: A general term for the anchor, anchor rodes, fittings, etc., used for securing a vessel at anchor.

HAWSPIPE: A cylindrical or elliptical pipe or casting in a vessel's hull through which the anchor rode runs.

HORIZONTAL LOAD: The horizontal force placed on an anchoring device by the vessel to which it is connected.

MOORING BITT: A post or cleat through or on the deck of a vessel used to secure an anchor rode or other line to the vessel.

RODE: The line connecting an anchor with a vessel.

SCOPE: The ratio of the length of the anchor rode to the vertical distance from the bow chocks to the bottom (depth plus height of bow chocks above water).

VERTICAL LOAD: The lifting force placed on the bow of the vessel by its anchor rode.

H.3. REASONS FOR ANCHORING

There are many reasons to anchor a vessel; the most important is for safety. Other reasons for anchoring are:

- engine failure,
- need to stay outside of a breaking inlet or bar,
- to weather a storm, or
- to hold your position while passing gear to a disabled vessel.

H.4. ANCHOR TYPES

There are different types of anchors, each with its own advantages. The type of anchor and size (weight) of anchor a boat uses depends upon the size of the boat. It is advisable for each boat to carry at least two anchors.

- A working or service anchor should have the holding power to equal to approximately 6 percent of the boat's displacement.

- A storm anchor should be at least 150–200 percent as effective as the service anchor.

Suggested Anchor Weights for Danforth Anchors

Maximum Boat Length	Working Anchor	Storm Anchor
20 feet (approx. 7 meters)	5 lbs.	12 lbs.
30 feet (approx. 10 meters)	12 lbs.	18 lbs.
40 feet (approx. 12 meters)	18 lbs.	28 lbs.

H.5. MAIN PARTS OF THE DANFORTH ANCHOR

Since most small boats use a Danforth type anchor, its parts are described below (see Figure 10-28):

SHANK: Aids in setting and weighing the anchor. Attachment point for the anchor line.

FLUKES: Dig in the bottom and bury the anchor, providing holding power.

STOCK: Prevents the anchor from rolling or rotating.

CROWN: Lifts the rear of the flukes, and forces the flukes into the bottom.

Ground Tackle

H.6. GENERAL

The complete anchor system consists of the anchor, the rode, and the various fittings connecting the rode to the anchor.

H.7. ANCHOR RODE

The rode is the line from the boat to the anchor and is usually made up of a length of line plus a short length of chain. Large boats may use an all-chain rode. Each element of the system must be connected to its neighbor in a strong and dependable manner.

TYPE OF LINE USED The most commonly used line for rode is nylon. The line may be either cable laid or braided. It must be free of cuts and abrasions. Foot or fathom markers may be placed in the line to aid in paying out proper lengths.

NYLON AND CHAIN Chain added with the rode has several advantages:

- It lowers the angle of pull (the chain tends to lie on the bottom.

- It helps to prevent chafing of the line on a coral or rocky bottom.

- It does not suffer the problems of line when sand penetrates strands of the fiber. line higher up.

- Sand doesn't stick to chain.

- Mud is easily washed off chain. (Nylon gets very dirty in mud.)

Chain diameter starts at one-quarter inch for small boats (20 feet) and can be significantly larger for heavy displacement craft. Chain should be galvanized to protect against rust. Neoprene-coated chain has the benefit of not marring the boat, but such coating has a limited life in active use. Generally Danforth and Northill type anchors need more scope than a Navy or yachtsman type anchors.

NOTE

SCOPE of the anchor rode should have a ratio range between 5:1 and 7:1. For heavy weather use 10:1.

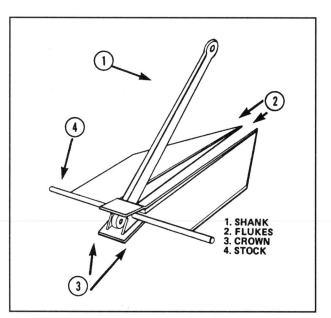

Figure 10-28 Main Parts of a Danforth Anchor

1. SHANK
2. FLUKES
3. CROWN
4. STOCK

Fittings

H.8. GENERAL

There are various methods for securing the rode to the anchor ring. With fiber line, the preferred practice is to work an eye splice around a thimble and use a shackle to join the thimble and ring. (See Figure 10-29.)

H.9. DESCRIPTION

The following list describes the different fittings used to connect the rode to the anchor.

SHACKLE: Bends the length of chafing chain to the shank of the anchor.

SWIVEL: Attaches the chafing chain to the detachable link. Allows the line to spin freely.

THIMBLE: Protects the anchor line from chafing at the connection point. Use synthetic line thimbles for lines 2¾" in circumference (⅞" diameter) and larger.

CHAFING CHAIN: Tends to lower the angle of pull of the anchor and assists in preventing chafing of the anchor line on the bottom.

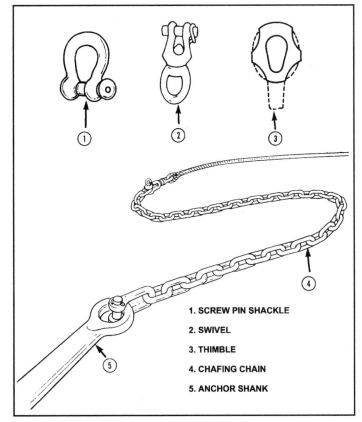

1. SCREW PIN SHACKLE
2. SWIVEL
3. THIMBLE
4. CHAFING CHAIN
5. ANCHOR SHANK

Figure 10-29 Anchor Fittings

DETACHABLE LINK: Attaches the anchor and associated ground tackle to the anchor line (not mandatory).

EYE SPLICE: Used around a thimble to connect it to a ring on the anchor by a shackle.

Anchoring Techniques

H.10. GENERAL

Before the need arises, the coxswain should brief the crew members on procedures for anchoring.

Anchoring involves good communication between the coxswain and the crew. With noise from the engine and exhaust, and sometimes the wind, it is usually difficult to hear voice communication. Have a pre-arranged set of hand signals that the crew understands. Keep the signals as simple as possible

NOTE

PFDs must be worn during the anchoring operation.

H.11. PRECAUTIONS FOR SELECTING ANCHORAGE AREA

Sometimes it may be possible to choose a sheltered anchorage area in shallow water (40' or less).

- Check charts to ensure that the anchorage area avoids any submerged cables or other obstructions.
- If other boats are in the same area, be careful not to anchor too close to them.
- Never drop within the swing area of another boat (see Figure 10-30).
- Always approach the anchorage into the wind or current (see Figure 10-31).

NOTE

Never anchor by the stern especially with small boats. Weather and seas may swamp the craft.

H.12. APPROACHING THE ANCHORAGE

Having selected a suitable spot, run in *slowly*, preferably on some range ashore selected from marks identified on the chart, or referring to your position to visible buoys and landmarks to aid you in locating a chosen spot. Use of *two* ranges will give the most precise positioning. Later these aids will be helpful in determining whether the anchor is holding or dragging.

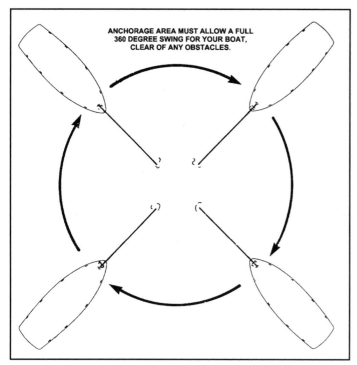

Figure 10-30 Anchorage Swing Area

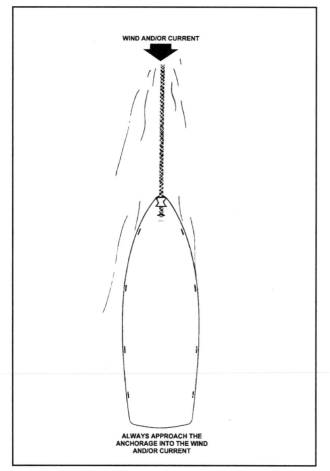

Figure 10-31 Approaching an Anchorage

BOTTOM CHARACTERISTICS Bottom characteristics are of prime importance. Characteristics of the bottom are normally shown on nautical charts.

FIRM SAND: Excellent holding quality and is consistent.

CLAY: Excellent holding quality if quite dense, but sufficiently pliable to allow good anchor engagement.

MUD: Varies greatly from sticky, which holds well, to soft or silt that is of questionable holding power.

LOOSE SAND: Fair, if the anchor engages deeply.

ROCK AND CORAL: Less desirable for holding an anchor unless the anchor becomes hooked in a crevice.

GRASS: Often prevents the anchor from digging into the bottom, and so provides very questionable holding for most anchors.

H.13. LOWERING THE ANCHOR

As the anchor is lowered into the water, it is important to know how much rode is paid out when the anchor hits the bottom. It is advisable to take a round turn on the forward bitt or cleat to maintain control of the rode. If anchoring in a strong wind or current, the anchor rode may not be held with hands alone.

Unless you must work single-handed:

1. Station one person on the forward deck.

2. Haul out enough line from the locker so as to run freely without kinking or fouling. If previously detached, the line must be shackled to the ring, and the stock set up (if of the stock type) and keyed.

Many an anchor has been lost for failure to attach the rode properly. Rodes too, have gone with the anchor when not secured at the bitter end.

Lightweight anchors are always ready for use and do not have to be set up, but always check to see that the shackle is properly fastened.

NOTE

Never stand in the coils of line on deck and don't attempt to "heave" the anchor by casting it as far as possible from the side of the boat. Lower hand over hand until it reaches the bottom.

LENGTH OF ROPE (SCOPE) The scope is a ratio of the length of rode paid out to the depth of the water. Pay out enough rode so the lower end of the rode forms an angle of 8° (or less) with the bottom. This helps the anchor dig-in and give good holding power.

NOTE

Generally, anchors with greater holding power per anchor weight (i.e., Danforth and Northill) need more anchor scope than Navy Yachtsman anchors.

MARKERS Markers along the line, similar to those on a lead line, show the amount of rode that is out. They also help to decide the scope necessary for good holding of the anchor

H.14. SETTING THE ANCHOR

An anchor must be "set" properly if it is to yield its full holding power. The best techniques for setting an anchor will vary from type to type; only general guidelines can be given here. Experiment to determine the best procedures for your boat, your anchors, and your cruising waters.

1. With the anchor on the bottom and the boat backing down slowly, pay out line as the boat takes it, preferably with a turn of line around the bitt or cleat.

2. When the predetermined scope has been paid out, snub the line quickly and the anchor will probably get a quick bite into the bottom.

If the anchor becomes shod with mud or bottom grass adhering to the flukes, lift it, wash it off by dunking at the surface, and try again.

H.15. AFTER ANCHOR IS SET

After the anchor is set, you can pay our or take in rode to the proper length for the anchorage, and for the prevailing and expected weather conditions. Scope must be adequate for holding, but in a crowded anchorage you must also consider the other boats.

Attach chafing gear to the rode at the point where it passes through the chocks and over the side to prevent abrasion, wear, and tear on the rode and boat.

H.16. CHECKING THE ANCHOR HOLDING

Make a positive check that the anchor is holding, and not dragging. There are several ways to do this.

- If the water is clear enough that you can see the bottom, you can detect any movement easily.

- If there is a jerk, or a vibration, the anchor is most likely not holding.

- Monitor bearings taken on at least two landmarks (if available) that are a minimum of 45° apart or use radar ranges and bearings. Small changes usually mean that the wind, tide, or current has caused the boat to swing around the anchor. If the compass heading is constant, but the bearings change, the anchor is dragging.

- If using a buoyed trip line from the crown of your anchor, apply reverse power to test the anchor's holding. The float on this line should continue to bob up and down in one spot unaffected by the pull on the anchor rode.

H.17. MAKING FAST

After the anchor has gotten a good bite, with proper scope paid out, make the line fast and shut off the motor. The fundamental idea in making fast is to secure in such a manner that the line can neither slip nor jam.

FORWARD BITT On boats with a forward bitt (samson post), an excellent way to secure the anchor line is to make two full turns around the bitt, and then finish off with a half-hitch around each end of the pin through the bitt. The bitt takes the load and the pin secures the line, and the line is more easily taken off the bitt than with any other hitch.

STOUT CLEAT Where a stout cleat is used to make fast, take a full turn around the base, one turn over each horn crossing diagonally over the center of the cleat, and finish with a half hitch around one horn.

H.18. NIGHT ANCHORING

Put extra line (scope) out before securing for the night, just in case the wind increases. Also, check the weather report before retiring. Don't forget anchor lights where required.

H.19. ANCHOR WATCH

Whenever the situation is questionable (forecast weather, potentially hazardous location, extreme tide range, etc.), an anchor watch should be assigned to protect against disaster. See Chapter 1—Boat Crew Duties and Responsibilities, for a description of the duties of an anchor watch.

H.20. WEIGHING ANCHOR

When you are ready to weigh anchor and get underway, go forward slowly and take in the anchor rode to prevent fouling the screws. Fake the line on the deck as it comes on board. When the boat approaches the spot directly over the anchor, and the rode is tending straight up and down, the anchor will usually free itself from the bottom.

H.21. CLEARING A FOULED ANCHOR

If the anchor refuses to break free, snub the anchor line around the forward bitt or cleat and advance the boat a few feet. Sometimes even this will not free the anchor, and the operator should run in a wide circle, slowly, to change the angle of pull. Take extreme care to ensure the anchor line does not tangle in the screws during this operation.

Another way to break out an anchor is with a "trip line," if one was rigged during anchoring. A "trip line" is a line strong enough to stand the pull of a snagged anchor (a ⅜-inch line is a typical size). Attach the "trip line" to the crown of the anchor (some anchors have a hole for this purpose). The "trip line" should be long enough to reach the surface in normal anchoring waters, with allowance for tidal changes. Pass the "trip line" through a float and end the line in a small eye-splice that can be caught with a boathook. If the anchor doesn't trip in the normal manner, pick up the trip line and haul the anchor up crown first.

H.22. CLEAN THE ANCHOR

Clean the anchor before bringing it on board. The anchor may have some "bottom" on it. Check the condition of the equipment and, before departure from the area, be sure the anchor is adequately secured to prevent shifting and damage to the boat.

Anchor Stowage

H.23. GENERAL

Stowage of ground tackle depends upon the size of the boat. In smaller boats, it may be on deck, with the anchor secured in chocks to prevent shifting as waves cause the boat to roll. Some boats have the working anchor attached to a pulpit and the rode in a forward locker. The ground tackle should always be ready for use when the boat is underway.

H.24. MAINTENANCE

After anchoring in salt water, rinse ground tackle off with fresh water before stowing it, if possible.

Nylon—Nylon rode dries quickly and can be stowed while damp.

All-chain rode—If using an all-chain rode, drying on deck before stowing will help to prevent rust.

Natural fiber—A natural fiber, like manila, must be thoroughly dried before stowage to prevent rot.

H.25. SECOND ANCHOR

Some boats carry a second anchor to use as a storm anchor. It is stowed securely, but in a readily accessible place with a rode nearby. Inspect the second anchor from time to time to make sure all is in good condition.

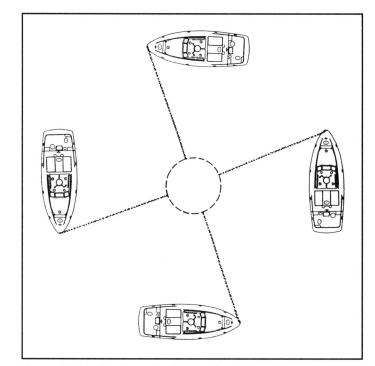

Figure 10-32 Freeing a Fouled Anchor

Communications

Editor's Note: The ability to communicate professionally and concisely could save your boat or even the lives of those on board. The procedures discussed in this chapter are used by professional government and civilian mariners. You should be professional when you use your VHF and HF radios, and you can be with a bit of study and a little practice. The use of prowords and the phonetic alphabet can help you make a vital communication at the outer edge of reception range. And, knowing how to send or relay a distress message could make all the difference for you or someone else in trouble on the water. This section provides the basics. You may want to copy the phonetic alphabet and proword list and post it near your radio. You'll also want to be sure others on your vessel are trained in basic radio use. After all, if you become disabled, someone else on your boat will have to call for help.

Most marine communications are done by using voice radio transmissions. These are very much like two people talking on the telephone, but with significant differences that boat crew members must understand.

Typically, voice radio communications are "simplex," or one way at a time—when one person is speaking, the second person must wait. This differs from face-to-face and telephone conversations where voices may overlap. Simplex communication is the reason for many of the procedural regulations for voice radio communications.

NOTE

All operators should check all of their radio equipment for proper operation before getting underway and immediately report any malfunctions.

Overview

Introduction

Communication between mariners has long been recognized as a necessity. Using the radio proficiently and knowing proper radio protocol reflects well upon the boat crew's and the radio operator's professionalism. It is essential that each boat crew member is completely aware of the common distress signals and how they are used in emergencies. This chapter will provide you with the basic knowledge of voice communication conventions, procedures, and the various distress signals.

NOTE

For additional information on Coast Guard communications, refer to the *Telecommunication Manual*, COMDTINST M2000.3 (series) and *Radiotelephone Handbook*, COMDTINST 2300.7 (series).

In this chapter

Radio Signal Characteristics

Overview

Introduction

Type of modulation and frequencies are the two basic characteristics shared by radio signals. To understand radio communications, it is fundamental for all crew members who use the radio to know about types of modulations, use of the different radios, and frequencies.

In this section

Modulation and Frequency

A.1. TYPES OF MODULATION

Modulation is a variation in radio wave amplitude or frequency. The Coast Guard uses the common types of modulation:

- Amplitude Modulation (AM)—Single Side Band (SSB) MF/HF, some VHF systems and UHF

- Frequency Modulation (FM)—very high frequency (VHF) systems

A.2. FREQUENCIES, TYPES, AND RANGES

The Coast Guard uses several types of frequencies, each generally capable of AM (SSB) and FM modulation. For maritime use, the most commonly used radio frequencies are in the following ranges:

Band	Frequency Range
Medium Frequency (MF)	0.3 to 3 MHz
High Frequency (HF)	3 to 30 MHz
Very High Frequency (VHF)	30 to 300 MHz
Ultra High Frequency (UHF)	300 to 3000 MHz

Radio Systems

A.3. GENERAL

Several basic types of voice radios are used on boats. Frequently they are MF/HF and VHF-FM and usually, they are identified by the radio's mode of transmission. Understanding the basic differences of the types of radios and their use will assist crew members in using them effectively and professionally.

A.4. RADIO SYSTEMS USE AND PERFORMANCE

Every Coast Guard boat carries a VHF-FM radio; many will also carry an MF-HF radio. There are several differences in usage and performance of MF-SSB and VHF-FM radios.

VHF LINE OF SIGHT RADIO VHF-FM (156–162 MHz) is used for local, short range marine communications. Frequencies in this band operate on the line-of-sight principle (LOS). Range depends mainly on the height of antennas for both the receiving and transmitting stations, and to some extent on the power output of the transmitting station. VHF equipment is called "line-of-sight radio" because its radio waves travel in nearly a straight line, meaning, if one antenna can "see" another antenna, communication between the two is possible. Occasionally, atmospheric conditions allow VHF signals to bounce or bend in their line of travel, increasing the transmission's range farther than normal.

VHF-FM NATIONAL DISTRESS SYSTEM The Coast Guard VHF-FM National Distress System (NDS) provides distress, safety, and command and control communications coverage in most areas of boating activity (including inland waters) in which the Coast Guard has SAR responsibilities. The NDS is designed to provide coverage for, or "see," a radio with an antenna 6 feet above the water and up to 20 miles offshore for most areas in U.S. coastal waters (see Figure 11-1).

MF AND HF BANDS Boats use the MF band typically to communicate with the Group when out of VHF radio range. The MF band uses low frequencies, so the ground wave travels along the surface of the earth permitting communications at distances up to 100 miles during daylight hours. The low frequency also makes communications at much greater distances at night possible. MF and HF radios of any modulation type usually have greater range than VHF. The operating range for MF and HF radios can shift as conditions change, and the conditions that

Figure 11-1 Line-of-Sight

affect the operating range will typically vary from hour to hour. As a consequence, communications between two vessels can be lost due to a number of factors, including changing weather.

VHF-FM AND MF/HF COMPARISON This table summarizes the major advantages and disadvantages of the radio systems discussed above:

Radio System	Advantages	Disadvantages
VHF-FM	• Relatively static free signal transmission • Offers a wide range of frequencies	• Limited range • Overcrowding causing interruptions
MF and HF	• Greater range • Less traffic and fewer interruptions than VHF-FM	• Interference (caused by atmospheric conditions)

Radio Frequencies

A.5. GENERAL

The following are the most common frequencies for VHF-FM and MF/HF bands and the purpose assigned to each.

A.6. VHF-FM

This is a list of the most common VHF-FM channels used for marine operations. It is organized by channel and frequency in megahertz (MHz), followed by their use.

NOTE

All vessels equipped with a VHF-FM radio are required to monitor Channel 16. Use this channel only when unsuccessful in establishing contact with units on a working frequency.

NOTE

Usually radio communications checks are done on working frequencies.

A.7. MF/HF (SSB)

Outlined below is a list of common MF/HF frequencies used for marine operations followed by their use.

Prowords and Common Abbreviations

B.1. GENERAL

Prowords speed the handling of radio messages by abbreviating single word or phrases to replace common words, phrases, sentences, and even paragraphs. Among other things, knowing and using Prowords help to reduce radio traffic by performing radio transmissions efficiently. The following list contains the most common Prowords and their meanings.

AFFIRMATIVE: Yes.

ALL AFTER: The portion of the message to which I make reference is all which follows.

ALL BEFORE: The portion of the message to which I make reference is all which comes before.

BREAK: I hereby indicate the separation of text from other portions of the message.

CORRECT: You are correct, or what you have transmitted is correct.

CORRECTION: An error has been made in this transmission. Transmission will continue with the last word correctly sent. The correct version is . . .

ETA: Estimated time of arrival.

ETD: Estimated time of departure.

ETR: Estimated time of return or repair.

FIGURES: Indicates numbers or numerals to follow. Used when numbers occur in the text of a message.

FROM: The originator of this message.

I SPELL: I shall spell the next word phonetically.

OPS NORMAL: Used to say the patrol is normal in all respects, "operations normal."

Channel	Frequency (MHz)	Use
6	156.300	Intership safety and SAR communications for ships and aircraft.
9	156.450	Alternate calling channel for non-commercial vessels. (Some Coast Guard districts have high level radio sites with Channel 9 capability.)
12	156.600	Used for port operations.
13	156.650	Bridge-to-Bridge VHF-FM frequency. Transmissions on this frequency are limited to one–watt output, with few exceptions. This frequency is to clarify a vessel's intent in meeting and passing situations, as described in the Navigation Rules (COLREGS). **Do not use for communications between Coast Guard boats and stations.**
16	156.800	International calling and distress frequency use by vessels in emergencies or to establish contact with others. Shore stations use it to announce broadcasts of general information on other frequencies, boat crew use Channel 16 to: • Transmit/receive distress calls and distress messages. • Transmit/receive urgent safety broadcasts and messages. • Identify vessel traffic concerns. • Place a preliminary call to other units in order to establishcommunications and shift to a working frequency to after contact. **Do not use this channel to deliver general information messages.**
21A	157.05	Intra-Coast Guard VHF-FM working frequency for units in maritime mobile operations.
22A	157.100	Primary VHF-FM liaison frequency for communications between Coast Guard units and civilian stations. It is also used for making Coast Guard Marine Information and Marine Assistance Request Broadcasts (MARBs). The Coast Guard may permit nongovernment use to conduct short business transactions on 22A on a not-to-interfere basis with Coast Guard communications.
23A	157.15	Intra-Coast Guard VHF-FM working frequency used for communications between Coast Guard units working in maritime mobile operations.
81A	157.075	Intra-Coast Guard VHF-FM working frequency for units in maritime mobile operations.
83A	157.175	Intra-Coast Guard VHF-FM working frequency for units in maritime mobile operations.

OUT: Used following the last line of the message transmitted, signifying the end of the transmission and nothing follows. No reply is required or expected.

OVER: Used following a transmission when a response from the other station is necessary. It is an invitation to the other station to transmit.

NEGATIVE: No.

ROGER: I have received your transmission satisfactorily.

I SAY AGAIN, or REQUEST YOU SAY AGAIN: I am repeating transmission or the portion indicated, or you should repeat your transmission or the portion indicated.

SILENCE (Spoken 3 times and pronounced SEE LONS): Cease all transmissions immediately. Silence will be maintained until lifted. Used to clear routine transmissions from a channel only when an emergency is in progress.

SILENCE FINI (Pronounced SEE LONS FEE NEE): Silence is lifted. Indicates the end of an emergency and resumption of normal traffic.

THIS IS: This transmission is from the station whose designator immediately follows.

TO: The addressees immediately following are addressed for action.

UNKNOWN STATION: The identity of the station

Frequency (kHz)	Use
2003	Intership safety frequency for the Great Lakes only.
2082.5	Intership safety frequency for all areas.
2142	Intership safety frequency for the Pacific coast area south of latitude 42° North (daytime only).
2182	International distress and calling frequency used world-wide for distress calls and for urgent message traffic. Also, ship and shore stations may use it to establish initial contact, then shift to a proper working frequency for passing operational traffic. All units must maintain radio silence on this frequency for three minutes, twice each hour; radio silence should begin on the hour and half hour, except for transmitting distress, or urgency messages, or vital navigation warnings.
2203	Intership safety frequency for the Gulf of Mexico only.
2638	International intership safety frequency.
2670	Coast Guard working frequency used to broadcast urgent safety messages; precede messages on 2670 kHz with a preliminary announcement on 2182 kHz. Primary MF/HF Coast Guard/civilian liaison frequency.
2738	International intership safety frequency. Coast Guard and Auxiliary boats may use this frequency to communicate with other vessels in all areas, except the Great Lakes and Gulf of Mexico.
2830	Intership safety frequency for the Gulf of Mexico only.
3023 and 5680	International SAR on-scene frequencies. Use either of these frequencies to conduct communications at the scene of an emergency or as the SAR control frequency.
4125	International distress and safety; used in Alaska.
5680 and 3023	International SAR on-scene frequencies. Use either of these frequencies to conduct communications at the scene of an emergency or as the SAR control frequency.
5692	Aircraft working frequency.
5696	Coast Guard Aircraft primary frequency (air to ground).

which you are trying to establish communications with is unknown.

WAIT: I must pause for a few seconds.

WAIT OUT: I must pause longer than a few seconds.

WILCO: Will comply with your last order or request.

WORD AFTER: The word to which I have reference is that which follows.

WORD BEFORE: The word to which make reference is that which precedes.

WRONG: Your last transmission was not correct. The correct version is . . .

Verbal Communications

Overview

Introduction

Letters and numbers spoken over a radio are often difficult for others to understand. Spelling out words and numbers that may be easily confused over a radio help clarify their meaning. Knowing how to pronounce the Phonetic Alphabet and numbers over the radio increases the chance that all voice communications between your boat and others are successful.

In this section

The Phonetic Alphabet

C.1. SPEAKING THE PHONETIC ALPHABET

The Phonetic Alphabet is based on the assumption that it is easier to understand a word than a letter. The Phonetic Alphabet is a series of words, each standing for a letter in the alphabet. Boat crew members should memorize each word of the Phonetic Alphabet listed below and always be ready to pair them to the correct letter in the alphabet.

C.2. USING THE PHONETIC ALPHABET

To use the phonetic alphabet to spell out difficult words within a message, always precede the actual spelling with the procedural words (prowords) "I spell."

Example: "Search from Saugatuck, I spell, Saugatuck—SIERRA, ALPHA, UNIFORM, GOLF, ALPHA, TANGO, UNIFORM, CHARLIE, KILO—Saugatuck to King's Point."

Numbers and Decimal Points

C.3. USING NUMBERS AND DECIMAL POINTS

Numbers and the term "decimal point" can be misunderstood when spoken over a radio. To reduce confusion, pronounce numbers differently over the radio than when speaking in normal conversation. Table 11-3 contains the radio pronunciation.

PROWORDS PRECEDING NUMBERS Always precede numbers with the proword "FIGURES," except in the heading of a message.
Example: "The master indicates he has FIGURES WUN, ZERO PERSONS ON BOARD, INCLUDING SELF."

MULTIPLE NUMBERS When a number consists of more than one numeral or digit, pronounce it one numeral at a time with a short pause between numerals.

Phonetic Alphabet

Alphabet	Phonetic Alphabet	Pronounced
A	ALPHA	AL-FA
B	BRAVO	BRAH-VOH
C	CHARLIE	CHAR-LEE
D	DELTA	DEL-TAH
E	ECHO	ECK-O
F	FOXTROT	FOKS-TROT
G	GOLF	GOLF
H	HOTEL	HOH-TEL
I	INDIA	IN-DEE-AH
J	JULIETT	JEW-LEE-ETT
K	KILO	KEY-LOH
L	LIMA	LEE-MAH
M	MIKE	MIKE
N	NOVEMBER	NO-VEM-BER
O	OSCAR	OSS-CAR
P	PAPA	PAH-PAH
Q	QUEBEC	KAY-BECK
R	ROMEO	ROW-ME-OH
S	SIERRA	SEE-AIR-RAH
T	TANGO	TANG-GO
U	UNIFORM	YOU-NEE-FORM
V	VICTOR	VIK-TAH
W	WHISKEY	WISS-KEY
X	XRAY	ECKS-RAY
Y	YANKEE	YANG-KEY
Z	ZULU	ZOO-LOO

Example: 52—Say, "Figures FI-YIV, TOO;" do not say, "FIFTY-TWO."

DECIMALS Include decimals in a spoken number by saying the word decimal ("DAY-SEE-MAL") in the proper location.
Example: 156.8 is pronounced: "Figures WUN, FI-YIV, SIX, DAY-SEE-MAL, ATE," **not** "ONE FIFTY-SIX DECIMAL EIGHT."

SECTION D

Radio Operating Procedures

D.1. GENERAL

As a boat crew member, operating a voice radio will be a frequent task for you, so you should be familiar and comfortable with using a radio. It is important to learn basic procedures and ways for properly using the radio so that messages are sent and received in the most effective and professional manner.

Table 11-3 Radio Pronunciation	
Numeral	**Spoken As**
0	ZE-RO
1	WUN
2	TOO
3	THUH-REE
4	FO-WER
5	FI-YIV
6	SIX
7	SEVEN
8	ATE
9	NIN-ER
Decimal	DAY-SEE-MAL

D.2. BASIC RADIO DISCIPLINE

Learning and understanding the following will help you use voice radios effectively:

CHECK SETTING: Be certain the radio is set on the proper frequency.

SQUELCH CONTROL: Squelch control blocks out weak signals. Adjust the squelch control until the noise can be heard, then adjust it slightly in the opposite direction until the noise stops. Setting the squelch control adjusts the receiver so only signals strong enough to pass the level selected will be heard and reduces the amount of static noise on the speaker.

DO NOT INTERRUPT OTHERS: Before beginning a transmission, listen for a few seconds to avoid interrupting other communications that are already in progress.

MICROPHONE PLACEMENT: Keep the microphone about one to two inches from your lips. When transmitting, shield the microphone by keeping your head and body between noise generating sources (such as engine noise, wind, helicopter, etc.) and the microphone.

KNOW WHAT YOU WILL SAY: Before keying the transmitter, know how to say what you are going to say. Keep all transmissions short and to the point. Never "chit-chat" or make unnecessary transmissions on any frequency.

SPEAKING: Speak clearly, concisely, and in a normal tone of voice, maintaining a natural speaking rhythm.

PHONETIC ALPHABET: Use the Phonetic Alphabet to spell out a word or a group of letters.

SPEAK SLOWLY SO OTHERS CAN WRITE: Send messages only as fast as the receiving operator can write.

PROPER PROWORDS: Use proper prowords, ending each transmission with "over" and the last with "out." Never say "over and out."

PROWORD FOR PAUSES: In cases where a pause for a few seconds between transmissions is necessary, use the proword "wait." If the pause is to be longer than a few seconds, use prowords "wait, out." Do not use "wait one" or "stand by."

MESSAGES ARE NOT PRIVATE: Remember, your transmission may be heard by anyone with a radio or scanner.

Learning to use the VHF radio properly is critically important for safe boating.

NOTE

When transmitting, the microphone may pick up the conversations of people talking near you.

D.3. USE OF APPROPRIATE RADIO LANGUAGE

The following is a list of things NOT to do while using the radio. Items on this list are either not protocol, they are illegal, or they cause misunderstandings of messages.

Do not . . .

- Break Radio Silence! Break it only for emergencies or ensuring safe navigation under the Bridge-to-Bridge Radiotelephone Act.

- Use profane or obscene language.

- Use unauthorized prowords, abbreviations, and procedures.

- Speak using extremes of voice pitch, this will cause distortion.

- Slur syllables or clip your speech, they are hard to understand.

- Use phrases such as "would you believe," "be informed," or "be advised." They are unprofessional and not correct procedure.

- Key the microphone unless you are ready to transmit. Keying the microphone also transmits a signal, causing interference on that frequency.

- Use "10 Codes" such as those used by many law enforcement agencies.

SECTION E

Communicating Between Coast Guard Facilities

Overview

Introduction

Communicating with other units within the Coast Guard will be a common task required of you. Knowing proper call signs and reporting procedures will become "second-nature" to you, even so, be careful to always use the military message formats. Radio communications are an official record. They reflect upon the ability of the entire boat crew, and the information you report to other units is important, especially in emergencies.

Coast Guard Voice Call Signs and Ops Normal Reports

E.1. GENERAL

Voice call signs are used to identify the craft that is calling or being called over voice radio. A Coast Guard boat's number or an Auxiliary boat's number serves as voice call sign for radio communications. This table summaries the different Coast Guard facilities and how to state each call sign you may encounter in the field.

Facility	Call Sign
Coast Guard Boat	"COAST GUARD FO-WER WUN THUH-REE ZE-RO ZE-RO" (41300)
Auxiliary Boat	"COAST GUARD AUXILIARY VESSEL TOO TOO SEVEN ATE TOO (22782)"
Cutter	"COAST GUARD CUTTER DILIGENCE"
Shore Radio Facilities	"COAST GUARD" followed by the type of facility air, radio, or station, and the geographical location if necessary; e.g., COAST GUARD GROUP KEY WEST
Aircraft	"COAST GUARD SIX FI-YIV ZE-RO ATE" (6508)
Aircraft Involved in SAR	"RESCUE" shall be included as part of the call sign "COAST GUARD RESCUE SIX FI-YIV ZE-RO ATE." (6508)

NOTE

"COAST GUARD" may be dropped once establishing communications with other Coast Guard units on Coast Guard frequencies. Number call signs may be shortened to the last three digits, if it doesn't cause confusion. For example, Coast Guard Boat 41357, already communicating with another Coast Guard unit, could refer to themselves simply as "THUH-REE FI-YIV SEVEN."

E.2. OPs NORMAL REPORTS

When underway, boat crews are required to provide an operations normal (Ops Normal) report every 60 minutes or according to local policy. The information to report is:

- Current position
- Operational status
- Significant changes in weather, wind and sea

Example: "Coast Guard Station Neah Bay, this is Coast Guard Four Seven Three One Five. Operations normal. My position is one mile north of Tatoosh Island. Wind has increased to 25 knots, seas have increased to 6 feet. Over."

If a boat is unable to establish communications with its command, it should use alternate methods, this may include:

- Relaying information through another unit
- Using cellular telephones, if available
- Using the marine operator

Bridge-To-Bridge Communications Required

E.3. GENERAL

Coast Guard boats shall follow the requirements of the Bridge-to-Bridge Radiotelephone Act of 1971 ("bridge" meaning the bridge or conning station of a ship). This Act was written mainly for ships but the *Coast Guard Telecommunications Manual* discusses those requirements that apply to boats.

E.4. BRIDGE-TO-BRIDGE COMMUNICATIONS REQUIRED

Both the Radiotelephone Act and the *Telecommunications Manual* require the following boats to use Bridge-to-Bridge communications:

- Every buoy boat and aids-to-navigation boat, or any other boat 26 feet or greater in length, when operating in or near a channel or fairway and conducting operations likely to restrict or affect navigation.
- Every towing vessel 26 feet or greater in length while navigating.

E.5. OTHER USE CHANNEL 13

All other Coast Guard boats shall use Channel 13 for the exchange or monitoring of navigational information. This information includes only that necessary for mission requirements or necessary to assure safe navigation.

E.6. LIMITING TRANSMISSION POWER

For bridge-to-bridge communications, limit the transmission power to one watt or less except in the following situations, when use of more power may be considered:

- Any emergency situation
- When the vessel called fails to respond to a second call at low power
- When making a broadcast in the blind (e.g., rounding a bend in a river)

SECTION F

Emergency Voice Communications and Distress Signals

Overview

Introduction

Whether your are providing emergency assistance or in need of it yourself, your knowledge of the correct procedures and available equipment can save lives.

In this section

Topic	See Page(s)
Standard Voice Radio Urgency Calls	213–15
Emergency Position-Indicating Radiobeacon (EPIRB) and Emergency Locator Transmitter (ELT)	215–16
Global Marine Distress and Safety System (GMDSS)	216
Distress Signals	217–18

Standard Voice Radio Urgency Calls

F.1. GENERAL

When an emergency occurs, use the proper prowords to show the degree of urgency. Hearing one of these urgency calls should trigger specific responses in a listener, such as, preparing to collect information on an emergency or refraining from transmitting on the frequency until all is clear. The meaning of each urgency call is outlined below.

F.2. MAYDAY

MAYDAY is a distress call of the highest priority. Spoken three times, it shows that a person, boat, or aircraft is threatened by grave or imminent danger and requires immediate assistance. Broadcast on 2182 kHz or Channel 16.

PRIORITY A MAYDAY call has absolute priority over all other transmissions and shall not be addressed to a particular station.

STATION RESPONSES All units hearing a MAYDAY call should immediately cease transmissions that may interfere with the distress traffic, and continue to listen on the distress message's frequency.

NOTE

If the unit transmitting the distress call is determined to be some distance from you, pause a few moments to allow ships or stations nearer the scene to answer.

NOTE

When working a distress situation on Channel 16, do not attempt to change (shift) to a working channel until enough information is obtained to handle the distress in case communications are lost during the act of shifting.

F.3. PAN-PAN

Broadcast on 2182 kHz or Channel 16, this urgency signal consists of three repetitions of the group of words "PAN-PAN" *(PAHN-PAHN)*. It means that the calling station has a very urgent message to transmit concerning the safety of a ship, aircraft, vehicle, or person.

F.4. SECURITÉ

"SECURITÉ" *(SEE-CURE-IT-TAY)* is a safety signal spoken three times and transmitted on 2182 kHz on Channel 16. It indicates a message on the safety of navigation, or important weather warnings will be transmitted on 2670 kHz or Channel 22.

F.5. RADIO ALARM SIGNAL

The radio alarm signal consists of two audible tones of different pitch sent alternately, producing a warbling sound. If used, the alarm continuously sends the signal for not less than 30 seconds or more than one minute, and the recipient of the signal should follow the signal by the radio distress signal and message. There are two primary reasons to use a radio alarm signal:

- To attract the attention of listeners on the frequency
- To actuate the automatic listening devices found on large ships and occasionally at shore stations

F.6. RECEIPT OF DISTRESS MESSAGES

When a distressed unit is in your vicinity, acknowledge receipt of the message immediately. However, if the unit is determined to be some distance from you, pause a few moments to allow ships or stations nearer the scene to answer. In the areas where communications with one or more shore stations are practicable, ships should wait a short period of time to allow them to acknowledge receipt.

RECEIPT PROCEDURE The receipt of distress messages should be acknowledged in the following manner.

- The distress signal MAYDAY
- The call sign of the unit in distress (spoken three (3) times)
- The words THIS IS (spoken once)
- The call sign of your unit (spoken three (3) times)
- The words RECEIVED MAYDAY
  Use SAR Incident check-off sheet

  Request essential information needed to effect assistance, (position, number of people on board, nature of distress, vessel's description) obtain less important information in a later transmission.
- The proword OVER.

INFORM DISTRESSED UNIT OF CG ASSISTANCE Inform THE DISTRESSED UNIT of any Coast Guard assistance being dispatched and to stand by.

VESSEL AND SHORE STATIONS Vessels and shore stations receiving distress traffic should by the most rapid means:

- Forward the information to the Operations Center (OPCEN).
- Set a continuous radio watch on frequencies of the distress unit.
- Maintain communications with the distressed unit.
- Maintain distress radio log.
- Keep the OPCEN informed of new developments in the case.

- Place additional people on watch if necessary.

- Obtain radio direction finder bearing of distressed unit if equipment and conditions permit.

TRANSMIT INFORMATION Every Coast Guard ship or aircraft which acknowledges receipt of distress messages, ensuring it will not interfere with stations in a better position to render immediate assistance, shall on the order of the Commanding Officer or Officer-in-Charge, transmit as soon as possible the following information to the unit in distress:

- Acknowledgment of unit's name and position

- Speed of advance of assisting unit to scene

- Estimated time of arrival at scene

KEEPING DISTRESSED UNIT INFORMED Keep the distressed unit informed of any circumstances that may affect your assistance to him such as speed, sea conditions, etc. Speak in a tone of voice that expresses confidence. After receiving a distress call or information pertaining to one, Coast Guard units shall, within equipment capabilities, set a continuous radio guard on the frequency of the distressed unit and set up a radio schedule if the distressed unit is unable to stand a continuous watch.

> **CAUTION!**
> Needless shifting of frequencies by you or the distressed unit may end in a loss of communications.

Emergency Position-Indicating Radiobeacon (EPIRB) and Emergency Locator Transmitter (ELT)

F.6. GENERAL

The emergency position-indicating radio beacon (EPIRB) is carried on vessels to give a distress alert. Aircraft have a similar device called an emergency locator transmitter (ELT). Originally, EPIRBs and ELTs transmitted on 121.5 MHz. However, newer devices operate on 406.025 MHz so COSPAS-SARSAT satellites can detect distress alerts. A global satellite detection network, COSPAS-SARSAT, has been established for detecting both 121.5 and 406 MHz distress beacons. (See Figure 11-2.) The 121.5 MHz can be detected by facilities that tune onto that frequency, typically aircraft and their support facilities. Coast

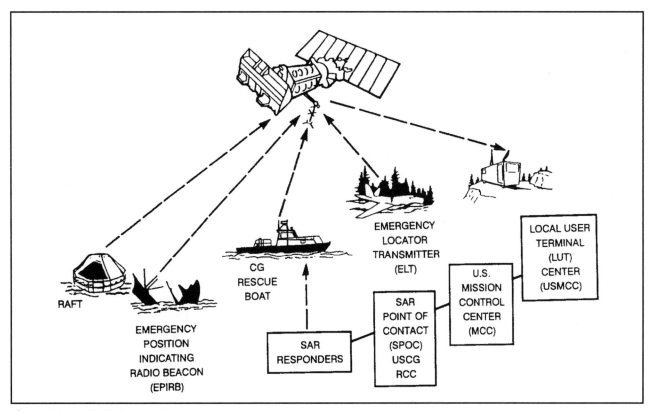

Figure 11-2 EPIRB System Operation

Guard boats carry the 406 MHz EPIRB. Requirements to carry EPIRBs vary:

- All Coast Guard cutters and most boats have been equipped.
- Optional for Coast Guard Auxiliary vessels.
- Encouraged for recreational vessels.
- Required for U.S. commercial vessels and many commercial fishing vessels.

NOTE

Additional information on EPIRBs, ELTs, and the COSPAS-SARSAT system, are found in Chapter 3 of the *National Search and Rescue Manual, Volume I.*

F.7. TYPES OF EPIRBS

There are two main types of EPIRBs.

- 121.5 MHz
- 406 MHz

121.5 MHZ These beacons transmit anonymously and generate positions accurate to within about 15 nautical miles. 121.5 MHz coverage is limited by the locations of sites selected for ground stations. 121.5 MHz beacons are plagued by a high false alarm rate. 121.5 MHz EPIRBs are categorized as follows:

- Class A 121.5 MHz EPIRBs are designed to float free and may be activated automatically or manually.
- Class B 121.5 MHz EPIRBs must be manually activated.

406 MHZ The EPIRB transmits a digital signal with a beacon-unique identifier. Owner registration allows automatic distressed vessel identification and provides case prosecution critical information. 406 MHz EPIRBs generate positions accurate to within about three nautical miles. 406 MHz EPIRBs have a 121.5 MHz homing signal and strobe. The false alarm rate is much lower for 406 MHz EPIRBs and registration makes it possible to identify false alarms, often before resources launch. 406 MHz EPIRBs are categorized as follows:

- Category I 406 MHz EPIRBs are designed to float free and may be activated automatically or manually.
- Category II 406 MHz EPIRBs must be manually activated.

F.8. EPIRB TESTING

Different models exist, so test your EPIRB by following manufacturer instructions printed on the beacon. Any test emitting a 121.5 MHz signal must be performed within the first five minutes after the hour and be limited to not more than ten seconds.

Global Marine Distress and Safety System

F.9. GENERAL

The Global Marine Distress and Safety System (GMDSS) was developed mainly for larger vessels. However, there will be times when boats have to respond and assist these vessels or to contact them. GMDSS has three key elements which assist SAR:

- Reliable timely distress alerting
- Accurate position indicating, and
- Efficient locating (visual and electronic)

F.10. GMDSS SYSTEM CONCEPT

GMDSS relies on ship-to-shore as well as ship-to-ship distress alerts by satellites and land based radio systems. GMDSS defines four worldwide sea areas and requires ships to have two of the following means to send a distress message:

- 406 MHz EPIRB
- Satellite communications (SATCOM)
- HF voice radio
- Error correcting teletype
- Digital selective calling capability

F.11. DIGITAL SELECTIVE CALLING (DSC)

Once GMDSS becomes fully operational after 1 February 1999, GMDSS-equipped ships do not have to maintain a live radio watch on Channel 16, VHF-FM. The ship will rely upon digital selective calling (DSC), an automated non-voice feature, to advise the crew of an incoming call. The ship would then communicate on a working frequency. For now, there is no requirement that all VHF-FM radios must have the DSC feature installed. This could create a problem for vessels without DSC to contact GMDSS-equipped vessels. The U.S. is developing additional guidance to address this concern.

Distress Signals

F.12. GENERAL

If voice communication is not possible or not effective, you will have to use other means of communication. These may include signals using pyrotechnics, flag hoist signals, hand signals, or a flashing light S-O-S (see Figure 11-3). These signals can be found in the publication called *Navigation Rules*.

F.13. PYROTECHNICS

The following are some pyrotechnic emergency signals you may encounter:

- Gun or explosive signal fired at about one minute intervals

- Red or orange flare fired one at a time in short intervals

- Rocket parachute showing a red light

- Smoke

- Any flame on a vessel may be used for signaling

F.14. FLAG HOISTS

Flag hoists are a quick way of emergency signaling, but can only be used in the daytime. These are some of the best known examples:

- A square flag with a ball, or ball-shaped object above or below the flag

- Hoisting an orange flag

- November Charlie Flag

Figure 11-3 Distress Signals

F.15. HAND SIGNALS

Possibly the oldest form of signaling are hand signals, but like other methods of visual communications, the signals are not standardized and can be easily misunderstood. Boat crew members must be constantly alert for hand signals from other mariners that are not standard distress signals, but that may be attempts to indicate an emergency situation. These are three standard hand signals that are used as distress signals:

- Slowly raising and lowering an outstretched arm
- Signaling with an oar raised in the vertical position
- Holding a life jacket aloft

F.16. FLASHING LIGHT/ STROBE (50–70/MIN.)

The Morse Code symbols 'SOS' (Save Our Ship) transmitted by a flashing light may be used to communicate distress.

S O S

● ● ● — ● ● ●

a strobe light (may be attached to a personal flotation device).

NOTE

Any unusual signal or action you see could be a signal that a craft is in trouble. You should investigate any peculiar or suspicious signals such as, the U.S. flag flown upside down or continuous sounding of a horn or fog signaling device.

SECTION G

Radio Checks

G.1. GENERAL

Radio checks test the signal strength and readability of transmitted radio signals. Checks are a simple way to determine that the radio used to send and receive messages is working properly. This is accomplished by transmitting a request for a radio check and receiving a response from any other station that provides a standardized description of the strength and readability of a transmitted signal. If you are ever in doubt about the readability of the signal you are sending out, you should initiate a radio check to confirm the strength and readability of your signal.

G.2. REPORTING PROCEDURES

Any station transmitting voice traffic assumes that its signal is clearly readable unless another station responds and reports that the signal strength and readability is less than loud and clear. If you respond to requests for a radio check, always be concise and use a combination of the following standard terms.

Signal Strength

"LOUD": means your signal is strong.

"GOOD": means your signal is readable.

"WEAK": means your signal is poor but readable.

"VERY WEAK": means your signal is unreadable.

Signal Readability

"CLEAR": means excellent signal quality.

"READABLE": means satisfactory quality.

"DISTORTED": means having difficulty in reading the transmission because of signal distortion.

"UNREADABLE": means the quality of your transmission is so bad I can not understand you.

"WITH INTERFERENCE": means having great difficulty in reading the transmission because of interference.

Weather and Oceanography

Editor's Note: *The study of weather and the water environment has long been the basic stuff of the mariner's kit. To the extent you master these subjects, they will not be able to master you. It's usually fun to be on the water, but any patch of water can turn into a hostile place in a matter of minutes given the right (or wrong) set of conditions. A late afternoon squall line, for example, can turn a gentle summer breeze into a 40-knot blow almost instantaneously. Coastal fog can drop like a curtain, leaving you stranded in a busy commercial channel waiting for the bows of a freighter to punch out of the mist. Most of the terrors that come with severe weather can be avoided if you understand its genesis. And just as important, you are better equipped to deal with weather challenges when they cannot be avoided if you understand their nature. Understanding the weather and the sea is what this chapter is about. You'll find the rules of thumb for spotting deteriorating weather conditions particularly valuable.*

Overview

Introduction

Boat crews operate in constantly changing environments. Weather and sea conditions interact causing many different types of situations. It is important to understand these conditions and how to operate in them. The information in this chapter will concentrate on the effects the environment has on the water and the problems these effects can cause. It will not provide an explanation of advanced meteorology or oceanography.

Wind, fog, rain, and cold temperatures (sea and air) can be very dangerous. Any of these phenomena can complicate the simplest mission, not only increasing the danger, but also lessening the survival probability of persons in distress.

Effects of wind, current, and tide can also dramatically affect a boat's behavior. A coxswain must understand how outside influences cause the boat to react in different ways.

In this chapter

Section	Title	See Page(s)
A	Weather	219–26
B	Oceanography	226–33

Weather

Overview

Introduction

One of the greatest hazards to the boat crew occurs when its members must work close inshore or in heavy weather. The waves, seas, and surf can present the greatest challenges to seamanship and survival skills. Your operating area of responsibility (AOR) will provide its own unique weather characteristics. Some major distinct conditions occur in various regions of the United States in predictable patterns. For example:

- *Bermuda High.* A semi-permanent high pressure area off of Bermuda. It affects the general wind circulation and the weather of the East Coast, especially summer heat waves.

- *Santa Ana Wind.* On the southern California coast, a dry, warm wind that blows through a pass and down the Santa Ana valley. It may blow so strongly that it threatens small craft near the coast.

- *Taku Wind.* A strong east-northeast wind in the vicinity of Juneau, Alaska, between October and March that can threaten small craft near the coast. It sometimes reaches hurricane force at the mouth of the Taku River.

In this section

Wind

A.1. GENERAL

High winds account for considerable destruction in the marine environment every year. Everyone knows water seeks its own level; the same is true with air. Air tends to equalize its pressure by flowing from a high-pressure area to a low-pressure area, producing wind.

A.2. AFTERNOON WIND INCREASES

Members of the boating public often get underway in the calm waters of the cool early morning. By afternoon, when they try to get home, the bay or ocean is so choppy that they may find themselves in need of assistance. The wind changes so drastically because the sun warms the Earth. The land warms faster than the surface of the water and radiates heat to the overlying air, warming it. This warm air rises, reducing the atmospheric pressure in the local area. The air offshore over the ocean is cool, and cool air is dense and heavy.

The cool air from offshore flows inland in an attempt to equalize the pressure differential caused by the rising warm air. This flow produces wind known as sea breeze. After sunset, the inland area cools more quickly than the water, and the wind diminishes.

Sea breezes typically reach their highest speeds during the period of maximum heating (i.e., during mid-afternoon). In some areas a land breeze can be established late at night or early in the morning. For this breeze to occur, the sea surface temperature must be higher than the air temperature over land, along with weak winds prior to the breeze.

NOTE

Wind direction is the compass heading from which the wind blows.

A.3. BEAUFORT WIND SCALE

The Beaufort Wind Scale (Figure 12-1) numbers define a particular state of wind and wave. The scale allows mariners to estimate the wind speed based on the sea state.

NOTE

The Beaufort Scale extends to force 18. For boat operating purposes, Figure 12-1 is limited to force 10.

A.4. WEATHER WARNING SIGNALS

The National Weather Service provides radio weather broadcasts. Although no longer required to be displayed, various shore activities may still use a system of flag and light signals to announce weather warnings. These weather warnings and their flags and lights signals are summarized below.

Storm Warnings	Winds	Day Signal On Shore	Night Signal On Shore
Small craft advisory (conditions dangerous to small craft operations)	Up to 33 knots	Red pennant	Red-over-white light
Gale	34–47 knots	Two red pennants	White-over-red lights
Storm	48–63 knots	Square red flag with black center	Two red lights
Hurricane	64 knots and above	Two square red flags with black centers	Three vertical lights—red, white, red

Figure 12-1 Beaufort Wind Scale

Beaufort Scale	Wind Speed (knots)	Indications	Approximate Wave Height (feet)	(meters)	Davis Sea State
0	calm	Mirror like.	0	0	0
1	1–3	Ripples with appearance of scales.	0.25	0.1	0
2	4–6	Small wavelets that do not break. Glassy appearance.	0.5–1	0.2–0.3	1
3	7–10	Large wavelets. Some crests begin to break. Scattered whitecaps.	2–3	0.6–1	2
4	11–16	Small waves becoming longer. Fairly frequent whitecaps.	3.5–5	1–1.5	3
5	17–21	Moderate waves. Pronounced long form. Many whitecaps.	6–8	2–2.5	4
6	22–27	Large waves begin to form. White foam crests are more extensive. Some spray.	9.5–13	3–4	5
7	28–33	Sea heaps up. White foam from breaking waves begins to blow in streaks along the direction of the waves.	13.5–19	4–5.5	6
8	34–40	Moderately high waves of greater length. Edges of crests break into spindrift foam blown in well marked streaks in the direction of the waves.	18–25	5.5–7.5	6
9	41–47	High waves. Dense streaks of foam. Sea begins to roll. Spray affects visibility.	23–32	7–10	6
10	48–55	Very high waves with over-hanging crests. Foam in great patches blown in dense white streaks. Whole surface of sea takes on a white appearance. Visibility affected.	29–41	9–12.5	7

Thunderstorms and Lightning

A.5. THUNDERSTORMS

Thunderstorms have violent vertical movement of air. They usually form when air currents rise over locally warmed areas or a cold front forces warm moist air aloft. Thunderstorms are dangerous not only because of lightning, but also because of the strong winds and the rough, confused seas that accompany them. Sharp intermittent static on the AM radio often indicates a thunderstorm.

A.6. LIGHTNING

Lightning is a potentially life-threatening phenomenon associated with some storms. Not all storms are thunderstorms, but all thunderstorms have lightning. Lightning occurs when opposite electrical charges within a thundercloud, or between a cloud and the earth, attract. It is actually a rapid equalization of the large static charges built up by air motion within the clouds. Lightning is very unpredictable and has immense power. A lightning "bolt" usually strikes the highest object on the boat, generally the mast or radio antenna. A mast with a full grounding harness affords excellent protection.

GROUNDING SYSTEMS Coast Guard standard boats have a **grounding system** (most commercially available vessels do not). A boat can minimize being struck by lightning by staying in port (assuming there are higher objects about) during thunderstorms and by installing a grounding system similar to those found on buildings and other land structures. The grounding system provides a path for lightning to reach ground without causing damage to property or injury to personnel. Figures 12-2 and 12-3 show the lightning-protected zones for a motorboat and a sailboat. Figure 12-4 shows how a grounding system can be installed on a boat.

NOTE

A grounding system on a boat provides lightning with a path to reach the water without causing severe damage or injury. Despite the high number of boats on the water, reports of lightning strikes on boats are rare.

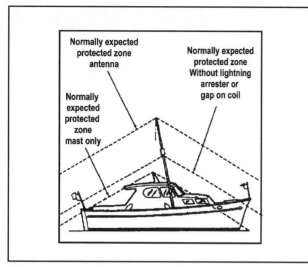

Figure 12-2 Lightning Protected Zone on a Motorboat

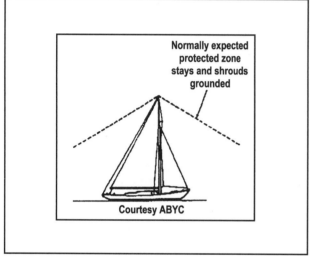

Figure 12-3 Lightning Protected Zone on a Sailboat

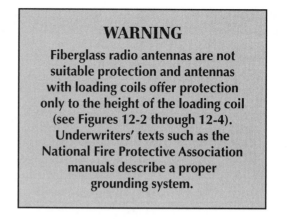

A.7. DISTANCE FROM A THUNDERSTORM

The boat's distance from a thunderstorm can be estimated by knowing it takes about five seconds for the sound of thunder to travel each mile.

- Observe the lightning flash.
- Count the number of seconds it takes for the sound of its thunder to arrive.
- Convert to miles by dividing the number of seconds by 5.

NOTE

Counting "one thousand one, one thousand two, one thousand three, one thousand four, one thousand five" will aid you in correctly counting seconds.

A.8. SAFETY

If caught in a lightning strike area, head for shore or the nearest shelter. While underway, stay

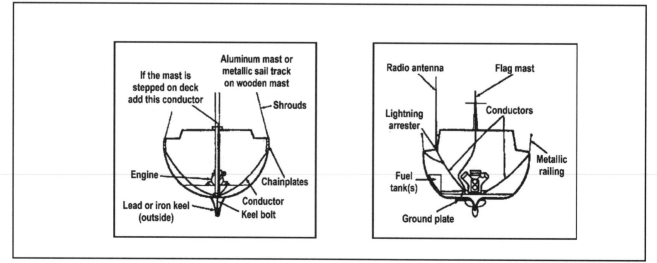

Figure 12-4 Grounding System on a Sailboat and a Motorboat

inside the boat, keep crew members low, and stay dry. Avoid touching metal, such as metal shift and throttle levers and metal steering wheels. Avoid contact with the radio. If lightning strikes, expect your compass to be inaccurate and onboard electronics to suffer extensive damage.

A.9. WATERSPOUTS

A **waterspout** is a small, whirling storm over water or inland waters. There are two types of waterspouts:

- violent convective storms over land moving seaward (tornadoes), and
- storms formed over sea with fair or foul weather (more common than tornadoes).

Waterspouts develop as a funnel-shaped cloud and when fully developed extend from the water's surface to the base of a cumulus cloud. The water in a waterspout is mostly confined to its lower portion. The air in waterspouts may rotate clockwise or counter-clockwise, depending on the manner of formation. Waterspouts vary in diameter, height, strength and duration and are found most frequently in tropical regions.

NOTE

While waterspouts are found more frequently in tropical areas, they are not uncommon in higher latitudes.

Fog

A.10. GENERAL

Fog is a multitude of minute water droplets hanging in the atmosphere, sufficiently dense to scatter light rays and reduce visibility. Fog makes locating anything more difficult, and also makes the voyage to and from the scene more hazardous.

A.11. ADVECTION FOG

The most troublesome type of fog to mariners is **advection fog**. Advection means horizontal movement. This type of fog occurs when warm air moves over colder land or water surfaces. The greater the difference between the air temperature and the underlying surface temperature, the denser the fog. Sunlight hardly affects advection fog. It can occur during either the day or night. An increase in wind speed or change in direction may disperse advection fog; however, a slight increase in wind speed can actually make the fog layer thicker.

A.12. RADIATION (GROUND) FOG

Radiation fog occurs mainly at night with the cooling of the earth's surface and the air, which is then cooled below its dew point as it touches the ground. It is most common in middle and high latitudes, near the inland lakes and rivers which add water vapor to the fog. It clears slowly over water because the water warms less from night to day than does land. Sunlight burns off radiation fog.

A.13. FOG FREQUENCY

Pacific Coast fog appears most frequently in areas from the northern tip of Washington State to around Santa Barbara, California. Atlantic Coast fog is most common from the northern tip of Maine to the southern tip of New York. Fog appears, on the average, more than 10% of the time in these waters. Off the coasts of Maine and Northern California it averages more than 20%. The fog frequency near Los Angeles, California, on the other hand, is about three times that of Wilmington, North Carolina.

A.14. OPERATING IN FOG

When operating in fog, slow down to allow enough time to maneuver or stop (i.e., operate your boat at a safe speed). When engaged in towing extra caution should be exercised. Display the proper navigation lights and sound appropriate sound signals. Employ all available navigation aids.

Station a lookout well forward and away from the engine sounds and lights to listen and look for other signals. *Navigation Rules* requires the use of a proper lookout. Besides listening for other boats, the lookout should listen for surf in case the navigational plot is incorrect. If the facility has dual steering stations, one inside and one exposed, use the exposed one in restricted visibility conditions. Being outside allows the lookout or operator the best chance to hear dangers to the boat.

NOTE

Consider anchoring to await better visibility, especially if transiting congested areas or narrow channels. Remember, fog increases the chance of a collision or grounding.

Figure 12-5 *Generalized Weather Indicators*

Condition	Deteriorating Weather	Impending Precipitation	Clearing Weather	Continuing Fair Weather	Impending Strong Winds
CLOUDS					
Clouds lowering and thickening	X				
Puffy clouds beginning to develop vertically and darkening	X				
Sky is dark and threatening to the west					X
Clouds increasing in numbers, moving rapidly across sky	X				X
Clouds moving in different directions at different heights	X				X
Clouds moving from east or northeast toward the south	X				
Transparent veil-like cirrus clouds thickening; ceiling lowering		X			
Increasing south wind with clouds moving from the west		X			
Cloud bases rising			X		
Rain stopping, clouds breaking away at sunset			X		
Clouds dotting afternoon summer sky				X	
Clouds not increasing, or instead decreasing				X	
Altitude of cloud bases near mountains increasing				X	
SKY					
Western sky dark and threatening	X				
A red sky in morning	X				X
Red western sky at dawn		X			
Gray early morning sky showing signs of clearing			X		X
Red eastern sky with clear western sky at sunset				X	
Clear blue morning sky to west				X	
PRECIPITATION					
Heavy rains occurring at night	X				
Rain stopping, clouds breaking away at sunset			X		
Temperatures far above or below normal for time of year	X				
A cold front passing in the past four to seven hours (in which case the weather has probably already cleared)			X		

Figure 12-5 *Generalized Weather Indicators*

Condition	Deteriorating Weather	Impending Precipitation	Clearing Weather	Continuing Fair Weather	Impending Strong Winds
FOG, DEW, AND FROST					
Morning fog or dew			X		
Early morning fog that clears				X	
Heavy dew or frost				X	
No dew after a hot day		X			
WIND					
Wind shifting north to east and possibly through east to south	X				
Strong wind in morning	X				
Increasing south wind with clouds moving from the west		X			
Gentle wind from west or northwest				X	
Bright moon and light breeze				X	
Winds (especially north winds) shifting to west and then to south		X			
BAROMETER					
Barometer falling steadily or rapidly	X				
Steadily falling barometer		X			
Barometer rising			X		
Barometer steady or rising slightly				X	
VISUAL PHENOMENA					
A ring (halo) around the moon	X				
Smoke from stacks lowers					X
Distant objects seeming to stand above the horizon		X			
If on land, leaves that grow according to prevailing winds turn over and show their backs					X
Halo around sun or moon		X			
Smoke from stacks rising			X		
Smoke from stacks lowering	X				
Bright moon and light breeze				X	
AUDIBLE PHENOMENA					
Very clear sounds that can be heard for great distances		X			
Dull hearing, short range of sound				X	
Static on AM radio	X				

Ice

A.15. GENERAL

Temperature and salinity govern the freezing point of water; however, winds, currents, and tides can slow the formation of ice by mixing in warmer water from below the surface. Fresh water freezes at 0°C/32°F, but the freezing point of seawater decreases because of salinity, the dissolved solid material in water often referred to as salt. Typically, seawater freezes at or below –1°C/30°F.

Shallow bodies of low-salinity water freeze more rapidly than deeper basins because a lesser volume must be cooled. Once the initial cover of ice has formed on the surface, no more mixing can take place from wind/wave action, and the ice will thicken. As a result, the first ice of the season usually appears in the mouths of rivers that empty over a shallow continental shelf. During the increasingly longer and colder nights of late autumn, ice forms along the shorelines as a semi-permanent feature and widens by spreading into more exposed waters. When islands are close together, ice can cover the sea surface between the land areas.

A.16. TOPSIDE ICING

One of the most serious effects of cold weather is that of topside icing, caused by wind-driven spray, particularly if the ice continues to accumulate. Ice grows considerably thicker because of splashing, spraying and flooding. It causes an increase in weight on decks and masts (the outer structure). It also produces complications with the handling and operation of equipment, it and creates slippery deck conditions. The ice accumulation causes the boat to become less stable and can lead to capsizing.

NOTE

The easiest and most effective way to minimize icing is to slow down.

NOTE

Ice can be broken away by chipping it off with mallets, clubs, scrapers, and even stiff brooms. Use special care to avoid damage to electrical wiring and finished surfaces.

Forecasting

A.17. GENERAL

Listening to either a news media broadcast meteorologist or NOAA Weather Radio, coupled with local knowledge, should make everyone safe weather-wise. However, many old common weather "thumb-rules" are often correct, but only with some basic weather knowledge and a tool (e.g., barometer or thermometer) with which to cross-check the belief.

A.18. WEATHER INDICATORS

Even experts are far from 100% correct. However, Figure 12-5 on pages 224–25 can assist in forecasting weather changes.

A.19. LOCAL CONDITIONS

Learn how conditions in your locality tend to vary because of nearby mountains, lakes, or oceans. The National Weather Service Table of Average Conditions, Figure 12-6, also can assist in forecasting weather conditions.

NOTE

Barometric pressure is in inches of mercury, corrected to sea level pressure. A rapid rise or fall in barometric pressure is defined as greater than or equal to 0.04 inches in three hours.

SECTION B

Oceanography

Introduction

Oceanography is a broad field encompassing the study of waves, currents, and tides. It includes the biology and chemistry of the oceans and the geological formations that affect the water. Boat crew members must have an appreciation of all these factors to safely operate in an ever-changing environment. Some major distinct conditions occur in various regions of the United States. For example:

- The freezing over of the Great Lakes.
- The *Gulf Stream*. A powerful, warm ocean current flowing along the East Coast. In the Straits of Florida, it greatly affects the speed of advance of vessels underway and drifting objects; off of Cape Hatteras, North Carolina, it "collides" with weather systems and can cause dangerous wave conditions.
- The West Coast, in general, has a narrow continental shelf (a gentle bottom slope) followed by a sharp drop into great ocean depth.

Figure 12-6 *National Weather Service Table of Average Conditions*

Wind Direction	Barometric Pressure	General Forecast
SW to NW	30.10 to 30.20—steady	Fair, with little temperature change for 1 to 2 days.
SW to NW	30.10 to 30.20—rising rapidly	Fair, with warmer weather and rain within 2 days.
SW to NW	30.20 or above—steady	Remaining fair with little temperature change.
SW to NW	30.20 or above—falling slowly	Fair and slowly rising temperature for about 2 days.
S to SE	30.10 to 30.20—falling slowly	Rain with 24 hours.
S to SE	30.10 to 30.20—falling rapidly	Rain within 12 to 24 hours. Wind will rise.
SE to NE	30.10 to 30.20—falling slowly	Rain within 12 to 18 hours. Wind will rise.
SE to NE	30.10 to 30.20—falling rapidly	Rain within 12 hours. Wind will rise.
SE to NE	30.00 or below—falling slowly	Rain will continue 1 or more days.
SE to NE	30.00 or below—falling rapidly	Rain with high winds in a few hours. Clearing within 36 hours—cooler in winter.
E to NE	30.10 or above—falling slowly	Summer: light winds and rain in 2 to 4 days. Winter: rain or snow within 24 hours.
E to NE	30.10 or above—falling rapidly	Summer: probable rain in 12 to 24 hours. Winter: rain and snow within 12 hours.
S to SW	30.00 or above—rising slowly	Clearing within a few a hours; then fair for several days.
S to E	29.80 or below—falling rapidly	Severe storm within a few hours; then clearing within 24 hours, colder in winter
E to N	29.80 or below—falling rapidly	Severe storm in few hours. Heavy rains or snowstorm, followed by colder air in winter.
Swinging	29.30 or below—rising rapidly	End of storm—clearing to West and colder.

In this section

Waves

B.1. GENERAL

By understanding how **waves** form and behave, boat crew members know what to expect and how to minimize danger to both boat and crew.

B.2. DEFINITIONS

The following definitions will help in understanding waves:

WAVES: Waves are periodic disturbances of the sea surface, caused by wind (and sometimes by earthquakes).

CREST: The top of a wave, breaker, or swell.

FOAM CREST: Top of the foaming water that speeds toward the beach after the wave has broken, popularly known as white water.

WAVE LENGTH: The distance from one wave crest to the next in the same wave group or series.

TROUGH: The valley between waves.

WAVE HEIGHT: The height from the bottom of a wave's trough to the top of its crest; measured in the vertical, not diagonal.

FETCH: The unobstructed distance over which the wind blows across the surface of the water.

SERIES: A group of waves that seem to travel together, at the same speed.

PERIOD: The time, in seconds, it takes for two successive crests to pass a fixed point.

FREQUENCY: The number of crests passing a fixed point in a given time.

WAVE REFRACTION: Refraction means bending. Wave refraction occurs when the wave moves into shoaling water, interacts with the bottom and slows. The first part of the wave slows, causing the crest of the wave to bend toward the shallower water. As a result the waves tend to become parallel to the underwater contours. The key to the amount of refraction that occurs is the bottom terrain. Refraction also can occur when a wave passes around a point of land, jetty, or an island.

While different segments of the wave travel in different depths of water, the crests bend and the waves change direction constantly. This is why wave fronts become parallel to the underwater contours and the shoreline, and why an observer on the beach sees larger waves coming in directly toward the beach while offshore they approach at an angle. Waves refracted off shoals can produce very dangerous seas. As the waves pass on each side of the shoal, they refract from their original line of travel toward each other. The angle where they meet behind the shoal produces a pyramid-type sea where the wave crests meet (see Figure 12-7).

WAVE REFLECTION: Any obstacle can reflect part of a wave. This includes under water barriers (e.g., submerged reefs or bars), although the main waves may seem to pass over them without change. These reflected waves move back towards the incoming waves. When the obstacles are vertical or nearly so, the waves may be reflected in their entirety.

INTERFERENCE: Waves refracted or reflected can interact with other waves. This action may increase or decrease wave height, often resulting in unnaturally high waves. Interference may even result in standing-wave patterns (waves that consis-

tently appear to peak in the same spot). Interference can be of particular concern because it may result in a boat being subjected to waves from unexpected directions and of unexpected size.

SWELL: Swells are the waves that have moved out of the area in which they were created. The crests have become lower, more rounded, and symmetrical. They can travel for thousands of miles across deep water without much loss of energy. Generally, a swell's direction of travel differs from the wind direction by at least 30°.

BREAKER: A breaking wave.

SURF: Several breakers in a continuous line.

SURF ZONE: The area near shore in which breaking occurs continuously in various intensities.

BREAKER LINE: The outer limit of the surf. All breakers may not present themselves in a line. Breakers can occur outside the breaker line and seem to come from nowhere.

COMBER: A wave on the point of breaking. A comber has a thin line of white water upon its crest, called feathering.

B.3. WAVE TYPES

The wind generates waves by moving over the water's surface. As wind speed increases white

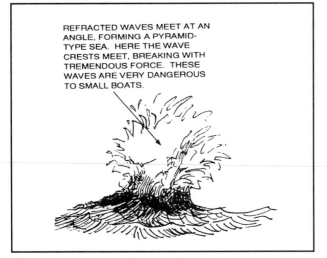

Figure 12-7 Wave Refraction

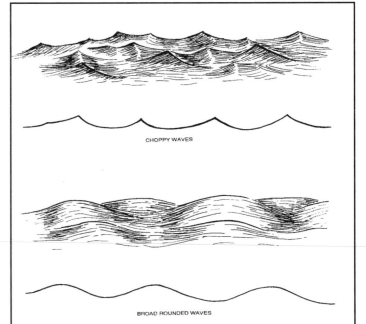

Figure 12-8 The Two Major Types of Waves

caps appear. As the wind continues, the waves become higher and longer. The Beaufort wind scale (see Figure 12-1) shows the size of waves in open water for a given wind strength. There are two major types of waves: the broad, rounded waves associated with deep water, and the more choppy waves found in shallow water (e.g., in bays and inland lakes) (see Figure 12-8).

B.4. BREAKING WAVES

Breaking waves are the most dangerous kind of wave for boat operations. How dangerous the wave is depends on the ratio of wave height to length, and on wave frequency. Steep sloped waves are the most dangerous. There are three main types of breaking waves: **plunging, spilling, and surging breakers**.

WARNING

A 6-meter/20-foot breaker will drop 1,362,000 kilograms/1,500 tons of water on a boat and can swamp and/or severely damage it.

PLUNGING WAVES Plunging waves result when there is a sudden lack of water ahead of the wave, such as in a steep rise of the ocean floor. This situation prevents the wave from traveling along, and causes the crest to be hurled ahead of the front of the wave and break with tremendous force (see Figure 12-9).

DEPTH IS EQUAL TO DISTANCE BETWEEN CRESTS

RAISES UP SUDDENLY AND BREAKS WITH TREMENDOUS FORCE

PLUNGING WAVES

SMALL CREST OF EVEN WHITE WATER BREAKING GENTLY

SPILLERS

Figure 12-9 Plunging and Spilling Waves

SPILLING BREAKERS Spilling breakers result from waves of low steepness moving over a gentle sloping ocean floor. They normally have a small crest of white water spreading evenly down the wave, and break slowly without violence (see Figure 12-9).

SURGING BREAKERS A surging breaker occurs on very steep beaches. The wave builds very quickly and expends its energy on the beach. It is very unlikely that you will encounter a surging breaker while aboard a boat unless you are beaching it on a very steep beach.

B.5. DEEP WATER WAVES

A **deep water wave** is a wind wave where the depth of the water is greater than one-half the wave length.

B.6. SHALLOW WATER WAVES

A **shallow water wave** travels in water where the depth is less than one-half the wave length. If the depth of water is small in comparison to the wave length, the bottom will change the character of the wave.

NOTE

As the waves travel out from their origin, they become swells developing into a series of waves equidistant apart which track more or less at a constant speed. Consequently, it is possible to time series of breakers.

B.7. WAVE SERIES

Wave series are irregular because of constant shifting of wind direction and speed. Storms at sea create masses of waves that build up in groups higher than other waves. Breakers vary in size and there is no regular pattern or sequence to their height. But while the space or interval between series of breakers may vary, the interval often is fairly regular. Breakers tend to stay the same for hours at a time.

The **height and period** of a wave depends on:

- The speed of the wind.
- The amount of time the wind has been blowing.
- The unobstructed distance over which the wind travels, known as fetch. Nearness to land will limit fetch, if the wind is blowing offshore.

NOTE

Tidal currents going against the waves will make the waves steeper.

The **lifecycle** of a wave consists of its:

• Generation by a wind.

• Gradual growth to maximum size.

• Distance traveled across the sea.

• Dissipation as wind decreases or when the wave impacts against the shore or an object.

B.8. SURF

Irregular waves of deep water become organized by the effects of the contact with the bottom. They move in the same direction at similar speeds. As the depth of water decreases to very shallow, the waves break and the crests tumble forward. They fall into the trough ahead usually as a mass of foaming white water. This forward momentum carries the broken water forward until the wave's last remaining energy becomes a wash rushing up the beach. The zone where the wave gives up this energy and the systematic water motions, is the **surf** (see Figure 12-10).

Sometimes there are two breaks of surf between the beach and the outer surf line. These breaks result from an outer sand bar or reef working against the wave causing the seas to pile up. The movement of water over such outer bars forms the inner surf belt as the water rolls toward the shore. The type of surf that forms around an inlet depends on the size of approaching swells and the bottom contours. Waves change in speed and shape as they approach shallow coastal waters. They become closer together (as their speed slows) and steeper as they contact the bottom. This change typically

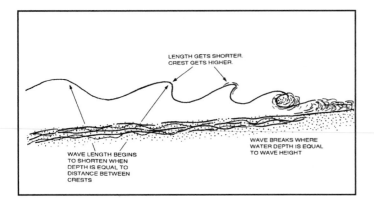

LENGTH GETS SHORTER. CREST GETS HIGHER.

WAVE BREAKS WHERE WATER DEPTH IS EQUAL TO WAVE HEIGHT

WAVE LENGTH BEGINS TO SHORTEN WHEN DEPTH IS EQUAL TO DISTANCE BETWEEN CRESTS

Figure 12-10 Surf

develops at a point where the water depth is approximately one half as deep as the wave' length.

The momentum caused by the breaking top of a wave will cause the water to fall ahead or curl because the water mass is not actually going forward. Momentum is what gives the curl of breakers its tremendous force.

NOTE

Operators can size up the surf situation by comparing the swell height and length with the water depth.

> **WARNING**
>
> **Stay out of the wave's curl. Coast Guard utility boat operations are not permitted in breaking surf or bar conditions. Auxiliarists are not authorized to operate in surf.**

Currents

B.9. GENERAL

Tide is the vertical rise and fall of the ocean water level caused by the gravitational attraction of the sun and moon. A **tidal current** is the horizontal motion of water resulting from the change in the tide. It is different from ocean currents, river currents, or those created by the wind. Tidal currents are of particular concern in boat operations.

NOTE

Current direction is the compass heading toward which the water moves.

B.10. FLOOD, EBB, AND SLACK CURRENTS

Flood current is the horizontal motion of water toward the land, caused by a rising tide. **Ebb current** is the horizontal motion away from the land, caused by a falling tide. **Slack water** is a period when current is changes direction. An outgoing or ebb current running across a bar builds up a more intense sea than the incoming or flood current. The intense sea results because the rush of water out against the incoming ground swell slows the wave speed and steepens the wave prematurely.

B.11. LONGSHORE CURRENTS

Longshore currents run parallel to the shore and inside the breakers. They are the result of the water transported to the beach by the waves.

> ## CAUTION!
> **Pay close attention to longshore currents—they can cause a boat to broach or the object of a search to move further than expected.**

B.12. EDDY CURRENTS

Eddy currents (eddies) occur at channel bends, near points of land, and at places where the bottom is uneven.

> ## CAUTION!
> **Watch for and avoid eddies—they can abruptly change speed and steering control of boats.**

B.13. WIND EFFECTS ON CURRENT

Wind affects the speed of currents. Sustained wind in the same direction as the current increases the speed of the current by a small amount. Wind in the opposite direction slows it down and may create a chop. A very strong wind, blowing directly into the mouth of an inlet or bay, can produce an unusually high tide by piling up the water. Similarly, a very strong wind blowing out of a bay can cause an unusually low tide and change the time of the high or low water.

B.14. EFFECTS ON BOAT SPEED

When going with the current, a boat's speed over ground is faster than the speed/rpm indication. When going against the current, a boat's speed over ground is slower than the speed/rpm indication.

B.15. EFFECTS ON BOAT MANEUVERABILITY

When working in current, the boat's maneuverability depends on its speed through the water. Although a boat has significant speed in relation to fixed objects (e.g., a pier) when going with the current, a boat lacks maneuverability unless there is sufficient water flow past the rudder. When going into the current, maneuverability is usually improved as long as enough headway is maintained. However, at slow speeds, even a small change in course can have the bow swing greatly as the water flow pushes on one side of the bow.

B.16. CROSSING THE CURRENT

When crossing the current to compensate for the set, a boat may be put into a **crab**, i.e., the boat may be forced off course by the current or wind. Because of this maneuver, the boat heading and the actual course made good will be different. When the boat is crabbing, the heading will not be the intended course of the boat. Therefore, navigate the current or wind by sighting on a fixed object (such as a range) or by marking the bearing drift on an object in line with the destination. Piloting in currents is covered in more detail in Chapter 14—Navigation.

B.17. TIDE AND TIDAL CURRENT CHANGES

The change of direction of the tidal current always lags behind the turning of the tide. This time difference varies according to the physical characteristics of the land around the body of water, as well as the bottom topography. For instance, with a straight coast and only shallow indentations, there is little difference between the time of high or low tide and the time of slack water. However, where a large body of water connects with the ocean through a narrow channel, the tide and the current may be out of phase by several hours. In a situation such as this, the current in the channel may be running at its greatest velocity when it is high or low water outside.

B.18. TIDAL CURRENT TABLES

When you are operating in tidal waters, it is important to know the set (direction toward) and drift (speed expressed in knots) of the tidal currents in the area. Obtain this information from the *Tidal Current Tables*. The National Ocean Survey (NOS) annually publishes the *Tidal Current Tables* (also available from International Marine/McGraw-Hill). It contains a table for reference stations and a table for subordinate stations.

TABLE 1 Table 1 lists the daily times of slack water and the times and velocities of maximum flood and ebb at the reference stations (see Figure 12-11).

TABLE 2 Table 2 includes the latitude and longitude of each subordinate station (and reference stations). It also includes the time and differences for slack water and maximum current, the speed ratios for maximum flood and ebb, and the direction and average speed for maximum flood and ebb currents (see Figure 12-12).

TIME AND SPEED Select the station closest to your area of concern. (Sometimes it may be a reference station which means no calculation is needed.) If you are using a subordinate station, apply its time differences to the time of slack and maximum current at the reference station to obtain the corresponding times at the subordinate station.

Calculate the maximum speed at the subordinate station, by multiplying the maximum speed at the reference station by the appropriate flood or ebb ratio.

Bay of Fundy Entrance (Grand Manan Channel), 1995

F–Flood, Dir. 032° True E–Ebb, Dir. 212° True

April

Day	Slack h m	Maximum h m	knots
1 Sa	0035	0345	3.1E
	0640	0940	3.0F
	1250	1555	2.8E
	1845	2150	3.2F
2 Su	0105	0415	3.0E
	0715	1010	3.0F
	1325	1625	2.6E
	1915	2220	3.1F
3 M	0130	0445	2.9E
	0745	1040	2.8F
	1355	1655	2.4E
	1945	2250	2.9F
4 Tu	0200	0515	2.7E
	0820	1110	2.6F
	1425	1725	2.1E
	2015	2320	2.6F
5 W	0225	0545	2.4E
	0850	1145	2.4F
	1455	1800	1.8E
	2050	2350	2.3F
6 Th	0255	0615	2.1E
	0925	1220	2.1F
	1535	1835	1.4E
	2125		
7 F		0030	2.0F
	0330	0655	1.8E
	1005	1305	1.8F
	1625	1920	1.1E
	2210		
8 Sa		0115	1.6F
	0420	0745	1.4E
	1100	1400	1.5F
◐	1730	2035	0.9E
	2320		
9 Su		0215	1.3F
	0525	0905	1.2E
	1210	1515	1.4F
	1900	2210	0.9E
10 M	0045	0340	1.2F
	0700	1035	1.3E
	1325	1640	1.5F
	2025	2330	1.3E
11 Tu	0210	0510	1.4F
	0825	1145	1.6E
	1435	1750	1.9F
	2120		
12 W		0025	1.8E
	0320	0620	1.8F
	0930	1245	2.0E
	1535	1845	2.4F
	2210		
13 Th		0115	2.3E
	0410	0710	2.4F
	1020	1330	2.5E
	1620	1930	2.9F
	2250		
14 F		0200	2.8E
	0455	0755	2.9F
	1105	1415	2.8E
	1705	2015	3.4F
	2330		
15 Sa		0240	3.3E
	0540	0840	3.3F
	1150	1455	3.1E
○	1750	2055	3.7F
16 Su	0005	0320	3.6E
	0620	0920	3.6F
	1230	1535	3.3E
	1830	2135	3.8F
17 M	0045	0400	3.7E
	0700	1000	3.7F
	1310	1615	3.3E
	1910	2215	3.8F
18 Tu	0125	0440	3.6E
	0745	1040	3.6F
	1355	1700	3.1E
	1955	2255	3.6F
19 W	0205	0520	3.4E
	0825	1125	3.4F
	1440	1745	2.8E
	2040	2340	3.2F
20 Th	0250	0605	3.1E
	0915	1210	3.1F
	1530	1835	2.4E
	2130		
21 F		0030	2.8F
	0340	0700	2.6E
	1005	1305	2.6F
◑	1630	1935	2.0E
	2225		
22 Sa		0125	2.3F
	0435	0800	2.2E
	1105	1405	2.3F
	1740	2045	1.7E
	2335		
23 Su		0230	1.8F
	0550	0915	1.9E
	1215	1520	2.0F
	1905	2205	1.8E
24 M	0055	0355	1.6F
	0715	1035	1.8E
	1325	1645	2.0F
	2020	2320	1.8E
25 Tu	0215	0520	1.7F
	0835	1145	1.9E
	1435	1755	2.2F
	2125		
26 W		0025	2.1E
	0320	0630	2.0F
	0940	1245	2.1E
	1535	1850	2.4F
	2210		
27 Th		0115	2.4E
	0415	0720	2.3F
	1030	1330	2.3E
	1625	1935	2.6F
	2255		
28 F		0200	2.6E
	0500	0805	2.5F
	1115	1415	2.5E
	1705	2015	2.8F
	2330		
29 Sa		0240	2.8E
	0540	0840	2.7F
	1155	1455	2.5E
●	1740	2050	2.9F
30 Su	0000	0315	2.9E
	0615	0910	2.8F
	1225	1530	2.5E
	1815	2120	2.9F

May

Day	Slack h m	Maximum h m	knots
1 M	0030	0345	2.8E
	0645	0945	2.8F
	1300	1600	2.4E
	1850	2150	2.8F
2 Tu	0100	0415	2.7E
	0720	1015	2.7F
	1330	1630	2.2E
	1920	2220	2.7F
3 W	0130	0445	2.6E
	0750	1045	2.6F
	1400	1705	2.0E
	1955	2255	2.5F
4 Th	0200	0515	2.4E
	0825	1120	2.5F
	1435	1735	1.8E
	2030	2330	2.3F
5 F	0235	0550	2.2E
	0900	1200	2.3F
	1515	1815	1.6E
	2110		
6 Sa		0010	2.1F
	0310	0635	1.9E
	0945	1245	2.1F
	1605	1905	1.4E
	2200		
7 Su		0100	1.8F
	0400	0725	1.7E
	1035	1335	1.9F
◐	1705	2015	1.3E
	2305		
8 M		0200	1.6F
	0505	0835	1.5E
	1135	1440	1.8F
	1815	2130	1.3E
9 Tu	0020	0310	1.5F
	0625	0955	1.5E
	1245	1555	1.9F
	1930	2240	1.6E
10 W	0135	0430	1.6F
	0745	1105	1.7E
	1355	1705	2.1F
	2035	2345	2.0E
11 Th	0240	0540	2.0F
	0855	1205	2.0E
	1455	1805	2.5F
	2125		
12 F		0040	2.4E
	0340	0640	2.4F
	0950	1300	2.4E
	1550	1900	2.9F
	2215		
13 Sa		0125	2.9E
	0430	0730	2.9F
	1040	1345	2.7E
	1640	1945	3.2F
	2300		
14 Su		0210	3.2E
	0515	0815	3.2F
	1130	1430	3.0E
○	1725	2030	3.5F
	2340		
15 M		0255	3.5E
	0600	0900	3.5F
	1215	1515	3.1E
	1810	2115	3.6F
16 Tu	0025	0340	3.6E
	0645	0945	3.6F
	1300	1600	3.1E
	1855	2200	3.5F
17 W	0105	0425	3.5E
	0725	1025	3.5F
	1345	1645	3.0E
	1940	2240	3.4F
18 Th	0150	0510	3.3E
	0810	1110	3.4F
	1430	1735	2.8E
	2030	2325	3.1F
19 F	0235	0555	3.0E
	0900	1200	3.1F
	1520	1825	2.5E
	2120		
20 Sa		0015	2.7F
	0325	0645	2.6E
	0950	1250	2.8F
	1615	1925	2.2E
	2215		
21 Su		0110	2.3F
	0425	0745	2.3E
	1045	1345	2.4F
◑	1720	2025	1.9E
	2320		
22 M		0210	1.9F
	0530	0850	1.9E
	1145	1450	2.1F
	1830	2135	1.8E
23 Tu	0030	0325	1.7F
	0645	1000	1.7E
	1250	1600	2.0F
	1940	2245	1.8E
24 W	0140	0440	1.6F
	0800	1105	1.7E
	1355	1710	2.0F
	2040	2345	1.9E
25 Th	0245	0550	1.8F
	0910	1205	1.8E
	1455	1810	2.1F
	2135		
26 F		0040	2.1E
	0340	0645	2.0F
	1005	1300	1.9E
	1545	1900	2.2F
	2220		
27 Sa		0125	2.3E
	0430	0730	2.2F
	1050	1345	2.0E
	1630	1940	2.3F
	2255		
28 Su		0210	2.4E
	0510	0810	2.3F
	1130	1425	2.0E
	1710	2020	2.4F
	2330		
29 M		0245	2.5E
	0545	0845	2.5F
	1205	1505	2.1E
●	1750	2050	2.5F
30 Tu	0005	0320	2.5E
	0620	0920	2.5F
	1240	1540	2.1E
	1825	2125	2.5F
31 W	0035	0350	2.6E
	0655	0955	2.6F
	1310	1615	2.1E
	1900	2200	2.5F

June

Day	Slack h m	Maximum h m	knots
1 Th	0105	0425	2.5E
	0725	1025	2.7F
	1345	1645	2.1E
	1935	2235	2.5F
2 F	0140	0500	2.5E
	0805	1105	2.7F
	1420	1725	2.0E
	2015	2315	2.4F
3 Sa	0215	0535	2.3E
	0840	1140	2.6F
	1500	1805	2.0E
	2100	2355	2.3F
4 Su	0300	0620	2.2E
	0925	1225	2.5F
	1545	1850	1.9E
	2150		
5 M		0045	2.2F
	0350	0710	2.0E
	1010	1315	2.4F
	1635	1945	1.8E
	2245		
6 Tu		0140	2.0F
	0445	0805	1.9E
	1105	1410	2.3F
◐	1735	2050	1.8E
	2345		
7 W		0240	1.9F
	0555	0910	1.8E
	1205	1515	2.2F
	1840	2155	1.9E
8 Th	0055	0350	1.9F
	0705	1020	1.8E
	1310	1620	2.3F
	1945	2300	2.1E
9 F	0200	0500	2.1F
	0820	1125	2.0E
	1415	1725	2.4F
	2045		
10 Sa		0000	2.4E
	0305	0605	2.4F
	0925	1230	2.2E
	1515	1825	2.7F
	2140		
11 Su		0100	2.7E
	0400	0705	2.7F
	1020	1325	2.5E
	1615	1920	2.9F
	2235		
12 M		0150	3.0E
	0455	0755	3.0F
	1115	1415	2.7E
	1705	2010	3.1F
	2325		
13 Tu		0240	3.3E
	0540	0845	3.3F
	1200	1505	2.9E
○	1755	2100	3.3F
14 W	0010	0325	3.4E
	0630	0930	3.5F
	1250	1550	3.0E
	1845	2145	3.3F
15 Th	0055	0410	3.4E
	0715	1015	3.5F
	1335	1640	3.0E
	1935	2230	3.2F
16 F	0140	0455	3.3E
	0800	1100	3.4F
	1420	1725	2.9E
	2020	2315	3.0F
17 Sa	0225	0545	3.0E
	0845	1145	3.2F
	1510	1815	2.7E
	2110		
18 Su		0005	2.8F
	0315	0630	2.7E
	0930	1230	3.0F
	1555	1905	2.4E
	2200		
19 M		0050	2.5F
	0405	0720	2.4E
	1015	1320	2.6F
◑	1650	2000	2.2E
	2250		
20 Tu		0145	2.1F
	0500	0815	2.0E
	1105	1410	2.3F
	1745	2055	1.9E
	2350		
21 W		0240	1.8F
	0605	0915	1.7E
	1200	1510	2.0F
	1845	2155	1.8E
22 Th	0055	0350	1.6F
	0715	1020	1.4E
	1300	1610	1.8F
	1945	2300	1.7E
23 F	0200	0500	1.5F
	0830	1125	1.4E
	1405	1715	1.7F
	2045		
24 Sa		0000	1.7E
	0300	0605	1.6F
	0930	1225	1.4E
	1505	1815	1.7F
	2135		
25 Su		0050	1.9E
	0355	0700	1.7F
	1025	1320	1.5E
	1600	1905	1.8F
	2225		
26 M		0140	2.0E
	0440	0745	2.0F
	1110	1405	1.6E
	1645	1950	2.0F
	2305		
27 Tu		0220	2.2E
	0520	0825	2.2F
	1150	1445	1.8E
●	1730	2030	2.1F
	2340		
28 W		0300	2.3E
	0555	0900	2.4F
	1220	1520	2.0E
	1810	2105	2.3F
29 Th	0015	0335	2.5E
	0630	0935	2.6F
	1255	1600	2.2E
	1845	2145	2.5F
30 F	0050	0410	2.6E
	0705	1010	2.8F
	1330	1635	2.3E
	1925	2220	2.6F

Time meridian 60° W. 0000 is midnight. 1200 is noon.

Figure 12-11 Table 1 of the Tidal Current Tables

TABLE 2 – CURRENT DIFFERENCES AND OTHER CONSTANTS

No.	PLACE	Meter Depth	POSITION Latitude	POSITION Longitude	Min. before Flood	Flood	Min. before Ebb	Ebb	Flood	Ebb	Minimum before Flood knots	Dir.	Maximum Flood knots	Dir.	Minimum before Ebb knots	Dir.	Maximum Ebb knots	Dir.
		ft	North	West	h m	h m	h m	h m			knots	Dir.	knots	Dir.	knots	Dir.	knots	Dir.
	BAY OF FUNDY Time meridian, 60° W					on Bay of Fundy Entrance, p.4													
1	Brazil Rock, 6 miles east of		43° 22'	65° 18'	−2 02	−2 00	−1 56	−2 00	0.4	0.4	0.0	− −	1.0	275°	0.0	− −	1.0	050°
6	Cape Sable, 3 miles south of		43° 20'	65° 38'	−3 02	−2 10	−1 21	−2 10	1.0	0.8	0.0	− −	2.2	275°	0.0	− −	2.0	095°
11	Cape Sable, 12 miles south of		43° 11'	65° 37'	−1 12	−1 00	−0 46	−1 00	0.7	0.7	0.0	− −	1.7	285°	0.0	− −	1.6	090°
16	Blonde Rock, 5 miles south of		43° 15'	65° 59'	−1 02	−0 50	−0 36	−0 50	0.9	0.8	0.0	− −	2.0	310°	0.0	− −	2.0	125°
21	Seal Island, 13 miles southwest of		43° 16'	66° 15'	−0 17	+0 10	+0 39	+0 10	1.1	0.7	0.0	− −	2.6	325°	0.0	− −	1.6	140°
26	Cape Fourchu, 17 miles southwest of		43° 34'	66° 24'	−0 38	+0 45	+0 44	+0 45	0.5	0.5	0.0	− −	1.2	355°	0.0	− −	1.2	145°
31	Cape Fourchu, 4 miles west of		43° 47'	66° 15'	−0 12	0 00	−0 09	0 00	0.9	0.7	0.0	− −	2.0	000°	0.0	− −	1.7	175°
36	Lurcher Shoal, 6 miles east of		43° 52'	66° 21'	+0 08	+0 30	+0 39	+0 30	0.9	0.8	0.0	− −	2.0	355°	0.0	− −	1.8	175°
41	Lurcher Shoal, 5 miles west of		43° 46'	66° 42'	+0 23	+0 30	−0 34	+0 30	0.6	0.7	0.0	− −	1.4	000°	0.0	− −	1.6	160°
46	Lurcher Shoal, 10 miles northwest of		43° 59'	66° 37'	−0 02	+0 30	+0 49	+0 30	0.8	0.5	0.0	− −	1.8	005°	0.0	− −	1.2	175°
51	Brier Island, 5 miles west of		44° 15'	66° 30'	+0 43	+0 50	+0 54	+0 50	1.2	1.0	0.0	− −	2.7	005°	0.0	− −	2.5	185°
56	Brier Island, 15 miles west of		44° 17'	66° 44'	−0 42	−0 15	+0 14	−0 15	0.6	0.5	0.0	− −	1.4	060°	0.0	− −	1.2	250°
61	Gannet Rock, 5 miles southeast of		44° 29'	66° 41'	+0 38	+0 30	−0 09	+0 30	1.1	1.6	0.0	− −	2.6	040°	0.0	− −	3.9	230°
66	Boars Head, 10 miles northwest of		44° 31'	66° 23'	+0 48	+0 55	+0 59	+0 55	0.8	0.8	0.0	− −	1.9	020°	0.0	− −	2.0	205°
71	Prim Point, 20 miles west of		44° 44'	66° 15'	+0 38	+0 45	+0 54	+0 45	0.7	0.6	0.0	− −	1.6	040°	0.0	− −	1.4	235°
76	Cape Spencer, 14 miles south of		44° 58'	65° 57'	+0 51	+0 55	+0 57	+0 55	0.7	0.7	0.0	− −	1.7	050°	0.0	− −	1.6	245°
81	BAY OF FUNDY ENTRANCE		44° 45.2'	66° 55.9'		Daily predictions					0.0	− −	2.3	032°	0.0	− −	2.4	212°
	MAINE COAST Time meridian, 75° W																	
86	Eastport, Friar Roads		44° 54'	66° 59'	0 00	0 00	0 00	0 00	1.2	1.2	0.0	− −	3.0	210°	0.0	− −	3.0	040°
91	Western Passage, off Kendall Head		44° 55.9'	67° 00.0'	+0 27	+0 11	+0 13	+0 40	1.4	1.3	0.0	− −	3.2	319°	0.0	− −	3.1	142°
96	Western Passage, off Frost Ledge		44° 57.9'	67° 01.9'	+0 33	+0 04	−0 16	+0 15	0.9	0.7	0.0	− −	2.1	330°	0.0	− −	1.7	150°
101	Pond Point, 7.6 miles SSE of		44° 20.1'	67° 30.2'	+0 13	−0 20	−1 93	−0 05	0.2	0.5	0.0	− −	0.5	015°	0.0	− −	1.2	215°
106	Moosabec Reach, east end		44° 31.71'	67° 34.36'	−2 45	−3 08	−3 13	−3 39	0.4	0.4	0.0	− −	1.0	110°	0.0	− −	1.0	258°
111	Moosabec Reach, west end		44° 31.25'	67° 39.00'	−1 43	−1 43	−2 00	−1 44	0.4	0.5	0.0	− −	1.0	092°	0.0	− −	1.2	253°
116	Bar Harbor, 1.2 miles east of <1>		44° 23.0'	68° 10.0'	− − −	+0 30	− − −	+0 48	0.1	0.3	0.0	− −	0.2	328°	0.0	− −	0.7	148°
121	Casco Passage, east end, Blue Hill Bay		44° 11.7'	68° 27.9'	−1 49	−1 44	−1 02	−1 58	0.3	0.3	0.0	− −	0.7	086°	0.0	− −	0.7	284°
126	Hat Island, SE of, Jericho Bay		44° 08.0'	68° 29.7'	−1 02	−0 35	−0 50	−1 20	0.4	0.5	0.0	− −	0.9	318°	0.0	− −	1.0	124°
131	Clam I., NW of, Deer I. Thorofare	14	44° 09.87'	68° 36.23'	−2 14	−0 15	−0 57	−2 46	0.1	0.1	0.0	− −	0.2	004°	0.0	− −	0.2	199°
136	Grog Island, E of, Deer Island Thorofare	14	44° 09.72'	68° 37.23'	−2 16	−2 22	−2 27	−3 31	0.1	0.1	0.0	− −	0.2	020°	0.1	302°	0.3	235°
141	Russ Island, N of, Deer Island Thorofare	14	44° 09.18'	68° 38.78'	−2 12	−2 10	−2 29	−3 16	0.2	0.2	0.0	− −	0.4	074°	0.0	− −	0.6	265°
146	Crotch Island—Moose Island, between <58>	14	44° 08.85'	68° 40.58'		Currents are unidirectional												
151	Isle au Haut, 0.8 mile E of Rich's Pt	11	44° 05'	68° 35'	−0 53	−1 07	−1 07	−1 19	0.6	0.6	0.0	− −	1.4	336°	0.0	− −	1.5	139°
	East Penobscot Bay																	
156	Mark Island, north of	14	44° 08.20'	68° 42.17'	−0 18	−1 01	−2 27	−0 22	0.1	0.2	0.0	− −	0.3	013°	0.1	300°	0.4	164°
161	Widow Island—Stimpson Island, between	14	44° 07.95'	68° 49.50'	−0 43	−0 49	+0 04	−1 08	0.3	0.2	0.0	− −	0.6	302°	0.0	− −	0.5	118°
166	Eagle Island, 0.4 nautical mile S of	14	44° 11.63'	68° 46.93'	−0 18	−0 55	−2 20	−1 46	0.4	0.4	0.2	030°	0.9	336°	0.3	050°	1.0	147°
171	Burnt Island—Oak Island, between	14	44° 11.47'	68° 49.13'	−0 18	−1 19	−2 22	−0 57	0.3	0.5	0.1	347°	0.7	290°	0.0	− −	1.0	098°
176	Butter I., 0.3 nautical mile SE of	14	44° 13.33'	68° 46.67'	−2 43	−2 14	−0 25	−1 36	0.1	0.3	0.0	− −	0.3	050°	0.1	150°	0.6	194°
						−1 31			0.1		0.2	032°						
						−0 23			0.2		0.4	077°						
181	Bradbury Island, ESE of	14	44° 14.03'	68° 44.07'	+0 11	−0 17	−0 53	−0 56	0.2	0.3	0.2	305°	0.5	025°	0.1	304°	0.7	225°
186	Compass Island, 0.4 nmi. ENE of	14	44° 13.00'	68° 51.33'	−1 44	−1 22	−1 25	−1 01	0.1	0.1	0.2	092°	0.3	015°	0.0	− −	0.3	175°
191	Scrag Island, 0.3 nautical mile SW of	14	44° 13.33'	68° 50.62'	−0 45	−0 27	−0 55	−0 55	0.2	0.1	0.0	− −	0.4	010°	0.1	078°	0.3	197°
196	Great Spruce Head Island, west of	14	44° 14.30'	68° 50.18'	−1 14	−0 04	−0 26	−1 19	0.2	0.1	0.0	− −	0.3	003°	0.0	− −	0.3	174°
201	Horse Head Island, 0.2 nmi. ENE of	14	44° 15.07'	68° 50.67'		See Rotary tidal currents, table 2.												
206	Pickering Island, NE end	14	44° 15.63'	68° 45.38'	−2 45	−1 37	−1 56	−2 37	0.2	0.2	0.2	203°	0.6	300°	0.3	201°	0.6	100°
211	Little Eaton Island, NNE of	14	44° 16.45'	68° 43.87'	−0 43	+0 12	+0 02	−0 19	0.2	0.1	0.0	− −	0.4	300°	0.2	224°	0.3	106°
216	Pickering Island, north of	14	44° 16.48'	68° 45.28'		See Rotary tidal currents, table 2.												
221	Hog Island, ESE of	14	44° 16.52'	68° 46.87'	−0 13	−0 02	−0 33	−0 51	0.1	0.2	0.0	− −	0.3	024°	0.2	105°	0.5	180°
226	Little Deer I.—Sheep I., between	14	44° 16.78'	68° 43.43'	−0 13	−0 37	+0 33	−0 52	0.2	0.2	0.1	231°	0.6	310°	0.0	− −	0.6	124°
231	Swains Ledge, WSW of	14	44° 16.90'	68° 45.28'		See Rotary tidal currents, table 2.												
236	Swains Ledge, 0.3 nautical mile SW of	14	44° 17.13'	68° 43.87'	−0 46	−0 22	−0 55	−1 07	0.2	0.2	0.0	− −	0.5	358°	0.0	− −	0.4	170°
241	Pond Island—Western Island, between	14	44° 17.58'	68° 49.00'	−1 44	−1 13	−1 56	−1 34	0.2	0.2	0.0	− −	0.4	356°	0.0	− −	0.6	172°

Figure 12-12 Table 2 of the Tidal Current Tables

CURRENT VELOCITY Flood direction is the approximate true direction toward which the flooding current flows. Ebb direction is generally close to the reciprocal of the flood direction. Average flood and ebb speeds are averages of all the flood and ebb currents. Use Table 3 in the *Tide Tables* to find the velocity of the current at a specific time.

ACTUAL VS. PREDICTED CONDITIONS NOS also publishes the *Tide Tables* for determining height and times of the tides. Procedures for determining tide heights are similar to those used for tidal current calculations. In using both the *Tide Tables* and the *Tidal Current Tables*, actual conditions frequently vary considerably from predicted conditions in the tables. Changes in wind force and direction, or variations in atmospheric pressure, produce variations in the ocean water level, especially the high-water height. The actual heights of both high-water and low-water levels are higher than the predicted heights with an on-shore wind or a low barometer. With a high barometer or off-shore wind, those heights usually are lower than predicted.

The actual times of slack or maximum current shown in the *Current Tables* sometimes differ from the predicted times by a half hour and occasionally by as much as an hour. However, a comparison between predicted and observed times of slack shows that more than 90 percent of slack water predictions are accurate to within half an hour. To get the full advantage of a favorable current or slack water, the navigator should plan to reach an entrance or strait at least half an hour before the predicted time of the desired current condition.

CHAPTER 13

Aids to Navigation

Overview

Introduction

This chapter introduces the aids to navigation (ATON) used in the United States. ATONs are devices or marks that assist mariners in determining their vessel's position or course or warn of dangers, obstructions, or regulatory requirements affecting safe navigation. In the U.S., the Coast Guard is responsible for servicing and maintaining ATONs under federal jurisdiction. This includes both short- and long-range navigation systems found in the navigable waters, along U.S. coasts, the Intracoastal Waterway (ICW) system, and the Western Rivers system.

Lakes and inland waterways that fall under state jurisdiction use the Uniform State Waterway Marking System (USWMS).

In this chapter

SECTION A

U.S. Aids to Navigation System

Overview

Introduction

Buoys, beacons and other short-range ATONs are used to guide mariners the same way signs, lane separations, and traffic lights are used to guide motor vehicle drivers. Together, these ATONs comprise the short-range ATON system, which uses charted reference marks to provide mariners with information required for navigating waterways safely. In the U.S., short-range aids conform to IALA Region B. This can be called System B, the U.S. Lateral System, or the U.S. Aids to Navigation System. The Coast Guard maintains short-range aids to provide:

- daytime visual system of daymarks, beacons and buoys;
- nighttime visual system of lights and retroreflective signals;

- radar system of radar reflectors and RACONs (radar beacons); and
- a sound system of various non-directional sound producing devices (not required by IALA).

Appendix A provides color representations of ATONs for the various U.S. system components and how they would appear on a nautical chart.

NOTE

"Natural ATONs" are charted prominent structures or landmarks that supplement the short-range ATON system. They are not a part of IALA System B, and are not a Coast Guard responsibility to service or maintain.

In this section

Lateral and Cardinal Significance

A.1. GENERAL

Prior to the mid-1970's, the world's nations employed over 30 different navigation systems. To reduce confusion, the International Association of Lighthouse Authorities (IALA) established two systems of buoyage for conveying navigation information to mariners—IALA System A and B. The U.S. complies with the IALA B system.

The IALA-A and IALA-B systems use the Lateral and Cardinal systems to define the conventions of buoyage and to mark channels with ATONs. "Lateral significance" or "cardinal significance" means that the rules for the Lateral or Cardinal System apply in that instance. But, if something has no lateral or cardinal significance, the respective system's rules do not apply to the situation. The differences between the markings and conventions used in the Lateral and Cardinal Systems are discussed in the following paragraphs. The following table briefly describes the IALA Systems A and B:

	IALA-A System	IALA-B System
Location	Europe, Africa, Australia, New Zealand and most of Asia	North and South America, Japan, South Korea, and the Philippines
Information shown by	Buoy shapes, colors, and if lighted, rhythm of flashes and colored lights	
Topmarks	Small distinctive shapes above the basic aid that assist in identification of the aid.	
Marks	Cardinal and lateral marks	Mostly lateral, some cardinal in the USWMS

Cardinal marks have black and yellow horizontal bands regardless of the IALA system.

When entering from seaward:

Keep Red Buoys to	Port	Starboard, "red-right-returning"
Keep Green Buoys to	Starboard	Port

A.2. LATERAL SYSTEM

In the Lateral System, buoys and beacons indicate the sides of the channel or route relative to a conventional direction of buoyage (usually upstream). They also mark junctions, a point where two channels meet for vessel is proceeding seaward; or bifurcations, a point where a channel divides for vessels proceeding from seaward, or the place where two tributaries meet.

In U.S. waters, ATONs use the IALA-B system of lateral marks with few exceptions (see Cardinal System), arranged in geographic order known as the "conventional direction of buoyage (CDB)." Use the "3R" memory aid—"Red, Right, Returning"—to orient yourself in the CDR. It applies when a vessel is returning from seaward, and means, when returning from sea, keep red markers to the right of the vessel. A vessel is considered to be returning when it is navigating from:

- north to south along the Atlantic Coast
- south to north and east to west along the Gulf Coast
- south to north and east to west along the Pacific Coast.
- east to west in the Great Lakes except for Lake Michigan which is north to south.

A.3. CARDINAL SYSTEM

The Cardinal System uses a buoy to indicate the location of a danger relative to the buoy itself. In the U.S., the Uniform State Waterway Marking System (USWMS) uses cardinal marks on waters where a state exercises sole jurisdiction. For instance, a white buoy with a black top indicates unsafe water to the south and west. Various countries throughout the world, including Canada, Bermuda, and the Bahamas, also use Cardinal marks along with Lateral marks. Cardinal marks are not used on waters where the U.S. Coast Guard maintains short-range ATONs.

General Characteristics of Short-Range ATONs

A.4. GENERAL

Aids to navigation have many different characteristics. An aid's color, size, light or sound signals signify what mariners should do when they encounter it. Characteristics of short-range aids used in the U.S. are described in the following paragraphs.

NOTE

While reading the following section, refer to Appendix A to see how the characteristics of color, numbering, lighting and light rhythms are used on ATONs to mark a waterway.

A.5. TYPE

The location and the intended use determine which one of the two types of ATON will be placed in a spot or waterway:

- floating (buoy); or
- fixed (beacon).

A.6. NUMBERING

Solid red ATON buoys and beacons bear even numbers and all solid green ATONs bear odd numbers. No other ATONs are numbered. When proceeding from seaward toward the direction of conventional navigation, the numbers increase. Numbers are kept in approximate sequence on both sides of the channel. Letters may be used to augment numbers when lateral ATONs are added to channels with previously completed numerical sequences. For instance, a buoy added between R"4" and R"6" in a channel would be numbered R"4A". Letters will also increase in alphabetical order.

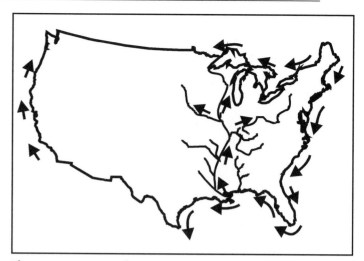

Figure 13-1 Proceeding From Seaward

NOTE

Preferred channel, safe water, isolated danger, special marks, and information/regulatory ATONs use only letters.

A.7. COLOR

During daylight hours, the color of an ATON indicates the port or starboard side of a channel, preferred channels, safe water, isolated dangers and special features. Only red or green buoys (or beacons fitted with red or green dayboards) have lateral significance.

A.8. SHAPE

Shapes of buoys and beacons help identify them from a distance or at dawn or dusk when colors may be hard to see. Like other characteristics of ATONs, mariners should not rely solely on shape to identify an aid.

CYLINDRICAL BUOYS (CANS) Cylindrical buoys, often referred to as "can buoys," are unlighted ATONs. When used as a lateral mark, they indicate the left side of a channel or of the preferred channel when returning from seaward. They are painted solid green or have green and red horizontal bands. The topmost band is always green. Can buoys are also used as unlighted special marks and will be colored based on their use. (See Figure 13-2.)

CONICAL BUOYS (NUN) Conical buoys, often referred to as "nun buoys," are unlighted ATONs. When used as a lateral mark, nun buoys indicate the right side of a channel or of the preferred channel when returning from seaward. They are painted solid red or red and green with horizontal bands. In this case, the topmost band is always red. Nun buoys are also used as unlighted special marks and will be colored based on their use. (See Figure 13-2.)

NOTE

Buoys other than a "can" and "nun" or buoys fitted with a top mark, such as isolated danger or safe-water buoys, have no shape significance. Their meanings are shown by numbers, colors, top marks, lights, and sound signal characteristics.

MISCELLANEOUS BUOYS The Coast Guard and other agencies place (station) specialty buoys for operational and developmental uses, and for research purposes. In many instances, the buoy used is a standard buoy modified for specialized use. There are several examples of specialty buoys:

- Fast water buoys
- Discrepancy buoys
- Weather/oceanographic buoys
- Mooring buoys

BEACONS Beacons have dayboards attached to a structure. When returning from sea, a triangular shaped dayboard marks the starboard side, and a rectangular shaped dayboard marks the port side of the channel. (See Figure 13-3.)

A nun buoy is prepared to be put on station.

A.9. LIGHT COLORS

Though you will see white and yellow lights, only ATONs with green or red lights have lateral significance. When proceeding in the conventional direction of buoyage, ATONs will display the following light colors.

GREEN Green lights mark port sides of channels and wrecks or obstructions. When proceeding from seaward, these aids are passed by keeping them on your port side. Green lights are also used on preferred channel marks where the preferred channel is to starboard. When proceeding along the conventional direction of buoyage (from seaward), a preferred channel mark fitted with a green light would be kept on your port side.

RED Red lights mark starboard sides of channels and wrecks or obstructions. When proceeding from seaward, these aids would be passed by keeping them on your starboard side. Red lights are also used on preferred channel marks where the preferred channel is to port. When proceeding along the conventional direction of buoyage (from

Figure 13-2 Can Buoy (left) Nun Buoy (right) "When Returning From Sea"

Figure 13-3 Daybeacon "When Returning From Sea"

seaward), a preferred channel mark fitted with a red light would be kept on your starboard side.

WHITE AND YELLOW White and yellow lights have no lateral significance. However, the characteristic (rhythm) of the light does give information such as safe water, danger, or special purpose. The publication called *Light List*, discussed in another section of this chapter, provides more details.

A.10. LIGHT SIGNALS

Lights are installed on ATONs to provide signals to differentiate one navigation light from another navigation light or from the general background of shore lights.

LIGHT CHARACTERISTICS Lights displayed from ATONs have distinct characteristics which help you identify them (see Figure 13-4). ATONs with lateral significance display flashing, quick, occulting or isophase light rhythms.

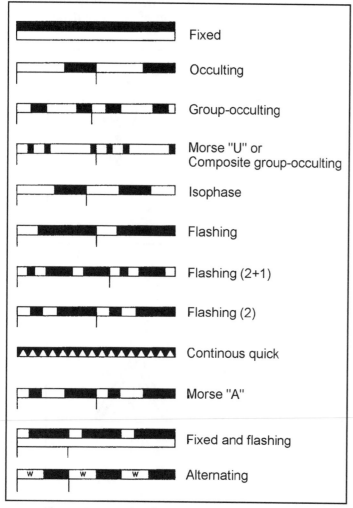

Figure 13-4 Light Characteristics

LIGHT IDENTIFICATION To identify a light, determine the following information:

COLOR: Color of the light beam (color of its lens).

CHARACTERISTIC: Pattern of flashes or eclipses (dark periods) observed from the start of the one cycle to the start of the next cycle.

DURATION: Length of time for the light to go through one complete cycle of changes.

Example: Buoy "8" displays one single flash of red every 4 seconds. That light color and rhythm information is indicated on the chart as shown below (it is underlined here for ease of identification; it is not underlined on a chart):
R"8"
Fl R 4s

A.11. SOUND SIGNALS

Though not a requirement of IALA B system, some ATONs in the U.S. have sound signals to provide information to mariners during periods of restricted visibility. Different types of devices are used to produce these sounds. Sound signals may be activated:

- continuously (bell, gong, or whistle buoy),
- manually,
- remotely, or
- automatically (when equipped with a fog detector).

Sound signals can be identified by their tone and phase characteristics. Horns, sirens, whistles, bells, and gongs produce distinct sound signals. The sound signal characteristics for specific ATONs are described briefly on the chart, and in detail in Column 8 of the *Light List*. Unless it is specifically stated that a signal "Operates Continuously" or the signal is a bell, gong, or whistle, signals will only operate in fog, reduced visibility, or adverse weather.

NOTE

A bell, gong or a whistle buoy may not produce a sound signal in calm seas.

NOTE

Distance and direction cannot be accurately determined by sound intensity. Occasionally, sound signals may not be heard in areas close to their location.

Device	Characteristic
Tone Characteristics	
Electronic horns	Pure tone
Sirens	Wail
Whistle buoys	Loud moaning sound
Bell buoys	One tone
Gong buoys	Several tones
Phase Characteristics	
Fixed structures	produce a specific number of blasts and silent periods every minute.
Buoys with a bell, gong, or whistle	are wave actuated and do not produce a regular characteristic.
Buoys with electronic horn	operate continuously.

A.12. RETROREFLECTIVE MATERIAL

Most minor ATONs (buoys and beacons) are fitted with retroreflective material to increase their visibility at night, especially if a searchlight is shined on them. The color of the reflective material is the same as the surface it covers (red has red, white has white material). All numbers and letters used on ATONs and the outline of daymarks are retroreflective.

Summary of Lateral Significance of Buoys and Beacons

A.13. GENERAL

While proceeding in the conventional direction of buoyage in IALA System B, you will see the following ATONs.

MEMORY AID

Red, Right, Returning.

A.14. MARKING STARBOARD SIDE

Red buoys and beacons with triangular shaped red dayboards mark the starboard side of a channel when you are returning from seaward. This is the "red-right-returning" rule. Keep ATONs displaying these characteristics to starboard when you are returning from seaward.

A.15. MARKING PORT SIDE

Green buoys and beacons with square shaped green dayboards mark the port side of a channel when you are returning from seaward.

A.16. MARKING CHANNEL JUNCTION OR BIFURCATION

Horizontally banded buoys and beacons—red over green, or green over red—are called preferred-channel marks. They indicate a channel junction or bifurcation, a point where a channel divides or where two tributaries meet. They may also mark wrecks or obstructions and may be passed on either side. When you are returning from sea, and the topmost band is:

- green, keep the aid to port to follow the preferred channel, or
- red, keep the aid to starboard to follow the preferred channel.

A.17. SAFE WATER MARKS

Safe Water Marks are buoys with alternating red and white vertical stripes, and beacons with red and white vertically striped dayboards (see Figure 13-5). They mark a mid-channel, fairway, channel approach points and the "In" and "Out" channels of a Traffic Separation Scheme. See buoy "N" in Figure 13-5. If lighted, safe water marks display a white light with the characteristic Morse Code "A." Lighted marks are fitted with a red sphere as a visually distinctive top mark. Safe water marks are not laterally significant.

Figure 13-5 Safe-Water Mark

A.18. ISOLATED DANGER MARKS

Black and red horizontally banded buoys are called "Isolated Danger Marks." They are used to mark isolated dangers (wrecks or obstructions) which have navigable water all around. Isolated danger marks display a white light with a "group-flashing" characteristic; and are fitted with a visually distinctive topmark, consisting of two black spheres, one above the other.

NOTE

This buoy marking system is not used in the Western River System.

A.19. SPECIAL MARKS

Yellow buoys and beacons are called "Special Marks." They mark anchorages, dredging/spoil areas, fishnet areas, and other special areas or features. When lighted, special-purpose marks display a yellow light with a Fixed ("F") or Flashing ("Fl") characteristic. Special marks also may be used to mark the center of the traffic separation scheme (see Figure 13-6).

A.20. MARKING REGULATED AREAS

Information and Regulatory buoys and beacons display various warnings or regulatory information. They are colored with white and orange shapes. (See Appendix A.) They will display only white lights and may display any light rhythm except "Quick Flashing."

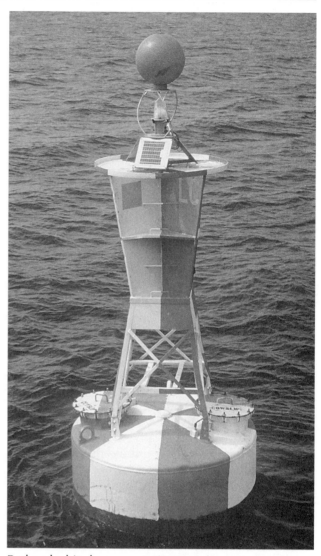

Red and white buoy on station.

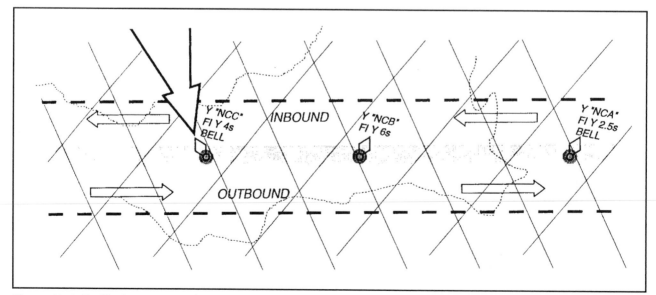

Figure 13-6 Traffic Separation Scheme

A.21. MARKING OUTSIDE NORMAL CHANNELS

Beacons with no lateral significance may be used to supplement lateral ATONs outside normal routes and channels. Daymarks for these aids are diamond shaped and will either be red and white, green and white, or black and white. (See Appendix A.)

Buoys

A.22. GENERAL

Buoys are floating ATONs anchored at specific positions for the guidance of mariners. The significance of an unlighted buoy can be determined by its shape. These shapes are only laterally significant when associated with laterally significant colors such as green or red. Buoys are useful ATONs, but should never be relied upon exclusively for navigation.

When a buoy is "watching properly" it is marking its charted position "on station" and properly displaying all other distinguishing characteristics. Heavy storms, collisions with ships, and severe ice conditions may move a buoy "off station." Heavy storms may also shift the shoal a buoy marks into the channel. Remember, even heavily anchored buoys fail.

NOTE

Remember the warning printed on nautical charts: "The prudent mariner will not rely solely on any single aid to navigation, particularly on floating aids."

NOTE

U.S. Coast Guard Regulations state: "Coxswains shall make every effort to observe and report any ATON that is out of order or off station within a unit's area of operations."

The crew of the Coast Guard Redwood prepares to bring a pillar buoy on deck.

A red pillar buoy on station.

Beacons

A.23. GENERAL

Beacons are fixed ATON structures that are attached directly to the earth's surface. The design, construction, and characteristics of these beacons depend on their location and relationship to other ATONs in the area. Strictly defined, a beacon is any fixed unlighted ATON (daybeacon) or minor light (lighted) ATON of relatively low candlepower. The following types of beacons are used in the U.S.:

- Daybeacons
- Lighted beacons (minor lights)
- Articulated lights
- Major lights
- Light towers

NOTE

Fixed aids (beacons) provide more accurate position information than floating aids (buoys).

A.24. DAYBEACONS

Daybeacons are unlighted fixed structures fitted with dayboards for daytime identification. Dayboards are fitted with retroreflective material to increase their visibility in darkness. They are mounted on different types of structures:

- Single pile with a dayboard on the top
- Multi-pile structure
- Tower
- Structure of masonry or steel

A.25. LIGHTED BEACONS (MINOR LIGHTS)

Just as daybeacons are sometimes substituted for unlighted buoys, lighted beacons are substituted for lighted buoys. Their structures are similar to daybeacons (see Figure 13-7). Lighted beacons are used with other lateral aids (buoys) marking a channel, river or harbor. In most instances, the lights have similar candlepower to those lights on buoys in the same area. Lighted beacons also are used to mark isolated dangers.

A.26. ARTICULATED LIGHTS

Articulated lights (beacons) are ATON structures in the water consisting of cylinders fixed to the bottom by sinkers. The cylinders are fitted with buoyant collars to keep them upright. The overall cylinder length is equal to the tidal range plus 10 to 15 feet. They are considered minor lights and fitted with the same signaling equipment as lighted beacons. When these structures are not fitted with lights, they are considered articulated daybeacons.

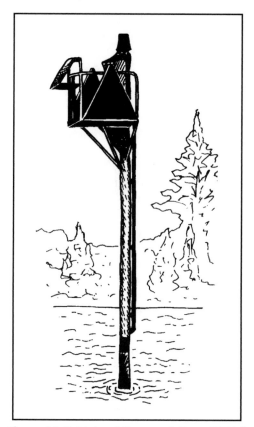

Figure 13-7 Lighted Beacon (Minor ATON)

A lighted daybeacon.

A.27. MAJOR LIGHTS

Major lights display a light of moderate to high candlepower. They may also be equipped with high-intensity audible signaling devices, radiobeacons and radar beacons (RACONs). Major light structures, lighthouses for instance, enclose, protect and house their signaling devices. Major light structures have visually distinctive appearances (see Figure 13-8). The designation of a light as "major" or "minor" depends on its candlepower and luminous range. Lights will be reclassified if they are refitted with higher or lower candlepower lights.

Major lights rarely have lateral significance and fall into two broad categories. They are used as "Coastal" or "Seacoast" lights and are often referred to as "Primary ATONs." They mark headlands and landfalls and are designed to assist vessels during coastal navigation or when approaching from seaward. They are also used as "Inland Major Lights" found in bays, sounds, large rivers, and coastal approaches. Inland major lights serve a variety of functions including:

- Obstruction mark
- Sector light
- Reference mark from which a visual bearing or range can be obtained

A.28. FEATURES

Major lights have the following additional features:

SECTOR LIGHTS Sector lights are sectors of color that are displayed on lantern covers of certain lighthouses to indicate danger bearings. Sector bearings are true bearings and are expressed as "BEARINGS FROM THE VESSEL TOWARDS THE LIGHT." A red sector indicates a vessel would be in danger of running aground on rocks or shoals while in the sector. Red sectors may be only a few degrees

in width when marking an isolated obstruction (see Figure 13-9).

EMERGENCY LIGHTS Reduced intensity emergency lights are displayed if the primary lights are extinguished. They may or may not have the same characteristics as the primary lights. The characteristics of emergency lights are listed in Column 8 of the *Light List* (see Figure 13-9).

A.29. LIGHT TOWERS

Light towers replaced lightships and are located in deep water to mark shoals and heavily traveled sea lanes. The foundation or legs of these towers are fixed to the bottom. They are equipped with signals comparable to major lights.

A.30. RANGES

Ranges are pairs of beacons located to define a line down the center of a channel or harbor entrance. They are usually lighted and arranged so that one mark is behind and higher than the other mark. When both markers of the range are in line, a vessel's position is along a known line of position. Ranges are located on specially built structures, existing ATON structures, or on structures such as buildings or piers. Ranges are found in entrance channels to harbors, piers, or successive straight reaches. Again, range marks are located so that when viewed from the channel the upper mark is

Figure 13-8 Lighthouse and Light Tower

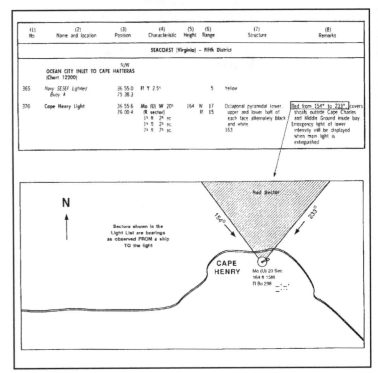

Figure 13-9 Sector Light

above and a considerable distance beyond the lower mark.

IF . . .	THEN . . .
the two marks are vertically aligned	the upper (rear) mark appearing directly above the lower (front) mark, the vessel is in the center of the channel (see Figure 13-10).
the upper mark is seen to the left of the lower mark,	the vessel is to the left of the center of the channel.
the upper mark is to the right of the lower mark	the vessel is to the right of the center of the channel.

CHARACTERISTICS Ranges are identified by rectangular daymarks that are striped in various colors. They are non-lateral ATONs and, when lighted, may display either red, green or white lights or combinations of the same. Consult the *Light List* for the light characteristics and color combinations displayed on the daymarks.

> **CAUTION!**
>
> The limits of a range can only be determined by checking the appropriate chart. They indicate a fairway or reach of the channel. On the chart, this area will be marked by a "Leading Line" (solid line). At a turn, the range will be marked by a spaced line (see Figure 13-10).

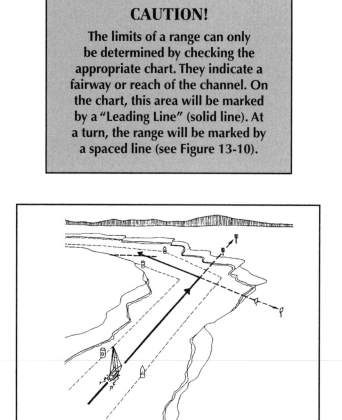

Figure 13-10 Using Range Lights

DIRECTIONAL LIGHTS Some structures are equipped with a directional light—a single light with a special lens that projects a narrow white light beam in a specific direction. On either side of the white beam is a red or green light. The width of the white sector varies with the location. The *Light List* and chart should be checked for specific information.

U.S. ATON System Variations

Introduction

Though the system of ATONs used in the U.S. and its territories consists of buoys and beacons conforming to IALA System B requirements; there are some variations in the U.S. waterways. See the following:

- Appendix A, page 421: How the Visual Guide Would Appear on a Nautical Chart.
- Appendix A, page 422: A Visual Buoyage Guide for System B.
- Appendix A, page 423: The U.S. Aids to Navigation System as Seen Entering From Seaward.
- Appendix A, page 424: Aids to Navigation Used on the *Western River System* and the *Uniform State Waterway Marking System*.

In this section

Intracoastal Waterway and Western Rivers

B.1. INTRACOASTAL WATERWAY

Extending some 2,400 miles along the Atlantic and Gulf coasts of the U.S., the Intracoastal Waterway (ICW) is a largely sheltered waterway suitable for year-round use. ATONs used to mark the ICW have the following characteristics:

- Special markings consisting of yellow squares and triangles are used so that vessels may readily follow the ICW.
- A yellow square indicates that the aid should be kept on the left side when traveling north-to-south or east-to-west.
- A yellow triangle indicates that the aid should be kept on the right side when traveling north-to-south or east-to-west.

The coloring, numbering, and conventional direction of buoyage conform to marks used in the U.S. ATON System with one exception—

- non-lateral aids in the ICW, such as ranges and safe-water marks, are marked with yellow horizontal bands.

B.2. WESTERN RIVERS

The "Western Rivers" marking system is used on the Mississippi River and tributaries above Baton Rouge, Louisiana, and certain other rivers which flow toward the Gulf of Mexico. The Western Rivers system varies from the U.S. ATON System in the following ways:

- Buoys are not numbered.
- Lighted beacons and daybeacons are numbered but have no lateral significance. (The numbers relate to the distance up or downstream from a given point in statute miles.)
- Red and green diamond-shaped daymarks as appropriate are used to indicate where the channel crosses from one side of a river to the other.
- Lights on green buoys and beacons are colored green or white (for crossings) and have a flashing (Fl) characteristic.
- Lights on red buoys and beacons are colored red or white (for crossings) and have a group flashing (Gp Fl) characteristic.
- Isolated danger marks are not used.

Uniform State Waterway Marking System

B.3. GENERAL

The Uniform State Waterway Marking System (USWMS) is designed for use by many types of operators and small vessels on lakes and inland waterways not shown on nautical charts. The conventional direction of buoyage in the USWMS is considered upstream or towards the head of navigation. This system has two categories of aids:

- In state waters outside of federal jurisdiction, a system of ATONs compatible with, and supplemental to the U.S. lateral system.
- System of regulatory markers that warn of danger or provide general information and directions (see B.6. below).

NOTE

USWMS marks may be used by the state or private individuals on waters where both state and federal governments have jurisdiction. These marks are classified as "Private" ATONs and require Coast Guard authorization prior to establishment. The location or characteristics of these marks are often found in the *Light List*.

B.4. USWMS VARIATIONS

There are three USWMS variations to the U.S. ATON System:

- On a well-defined channel, solid colored red and black buoys are established in pairs (gate buoys), marking each side of the navigable channel.
- The color black is used instead of green.
- The shape of the buoy has no significance.

B.5. USWMS CARDINAL MARKS

ATONs with cardinal marks may be used when no well-defined channel exists or when there is an obstruction whose nature and location allows it to be approached by a vessel from more than one direction. The USWMS provides for three aids with marks that have cardinal significance:

- A white buoy with a red top represents an obstruction and the buoy should be passed on the south or west.
- A white buoy with a black top represents an obstruction and the buoy should be passed to the north or east.
- A red and white vertically striped buoy indicates an obstruction exists between that buoy and the nearest shore.

B.6. USWMS REGULATORY MARKS

USWMS regulatory marks are white with two international orange horizontal bands completely around the buoy circumference. One band is near the top of the buoy while the second band is just above the waterline. Geometric shapes are placed on the buoy's body and are colored international

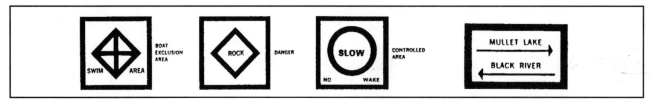

Figure 13-11 Regulatory Mark Information Mark

orange (see Figure 13-11). There are four basic geometric shapes authorized for these marks and each one has a specific meaning associated with it. These are:

- A vertical open-faced diamond shape means danger.

- A vertical open-faced diamond shape having a cross centered in the diamond means that vessels are excluded from entering the marked area.

- A circular shape indicates a control zone where vessels in the area are subject to certain operating restrictions.

- A square or rectangular shape is used to display information such as direction and/or distances to a location. (Information and regulatory marks can also be used in waters outside USWMS waters, e.g., federal channels which use the U.S. ATON system.)

NOTE

Regulatory marks are displayed on beacons as well as buoys.

B.7. USWMS MOORING BUOYS

Mooring buoys in USWMS are white with a horizontal blue band midway between the waterline and the top of the buoy, and display a slow-flashing white light when lighted. Mooring buoys in federal waters (U.S. ATON system) also display white with a horizontal blue band.

SECTION C

Short-Range Electronic Aids

C.1. GENERAL

Electronic systems are supplemental systems that are very useful when visibility is restricted or when mariners are beyond the sight of land. There are two commonly used types of short-range electronic aids to navigation:

- Radiobeacons
- Radar Beacon

NOTE

All navigation systems are not perfect, so a rhyme for the wise: "A mariner who relies solely on one navigation system, may soon find they are way off position."

C.2. RADIOBEACONS

Marine radiobeacons are the oldest electronic aids to navigation. They are homing beacons whose signals are received by radio direction finders. They transmit a distinctive Morse code radio signal in the low-to-medium frequency band of 285 to 325 kilohertz (kHz).

The location of radiobeacons is shown on nautical charts by the abbreviation "RBn" and a circle. The transmission characteristics of radiobeacons are found in the appropriate *Light List*.

Marine radiobeacons provide only bearing information to the transmitter site. These radiobeacons are being phased out by the Coast Guard. In the year 2000, the only remaining marine radiobeacons will be those used for transmitting Differential Global Positioning System (DGPS) corrections. (DGPS is discussed later in this chapter.)

C.3. RADAR BEACONS

RACON is an acronym for Radar Beacon. These beacons transmit a Morse Code reply when triggered by a boat's radar signal. This reply "paints" the boat's radar screen in the shape of dashes and dots representing a specific Morse Code letter, usually beginning with a dash. The "paint" signal appears on the radar screen showing the Morse Code signal beginning at a point just beyond the location of the RACON transmitter location and extending radially for one to two nautical miles.

Transmission characteristics of RACONs may be found in the appropriate *Light List*. RACONs are shown on nautical charts with the letters "RACON" and a circle. RACONs are more useful than radiobeacons because they provide information on both bearing and range to the transmitter site.

Radionavigation Systems

Overview

Introduction

Radionavigation systems are used by mariners for obtaining a position fix. Depending upon their range and accuracy, some systems can be used in the middle of an ocean or while entering a difficult harbor approach. All of the systems transmit a signal from a land or space-based transmitter to a shipboard receiver allowing mariners to determine their position. The most widely-used systems are Loran-C, the Global Positioning System (GPS), and the Differential Global Positioning System (DGPS).

In this section

Loran-C

D.1. GENERAL

Derived from the words LOng RAnge Navigation, Loran-C is a navigation system based on a network of transmitters consisting of one master station and two or more secondary stations. Loran-C is a pulsed, hyperbolic (uses curved lines) system. Loran-C receivers measure the Time Difference (TD) between the master transmitter site signal and the secondary transmitter site signal to obtain a single Line of Position (LOP). A second pair of Loran-C transmitting stations produces a second LOP. Plotting positions using TDs requires charts overprinted with Loran-C curves. However, many modern Loran-C receivers convert Loran-C signals directly into a readout of latitude and longitude. The mariner can use this information directly with a standard nautical chart without Loran-C curves.

D.2. ACCURACY

Loran-C is accurate to better than 0.25 nautical miles (NM) and available more than 99.9 percent of the time for each station. When used to return to a position with known TDs, Loran-C can produce an accuracy to within 20 meters (60 feet).

D.3. AREA COVERAGE

U.S. and Canadian coastal areas are covered by Loran-C transmitter sites controlled by the U.S. Coast Guard. Loran-C is used by other countries making coverage available for most of the North Atlantic, Europe, Mediterranean Sea, Japan, China, and Korea.

Global Positioning System (GPS)

D.4. GENERAL

The Global Positioning System (GPS) is a system of 24 satellites operated by the Department of Defense (DoD). It is available 24 hours per day, worldwide, in all weather conditions. Each GPS satellite transmits its precise location (position and elevation). In a process called "ranging," a GPS receiver on the boat uses the signal to determine the distance between it and the satellite. Once the receiver has computed the range for at least four satellites, it processes a three-dimensional position that is accurate to about 100 meters. GPS provides two levels of service—Standard Positioning Service (SPS) for civilian users, and Precise Positioning Service (PPS) for military users.

D.5. STANDARD POSITIONING SERVICE

The civilian SPS is available on a continuous basis to any user worldwide. It is accurate to a radius within 100 meters of the position shown on the receiver about 99 percent of the time.

D.6. PRECISE POSITIONING SERVICE

PPS provides positions fixes accurate to within 21 meters. This service is limited to approved U.S. Federal government, allied military, and civil users.

Differential Global Positioning System (DGPS)

D.7. GENERAL

The Coast Guard developed Differential Global Positioning System (DGPS) to improve upon SPS signals of GPS. It uses a local reference receiver to correct errors in the standard GPS signals. These corrections are then broadcast and can be received by any user with a DGPS receiver. The corrections are applied within the user's receiver, providing mariners with a position that is accurate within 10 meters, with 99.7 percent probability. While DGPS is accurate to within 10 meters, improvements to receivers will make DGPS accurate to within a centimeter, noise-free and able to provide real-time updates.

The Coast Guard uses selected marine radiobeacons to send DGPS corrections to users. DGPS provides accurate and reliable navigating information to maritime users in Harbor Entrance and Approach (HEA), along U.S. coastal waters, the Great Lakes, navigable portions of the western rivers, Puerto Rico, Hawaii, and Alaska.

Radionavigation System Summary

D.8. GENERAL

The following is a summary of the different long-range ATONs used by mariners.

The *Light List*

E.1. GENERAL

The *Light List* is a seven volume, annual publication providing information on ATONs maintained or authorized by the U.S. Coast Guard located on coastal and inland waters. The volumes cover the U.S. and its possessions, including the Intracoastal Waterway, Western Rivers, and the Great Lakes for both U.S. and Canadian waters. Each volume contains information on ATONs within its region maintained under the authority of the Coast Guard, including authorized private aids.

E.2. CONTENTS

This publication includes detailed descriptions of both short-range ATONs and radionavigation systems, complete lists of lights for the area, Loran-C chains not shown on a nautical chart, and more.

Summary of Radionavigation Systems

System Parameters	Loran-C	GPS	DGPS
Signal Characteristics	Pulsed Hyperbolic (curved line), operating in the 90 to 110 kHz range.	Messages broadcast from satellites on two L-band frequencies: L1, 1575.42 MHz & L2, 1227.6 MHz.	Data messages broadcast from radiobeacon sites in 283 kHz to 325 kHz frequency band.
Predictable Accuracy	0.25 NM	100 m	10 m
Availability	99%+	99%+	99.7%
Coverage	U.S. Coastal areas, selected overseas areas.	Worldwide	U.S. coastal waters, Great Lakes, western rivers, P.R., HI, and AK.
Reliability	99.7% (Triad reliability).	99.79%	99.7%
Fix Rate	13–20 fixes/in.	Continuous	Continuous
Integrity	Steady monitoring: "stations" blink notifies pair is unusable, and detects flaws.	None	Yes, site monitored.
Advantages	Monitored, excellent integrity; some charts overlay Loran lines.	Accurate; available—worldwide.	Extremely accurate and monitored.
Common Interference	Electromagnetic irregularities.	Shadows, signals blocked due to natural or man-made obstructions.	Shadows, signals blocked due to natural or man-made obstructions.

Caution: System specifications noted here may change at any time.

E.3. NUMBERING SEQUENCE

The aids in the *Light List* are listed so that seacoast aids appear first, followed by entrance and harbor aids from seaward to the head of navigation. *Light List* Numbers (LLNR) are assigned to aids for easy reference and appear in sequence from:

- north to south along the Atlantic Coast
- south to north and east to west along the Gulf Coast
- south to north along the Pacific Coast

E.4. GENERAL INFORMATION SECTION

The general information section offers information about the layout and organization of the *Light List*. It describes the U.S. system of ATONs and its characteristics, and provides a glossary of terms.

E.5. EXAMPLE OF USING THE *LIGHT LIST*

Determine the position and characteristic of Ocean City Inlet Jetty Light.

Take these steps to find this information in the *Light List*:

1. Use the *Light List* for that location (Volume II, Atlantic Coast).

2. Look up "Ocean City Inlet Jetty Light" in the index and note the LLNR. (See Figure 13-12). In this example, the LLNR is "230."

3. Find the correct page, listing LLNR 230. (See Figure 13-13.) Each ATON is listed numerically by LLNR.

4. Extract the information you need for the aid.

In this case, the position of the light is 38°19.5' N, 75°05.1' W; and the light characteristic is Isophase white 6 seconds. Note that across the top of each page is a column heading which explains the information listed in the column.

O	
Oak Creek	26205
Oak Island Channel	30415
Oak Island Light	810
Oak Island Radiobeacon	815
Occohannock Creek	21695
Occoquan River	18265
Ocean City Inlet	4720
OCEAN CITY INLET JETTY LIGHT	225
Ocean City Inlet Radiobeacon	230
Ocean City Inlet Lighted Bell Buoy 2	240
Ocean City Research Buoy	235
Ocean City Wreck Buoy WR2	245
OCEAN PINES YACHT CLUB	4925
Ocracoke Inlet	28895
Ocracoke Light	660

Figure 13-12 *Light List* Index

In this example, the Ocean City Inlet Jetty Light has what appears to be two LLNRs, 230 and 4485. Having two LLNRs means that this aid will be listed as a "seacoast" aid using LLNR 230 and again as a "harbor entrance" aid under Ocean City Inlet Jetty Light using LLNR 4485. Seacoast. ATONs are indexed in the beginning of the *Light List*.

E.6. CORRECTIONS

Corrections to *Light List* are made in the "Local Notice to Mariners" published by each Coast Guard district. These notices are essential for all navigators to keep their charts and *Light List*, current.

(1) No.	(2) Name and location	(3) Position	(4) Characteristic	(5) Height	(6) Range	(7) Structure	(8) Remarks
			SEACOAST (Maryland) – Fifth District				
	OCEAN CITY INLET TO CAPE HATTERAS (Chart 12200)						
225 4720	OCEAN CITY INLET JETTY LIGHT	38 19.5 75 05.1	Iso W 6ˢ	28	8	NB on skeleton tower.	HORN: 1 blast ev 15ˢ (2ˢ bl).
230 4725	**Ocean City Inlet Radiobeacon**	38 19.5 75 05.3	OC (--- --•••)		10		FREQ: 293 kHz. Antenna located on Ocean City Inlet Jetty Light.
235	Ocean City Research Buoy	38 20.8 75 01.1				Yellow.	Maintained by U.S. Army Corps of Engineers.

Figure 13-13 *Light List* Excerpt

CHAPTER

14

Navigation

Overview

Introduction

The art and science of navigation is an ancient skill. For thousands of years sailors navigated using the stars as their guides. In the distant past only a select few individuals were allowed access to the "mysteries" of navigation for possession of them gave one considerable power. A person who could safely follow the stars and navigate a ship— from one point to another—exercised significant influence over crew members who could not.

The art of navigation has expanded from using the stars and planets (celestial navigation) to the use of sophisticated electronic systems (electronic navigation). The safe and confident navigation of your boat is an absolute necessity, not only for the welfare of your fellow crew members, but also for the welfare of those you are sent to assist. Boat navigation falls into three major categories:

- Piloting: use of visible landmarks, aids to navigation (ATONs) and soundings.

- Dead Reckoning: use of a compass and a clock to set a true or magnetic course steering and, knowing speed, to determine distance and direction traveled from a known point or fix.

- Electronic Navigation: use of received radio signals to determine position. The most commonly used systems are Loran, GPS and radio direction finding.

As a coxswain, you are responsible for knowing the position of your boat at all times. Additionally, you have been entrusted with the safety of your boat, all crew members and people from distressed vessels.

Each crew member on a Coast Guard boat is a coxswain in training. If you are a crew member, you must learn all landmarks, charts and navigation aids used for the waters on which you are operating. Through experience, you will become proficient in the various skills necessary to perform any essential task in an emergency.

In this chapter

The Earth and Its Coordinates

Overview

Introduction

Navigation is concerned with finding your position and calculating distances measured on the surface of the earth which is a sphere. However, the earth is not a perfect sphere—the diameter through the equator is about 23 nautical miles longer than is the diameter through the North and South Poles. This difference is so small that most navigational problems are based on an assumption that the earth is a perfect sphere. Charts are drawn to include this slight difference. Distance is figured from certain reference lines. Your position at any given time, while underway, may be determined by your location relative to these lines as well as visible landmarks in your local area. You must know what these lines are and how to use them.

In this section

Lines and Circles

A.1. REFERENCE LINES OF THE EARTH

The earth rotates around an axis defined as a straight line drawn through the center of the earth. The axis line meets the surface of the earth at the

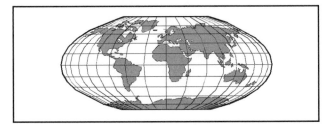

Figure 14-1 Earth with Reference Lines

North Pole and at the South Pole. To determine your location, a system of reference lines is placed on the surface of the earth as shown in Figure 14-1. This figure reveals the difficulty a boat navigator faces—the earth is curved as a sphere but navigation is typically done on a flat chart with straight reference lines running top to bottom and left to right.

A.2. GREAT CIRCLES

A great circle is a geometric plane passing through the center of the earth which divides the earth into two equal parts. A great circle always passes through the "widest" part of the earth. The equator is a great circle. All circles that pass through both the North and South Poles are great circles. The edge of a great circle conforms to the curvature of the earth. Just as if you look up at a full moon you see a circle.

NOTE

The earth's circumference is 21,600 nautical miles. You determine a degree of arc on the earth's surface by dividing the earth's circumference (in miles) by 360 degrees

---

CIRCLE PROPERTIES The outline of the moon also reveals another fact about great circles which is a property of all great circles: each circle possesses 360 degrees around its edge, which passes through a sphere so as to divide the sphere into two equal half-spheres. There are an infinite number of great circles on a sphere.

DEGREES Great circles have 360 degrees of arc. In every degree of arc in a circle there are 60 minutes. 60 minutes is equal to one degree of arc and 360 degrees are equal to a complete circle. When degrees are written, the symbol (°) is used.

MINUTES For every degree of arc, there are 60 minutes. When minutes of degrees are written, the symbol (') is used, 14 degrees and 15 minutes is written: 14°15'.

When written, minutes of degrees are always expressed as two digits. Zero through nine minutes are always preceded with a zero. Three minutes and zero minutes are written as 03' and 00' respectively.

SECONDS For every minute of arc, in a circle, there are 60 seconds of arc. 60 seconds is equal to one minute of arc and 60 minutes is equal to one degree of arc.

For every minute of arc there are 60 seconds. When seconds are written the symbol (") is used. 24 degrees 45 minutes and 15 seconds is written: 24°45'15".

When seconds are written they are always expressed as two digits. Zero through nine seconds are always preceded with a zero. Six seconds and zero seconds are written as 06" and 00" respectively.

Seconds may also be expressed in tenths of minutes. 10 minutes, 6 seconds (10'06") can be written and 10.1'.

The relationship of units of "arc" can be summarized as follows:

Circle = 360 degrees (°)

1 degree (°) = 60 minutes (')

1 minute (') = 60 Seconds (")

Parallels

A.3. GENERAL

Parallels are circles on the surface of the earth moving from the Equator to the North or South Pole. They are parallel to the Equator and known as Parallels of Latitude, or just latitude.

Parallels of equal latitude run in a West and East direction (left and right on a chart). They are measured in degrees, minutes, and seconds, in a north and south direction, from the equator. (0 Degrees at the equator to 90 degrees at each pole.)

The North Pole is 90 degrees North Latitude and the South Pole is 90 degrees South Latitude. The equator itself is a special parallel because it is also a great circle. One degree of latitude (arc) is equal to 60 nautical miles (NM) on the surface of the earth, one second (") of latitude is equal to 1 NM. The circumferences of the parallels decrease as they approach the poles. (See Figure 14-2.)

On charts of the northern hemisphere, True North is usually located at the top. Parallels are normally indicated by lines running from side to side and latitude scales are normally indicated along the side margins as shown in Figure 14-2.

A.4. TO MEASURE LATITUDE

To measure the latitudinal position of an object on a nautical chart follow this procedure:

1. Put one point of a pair of dividers on the parallel of latitude nearest to the object.

2. Place the other point of the dividers on the object.

3. Move the dividers to the nearest latitude scale, keeping the same spread on the dividers.

4. Place one point on the same parallel of latitude that you used before (step 1). The second point

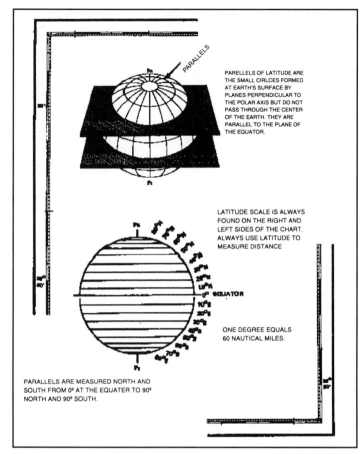

PARELLELS OF LATITUDE ARE THE SMALL CIRLCES FORMED AT EARTH'S SURFACE BY PLANES PERPENDICULAR TO THE POLAR AXIS BUT DO NOT PASS THROUGH THE CENTER OF THE EARTH. THEY ARE PARALLEL TO THE PLANE OF THE EQUATOR.

LATITUDE SCALE IS ALWAYS FOUND ON THE RIGHT AND LEFT SIDES OF THE CHART. ALWAYS USE LATITUDE TO MEASURE DISTANCE

ONE DEGREE EQUALS 60 NAUTICAL MILES.

PARALLELS ARE MEASURED NORTH AND SOUTH FROM 0° AT THE EQUATER TO 90° NORTH AND 90° SOUTH.

Figure 14-02 Parallels of Latitude

of the dividers will fall on the correct latitude of the object.

5. Read the latitude scale.

NOTE

- Always use the latitude scale to measure distance in navigation.

- A degree of latitude is measured "UP" or "DOWN."

NOTE

On a mercator projection chart (normally used for boat navigation), the scale varies along the latitude scale but will always remain accurate in relation to actual distance within the latitude bounded by that scale.

Meridians

A.5. GENERAL

A meridian is a great circle formed by a plane which cuts through the earth's axis and its poles. Such circles are termed meridians of longitude.

The meridian which passes through Greenwich, England, by international convention, has been selected as 000 degrees and is called the Prime Meridian. From this point, Longitude is measured both East and West for 180 degrees.

The 180 degree meridian is on the exact opposite side of the earth from the 000 degree meridian. The International Date Line generally conforms to the 180th meridian. The great circle of the Prime Meridian and the International Date Line divide the earth into eastern and western hemispheres.

A degree of longitude equals 60 miles at the equator and is undefined at the poles where all meridians meet. Meridians of Longitude run in a North and South direction (top to bottom on a chart) and are measured in degrees, minutes and seconds, East or West of the prime meridian at Greenwich. (See Figure 14-3.)

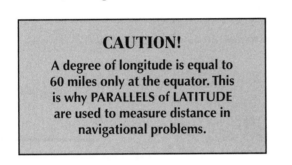

CAUTION!

A degree of longitude is equal to 60 miles only at the equator. This is why PARALLELS of LATITUDE are used to measure distance in navigational problems.

A.6. TO MEASURE LONGITUDE

To measure the longitude of an object on a nautical chart, follow the same procedures as in measuring a latitude position using the longitude scale.

A.7. RHUMB LINE

Typical boat navigation is done by plotting rhumb lines on a Mercator chart. A rhumb line is an imaginary line that intersects all meridians at the same angle. The rhumb line on the surface of a sphere is a curved line. On most nautical charts the rhumb is represented as a straight line.

A course line, such as a compass course, is a rhumb line which appears as a straight line on a mercator chart. Navigating with a rhumb line course allows the helmsman to steer a single compass course.

Chart Projections

A.8. GENERAL

For the purpose of coastal navigation, the earth is considered to be a perfect sphere. To represent the features of the earth's spherical surface on the flat surface of a chart, a process termed "projection"

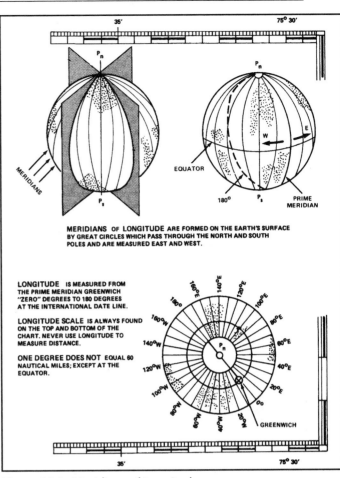

Figure 14-3 Meridians of Longitude

is used. Two basic types of projection used in making piloting charts are Mercator and Gnomonic.

A.9. MERCATOR PROJECTION

Mercator charts are the primary charts used aboard boats. A mercator projection is made by transferring the surface of the globe (representing the earth) onto the surface of cylinder.

The equator is the reference point for accomplishing the 'projection' from one geometric shape to another. The distinguishing feature of the mercator projection is that the meridians are projected so they appear to be equal distance from each other and parallel. (See Figure 14-4.)

NOTE

Only the latitude scale is used for measuring distance.

A.10. GNOMONIC PROJECTION

Gnomonic projections aid in long distance navigation by allowing navigators to use great circle courses. On this projection, meridians appear as

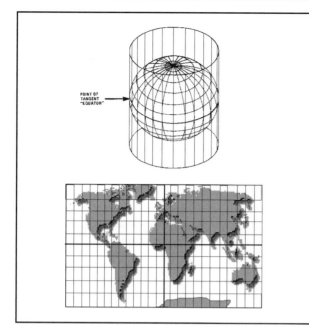

Figure 14-4 Mercator Projection

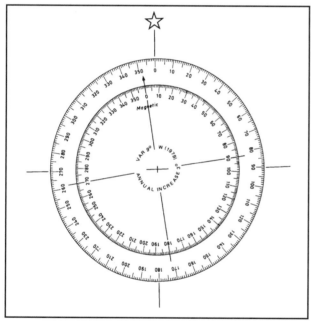

Figure 14-5 Compass Rose

straight lines that converge as they near the closest pole. The equator is represented by a straight line, all other parallels appear as curved lines.

NOTE

Gnomonic charts are not normally used for small boat navigation.

Nautical Charts

Overview

Introduction

The nautical chart is one of the mariner's most useful and most widely used national aids. Navigational charts contain a lot of information of great value to a boat coxswain.

In this section

The Compass Rose

B.1. GENERAL

Nautical charts usually have one or more compass roses printed on them. These are similar in appearance to the compass card and, like the compass card, are oriented with North at the top. Directions on the chart are measured by using the compass rose (see Figure 14-5). Direction is measured as a straight line from the center point of the circle to a number on the compass rose. Plotting the direction and explanation of the terms is discussed later.

B.2. TRUE DIRECTION

True direction is printed around the outside of the compass rose.

B.3. MAGNETIC DIRECTION

Magnetic direction is printed around the inside of the compass rose. An arrow points to magnetic North.

B.4. VARIATION

Variation, the difference between true and magnetic north, for the particular area covered by the

---

chart is printed in the middle of the compass rose along with any annual change.

Soundings

B.5. GENERAL

One of the more vital services a chart performs is to describe the bottom characteristics to a boat operator. This is accomplished through the use of combinations of numbers, color codes, underwater contour lines and a system of symbols and abbreviations.

B.6. DATUM

The nautical chart water depth is measured downward from sea level at low water (soundings). Heights or landmarks are given in feet above sea level. In the interest of navigation safety the mean, or average, of the lower of the two tides in the tidal cycle is used for soundings.

MEAN LOW TIDE Most of the numbers on the chart represent soundings of the water depth at Mean Low Tide. Datum refers to a base line from which a chart's vertical measurements are made.

MEAN LOW WATER On the East and Gulf Coasts the tidal datum is Mean Low Water (the average low tide). The tidal cycle on the East and Gulf Coasts produces tides approximately equal in highness and lowness (range).

AVERAGE LOW TIDE Since the greatest danger to navigation is during low tide, a number of the depths of low tide are averaged to produce the Average Low tide.

MEAN LOW WATER MARK On the Pacific Coast the datum is the mean lower low water mark. The reason for the mean lower of the two low tides being the West Coast datum is because their low tides can differ by several feet.

B.7. COLOR CODE

Generally, the shallow water is tinted darker blue on a chart, while deeper water is tinted light blue or white.

B.8. CONTOUR LINES

Contour Lines, also called fathom curves, connect points of roughly equal depth and provide a profile of the bottom. These lines are either numbered or coded, according to depth, using particular combinations of dots and dashes.

EQUATING DEPTH Depth of water may either be in feet, meters or fathoms (a fathom equals six feet). The chart legend will indicate which unit (feet, meters or fathoms) is used.

Basic Chart Information

B.9. GENERAL

The nautical chart shows channels, depth of water buoys, lights, lighthouses, prominent landmarks, rocks, reefs, sandbars and much more useful information for the safe piloting of your boat. The chart is the most essential part of all piloting equipment. Below are some basic facts you should know about charts:

- Charts usually are oriented with North at the top.
- The frame of reference for all chart construction is the system of latitude and longitude.
- Any location on a chart can be expressed in terms of latitude and longitude. (See Figure 14-6.)
- The latitude scale runs along both sides of the chart.

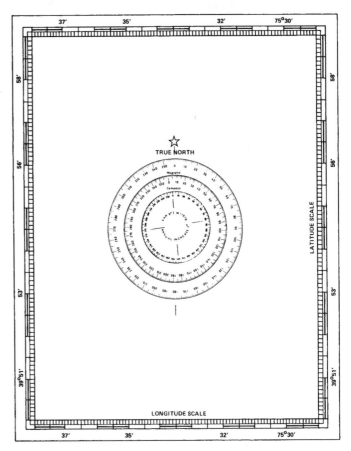

Figure 14-6 Chart Orientation

- The longitude scale runs across the top and bottom of the chart.
- Latitude lines are reference points in a North and South direction with the equator as their zero reference point.
- Longitude lines are the East and West reference points with the prime meridian as the zero point.

B.10. GENERAL INFORMATION BLOCK

The general information block (see Figure 14-7) contains these items:

- The chart title which is usually the name of the prominent navigable body of water within the area covered in the chart;
- A statement of the type of projection and the scale; and
- The unit of depth measurement (feet, meters or fathoms).

B.11. NOTES

Closely read the notes. They may contain information that can not be presented graphically, such as:

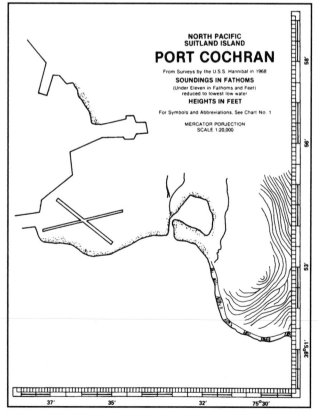

Figure 14-7 Title Block of a Chart

- The meaning of abbreviations used on the chart;
- Special notes of caution regarding danger;
- Tidal information; and
- Reference to anchorage areas.

B.12. EDITION NUMBER

The edition number of a chart and latest revisions tell you when information on the chart was updated.

- The edition number and date of the chart is located in the margin of the lower left hand corner.
- The latest revision date immediately follows in the lower left hand corner below the border of the chart. Charts show all essential corrections concerning lights, beacons, buoys and dangers which have been received to the date of issue.

Corrections occurring after the date of issue are published in the Notice to Mariners and must be entered by hand on the chart of your local area upon receipt of the notice.

Scale of the Nautical Chart

B.13. GENERAL

The scale of a nautical chart is a ratio. It compares a unit of distance on the chart to the actual distance on the surface of the earth.

For example: The scale of 1:5,000,000 means that one of some kind of measurement of the chart is equal to 5,000,000 of the same kind of measurement on the earth's surface. For example, one inch on the chart would equal 5,000,000 inches on the earth's surface. This would be a *small scale*, chart, since the ratio 1/5,000,000 is a very small number.

NOTE

Navigate with the *largest* scale chart available.

Large scale chart represents a smaller area than does a *small scale* chart. There is no firm separation between large scale and small scale. Remember "large scale—small area," and "small scale—large area."

For example: The scale of 1:2,500 (one inch on the chart equals 2,500 inches on the earth's surface) is a much larger number and is referred to as a large scale chart.

B.14. SAILING CHARTS

Sailing Charts are produced at scales of 1:600,000 and smaller. They are used in fixing the mariners position for approach to the coast from the open ocean or for sailing between distant coastal ports.

On such charts the shoreline and topography are generalized; only off shore soundings, such as the principal lights, outer buoys and landmarks visible at considerable distances, are shown.

B.15. GENERAL CHARTS

General Charts are produced at scales between 1:150,000 and 1:600,000. They are used for coastwise navigation outside of outlying reefs and shoals when the ship or boat is generally within sight of land or aids to navigation and its course can be done by piloting techniques.

B.16. COASTAL CHARTS

Coastal Charts are produced at scales between 1:50,000 and 1:150,000. They are used for inshore navigation, for entering bays and harbors of considerable width, and for navigating large inland waterways.

B.17. HARBOR CHARTS

Harbor Charts are produced at scales larger than 1:50,000. They are used in harbors, anchorage areas, and the smaller waterways.

B.18. SMALL CRAFT CHARTS

Small Craft Charts are produced at scales of 1:40,000 and larger. There are special charts of inland waters, including the Intracoastal Waterways. Special editions of conventional charts, called small craft charts, are printed on lighter weight paper and folded.

These "SC" charts contain additional information of interest to small craft operators, such as data on facilities, tide predictions, and weather broadcast information.

Chart Symbols and Abbreviations

B.19. GENERAL

Many symbols and abbreviations are used in charts. It is a quick way to tell you the physical characteristics of the charted area and information on aids to navigation.

These symbols are uniform and standardized, but may vary depending on the scale of the chart or chart series. These standardized chart symbols and abbreviations are shown in the Pamphlet "CHART No. 1" published jointly by the Defense Mapping Agency Hydrographic Center and the National Ocean Service. (Also available as *How to Read a Nautical Chart*, by Nigel Calder, published by International Marine/McGraw-Hill.)

B.20. COLOR

Nearly all charts employ color to distinguish various categories of information such as shoal water, deep water, and land areas. Color is also used with aids to navigation (ATON) to make them easier to locate and interpret.

Nautical purple ink (magenta) is used for most information since it is easier to read under red light normally used for navigating at night.

B.21. LETTERING

Lettering on a chart provides valuable information. Slanted Roman lettering on the chart is used to label all information that is affected by tidal change or current (with the exception of bottom soundings). All descriptive lettering for floating ATON is found in slanted lettering.

Vertical roman lettering on the chart is used to label all information that is not affected by the tidal changes or current. Fixed aids such as lighthouses and ranges are found in vertical lettering. (See Figure 14-8.)

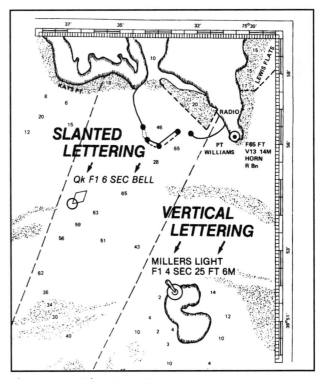

Figure 14-8 Chart Lettering

Buoy Symbols

B.22. SYMBOL DESCRIPTION

Buoys are shown with the following symbols:

- The basic symbol for a buoy is a diamond and small circle.
- A dot will be shown instead of the circle on older charts.
- The diamond may be above, below or alongside the circle or dot.
- The small circle or dot denotes the approximate position of the buoy mooring.
- The diamond is used to draw attention to the position of the circle or dot and to describe the aid.

See Chapter 13—Aids to Navigation, for ATON chart symbols, additional information and color pictures of ATON.

Other Chart Symbols

B.23. LIGHTHOUSES AND OTHER FIXED LIGHTS

The basic symbol is a black dot with a magenta "flare" giving much the appearance of a large exclamation mark (!). Major lights are named and described; minor lights are described only.

B.24. RANGES AND BEACONS

Chapter 13—Aids to Navigation, has chart symbols and color pictures of these ATON.

RANGES Ranges are indicated on charts by symbols for the lights (if lighted) and dashed line indicating the direction of the range.

DAY BEACONS Day beacons are indicated by small triangles, which may be colored to match the aid. Day beacons, commonly called day marks, are always fixed aids. That is, they are on a structure secured to the bottom or on the shore. They are of many different shapes.

B.25. PROMINENT LANDMARKS

Prominent landmarks such as water towers, smoke stacks, and flag poles are pinpointed by a standard symbol of a dot surrounded by a circle. A notation next to the symbol defines the landmark's nature. The omission of the dot indicates the location of the landmark is only an approximation. (See Figure 14-9.)

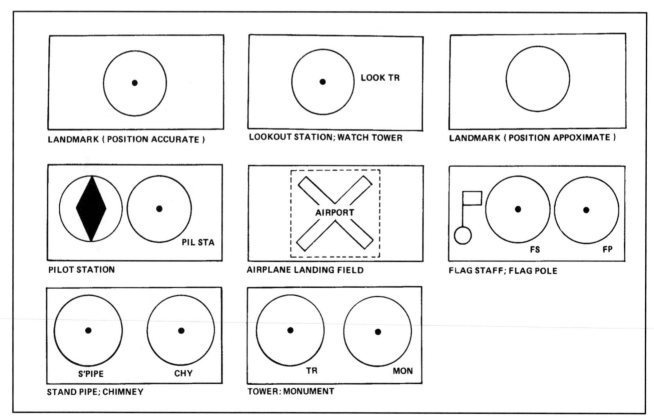

Figure 14-9 Symbols for Prominent Landmarks

B.26. WRECKS, ROCKS, AND REEFS

These are marked with standardized symbols, for example, a sunken wreck may be shown either by a symbol or by an abbreviation plus a number that gives the wreck's depth at mean low or Lower low water. A dotted line around any symbol calls special attention to its hazardous nature. (See Figure 14-10.)

B.27. BOTTOM CHARACTERISTICS

A system of abbreviations, used alone or in combination, describes the composition of the bottom allowing you to select the best holding ground for anchoring. (See Figure 14-11.)

NOTE

Knowledge of bottom quality is very important in determining an anchorage.

B.28. STRUCTURES

Shorthand representations have been developed and standardized for low-lying structures such as jetties, docks, drawbridges and waterfront ramps. Such symbols are drawn to scale and viewed from overhead. (See Figure 14-12.)

B.29. COASTLINES

Coastlines are represented at both low and high water. Landmarks that may help you fix your position are noted and labeled. (See Figure 14-13.)

Accuracy of Charts

B.30. GENERAL

A chart is only as accurate as the survey on which it is based. Major disturbances such as hur-

Hre	Hard	M	Mud; Muddy
Sft	Soft	G	Gravel
S	Sand	Stk	Sticky
Cl	Clay	Br	Brown
St	Stone	Gy	Gray
Co	Coral	Wd	Seaweed
Co Hd	Coral Head	Grs	Grass
Sh	Shells	Oys	Oysters

Figure 14-11 Bottom Composition

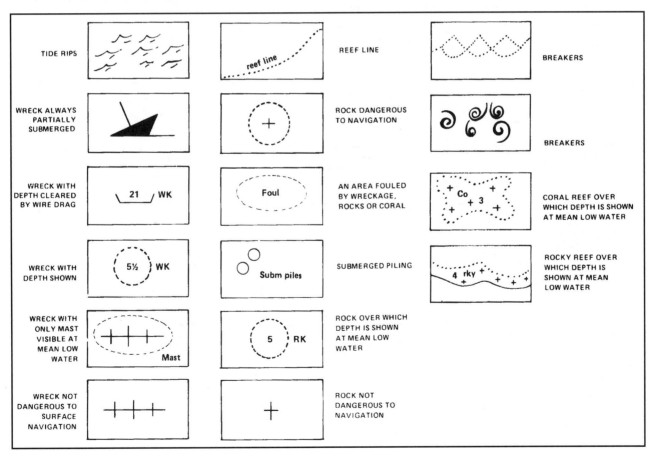

Figure 14-10 Breakers, Rocks, Reefs, Pilings

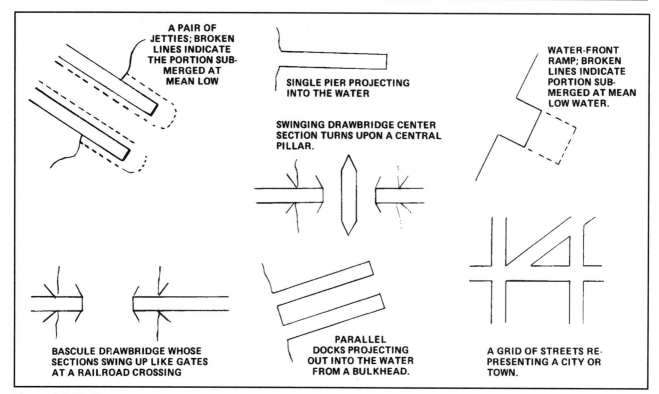

Figure 14-12 Structures

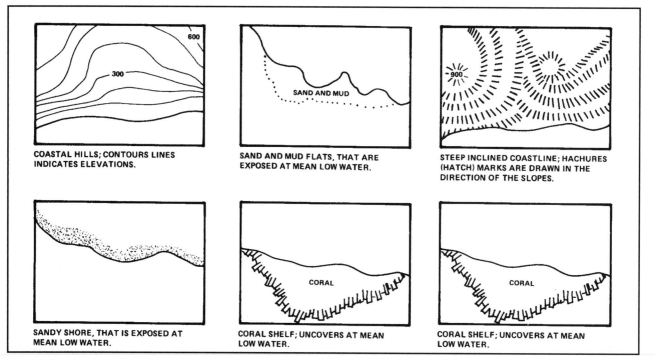

Figure 14-13 Coastlines

ricanes and earthquakes, cause sudden and extensive changes in the bottom contour. Even everyday forces of wind and waves cause changes in channels and shoals. The prudent sailor must be alert to the possibilities of changes in conditions and inaccuracies of charted information.

B.31. DETERMINING ACCURACY

Compromise is sometimes necessary in chart production as various factors may prevent the presentation of all data that has been collected for a given area. The information shown must be presented so that it can be understood with ease and certainty.

In order to judge the accuracy and completeness of a survey, note the following:

SOURCE AND DATE The source and date of the chart are generally given in the title along with the changes that have taken place since the date of the survey. The earlier surveys often were made under circumstances that precluded great accuracy of detail.

TESTING Until a chart based on such a survey, is tested, it should be regarded with caution. Except in well-frequented waters, few surveys have been so thorough as to make certain that all dangers have been found.

FULL OR SPARSE SOUNDINGS Noting the fullness or scantiness of the soundings is another method of estimating the completeness of the survey, but it must be remembered that the chart seldom shows all soundings that were obtained. If the soundings are sparse or unevenly distributed, it should be assumed, as a precautionary measure, that the survey was not made in great detail.

BLANK SPACES AMONG SOUNDINGS Large or irregular blank spaces among soundings mean that no soundings were obtained in those areas. Where the nearby soundings are "deep," it may logically be assumed that in the blanks the water is also deep. When the surrounding water is "shallow," or if the local charts shows that reefs are present in the area, such blanks should be regarded with suspicion. This is especially true in coral areas and off rocky coasts. These areas should be given wide berth.

Magnetic Compass

Overview

Introduction

Even though it has been around for centuries, the magnetic compass remains a vitally important tool for safe marine navigation. Whether you are steering a course far out of sight of land or operating in poor visibility, the magnetic compass will be your primary tool for guiding your boat to its destination.

In this section

Topic	See Page(s)
Components of a Magnetic Compass	**261–62**
Direction	**262–63**
Compass Error	**263**
Variation	**263**
Deviation	**263–67**
Compass Adjustment	**267–68**
Applying Compass Error	**268–70**

Components of a Magnetic Compass

C.1. GENERAL

The magnetic compass is standard equipment on all boats. Mechanically, it is a simple device. The magnetic compass is used to determine the boat's heading. A prudent seaman will check its accuracy frequently realizing that the magnetic compass is influenced, not only by the earth's magnetic field, but also by fields radiating from magnetic materials aboard the boat. It is also subject to error caused by violent movement as might be encountered in heavy weather.

C.2. COMPASS CARD

The arc of the compass card is divided into 360 degrees (°) and is numbered all the way around the card from 000° through 360° in a clockwise direction. Attached to the compass card is a magnet that aligns itself with the magnetic field around it. The "ZERO" (North) on the compass card is in line with the magnet or needle attached to the card. When the boat turns, the needle continues to align itself

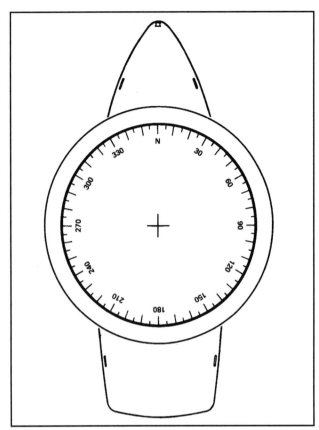

Figure 14-14 Compass Card

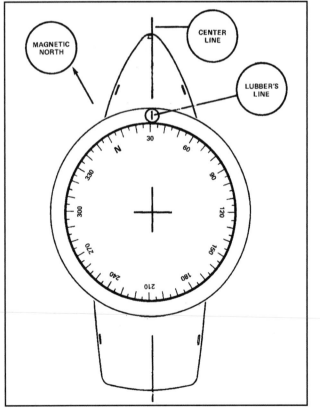

Figure 14-15 Lubber's Line and Magnetic North

with the magnetic field. This means the compass card stays stationary and the boat turns around it. (See Figure 14-14.)

C.3. LUBBER'S LINE

The lubber's line is a line or mark scribed on the compass housing to indicate the direction in which the boat is heading. The compass is mounted in the boat with the lubber's line on the boat's center line and parallel to its keel. (See Figure 14-15.)

Direction

C.4. GENERAL

Direction on the earth is measured clockwise from 000° to 360°. When speaking of degrees representing a course or heading, always use three digits, such as 270° or 057°.

C.5. TRUE AND MAGNETIC

Directions measured on a chart are in true degrees or magnetic degrees.

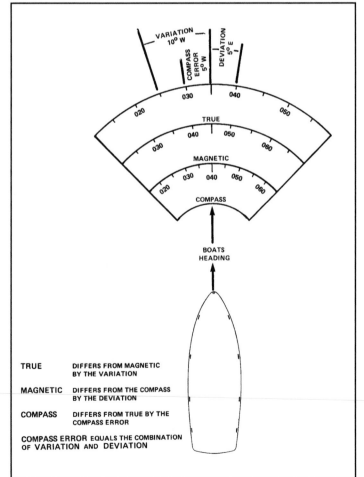

Figure 14-16 True, Magnetic, and Compass Courses

- True direction uses the North Pole as a reference point.
- Magnetic direction uses the Magnetic North as a reference point.
- True direction differs from magnetic direction by variation.

Directions steered by reference to the boat's compass are magnetic degrees. The difference between the true and magnetic heading is compass error. Compass error also includes internal instrument error. This is discussed later. (See Figure 14-16.)

Compass Error

C.6. GENERAL

Compass error is the angular difference between a compass direction and its corresponding true direction. The magnetic compass reading must be corrected for variation and deviation to get true direction.

Variation

C.7. GENERAL

Variation is the angular difference in degrees between true north and magnetic north. It varies according to location on the earth's surface.

C.8. AMOUNT OF VARIATION

The amount of variation changes from one point to the next on the earth's surface. Variation is measured in degrees east or degrees west. Variation for any area is shown on the appropriate charts as the inside ring of each compass rose.

C.9. VARIATION INCREASES/DECREASES

Variation changes irregularly with time at any given location. For example, variation at one location may increase for many years, then remain static for a few years, and then and then reverse its change trend and begin to decrease. Therefore, predictions of the change of variation printed on nautical charts are intended for short term use—a period of only a few years. The latest available charts should always be used. Notes in the compass roses will show the magnitude and direction of predicted change.

C.10. CALCULATING THE VARIATION

Follow the procedures below for determining the amount of annual increase or decrease of variation:

1. Locate the compass rose nearest to area of operation on the chart.
2. Locate the variation and annual increase/decrease from the center of the compass rose.
3. Locate the year from the center of the compass rose where variation and the year are indicated.
4. Subtract year indicated in the compass rose from the present year.
5. Multiply the number of years difference by the annual increase or decrease.
6. Add or subtract the amount from step 5 to the variation within the compass rose.

NOTE

Since variation is caused by the earth's magnetic field, its value changes with the geographic location of the boat. Variation remains the same for all headings.

Deviation

C.11. GENERAL

Deviation is the amount the magnetic compass needle is deflected by magnetic influences in the boat. Deviation can be caused by:

- metal objects near the compass,
- electrical motors, and
- the boat itself.

Deviation creates an error in the compass indication and, if uncorrected, an error in the course that helmsman attempts to steer. For navigational accuracy and the safety of the boat and crew, the boat's compass heading must be corrected for deviation so that the actual magnetic course can be accurately steered.

NOTE

Deviation changes with the boat's heading; it is not affected by the geographic location of the boat.

C.12. DEVIATION TABLE

Coast Guard regulations require unit commanders to ensure compass errors are accurately known and properly recorded and posted. This is accomplished for a magnetic compass by "swinging ship" to determine deviation. A deviation table may be created or the Coast Guard Deviation Table used by ships may be altered for use by boats. (Boats do not fill in the "Degaussing On" column since they do not carry this equipment.) Unit commanders are also required to develop procedures to compensate or calibrate compasses as necessary.

A new deviation table must be completed and approved by the unit commander annually, after yard availabilities, and after installation or removal of equipment or completion of structural alternations that affect the magnetic characteristics of the boat. The original updated deviation table shall be placed in the permanent boat record and a copy posted on the boat near the compass.

C.13. PREPARING A DEVIATION TABLE

Since deviation varies from boat to boat, you need to know the effect of deviation on your compass. Deviation is measured tabulated for each 15° of the compass. Deviation varies for different courses you steer and can be either easterly (E), westerly (W), or no error. Deviation is applied to the boat's compass heading to determine the correct magnetic course.

C.14. DEVIATION BY RUNNING A RANGE

A commonly used practice to determine deviation is running a range. A range is a line of bearing made by two fixed objects. Sometimes, specific range marks are installed so that when they are lined up, you are on the center of a channel (and moving in a true or magnetic direction that can be read on the compass rose). Alternatively, prominent landmarks can be found that line up to form natural ranges.

FINDING BEARING OF A RANGE When running ranges to check compass deviation, work in an area where your activities will not interfere with normal shipping traffic. To find the magnetic bearing of the range on a chart:

1. Align the edge of the parallel rulers (or course plotter) so that it passes through the charted positions of the two objects.

2. Line up the edge of the parallel rulers with the center of the nearest compass rose.

3. Read the magnetic bearing off of the inner ring of the compass rose.

Be sure to read the correct side of the compass rose—going in the wrong direction will give the reciprocal bearing which is 180° in the wrong direction. To be sure you've selected the proper orientation, imagine the boat positioned in the center of the compass rose with its bow pointed toward the range.

Example: The magnetic bearing (M) of the range measured on the chart is 272°. The bearing of the range read off of the magnetic compass (C) is 274°. (See Figure 14-17.)

Answer: 2°W is the deviation

The amount of deviation is the difference between C and M, this is 2°. The direction of deviation is based upon "Compass Best, Error West." Since C is greater than M, the error is west. (This will be discussed in more detail later.)

NOTE

The directions of man-made ranges may be marked on the chart. If so, the bearing will be marked in degrees true NOT degrees magnetic.

NOTE

To correct the compass, subtract Easterly errors; add Westerly errors.

EXERCISE Use the example above and Figure 14-17 for guidance in developing a deviation table. Prepare a work table using the procedures as follows:

1. Enter the boat's compass headings for every 15° in the first column.

2. Enter in the third column the range's magnetic bearing as measured on the chart (272°). It is the same value for all entries.

3. Get the boat underway, at slow speed and in calm water. Steer the boat's compass heading

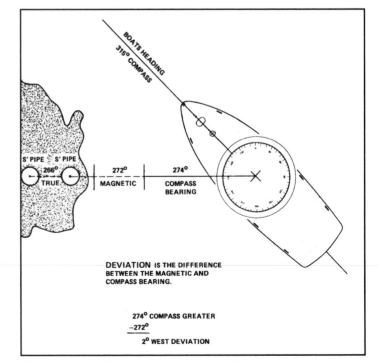

Figure 14-17 Obtaining Deviation Using Ranges

listed in the first column, normally starting with a compass heading of 000°. Steer a steady heading and cross the range.

4. Observe the compass bearing of the range at the instant you cross the range. Use 266° for this exercise. Enter the range's bearing by compass in the second column on the same line as the "Boat's Compass Heading" of 000°.

5. Come around to the boat's compass heading of 015°. Steer a steady heading and cross the range.

6. Observe the compass bearing of the range at the instant you cross the range. Use 265° for this exercise. Enter the range's bearing by compass in the second column on the same line as the "Boat's Compass Heading" of 015°.

7. Come around to the boat's compass heading of 030°. Steer a steady heading and cross the range.

8. Observe the compass bearing of the range at the instant you cross the range. Use 265° for this exercise. Enter the range's bearing by compass in the second column on the same line as the "Boat's Compass Heading" of 030°.

9. Continue changing course by 15° increments until you have crossed the range and noted the

compass bearing of the range for each for each boat's compass heading. The table is already filled in for this exercise.

10. Having completed "swinging ship", determine deviation for each heading by taking the difference between the magnetic bearing and the compass bearing. (See Figure 14-18.)

11. Prepare a smooth deviation table to be placed next to the boat's compass. The table must give the deviation for a magnetic course so you can use the table to correct courses. (See Figure 14-19, next page.) As noted before, the deviation table used by ships can be altered for use by boats.

NOTE

Enter all compass bearings to the nearest whole degree.

NOTE

When the compass bearing is LESS than the magnetic bearing, deviation (error) is East. When the compass bearing is GREATER than the magnetic bearing, deviation (error) is West.

MEMORY AID

Determining the direction of deviation: "Compass least, error East; compass best, error West."

C.15. DEVIATION BY MULTIPLE OBSERVATIONS FROM ONE POSITION

An accurately charted object, such as solitary piling, with maneuvering room, and depth, around it must be available. In addition, there must be charted and visible objects, suitable for steering on with accuracy, at a distance of greater than ½ mile. Use the largest scale chart possible.

PREPARING Determine and record the magnetic bearing from the chart (from piling to object) of various selected objects. Ideally, the objects should be 15° apart. However, this is not necessary as long as a minimum of ten objects/bearings, evenly separated through the entire 360°, are available. For ready reference, record this information as shown in columns (1) and (2) in the table next page.

Boat's Compass Heading	Compass Bearing of Range	Magnetic Bearing of Range	Deviation	Magnetic Course
000°	266°	272°	6°E	006°
015°	265°	272°	7°E	022°
030°	265°	272°	7°E	037°
045°	267°	272°	5°E	050°
060°	270°	272°	2°E	062°
075°	269°	272°	3°E	078°
090°	271°	272°	1°E	091°
105°	272°	272°	0°	105°
120°	267°	272°	5°E	125°
135°	273°	272°	1°W	134°
150°	268°	272°	4°E	154°
165°	275°	272°	3°W	162°
180°	274°	272°	2°W	178°
195°	277°	272°	5°W	190°
210°	278°	272°	6°W	204°
225°	279°	272°	7°W	218°
240°	275°	272°	3°W	237°
255°	279°	272°	7°W	244°
270°	279°	272°	7°W	263°
285°	277°	272°	5°W	280°
300°	270°	272°	2°E	302°
315°	274°	272°	2°W	313°
330°	269°	272°	3°E	333°
345°	266°	272°	6°E	351°

Figure 14-18 Completed Work Table, Deviation

(1) Object (on chart)	(2) Magnetic Heading (plotted)	(3) Compass Heading (measured)	(4) Deviation (calculated)
Steeple	013°	014.0°	1.0°W
Stack	040°	041.5°	1.5°W
R. Tower	060°	062.0°	2.0°W
Lt. #5	112°	115.0°	3.0°W
Left Tangent Pier	160°	163.0°	3.0°W
Water Tower	200°	201.0°	1.0°W
Right Tangent Jetty	235°	235.0°	0.0°W
Light House	272°	271.0°	1.0°E
Flag Pole	310°	309.0°	1.0°E
Lookout Tower	345°	344.5°	0.5°E

OBSERVING

- With the above information (columns (1) and (2)) proceed to and tie off to the piling.

- With the piling amidships, pivot around it and steer on the objects that were identified, then record the compass heading in column (3). Comparing columns (2) and (3) will yield the deviation for that heading (4).

Compass Course	Deviation	Magnetic Course
000°	6°E	006°
015°	7°E	022°
030°	7°E	037°
045°	5°E	050°
060°	2°E	062°
075°	3°E	078°
090°	1°E	091°
105°	0°	105°
120°	5°E	125°
135°	1°W	134°
150°	4°E	154°
165°	3°W	162°
180°	2°W	178°
195°	5°W	190°
210°	6°W	204°
225°	7°W	218°
240°	3°W	237°
255°	7°W	244°
270°	7°W	263°
285°	5°W	280°
300°	2°E	302°
315°	2°W	313°
330°	3°E	333°
345°	6°E	351°

Figure 14-19 Deviation Table (Mounted Close to Compass)

- Use the observed deviation (4) for the indicated magnetic heading (2) as reference points, then draw a deviation curve on the graph as is shown in table top of next page.

DETERMINING Extract deviation from the deviation curve for any heading.

NOTE

The graph is divided vertically in 15° increments and horizontally in half (for east and west deviation) and then further divided according to amount of deviation. This later subdivision may be greater than the 4° depicted. However, do not tolerate deviations of more than 3°. If excessive deviations are noted, the compass should be adjusted by the technique discussed later or by a professional compass adjuster.

C.16. DEVIATION BY MULTIPLE RANGES

Use the largest scale chart available covering the local area. With parallel rules, triangles, etc., identify as many terrestrial ranges as possible that will be visible when underway, and that also will provide LOPs across expanses of water with adequate maneuvering room and depth. As far as possible, the ranges should be in the same area, so that variation remains constant.

PREPARING The number of terrestrial ranges available may be limited. However, for each range, deviation will be for both the "steering toward" and the "steering away" (reciprocal) heading. Be careful when "running" the reciprocal heading that the lubber's line of the compass aligns with the axis of the range. Make every effort to identify no less than four ranges to yield deviation values for the cardinal points (N, S, E, W) and intercardinal points (NE, SE, SW, NW).

CAUTION!

Ensure that there are no local magnetic anomalies (such as wrecks, pipe lines, bridges or steel piers) near the boat that could affect the local variation indicated on the chart. Check the chart for any indication of local disturbances.

Determine the magnetic bearing from the chart. Record this information in the format shown.

(1) Range (on chart)	(2) Magnetic Heading (plotted)	(3) Compass Heading (measured)	(4) Deviation (calculated)
Steeple— Jetty Lt#4	015°/195°	014°/195°	1°E/0°
R. Tower— Tank	103°/283°	104°/282°	1°W/1°E
Flag Pole— Lt#5	176°/356°	177°/355.5°	1°W/.5°E
Stack—Left Tangent Pier	273°/093°	272°/094°	1°E/1°W
Ent. Channel Range	333°/153°	332°/154.5°	1°E/1.5°W

OBSERVING Observing with the information from columns (1) and (2) get underway and "run" the various ranges. Record the compass heading in column (3), as appropriate. Take care not to become so preoccupied with running the range that the boat is in jeopardy of collision, grounding, etc. Comparing columns (2) and (3) will yield the deviation from that heading (4).

DETERMINING The deviation for the indicated headings may be plotted on the deviation graph resulting in a deviation curve. With the resulting deviation curve, deviation for any heading is possible. (See chart below.)

Compass Adjustment

C.17. PROCEDURE

The following is one procedure for adjusting a small boat compass.

1. Steer a course in a northerly direction as close to magnetic north as possible as defined by the known objects on the chart. With a nonmagnetic tool, adjust the N/S compensating magnet to remove half the observed error. (Do not try to short cut. Removing all the error in the first step will just overcompensate the error.)

2. Steer a course in a southerly direction. Again remove half the observed error.

3. Steer a course in an easterly direction. Adjust the E/W compensating magnet to remove half the observed error.

4. Steer a course in a westerly direction. Again remove half the observed error.

5. Repeat the above steps, as often as needed, to reduce observed error to the minimum achievable.

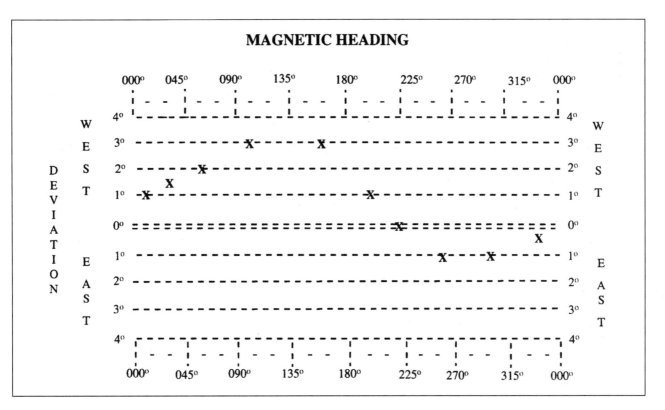

MAGNETIC HEADING

6. Record the final observed instrument error for N, S, E, and W.

7. Determine the observed error for NE, SE, SW, and NW. Record these but do not try to adjust these errors manually.

8. Use the recorded values for compass corrections.

This simple procedure is sufficiently precise for most boats. To gain greater precision, consult a qualified compass adjuster or consult a book on the subject.

Applying Compass Error

C.18. PROCEDURE

"Correcting" is going from magnetic direction (M) to true (T), or going from the compass direction (C) to magnetic (M). To apply compass error to correct your course or direction:

1. start with the *compass course*

2. apply deviation to obtain the *magnetic course*

3. apply variation to obtain *true course*

The sequence of the procedure is outlined below: (See Figure 14-20.)

a. Compass (C)

b. Deviation (D)

c. Magnetic (M)

d. Variation (V)

e. True (T)

MEMORY AID

Applying compass error:
Can **D**ead **M**en **V**ote **T**wice **A**t **E**lection
(**C**ompass) (**D**eviation) (**M**agnetic) (**V**ariation) (**T**rue) (**A**dd) (**E**asterly error)
Add Easterly Errors—Subtract Westerly Errors

C.19. OBTAINING TRUE COURSE

For Figure 14-20, the compass course is 127°, variation from the compass rose is 4°W, and the deviation from the boat's deviation table is 5°E. Then, the true course is obtained as follows:

1. Write down the correction formula:

$$C = 127°$$
$$D = 5°E$$
$$M = 132°$$
$$V = 4°W$$
$$T = 128°$$

2. Compute the information you have opposite the appropriate letter in the previous step.

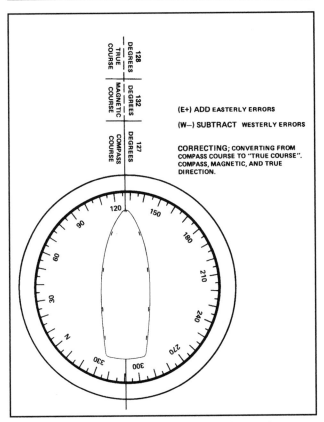

Figure 14-20 Applying Compass Error, Correcting

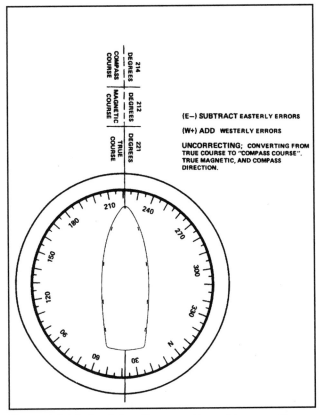

Figure 14-21 Applying Compass Error, Uncorrecting

3. Add the Easterly error of 5°E deviation to the compass course (127°) and you have the magnetic course (132°).

4. Subtract the Westerly error of 4°W variation from the magnetic course (132°).

The true course is 128°.

C.20. CONVERTING TRUE COURSE TO COMPASS COURSE

Converting from true (T) direction to magnetic (M), or going from magnetic (M) to compass (C) is "uncorrecting." For converting from True Course to Compass Course:

1. Obtain your *true course*.

2. Apply variation to obtain the *magnetic course*.

3. Apply deviation to obtain your *compass course*.

The sequence of the procedure is outlined below:

a. True (T)

b. Variation (V)

c. Magnetic (M)

d. Deviation (D)

e. Compass (C)

MEMORY AID

Converting true course to compass course:
True Virtue Makes Dull Company After Wedding
(True) (Variation) (Magnetic) (Deviation) (Compass) (Add) (Westerly error)
Subtract Easterly Errors—Add Westerly Errors

C.21. OBTAINING COMPASS COURSE

For Figure 14-21, by using parallel rules, the true course between two points on a chart is measured as 221°T, variation is 9°E and deviation is 2°W.

To obtain the compass course (C)—follow the procedure given below:

1. Write down the conversion formula:

$$T = 221°$$
$$V = 9°E$$
$$M = 212°$$
$$D = 2°W$$
$$C = 214°$$

2. Compute the information you have opposite the appropriate letter in the previous step.

3. Subtract the Easterly error of 9°E variation from True Course of 221° and obtain the Magnetic Course of 212°.

4. Add the Westerly error of 2°W deviation to the Magnetic Course (212°).

The compass course (C) is 214°.

SECTION D

Piloting

Overview

Introduction

Piloting is directing a vessel by using landmarks, other navigational aids and soundings. Safe piloting requires the use of corrected, up-to-date charts. Piloting deals with both present and future consequences. Be alert and attentive. You must be consciously aware of where you are and where you soon will be.

In this section

Basic Piloting Equipment

D.1. GENERAL

Adequate preparation is very important in piloting a boat. Piloting is the primary method of determining a boat's position. In order for a boat cox-

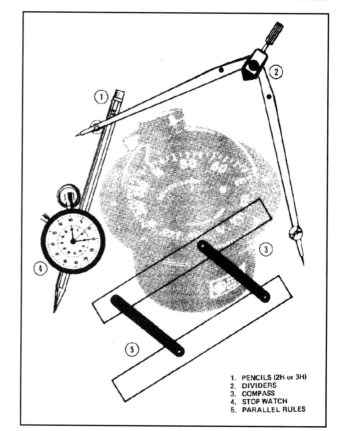

1. PENCILS (2H or 3H)
2. DIVIDERS
3. COMPASS
4. STOP WATCH
5. PARALLEL RULES

Figure 14-22 Basic Piloting Tools

swain to make good judgments on all decisions in navigation, tools such as compasses, dividers, stopwatches, parallel rulers, pencils and publications must be available. (See Figure 14-22.)

D.2. COMPASS

The magnetic compass is used to steer your course. It gives you a continual report on your boat's heading and can be used as a sighting instrument to determine bearings.

A mark, called a "lubber's line," is fixed to the inner surface of the compass housing. Similar marks, called "90-degree lubber's line," are usually mounted at ninety degree intervals around the compass card. They are used to determining when an object is bearing directly abeam or astern. A pin (longer than the lubber's line pins) is centered on the compass card and is used to determine a position by taking bearings on visible objects

D.3. PARALLEL RULERS

Parallel rulers are two straight edges connected by straps that allow the rulers to separate while remaining parallel. They are used in chart work to transfer directions from a compass rose to various plotted courses and bearing lines and vice versa.

Parallel rulers are always walked so that the top or lower edge intersects the compass rose center to obtain accurate courses.

D.4. COURSE PLOTTER

A course plotter may be used for chart work in place of the parallel rulers discussed above. It is a rectangular piece of clear plastic with a set of lines etched parallel to the long edges, and semi-circular protractor-like scales. The center of the scales is at or near the center of one of the longer sides and has a small circle or bull's eye. The bull's eye is used to align the plotter on a meridian so that the direction (course or bearing) can be plotted or read off of the scale. A popular model is the "Weems Plotter" which is mounted on a roller for ease of moving.

D.5. PENCILS

It is important to use a correct type of pencil for plotting. A medium pencil (No. 2) is best. Keep your pencils sharp; a dull pencil can cause considerable error in plotting a course due to the width of the lead.

D.6. DIVIDERS

Dividers are instruments with two pointed legs, hinged where the upper ends join. Dividers are used to measure distance on a scale and transfer them to a chart.

D.7. STOPWATCH

A stopwatch or navigational timer, which can be started and stopped at will, is very useful for speed checks and determining the lighted periods of a navigational aids.

D.8. NAUTICAL SLIDE RULE

The Nautical Slide Rule will be discussed in the section of this chapter dedicated to time, distance and speed calculations.

D.9. DRAFTING COMPASS

The drafting compass is an instrument similar to dividers. One leg has a pencil attached. This tool is used for swinging arcs and circles.

D.10. SPEED CURVE (SPEED VS. RPM)

A speed curve is used to translate tachometer readings of revolutions per minute (RPM) into the boat's speed through the water. A speed curve is obtained by running a known distance at constant RPM in one direction and then in the opposite direction. The time for each run is recorded and averaged to account for current and wind forces. Using distance and time, the speed is calculated for each RPM run. (See Figure 14-23.)

D.11. CHARTS

Charts are essential for plotting and determining your position, whether operating in familiar or unfamiliar waters. Never get underway without appropriate charts.

D.12. DEPTH SOUNDER

There are several types of depth sounder but they operate on the similar principles. The depth sounder transmits a high frequency sound wave that reflects off the bottom and returns to a receiver. The echo is converted to an electrical impulse that can be read from a visual scale on the depth sounder instrument. The indicator displays the depth of water you are in, but it does not show the depth of water you are heading for.

TRANSDUCER The sound wave is transmitted by a device called a transducer. The transducer is usually mounted through the hull and sticks out a very short distance. It is not mounted on the lowest part of the hull. The distance from the transducer

Speed, Kts Calm Water	Approx. RPM	Fuel Gal/Hour	Consumption Gal/Mile	Cruise Radius/Miles
7.60	760	3.86	.51	882
7.89	1000	4.99	.63	712
9.17	1250	7.50	.82	550
9.48	1500	12.75	1.31	335
12.50	1750	16.80	1.35	333
15.53	2000	21.00	1.35	333
19.15	2250	33.00	1.72	261
21.34	2400	33.75	1.58	284

Figure 14-23 Sample Speed vs. RPMs Conversion Table

to the lowest point of the hull must be known. This distance must be subtracted from the depth sounding reading to determine the actual depth of water under the boat.

Example: Depth sounder reading is six feet. The transducer is mounted one foot above the lowest point of the hull; thus boat extends one foot below the transducer. You subtract the one-foot difference from the depth sounder reading of six feet to arrive at the actual depth of water beneath the boat—five feet in this case.

NOTE

Always consider the location of the transducer. It is usually mounted above the lowest point of the hull.

VIEWING THE DEPTH Water depth is indicated by a variety of methods:

1. Indicator: A digital display or a flashing light that rotates clockwise around a scale on a visual screen in the pilothouse. In the flashing light type, the first "flash" is when the pulse leaves the transducer, and the second flash represents the arrival of the echo return.

2. Recorder: Depths are recorded on paper tape.

3. Video display screen: The display is similar to a small television set with brightness on the bottom of the screen indicating the sea floor.

NOTE

To determine the water depth below the boat's hull, subtract the distance between the transducer and the lowest point of the hull from all readings.

VIEWING BOTTOM CONDITIONS With practice and experience, you can also tell what the bottom characteristics and conditions are. Flashing light and video display sounders may be generally interpreted as:

- Sharp, clear flash—hard bottom
- Broad, fuzzy flash—soft, muddy bottom
- Multiple, fairly sharp flashes—rocky bottom
- Additional flashes or displays at multiples of the least depth indicated may reveal the need to turn down the sensitivity control.

ADJUSTMENT CONTROLS Adjustment controls depend on the type of depth sounder. The operator's manual should be reviewed for correct use.

Typical adjustment controls include depth scales (which may include feet and fathoms) and a sensitivity control.

D.13. LEAD LINE

Knowledge of the depth of water is one of the most important dimensions of piloting. A hand-held lead line is used for ascertaining the depth of water when you don't have a depth sounder, when the depth sounder is not operational or when you are operating in known shallow water.

A lead line consists of a line marked in fathoms and a lead weight of 7 to 14 pounds, hollowed at one end in which tallow is inserted to gather samples of the bottom. It is simple and not subject to breakdown. Lead line limitations include:

- not useable in adverse sea conditions
- awkward to use
- usable only at slow speed

NOTE

Always keep a lead line neatly stowed and ready for use in the event the depth sounder becomes inoperative.

LEAD LINE MARKINGS Lead lines are marked as follows (see Figure 14-24):

2 FATHOMS: two (2) strips of leather

8 FATHOMS: three (3) strips of leather

5 FATHOMS: one (1) white rag (usually cotton)

7 FATHOMS: one (1) red rag (usually wool)

10 FATHOMS: one (1) strip of leather with a hole

18 FATHOMS: three (3) strips of leather

15 FATHOMS: one (1) white rag (usually cotton)

17 FATHOMS: one (l) red rag (usually cotton)

20 FATHOMS: two (2) knots

26 FATHOMS: one (1) knot

NOTE

Lead lines should be wetted and stretched prior to marking.

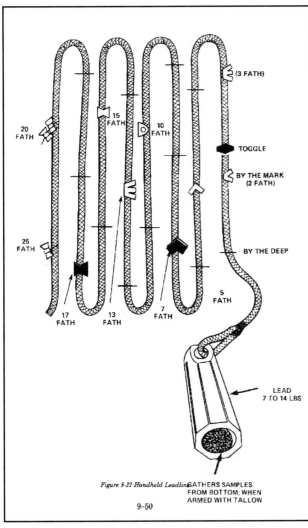

Figure 14-24 Handheld Lead Line

CASTING THE HAND-HELD LEAD LINE The procedure below should be followed in casting a lead line:

1. Grasp the line by the toggle.

2. Swing the lead in a fore-and-aft arc.

3. When sufficient momentum is obtained and at shoulder level, throw the lead as far forward as possible.

4. Pull the slack out of the line until you feel the lead on the bottom.

5. When the line is straight up and down read the sounding.

REPORTING THE SOUNDINGS There are two ways to report soundings, depending upon where the watermark is located on the lead line.

1. Depth that corresponds to any mark on the lead line is reported: "By the Mark," that is, should

the depth align with the two strips of leather it would be reported "By the Mark 2."

2. Intermediate whole fathoms are called deeps. Report fractions of a fathom as halves and quarters, such as, (and a half seven) or (less a quarter ten).

D.14. RDF AND ADF

A radio direction finder (RDF) will allow you to take bearings on radio transmitters which are well beyond your visual range. One type of RDF requires manual operation to obtain bearings. The automatic radio direction finder (ADF) automatically takes and displays the bearings.

Radio bearings are not as accurate as visual bearings. It takes a great deal of experience to be able to effectively use RDF equipment. Be very careful when plotting radio bearings. Watch for reciprocal errors.

D.15. VHF-FM HOMER

The VHF-FM homer (direction finder homing device) allows you to aim in on the source of any FM radio signals you are receiving. This unit can also function as a backup VHF-FM receiver.

The VHF-FM homer has several antennas. It measures the small difference in angle of signal received at each antenna from a known source then converts this electronic measurement into a bearing indication. The bearing to the radio station is displayed by a needle/compass rose indicator mounted in the pilothouse. The radio source must continue to transmit for you to track it over a period of time.

The procedure for using the homer is outlined below:

1. The homer has six channels (6, 12, 13, 14, 16, and 22) in addition to the weather channels. Set the channel switch to the channel receiving the signal.

2. Request a long count.

3. Turn the squelch control fully counterclockwise.

4. Set volume to a comfortable level.

5. Rotate squelch control to remove speaker noise.

6. Push squelch control IN for homing, OUT for monitoring.

7. Turn the boat in the direction of the pointer until it centers itself.

8. Turn 30 degrees to be sure the source is ahead, not aft.

9. Change course as indicated by the needle and proceed to the source of the signals, giving due caution to navigation hazards that may be between you and your destination.

NOTE

A needle centered in the middle of the screen may indicate a source dead ahead or dead astern. The homer cannot distinguish this since both signals would arrive at 90 degrees to each antenna.

To determine whether the transmitter is ahead or behind, turn off course 30 degrees and observe the needle. If the needle directs you to return to your original heading, the source is ahead.

If the needle points elsewhere, follow it. The indicator needle is affected by radio wave reflections and may bounce around when passing near large metal objects.

D.16. LIGHT LIST

Light Lists provide more complete information concerning aids to navigation than can be shown on charts. They are not intended to replace charts for navigation and are published in seven volumes:

VOLUME I: Covers Atlantic Coast, from St. Croix River; Maine to Toms River, New Jersey

VOLUME II: Covers Atlantic Coast, from Toms River, New Jersey to Little River Inlet, South Carolina

VOLUME III: Covers Atlantic Coast, from Little River Inlet, South Carolina, to Econfina River, Florida, and the Greater Antilles

VOLUME IV: Covers Gulf of Mexico, from Econfina River, Florida, to Rio Grande, Texas

VOLUME V: Covers Mississippi River System

VOLUME VI: Covers Pacific Coast and Pacific Islands

VOLUME VII: Covers Great Lakes

D.17. TIDE TABLES

Tide tables give daily predictions of the height of water at almost any place at any given time, and are published annually in four volumes. Instructions are provided within the publication on how to use the tables.

VOLUME I: Covers Europe and West Coast of Africa (including the Mediterranean Sea)

VOLUME II: Covers East Coast of North and South America (including Greenland)

VOLUME III: Covers West Coast of North and South America (including the Hawaiian Islands)

VOLUME IV: Covers Central and Western Pacific Ocean and Indian Ocean.

D.18. TIDAL CURRENT TABLES

These tables provide the times of maximum flood and ebb currents, and times of the two slack waters when current direction reverses. They also tell the predicted strength of the current in knots. The time of slack water does not correspond to times of high and low tide. The tide tables cannot be used to predict current predictions. The tables are published in two volumes. Instructions are provided within the publication on how to use the tables.

VOLUME I: Covers Atlantic Coast of North America

VOLUME II: Covers Pacific Coast of North America and Asia

D.19. COAST PILOTS

The amount of information that can be printed on a nautical chart is limited by available space and the system of symbols that is used. Additional information is often needed for safe and convenient navigation. Such information is published in the *Coast Pilot*. *Coast Pilot* volumes are printed in book form covering the coastline and the Great Lakes in nine separate volumes.

Each *Coast Pilot* contains sailing directions between points in its respective area, including recommended courses and distances. Channels with their controlling depths and all dangers and obstructions are fully described. Harbors and anchorages are listed with information on those points at which facilities are available for boat supplies and marine repairs. Information on canals, bridges, docks, and more is included.

ATLANTIC COAST

VOLUME NO. 1: Covers Eastport to Cape Cod

VOLUME NO. 2: Covers Cape Cod to Sandy Hook

VOLUME NO. 3: Covers Sandy Hook to Cape Henry

VOLUME NO. 4: Covers Cape Henry to Key West

VOLUME NO. 5: Covers Gulf of Mexico, Puerto Rico, and Virgin Islands

GREAT LAKES

VOLUME NO. 6: Covers Great Lakes and connecting waterways

PACIFIC COAST

VOLUME NO. 7: Covers California, Oregon, Washington, and Hawaii

ALASKA

VOLUME NO. 8: Covers Dixon Strait to Cape Spencer

VOLUME NO. 9: Covers Cape Spencer to Beaufort Sea

D.20. NAVIGATION RULES (COLREGS)

The Rules of the Road set forth regulations of navigational waters. The Rules of the Road are covered in COMDTINST M16672.2 (series).

Distance, Speed, and Time

D.21. GENERAL

Distance, speed, and time are critical elements in navigational calculations. Each has its own importance and use in piloting. And all three are closely associated in the way they are calculated. In planning a sortie or while underway, the typical navigation problem involves calculating one of these elements based on the value of the other two elements.

D.22. EXPRESSING DISTANCE, SPEED, AND TIME

Units of measurement are:

- distance in nautical miles (NM) except statute miles on the western rivers,
- speed in knots, and
- time in minutes.

In calculations and answers express:

- distance to the nearest tenth of a nautical mile,
- speed to the nearest tenth of a knot, and
- time to the nearest minute.

D.23. FORMULAS

There are three related equations used to determine distance (D), speed (S) and time (T) in navigation problems. When two of the three variables are known, the third can be found. The equations are:

- $D = S \times T \div 60$
- $S = 60D \div T$
- $T = 60D \div S$

The constant "60" in the equations represents the 60 minutes in an hour.

The following examples demonstrate how these equations are used:

Example #1:
If your boat is traveling at 10 knots, how far will it travel in 20 minutes? Solve for distance (D).

$$D = S \times T \div 60$$
$$D = 10 \times 20 \div 60$$
$$D = 200 \div 60$$
$$D = 3.3 \text{ nautical miles (NM)}$$

Example #2:
At a speed of 10 knots, it took the boat 3 hours and 45 minutes to go from your station to the shipping channel. What was the distance traversed?

1. Convert the hours to minutes for solving this equation. First, multiply the 3 hours by 60 (60 minutes in an hour), add the remaining 45 minutes, that is:

$$3 \times 60 + 45 = 225 \text{ minutes.}$$

2. Write the equation.

$$D = S \times T \div 60$$

3. Substitute information for the appropriate letter and calculate the distance.

$$D = 10 \text{ knots} \times 225 \text{ minutes} \div 60$$

4. $$D = 2250 \div 60$$

$$D = 37.5 \text{ NM (nearest tenth)}$$

Example #3:
Your boat has traveled 12 NM in 40 minutes. What is your speed (S)?

$$S = 60D \div T$$
$$S = 60 \times 12 \div 40$$
$$S = 720 \div 40$$
$$S = 18 \text{ knots}$$

Example #4:

Speed can be calculated when distance and time are known. Your departure time is 2030, the distance to your destination is 30 NM. Calculate the speed you must maintain to arrive at 2400.

1. Calculate the time interval between 2030 and 2400. To determine the time interval, convert time to hours and minutes and then subtract.

$$23 \text{ hours } 60 \text{ minutes } (2400)$$
$$- 20 \text{ hours } 30 \text{ minutes } (2030)$$
$$3 \text{ hours } 30 \text{ minutes}$$

2. Distance-Speed-Time equations are computed in minutes. Convert the 3 hours to minutes, add the remaining 30 minutes.

$$3 \times 60 = 180 \text{ minutes}$$
$$+ 30$$
$$210$$

3. Write the equation.

$$S = 60D \div T$$

4. Substitute information for the appropriate letter and calculate your speed.

$$S = 60D \div T$$
$$S = 60 \times 30 \text{ nautical miles} \div 210 \text{ minutes}$$

5.
$$S = 1800 \div 210$$
$$S = 8.6 \text{ knots}$$

Example #5:

You are cruising at 15 knots and have 12 NM more to go before reaching your destination. Determine the time to go to your destination.

$$T = 60D \div S$$
$$D = 12 \text{ NM}$$
$$S = 15 \text{ knots}$$
$$T = 60 \times 12 \div 15$$
$$T = 720 \div 15$$
$$T = 48 \text{ minutes}$$

D.24. NAUTICAL SLIDE RULE

The nautical slide rule was designed to solve speed, time and distance problems. Using the nautical slide rule can increase reduce the chance of error in calculations and is often faster than manual calculations. There are several types of nautical slide rule but all work on the same principle.

The nautical slide rule has three rotating scales. The scales are clearly labeled for:

- speed,
- time, and
- distance.

When any two of the values are set on opposing scales, the third is read from the appropriate index. (See Figure 14-25 which is set for the approximate values of SPEED of 18.2 knots, TIME of 62 minutes and DISTANCE of 18.4 NM or 36,800 yards.)

Fuel Consumption

D.25. GENERAL

In calculating solutions for navigation problems it is important to know how much fuel your boat consumes. Of course, you must ensure that you will have enough fuel on board to complete the sortie—to arrive on scene, conduct operations, and then return to base (or a refueling site).

D.26. CALCULATING FUEL CONSUMPTION

Calculate fuel consumption by the following procedures:

1. Ensure fuel tank(s) are topped off.
2. Measure and record total gallons in fuel tank(s).
3. Start engine(s).

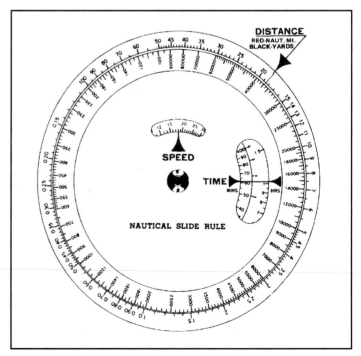

Figure 14-25 Nautical Slide Rule

4. Record time engine(s) were started.

5. Set desired RPMs for engine(s).

6. Record set RPMs.

7. Maintain set RPMs.

8. Stop engine(s) at a specified time (usually one hour).

9. Record time.

10. Measure and record total gallons of fuel in tank(s).

11. Subtract total gallons in tank(s) after running one (1) hour from total gallons recorded on boat at beginning of underway period.

12. Record the difference.

13. Measure the distance traveled and record.

14. Compute boat speed and record.

15. Apply the equation: Time (T) times gallons per hour (GPH) equals total fuel consumption (TFC); or

$$T \times GPH = TFC$$

16. Calculate TFC for other selected RPM settings. (Change RPM setting and repeat steps 6 through 15.)

Terms Used In Piloting

D.27. GENERAL

The following terms and their definitions (shown with their abbreviations) are commonly used in the practice of piloting.

BEARING (B, BRG.): The horizontal direction of one terrestrial (earth bound) point from another (the direction in which an object lies from you) is its bearing, expressed as the angular distance (degrees) from a reference direction (a direction used as a basis for comparison of other direction). A bearing is usually measured clockwise from 000° through 360° at the reference direction—true north, magnetic north or compass north.

COURSE (C): The intended horizontal direction of travel (the direction you intend to go), expressed as angular distance from a reference direction clockwise through 360°. For marine navigation, the term applies to the direction to be steered.

HEADING (HDG.): The actual direction the boat's bow is pointing at any given time.

COURSE LINE: Line drawn on a chart going in the direction of a course.

CURRENT SAILING: Current sailing is a method of allowing for current in determining the course made good, or of determining the effect of a current on the direction or motion of a boat.

DEAD RECKONING (DR): Dead reckoning is the determination of approximate position by advancing a previous position for course and distance only, without regard to other factors, such as, wind, sea conditions and current.

DEAD RECKONING PLOT: A DR plot is the plot of the movements of a boat as determined by dead reckoning.

POSITION: Position refers to the actual geographic location of a boat. It may be expressed as coordinates of latitude and longitude or as the bearing and distance from an object whose position is known.

DR POSITION: A DR position is a position determined by plotting a single or a series of consecutive course lines using only the direction (course) and distance from the last fix, without consideration of current, wind, or other external forces on a boat.

ESTIMATED POSITION (EP): A DR position modified by additional information which in itself is insufficient to establish a fix.

ESTIMATED TIME OF ARRIVAL (ETA): The ETA is the best estimate of predicted arrival time at a known destination.

FIX: A fix is a position determined from terrestrial, electronic or celestial data at a given time with a high degree of accuracy.

LINE OF POSITION (LOP): A line of bearing to a known object which a vessel is presumed to be.

COAST PILOTING: Coast Piloting refers to directing the movements of a boat near a coast.

RANGE: There are two types of ranges used in piloting:

1. Two or more fixed objects in line. Such objects are said to be in range.

2. Distance in a single direction or along a great circle. Distance ranges are measured by means of radar or visually with a sextant.

RUNNING FIX (R FIX): A running fix is a position determined by crossing LOPs obtained at different times.

SPEED (S): The rate of travel of a boat through the water measured in knots is the speed. A knot is a unit of speed equal to one nautical mile per hour. A nautical mile is 2,000 yards or one minute of latitude.

Speed of Advance (SOA) is the average speed in knots which must be maintained to arrive at a destination at any appointed time.

Speed made good: Speed over ground (SOG) is the speed of travel of a boat along the track, expressed in knots;

The difference between the estimated average speed (SOA) and the actual average speed (SOG) is caused by external forces acting on the boat (such as wind, current, etc.).

TRACK (TR): A track is the course followed or intended to be followed by a boat. The direction may designated true or magnetic.

SET: The direction toward which the current is flowing expressed in degrees true.

DRIFT: The speed of the current usually stated in knots.

COURSE OVER GROUND/COURSE MADE GOOD (COG/CMG): The resultant direction of movement from one point to another.

Laying the Course

D.28. PROCEDURE

A navigation plot typically includes several course lines to steer from your beginning point to arrival at your destination. The technique for laying each course line is the same and is summarized as follows (see Figure 14-26):

1. Draw a straight line from your departure point to the intended destination. This is your course line.

2. Lay one edge of your parallel rulers along the course line.

3. Walk the rulers to the nearest compass rose on the chart, moving one ruler while holding the other in place.

4. Walk the rulers until one edge intersects the crossed lines at the center of the compass rose.

5. Going from the center of the circle in the direction of the course line, read the INSIDE degree circle where the ruler's edge intersects. This is your magnetic course (M).

6. Write your course along the top of the penciled trackline as three digits followed by the letter (M) Magnetic, for example, C 068 M.

Figure 14-26 shows a course of 068° M between two buoys as measured by parallel rulers on a chart's compass rose.

NOTE

Ensure the rulers do not slip. If they do, the original line of direction will be lost.

Dead Reckoning (DR)

D.29. GENERAL

Dead reckoning (DR) is widely used in navigation. It is the process of determining a boat's approximate position by applying its speed, time and course from its last known position.

D.30. KEY ELEMENTS OF DEAD RECKONING

The key elements of dead reckoning are the course steered and the distance traveled without consideration to current, wind or other external forces.

COURSE STEERED Only courses steered are used to determine a DR. Course for a boat is normally stated in degrees magnetic (M) since small vessels usually do not carry gyrocompasses that indicate true (T) direction.

DISTANCE TRAVELED Distance traveled is obtained by multiplying speed (in knots) by the time underway (in minutes).

$$D = S \times T \div 60$$

(On the western rivers, distance is computed in statute miles.)

D.31. STANDARDIZED PLOTTING SYMBOLS

All lines and points plotted on a chart must be labeled. The symbols commonly used in marine navigation are standardized and summarized as follows:

- **Labeling the fix:** The plotter should clearly mark a visual fix with a circle or an electronic fix with a triangle. Clearly label the time of each fix. A visual running fix should be circled, marked "R Fix" and labeled with the time of the second LOP. Maintain the chart neat and uncluttered when labeling fixes.

- **DR position:** A point marked with a semicircle and the time.

- **Estimated position (EP):** A point marked with a small square and the time.

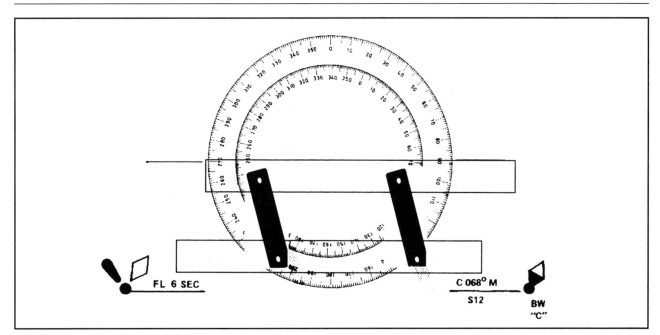

Figure 14-26

See Figure 14-27 for examples of the plotting symbols.

NOTE

Only standard symbols should be used to make it possible for every crew member to understand the plot.

D.32. LABELING A DR PLOT

The DR plot starts with your last known position (usually a fix). The procedure for labeling a DR plot is given below. (See Figure 14-27.)

Figure 14-27 shows a DR plot starting in the upper left corner from a 0930 fix. (The compass rose is shown for information purposes and is not always so obvious on the chart.) At 1015 a fix is taken and a new DR plot started. Also, at 1015, the course is adjusted to C 134 M to get to the intended destination at the 1200 DR plot. Then, the 1200 fix is plotted and the new DR plot (C 051 M and S 16) is started.

1. Plot your course line, label it clearly and neatly.

   • **Course:** Above the course line place a capital C followed by the ordered course in three digits.

   • **Speed:** Below the course line place a capital S followed by the speed

2. Use standard symbols to label a DR plot:

   • Circle for a fix.

   • Semicircle for a DR position.

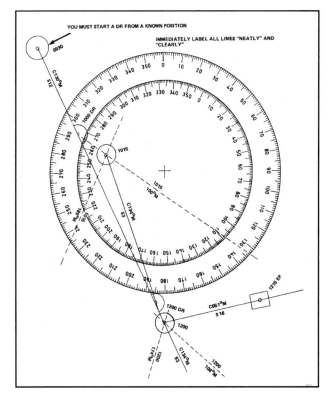

Figure 14-27 Labeling a DR Plot

   • Square for an estimated position.

3. Plot a DR position:

   • At least every half hour.

   • At the time of every course change.

   • At the time of every speed change.

4. Start a new DR plot from each fix or running fix (plot a new course line from the fix).

5. **Time** is written as four digits.

The course can be magnetic (M), true (T) or compass (C) and is always expressed in three digits. If the course is less than 100 degrees, zeros are prefixed to the number—for example, 009°.

Basic Elements of Piloting

D.33. GENERAL

Direction, distance, and time are the basic elements of piloting. With these elements, an accurate navigation plot can be maintained.

D.34. DIRECTION

Direction is the relationship of one point to another point (known as the reference point). Direction, referred to as bearing, is measured in degrees from 000 through 360.

REFERENCE POINT/REFERENCE DIRECTION The usual reference point is 000°. The relationships between the reference points and reference directions are listed below:

Reference Direction	Reference Point
True (T)	Geographical North Pole
Magnetic (M)	Magnetic North Pole
* Compass (C)	Compass North
* Relative (R)	Boat's Bow

* Not to be plotted on a chart.

D.35. BEARINGS

A bearing is a direction expressed in degrees from a reference point. Bearings may be true, magnetic, compass or relative. You may use all of the above reference directions except relative direction to designate headings or courses. Relative direction, which uses the boat's bow as the reference direction, changes constantly.

In boat navigation, you will usually use magnetic courses and bearings since true bearings are obtained from gyro compasses which are not normally found on boats.

OBTAINING BEARINGS Bearings are obtained primarily by using your magnetic compass (compass bearings) or radar (relative bearings). Bearings of fixed, known, objects are the most common sources for lines of position (LOPs) in coastal navigation. When using your compass to take bearings, sight the object across the compass.

D.36. COMPASS BEARINGS

In the section on compass and compass error, we discussed how to convert from a compass course to magnetic and true courses by correcting the compass indication. A compass bearing must be corrected before it can be plotted.

NOTE

DEVIATION always depends on your boat's heading.
The BEARING (compass or relative) of any object is not your course.
Enter the deviation table with the COMPASS HEADING you are steering to obtain proper deviation.

OBTAINING COMPASS BEARINGS You are on a heading of 270° M. You observe that the compass bearing to Kays Pt. Light is 060°. Deviation from the deviation table on the boat's heading of 270° M is 7°W. Obtain magnetic bearing of Kays Pt. Light. (See Figure 14-28.)

1. Correct your compass bearing of 60° magnetic. Write down the correction formula in a vertical line.

    C = 060° compass bearing of light.

    D = 7°W (+E, –W) from deviation table for boat's heading

    M = What is the magnetic bearing of the light?

2. Compute information you have opposite appropriate letter in step 1.

3. Subtract 7°W deviation, the westerly error, from the compass bearing (060°) to obtain magnetic bearing (053°).

    M = 053°

D.37. RELATIVE BEARINGS

Relative bearing of an object is its direction from the boat's bow at 000 degrees measured clockwise through 360 degrees.

CONVERTING TO MAGNETIC BEARINGS Relative bearings must be converted to magnetic bearings before they can be plotted. The steps are:

1. Convert your heading to a magnetic course. Based on the boat's heading at the time the bearing was taken, use the deviation table to determine the deviation. (Deviation depends on your boat's heading, not that of the relative bearing.)

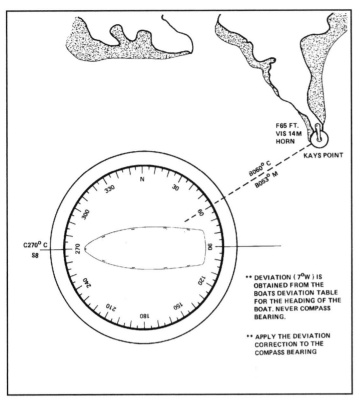

Figure 14-28 Converting Compass Bearing to Magnetic

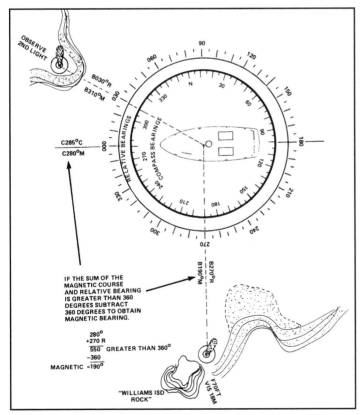

Figure 14-29 Converting Relative Bearings to Magnetic; Sums Greater than 360 Degrees

2. Add the relative bearing.

3. If this sum is more than 360 degrees, subtract 360 degrees to obtain the magnetic bearing.

Three examples follow to demonstrate these steps.

Example #1:

You are on a heading of 150°. You observed that the relative bearing to a standpipe was 125 degrees relative. Deviation (from the boat's deviation table) on the boat's heading is 4°E. Obtain the magnetic bearing of the standpipe.

1. Correct your heading of 150° to magnetic. Write down the correction formula in a vertical line.

$$C = 150°$$
$$D = 4°E\ (+E, -W)$$
$$M = 154\ degrees$$
$$V = Not\ applicable\ in\ this\ problem$$
$$T = Not\ applicable\ in\ this\ problem$$

2. Compute information you have opposite appropriate letter in step 1.

3. Add the easterly error, 4°E deviation from the compass heading to obtain magnetic heading (154°).

4. Add the observed relative bearing (125 degrees) and the magnetic heading (154°) to obtain magnetic bearing (279°M) of the standpipe.

Example #2:

Your boat is on a heading of 285°. You observed that the relative bearing to Williams ISD Rock Light is 270 degrees relative. You also observed that the relative bearing to another light is 030 degrees relative. Deviation from the boats deviation table on the boats heading is 5°W. Obtain magnetic bearing of both lights. (See Figure 14-29.)

1. Correct your heading of 285 to the magnetic heading. Write down the correction formula in a vertical line.

$$C = 285°$$
$$D = 5°W\ (+E, -W)$$
$$M = 280°$$
$$V = not\ applicable\ to\ this\ problem$$
$$T = not\ applicable\ to\ this\ problem$$

2. Compute information you have opposite appropriate letter in step 1. Subtract the westerly error, 5°W deviation from the compass heading (285°) to obtain magnetic heading (280°).

3. Add each of the observed relative bearings (270 degrees relative and 030 degrees relative) to the magnetic heading (280°) to obtain the magnetic bearings.

WILLIAMS ISD ROCK

280° M
+ 270° relative bearing
550 degrees (greater than 360 degrees)
−360
190° magnetic bearing

OTHER LIGHT

280° M
+ 030° relative bearing
310° magnetic bearing

D.38. DISTANCE

The second basic element in piloting is the special separation of two points measured by the length of a straight line joining the points without reference to direction. In piloting, it is measured in miles or yards. There are two different types of miles used: nautical miles and statute miles.

NAUTICAL MILE The nautical mile is used for measurement on most navigable waters. One nautical mile is 6,076 feet or approximately 2,000 yards and is equal mile to one minute of latitude.

STATUTE MILE The statute mile is used mainly on land, but it is also used in piloting inland bodies of water such as the Mississippi River and its tributaries, the Great Lakes and the Atlantic and Gulf Intracoastal waterways.

MEASURING DISTANCE Measure the distance by:

1. Place one end of pair of dividers at each end of the distance to be measured; being careful not to change the span of the dividers.

2. Transfer them to the latitude scale closest to the latitude being measured, read the distance in minutes. (See Figure 14-30.)

3. When the distance to be measured is greater than the span of the dividers, the dividers can be set at a minute or number of minutes of latitude from the scale and then "stepped off" between the points to be measured.

4. The last span, if not equal to that setting on the dividers, must be separately measured. To do

this, step the dividers once more; closing them to fit the distance.

5. Measure this distance on the scale and add it to the sum of the other measurements.

6. The latitude scale nearest the middle of the line to be measured should be used.

NOTE

The longitude scale is never used for measuring distance.

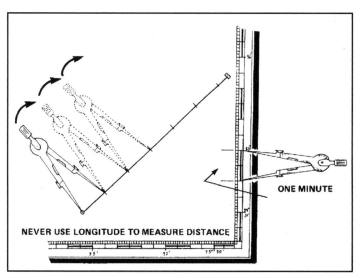

Figure 14-30 Measuring Distance, Latitude

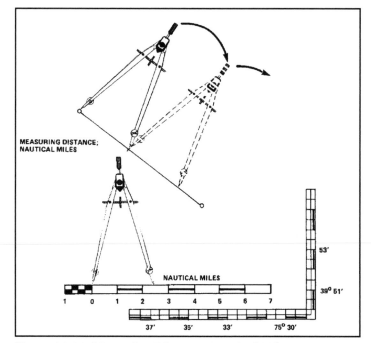

Figure 14-31 Measuring Distance, Nautical Miles

To measure short distances on a chart the dividers can be opened to a span of a given distance, then compared to the nautical mile or yard scale on the chart. (See Figure 14-31.)

D.39. TIME

Time is the third basic element in piloting. Time, distance, and speed are related. Therefore, if any two of the three quantities are known, the third can be found. The basic equations for distance, speed, and time, the speed curve and nautical slide rule and their use have been discussed earlier.

Plotting Bearings

D.40. GENERAL

A bearing or series of bearings can be observed as compass (C), magnetic (M), true (T), or as a relative bearing (visual or radar). The compass bearing reading usually needs to be converted for plotting and then drawn on the chart as a line of position (LOP).

D.41. PARALLEL

One common method of plotting bearings on a chart is using parallel rulers or a course plotter. Follow the procedures below for plotting the bearing on to the chart.

Example:

Your boat is on a heading of 192° compass. At 1015 you obtain a bearing of 040 degrees relative on a water tower. Deviation from the boat's deviation table on the boat's heading is 3°W.

1. Correct your compass heading of 192° to the magnetic heading.

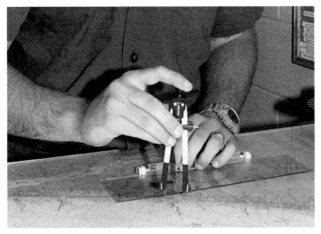

When plotting a course, dividers are used to measure distance.

Write down the correction formula in a vertical line.

C = 192°

D = 3W° (+E, –W when correcting)

M = 189°

V = not applicable to this problem

T = not applicable to this problem

2. Compute information you have opposite appropriate letter in STEP 1. Subtract the westerly error, 3°W deviation from the compass heading (192°) to obtain magnetic heading (189°)

3. Add the relative bearing (040 degrees) to the magnetic heading (189°) to obtain the magnetic bearing (229°); or

$$\begin{array}{r} 189° - (M) \\ + \, 040° \\ \hline 229° \text{ magnetic bearing} \end{array}$$

4. Place the parallel rulers with their edge passing through the crossed lines at the center of the compass rose and the 229° mark on the inner ring (magnetic) of the compass rose. (See Figure 14-32.)

5. Walk the parallel rulers to the dot marking the exact position of the water tower.

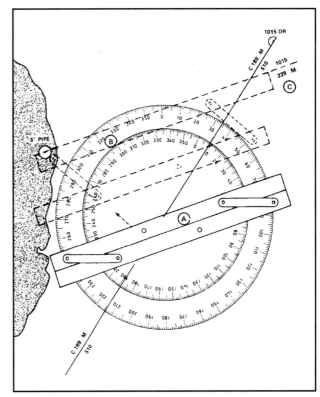

Figure 14-32 Plotting Bearings

6. Draw a broken line and intersect your course Line (C 189 M).

7. Label a segment of line with the time of the bearing along the top. The segment is drawn near the course line, not the entire length from the water tower.

8. Below the line label the magnetic bearing 229 M.

At 1015 your boat was somewhere along your LOP. A single line of bearing gives you a line of position but you cannot accurately fix your boat's location by a single LOP.

Line of Position (LOP)

D.42. GENERAL

The position of a boat can be determined by many methods of piloting. The line of position (LOP) is common to all methods of piloting. For example, if you observe a standpipe and a flagstaff in a line, you are somewhere on a line extended from the standpipe through the flagstaff and towards your boat. This line is called a range or a visual range.

If the bearing is taken on a single object, the line

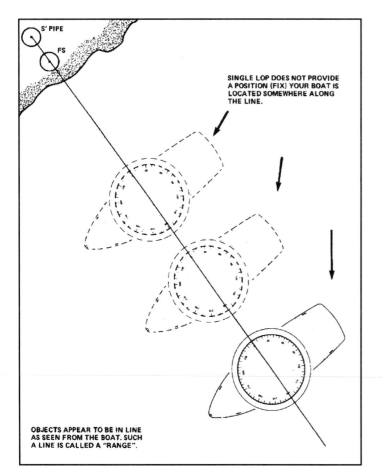

OBJECTS APPEAR TO BE IN LINE AS SEEN FROM THE BOAT. SUCH A LINE IS CALLED A "RANGE".

Figure 14-33 Visual Range LOP

drawn is called a bearing line of position. The observed bearing direction must be corrected to magnetic or true direction and plotted. The compass rose can be used to provide the direction.

A single observation gives an LOP, not a position—you are located somewhere along that LOP. (See Figure 14-33.)

NOTE

A boat's position is somewhere along the line of position.

D.43. SELECTING OBJECTS TO OBTAIN A FIX

The primary consideration in selecting charted objects to obtain a fix is the angle between the bearings. Also, always attempt to take bearings on object as close as possible to your boat because minor errors in reading are magnified as you increase your distance from the object.

NOTE

An error of 1 degree at 1 mile will result in an error of 100 feet.

TWO LINES OF POSITION When you have only two LOPs for a fix, the accuracy of the fix will be best when there is a 90 degree difference in the lines. Serious error in position can result if the angular difference between the LOPs is less than 60 degrees or more than 120 degrees. Therefore, two LOPs should intersect at right angles or near-right angles wherever possible.

THREE LINES OF POSITION An ideal fix has three or more LOPs intersecting at a single point AND with separations of at least 60 degrees but not more than 120 degrees.

D.44. OBTAINING FIXES

A single line of bearing gives an LOP, and your boat is somewhere along that LOP. You cannot accurately fix your position by a single line of position. Two or more intersecting LOPs or radar ranges must be plotted to obtain an accurate fix. The greater the number of lines of position or radar ranges intersecting at the same point, the greater the confidence you can have in the accuracy of the fix. For a fix to be accurate, LOPs must be observed at the same time. However, in practical boat navigation you can take two or more bearings, one after the other, and consider them observed simultaneously.

NOTE

For a fix to be accurate, LOPs must be from simultaneous observation (exact same time). Two or more bearings taken one immediately after the other are considered simultaneous.

OBTAINING BEARINGS Bearings are obtained by visual sightings across a mounted compass, a hand held bearing compass, the boat itself (relative bearings or "Dumb Compass") or by radar. The direction to the object sighted is then recorded, converted to magnetic or true direction and plotted.

USING CROSS BEARINGS A fix is obtained using cross bearings by taking bearings on two well defined objects and plotting the observed bearings on the chart. A more accurate fix can be obtained by taking a third bearing on another well defined object. The three lines of position should form a single point or a small triangle. Your boat's position is then considered to be on the point or in the center of the small triangle.

A large triangle is an indication than an inaccurate bearing was taken, double check your measurements.

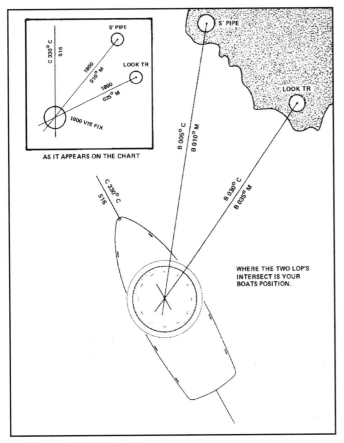

Figure 14-34 Two Ranges

Example:

While cruising on a compass heading of 330°, you sight a lookout tower and a standpipe and decide to take a fix. You observe the lookout tower to bear 030° (compass) and the standpipe bearing 005° (compass). Deviation from the deviation table, on the boat's compass heading (330° C), is 5°E. Plot your fix. (See Figure 14-34.)

1. Correct your compass bearing (030°) and (005°) to magnetic bearings.
   Write down the correction formula in a vertical line.

Lookout Tower	Standpipe
C = 030°	C = 005°
D = 5°E (+E, −W)	D = 5°E (+E, −W)
M = 035°	M = 010°
V = not applicable	V = not applicable
T = not applicable	T = not applicable

2. Compute information you have opposite the appropriate letter in step 1. Add the easterly error 5°E deviation to the compass bearing 030° and 005° to obtain magnetic bearings of 035° and 010°.

3. Plot the two magnetic bearings. The prudent sailor will recognize that the accuracy of this fix is doubtful due to the angle between the bearings being considerably less than the desired 60–120 degrees.

RANGES When two charted objects are in range, as seen from a boat, the boat is located somewhere on a straight line through these objects. Frequently a range will mark the center of a channel. The boat is steered so as to keep the range markers in line.

Ranges may be established navigational aids or natural ranges such as a church steeple and a water tower. When entering or leaving a harbor, it is often possible to fix your position by means of ranges.

Example:

You are steering on a range. While steering on this range (keeping the bow lined up with the two range marks), you note the time is 0800 when two charted objects (for example, a water tank and smoke stack) line up on the starboard side. The boat's position is at the intersection of the lines drawn through each set of ranges. (See Figure 14-35.) After having observed two sets of ranges which determined a fix, you come to a magnetic course of 330° M to stay in safe water.

RUNNING FIX (R FIX) Often it is impossible to obtain two bearing observations within close enough interval time to be considered simultaneous. A running fix (R Fix) can be obtained by using two lines of position acquired at different times. A running fix is determined by advancing an earlier LOP by using dead reckoning calculations of the boats direction and distance traveled during an interval. (See Figure 14-36.)

Plot a running fix by following these steps:

1. Plot the first LOP. Plot the second LOP.

2. Advance the first LOP along your DR plot to the time of second LOP. (The first LOP is advanced by moving it parallel to itself, forward along the course line for the distance the boat will have traveled to the time of the second bearing.)

3. Where the two LOPs intersect is your running fix.

4. Avoid advancing a LOP for more than 30 minutes.

NOTE

The shorter the time interval between LOPs, the more accurate the running fix.

Example:

At 1000 you observed a light on a compass bearing of 240°. At that time, there were no other well defined objects from which to obtain a bearing. Since plotting the first LOP you have run at 28 knots on a compass course of 030° C

At 1030 you observe a second compass bearing of 325° to the light. Plot this as a second LOP and advance your first LOP. The position where they cross is your running fix.

1. Obtain the time interval and the distance your boat traveled since your 1000 LOP.
   (A Nautical Slide Rule may be used.)

$$\begin{array}{r} 10 \text{ hours } 30 \text{ minutes} \\ -10 \text{ hours } 00 \text{ minutes} \\ \hline 30m - \text{time interval} \end{array}$$

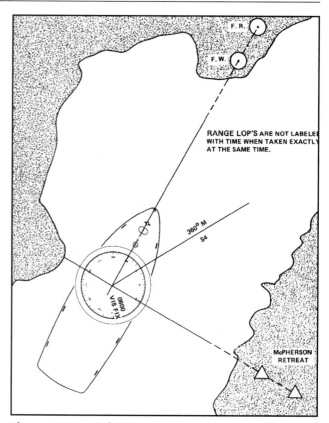

Figure 14-35 Fix by Two Ranges

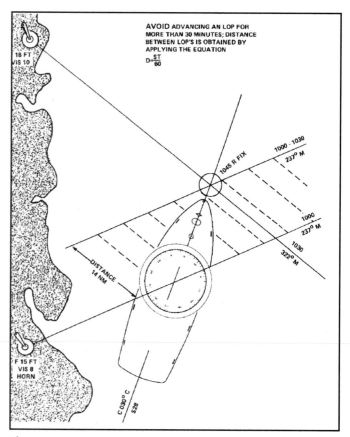

Figure 14-36 Running Fix

Apply the equation for Distance (Nautical slide Rule may be used).

$$D = S \times T \div 60$$
$$D = 28 \times 30 \div 60$$
$$D = 840 \div 60$$
$$D = 14 \text{ nautical miles}$$

2. Using your dividers measure the distance (14 NM) off of the latitude or nautical mile scale along the course line in the direction traveled.

3. Advance your first LOP, ensuring it is moved parallel to itself, forward along the course line for the distance traveled (14 NM). Draw the LOP labeling the new line (1000–1030) to indicate that it is an advanced LOP.

4. Correct the compass bearing of the second light (325° C) to obtain the magnetic bearing (322° M)

5. Plot the bearing. You now have established a running fix by advancing an LOP.

DANGER BEARINGS Danger bearings are used to keep a boat clear of a hazardous area in the vicinity of your track. Danger bearings are the maximum or minimum bearing of a point used for safe pas-

sage. They indicate a charted object whose bearing will place you outside that hazardous area. Examples of such dangers are submerged rocks, reefs, wrecks and shoals. A danger area must be established in relation to two fixed objects, one of which is the danger area. The other object must be selected to satisfy three conditions:

- visible to the eye
- indicated on the chart; and
- bearing from the danger area should be in the same general direction as the course of the boat as it proceeded past the area.

Plot a danger bearing with the steps below (see Figure 14-37):

1. On a chart, draw a line from the object selected (the leading object) to a point tangent to the danger area closest to where you intend to pass. The measured direction of the line from the danger area to the leading object is the danger bearing. Figure 14-37 indicates that 311° M is a danger bearing.

2. Label the danger bearing with the abbreviation "DB" followed by the direction (DB 311 M). Frequent visual bearings should be taken. If the bearings are greater than the danger bearing, your boat is in safe water.

When a bearing is observed to be less than the danger bearing, such as 300° M, your boat is standing into danger. Danger bearings should have a series of short lines drawn on the danger side for easy identification as shown in Figure 14-37.

The label DB may be proceeded by the letters NMT (not more than) or NLT (not less than) as appropriate.

The coxswain should ensure that all crew members are aware of where the danger lies. That is, whether the danger includes all degrees less than the danger bearing or all the degrees greater than the danger bearing.

Set and Drift (Current Sailing)

D.45. GENERAL

Current sailing is the method of computing course and speed through the water, considering the effects of current so that, upon arrival at your destination, the intended course (track) and the actual course made good are the same. The difference in position between a DR position and a fix taken at the corresponding time is due to various external forces acting on the boat. These forces are usually accounted for as set and drift.

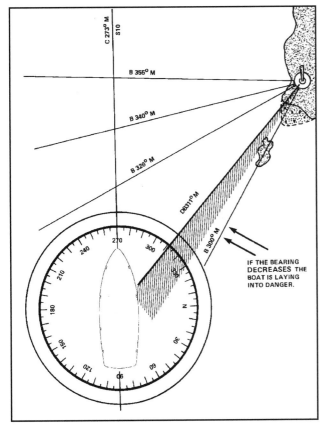

Figure 14-37 Danger Bearings

D.46. DEFINITION

Set is the direction of these forces and includes factors such as wind, current and sea condition. Set is expressed in degrees. "Set 240° magnetic" means that the boat is being pushed towards 240° magnetic.

Drift is the strength of the set and is expressed in knots. "Drift 1.5 knots" means that the boat is being pushed in a given direction (set) at a speed of 1.5 knots.

D.47. MAKING ALLOWANCES

In working problems involving set and drift you must allow for their effect upon your boat. This can be accomplished by comparing actual fix position information with your DR track and determining the difference. However, conditions do not always allow for this. Also, this can only be done after some portion of your voyage has already occurred.

D.48. TIDAL CURRENT CHARTS

Tidal Current Charts are available for certain bodies of water such as Boston Harbor or San Francisco Bay. They indicate graphically the direction and velocity of tidal currents for specific times with respect to the state of the current predictions for major reference stations. These charts make it possible to visualize how currents act in passages and channels throughout the 12-hour tidal cycle. By referring to the current charts you can plan a passage which is made quicker by either taking advantage of a favorable current or picking a track which reduces the effect of a head current.

D.49. TIDAL CURRENT TABLES

Tidal Current Tables are used to predict tidal currents. Examples of how to apply predicted currents are found in the back of the publication. This allows you to apply the corrections well in advance so that you may avoid the dangers along the way and safely arrive at your destination. This method involves the use of a vector diagram called a current triangle.

NOTE

The tidal current directions are shown in degrees true and must be converted to magnetic before plotting the set and drift problem.

D.50. CURRENT

The current triangle is a vector diagram from which you can find the course and speed your boat will make good when running a given course at a given speed. (See Figure 14-38.) It can also be used to determine the course to steer and the speed necessary to remain on your intended track. You may obtain this information by using the chart's compass rose for constructing a current triangle to provide a graphic solution.

- The first line (AB) on a current triangle indicates your boat's intended direction and the distance to travel in a given period of time. The length of this line represents your boat's speed in knots.

- The second line (CB) laid down to the destination end of the intended direction (the first line), shows the set (direction) of the current. The length of this line represents the drift (speed) of the current in knots.

- The third line (AC) provides the resulting corrected course to steer and the speed of advance to arrive safely at your destination. If any two sides of the triangle are known the third side can be obtained by measurement.

Example:

The intended track to your destination is 093° magnetic (093M), your speed is 5 knots, the *Tidal Current Table* for your operating area indicates that the current will be setting your boat 265° true (265T), drift (speed) 3 knots. The local variation is 4 degrees (W). Obtain the corrected course to steer and speed of advance (SOA) to allow for set and drift. (See Figure 14-39, the nautical miles scale is provided as an example for measuring "units" of length.)

1. Lay out your chart. Think of the center of the compass rose as your departure point. Draw your boat's intended track (093° M) from the center of the compass rose: Make this line 5

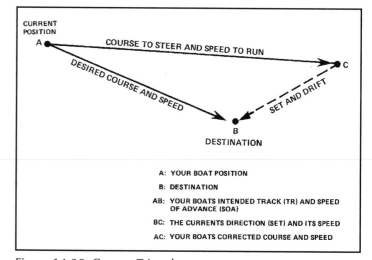

Figure 14-38 Current Triangle

units in length to represent 5 nautical miles from the center of the compass rose. Put a small arrowhead at this point. This is your desired course and speed vector.

2. Draw your line for the set and drift of the current from the center of the compass rose towards 261° magnetic

(265°T – 4°W (variation) = 261° M).

Set in the *Tidal Current Tables* is given in degrees true and must be converted to degrees

magnetic to be used. Make this line 3 units long putting an arrowhead at the outer end. This is your set and drift vector.

3. Draw a straight line to connect the arrowheads of the desired course and speed vector and the set and drift vector. This line is your corrected course to steer and speed of advance.

4. Measure the length of this line to obtain the speed (8.7 knots) from the nautical miles scale.

5. Advance the line to the center of the compass rose and read the corrected magnetic course to steer (088° M) from the inner circle of the compass rose.

Using the same figures as shown in the above example, Figure 14-40 shows what the effect would be if you do not correct for set and drift by using a current triangle.

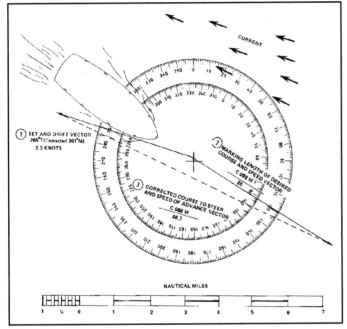

Figure 14-39 Plotting Set and Drift to Set Course to Steer

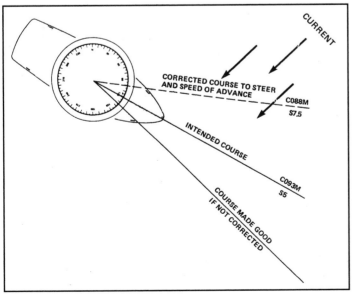

Figure 14-40 Compensating for Set and Drift

Radar

D.51. GENERAL

Radar is an aid in navigation. It is not the primary means of navigation. The success of boat navigation using radar in limited visibility depends on the coxswain's experience with radar operation. It also depends on the coxswain's knowledge of the local operating area and is not a substitute for an alert visual lookout.

D.52. BASIC PRINCIPLE

Radar radiates radio waves from its antenna to create an image that can give direction and distance to an object. Nearby objects (contacts) reflect the radio waves back and appear on the radar indicator as images (echoes). On many marine radars, the indicator is called the plan position indicator (PPI).

D.53. ADVANTAGES

Advantages of radar include:

• Use at night and low visibility conditions.

• Obtain a fix by distance ranges to two or more charted objects. An estimated position can be obtained from a range and a bearing to a single charted object.

• Rapid fixes.

• Fixes may be available at greater distances from land than by visual bearings.

• Assistance in preventing collisions.

D.54. DISADVANTAGES

The disadvantages of radar include:

- Mechanical and electrical failure.
- Minimum and maximum range limitations.

MINIMUM RANGE The minimum range is primarily established by the radio wave pulse length and recovery time. It depends on several factors such as excessive sea return, moisture in the air, other obstructions and the limiting features of the equipment itself. The minimum range varies but is usually 20 to 50 yards from the boat.

MAXIMUM RANGE Maximum range is determined by transmitter power and receiver sensitivity. However, radar radio waves are line of sight (travel in a straight line) and do not follow the curvature of the earth. Therefore, anything below the horizon usually will not be detected.

OPERATIONAL RANGE The useful operational range boat radar is limited mainly by the height of the antenna above the water.

D.55. READING THE RADAR INDICATOR

Interpreting the information presented on the indicator takes training and practice. The radar indicator should be viewed in total darkness, if possible, for accurate viewing of all echoes. Also, charts do not always give information necessary for identification of radar echoes, and distance ranges require distinct features.

It may be difficult to detect smaller objects (e.g., boats and buoys) in conditions such as:

- heavy seas;
- near the shore; or
- if the object is made of nonmetallic materials.

D.56. OPERATING CONTROLS

Control arrangement differs from radar to radar, but control functions are basically similar. The boat crew should become familiar with the operation of the radar by studying its operating manual and through the unit training program.

D.57. READING AND INTERPOLATING RADAR IMAGES

The plan position indicator (PPI) is the face or screen of the CRT (Cathode Ray Tube) which displays a bright straight radial line (tracer sweep) extending outward from the center of a radar screen. It represents the radar beam rotating with the antenna. It reflects images on the screen as patches of light (echoes).

In viewing any radar indicator, the direction in which the boat's heading flasher is pointing can be described as "up the indicator." The reciprocal of it is a direction opposite to the heading flasher, or down the indicator. A contact moving at right angles to the heading flasher anywhere on the indicator would be across the indicator.

The center of the radar screen represents the position of your boat. The indicator provides relative bearings of a target and presents a map-like representation of the area around the boat. The direction of a target is represented by the direction of its echo from the center, and the target's range is represented by its distance from the center. (See Figure 14-41.)

The cursor is a movable reference and is controlled by the radar cursor control. The cursor is used to obtain the relative bearings of a target on the indicator.

RADAR BEARINGS Radar bearings, like visual bearings, are measured relative to the boat with 000 degrees relative being dead ahead. (See Figure 14-41.) In viewing any radar indicator, the dot in the center indicates your boat's position. The line from the center dot to the outer edge of the indicator is called the heading flasher and indicates the direction your boat is heading.

To obtain target relative bearings, adjust cursor control until the cursor line crosses the target. The radar bearing is read from where the cursor line crosses the bearing ring.

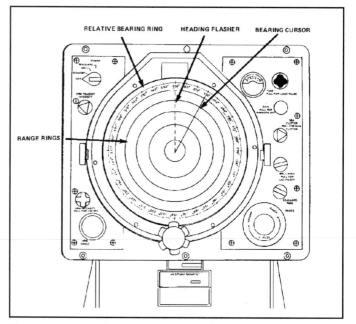

Figure 14-41 Radar Range Rings, Relative Bearing Ring, Heading Flasher and Bearing Cursor

As is the case with visual observations, radar relative bearing measurements must be converted to magnetic bearing before you plot them on a chart.

TARGET RANGE Many radars have a variable range marker. You dial the marker out to the inner edge of the contact on the screen and read the range directly.

Other radars may have distance rings. If the contact is not on a ring, you would estimate (interpolate) the distance by its position between the rings.

Example:

The radar is on the range scale of 2 nautical miles, and has 4 range rings. Range information is desired for a target appearing halfway between the third and fourth rings.

1. Range rings on the two mile scale are ½ mile or 1,000 yards apart (4 rings for 2 miles means each ring equals ¼ of the total range of 2 miles).

2. Calculate range as

   $1,000 + 1,000 + 1,000 + ½ \times 1,000$ or 3,500 yards.

D.58. RADAR CONTACTS

Even with considerable training you may not always find it easy to interpret a radar echo properly. Only through frequent use and experience will you be able to become proficient in the interpretation of images on the radar screen.

Knowledge of the radar picture in your area is obtained by using the radar during good visibility and will eliminate most doubts when radar navigating at night and during adverse weather. Images on a radar screen differ from what is seen visually by the naked eye. This is because some contacts reflect radio waves (radar beams) better than others.

COMMON RADAR CONTACTS

A list of common radar contacts and reflection quality follows:

REEFS, SHOALS, AND WRECKS: May be detected at short to moderate ranges, if breakers are present and are high enough to return echoes. These echoes usually appear as cluttered blips.

SANDY SPITS, MUD FLATS AND SANDY BEACHES: Return the poorest and weakest echoes. The reflection, in most cases, will come from a higher point of land from the true shoreline such as bluffs or cliffs in back of the low beach. False shorelines may appear because of a pier, several boats in the area, or heavy surf over a shoal.

ISOLATED ROCKS OR ISLANDS OFF SHORE: Usually return clear and sharp echoes providing excellent position information.

LARGE BUOYS: May be detected at medium range with a strong echo; small buoys sometimes give the appearance of surf echoes. Buoys equipped with radar reflectors will appear out of proportion to their actual size.

PIERS, BRIDGES AND JETTIES: Provide strong echoes at shorter ranges.

RAIN SHOWERS, HAIL AND SNOW: Will also be detected by radar and can warn you of foul weather moving into your area. Bad weather appears on the screen as random streaks known as 'clutter.'

D.59. RADAR FIXES

Radar navigation provides a means for establishing position during periods of low visibility when other methods may not be available. A single prominent object can provide a radar bearing and range for a fix, or a combination of radar bearings and ranges may be used. Whenever possible, obtain more than one object. Radar fixes are plotted in the same manner as visual fixes.

NOTE

If a visual bearing is available it is more reliable than one obtained by radar.

Example:

On a compass heading of 300°, you observe a radar contact (image) bearing 150 degrees relative. Deviation, from the deviation table, for the boat's compass heading (300° C) is 3'E.

Obtain the magnetic bearing of the contact.

1. Correct your compass heading of 300 degrees to magnetic heading.

   Write down the correction formula in a vertical line.

   C = 300°

   D = 3° E (+E, –W when correcting)

   M = 303° M

   V = not applicable in this problem

   T = not applicable in this problem

2. Compute information you have opposite appropriate letter in STEP No. 1. Add the easterly error 3°E deviation to the compass heading (300° C) to obtain the magnetic course of 303° M).

3. Add the radar relative bearing (150 degrees relative) to the magnetic heading (303° M) to obtain magnetic bearing of the radar contact (093° M).

$$303°$$
$$+150°$$
$$453° \text{ degrees (greater than } 360°)$$

$$453°$$
$$+360°$$
$$093° \text{ M bearing of contact}$$

RANGE RINGS Radar range rings are displayed as circles of light on the screen. Major range scales are indicated in miles and are then subdivided into range rings. Typical range scales for boat radar are ½, 1, 2, 4, 8, and 16 nautical miles (NM). Typical number of range rings for a particular range scale are shown in the table below.

Scale/Miles	Rings	NM Per Ring
½	1	½
1	2	½
2	4	½
4	4	1
8	4	2
16	4	4

LINES OF POSITION Radar lines of position (LOPs) may be combined to obtain fixes. Typical combinations include two or more bearings; a bearing with distance range measurement to the same or another object; two or more distance ranges. Radar LOPs may also be combined with visual LOPs.

Care should be exercised when using radar bearing information only since radar bearings are not as precise as visual bearings. A fix obtained by any radar bearing or by distance measurement is plotted on the chart with a dot enclosed by a circle to indicate the fix and label with time followed by "RAD FIX", such as, 1015 RAD FIX.

DISTANCE MEASUREMENTS EXAMPLE At 0215, you are on a course of 303' (303' M). Your radar range scale is on 16 miles. You observe two radar contacts (land or charted landmark). The first has a bearing of 330 degrees relative at 12 NM. This

target is on the third range circle. The second target is bearing 035 degrees relative at 8NM. This target is on the second range circle. Obtain a distance measurement fix. (See Figure 14-42.)

1. Locate the objects on the chart.

2. Spread the span of your drawing compass to a distance of 12 NM (distance of first target), using the latitude or nautical mile scale on the chart.

3. Without changing the span of the drawing compass, place the point on the exact position of the object and strike an arc towards your DR track, plotting the distance.

4. Repeat the above steps for the second object (distance of 8 NM). Where the arcs intersect is your fix (position). Label the fix with time and "RAD FIX" (0215 RAD FIX).

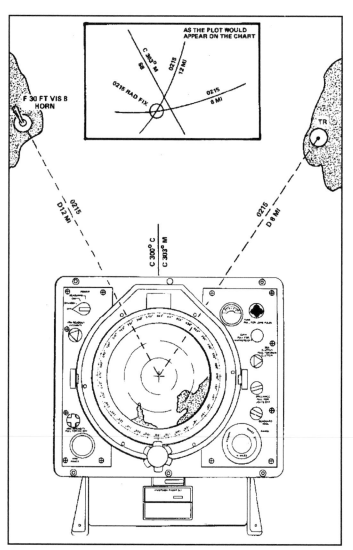

Figure 14-42 Obtaining a Radar Fix Using Two Distance Measurements

NOTE

Radar ranges are usually measured from prominent land features such as cliffs or rocks. However, landmarks such as lighthouses and towers often show up at a distance when low land features do not.

A DR plot typically includes many types of LOPs and fixes. Figure 14-43 is provided as an example of what could appear on a properly maintained DR plot. Some of the fixes within the figure have not been discussed within the text.

Loran

D.60. GENERAL

Derived from the words LOng RAnge Navigation, Loran-C is a navigation system network of transmitters consisting of one master station and two or more secondary stations. Loran-C is a pulsed, hyperbolic (uses curved lines) system. Loran-C receiver's measure the Time Difference (TD) between the master transmitter site signal and the secondary transmitter site signal to obtain a single line of position (LOP). A second pair of Loran-C transmitting stations produces a second LOP. Plotting positions using TDs requires charts overprinted with Loran-C curves. However, many modern Loran-C receivers convert Loran-C signals directly into readouts of latitude and longitude. The mariner then can use a standard nautical chart without Loran-C curves. Loran is accurate to about 0.25 nautical mile (NM).

D.60. RECEIVER CHARACTERISTICS

Control locations vary on different Loran receivers, but their functions are similar. The boat crew should become familiar with the operation of the Loran receiver by studying its operating manual and through the unit training program.

NOTE

Loran-C is not accurate enough for precise navigation, such as staying within a channel.

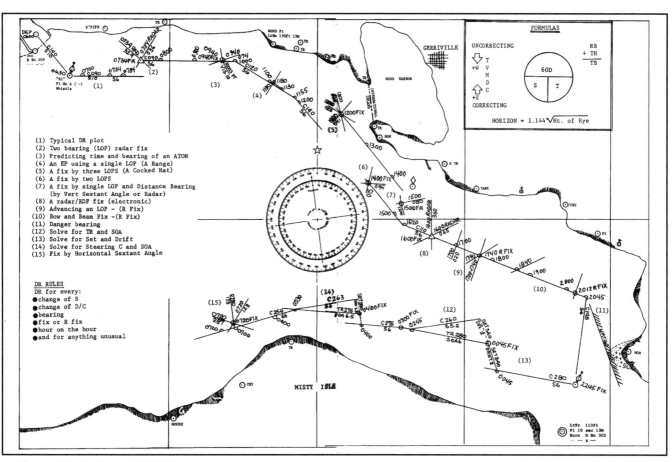

Figure 14-43 Sample DR Plot

D.61. DETERMINING POSITION

Many Loran-C receivers give direct readouts of latitude and longitude position which can be plotted on the chart. Depending on the receiver, some position accuracy may be lost during the conversion of Loran TDs to latitude and longitude. Loran position readout typically displays two decimal places (hundredths), but plotting normally only goes to the first decimal place (tenths).

Older Loran-C receivers display only a TD for each pair of stations. By matching these TD numbers to the chart's Loran-C grid you determine an LOP. Intersecting two or more of these LOPs gives you a fix.

TDs represent specific intersecting grid lines on a Loran-C chart. (See Figure 14-44.) Each line is labeled with a code such as SSO-W and SSO-Y that identifies particular master-secondary signals. Following the code is a number that corresponds to the TDs that would appear on a Loran receiver on a boat located along the line. Note the TDs and find the two intersecting grid lines that most nearly match the readings on your boat's receiver—one on the SSO-W axis, the other on the SSO-Y Axis.

The first step in plotting a Loran position is to match the numbers on the receiver with the Loran grid on the chart. The point where the two lines meet gives you a fix of your position.

D.62. REFINING A LORAN-C LINE OF POSITION

You have two Loran readings: SSO-W-13405.0 and SSO-Y-56187.5. The first axis lies between SSO-W-13400.0 and SSO-W-13410.0 and the second axis lies between SSO-Y-56180.0 and SSO-Y-56190.0.

Refine your Loran-C fix. (See Figure 14-45.)

1. Use dividers and measure the exact distance between the Loran lines of position SSO-W-13400.0 and SSO-W-13410.0 on your chart. (See Figure 14-45.)

2. Without changing the span of your dividers, find the points where the distance between the base of the wedge-shaped interpolator scale on the chart and the topmost sloping edge of the interpolator matches the span of the dividers. Connect these two points with a vertical line. (See Figure 14-45.)

3. Along the vertical edge of the interpolator are the numbers 0, 1, 2, 3, 4, 5, 6, 7, 8, 9, 10. Beginning at the base, read UP. Each number makes an immediate sloping line on the interpolator. The difference between SSO-W- 1 3405.0 and SSO-W-18410.0 is five. Select line five of the interpolator and follow it to the vertical line drawn in step 2.

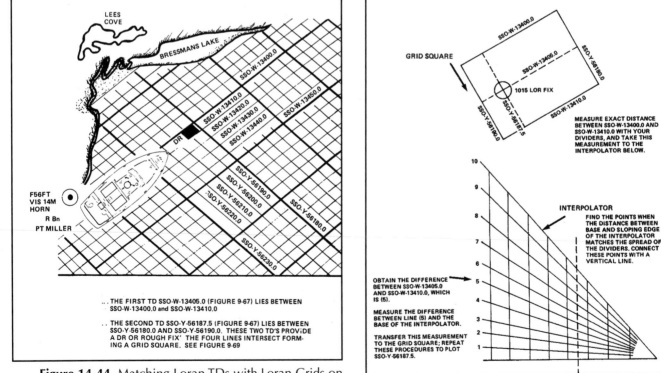

Figure 14-44 Matching Loran TDs with Loran Grids on a Chart

... THE FIRST TD SSO-W-13405.0 (FIGURE 9-67) LIES BETWEEN SSO-W-13400.0 and SSO-W-13410.0

.. THE SECOND TD SSO-Y-56187.5 (FIGURE 9-67) LIES BETWEEN SSO-Y-56180.0 AND SSO-Y-56190.0. THESE TWO TD'S PROViDE A DR OR ROUGH FIX' THE FOUR LINES INTERSECT FORMING A GRID SQUARE. SEE FIGURE 9-69

Figure 14-45 Obtaining a Loran Fix on a Grid Square

4. Take your dividers and measure the distance between line five and the base of the interpolator. Without changing the span of the dividers measure the same distance, away and perpendicular to the line SSO-W-13400.0 on the chart nearest your DR.

Measure the direction toward the line SSO-W-13410.0. Take your parallel rulers and draw a line parallel to S SO-W- 1 8400.0 at this point. Your SSO-W- 1 3405.0 TD is now plotted.

5. Plot the SSO-Y-56187.5 between SSO-Y-56180.0 and SSO-Y-56190.0 using the above procedure.

Global Positioning System (GPS)

D.63. GENERAL

The Global Positioning System (GPS) is a radionavigation system of 24 satellites operated by the Department of Defense (DoD). It is available 24 hours per day, worldwide, in all weather conditions. Each GPS satellite transmits its precise location—position and elevation. In a process called "ranging," a GPS receiver processes the signal to determine the distance between it and the satellite. Once the receiver has computed the range for at least four satellites, it processes a three-dimensional position that is accurate to about 100 meters. GPS provides two levels of service—Standard Positioning Service (SPS) for civilians users, and Precise Positioning Service (PPS) for military users.

D.64. STANDARD POSITIONING SERVICE

The civilian SPS is available on a continuous basis to any user worldwide. It is accurate to a radius within 100 meters of the position shown on the receiver about 99% of the time.

D.65. PRECISE POSITIONING SERVICE

PPS provides position fixes accurate to within 21 meters. This service is limited to approved U.S. Federal government, allied military, and civil users.

D.66. EQUIPMENT FEATURES

GPS receivers are small, with small antennas and low power consumption. Hand-held units are available. Positional information is shown on a liquid crystal display (LCD) screen as geographical coordinates (latitude and longitude readings). These receivers are designed to interface with and provide position information to other devices such as autopilots, EPIRBs and other distress alerting devices. Navigational features available in the typical GPS receiver include:

- entry of waypoints and routes in advance
- display of course and speed made good
- display of cross-track error
- availability of highly accurate time information

Differential Global Positioning System (DGPS)

The Coast Guard developed Differential Global Positioning System (DGPS) to improve upon GPS SPS signals. DGPPS uses a local reference receiver to correct errors in the standard GPS signals. These corrections are then broadcast and can be received by any user with a DGPS receiver. The corrections are applied within the user's receiver, providing mariners with a position that is accurate within 10 meters, with 99.7 percent probability. While DGPS is accurate to within 10 meters, improvements to receivers will make DGPS accurate to within a centimeter, noise-free and able to provide real-time updates.

The Coast Guard uses selected marine radiobeacons to send DGPS corrections to users. DGPS provides accurate and reliable navigating information to maritime users in Harbor Entrance and Approaches (HEA), along U.S. coastal waters, the Great Lakes, navigable portions of the western rivers, Puerto Rico, Hawaii, and Alaska.

<hr>

SECTION E

River Sailing

Overview

Introduction

This section provides general information for operating on rivers, with emphasis on the western rivers. The western rivers (Mississippi River system) pose navigational concerns that often are not seen in harbor, coastal or high seas sailing. Local knowledge is very important. Riverine navigational techniques and nautical lexicon both have differences that must be learned to become a competent river sailor.

In this section

Major Piloting Differences

E.1. GENERAL

Some of the special considerations for river navigation include:

- Charts
- Mile marks
- Fixed aids
- Buoyage
- Compass
- Dead reckoning (DR) plot

E.2. CHARTS

Simple, line-drawn "maps" that show the main geographical features of the waterway, the channel or sailing line, prominent manmade objects, and the various aids. River charts do not show landmarks such as stacks, water towers, or antennas. These charts do not always show the geographical names for areas along the bank. River charts only show structures immediately on the banks by symbol and footnote. Figure 14-46 provides a good example.

NOTE

A road map of the operating area is a good supplement for identifiable geographical names.

E.3. MILE MARKS

The Western Rivers have mile marks (beginning at the mouth or at the headwaters of the stream).

E.4. FIXED AIDS

Fixed aids (daymarks and lights) display the mile (usually statute miles) on a "mile" board for that point of the river. Where no aid exists, landmarks such as bridges, creeks, islands, and overhead power lines, provide the mile-mark reference.

E.5. BUOYAGE

The U.S. lateral system of buoyage has differences when used on these rivers.

E.6. COMPASS

Compasses are not normally very useful on western rivers due to no plotting references on the chart and the fact that many rivers meander. However, boat-mounted compasses must be installed. There will be situations in which the use of a compass can help determine a position. For example, on a meandering river with no prominent landmarks, comparing the compass heading with the north arrow on the chart will help identify the bend or reach where the boat is operating. A log is to be maintained showing each position.

E.7. DEAD RECKONING (DR) PLOT

As in coastal sailing, a boat's approximate position is determined by dead reckoning–applying its speed, time and course from its last known position. However, because many rivers have numerous bends, it often is not possible to maintain a complete DR plot with precise course changes.

Conditions and Effects

E.8. GENERAL

Surface and bottom conditions of a river are unpredictable and can change quickly. Some of the unique situations you will have to deal with include:

- Silting and shoaling
- Drift
- Flood or drought

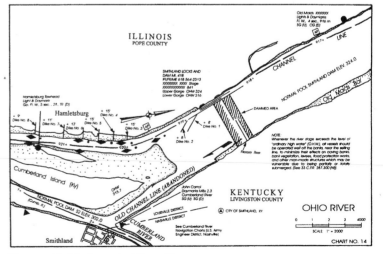

Figure 14-46 Sample River Chart

E.9. SILTING AND SHOALING

Silt is a mass of soil particle carried in water. It can clog boat cooling water intakes and wear out strut bearings and shafts. Silt settles on the bottom as shoaling, either adding to or creating sand bars or mud banks.

E.10. DRIFT

"Drift" or "driftwood" is floating debris carried by the river flow and washed or lifted from the banks. Running drift can damage a boat.

E.11. FLOOD OR DROUGHT

Tides affect rivers near the coast, but flooding or drought will greatly affect the vertical level (depth) of the entire river.

FLOOD Flooding is created by runoff or drainage from heavy rains or melting snow. A waterway will contain strong currents and a lot of running drift during flooding. Navigating outside the river banks requires caution and local knowledge.

DROUGHT Drought is low water level. This can result in the closing of channels. Snags and obstructions that once could be cleared easily become hazards to navigation. Also, sandbars and mud flats will appear where it was once safe to operate.

NOTE

Refer to Chapter 10—Boat Handling, for information on operating boats in narrow channels.

Locks and Dams

E.12. GENERAL

Locks and dams provide a navigable channel for river traffic. Navigation dams release water, as necessary, to maintain a navigable channel during the navigation season. Locks release water as a part of their normal operation. Both dams and locks can present safety problems for boat operators. Knowledge of locks and dams, including location, use and associated hazards, is essential for safe boat operations.

E.13. CONSTRUCTION AND OPERATION

The navigation dams on the Mississippi, Illinois and Ohio rivers vary in construction. Two common types of dam construction are the Tainter gate and the Roller gate. Also, some dam releases are controlled remotely. The type of dams that will be en-

countered and how they are controlled is the kind of local knowledge boat crews needs to check.

Most people know that water released from a dam can create a powerful, turbulent current downstream. However, an upstream water current can exist close to the lower or downstream side of a dam. Operating too close to the downstream side of a dam can result in the boat being drawn into the dam.

A strong suction is created by the rush of water underneath the upper side of a roller-gate dam. (See Figure 14-47.) A boat drifting into the dam on the upper side is in no danger on the surface of being drawn into the gate but personnel should not enter the water.

E.14. NAVIGATION DISPLAYS

When locks at fixed damns and moveable dams have their dams up, they will show navigation lights during hours of darkness. These lights are green, red, or white and are displayed in groups of one, two or three. A circular disc may also be shown. The significance of these displays is explained in local guidance.

E.15. LOCK OPERATIONS

The purpose of a lock is to raise or lower the boat to the level of the channel that it wants to navigate. Locks come in all shapes and sizes, but they all operate on the principle that water seeks its own level. A lock is an enclosure with accommodations at both ends (generally called gates) to allow boats to enter and exit. The boat enters, the gates are closed, and by a system of culverts and valves, the water level in

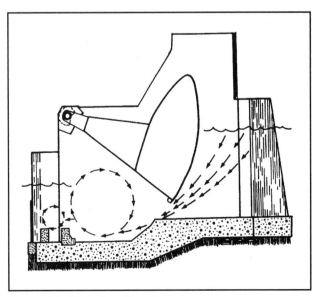

Figure 14-47 Roller Gate Dam

the lock aligns with the pool level of the upstream or downstream side of the lock. The gate then opens and the boat can continue on its way.

E.16. LOCKING PROCEDURES

There are many common locking procedures, and local regulations can vary. The boat crew must check local guidance for correct locking procedure for each lock. Standard locking signals are shown in Figure 14-48. Precautions to take in locking include:

- do not come closer than 400 feet of the lock wall until the lockman signals you to enter
- moor to the side of the lock wall as directed
- if using your own mooring lines, they should be at least 50 feet long with a 12-inch eye splice
- do not tie mooring lines to the boat; tend the lines as the water level changes
- be prepared to cast off lines in an emergency; a small hand axe or hatchet should be available
- use fenders
- do not moor to ladder rungs embedded in the lock walls
- wait for the lockman's signal (an air horn) to depart
- depart in the same order that you entered the lock with other boats
- steer for the channel and keep a sharp lookout for craft approaching from the other direction

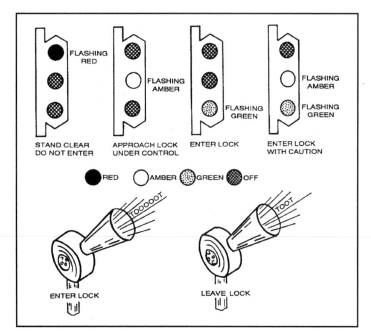

Figure 14-48 Standard Locking Signals

At locks with "small craft signals," you may signal the lockman that you want to pass. After signaling, stand clear and wait for instructions. Many locks are radio-equipped to receive requests that way. Consult the appropriate navigation charts for radio-equipped locks, the frequency, and the call sign.

E.17. GENERAL CONSIDERATIONS

General considerations around locks include:

- The Secretary of the Army sets the priorities for safe and efficient passage of the various types of craft on inland waterways. Priorities, listed in descending order with the highest priority on top, are:

  U.S. military craft

  vessels carrying U.S. mail

  commercial passenger craft

  commercial tows

  commercial fisherman

  recreational craft

- Under certain conditions, boats may be locked through with other crafts having a higher priority. This occurs only when there is no delay and neither craft is placed in jeopardy.
- Lockmen have the same authority over a boat in a lock as the traffic police have over a car at an intersection. For safety purposes, obey the lockman's instructions.
- Every boat should carry a copy of, and the crew should be familiar with the regulations governing navigation on the rivers in its AOR.

Safety Considerations Around Navigation Dams

E.18. GENERAL

General safety considerations include:

- Stay clear of danger zones—600 feet above and 100 feet below dams.
- Approach dams at reduced speed, along the shore at the lock.
- Be "dam" conscious:

1. It is dangerous to approach near the intake ports in the lock walls above the upstream lock gates during the filling process. The filling process creates a powerful suction as water rushes into the culverts. Boats must stay clear of the locks until signaled to approach.

2. During the emptying process, a strong undercurrent and suction is created in the lock chamber. This suction occurs next to the lock walls and is created by the water rushing into the filling and emptying ports of the lock.

3. Wearing a PFD may not keep you from being pulled under the water in these circumstances.

Flood Warnings

E.19. GENERAL

During flood condition, do not use the waterway if you do not have to go out. Dangers include:

- currents are much stronger,
- channels can shift,
- obstructions can be hidden under the water,
- hazards (trees and other debris) increase;
- aids to navigation can be broken; and
- bridge clearances are reduced.

Common River Sailing Terms

E.20. GENERAL

The following terms and their definitions are the most commonly used in river sailing.

AUXILIARY LOCK: A small secondary lock next to the main lock.

BACKWATER: The water backed up a tributary system.

BAR: A deposit of sand or gravel in or near the channels that, at times, prevents boat traffic from passing.

BEND: A bend of the river is like a curve in a highway.

BERM: The sharp definitive edge of a dredged channel such as in a rock cut.

BIGHT OF A BEND: Sharpest part of a curve in a river or stream.

BITTS, FLOATING: Part of a lock system for securing a boat waiting in a lock, recessed in lock walls.

BOIL: Turbulence in the water resulting from deep holes, ends of dikes, channel changes, or other underwater obstructions.

CAVAL OR KEVEL: A steel cleat of special design on barges and towboats for making aft mooring and towing lines.

CHUTE: Section of river that is narrower than ordinary and through which the river current increases. It is also the passage behind an island that is not the regular channel.

DEADHEAD: A water soaked wooden pile, tree, or log that floats at the surface of the water (barely awash), usually in a vertical position.

DIKE: A structure of pilings or stone that diverts the current of a river.

DOWN DRAFT: The natural tendency of a river current to pull the boat downstream when making a river crossing.

DRAFT: A crosscurrent that is usually designated as an out draft, or as a left or right-handed draft.

DRAW DOWN: The release of water through one dam before the arrival of a significant increase in water from the upper reaches of the river.

DRIFT: It is debris floating in or lodged along the banks of the river. (Also known as driftwood.)

FLAT POOL: The normal stage of water in the area between two dams. It is maintained when little or no water is flowing; therefore the pool flattens out.

FLOOD STAGE: A predetermined level or stage along the main river bank where flooding will occur or may overflow in the particular area.

FOOT OF ____: The downstream end or lower part of a bend or island.

GAUGE: A scale graduated in tenths of a foot which shows the water level or river stage. A lower gauge is one which shows the downstream side of a dam and an upper gauge is one on the upstream side.

HEAD OF ____: The upstream end or beginning of a bend or island.

LEFT BANK: The left bank of a river when going down stream, properly termed left bank descending.

LEVEE: An embankment or dike constructed for flood protection.

LOCK: A chamber built as part of a river dam to raise or lower boat traffic that wants to pass the dam.

LOCK GATE: A moveable barrier that prevents water from entering or leaving a lock chamber.

MILE BOARD: A 12" x 36" board above a river aid and with the river mileage at that point from a given location.

OPEN RIVER: Any river having no obstructions such as dams, or when the river stage is high enough to navigate over movable dams.

POOL STAGE: The stage of water between two successive dams. It is usually at the minimum depth to maintain the depth in the channel at the shallowest point.

REACH: Usually a long, straight section of a river.

RIGHT BANK: The right bank of a river when going downstream, properly termed as right bank descending.

SLACK WATER: A location where there is a minimum current.

SNAG: Tree or log embedded in the river bottom.

STERN LINE TALK: Supposedly factual information about anything passed between river people.

TOW: One or more barges made up to be transported by a boat.

TOWBOAT: A river boat that push barges ahead.

Search and Rescue

Editor's Note: *With the skills you've learned in previous chapters (and a little luck), you'll probably never be the object of a Coast Guard search and rescue (SAR) operation. But you may be called upon to help out the Coasties in their efforts to help someone else on the water. This chapter is designed to introduce Coast Guard personnel to basic search and rescue skills and procedures. It's important to understand that the Coast Guard will render what aid it can whenever life or property are in peril on the water. However, federal legislation prohibits the Coast Guard from competing with commercial tow operators when there is no threat to persons on board. So, if you run out of gas on a sunny afternoon in calm seas, the Coasties will be happy to initiate a Marine Assistance Radio Broadcast seeking tow operators or Good Samaritans willing to come to your aid, but don't expect a motor lifeboat to come running. On the other hand, if you run out of gas and the weather is rough, or darkness is approaching, or someone aboard is ill, or you flag down an auxiliary vessel passing by, you are very likely to get assistance. It never hurts to ask.*

Overview

Introduction

This chapter provides a general overview of the Search and Rescue (SAR) organization and basic skills and knowledge required to conduct SAR operations as a boat crew member.

A successful rescue mission depends on correct search planning and execution. The dramatic image of a Coast Guard boat battling wind and sea in the dead of night to save a helpless mariner is only part of the story. The rest of the story involves collecting essential information, planning the correct response, assessing the risk, selecting the proper search and rescue unit, and exercising proper safety precautions.

NOTE

Specific policies, guidance, and technical information for SAR operations are in the *National Search and Rescue Manual,* COMDTINST M16120.5 & 6, and the *Coast Guard Addendum to the National Search and Rescue Manual* COMDTINST M16130.2 (series).

In this chapter

Organization and Responsibility

Overview

Introduction

The boat responding to a SAR incident is an operational facility that is one part of the overall SAR system. To enable the boat to effectively perform its operation as a search and rescue unit (SRU), an organization and assignment of responsibilities have been established on a national and international level. This section presents SAR information on the national system.

In this section

Coast Guard Responsibility

A.1. GENERAL

SAR coordination responsibility in the United States is divided between the Air Force and the Coast Guard. The Air Force is responsible for inland SAR. The Coast Guard is responsible for maritime SAR which includes:

- interior river systems,
- inland waterways,
- coastal waters, and
- parts of the high seas.

Memorandums of understanding (MOU) with Guam, Alaska and Hawaii, state that Coast Guard resources are also responsible for land SAR in these areas (only portions of Alaska).

A.2. THE LAW AS IT APPLIES TO THE COAST GUARD

The Coast Guard promotes safety on, over, and under the high seas and all waters subject to the jurisdiction of the United States. U.S. law states that the Coast Guard **shall** develop, establish, maintain, and operate search and rescue facilities and **may** render aid to distressed persons and protect and save property. It also states that the Coast Guard may utilize its resources to assist other federal and state entities.

A.3. AREAS OF RESPONSIBILITY

Maritime SAR is divided into two major areas of responsibility (AORs):

- Atlantic maritime region
- Pacific maritime region

The two regions are further subdivided into smaller geographical AORs for better distribution and management of personnel and facilities.

A.4. OBJECTIVES

Two SAR program objectives are of direct importance to boat crews:

- To minimize loss of life, personal injury, and property loss and damage in the maritime environment.
- To minimize search duration and crew risk during SAR missions.

A.5. SAR FACTS

The majority of SAR cases occurs within 20 miles of shore. Coast Guard helicopters and boats, the primary quick response assets, handle most of these cases. About 90% of all cases do not require searching. A small percentage of cases involve minor searches (less than 24 hours) and an even smaller percent of these cases involve major searches lasting over 24 hours. Despite being a small percentage of SAR operations overall, the annual cost for searches is millions of dollars. Boats may conduct operations with helicopters, especially searches or medical evacuations (MEDEVACs). Chapter 19—Air Operations, provides more information on operating with aircraft.

Search and Rescue Coordination

A.6. GENERAL

Your boat is part of a unit; your unit is part of a group; your group is part of a district; and your district is part of an area. Each link going up this chain of command controls more SAR resources and has wider geographic responsibility than the link below it. The SAR system has three levels of coordination—the SAR coordinator, the SAR mission coordinator, and the on-scene coordinator.

A.7. SAR COORDINATOR (SC)

The Coast Guard is designated **SAR coordinator (SC)** for the Maritime Area and the Air Force for the Inland Area. Coast Guard area commanders are designated SCs for each of the two maritime SAR regions and so are district commanders for their SAR regions. The SCs are the top level SAR managers. The SC is responsible for:

- Establishing, staffing, equipping, and managing the SAR system
- Establishing rescue coordination centers (RCCs)
- Providing or arranging for SAR facilities
- Coordinating SAR training
- Developing SAR policies

A.8. SAR MISSION COORDINATOR (SMC)

Each SAR operation is carried out under the guidance of an **SMC**. The SMC is usually the district RCC or the Group (activity) operations center (OPCEN). The SMC has several duties and responsibilities:

- Obtain and evaluate all data on the emergency.
- Dispatch search and rescue units (SRUs) based on this information.
- Develop search plans which include determining limits for the search area, selecting the search pattern, and designating the on-scene coordinator (OSC).
- Control the SAR communication network for the assigned mission.
- Monitor progress of the SAR mission and request additional SAR resources as necessary.

A.9. ON-SCENE COMMANDER (OSC)

The **OSC** is designated by the SMC to coordinate the activities of all units when two or more SRUs are on scene for the same incident. The first unit on scene usually assumes OSC until the SMC directs that the person be relieved. The OSC should be the most capable unit, considering SAR training, communications capabilities, and the length of time that the unit can stay in the search area. As the subordinate of the SMC, the OSC has several duties and responsibilities. These are:

- Inform the SMC through periodic situation reports (SITREPs)
- Coordinate the efforts of all SRUs on scene
- Implement the search action plan from the SMC

- Control all on-scene communications between those SRUs
- Monitor the endurance of all SRUs and call for replacement units as needed
- Provide initial briefings and search instructions to arriving SRUs

A.10. SEARCH AND RESCUE UNIT (SRU)

An **SRU** is a unit with trained personnel and provided with equipment for SAR operations. The **SRU** responsibilities include:

- Efficiently execute assigned SAR duties.
- Establish and maintain communications with the OSC or SMC, as appropriate, prior to arriving on scene and until released from the case.

REPORTING Unless you are designated OSC, or are the single SRU on scene, you will report to the OSC. If you are designated OSC or are the single SRU on scene, assume the duties of OSC and report to the SMC.

COMMUNICATION Communications and information flow is critical to good SAR planning and conducting of SAR operations. SRUs must continually keep the OSC, or if an OSC is not assigned, the SMC informed of any changes on scene so that proper, timely, and accurate changes can be made to the search plan (see Figure 15-1).

SECTION B

SAR Emergency Phases

B.1. GENERAL

Upon receiving an initial report of a distress situation, the SMC should evaluate all available information and, considering the degree of emergency, declare a SAR emergency phase. A boat underway may take these initial steps to respond as the SMC begins work on a search action plan, if needed.

B.2. EMERGENCY PHASES

Three emergency phases have been established for classifying incidents and to help in determining the actions to take. These are:

- Uncertainty Phase
- Alert Phase
- Distress Phase

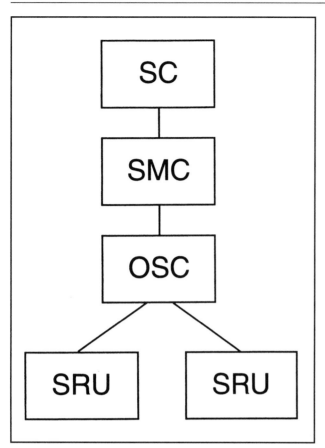

Figure 15-1 SAR Organization

Emergency phases are based on the level of concern for the safety of persons or craft which may be in danger. Each phase requires the collection of data that can assist in determining proper response actions. The emergency phase may be reclassified by the SMC as the situation develops. Also, if sufficient information is received from initial, or early reports, one or more phases may be skipped in determining the proper phase for a particular case. The ultimate action could be immediate dispatch of an SRU. Everything possible must be done to make certain that a unit sent on a SAR case is the proper response.

B.3. UNCERTAINTY PHASE

An **uncertainty phase** exists when there is knowledge of a situation that may need to be monitored, or have more information gathered, but does not require dispatching resources. When there is doubt about the safety of an aircraft, ship, or other craft or persons on board, or it is overdue or failed to make an expected position report, the situation should be investigated and information gathered. The key word is "**doubt**." A preliminary communications search (PRECOM), is normally conducted during the uncertainty phase. The PRECOM is conducted by contacting facilities or agencies within a specific area to either locate the vessel or determine if the vessel has been seen.

B.4. ALERT PHASE

An **alert phase** is assigned when an aircraft, ship, or other craft or persons on board are having difficulty and may need assistance, but are not in immediate danger. Apprehension is usually associated with the Alert Phase, but there is no known threat requiring immediate action. SRUs may be dispatched to provide assistance if it is believed that conditions might get worse. For overdue craft, the Alert Phase is considered when there is a continued lack of information about its position or condition. The key word is "**apprehension**." An extended communications search (EXCOM) is normally conducted during the alert phase. The EXCOM consists of extensive and repeated attempts to communicate with the missing vessel. The SMC may direct SRUs to conduct an EXCOM, this usually means you must try to establish radio contact with the vessel every four hours for a 24-hour period. Boat may also be deployed to check out any leads.

B.5. DISTRESS PHASE

The **distress phase** when there is reasonable certainty that an aircraft, ship, or other craft or persons on board is in danger and requires immediate assistance. This includes a direct report of an emergency or the continued lack of knowledge about a vessel's progress or position. The key word is "**danger**." SRUs are normally dispatched when this phase is reached.

Legal Aspects and U.S. Coast Guard Policy

Introduction

Numerous legal issues affect SAR. This section briefly covers situations that you should be aware of and general Coast Guard policy guidance. These issues are covered in greater detail in your district operation plan (OPLAN) or standard operating procedures (SOP).

In this section

SAR Agreements

C.1. GENERAL

"SAR agreements," formal written documents, are used to resolve coordination problems such as guidance for entering another AOR or providing SRUs to assist another agency or country. These agreements may be at the local level or on an international level. Check local regulations concerning the effect that any treaty or SAR agreement may have within your AOR. Each nation has final right to regulate entry into their territory regardless of treaties that have been signed. Always be familiar with current policies before conducting SAR outside your normally assigned AOR.

Distress Beacon Incidents

C.2. GENERAL

Distress beacons are one of the most important tools available to people in distress for assisting SAR authorities. The various types of distress beacons and their proper use are described in the *National Search and Rescue Manual*. Additional policy and general information are provided in the *Coast Guard Addendum to the National Search and Rescue Manual*.

C.3. GENERAL CONSIDERATIONS

Many ships and commercial fishing vessels are required to carry an Emergency Position-Indicating Radiobeacon (EPIRB); recreational boats are not required but are strongly encouraged to carry them. The original EPIRB, just like the aeronautical version (Emergency Locator Transmitter or ELT) operated on the 121.5 MHz frequency. However, the 406.025 MHz EPIRB and ELT were developed for satellites to detect these distress alerts. As implied, the receipt of a beacon alert is considered a distress. The response for 406 varies slightly from the 121.5 (see CG Addendum). The increased reliability of the 406 over the 121.5, due to its ability to transmit a data string of identification and contact information, and the sole use of the 406 MHz frequency for distress alerting, permit an immediate response by SAR forces.

C.4. REPORTS OF BEACON ALERTS

Reports of audible beacon alerts indicate a beacon has been activated. SAR response to an audible beacon signal should be similar to the type of response provided for orange or red flare sightings, discussed later in this chapter. In cases where Coast Guard resources hear the beacon, they normally respond immediately to determine the signal source. Most other audible signal reports come from aircraft.

NOTE

EPIRBs are distress beacons. These beacons shall not be used as datum marker buoys. The beacon's signal may prevent another distress beacon from being properly tracked or reported.

Flare Incidents

C.5. GENERAL

The Coast Guard responds to many **flare sightings**. Red and orange flares are recognized around the world as marine and aviation emergency signals and must be treated as a distress.

C.6. CONSIDERATIONS

The nature of flare distress signaling makes planning and execution of searches difficult due to the wide variation of flare types, possible altitudes, skill and position of the reporting source/observer, weather, and many other factors. For this reason, the accuracy of the information received from the reporting source and/or observer is critical. For example, a hand-held flare in a recreation boat seen on the horizon by a beach observer will be approximately four miles away while a parachute flare rising to 1,200 feet and seen on the horizon by the same beach observer could be more than 30 miles away. As with all SAR cases, a prompt, thorough, and proper response, including a thorough debrief of the reporting sources(s), yields the best chance for a successful rescue.

C.7. REPORTS OF FLARE SIGHTING

It is critical that correct, descriptive, and accurate information be obtained from persons sighting a flare. This requires careful and thorough questioning of the reporting source. The data gathering process requires patience and good interpersonal skills, since reporting sources are rarely familiar with the terms or procedures used by the Coast Guard when investigating flare sightings. A flare reporting checklist must be used to ensure all the proper information is obtained.

Additional information on flare signals and sightings is located in the *Coast Guard Addendum to the National Search and Rescue Manual*.

Hoaxes and False Alarms

C.8. GENERAL

False alarms and hoaxes waste valuable operational resource time and dollars, frustrate both search controllers and those required to respond, and may adversely affect the Coast Guard's ability to respond to real distress calls. It is often very difficult to determine with certainty whether an incident is a false alarm, hoax, or real distress due to sketchy and/or contradictory information.

C.9. HOAX

A hoax is a case where information is reported with the **intent to deceive**.

C.10. FALSE ALARM

A false alarm is when someone or something reported to be in distress is confirmed to be not in distress and not to be in need of assistance. In a false alarm case, the reporting source either misjudged a situation or accidentally activated a distress signal or beacon resulting in an erroneous request for help, but **did not deliberately act to deceive**.

C.11. COAST GUARD RESPONSE

Coast Guard units shall respond without delay to any notification of distress, even when a false alarm or hoax is suspected. Until proven differently, these cases should be treated as if they are real distress cases. A distress call which "sounds like a hoax" shall not be merely dismissed without further action. A distress shall be considered to exist until the case is closed, suspended, or downgraded by proper authority.

Maritime SAR Assistance Policy

C.12. GENERAL

The Coast Guard's primary concern in any SAR operation is that proper, timely, and effective assistance be provided. A key issue is that **it is always a Coast Guard priority to remove people from danger**. When commercial assistance resources are available or may be operating within your AOR, particular guidelines apply depending on the specific situation. These guidelines are published as the Maritime SAR Assistance Policy (MSAP) in the *Coast Guard Addendum to the National Search and Rescue Manual*. More specific guidance is available in your district OPLAN or SOP. The four paragraphs that follow outline some of these guidelines.

C.13. DISTRESS

Immediate response will be initiated for any situation when a mariner is known to be in imminent danger. This response may be provided by regular Coast Guard resources, Coast Guard Auxiliary resources, or resources belonging to other federal, private, state, local, or commercial entities; volunteers or good samaritans. The SMC may use all sources of assistance in a distress situation without concern for conflict with private enterprise.

C.14. NO CONFLICT CONCERN—ANY SITUATION

Private organizations (non-commercial), state and local organizations, and Good Samaritans are acceptable sources of SAR assistance. When volunteered or available, their help can be used without any concern for conflict with commercial providers. However, if their expertise is unknown, the SMC shall more closely monitor the assistance provided. This is especially true in the case of Good Samaritans.

C.15. NON-DISTRESS CASES

When specifically requested assistance, such as a commercial firm, marina, or friend is not available, a marine assistance request broadcast (MARB) may be broadcast. If a commercial provider is available and can be on scene within a reasonable time (usually one hour or less) or an offer to assist is made by any of the resources listed in the previous paragraph, no further action by the Coast Guard, beyond monitoring the incident, will be taken.

For a non-distress situation where an Auxiliary facility discovers a vessel requesting assistance but which has not contacted the Coast Guard, refer to the Coast Guard Addendum to the National SAR Manual and the Auxiliary Operations Policy Manual for guidance.

NOTE

If the commercial provider and the boater in need of assistance do not reach agreement, the Coast Guard must continue to monitor the case.

C.16. NON-DISTRESS USE OF COAST GUARD RESOURCES

Coast Guard resources normally do not provide immediate assistance in non-distress cases where there is alternative assistance available. The Coast Guard both supports efforts of private enterprise and encourages volunteerism in assisting mariners. Coast Guard resources will not unnecessarily interfere with private enterprise. A Coast Guard resource may assist in a non-distress situation when no higher priority missions exist and no other capable resource is reasonably available (see Figure 15-2).

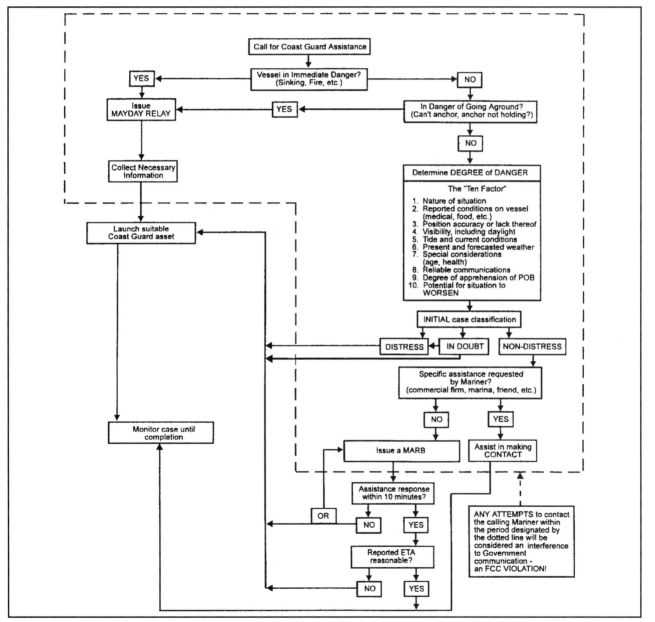

Figure 15-2 SAR Incident Decision Tree

General Salvage Policy (Other Than Towing)

C.17. GENERAL

Coast Guard units and resources are employed for SAR, not for salvage operations. However, if circumstances dictate that salvage operations must be undertaken, follow the guidance in the *Coast Guard Addendum to the National Search and Rescue Manual*. Additional guidance may be found in district and unit SOPs.

C.18. GENERAL CONSIDERATIONS

During a SAR operation, boat crew and SAR planners should be alert to see if the situation is changing:

- Has the incident changed from a distress (e.g., people are rescued) to an effort that is now more of a salvage operation?

- Will salvage by the Coast Guard reduce the threat of loss of life or the vessel becoming a hazard to navigation? What can be done to prevent a worsening condition or total loss of vessel?

- Is there a threat of injury to boat crew members or damage to the boat that would prevent the SRU from responding to another distress?

C.19. COMMERCIAL SALVAGE

When **commercial salvers** are on scene performing salvage, Coast Guard units may assist them if the salver requests, and the assistance is within the unit's capabilities. However, salvage operations shall be performed only at the discretion of the unit CO/OinC. When no commercial salvage facilities are on scene, Coast Guard units may engage in salvage, other than towing, only when such limited salvage operations (e.g. ungrounding, pumping, damage control measures, etc.) can prevent a worsening situation or complete loss of the vessel. Coast Guard units and personnel shall not unduly hazard themselves at any time by performing salvage operations.

NOTE

Firefighting policy is discussed in Chapter 18—Firefighting, Rescue, and Assistance.

SMALL CRAFT This policy applies to small craft which need salvage other than towing. However, when no commercial salvage companies are available within a reasonable time or distance, the district commander may modify the policy to provide for refloating a grounded boat which is not in peril of further damage or loss if:

- the Coast Guard units are capable of rendering the assistance;

- the owner requests the assistance and agrees to the specific effort to be made; and

- Coast Guard units and personnel are not unduly hazarded by the operation.

OPERATOR INSISTENCE Occasionally an operator will insist the Coast Guard take action, such as pulling a vessel from a reef, which the Coast Guard personnel on scene consider unwise. The Coast Guard is under no obligation to agree to any such request or demand. If a decision to comply with such a request is made, it should be made clear to the operator that he is assuming the risk of the operation and the fact that the action is undertaken at his request against Coast Guard advice should be logged.

General Issues

C.20. PUBLIC RELATIONS

A SAR operation often creates great interest with the general public and with radio, television and newspapers. Your responsibilities as a boat crew member do not include providing information to the news media. To avoid wrong information and misunderstandings for the public, you should direct all inquires to your Officer Of the Day (OOD), Officer in Charge (OinC), or Commanding Officer (CO). Relatives of missing persons may also seek information. You should show proper concern for their stressful situation but also refer them to the OOD, OinC, or CO for any information.

C.21. SEARCHES FOR BODIES

Chapter 4 of *Coast Guard Regulations* states that, "when it has become definitely established, either by time or circumstances, that persons are dead, the Coast Guard is not required to conduct searches for bodies. If, however, requests are received from responsible agencies, such as local police, military commands, etc., Coast Guard units may participate in body searches provided that these searches do not interfere with the primary duties of the units." Since boats are not provided the specific gear or training to conduct searches for bodies, their involvement is usually either as a surface search unit or support platform for other agencies to use their equipment.

C.22. TRESPASSING

SAR personnel should obtain permission from the owner or occupant prior to entering private property. If this is not possible, then permission must be granted by your operational commander **before** entering private property. Only when saving a person's life, can immediate action be taken.

SECTION D

SAR Incident Information

Overview

Introduction

Once aware of a distress, SAR units attempt to find out as much information about the incident as possible. Standard response procedures and report formats are very important.

Before SAR units are activated, a number of facts about the case must be recorded. These facts fall into two broad categories:

- Initial SAR information
- Additional SAR information

Initial SAR information is very important for several reasons. One use of SAR case information by SAR planners is to categorize the case to determine the most appropriate and effective response to provide. SAR planners use every available piece of information to plan the Coast Guard's response, including determining the type of SRU assigned, when it is dispatched, and what type of equipment is taken to the scene.

NOTE

For guidance and recommended format for standard incident checksheets, refer to Appendix E of the *Coast Guard Addendum to the National Search and Rescue Manual* and your district SOP.

In this section

Topic	See Page(s)
Initial SAR Information	309–11
Additional SAR Information	311

Initial SAR Information

D.1. DATA COLLECTING AND RECORDING

Initial notification that an emergency exists may come from many sources, including:

- relatives may report that a family member is overdue
- "MAYDAY" by radio
- witness to the distress

If the caller seems excited:

1. Calm the individual down enough to collect accurate, essential information.
2. Be courteous and show concern for the caller and their situation.
3. Be confident and professional, but not overbearing.
4. Speaking calmly will help ease people's concerns and assure them that the situation is well in hand.
5. Be prepared to write down information (have checklist and pen within reach).

D.2. COMMUNICATION WITH THE SOURCE

It is important to maintain communication with reporting sources, regardless of who they are or how the call was made. Also, keep callers advised of what actions are being taken to resolve the situation they reported.

RADIO SOURCE Most distress calls by radio come in on Channel 16, 156.8 MHz. This channel is the maritime VHF-FM international distress and calling frequency. To keep it open for other distresses, the caller is usually asked to move (shift) to a working channel, if possible. Since shifting could result in losing communications with your reporting source, the caller is asked to shift back to channel 16 if no reply is heard on the working channel within five minutes. The transmission may be as follows:

Example: "Vessel in distress, this is Coast Guard Station. Shift and answer channel 21. If no reply is heard on that channel within five minutes, shift back to this frequency, channel 16, over."

"Coast Guard, this is the vessel, shifting to channel 21, out."

TELEPHONE SOURCE If calls come in by telephone, **immediately take down the name and number of the person calling**. In the event you are disconnected, you will be able to return the call and obtain the needed information. Also try to identify how you may be able to try to communicate with the person or vessel that is reported to be in distress. Cellular telephone numbers, types of radio equipment and frequencies used may help establish communications with the distressed vessel or person.

D.3. INITIAL INFORMATION

Once stable and repeatable communications are established, the **most vital** information to record **immediately** is:

- Location
- Number of people on board (POB)
- Nature of distress
- Name, radio call sign of distressed craft
- Description of the craft

Response activity can be started once these items are known. Also, realize that this may be the only contact made with the distressed craft or reporting source (e.g., the radio broke, power was lost, or the boat sank).

D.4. DISTRESSED VESSEL INFORMATION

The identity of the distressed vessel should be established:

- Vessel name
- Vessel numbers
- Vessel type
- Vessel call sign
- Name of person calling
- Number of people on board (POB)
- Condition of all POB

When direct communications with the vessel in distress are not available, that is to say the information about the distressed vessel is being relayed, gather and record the same information about the relaying source.

NOTE

In this section, the term "vessel" includes aircraft, person, or any other source of initial SAR case information. In these instances, ALL appropriate identifying information should be obtained.

D.5. TYPE OF EMERGENCY

The nature of the emergency must be clearly and completely understood in order for responding units to be prepared to assist. The emergency may be any **one** of the following, or it may include **many** of these examples, or it may be some other type of emergency:

- Aground
- Sinking
- Collision
- Fire
- Disabled
- Overdue
- Medical

D.6. LOCATION OF EMERGENCY

The location of the emergency must be clearly established in the most detailed terms possible. This should include any or all of the following, plus all additional information received.

- Position (latitude and longitude) of the incident
- Bearing and distance from the incident to any points of land or landmarks known or observed
- Last known position of the incident or distressed vessel

D.7. PERSONS ON BOARD

- Number of people on board (POB)
- Condition of all POB
- Survival equipment
- Friends/Relatives

D.8. ADDITIONAL LOCATION INFORMATION

After the nature of the incident has been completely established, additional information about the location should be gathered. This additional information is needed when determining "datum," the position where the incident occurred or where the search will begin:

- Vessel's course and speed
- Date and time of the last known position
- Length of the time that the vessel has been drifting/disabled/aground

Additional SAR Information

D.9. GENERAL

Besides recording the SAR information described above, certain additional information is extremely valuable. Information in this category includes:

- Medical data
- On-scene weather data
- Overdue data

All radio frequencies the vessel can use or monitor, or cellular telephone if used.

D.10. MEDICAL DATA

If medical assistance is required, collect and record as much of the following additional information as possible. Check lists containing complete lists of information to collect can be found in your district OPLAN or SOP and should be used to avoid missing key information. Addition information includes:

- Patient's name, nationality, age, and sex
- Patient's symptoms and vital signs
- All medication given to patient
- All medication available aboard the vessel

All radio frequencies the vessel can use or monitor, or cellular telephone if used.

D.11. ON-SCENE WEATHER

Additional weather information can be useful. The weather on scene may differ from the weather at your location. **On-scene weather** information is important in determining:

- Type of SRU best suited to respond
- Datum (the probable location of the distressed vessel)
- Emergency phase

D.12. OVERDUES

Some reports received will involve people or vessels that are **overdue** at some location, but no distress will be evident at that time. Information collected at the time of the initial report may prove invaluable later if a search planning effort is begun.

D.13. GATHERING DATA

Gathering the following type of data will avoid possible delays if the person or vessel does not arrive at the destination and further action is required. Sometimes it becomes difficult to reestablish contact with the reporting source to gather additional information when that information is needed. Data collection includes:

- Period of time the vessel has been overdue
- Vessel's departure point and destination
- Places the vessel planned to stop during transit
- Navigation equipment aboard the vessel
- Survival equipment aboard the vessel
- Number of people aboard the vessel as well as their names, ages, sex, and general health
- Personal habits of the people aboard the vessel (e.g., dependability, reliability, etc.)
- License plate number and description of the towing vehicle and trailer, if the boat was trailered to the departure point
- Communications equipment on board including radio frequencies monitored
- Additional points of contact
- Pending commitments (work, appointments, etc.)

SECTION E

Search Planning

Overview

Introduction

Before SRUs are dispatched, careful planning is needed to accurately determine area where the survivors are or will be located when the boat arrives on scene. Good SAR planning significantly increases the probability of successfully locating and rescuing those in distress. Planning the search involves calculating datum and then outlining the boundaries of the search area. Most search planning would be done by the RCC or the Group OPCEN and results in a search action plan. The boat crew then conducts SAR operations based on this search action plan. However, there may be times where you would have to do basic search planning. Search planning also includes risk management to determine what response, if any, is appropriate and which resources are the right ones to respond.

For more information on search planning, calculation of datum, and the forces that affect datum see the *National Search and Rescue Manual* and the *Coast Guard Addendum to the National Search and Rescue Manual.*

In this section

Datum

E.1. GENERAL

The term "datum" refers to the most probable location of the distressed vessel, corrected for drift over a given period of time. Depending on the information available and its accuracy, datum may be:

- A point
- A line
- An area

As the case develops, datum must be corrected to account for wind and current. Datum is established by the SMC or OSC.

DATUM POINT A point at the center of the area where it is estimated that the search object is most likely located.

DATUM LINE If you cannot pinpoint the location of a distressed boat, you may be able to determine its intended trackline or a line of bearing. The **datum line** is the intended trackline or line of bearing plotted on the chart. Without more information, it is assumed that the distressed vessel may be anywhere along the length of the plot. The line could also be a direction finding line of position.

DATUM AREA When you cannot determine either the exact position of the distress or a datum line, a **datum area** is developed based on many factors, but including as a minimum:

- Fuel endurance of the vessel in distress
- Vessel's maximum cruising range
- Wind and currents which affect the search object

- Operator's intentions

E.2. FORCES AFFECTING DATUM

As time progresses, datum must be corrected to compensate for the effects of wind and current. Some of the many natural forces which affect a search object are listed below.

LEEWAY Leeway is the movement of a search object through the water. Leeway is caused by local winds blowing against the exposed surface of the vessel.

LOCAL WIND DRIVEN CURRENT Wind blowing over the water's surface tends to push the water along in the same direction the wind is blowing. This wind current affects the movement of a search object in open waters. Wind-driven current may not be a factor when searching in coastal waters, small lakes, rivers, or harbors because nearby land masses may block or reduce the effect of wind.

SEA CURRENT Sea current refers to the movements of water in the open sea.

TIDAL CURRENT Tidal current is caused by the rising and falling of tides.

RIVER CURRENT The flow of water in a river is called **river current**. These currents can quickly move a search object over a long distance. This should be considered in rivers or at the mouth of a large river.

NOTE

Drift, in search planning, is the movement of a search object caused by all of the environmental forces.

Search Area Description

E.3. GENERAL

The search area is a geographic area determined by the SMC as most likely to contain the search object. The amount of error inherent in drift calculations and navigational capabilities of both the distressed craft and the SRU are used to calculate a search **radius**.

NOTE

When response times are short, the SMC may use a standard radius, adjusted for physical surroundings. Where a search can begin in less than six hours, a six mile radius around a datum adjusted for drift is usually large enough to include most search objects.

E.4. METHODS

Search areas may be described by many methods, including the following:

CORNER POINT In this method the latitude and longitude (or geographic features) of each corner of the search area are given (see Figure 15-3).

TRACKLINE The latitude and longitude of the departure point, turn points, and destination point are given with a specific width along the track (see Figure 15-4).

CENTER POINT (CIRCLE) The latitude and longitude of datum are given along with a radius around datum (see Figure 15-5).

CENTER POINT (RECTANGLE) The latitude and longitude of datum are given with the direction of major (longer) axis plus the length and width of the area (see Figure 15-6).

CENTER POINT—LANDMARK (RECTANGLE, BEARING & DISTANCE) The center point, or datum, may also be designated by a bearing and distance from some geographic landmark (see Figure 15-7).

LANDMARK BOUNDARIES Two or more landmarks are given as boundaries of the search area along a shoreline (see Figure 15-8).

Search Patterns

E.5. GENERAL

Once a search area has been determined, a systematic search for the object must be planned. Which is the best search pattern to use?

E.6. CONSIDERATIONS

Consider the following to determine which search pattern to use:

- Weather conditions
- Size of search area
- Size of search object
- Number of search units involved
- Search area location
- Time limitations

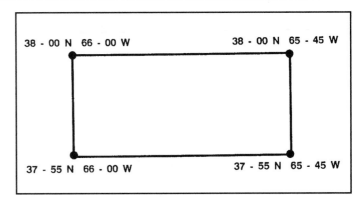

Figure 15-3 Corner Point

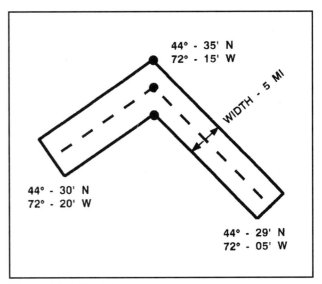

Figure 15-4 Trackline

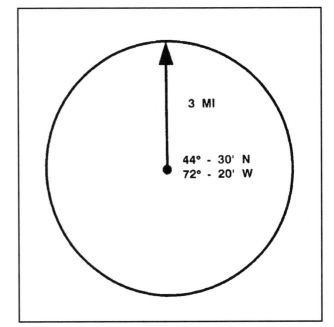

Figure 15-5 Center Point (Circle)

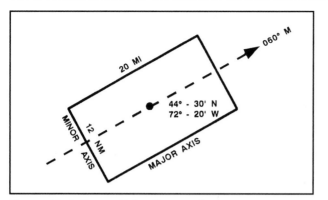

Figure 15-6 Center Point (Rectangle)

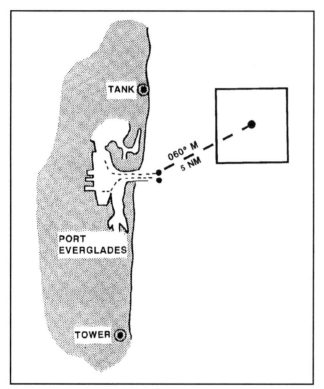

Figure 15-7 Center Point Method (Rectangle, Bearing & Distance)

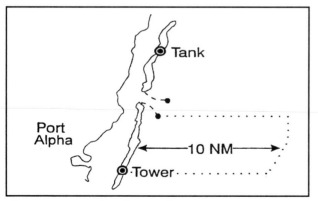

Figure 15-8 Landmark Boundaries

E.7. SEARCH PATTERN DESIGNATION

Search patterns are designated by letters. The first letter indicates the general pattern group:

- T = Trackline
- C = Creeping line
- P = Parallel
- V = Sector
- S = Square

The second letter indicates the number of search units:

- S = Single-unit search
- M = Multiunit search

The third letter indicates specialized SRU patterns or instructions, for example:

- R = Return
- N = Non-return

E.8. TYPES OF SEARCH PATTERNS

The most common types of search patterns are discussed below. Detailed descriptions of each pattern are available in the *Coast Guard Addendum to the National Search and Rescue Manual* and in the *National Search and Rescue Manual*.

SQUARE PATTERN (S) The **square search pattern** is used when the last known position of a search object has a high degree of accuracy, the search area is small, and a concentrated search is desirable. Sector patterns are good for man overboard searches.

- *Square Single-unit (SS).* In the **SS pattern** for boats, the first leg is normally in the direction of the search object's drift and all turns are made 90° to starboard (see Figure 15-9).

- *Square Multiunit (SM)* The **SM pattern** is used when two units are available. The second unit begins on a course 45° to the right of the first unit's course.

SECTOR PATTERNS (V) **Sector search patterns** are used when datum is established with a high degree of confidence but the search object is difficult to detect, such as a person in the water. The search unit passes through datum several times, each time increasing the chances of finding the search object. The pattern resembles the spokes of a wheel with the center of the wheel at datum. **Datum should be marked by the first SRU on scene with a Data**

Marker Buoy (DMB) or other floating object. By marking the center of the search pattern, the coxswain has a navigation check each time the boat passes near the center of the search area (datum). This pattern consists of nine legs. There are two types of sector search patterns.

- *Sector Single-unit (VS).* The **VS pattern** is used by a single boat. The first leg begins in the same direction that the search object is drifting toward. All legs and crosslegs of this pattern are of equal length. After running the first leg, your first turn will be 120° to starboard to

begin the first crossleg. All subsequent turns will be 120° to starboard to a course determined by adding 120° to your previous course (see Figure 15-10). Notice that after completing the first leg and crossleg, the second and third legs of the pattern are completed in sequence without turning between.

- *Sector Multiunit (VM).* The **VM pattern** is used when a second boat is available. The second boat starts at the same datum, but begins the first leg on a course 90° to the left of the first boat. The search is then the same as a VS pattern. The second boat should start the search at a slower speed than the first boat, if both boats start at the same time. When the first boat is one leg ahead of the second boat, the second boat accelerates to search speed. This slow start by the second boat will keep both boats from arriving at the center of the search pattern at the same time (see Figure 15-11).

NOTE

Course and leg identifiers should be carried in each SRU to calculate courses and times for each expanding square and sector search pattern leg. The course and leg identifiers can be easily obtained through the federal stock system, Stock Number SN 7530-01-GF2-9010 (see Figures 15-12 and 15-13).

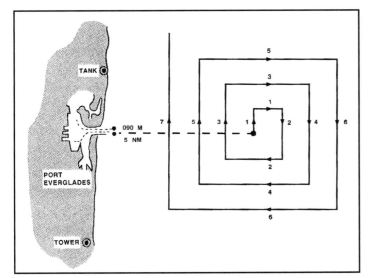

Figure 15-9 Square Single-unit (SS)

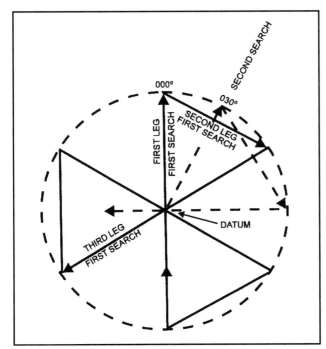

Figure 15-10 Sector Single-unit (VS)

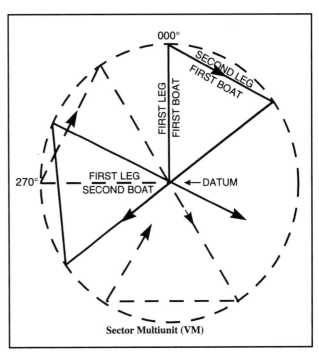

Figure 15-11 Sector Multiunit (VM)

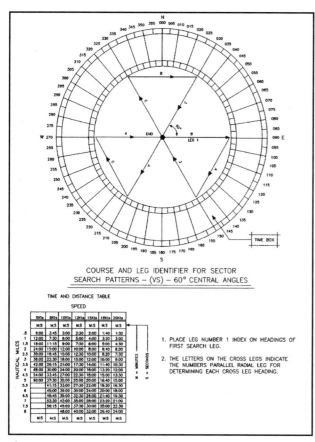

Figure 15-12 Course and Leg Identifier For Sector Search Patterns

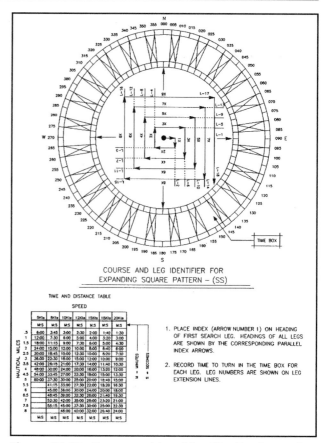

Figure 15-13 Course and Leg Identifier For Expanding Square Pattern

PARALLEL PATTERNS (P) Parallel track patterns are used when there is an equal probability that the search object could be anywhere in the search area. It is a good pattern to use when the approximate location of the search object is known and **uniform coverage is desired**. Parallel track patterns are the simplest of the search patterns. You steer straight courses on all legs. Each leg is one track spacing from the other. The legs are parallel to the long side or major axis of the search area. There are two types of parallel track patterns.

The Commence Search Point (CSP) for parallel patterns is located at a point ½ of the distance selected as the search track spacing inside a corner of the search area. The first and last search legs then run ½ track spacing inside the search area boundaries. This prevents excessive duplicate coverage, eliminates the possibility of leaving an unsearched track at the search area boundary, and gives SRUs in adjacent search areas a margin of safety.

- *Parallel Track Single-unit (PS).* The **PS pattern** is conducted by a single SRU. The legs of the search are run parallel to the long side (Major Axis) of the search area (see Figure 15-14).

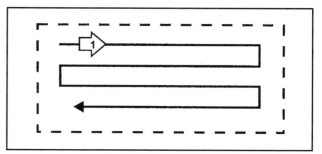

Figure 15-14 Parallel Track Single-unit (PS)

- *Parallel Track Multiunit (PM).* The **Multiunit (PM)** pattern is used under the same circumstances as the (PS) but with more than one SRU (see Figure 15-15). The SRUs are separated by a single track space. They search parallel to the long side of the search area. After completing the first search leg, they move over a distance equal to the track spacing times the number of SRUs, and then search back on the reciprocal heading of the first leg.

An example of a PM search is provided as Figure 15-16. The search area is from Hunter Inlet South Jetty Light on the north to 30 NM south and 18 NM

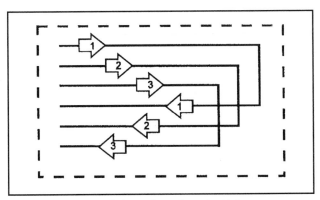

Figure 15-15 Parallel Track Multiunit (PM)

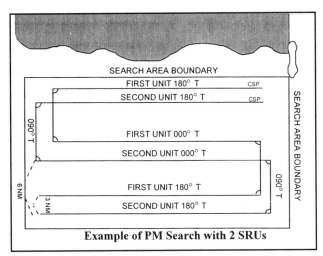

Figure 15-16 Example of PM Search with 2 SRUs

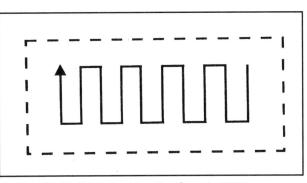

Figure 15-17 Creeping Line Single-unit (CS)

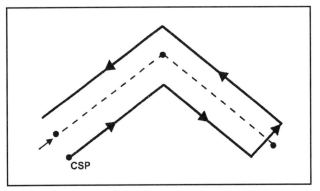

Figure 15-18 Trackline Single-unit Return (TSR)

offshore. Two SRUs are used with a track spacing of three NM and a search speed of 10 knots

CREEPING LINE SINGLE-UNIT (CS) The **CS pattern** is used when the probable location of the search object has been determined to be **more likely at one end of the search area** than at the other end. Creeping line search patterns are the same as parallel patterns with the exception that the legs are run parallel to the short side (minor axis) of the search area. This pattern's CSP and search legs are also located ½ track spacing inside the search area (see Figure 15-17).

TRACKLINE SINGLE-UNIT RETURN (TSR) The **Trackline Single-unit Return** (TSR) pattern is used to search when the only information available on the missing vessel is the intended track of the search object (see Figure 15-18).

NOTE

In darkness or extremely low visibility, surface search vessels should periodically stop their engines at selected points in the search area and conduct a listening search for a short period of time, then return to covering their assigned search area.

BARRIER The barrier pattern is used in areas with strong current, such as a river. The search lies along the path of the current. The boat moves back and forth over the same track. This can be done by steering on an object on each side of the river bank. The boat moves from one side of the search area to the other while the current carries the water and objects past the search barrier.

Since river currents can vary across the width of a river, a more effective barrier might be established by forming a line abreast. This is done by placing observers on each bank and a boat in the area of swiftest current holding station between the observers on shore. Additional boats, if available, could be added to the line abreast to reduce the effective track spacing and increase the effective coverage. This technique produces a more effective, and predictable, barrier.

Initial Response

E.9. SEARCH PATTERNS AND ACTIONS TO BE USED

The simplified patterns and initial search actions recommended in the Coastal search planning section for coastal incidents in the *CG Addendum to the National SAR Manual* are to be used when an SRU arrives on scene and the object of the SAR incident is not initially seen or located. The following patterns and initial search actions are to be used until a complete search plan has been developed by the SMC.

E.10. SRU ACTIONS

Whenever a case occurs which has a SRU on scene and the object of the distress is not immediately seen or located, report the situation to the SMC by the quickest means possible. The SMC will immediately start planning and then develop a search action plan of the SRU. In the meantime, the SRU shall be conducting either an expanding square or sector search using a search radius of 6 NM.

E.11. INITIAL RESPONSE SEARCH AREA

If the search object is not located on arriving on scene, the SRU is to assume it is adrift if the distressed boat did not indicate it was at anchor.

1. Draw a circle with a 6 NM radius centered at the last known position (LKP). If drift is considered to be significant, the SRU should estimate the drift based on local knowledge/on scene conditions, and center the 6 NM circle around the drifted LKP.

2. Communicate and confirm the new datum with the SMC. Remember that the time of datum must take into consideration the underway transit times for the SRU.

3. Next draw the search pattern within the tangent of the circle. Datum for the search is the commence search point (CSP). Track spacing is from Figure 15-21.

4. Orient the search area in the same direction of drift, that is, in the same direction as the total drift vector (Figures 15-19 and 15-20).

If the reported position of the distressed craft is in shallow water, it could be at anchor, and a search down the drift line may be appropriate.

E.12. KEEPING THE SMC UPDATED

The SRU shall also keep the SMC constantly updated on conditions, findings, and when nearing completion of initial response search. This direction should not preclude a SRU from using an alternate search pattern or area when it is clearly not practical (e.g., narrow waterway or other physical barrier).

E.13. APPROPRIATE SEARCH PATTERN

The preplanned operations and search procedures for the first SRU on scene should be to immediately report to station, or SMC the on scene conditions and findings. Next, begin appropriate search pattern.

SURFACE SRUs Usually an expanding square (SS) is used. This is because it concentrates the search closure to datum and usually there will only be a short period of time on the initial response before the SMC gives direction and information for conducting and starting a first search. If the search area is confined or there is reason to have a high degree of confidence for the selected datum (e.g., debris found), the surface SRU may use a sector

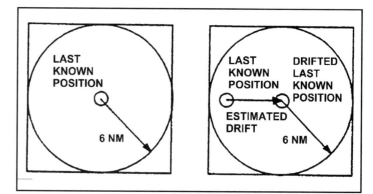

Figure 15-19 Initial Response Search Area

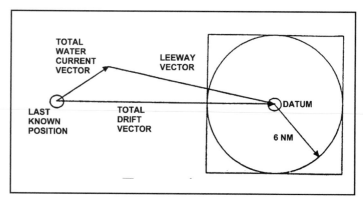

Figure 15-20 Vessel Adrift

search (VS). Other search patterns may be used as appropriate.

FOR HELICOPTER SRUs Helicopters are a suitable platform to execute SS and VS pattern searches. Depending on the proximity to the coast and environmental conditions, a radius larger than 6 NM may be appropriate for a helicopter during the initial search due to a higher search speed.

INITIAL TRACK SPACING Use Figure 15-21 to determine the track spacing for the initial response search by surface or helicopter SRUs.

Search Area Coverage

E.14. GENERAL

Search area coverage considers the area to be searched and the SRUs available to search. Once the search area has been determined and the search patterns selected, the next step is to have SRUs conduct the search. Based on the sweep width, an SRU will be assigned its own part of the overall areas to search. Essentially, your boat will start at an assigned commence search point (CSP), steer the track (search leg), and search (sweep down) on both sides of the boat.

E.15. SWEEP WIDTH (W)

Sweep width is a distance measured on both sides of an SRU. A sweep width of one mile means ½ mile to starboard and ½ mile to port for a total "width" of one mile. Sweep width is determined by:

- Search object type, size and construction
- Environmental conditions
- Sensor (e.g., visual or radar)

E.16. TRACK SPACING (S)

Track spacing is the distance between adjacent parallel legs within a search area. These tracks may be conducted simultaneously by multiple units separated by fixed intervals, or they may be the result of successive sweeps conducted by a single SRU. Most

Search object	Good Conditions Wind < 14 kts Seas < 3 ft	Poor Conditions Wind > 15 kts Seas > 3 ft
PIW	0.1*	0.1*
< 15 ft	0.5	0.2
> 15 ft	1.0	1.0

* > 0.1 up to SRUs minimum ability to navigate

Figure 15-21 Initial Track Spacing (NM)

of the search patterns described in this chapter consist of equally spaced, parallel search legs (tracks). The distance between adjacent search legs is called the track spacing (S). The best track spacing is a distance which permits maximum expectation of search object detection in the shortest period of time.

E.17. COMMENCE SEARCH POINT (CSP)

The **commence search point** is a point normally specified by the SMC for an SRU to begin its search pattern.

Search Preparations

Overview

F.1. GENERAL

Before beginning a search, you must collect all available facts about a case. The SMC should provide most of this information as the search action plan. The checklist below will help you determine whether you have everything you need to begin a mission. Once you have collected all available facts and have performed the required search planning, you are ready to get underway.

NOTE

In an emergency, this information can be passed to the boat crew while en route to a search area.

F.2. QUESTIONS

Answers to the following questions will help determine if you have done everything you need to do before getting underway:

What is the object of this search and what equipment do the personnel aboard have?

- How many people are involved?
- What is the assigned search area?
- What are the circumstances of their distress?
- What search pattern will be used?
- What is the desired search speed?
- What special equipment is required?
- What radio frequencies will you use?
- Are other units assigned? If so:
  What kind?

What are their search areas?

What are their search speeds?

What search patterns will they employ?

What radio frequencies will they use?

- Do you have all required charts aboard?
- What are the weather and sea conditions?
- Who is on-scene coordinator (OSC)?
- What unusual circumstances may be encountered? How will you correct for them?

F.3. BRIEF CREW

Crew members must be briefed before getting underway. Make sure all crew members:

- Understand the mission
- Know what they are looking for
- Know where the search will be conducted
- Understand how the search will be conducted

Conducting a Search

Overview

G.1. GENERAL

It is critical that an SRU perform all duties assigned in a correct and predictable fashion. In this case the term SRU includes the vessel, crew, and equipment. Search planners, OSCs, SMCs, and others all make plans based on assumptions they have made. These assumptions are considered when making decisions that could have life and death consequences for someone who may be the object of a major Coast Guard search effort. One assumption made by SAR planners is that the SRU, its crew, and equipment all perform as planned, completing all missions assigned unless advised otherwise.

In some instances, however, SRUs have failed to properly complete their assigned mission. Reasons may include not having proper equipment on board, or a crew member not fully prepared, trained, or qualified, or a failure to complete some task. There have been instances when an SRU failed to fully search an assigned area or, due to careless navigation, failed to search in the area assigned. Actual searches and rescues are typically carried out when conditions are at their worst, making even simple and routine tasks extremely difficult. Accurate navigation, observant lookouts, and trained and knowledgeable crew members can make the difference between successful cases and disasters.

All effort expended to gather carefully key information, to plan the most effective search, or to select exactly the right SRU is wasted if the SRU performing the search or rescue fails to do so in a professional manner to the best of its ability. If not able to complete the search (e.g., equipment failure, poor visibility, or worsening weather), advise the SMC what areas were searched.

CHAPTER

16

Person in the Water Recovery

Editor's Note: *Study this chapter and be sure other persons who regularly go out on the water with you also are familiar with its lessons. A person unintentionally overboard always presents an emergency. You should have a recovery plan tailored for your vessel and you and your crew should practice it regularly. Be sure your mates know how to handle the boat and call for help on the radio—you may be the one overboard. Retrieving people from the water is the Coasties' bread and butter. The techniques discussed in this section are proven—they work—but they only work if you have prepared ahead of time by equipping your vessel with the appropriate equipment—throwing lines, rings, PFDs, etc. Each man-overboard situation is different. Stay calm. Don't lose sight of the victim: assign at least one crew member to do nothing but watch and point to the victim continously. Punch the MOB button on your electronic nav gear. Think. Call for help, unless you can recover the person immediately. Review this chapter before the start of each boating season, and conduct regular drills.*

Overview

Introduction

Even the best of swimmers can become disoriented when unexpectedly falling into the water. Immediate action is of primary importance when a person falls overboard. Every second counts, particularly in heavy seas or cold weather. This chapter addresses man overboard and person in water (PIW) recovery procedures, as well as water survival skills. Lives depend on every crew member performing these procedures competently and effectively.

In this chapter

SECTION A

Recovery Methods

Overview

Introduction

All crew members must be prepared when someone falls overboard. Rehearsing how to react is vital to a successful and safe recovery of the individual. Assume the person who is in the water is suffering from shock, may be unconscious, and possibly is injured.

The information here is only a general guideline, as each boat and situation presents problems beyond the scope of this publication. A professional understands and rehearses each possibility remembering that the key to a successful rescue is preparation, practice, and alertness.

In this section

General Man Overboard Procedures

A.1. GENERAL

The action taken in the first few seconds after a crew member falls overboard determines the success of the recovery. An alert crew member can do much to save the life of someone who might otherwise drown. First actions should be swift and certain.

A.2. FIRST SIGHTING

If a person falls over the port side, the first crew member to realize someone has fallen overboard should follow these procedures:

1. Spread the alarm in a loud voice by repeatedly calling out, "MAN OVERBOARD, PORT SIDE" (or STARBOARD).

2. Throw a ring buoy with strobe light (or anything that floats) over the side towards the person in the water.

3. Maintain sight of, and continuously point (open handed), to the individual in the water while carefully moving to a position where you can be seen by the coxswain or operator. Give clear, loud verbal directions to the coxswain.

A.3. COXSWAIN OR OPERATOR ACTIONS

The coxswain should push the memory button on the Loran-C or GPS receiver (if so equipped) to mark the exact position (datum) of the distress.

Use all possible means to identify the position (dead reckoning, visual landmarks, radar, etc.). Note the location on the chart so that the boat can return to the vicinity of the person in the water.

NOTE

Where the correct equipment is available, a more precise position locked into the navigation receiver will be invaluable in determining datum.

A.4. TURNING THE BOAT AROUND

At the same time the position is being recorded, turn the boat in the direction the individual fell overboard (port or starboard) and simultaneously sound the danger signal (5 or more short blasts on the boat's whistle or horn). (See The Approach further in this Section.)

A.5. THROWING A FLOTATION DEVICE

Throw a ring buoy with strobe light (or anything that floats) over the side towards the person in the water. It does not matter if the person is visible at this time or not. The person in the water may see the flotation device and be able to get to it. Additionally, the ring buoy (see Figure 16-1) or any floating object thrown over the side (if a ring buoy is not available) serves as a reference point (datum) marking the general location of the incident and for maneuvering the boat during the search.

Do not throw the floatable object(s) at the person overboard. It could cause further injury if it hits the individual. Throw the object so that it or its line can drift down to the person while avoiding fouling the line in the propeller.

A.6. ASSIGN CREW DUTIES

Once a device is thrown, the coxswain will assign duties to each crew member.

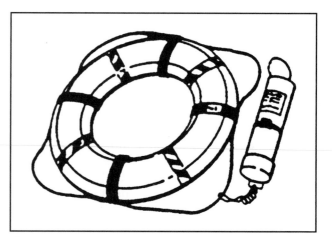

Figure 16-1 Ring Buoy with Strobe

- If weather conditions permit, a POINTER will be positioned on or near the bow of the boat.

- A RECOVERY/PICK-UP crew member will be assigned to prepare a heaving line to be used in retrieving the person from the water.

- A SURFACE SWIMMER will be made ready as needed, as well as another crew member on the tending line to the surface swimmer's safety harness whenever the swimmer is in the water.

THE POINTER The Pointer will visually search for the person overboard, and when located, will point to the person overboard at all times. The coxswain will guide on the Pointer's hand signals in maneuvering the boat for the recovery approach.

In smaller boats, anyone simultaneously can yell to the helm, keep their eyes on the person overboard, and throw something in the water. The larger the boat, the harder it becomes to do this and keep sight of the person overboard. Even given the maneuverability and short distances involved in smaller boats, sight of a head in the water can be quickly lost. The coxswain should ensure that the crew member keeping an eye on the person overboard is relieved of any other duties that could be distracting.

A.7. CREW BRIEFING

When the coxswain is ready to commence the recovery approach, he must brief the crew on how

If no ring buoy is available, throw some other flotation device toward the individual, taking care to throw it so it can drift toward the person. Throwing the object directly at the individual could cause further harm if the device struck the person.

the recovery will be made and whether it will be accomplished on the port or starboard side. The approach will be influenced by:

- wind,

- sea surf conditions,

- maneuverability of the boat, and

- maneuvering space restriction.

A.8. ALERTING BOATS IN THE GENERAL VICINITY

Sounding five or more short blasts on the sound signal, horn, or whistle alerts boats in the area that a danger exists (i.e., a man overboard is occurring). Boats in the vicinity may not be aware of what the signal means but at least they will realize something unusual is happening.

A.9. PAN PAN PAN

If the person overboard has not been located and immediately recovered and assistance of other boats is needed, transmit the emergency call signal Pan (pronounced PAHN) three times on channel 16 or 2182 kHz. Follow this with the boat's identification, position, and a brief description of the situation. Do not use "Mayday." A boat uses a Mayday call only when threatened by grave and imminent danger. After returning to datum and completing a quick scan of the area, if the PIW is not found, drop a datum marker and commence an initial search pattern. Continue the search until otherwise directed by the operational commander.

A.10. INFORMING THE OPERATIONAL COMMANDER

When circumstances and time permits, the coxswain must notify the operational commander of the man overboard situation. This should be done as soon as possible after the occurrence.

A.11. REQUESTING ADDITIONAL ASSISTANCE

Requests for additional assistance may be made to the operational commander by radio. Also, any craft near the scene may be requested by the coxswain to assist as needed.

A.12. SUMMARY

The general person in the water recovery procedure described above applies whether the individual fell overboard from your boat or from another boat. These steps are in a sequence as it occurs in time:

1. Someone falls over the side.

2. The first crew member to observe the incident or the person overboard calls out "MAN OVERBOARD" and follows this exclamation with the side from which the event occurred or the person was sighted; then maintains sight of and continuously points to the individual in the water.

- A crew member throws a ring buoy with strobe light over the same side that the person fell (or was sighted on) and in the general direction of the person in the water.

3. Events happening at approximately the same time:

- The coxswain turns the boat in the direction indicated in the alarm, depresses the Loran-C or GPS receiver memory button (if this equipment is on the boat), sounds 5 or more short blasts on whistle or horn, and notifies the station at the earliest possible moment.

4. The coxswain assigns crew member duties:

- The Pointer (or first person to see the member go overboard) moves forward near a pilothouse window, weather permitting, locates the person overboard and points to the location of the person at all times.

- The Recovery crew member makes preparation for the pickup.

5. The coxswain makes the recovery approach, briefs the crew as to how the recovery will be made and which side of the boat it will be made on. Based on existing conditions, the coxswain will select either a leeward or a windward approach.

The Approach

A.13. BASIC APPROACHES

The coxswain must select an approach that is suitable for the existing conditions. There are two basic approaches:

- A leeward approach (against the wind and current)

- A windward approach (with the wind and current

A.14. LEEWARD APPROACH

Perform the leeward approach with the bow facing into the greatest force of oncoming resistance at the time of pickup. (See Figure 16-2.) This may be the wind, current, seas, or any combination of the three. There are times when the wind and current are from different directions. Select the heading which will best ease the approach. The coxswain

must also balance the effect of any swell that might be present. The approach must be made rapidly but as the boat nears the person you must slow the boat and reduce your wake enough to where a short burst backing down stops your headway. The person in the water should be next to the recovery area on the boat and the boat should be dead in the water. Place the engines in neutral and, when the person overboard is alongside, have a crew member make the recovery. Make all pick ups into the prevailing weather and sea conditions. Take care not to overrun the person overboard or to have so much headway on that the boat drifts beyond the person overboard. If the person in the water does drift aft of the boat, do not back down to effect the recovery. The propeller could injure the person.

WARNING

If the person in the water does drift aft of the boat, do not back down to effect the recovery. The propeller could injure the person.

A.15. WINDWARD APPROACH

Perform the windward approach with the wind coming from behind the boat. Use the windward approach when the person overboard is in a confined space or a leeward approach is impossible. However, avoid a situation where the boat can not turn into the wind due to superstructure or bow sail area ("in irons"). The operator must maneuver into a position upwind and up current from the person over-

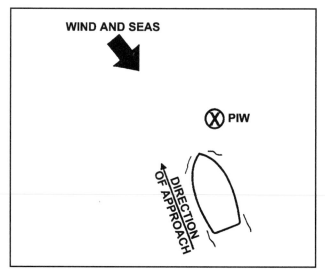

Figure 16-2 Placing Person in the Water on Leeward Side of Boat on Approach

board, place the engine in neutral, and drift down to the person. Ensure that the boat drifts so it places the person overboard along the "recovery" side but do not allow the boat to drift over the person.

A.16. WINDWARD TO LEEWARD OF MULTIPLE PERSONS

Depending upon skill and experience, a combination of the windward and leeward approaches may be necessary. One instance may be in the case of recovering multiple persons in the water. (See Figure 16-3.)

A.17. STOPPING IMMEDIATELY

There may be instances when stopping the boat and allowing the person overboard to swim back to the boat, or at least to reach the tethered floating object is the most appropriate action. Especially if the boat can be stopped quickly after the person falls overboard.

A.18. QUICK TURN

The boat can be turned in the quickest time with full rudder and full speed. The turn can be achieved with a short turning diameter on twin prop boats by backing the inboard propeller. Whether single or twin propeller, the coxswain will slow the boat on the final approach such that the boat will nearly be

DIW (dead in the water) when the person in the water comes abeam.

A.19. STOP PIVOT RETURN

Another option, particularly in a restricted waterway, is to stop, pivot/back and fill, then return to the PIW. The turning and backing characteristics of the boat and the prevailing wind and sea conditions will dictate how the approach is made. The coxswain will maneuver the boat to the weather side of the person in the water so that the boat is set by the wind or seas toward the person rather than away.

A.20. DESTROYER TURN

Except in a narrow channel, make the turn to either side that permits the tightest turn, in this case to port, to move the stern of the boat away from the person overboard. This maneuver can be modified for use by twin propeller boats. Twin propeller boats are pivoted by putting one engine ahead and the other in reverse. With a single propeller boat put the rudder hard over with the engine full ahead. (See Figure 16-4.)

1. Make the turn to either side that will permit the tightest turn for the boat.

2. Continue making a complete turn, coming around and approaching the person that fell overboard with the boat's bow directly into the wind/current.

3. Once pointed toward the person, proceed rapidly until close.

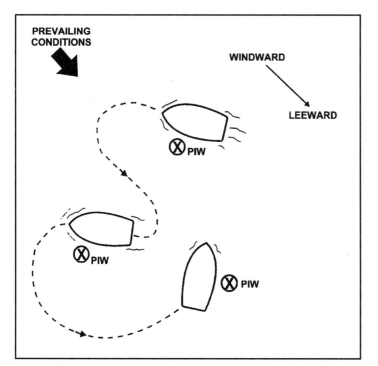

Figure 16-3 Windward to Leeward Approach of Multiple Persons in the Water

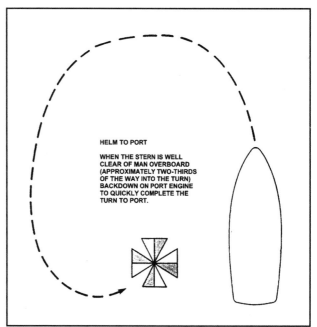

Figure 16-4 Destroyer Turn Man Overboard, Port Side

4. Then make a slow and deliberate approach to the person, coming to a stop when alongside.

A.21. APPROACHING IN SEVERE WEATHER CONDITIONS

Severe conditions may dictate that the approach be made from leeward with the bow dead into the seas and/or wind in order to maintain control of the boat. In severe conditions, particularly aboard single propeller boats, this will test the experience and skill of the coxswain. (See Section D in the Heavy Weather Addendum for more information.)

NOTE

Never have the propeller turning when the person overboard is next to the boat. If you have to add power and maneuver with the person in the water in close proximity to the boat, turn the bow toward the person, swinging the stern and propeller(s) away and at a safe distance.

Sailboat Approaches

A.22. GIVING COMMANDS

During periods of distress, such as a person in the water, take special care with the remaining crew members to assure their safety. Give clear commands to ensure that crew members keep clear of the boom.

A.23. MODERATE WIND, BOAT ON REACH

Carry out these preliminary procedures:

- pass the alarm
- throw flotation device
- point to the person in the water

ALTER THE COURSE TO BEAM REACH Alter the course to beam reach by doing the following:

1. Release the shaft lock.
2. Maintain silence, except the relative bearings given by the pointer.
3. Prepare the gybe.
4. Prepare to drop the headsail.
5. Start the engine (if so equipped).
6. Check for lines over the side.

GYBE If the conditions permit:

1. From the turning point, divide the knot minutes by the average speed on the return leg.

Example: 3 knots average speed, divide 12 by 3 equals 4 minutes for this leg.

2. Drop the headsail.
3. Rig the preventer on boom and rig the line through the block.

WEATHER SIDE APPROACH Approach to the weather side of the person in the water (see Figure 16-5).

1. Rig the ladder, slack the headsail.
2. Tighten the boom preventer, use the engine if possible.

A.24. HEAVY WIND/SEA APPROACHES

The procedures for heavy wind/sea, boat on beam reach or boat close hauled approach are the same as above except that it may be easier to tack with headsail up.

A.25. ALL CONDITION APPROACHES

All conditions, boat on a broad reach or run approach:

1. Carry out the preliminary procedures for person in the water recovery situations:

- pass alarm
- throw PFD
- point
- commence a navigation plot
- lower blooper and spinnaker in that order (if they are deployed)

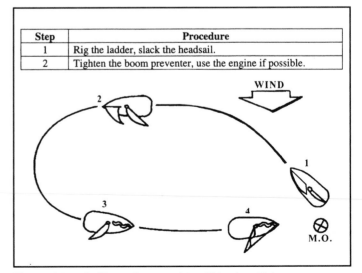

Step	Procedure
1	Rig the ladder, slack the headsail.
2	Tighten the boom preventer, use the engine if possible.

Figure 16-5 Sailboat Approaching Weather Side

2. Alter course to a beam reach and tack when possible.

3. Continue upwind, close hauled, until roughly abeam of the person in the water (see Figure 16-6).

   • Fall off the wind.

   • Drop the headsail, rig the preventer, and rig the line through block.

4. Make the approach as discussed in the preceding paragraphs.

Approaching in Low Visibility

A.26. GENERAL

During low visibility and night operations when a crew member sees another crew member go over the side the same general procedures apply. The crew member observing the person go overboard tosses a flotation device with a strobe (or any other light) attached, if available. They also continue to observe and point to the person overboard as long as possible. The coxswain presses the memory button on the Loran-C or GPS receiver, if so equipped, sounds signals, and goes to the datum using one of the following turns.

A.27. ANDERSON TURN

An advantage of the Anderson turn is that it is the fastest recovery method. A disadvantage is that it is not meant for use by a single propeller boat. The Anderson turn involves the following:

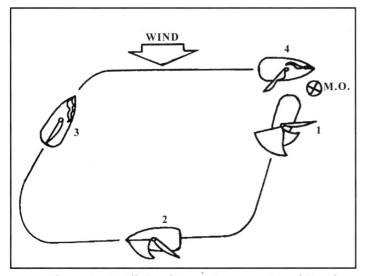

Figure 16-6 All Conditions, Boat on a Broad Reach or Run, Approach

1. Put the rudder over full in the direction corresponding to the side from which the person fell. Go ahead full on the outboard engine only.

2. When about ⅔ of the way around, back the inboard engine ⅔ or full.

3. Stop engines when the person overboard is within about 15° of the bow.

4. Ease the rudder and back the engines as require to attain the proper final position. (See Figure 16-7.)

A.28. RACE TRACK TURN

The final straight leg approach of the Race track turn helps for a more calculable approach. The race track turn involves the following:

1. Put the rudder over full in the direction corresponding to the side from which the person fell, going ahead full on all engines.

2. Use full rudder to turn to the reciprocal of the original course.

3. Steady up on this course for a short distance, then use full rudder to turn to the person overboard. (See Figure 16-8.)

A.29. WILLIAMSON TURN

If an individual falls overboard during periods of darkness or restricted visibility and the exact time of the incident is unknown, a maneuver known as the Williamson turn should be used to search for the person overboard. The advantage of the Williamson turn, when properly executed, is that it will position the boat on a reciprocal cause on its exact original track. This allows the search to commence on the track where the victim fell over, not from a parallel track. Of course, as soon as the alarm is spread the general person overboard procedure will be initiated.

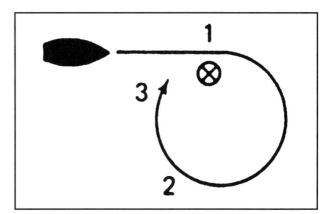

Figure 16-7 The Anderson Turn

PROCEDURE There are four steps in performing the Williamson turn:

1. Mark the original course when the alarm was initially spread. Put over a ring buoy strobe or other float to work datum.

2. Alter the course 60° to port or starboard from the original course. It does not matter which direction is chosen. Naturally, if turning to starboard, 60° will have to be added to the original course to know when the correct number of degrees have been transited. If turning to port, the 60° will be subtracted from the initial course.

3. The turn is actually executed while the first two steps are in progress. In this step, the reciprocal course must be calculated from the original course. That is to say, a new course which runs in the exact opposite direction (180°) from the original course must be figured.

4. Once the correct reciprocal has been calculated and the compass reaches the "60° mark" after turning off the initial course, shift the rudder in the opposite direction from the 60° turn and come to the reciprocal course.

STARBOARD TURN Figure 16-9 shows how the Williamson turn would look if the 60° turn was to starboard. Point "A" represents the initial course and is illustrated as 000°. At Point "B", the compass reads 060°. At this point, the reciprocal course (180°) has been figured. When the compass reaches the 060° mark, the rudder is shifted to the opposite direction (port) of the 60° turn and the boat comes around to the reciprocal. When the 180° course is marked, the boat will continue on this new course and if the person overboard has not been sighted by this time, the boat crew will conduct a search for the victim along this heading. If individual is not located, the boat should proceed along the track to a point where the member was last *known* to be aboard. At this point a second datum marker (ring buoy, fender, etc.) is deployed.

MAINTAIN SPEED Do not change speed during a Williamson turn. Speed changes may bring the boat around to the reciprocal course in a different position than the line of the initial course. The danger is that the person overboard may be too far away for you to locate. The idea behind the Williamson turn is to bring the boat around so that it is on the exact line of the original course but in the opposite direction.

CALCULATING THE 60° TURN Once the person overboard alarm is spread, the coxswain turns the boat 60° from the original course to either port or starboard.

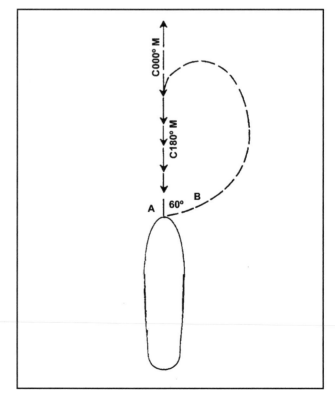

Figure 16-8 The Race Track Turn

Figure 16-9 The Williamson Turn

IF . . . THE TURN IS TO STARBOARD: **Then** . . . the 60° must be ADDED to the original course:

Original course marked when alarm was sounded	080°
Starboard turn	+ 060°
Shift rudder when compass reads	140°

IF . . . THE TURN IS TO PORT: **Then** . . . the 60 degrees must be SUBTRACTED from the original course:

Original course marked when alarm was sounded	080°
Port turn	− 060°
Shift rudder when compass reads	020°

CALCULATING THE RECIPROCAL OF A GIVEN COURSE Calculating the reciprocal of a given course is done by either adding 180° to the given course or subtracting 180° from the given course. To add or to subtract depends on whether the given course was less than 180° or more than 180°.

CALCULATING THE RECIPROCAL OF A COURSE LESS THAN 180° If the original course is less than 180°, add 180° to the original course to get the reciprocal.

Example 1

Original course	000°
Add 180°	+ 180°
Reciprocal course	180°

Example 2

Original course	080°
Add 180°	+ 180°
Reciprocal course	260°

CALCULATING THE RECIPROCAL OF A COURSE MORE THAN 180° If the original course is more than 180°, subtract 180° from the original course to get the reciprocal.

Example 1

Original course	200°
Subtract 180°	− 180°
Reciprocal course	020°

Example 2

Original course	320°
Subtract 180°	− 180°
Reciprocal course	140°

A.30. WHILE TOWING

If during a towing evolution a man overboard emergency occurs, boat crew members should be aware of the severity and danger of the situation. Several problems can occur when dealing with a simultaneous towing and man overboard situation.

VESSEL MANEUVERABILITY Boat Towing Astern:

- A decrease in speed could cause the towed boat to overrun the towing boat.
- Tripping can occur when a boat is towed sideways by an opposing force on the towline. If the towline is out of alignment (not in line) and pulls sideways, the towing boat will heel over, often beyond its ability to right itself.

NOTE

Tripping occurs more frequently when the tow is larger than the towing boat.

WARNING

The closer the towing bit is to amidships (if so equipped), the more serious the danger.

Boat Towing Alongside:

- Extra weight slows the ability to stop and makes it difficult to turn away from the side to which the tow is secured.

WEATHER CONDITIONS Current, wind, sea, or swell from astern can cause yawing and add to the problem of the tow overrunning the towing boat.

Current broadsides to the tow create difficulty in holding the tow due to side slip, causing the tow to yaw.

NOTE

Bar or inlet conditions will compound all these problems.

PRE-PLANNING Considering the number of potential problems that can occur, the operator should carefully assess all possible situations and conditions to preplan steps to take in case of a man overboard emergency.

ADDITIONAL PROCEDURES If a person falls overboard during a towing evolution, follow the steps discussed earlier in this section. The following are additional considerations to take which apply to man overboard situations specific to towing evolutions.

- If another boat is nearby, get that boat to make the pickup.
  Since tows are made at slow speeds, it may possible that the tow can make the pickup. The towing boat should aid in any way possible.

- If towing astern, advise the towed boat of the man overboard situation, and have the people on the tow assist in looking for the person in the water.

Be sure to advise the people on the tow that there is a real danger of tripping or broaching if the towed boat sheers away violently from alignment.

It might be necessary to drop the tow in order to perform a man overboard operation. Consider the environmental factors and water traffic when/if dropping the tow to minimize the possibility of a hazardous situation. Have the tow anchored.

- Never forget that the man overboard may be injured if hit by the tow.

A person who has fallen off the bow or side can be seriously injured or killed by the propellers. Any turns made should move the stern away from the person in the water.

CAUTION!
Slow calculated moves are better than a "knee jerk" response.

TOWING ALONGSIDE When towing a boat alongside, follow the guidelines discussed in earlier in this section. Keep in mind that towing alongside allows more freedom to turn. Consider the following points:

- Engines, while useful, will not respond as usual. Remember, the engines were designed to propel one boat, not two.

- When making a turn, turn slowly towards the side with the tow and pivot on the tow. Be careful not to swamp the tow.

- The best approach is to make the pickup on the free side since the operator can better observe the person in the water and the pickup.

- Again, consider dropping the tow.

The procedures will remain the same whether the person falls from the tow or towing vessel.

TOWING ASTERN If the person falls overboard from the tow, follow the procedures outlined above. Realize that if there is no boat to help, the towing boat will have no other choice but to drop the tow.

SUMMARY Always consider the effect of each action on all the boats and persons involved. **People before property.** People's safety is the number one priority. People on board the tow are just as important as the person in the water. Consider if the towed boat is not manned, drop the tow! Always inform all people and vessels involved of every situation.

The best way to handle a man overboard emergency is to prevent one from happening. Be aware of the crew: know where they are and what they are doing.

Approaching Under Surf Conditions

A.31. GENERAL

Recovering a person overboard in heavy weather requires special precautions beyond the routine described in the section on general person overboard procedure. The general procedure is put into effect as soon as the alarm is sounded. The Auxiliary is not authorized to operate in surf conditions. (See Section D in the Heavy Weather Addendum for more information.)

Recovery

A.32. GENERAL

Recovery techniques for a person in the water are the same for any distress—your own crew as a man overboard, passengers from a ditched aircraft, fisherman from a sinking boat, someone washed off of a jetty, or whatever emergency.

A.33. RECOVERY METHODS

The condition of the person in the water will dictate the type of recovery procedure used. Once the condition of the person in the water can be determined, that is, conscious, unconscious, or injured, the coxswain will select one of the procedures below and assign crew member duties accordingly. Generally, the pickup is completed at the lowest point of freeboard and away from the propellers.

When approaching persons needing rescue, try to assess their physical condition.

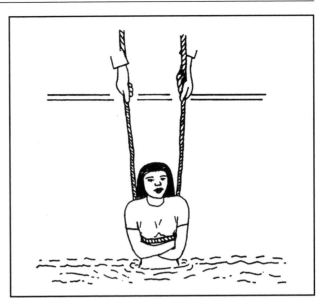

Figure 16-10 Person in the Water Recovery Strap

A.34. PERSON OVERBOARD IS UNINJURED AND CONSCIOUS

Recovery method when the person is conscious and able to move freely in the water.

1. Upon command of the coxswain, a crew member casts out a heaving line or a float line to the person in the water.

2. The person will hold on to the line and be hauled in for recovery by the crew member tending the line.

3. If the person needs assistance to board the boat, two crew members could be used to pull the person up out of the water and onto the boat by each placing a hand under the person's armpit (use the other hand to hold onto the boat);

     or

   the use of a recovery strap (see Figure 16-10) or a boarding ladder could be used if available.

A.35. ADDITIONAL PROCEDURES

The construction of some boats allows the rescue team to reach the victim at the surface of the water.

- The boat crew members should physically pick the person straight up out of the water to a sitting position on the gunwale (gunnel) (see Figure 16-11).

- Be careful not to drag the person's back across the rail.

Figure 16-11 Recovering the Person in the Water at the Surface of the Water

If only one person is available to lift an uninjured person from the water:

1. Position the victim facing the boat with both arms reaching upwards.

2. Boat crew member should reach down with arms crossed and grasp victim's wrists.

3. Boat crew member should lift the victim straight out of the water while simultaneously uncrossing the arms. This should extract the victim from the water in a corkscrew motion.

If the freeboard of the boat is too high to recover the victim safely:

- use a line under the armpits in a horse collar fashion;

- the line should cross the chest, pass under each arm, and up behind the head.
- Use padding for comfort, if available.

A person is light in the water due to buoyancy; however, once free from the water the person becomes "dead weight." Keep this in mind and be especially careful when recovering injured persons.

A.36. PERSON IN THE WATER IS UNCONSCIOUS OR INJURED

The procedure in the event the victim is unconscious or injured is slightly more complicated. The coxswain will designate one of the crew members as a surface swimmer.

1. The surface swimmer will don a wet suit, dry suit with a PFD (which one depends upon the water temperature and the weather), a helmet, and a swimming harness with tending line. (See Figure 16-12.)

2. For quick deployment, the line should be coiled and attached to the back of the swimmer's harness.

3. When the surface swimmer has reached the unconscious or injured victim and has obtained a secure hold on the person, the crew member tending the harness line will haul both back to the boat.

A flotation equipped Stokes Litter is employed to recover a person only if that person is seriously injured and seas are calm. (See Figure 16-13.)

SURFACE SWIMMER Surface swimmers are any swimmers not trained as rescue swimmers. Their training is accomplished through Personnel Qualification Standard (PQS). They are deployed from floating units, piers, or the shore. A surface swimmer must wear a PFD with dry suit or wet suit and a swimming harness with a tending line. Another crew member will tend the harness whenever the swimmer is in the water.

NOTE

Auxiliary does not have surface swimmers.

A.37. REQUESTING A RESCUE SWIMMER

The primary mission of the helicopter rescue swimmer is to provide rotary wing stations with the capability of deploying a properly trained and conditioned person to assist persons in distress in the marine environment. The rescue swimmer must have the flexibility, strength, endurance, and equipment to function for 30 minutes in heavy seas, and the skills to provide basic pre-hospital life support for the rescued individual(s). The rescue swimmer's Emergency Medical Technician (EMT) skills may also be used during other SAR cases in which the swimming ability is not required.

If medical assistance is needed, the parent station shall be advised. The station may arrange for medical assistance on-scene or at an agreed upon rendezvous point.

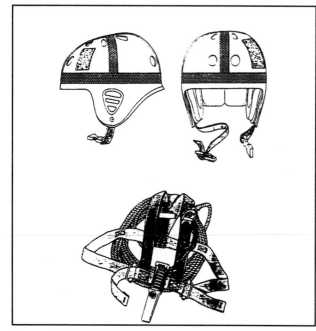

Figure 16-12 Surface Swimmer's Helmet and Harness

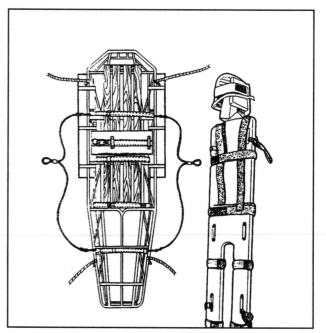

Figure 16-13 Stokes Litter and Miller Board

Figure 16-14 Multiple Person in the Water Recovery System

A.38. MULTIPLE PERSON IN THE WATER RECOVERY

For multiple persons in the water, the question becomes which person in the water is recovered first? The answer to this requires the coxswain's best judgment. An accurate assessment once on the scene will dictate the coxswain's response. Consideration should be given to the following:

1. Are one or more persons in the water injured?

2. Which persons in the water have on PFDs and which do not?

3. How close are the persons in the water to the beach or jetty?

4. How old are they and what is their physical condition?

A.39. MULTIPLE PERSON IN THE WATER RECOVERY (MPR) SYSTEM

The Multiple Person in the Water Recovery (MPR) System is an inflatable rescue device designed to assist in the retrieval of multiple survivors from the water to the deck of a rescue vessel. (See Figure 16-14.) The MPR was specifically designed for use on the 41' UTB. When installed and operated correctly, the MPR will inflate in less than 10 seconds and be ready for use. The unique design of this system allows rescuers to descend the ramp to assist in the recovery of multiple persons in the water or allows multiple persons in the water to easily climb from the water.

Specific instructions will be provided at the station to 41' UTB crew members on use and operation of the MPR system.

Water Survival Skills

Overview

Introduction

In the event a crew member enters or ends up in the water due to an emergency, survival procedures should be pre-planned. By doing so, the chances for a successful rescue are increased.

This section addresses the survival techniques that will greatly increase the likelihood of survival for a person in the water. Never forget that a PFD is the best insurance for survival.

In this section

Cold Water Survivability

B.1. COLD WATER SURVIVAL

The length of time a person can stay alive in cold water depends on the temperature of the water, the physical condition of the survivor, and the action taken by the survivor. Figure 16-16 illustrates the relationship between an uninjured victim's activity, water temperature, and estimated survival time. Swimming typically reduces a person's chance of survival due to more rapid loss of body heat.

B.2. CRITICAL FACTORS

Time is critical when forced to enter cold water. The loss of body heat is one of the greatest dangers to survival. Critical factors that increase the threat of hypothermia and other cold water injuries include prolonged exposure to cold water temperatures, sea spray, air temperature, and wind chill.

Survival Techniques

B.3. PREVENTATIVE MEASURES

There are several preventative measures that can be used to increase the chances for successful cold water survival including:

How Hypothermia Affects Most Adults		
Water Temperature °F (°C)	Exhaustion or Unconsciousness	Expected Time of Survival
32.5 (0.3)	Under 15 min.	Under 15 to 45 min.
32.5 to 40 (0.3 to 4.4)	15 to 30 min.	30 to 90 min.
40 to 50 (4.4 to 10)	30 to 60 min.	1 to 3 hrs.
50 to 60 (10 to 15.6)	1 to 2 hrs.	1 to 6 hrs.
60 to 70 (15.6 to 21)	2 to 7 hrs.	2 to 40 hrs.
70 to 80 (21 to 26.7)	2 to 12 hrs.	3 hrs. to indefinite
Over 80 (26.7)	Indefinite	Indefinite

Figure 16-16 Survival Times vs. Water Temperatures

1. Put on as much warm clothing as possible, making sure to cover head, neck, hands and feet.

2. If the hypothermia protective clothing does not have inherent flotation, put on a PFD.

3. Avoid entering the water if possible. If it is necessary to jump into the water, hold elbows close to your sides, cover nose and mouth with one hand while holding the wrist or elbow firmly with the other hand.

4. Before entering the water, button up clothing, turn on signal lights (only at night), locate your survival whistle and make any other preparations for rescue.

NOTE

For more information on cold water survival see COMDTPUB P3131.6, "A Pocket Guide to Cold Water Survival."

B.4. WATER SURVIVAL SKILLS

There are water survival skills that should be utilized to increase the chances for surviving cold water immersion including:

1. Immediately upon entering the water, become oriented to the surrounding area. Try to locate your sinking boat, floating objects, and other survivors.

2. Try to board a lifeboat, raft or other floating platform as soon as possible to shorten the immersion time. Body heat is lost many times faster in the water than in the air. Since the effectiveness of the insulation worn is seriously reduced by being water soaked, it is important to be shielded from wind to avoid a wind-chill effect. If able to climb aboard a survival craft, use a canvas cover or tarpaulin as a shield from the cold. Huddling close to the other occupants in the craft will also conserve body heat.

3. While afloat in the water, DO NOT attempt to swim unless it is necessary to reach a fellow survivor or a floating object which can be grasped or climbed onto.

Unnecessary swimming will pump out any warm water between the body and the layers of clothing and will increase the rate of body-heat loss. Also, unnecessary movements of arms and legs send warm blood from the inner core to the outer layer of the body resulting in a rapid heat loss.

1. The body position assumed in the water is very important in conserving heat. Float as still as possible with legs together, elbows close to your side and arms folded across the front of your PFD. This is called the HELP (Heat Escape Lessening Position) and minimizes exposure of the body surface to the cold water. Try to keep head and neck out of the water (see Figure 16-17). However, if you're wearing a Type III PFD, or if the HELP position turns you face down, bring your legs together tight and your arms tight to your sides and your head back.

Another heat conserving position is to huddle closely to others in the water making as much body contact as possible. A PFD must be worn to be able to maintain these positions in the water (see Figure 16-18).

1. Avoid drown-proofing in cold water. (Drown-proofing is a technique where you relax in the water and allow your head to submerge between breaths. It is an energy saver in warm water when a PFD is not worn.) The head and neck are high heat loss areas and must be kept above the water. That is why it is even more important to wear a PFD in cold water. If a PFD is

Figure 16-17 Single Person in the Water

not worn, tread the water only as much as necessary to keep your head out of the water.

2. Keep a positive attitude about your survival and rescue. This will extend your survival time until rescue comes. A will to live does make a difference.

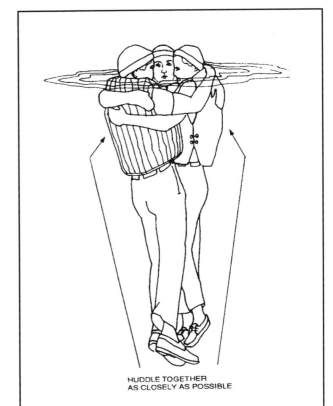

Figure 16-18 Multiple People in the Water

Towing

Editor's Note: *Sooner or later you'll be tempted to help out a fellow boater by playing "Good Sam" and helping him back to shore. But before you do, keep in mind that towing a boat is anything but simple. A towed boat can yaw uncontrollably and capsize the tow boat; towing stress can break loose hardware from either vessel, turning it into deadly missiles; lines can snap and whip across decks, tossing crew into the water; hands and feet can be crushed as crewmembers attempt to fend off. The list of hazards is long and grim. All of this does not mean you should avoid offering aid to a fellow mariner in distress, but it does mean you should know proper techniques and you should know your limits and your boat's limits and then you should add a large safety factor. This chapter is written for Coasties and Auxiliarists who train and recertify in towing maneuvers and techniques annually. Note that the Coast Guard puts safety ahead of all other considerations. Coasties will always take care of people before property. So, learn the lessons of this section well if you are tempted to engage in tow operations. Make modifications where appropriate for your boat and your capabilities. And then rethink the whole business before you pass a tow line.*

Overview

Introduction

As a boat crew member, towing will be one of the responsibilities you will execute for many types of maritime craft. This chapter covers forces in towing, towing equipment, safety, and procedures. Boat crews need a firm grasp of towing principles to ensure that a "routine" evolution does not result in injury, death or further damage to property. No two towing evolutions are exactly the same. Variations in technique and procedure will occur. Apply your knowledge of principles and standard procedures to account for weather and sea conditions, vessel types, and crew experience. Ensure the tow is within your and your vessel's capabilities.

The *Coast Guard Addendum to the National Search and Rescue Manual* states policy on vessel-assistance towing. Standard-Boat Operators Handbooks provide specific procedures for those types of boats. Individual manufacturers' boat owner's guides and product specification sheets provide equipment limitations and safety information. Boat Crew Qualification Guides address crew performance requirements. Chapter 1—Boat Crew Duties and Responsibilities, in this manual, outlines the towing watch responsibilities. Be familiar with and comply with the policies, direction and information in these sources.

In this chapter

Towing Safety

Overview

Introduction

SAFETY is always the most important concern. Every towing activity is potentially dangerous. The safety of your crew and the crew of the towed vessel is more important than property, and your primary responsibility in any towing situation is to maintain safety measures. Towing is a complex evolution. A safe and successful outcome hinges on crew professionalism, ability, and **teamwork**.

Chapter 4 is dedicated to safety-related items, including risk management and team coordination. Towing-specific applications are covered here.

In this section

Topic	See Page
Assessment and Awareness	337
Risk Management Planning	337

Assessment and Awareness

A.1. RISK ASSESSMENT

Every boat crew member is responsible for identifying and managing risks. Prevent towing mishaps by honestly evaluating risks involved in every step of any towing evolution. Communicate with the towed vessel's crew who may have important information necessary to complete a successful mission.

> **WARNING**
>
> Do not let a perceived need to engage in a towing mission override a complete, honest risk assessment process that emphasizes personnel safety.

A.2. SITUATIONAL AWARENESS

The dynamics of a towing situation continuously change from the time pre-towing preparations begin until mooring at the conclusion of the mission. All crew members must stay fully aware of the constantly changing situation at all times any given time during a towing evolution. Know what goes on around you and how things change. Reinforce crew awareness through communication: comment on what you think you see happening, and involve the towed vessel's crew. The "outside" view could provide information on things not visible from the towing vessel.

When clues indicate that situational awareness is being lost, a decision must be made whether or not to continue with the towing evolution. A decision takes the form of action/reaction and communication. Everyone in the crew has a responsibility in making decisions.

Risk Management Planning

A.3. RISK MANAGEMENT

Realistic towing training based on standardized techniques, critical analysis, and mission debrief will contribute to risk management and the development of a towing risk management plan. All crew members must contribute to risk management planning.

Standard precautions at the end of this chapter (Appendix 17-A) make up the basis for a towing risk management plan, but keep in mind that each towing evolution is unique, and revise the plan for whatever the situation dictates. Refer to Chapter 4 for discussion of Risk Assessment and Management.

Forces in Towing

Overview

Introduction

Boat crews must understand the forces, or types of resistance, which act on the towed vessel and how to handle the resistance safely. They are the same forces that affect all vessels, but a distressed vessel is limited in how it can overcome them. The towing vessel must provide the means to move the towed vessel. The towline or tow rig transfers all forces from the towed vessel to the towing vessel. Learn to recognize the different forces and each of their effects individually to effectively balance and overcome them when they act together.

In this section

Static Forces

B.1. GENERAL

Static forces cause a towed vessel to resist motion. The **displacement** or mass of a towed vessel determines the amount of force working against the vessel. The assisting vessel must overcome these forces before the towed vessel moves. **Inertia** and the **Moment of Inertia** are two different properties of static forces which cause resistance in towing vessels.

B.2. INERTIA

In this case, inertia is the tendency for a vessel at rest to stay at rest. The more mass a vessel has (the greater its displacement), the more inertia it has and the harder it is to get it moving.

B.3. MOMENT OF INERTIA

The Moment of Inertia occurs when a towed vessel resists effort to turn about a vertical axis to change heading. The larger the vessel, the more resistance there will be in turning the vessel. Unless necessary in a case of immediate danger, **do not** attempt to tow a distressed vessel ahead **and** change its heading at the same time. (See Figure 17-1.) Both inertia and the moment of inertia will be involved in the resistance of moving the distressed vessel, which can cause potentially dangerous situations and greater resistance for towing. Both vessels, their fittings, and the towing equipment take much less stress and strain when the two forces are conquered individually.

Overcome the effects of static forces by starting a tow **slowly**, both on the initial heading or when changing the towed vessel's heading. A large amount of strain is placed on both vessels, their fittings and the towing equipment when going from dead-in-the-water to moving in the desired direction and at the desired speed. Use extreme caution when towing a vessel of equal or greater mass than the assisting vessel. In such situations, the assisting vessel strains the capacity and capability of its equipment, requiring slow and gradual changes.

STARTING THE TOW ON THE INITIAL HEADING Apply the towing force on the initial heading to gradually overcome the towed vessel's inertia. As the towed vessel gains momentum, slowly and gradually increase speed. To change the tow direction, make any change slowly and gradually after the towed vessel is moving.

CHANGING THE TOWED VESSEL'S HEADING Apply the towing force perpendicular to the vessel's heading. Once the towed vessel starts to turn, resistance will develop. Apply turning force slowly and gradually. It is more difficult to change the initial heading of a heavy vessel (one with a high moment of inertia) than a light one. Now, begin to tow in the desired direction and gradually overcome inertia to get the towed vessel moving forward.

Once making way, the effects of static forces lessen. Until the tow achieves a steady speed and direction, apply effort to defeat any remaining in-

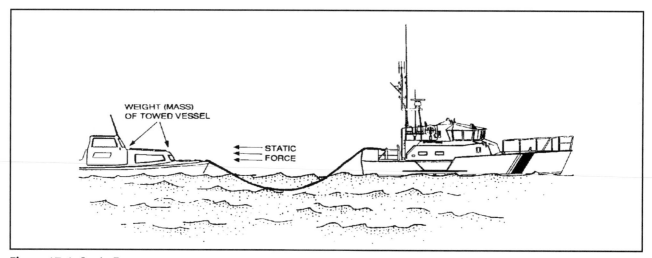

Figure 17-1 Static Forces

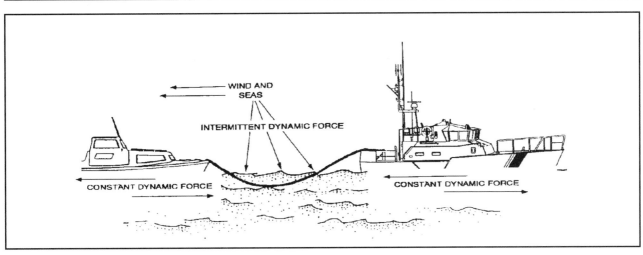

Figure 17-2 Dynamic Forces

ertia or to change the towed vessel's momentum gradually.

Dynamic Forces

B.4. GENERAL

Dynamic forces occur once the towed vessel is moving. They are based on the towed vessel's characteristics (shape, displacement, arrangement, rigging), the motion caused by the towing vessel, and the effects of waves and wind. (See Figure 17-2.)

B.5. MOMENTUM

Once a vessel moves in a straight line, it wants to keep moving in a straight line. The greater its displacement or the faster it is moving, the harder it is to stop or change the vessel's direction.

B.6. ANGULAR MOMENTUM

Once the vessel's heading begins to change, it wants to keep changing in that same direction. The faster the towed vessel's heading changes, the harder it is to get the tow moving in a straight line.

The towed vessel's momentum will gradually increase with towing speed. Momentum in a straight line will resist effort to change the towed vessel's direction and will tend to keep the towed vessel moving when tension in the towing rig is decreased. If necessary to first change the direction of the tow, the towed vessel will develop angular momentum while the vessel's heading is changing. You may need to apply towing force opposite the swing, before the towed vessel achieves the desired heading. The key to dealing with momentum is to anticipate how momentum will affect the towed vessel's motion and apply an offsetting force early and gradually.

B.7. FRICTIONAL RESISTANCE

As a vessel moves, the layer of water in immediate contact with the hull moves too. Due to friction between water molecules, the layers of water close to the hull try to drag along. The vessel appears to move "through" the water. This attempt to drag water alongside takes energy. As speed increases, the layers of water closest to the hull action become "turbulent." This turbulence takes additional energy to overcome, and more speed requires even more power.

NOTE

Frictional resistance also varies with hull shape. Greater underwater (wetted) surface area causes greater frictional resistance. Hull appendages, such as propellers, shafts, skegs, keel, and rudders contribute to wetted surface area and frictional resistance.

> **CAUTION!**
> Frictional resistance will constantly affect the tow, *normally* keeping some steady tension in the towing rig. Since the shape and wetted surface area of the towed vessel will not change, frictional resistance is managed with towing speed. Higher towing speed causes higher frictional resistance and more strain on the towing rig.

B.8. FORM DRAG

Form drag plays a large role in the ability to control changes in the towed vessel's movement. Different hull shapes react to motion through the water in different ways. The shape and size of the towed vessel's hull can either help or hinder effort to move in a straight line, when changing heading, and motion changes in response to waves due to buoyancy. The less water a hull shape has to *push* out of its way, the easier it will move through the water. A deep-draft, full-hulled vessel takes more effort to move than one with a fine, shallow hull. A large amount of lateral resistance, spread evenly over the length of the hull, will hinder effort to change a towed vessel's direction, but will help offset angular momentum in steadying up on a desired heading. A towed vessel may be able to help offset form drag by using its rudder.

B.9. WAVE MAKING RESISTANCE

A surface wave forms at the bow while the hull moves through the water. The size of the bow wave increases as speed increases, and this bow wave generates resistance to movement of the boat. The larger the bow wave system, the greater the resistance, causing the wave to create resistance for the bow to be pulled or propelled through the water.

Keep in mind the different hull types of maritime craft, including the towing vessel. In any towing evolution, the boat crew must be able to recognize a vessel's hull type, as well as its critical capabilities and limitations. Dependent on the type of hull, towing vessels must be careful not to tow a vessel faster than the design speed of its the towed vessel's hull. Refer to Chapter 8—Boat Characteristics, for discussion of different hull types.

CAUTION!

It is not always safe to tow a planing hull type of vessel above planing speed. Going from displacement speed to planing speed, or back, can decrease the towed vessel's stability and cause it to capsize. Also, wave drag (even one large wake) could slow the hull down to displacement speed and cause a severe "shock-load" to the towing gear as the towed vessel tries to get back on plane.

NOTE

"Shock-load" or "shock-loading" is the rapid, extreme increase in tension on the towline, which transfers through the tow rig and fittings to both vessels.

B.10. WAVE DRAG, SPRAY DRAG, AND WIND DRAG

These frictional forces act on the hull, topsides, superstructure, and rigging. They all have a major effect on the motion of the towed vessel, and the transfer of forces to and through the towing rig. These constantly changing forces all vary with the towed vessel's motion relative to the environmental elements and are directly related to the towed vessel's amount of exposure to them. These forces are cumulative and can add up and cause **shock loading**. Wind and wave drag also cause a distressed drifting vessel to make leeway, that is motion in a downwind direction.

WAVE DRAG **Wave drag** depends on the "normal" wetted surface area of the hull and the amount of freeboard exposed to wave action. Wave drag has a large effect on the strain of the tow rig.

- In large seas, be aware that:

  The combination of wave drag and form drag can overcome the towed vessel's forward momentum and cause the towed vessel to stop and transfer a large amount of strain to the tow rig.

  Shock-load can damage vessel fittings, part the towline, and endanger both vessel crews.

- In head seas, be aware that:

  The towing vessel can only control the effect of wave drag by adjusting the speed and angle that the towed vessel encounters the waves.

  Limiting vessel speed and towing at an angle to the seas can prevent seas from breaking over the bow of the towed vessel.

- In following seas, be aware that:

  Wave drag can cause the towed vessel to speed up as the crest approaches.

  Consider increasing tow speed to keep tension in the towing rig when this happens, and then reducing speed as the crest passes.

SPRAY DRAG **Spray drag** also provides resistance to the tow. The spray from a wave can slow the towed vessel and increase the amount of shock loading. Spray drag can also adversely affect the towed vessel's motion by imparting a momentary heel, pooling on deck or in the vessel cockpit, and forming ice in cold weather. Any of these phenomena can decrease stability.

WIND DRAG Wind drag can cause shock loading and have a bad effect on the towed vessel's motions and stability. A steady beam wind can cause list and leeway, while a severe gust can cause a threatening heel. List, heel, and leeway may cause the towed vessel to yaw. A headwind increases tow rig loading in a direct line with the towed vessel whenile the towed vessel crests a wave, causing shock-loading.

B.11. BUOYANCY RESPONSE AND GRAVITY EFFECTS

Develop a feel for the towed vessel's initial and reserve buoyancy characteristics, overall stability, sea keeping, response to the prevailing environmental conditions, and the response to being towed. Though a distressed vessel may seem stable and sound at rest, its response in tow could be a capsize. A towed vessel's bow may react to an oncoming wave by pitching skyward, or by "submarining." Buoyancy response to following seas could cause the towed vessel to yaw excessively or gravity may cause it to gain speed and "surf" down the face of a wave.

WARNING

Once making way, a vessel's buoyancy response or the effect of gravity in a seaway may cause severe shock-loading.

Combination of Forces and Shock-Load

B.12. GENERAL

A boat crew rarely deals with only one force acting on the tow. The crew usually faces a combination of all the forces, each making the situation more complex. Some individual forces are very large and relatively constant. Crews can usually deal with these safely, provided all towing force changes are made slowly and gradually. When forces are changed in an irregular manner, ten-

sion on the tow rig starts to vary instead of remaining steady.

Example:

In calm winds and seas, a towing vessel encounters a steady, large amount of frictional resistance, form drag and wave making resistance when towing a large fishing vessel with trawl lines fouling its propeller and net still down. The tow rig and vessel fittings will be under heavy strain, and the tow vessel engine loads will be rather high, but the tow proceeds relatively safely. If, suddenly, the net tangles and is caught on an unseen obstacle, this new "force" acting through the tow rig could immediately increase stress to a dangerous level. This shock-load could part the towline or destroy fittings.

(In the example above, the prudent solution would be have been to make a "safe" tow by recovering the net or marking it and letting it loose before starting the tow.)

Though the situation in this example began as a safe and steady tow, a single unexpected incident could have caused a very dangerous situation. Always keep in mind that some degree of shock-loading can occur during any tow evolution.

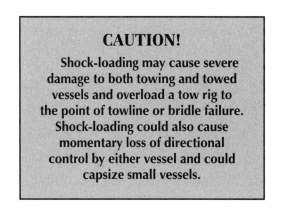

CAUTION!

Shock-loading may cause severe damage to both towing and towed vessels and overload a tow rig to the point of towline or bridle failure. Shock-loading could also cause momentary loss of directional control by either vessel and could capsize small vessels.

B.13. SHOCK-LOADING PREVENTION OR COUNTERACTION

Because of the potential dangers, the tow vessel must use various techniques to prevent or counteract shock-loading, or to reduce its effect.

REDUCE TOWING SPEED: Slowing down lowers frictional resistance, form drag, and wave-making resistance. Reducing these forces will lower the total tow rig tension. In head seas, reducing speed also reduces wave drag, spray drag, and wind drag, lowering the irregular tow rig loads. The total reduction in forces on the tow could be rather substantial. When encountering vessel wake in relatively calm conditions, decrease speed early enough so the towed vessel loses momentum before hitting the wake. A small towed vessel slamming into a large wake will shock-load the tow rig, and may even swamp.

GET THE VESSELS "IN STEP": Extreme stress is put on the tow rig in heavy weather when the tow vessel and the towing vessel do not climb, crest or descend waves together. Vessels in step will gain and lose momentum at the same time, allowing the towing force to gradually overcome the towed vessel's loss of momentum, minimizing shock-loading. To get the vessels in step, *lengthen* rather than shorten the towline if possible.

NOTE

When operating near bars and inlets, getting the vessels in step may be impractical due to rapidly changing water depth and bottom contours.

LENGTHEN THE TOWLINE: A longer towline reduces the effect of shock-loading in two ways. The weight of the line causes a dip in the line called a **catenary**. The more line out, the greater the catenary. When tension increases, energy from shock loading is spent on "flattening out" the catenary before it the load is transferred through the rest of the rig and fittings. The second benefit of a longer towline is more stretch length. Depending on the type of towline, another 50' of towline length will give 5'–20' more stretch to act as a shock-load absorber. Remember to lengthen the towline enough to keep the vessels in step and minimize the shock-load source.

SET A COURSE TO LESSEN THE EFFECT OF THE SEAS: Do not try to tow a vessel either directly into or directly down large seas. Tow on a course to keep the seas 30–45 degrees either side of dead ahead or dead astern. This may require "tacking" to either side of the actual desired course.

DEPLOY A DROGUE FROM THE TOWED VESSEL: This device (covered under Towing Equipment) may help to prevent the towed vessel from rapidly accelerating down the face of a wave. The drogue does add form drag to the tow, but could prevent shock-load.

CONSTANTLY ADJUST TOWING VESSEL SPEED TO MATCH THAT OF THE TOWED VESSEL: In large seas, constant "finesse" techniques may reduce shock-loading. This requires the coxswain to constantly observe the towed vessel, and to increase or decrease towing vessel speed to compensate for the effects on the towed vessel of approaching or receding seas. This takes much practice and experience.

NOTE

Safety demands emphasis on preventing shock-load and reducing its effects. Shock-loading presents a definite possibility of vessel fitting or tow rig failure. One of the more feared possibilities is towline snap-back. Think of this as a greatly magnified version of stretching a rubber-band until it breaks. Remember, some nylon

> ## CAUTION!
> **Shock-load can also capsize or swamp the towed vessel. The additional towing force from a shock-loaded towline could cause a smaller vessel to climb its bow wave and become unstable or it could pull the bow through a cresting wave.**

cordage can stretch up to an additional 40% of its length before parting.

Towing Equipment

Overview

Introduction

When towing a boat or other maritime craft, always use the proper equipment for the task. Using the proper equipment minimizes accidents and possible injuries. Towing equipment includes towlines, pendants and bridles, deck fittings, hardware for attaching the towline (skiff hooks, shackles, etc.), fenders, drogues, and alongside lines. This section discusses the design, use, and limits of towing equipment.

In this section

Towlines and Accessories

C.1. TOWLINES

Towlines are usually 2-in-1 (double-braided) nylon, two to four inches in circumference. Length can be up to 900 feet. Use nylon instead of other synthetic fiber cordage for a good combination of strength and stretch (elongation and elasticity). The Auxiliary will have and use a variety of types and sizes of tow lines.

NOTE

Refer to Chapter 7—Marlinespike Seamanship, for a complete table of breaking strength for various circumferences of rope.

The towing vessel's construction, power, size, and fittings determine towline size (circumference). The proper towline will allow a vessel to tow up to its design limits. The towline will part before damage occurs to a vessel's fittings, structure or hull.

> ### CAUTION!
>
> **Do not tow beyond the vessel's design limits by simply increasing towline size. If the towline's breaking strength exceeds the limits designed into the vessel's fittings and structure, damage and structural failure may result.**

Each Coast Guard boat type has an equipment list that specifies towline length and size. Towlines will usually have an eye spliced into the tow end. Towline length and size will vary on other vessels due to design limits and available space. Offshore or in heavy weather, a towing vessel may need 500 feet or more of towline to keep a towed vessel in step and to minimize the effect of shock-loading.

TOWLINE STORAGE Store towline on a **tow reel** with the bitter end secured to the reel with small stuff. The line will lie evenly on the reel. More importantly, to quickly slip (release) the towline in an emergency, just cut the small stuff with a knife, and the bitter end will run free. When putting new cordage in service as a towline, splice an eye at both ends. This will allow an "end-for-end" switch before part of the towline is beyond useful service.

Many tow reels have mechanical advantage (hand crank, gear train) or electric motors to ease towline retrieval. These devices are only to retrieve a slack towline. Do not try to take any tension with these devices. Inspect the tow reel frequently for easy rotation and adequate lubrication.

NOTE

Unless slipping the towline in an emergency, keep at least 4 four turns of towline on the reel. Paying out the entire length can result in loss of both tow and towline.

TOWLINE CONDITION AND INSPECTION Safe and efficient towing requires an undamaged, serviceable towline. Whenever any towline damage is found or suspected, remove or repair the damage. If removing damage shortens the towline to less than serviceable length, then replace the towline. Usable sections in good condition can be used for bridles, alongside lines, mooring lines, etc.

Inspect towlines on a regular basis to detect damage from:

- Cuts
- Chafing
- Flattening
- Fusing (caused by overheating or overstretching)
- Snags
- Hardening (heavy use will compact and harden a towline and reduce its breaking strength)

If a towline shows any of these characteristics, do not use it as a towline.

C.2. TOWING PENDANTS AND BRIDLES

It is not always possible, appropriate, or safe to attach a towline from the stern of a towing vessel to a single point on the bow of a distressed vessel. The distressed vessel's deck layout may not have a single direct run through a bull nose; there might not be a

Samson post or centered bitt; the towline might be too large for deck fittings; or deck fittings may be improperly mounted, rotted or corroded where they attach to the deck. In these cases, rig a **pendant** or **bridle**. The pendant or bridle forms part of the tow rig, leading from the eye or thimble of a towline to the appropriate location(s) or deck fitting(s) on the towed vessel. Towing pendants and bridles are made of double-braided nylon or wire rope. (Use wire rope for large vessels or steel hulls.) The two most common rigs are a pendant and a bridle. Auxiliary facilities will have a variety of pendants and bridles, not necessarily constructed of double braided nylon or wire rope.

When possible, use pendants and bridles with breaking strength equal to or greater than the towline. If the towed vessel's fittings (chocks or cleats limit bridle or pendant size, consider "doubling-up" (two bridles or pendants). When expected towing force threatens safe working load of the individual bridle legs, if doubling-up, all lengths must be exactly the same so each part shares an equal load.

PENDANTS Use a pendant to reduce wear and chafing at the towline end (particularly the eye and its splice). A pendant must be long enough so the towline connection is clear of obstructions on the towed vessel (see Figure 17-3).

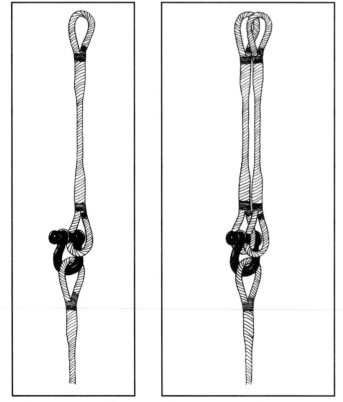

Figure 17-3 Pendant   **Figure 17-4** Bridle Connection

When attaching a bridle, use the following steps:

- Center the bridle with at least one round turn on the attachment point.
- Attach the bridle ends to the towline eye with a shackle.

BRIDLE Use a bridle (a "Y" bridle) when both legs can be rigged to exert an equal pull on the hull of a distressed vessel (see Figure 17-4). A bridle provides the best results where towed vessel deck fittings (chocks and cleats or bitts) are not right at the towed vessel's bow (as a bullnose), or where obstructions (bulwark or rigging) on the bow prevent a pendant or towline from making a direct lead back to the towing vessel. Use the following list as a guideline for attaching a bridle for towing:

- Use a long bridle when the best attachment points for the towed vessel are well aft to either side of the deck, but maintain a fair lead forward to reduce chafe.
- Remember that the amount of tension on each bridle leg increases with the size of the angle between the bridle legs.
- Keep the legs of the bridle long enough so the angle of the legs stays less than 30 degrees.
- The legs must be long enough to reduce towed vessel yaw.
- Protect bridles with chafing gear when necessary.
- Use thimbles in the bridle leg eyes where they meet.
- When shackled to the towline, remember to mouse the shackle pin.

A bridle is also used by towing vessels without centerline towing capability or with transom obstructions (outboard motors or rigging). Attach the bridle to fittings in a manner to clear the obstructions. Again, bridle leg lengths must be equal to share the strain of the tow.

PENDANT AND BRIDLE CONDITION AND INSPECTION Safe and efficient towing requires undamaged, serviceable pendants and bridles. Inspect pendants and bridles on a regular basis to detect damage. **Ensure bridle leg lengths are equal.** For nylon pendants and bridles, use the towline condition and inspection list provided earlier in this section.

Wire rope bridles must be inspected for:

- Broken wires
- Fish hooks (broken ends of wire protruding from the lay)

- Kinks
- Worn or corroded portions (worn portions of wire rope appear as shiny, flattened surfaces)

NOTE

Inspect towlines, pendants, and bridles after each tow and whenever shock-loading has occurred.

Messengers

C.3. GENERAL

A towline is too heavy to cast more than a few feet. In rough weather or when impossible to get close enough to throw a towline to a distressed vessel, use a **messenger** to reach the other vessel. A messenger is a length of light line used to carry a larger line or hawser between vessels.

C.4. PASSING A TOWLINE

To pass a towline with a messenger, attach one end of a small line to the end of the towline and cast the other end to the other vessel's crew.

Then use the lighter line to pull the towline across the distance between the vessels. Sometimes, multiple lines are used as messengers. An intermediate-sized line might be added between a heaving line and towline. The following may serve as a messenger for small vessel towing evolutions:

- Heaving Line and Heaving Ball
- Float Line
- Shot Line
- BOLO
- Shoulder Line Throwing Gear

HEAVING LINE AND HEAVING BALL A heaving line is made of light, flexible line with a monkey's fist at the thrown end. Sometimes, the monkey's fist is weighted. A variation of this is a heaving ball or heaving bag. Instead of a monkey's fist, there is a plastic or rubber ball permanently affixed to the end of a synthetic line. A heaving line must be in good condition, at least 75 feet long, and free of rot or weathering (see Figure 17-5).

The bitter end of a heaving line is attached to the towline with a clove hitch, bowline, small carbiners, or snap hook. Slip clove hitches may work best in very cold weather. The longest heaves are cast downwind, but this may not always be possible. Target the throw above the center of the vessel so the thrown line crosses over the deck and avoids breaking glass or injuring people.

FLOAT LINE To reach a vessel beyond the range of a heaving line or in an inaccessible position, a buoyant synthetic line may be floated from upstream or upwind. Tie one end to a ring buoy or float, the other end to the towline, and throw the float line downstream in the direction of the distressed vessel. Let the current or wind carry the float line toward the other vessel. This method is only effective if the wind or current can get the float within range of the other vessel.

Chafing Gear

C.5. GENERAL

Chafing gear protects towlines, bridles and pendants from wear caused by rubbing against deck edges, gunwales, bulwarks, chocks, taffrail or tow bars.

C.6. PREVENTING CHAFING DAMAGE

Tie layers of heavy canvas or leather with small stuff to the towline, bridle, or wire rope at contact points to prevent chafing damage. Sections of old fire hose also work well as chafing gear. Make sure the chafing gear stays in place for the duration of the tow.

C.7. THIMBLES

Thimbles are designed to equalize the load on an eye of a line and provide maximum chafing protection to the inner surface of the eye. On double

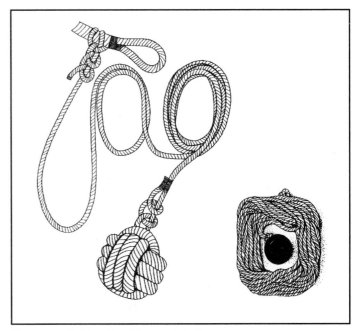

Figure 17-5 Heaving Line and Ball

braided nylon, use thimbles made specifically for synthetic lines (see Figure 17-6). Use galvanized "teardrop" shaped thimbles on wire rope.

Deck Fittings and Other Fittings

C.8. GENERAL

Fittings are attachments or fair lead points on vessels for towlines, anchor lines, and mooring lines. Many fishing and sailing vessels have other attachment points for standing and running rigging that could also provide tow rig attachment points or fair leads. For towing, only use attachment points and fair leads designed for horizontal loads.

Common fittings include bitts (mooring and towing), cleats, chocks, and Samson posts. A tow bar or taffrail acts as a fair lead. Do not overlook pad eyes, turning and snatch blocks, winch drums, capstans, and windlasses when considering attachment points or fair leads on a towed vessel. Trailer-able boats usually have an eye bolt or eye fitting at the bow for an attachment point.

C.9. CONDITION AND INSPECTION

Make regular inspections of towing vessel fittings. Check for cracks, fractures, rust, corrosion, wood rot, fiberglass core softening, or delamination. Inspect surfaces that are normally hidden from view, particularly backing plates and under-deck fasteners. Tow bars are subject to high vibration and may loosen or cause stress fractures around their foundations. Keep working surfaces free from paint and relieve any surface roughness. A smooth working surface reduces wear, friction and chafing on lines.

C.10. SKIFF HOOK

The typical **skiff hook** has a quick release safety buckle and snap hook clip that can be attached directly to the boathook handle (see Figure 17-7). Skiff hook assemblies are commercially available.

USING A SKIFF HOOK Attach the skiff hook line to a towline with a shackle or double becket bend.

> **WARNING**
>
> Do not over stress a skiff hook. Never use one for any operation that might be more of a load than towing small, trailer-able boats.

> **CAUTION!**
>
> Use extreme care when removing a skiff hook from a trailer eye fitting. Even at a dock, crew members risk injury from vessel movements.

Use the skiff hook assembly to reach down and place the hook into a small distressed vessel's trailer eye. The hook is snapped into the eye and the handle is slipped off the round stock and pulled back.

Drogues

C.11. GENERAL

A **drogue** is a device that acts in the water somewhat the way a parachute works in the air. The drogue is deployed from the stern of the towed vessel to help control the towed vessel's motions. Coxswains and boat crews must familiarize them-

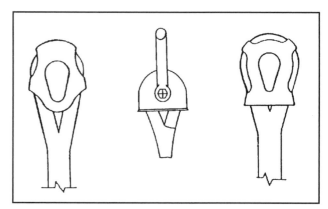

Figure 17-6 Thimble

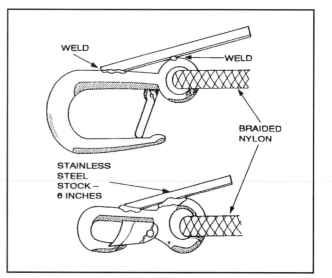

Figure 17-7 Skiff Hook (Older Style)

selves with the operating characteristics and effectiveness of available drogues. Train with and test drogues under various conditions to learn drogue capabilities. The time to learn about a drogue is before you need to deploy one.

While trailing a drogue from the towed vessel is not an unacceptable practice, and may be useful when a distressed vessel has lost rudder control, normally it is not deployed when well offshore. If necessary to tow a vessel with large swells directly on the stern, it may be more prudent to alter course or lengthen the towline rather than to deploy a drogue. Drogues are typically used when the tow is shortened as in preparing to tow into a bar or inlet. With a short hawser and large swells on the stern, the drogue is deployed to prevent the towed vessel from running up the stern of the towing vessel and to keep tension on the towline to help prevent the towed vessel from "surfing" down the face of a wave.

The idea of the drogue is to provide backward pull on the stern of the towed vessel so that the wave will pass under the boat. It is important to match the size of the drogue to the towed boat, its deck fittings, and its overall condition. The larger, well constructed cone drogues can exert a very large force on a boat's transom so the towed vessel's stern must be carefully examined.

There are numerous types, sizes and styles of drogues, all commercially available (Figure 17-8). Different-sized drogues are used for different conditions and different vessel sizes. A traditional drogue is a canvas or synthetic cloth cone, with the pointed end open. Drogues of this type have a ring in the

base of the cone (the leading edge) to which attaches a four-part bridle. The other ends of the bridle connect to a swivel, which in turn, connects to a line made fast to the stern of the towed vessel. The towed vessel "tows" the drogue. Drogues sometimes have another line attached to the tail end for retrieval.

NOTE

A large drogue can cause stress that will damage a small boat. For a small boat, the larger the drogue used, the slower the towing speed must be. A slight increase in speed causes a tremendous increase in drogue tension.

C.12. PREPARE THE DROGUE GEAR

For the drogue towline, use 200 feet of 2-inch double braided nylon. Mark the drogue line every fifty feet.

Transfer the drogue rig to a distressed boat before taking it in tow. The following checklist will help ensure that the drogue rig and related equipment are ready for transfer.

- Visually inspect the drogue rig for worn rusted, or corroded fittings and swivels, correct size shackles, and untangled bridles.

- Ensure that the drogue rig has 200 feet of two-inch, double-braided nylon line properly attached to the bridle swivel using a correctly sized shackle. Make sure it has no sharp fittings or exposed wires, and is stowed in a manner that will keep it intact until it is deployed.

- Provide all necessary equipment with a drogue rig such as extra shackles, bridles, straps, and chafing gear to achieve the best possible connection on the stern of a tow.

NOTE

Auxiliary facilities are not required to carry drogues.

- Place all equipment in a gear bag with laminated written instructions and illustrations on how to rig a drogue, both with and without a bridle. At night attach a chemical light to the bag and include a flashlight inside.

- Attach flotation to the bag, usually a fender (discussed in Section C.20.), and two lines, each 40 feet in length, to the handles of the gear bag. Bend a heaving line or buoyant rescue line onto one of the lines.

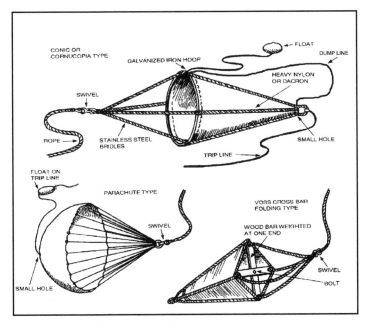

Figure 17-8 Drogue Types

NOTE

Determine what fittings the drogue will connect to, how to make the connection, and how much line to deploy BEFORE sending it to the tow. Always ask about backing plates, fitting sizes, and strength of materials involved. Be cautious if you cannot see an attachment point. Rely on your experience and judgment.

C.13. PASS THE DROGUE

Pass the drogue directly from the towing vessel to the towed vessel when in the best position. The drogue and line can be heavy and awkward for the crew of the distressed vessel. If possible, maneuver the rescue vessel to pass the drogue to an area on the distressed vessel where the crew will not have to lift the apparatus a long distance.

Instead of immediately taking a boat in tow, stand by and watch the distressed vessel crew ready the drogue rig for deployment. Provide visual inspection, verbal direction, and clarification if necessary.

NOTE

Unless a crew member from the towing vessel goes aboard the towed vessel, the towed vessel crew must carry out the following procedures. Provide them guidance and direction as needed.

C.14. RIG DROGUE FOR DEPLOYMENT

Use attachment fittings as near the centerline as possible. On many vessels, a bridle will be needed to spread the load between two separate fittings to center the drogue towline. Winches, motor mounts, masts, and davit bases are other possible locations for good strong connections. When trying to compensate for a jammed rudder, attach the drogue well off the centerline, close to the quarter, opposite the side where the rudder is jammed.

- Connect the bridle legs or the drogue lines to the appropriate fittings.

C.15. DEPLOY THE DROGUE

Start the tow moving, then direct the towed vessel crew to deploy the drogue.

- Move the tow forward slowly, just enough to control the tow.
- Direct the towed vessel's crew to recheck connections, put the drogue in the water and pay out the line slowly from a safe position. Un-

BEGIN OR RESUME TOWING Once the drogue sets and starts to pull, slowly increase speed while the distressed vessel's crew observes the rig. Check attachment points and the effectiveness of a drogue. If adjustments must be made, slow down and make them.

Once you deploy a drogue, pick the most comfortable course and speed. Control of the tow is more important than speed. Towing a drogue at too great a speed may damage the towed vessel or may cause the drogue rig to fail. One of the crew on the towed vessel should monitor the drogue.

WARNING

Drogue use does not justify towing through breakers. When in doubt, stay out.

C.16. SHORTEN-UP AND RECOVER DROGUE

Because a tripping line is not recommended, several alternate recovery methods are available. If recovery is not properly set up and controlled, a drogue may become fouled on the tow, a buoy, or other object.

- Slow or stop the tow, then haul it in. The primary method for shortening up or recovering a drogue is accomplished by slowing the tow or stopping it completely. Have people on board the tow slowly pull in the drogue. Provide enough maneuvering room to bring the tow around on a course causing little or no tension on the drogue line during recovery.

- Have another vessel come alongside and transfer the drogue line to it. The second vessel can recover the drogue rig.

- Attach a color coded **dumping line**, a short piece of line run from the bridle shackle to the tail of the drogue, outside the cone. Haul the drogue to the stern, recover the dumping line, and when pulled, it inverts the drogue making it easy to recover. A dumping line is only suitable for large drogues that drain slowly.

C.17. DROGUE STORAGE

A synthetic gear bag will hold the drogue for storage and deployment. The bitter end of the line feeds out through a grommet in the bottom and the

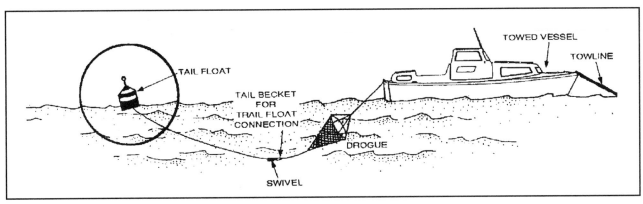

Figure 17-9 Drogue Deployed

remainder of the line is stuffed inside the bag. A drawstring at the top holds the bag closed. Ensure the line bag can hold 200 feet of 2-inch line.

C.18. DROGUE CONDITION AND INSPECTION

Inspect the drogue for tears, cuts and holes. Inspect the drogue towline and bridle using the same guidelines for towlines and bridles as listed in Sections C.1. and C.2. Also check for worn, rusted or corroded fittings, swivels and shackles. Ensure there are no sharp edges or points of hardware.

Other Equipment

C.19. ALONGSIDE LINES

At some point during a tow, the towing vessel most likely will need to tow the distressed vessel alongside in restricted waters or moor to the towed vessel. The tow vessel will usually need a combination of lines to allow for vessels of different size.

ALONGSIDE LINE STORAGE Each Coast Guard standard boat equipment list specifies number, length and size of **alongside lines** for vessel type. Stowage and weight considerations will guide other vessel types.

ALONGSIDE LINE CONDITION AND INSPECTION Alongside lines must be kept in the same condition as towlines and bridles (see Sections C.1. and C.2.).

C.20. FENDERS

Fenders are portable rubber, synthetic, or foam devices that protect a hull when maneuvering in close proximity to other vessels, docks or pilings. Fenders have either eye(s) or a longitudinal hole for attaching lines. They can be spherical, cylindrical, or rectangular prisms. Fender size varies greatly, and the appropriate size should be used depending on the situation. Use fenders that will keep space between vessel hulls or rub rails and hulls.

FENDER DEPLOYMENT Use plenty of fenders whenever there is the possibility of a hull making contact with another object. Strategically place fenders to account for different hull shapes (maximum beam, tumble-home, flare) or appendages (rub rails, spray rails, trawl rigs, platforms).

FENDER PLACEMENT Because vessels are shifted around by the water, fenders may need to be moved for best effectiveness, even after strategic placement. Most vessel crews are too small to have a dedicated fender tender, therefore you should try to minimize the need beforehand.

C.21. GENERAL HARDWARE

General hardware includes shackles, snap hooks, carbiners, swivels and other items. These items must be made of strong, low-maintenance materials. They must be easy to connect and disconnect or open and close by a crew member wearing gloves on a dark, icy night in heavy weather. All hardware should resist distortion. Shackles need a large enough throat to easily cross an eye or thimble. Use captive-pin shackles or attach the pin to the shackle with a lanyard to prevent pin loss.

Keep all hardware clean and lubricated. Inspect hardware after each use. Be particularly cautious of hardware that has been shock-loaded. Immediately replace any hardware that is distorted, spreading, excessively worn, or stripped.

Standard Towing Procedures

Overview

Introduction

The procedures listed below are derived from time-tested, experience-based techniques proven to be effective, safe, and efficient. They shall be real actions, performed by coxswain and crew. Some of the actions can be executed simultaneously to minimize duplication or avoid wasting time, but be sure to indicate that an action has been taken. In extreme conditions or emergencies, some actions may not be possible. If actions must be skipped, make sure to consider this in assessing and managing risk. If a problem occurs at any step in the procedures, it may be safer and easier to "back up" to the last successfully completed step and restart.

In this section

Pre-Towing Procedures

D.1. GENERAL

The amount of effort put into preparing ahead of time will pay off with safer, easier execution of the tow.

NOTE

Throughout the entire towing evolution, open communication among the coxswain and crew is absolutely necessary for safety.

D.2. RECEIVE NOTIFICATION AND ACCEPT TASKING

When notified of a potential towing mission, get as much information needed to do the job effectively. Write down critical information, and confirm what you have written.

- Get as much critical information as necessary.
- Write down the information.
- Develop a full understanding of the situation.
- Make a conscious decision to "accept" the tasking.

Make this a common practice. The coxswain is ultimately responsible for mission execution, so confirm the tasking in view of vessel and crew capability. If tasking exceeds vessel or crew capability, particularly if not an actual distress case, be assertive and describe your concerns. Consider vessel towing limits, maximum range, sea-keeping, crew fatigue, etc. Assess and manage potential risk.

NOTE

Keep a brief (plastic clipboard and grease pencil) written record of critical information. Include vessel information number of persons on the boat, position, and environmental conditions. A written record allows the crew to concentrate on task completion without having to later rely on memory for needed facts. Repeating information over the radio is frustrating and distracting. As information changes, update the record.

D.3. BRIEF THE CREW

Conduct a thorough boat crew briefing. Explain the situation and what might be expected. Use the facts. If there is any confusion or uncertainty, clear it up now. The crew must participate and ask relevant questions. Assign personnel to assist with preparations and collect any needed tow rig or assistance items not aboard the towing vessel. Ensure proper safety and personnel protective equipment is donned by the crew.

D.4. EVALUATE CONDITION

Note how the different environmental conditions will affect the operation. As conditions may change during the mission, estimate which phase of the mission will encounter which conditions and whether on-scene conditions will be different from those met en route. Keep a record of the present and forecast conditions (do not try to rely on memory) and update as necessary. Necessary condition information:

- Existing and forecast marine weather (including winds, seas, bar conditions).

- Currents and tide (next high/low, slack/maximum).

- Daylight/darkness (sunrise/sunset, twilight).

D.5. OPERATE AND NAVIGATE THE VESSEL SAFELY

The only way to perform the tow is get there safely. **Do not let a sense of urgency affect judgment.** Safe operation and navigation:

- Maintain safe speed for the conditions (seas, visibility, and other traffic).

- Keep constant awareness of navigational position and navigational hazards.

- Stay aware of the distressed vessel's position.

D.6. COMMUNICATE WITH DISTRESSED VESSEL

Make radio contact with the distressed vessel, if possible. Communication procedures:

- Provide the distressed vessel your estimated time of arrival.

- Advise persons on the distressed vessel to put on PFDs.

- Get details of deck layout and fittings. Ask about the size of chocks and cleats to determine size of towline, bridle or drogue line and bridle.

- Ask for any information the distressed vessel's crew think you will need to know before arriving on scene (lines or gear in the water, nearby vessels, etc.).

- Determine if anything has changed since the distressed vessel's initial contact with the operational commander.

- Ascertain any sense of heightened urgency.

- Inform the distressed vessel that once on scene, you will observe conditions and make final preparations before setting up the tow and will provide further instructions then.

- Establish and maintain a communications schedule.

D.7. PREPARE EQUIPMENT

With the information known, begin to plan a tow rig. Ready all necessary equipment and re-inspect it, i.e., towline, bridle, shackles, knife, messenger line, chafing gear, etc., as directed by the coxswain.

D.8. PERFORM AN ON-SCENE ASSESSMENT

Once on scene, use the following procedures:

- Watch the vessel's movement (pitch, roll) in the seas and determine the effect of wind and current on the distressed vessel's drift rate and lateral movement. Compare it to your own drift. Knowing the different drift rates will help determine the best approach.

- Evaluate the location and any abnormal condition of deck fittings.

- Confirm the number of persons on board.

- Note any unusual conditions that may affect towing procedures, i.e., loose gear, rigging, or debris in the water.

- Communicate any concerns to the distressed vessel and direct all personnel on the distressed vessel to put on PFDs.

- Decide whether to put one of your crew aboard the distressed vessel.

- Decide if it is best to remove the crew from the distressed vessel.

- Determine if an equipment transfer (drogue, pump, radio) will be necessary.

- After evaluating the on-scene situation and making risk assessment, decide whether to tow or not.

NOTE

This period of pre-tow, on-scene analysis is when crew experience and judgment on both vessels must mesh. Discuss concerns before directing action. The distressed vessel's crew may have information that you do not. The easiest way to get the big picture may be by circling the distressed vessel, if possible.

A method to check drift rate of the distressed vessel is to maneuver the towing vessel onto the same heading as the distressed vessel and stop astern of it. If the distance between the vessels increases, one vessel has a higher drift rate.

Note the different angles or aspects the towing vessel and the towed vessel hold towards the winds and seas. The only time the drift rate and aspect will be exactly the same is if the vessels are exactly the same.

D.9. MAKE-UP THE TOW RIG AND PREPARE FOR TRANSFER

Visualize the tow in progress, given all the factors identified in the on scene assessment. This may help identify any special considerations. Size elements of the tow rig appropriately for the specific distressed vessel, i.e., a 3-inch towline with eye might not fit through a bow chock or around a cleat of a 25-foot boat.

- Set up the tow vessel deck with all equipment staged and ready.

- Attach 2 heaving lines to the tow rig. If using a bridle, secure one heaving line to one eye (or end) and the second to the other eye (end).

- Assign crew members to each heaving line, and to bitt or line handler duties.

NOTE

Pass equipment (pump, drogue, etc.) and transfer personnel before making the approach to transfer the tow rig.

D.10. DETERMINE THE APPROACH

Though it is usally best to make your approach from down wind and down sea, the drift and aspect of the distressed vessel may determine another approach. A vessel with a large superstructure forward, will tend to lay stern-to the wind. (Many outboard-powered vessels exhibit this tendency to "weathervane.") A vessel with deep draft and low superstructure will generally lie broadside to the seas. Of course, there are any number of positions in between. The approach to a vessel drifting down wind and down sea, "stern to" the wind and seas will be different from the approach to a vessel lying "beam to." The usual approach by a boat to make a tow is with the bow into the seas.

Determine how you will make the approach and inform your crew. Specifically tell the crew from which side to pass the tow rig (or equipment), when (in what relative position of the two vessels) to pass the tow rig, and whether to use a heaving line.

D.11. BRIEF THE DISTRESSED VESSEL

Explain your plans and pass safety instructions. Include enough information so the distressed vessel's crew does not have to ask questions once the approach begins. Follow these steps when briefing the distressed vessel:

- If transferring crew or equipment before the tow, relate when and how.
- Describe the towing approach.
- Tell when and how you will pass the tow rig.
- Give tow rig connection instructions (how to lead, where to attach).
- List emergency break away procedures.
- Describe emergency signals.
- Instruct on general safety during the approach and passing the tow rig.

NOTE

Limit the content of this briefing to information the distressed vessel needs to know before the tow begins. Once hooked up and in tow, there will be opportunity to pass additional information.

Towing Astern

D.12. GENERAL

The most common towing technique is to tow the distressed vessel from astern of the rescue vessel.

D.13. MAKING THE APPROACH

The on-scene assessment gives you the knowledge of how conditions affect both vessels. Knowledge of and experience with the towing vessel's handling and maneuvering characteristics should allow you to overcome conditions and put the towing vessel in a safe position for the crew to pass the tow rig.

D.14. ESTABLISH A DANGER ZONE

Before starting the approach, establish an imaginary danger zone around the distressed vessel and approach outside of it. The size of a danger zone depends upon conditions and the arrangement of the distressed vessel. The poorer the conditions, the larger the danger zone.

D.15. MANEUVER TO AN OPTIMUM POSITION

Maneuver the towing vessel so the crew can maximize use of the best deck work area on the vessel for passing and working the tow rig. This will provide the opportunity for the most vessel control and visibility for the coxswain, while keeping a safe distance from the distressed vessel, and providing a safe "escape route" in case of emergency. This is the **optimum position**.

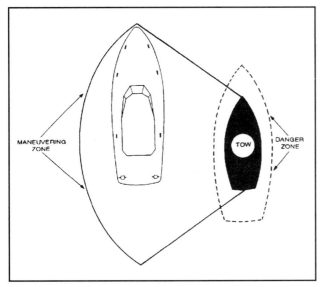

Figure 17-10 Danger Zone

- In calm conditions, make the approach at an angle that allows the crew the best opportunity to pass the tow rig.

In rough conditions make your approach into the prevailing wind and seas. If the wind is different from the seas, make your approach into the seas. This usually maximizes control for the coxswain and ensures the most stable platform for the crew.

Make the approach at the slowest speed necessary to maintain steerage.

CAUTION!

The coxswain must let crew members know before making correcting maneuvers so that they can tend lines and ready themselves.

- Once in the optimum position, **keep station** on the distressed vessel. Station keeping maintains the position and heading relative to the weather and seas, outside the danger zone. This is usually done by use of helm and engine control. To keep station, the coxswain must simultaneously focus on the seas, the bitt and line handlers, and the position with respect to the distressed vessel. Maneuver and apply power early and smoothly as distance and angle to the distressed vessel change. If the towing vessel begins to move towards the danger zone, maneuver to open the distance. If the distressed vessel begins to

get away from the towing vessel, close the gap. **Use correcting maneuvers (opening and closing) before a problem develops.** A small correction early can prevent a large problem later.

NOTE

Actual maneuvering techniques vary from vessel to vessel and are mastered by practice and experience. Actual station keeping techniques also vary as the specific wind and sea conditions affect the specific distressed vessel.

D.16. KEEP STATION

The coxswain now must keep station, outside the danger zone and in a maneuvering zone (usually a 90 degree arc, from 45 degrees off the bow to 45 degrees off the stern, with the distance between vessels no greater than the length of the heaving line) for the crew to pass the tow rig. The coxswain must continue station keeping until the tow rig is connected and the transition to towing astern begins. The crew must make every effort to ensure that passing the tow rig goes smoothly and quickly.

CAUTION!

Maneuver as required but it is preferable not to make opening and closing maneuvers when lines are over (except the heaving line). Avoid making correcting maneuvers on the face of a wave.

In calm conditions, station keeping may simply be holding the nearest safe position to take advantage of the best angle for the crew to pass the tow rig. However, even though conditions may be calm, a vessel's wake or a current can suddenly increase the chance of hull to hull contact with the distressed vessel. Plan a safe escape route for all approaches and while station keeping.

NOTE

A boat crew's teamwork, communications, and experience are keys to a safe, successful approach.

D.17. PASS THE TOW RIG

Once maintaining optimum position, pass the tow rig.

- All lines, equipment, and connections should already be inspected, made ready, and double-checked.

- Minimize loose towline on deck by paying out directly from the reel. If the towing vessel is not equipped with a towline reel, fake the towline carefully so that it will not kink or tangle. In heavy weather, use caution to ensure line is not washed over the side and into the screw.

NOTE

While passing and connecting the tow rig, and transitioning to stern tow, use loud and clear communication between crew members and coxswain to prevent accidents. Whenever the coxswain directs an action, a crew member must take that action and reply that the action has been taken. Whenever a crew member advises the coxswain of status or action, the coxswain must acknowledge same.

CALM CONDITIONS Passing the rig in calm conditions (no heaving line):

- Coxswain directs crew to pass the rig.

- Line handler hands over or carefully tosses the end of the rig to a person on the distressed vessel. The person receiving the rig must be physically able to haul it to the connecting point and then attach it properly.

- Line handler advises coxswain that the rig is away.

- Line handler pays out and takes in towline as required to eliminate any risk of fouling the propellers, rudders, rigging, or other fixtures. Crew members must advise the coxswain when the action has been successfully executed and the towline is properly secured on the towed vessel.

USING A HEAVING LINE Passing a rig using a heaving line:

- Wet both heaving lines to make them more flexible and minimize risk of them becoming tangled.

- Take two-thirds of a heaving line coil into the casting hand leaving the remainder in the other hand.

- Check that the area is clear of people and obstructions.

- Advise coxswain when ready and await direction before casting.

- Coxswain directs cast.

Call out "HEADS UP" as a warning to people on board the distressed vessel to take cover and watch out for the toss.

NOTE

It takes practice to cast a heaving line properly. Adapt technique to conditions for a safe and successful result.

CASTING Casting a heaving line:

- Cast a heaving line so it falls across the distressed vessel's deck.

- Tell coxswain "heaving line cast," then that it's retrieved, short, or missed. Advise the coxswain whenever a line is in the water, so no maneuvering will be done.

- If the first cast is not retrieved, quickly recover the line and advise coxswain when the second heaving line is ready. When coxswain directs, repeat the procedure.

- Untie the unused/unretrieved heaving line from the tow rig (take care to untie the correct line) and advise the coxswain that you're ready to transfer the rig.

- Coxswain will direct crew members to send the rig; the crew members reply and begin

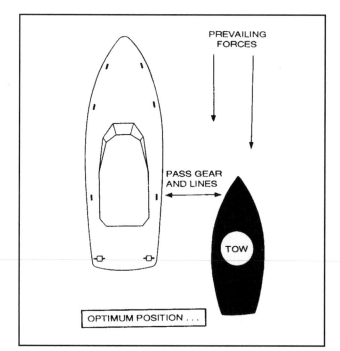

Figure 17-11 Optimum Position for Passing the Tow Rig

transferring the rig. Crew members tend the messenger to reduce the risk of it becoming fouled. Once the rig starts across, maneuvering opportunities are limited.

- Advise coxswain of tow rig transfer progress (when bridle is clear or aboard distressed vessel, when towline is going over or aboard, etc.).

D.18. CONNECT THE TOW RIG

Methods of tow rig connection generally available are:

- Tow rig to fittings.
- Tow rig to trailer eye.

Connecting Tow Rig to Fittings

D.19. GENERAL

The attachment point(s) for a tow rig must be sound. Towing places a tremendous strain on deck fittings, especially in rough conditions. Bow bitts, forward cleats and Samson posts on the distressed vessel usually will provide the best attachment points. Always use fittings secured to a deck with through bolts and backing plates or those secured to the keel or structural framing. Other fittings, such as pad eyes or capstans, may also provide solid attachment points.

Unless the towing vessel puts a crew member aboard the distressed vessel, the towed vessel crew is responsible for these actions. A good brief to the distressed vessel will address each item, but in the rush to get things set up aboard the distressed vessel, the crew may forget important steps. The towing vessel crew must closely watch and advise when necessary.

> **CAUTION!**
>
> Though deck fittings should be checked during pre-tow procedures, do not hesitate to stop the connection if something is wrong. If necessary, recover the rig and transfer a crew member to the distressed vessel to physically inspect the fittings.

> **CAUTION!**
>
> Transfer of people between vessels is not a common practice. Whenever this is considered, it must be conducted with extreme caution for the safety of people on both vessels.

D.20. ENSURE A FAIR LEAD

Lead a single point tow rig (pendant or towline) through or to a fitting as close to the center line as possible. Once led through a secure chock near centerline, the end of the rig can go to a suitable deck fitting (see Figure 17-12).

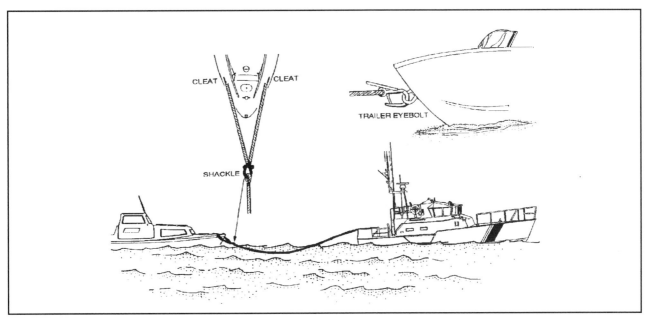

Figure 17-12 Bridle and Single Point Tow Rig Connection

- Lead the parts of a bridle through chocks, equally spaced from the centerline.

D.21. MAKE FAST TO FITTINGS

Connect the eye of a pendant or towline to posts, bitts, or cleats so that it will not come loose when a strain is placed on the rig.

Connect the bridle to fittings located at points that allow equal pull to be exerted on them. Check that the center of the bridle is on centerline or the extension of the centerline. Minimize the angle made where the bridle joins the towline by using fittings as far forward as possible. (See Figure 17-13.)

D.22. INSTALL CHAFING GEAR

Where necessary, try to protect the tow rig from abrasion or chafing, particularly if the rig takes a

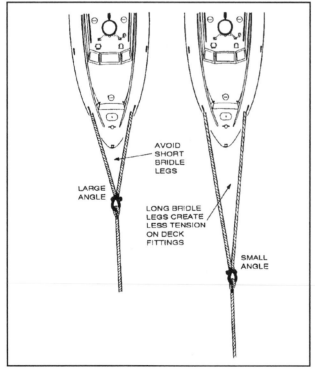

Figure 17-13 Towline Connection Showing Bridle Angle

sharp turn at chocks or comes close to contact with any obstructions.

Connecting Tow Rig to a Trailer Eye

D.23. GENERAL

On smaller, trailer-able boats, the trailer eye is frequently the sturdiest fitting available to attach a tow rig. Attaching a towline to the trailer eye is a dangerous technique. It requires the towing vessel to maneuver very close to a distressed boat and requires crew members to extend themselves over the side between two vessels, or under the flared bow sections of the distressed boat.

D.24. ATTACH THE SKIFF HOOK

A newer style of skiff hook with a quick release safety buckle and snap hook clip is in common use. Manufacturer instructions should be reviewed for its proper use. The older style skiff hook requires these steps:

- Connect the skiff hook pendant to the towline using a double becket bend or shackle.
- Slide the skiff hook into the boat hook handle.
- While keeping the pendant taut, extend the boat hook and snap the skiff hook into the trailer eye.

D.25. HOOK UP TO THE TRAILER EYE

While keeping the pendant taut, extend the boat hook and snap the skiff hook into the trailer eye.

Transition to Stern Tow

D.26. START MOVING AWAY

- Slowly move the towing vessel out of optimum position and the maneuvering zone.

- Give particular attention to the direction the towline tends and the amount of slack.

- Pay out towline gradually in conjunction with the towing vessel's movement.

> **CAUTION!**
>
> **Do not put a working turn on the bitt until the rig is securely fastened to a tow AND persons on board are clear of the bow.**

D.27. PUT A WORKING TURN ON THE BITT

Once the towline is secured on the distressed vessel and persons on the towed vessel have cleared the bow, the coxswain instructs the crew member to take a working turn on the bitt. Different towing bitts require different types of working turns. Use a method to provide enough towline-to-bitt contact surface to ensure control of the towline. Smooth towline pay out keeps the towed vessel from being pulled around.

D.28. MANEUVER TO BEGIN TOW

Slowly maneuver to a position either in line with the towed vessel's centerline (to tow ahead) or perpendicular to the towed vessel's bow (to change the initial heading).

D.29. MANEUVER TO "PAY OUT" COURSE

Once the distance allows clear movement of a tow, maneuver the towing vessel to allow a smooth pay out of the towline. As tension increases in the tow line, static forces will be felt as the tow rig tries to move the towed vessel. Transitioning is the initial test of strength and performance for the tow rig and connections. Each towing vessel will react uniquely to this initial resistance. The pivot point distance, propulsion and steering, and size difference between towing and towed vessels and weather will determine how the towed vessel will react. Actual maneuvering techniques are mastered through practice and experience. Minimize surge and shock loading.

> **CAUTION!**
>
> *Gradually* **come to a pay out course. Rapid movements or changes in direction increase the risk of:**
>
> - fouling the towline in propellers or on deck fittings
> - shock loads
> - loss of towline control

The bitt person must have complete control of the towline. Too much towing vessel headway may cause the bitt person to lose control of towline tension, and the towline will start to run.

> **WARNING**
>
> **Crews risk injury from a running towline, with the possibilities of injuring their hands and arms in the tow bitt, tow reel, or in bights of line faked on deck. If the towline starts to run, reduce speed immediately. Regain towline control after the line stops running.**

D.30. PAY OUT THE TOW LINE

Continue paying out towline until satisfied with the initial amount of towline scope.

D.31. MAKE UP THE BITT

- Once the desired scope of towline is deployed, the coxswain directs the crew to make up the bitt.

- Slow the forward motion enough to slack the towline, and then apply the proper turns.

> **WARNING**
>
> **Do not attempt to make up the bitt with a strain on a towline. This increases risk of injury by catching hands, fingers, and arms between the bitt and the towline.**

It is vital to maintain a constant watch when towing.

Here the tow slides down a wave crest, producing unwanted slack. The two vessels should be "in step."

D.32. SET A TOWING WATCH

The towing watch has a critical responsibility. In addition to the crew member assigned, it is a collateral duty for all other crew members. The condition of the vessel in tow and the towline must be constantly monitored.

Underway with Stern Tow

D.33. GENERAL

The best course to safe haven is not always the shortest distance. Choose a course that gives the best ride for both vessels. At times, you may have to tack (run a zigzag type course) to maintain the best ride. Put into practice your understanding of the dynamic forces in towing to ensure a safe tow.

D.34. BRIEF THE TOWED VESSEL

Pass instructions and information that will apply to each step of the tow astern.

- General safety (PFDs, staying clear of tow rig, tow rig chafe, location of crew).

- Equipment (pumps, drogues).
- Steering (whether to man helm or lock rudder amidships, whether to steer on towing vessel stern).
- Route you will take, expected weather and seas, destination, estimated time of arrival.
- Lighting, sound signals.
- Communications (primary/secondary radio frequencies, times of status reports).
- Emergencies (breakaways, signals).

D.35. DEPLOY DROGUE

If drogue deployment is necessary, i.e., to counteract a jammed rudder or other condition, deploy the drogue while barely making way before increasing speed to the planned towing speed. (See Section C, Towing Equipment, for procedure.)

D.36. MAINTAIN A CATENARY

Once underway with a tow astern, maintain a proper length of towline. As discussed in Section 17.B.12. (Combination of Forces and Shock-Load), gravity causes a "dip" or downward sag to form in the middle of the towline as it is lengthened. This catenary acts as a natural shock absorber for a tow rig and is a major factor in counteracting shock-loading.

D.37. STAY IN STEP

Keep the tow in step at a proper distance behind the towing vessel. When the towing vessel is on a wave crest, the towed vessel should also be on a wave crest 2 to 3 waves behind.

If the towing vessel is riding up a crest while the tow is sliding down a crest, the towline slackens. Control of the tow may be lost. If an adjustment is not made, when the towing vessel starts to slide down the crest into the trough as the towed vessel starts to climb a crest, the towline becomes taut, shock-loading the tow rig.

- Increase towline scope to get the tow on crest at the same time as the towing vessel.
- Careful manipulation of power (increase or decrease) to vary towing vessel speed may also help.

Other measures that may help to stay in step include:

- Alter course to increase the angle of the tow to the waves (to approximately 45 degrees).
- Deploy a drogue. In really confused seas, drogue deployment could help by preventing the towed vessel from surfing down the face of a wave.

Sometimes conditions make staying in step impossible. In such cases, use the techniques above and reduce speed to counteract shock loading.

D.38. MINIMIZE YAW

The tow is said to yaw when it veers to one side or the other. Yaw can be caused by trim (including list, heeling or rolling, or by a bow-down attitude), rudder problems and wave action. Severe yawing is extremely dangerous and if not corrected, may cause one or both vessels to capsize. Yawing also places tremendous strain on deck fittings and connections. Ways to reduce or minimize towed vessel yaw include:

- Change towline scope.
- Adjust trim (more easily done on a smaller vessel) to raise the bow or counteract list.
- Decrease speed or alter course to reduce effect of waves and wind.
- Deploy a drogue (particularly to overcome rudder problems).

Keep close watch on the action of the tow and immediately report any unusual movements to the coxswain. If yawing cannot be reduced or controlled, it may be prudent to heave to until sea conditions improve or the source of the yaw is corrected.

NOTE

Currents can cause a relatively constant or gradual offset of the towed vessel from the towing vessel's intended track or heading. Do not mistake this for yaw. (See Compensating for Current, below.)

D.39. TOW AT A SAFE SPEED

A safe and comfortable towing speed maximizes towing efficiency. Damage, sinkings and loss of life have occurred as a direct result of towing too fast. Maximum safe towing speed is based on the vessel's waterline length and hull shape, but wind and sea conditions can dictate a much slower speed. The following formula shows how to calculate maximum safe towing speed.

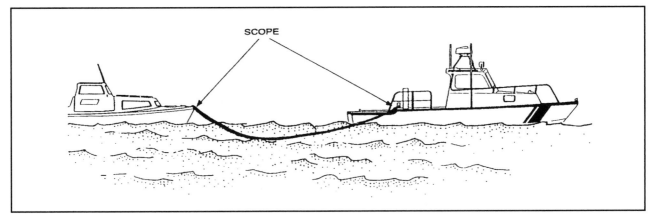

Figure 17-14 Scope of Towline with Catenary

- Towing Speed Formula. For the purposes of the following calculations:

S = Maximum towing speed (hull design speed)

Ss = Maximum Safe towing speed

$\sqrt{Lw}$ = Square Root of Length at waterline

$$S = 1.34 \times {}^*Lw$$

Ss = S − (10% × S) a 10% reduction in the maximum towing speed.

For example, to determine a safe towing speed for a boat that has a 36-foot waterline length, do the following:

$$S = 1.34 \times \sqrt{Lw}$$

$$S = 1.34 \times (\text{square root of } 36)$$

$$S = 1.34 \times 6$$

$$\textbf{S = 8.0 knots}$$

$$Ss = 8.0 − (0.1 \times 8.0)$$

$$Ss = 8.0 − 0.8$$

$$\textbf{Ss = 7.2 knots}$$

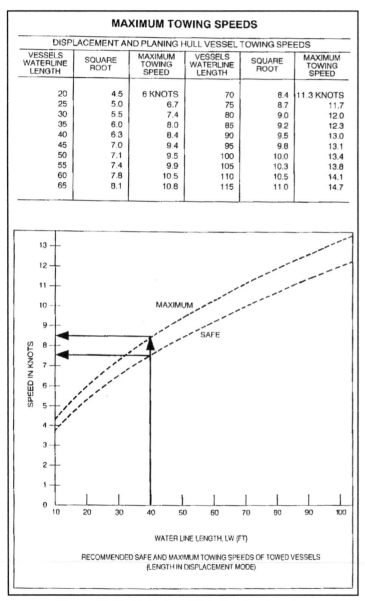

MAXIMUM TOWING SPEEDS

DISPLACEMENT AND PLANING HULL VESSEL TOWING SPEEDS

VESSELS WATERLINE LENGTH	SQUARE ROOT	MAXIMUM TOWING SPEED	VESSELS WATERLINE LENGTH	SQUARE ROOT	MAXIMUM TOWING SPEED
20	4.5	6 KNOTS	70	8.4	11.3 KNOTS
25	5.0	6.7	75	8.7	11.7
30	5.5	7.4	80	9.0	12.0
35	6.0	8.0	85	9.2	12.3
40	6.3	8.4	90	9.5	13.0
45	7.0	9.4	95	9.8	13.1
50	7.1	9.5	100	10.0	13.4
55	7.4	9.9	105	10.3	13.8
60	7.8	10.5	110	10.5	14.1
65	8.1	10.8	115	11.0	14.7

RECOMMENDED SAFE AND MAXIMUM TOWING SPEEDS OF TOWED VESSELS
(LENGTH IN DISPLACEMENT MODE)

Figure 17-15 Calculated Safe Towing Speeds

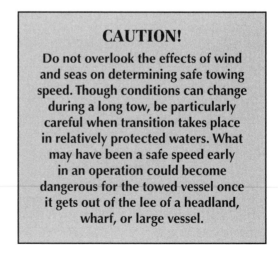

WARNING

Due to safety concerns, never try to tow a hull faster than the hull design speed. When moving at a speed higher than hull speed, the vessel will try to ride up on its bow wave, becoming unstable and, in extreme cases, could capsize. Also, wave drag (even one large wake) could slow the hull to displacement speed and cause a severe shock-load in the tow rig as the towing force tries to pull the towed vessel back on plane. In response to this shock-load, the towed vessel could plow its bow into another wave and swamp or capsize.

Figure 17-15 shows calculated safe towing speeds based on waterline length.

If it is possible to tow fast enough to get the vessel up to hull design speed, you can reduce the strain and stress of the tow for both vessels. Often, due to weather, seas, and other conditions, you will not be able to tow a hull fast enough to take advantage of its design.

CAUTION!

Do not overlook the effects of wind and seas on determining safe towing speed. Though conditions can change during a long tow, be particularly careful when transition takes place in relatively protected waters. What may have been a safe speed early in an operation could become dangerous for the towed vessel once it gets out of the lee of a headland, wharf, or large vessel.

Compensating for Current

D.40. GENERAL

Handling a tow becomes more of a challenge when traveling in a river, estuary or other area where tidal currents affect navigation or in areas where major coastal currents or wind-driven currents come into play. This is particularly true near inlets, bars, river mouths, river bends, and areas where currents diverge or converge. Generally, there are four conditions encountered while towing in current:

- Head Current
- Tail Current
- Cross Current
- Combinations of the above

To effectively deal with any of these, you must navigate not only the towing vessel, but the towed vessel as well. One way to do this is to look at a stern tow as a single long vessel, with the propeller(s) and rudder(s) at the bow, and the pivot point at the stern. Though not a totally accurate picture, it shows that just because the towing vessel (the bow) changes direction, the towed vessel (the stern) will not immediately and automatically follow. Momentum will try to keep the towed vessel going in the original direction. Also, though you may frequently "crab" against the current with the towing vessel alone, now you must crab a vessel that becomes longer than the towline.

"Local knowledge" becomes extremely important when dealing with current. The effect of current on vessel navigation at 12–30 knots is far less than the effect while towing at 6–8 knots.

> **CAUTION!**
> Regardless of speed over the ground, the tow is still moving through the water. Safe towing speed is based on speed through the water. Avoid towing a vessel above its hull speed and do not exceed the safe limits imposed by wind and sea conditions. If the current opposes winds and seas, the seas get steeper and break more readily. Increasing the speed through the water places excessive strain on a tow rig and deck fittings. Dynamic forces are still at work.

> *NOTE*
> Keep overall tow length in mind. In current, even though the towing vessel may be well clear of obstructions or buoys, the tow rig and towed vessel may be set into them.

D.41. HEAD CURRENT

This is a current flowing directly against the steered course. Depending on the velocity of the current and the speed of the tow, speed over the ground may be reduced, stopped, or even reversed.

NARROW AND STRAIGHT WATERWAYS A head current in a "narrow" waterway poses other concerns. In a perfectly straight waterway, shallower water outside a deep channel will provide some relief, provided that the tow remains in deep enough water for safe navigation.

> **CAUTION!**
> Make sure that both the towing vessel and the tow stay in water deep enough so neither vessel grounds.

BENDS AND TURNS When towing in a waterway with bends and turns, the greatest current will be to the outside of the bend or turn. Accordingly, the water will be deepest on the outside. When towing around a bend, the direction of the head current acting on the towing vessel may differ from that on the towed vessel. At a bend, the towed vessel may sheer (or yaw) to the outside of the bend.

- To deal with a very strong head current, consider waiting for the current to slacken, waiting offshore for tidal conditions to change, or changing destination. Also, you may find an area out of the main current flow in which to make progress.
- Determine conditions in the river prior to entering. It may be prudent to remain in open water until currents slacken or tidal conditions change.

> *NOTE*
> Prevent towed vessel sheer by reducing towline length before entering narrower sections of a waterway.

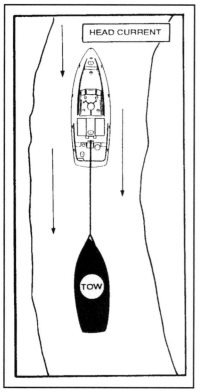

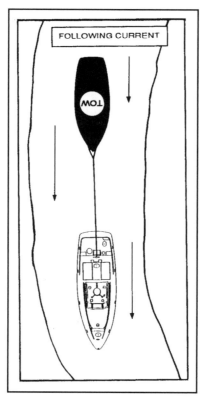

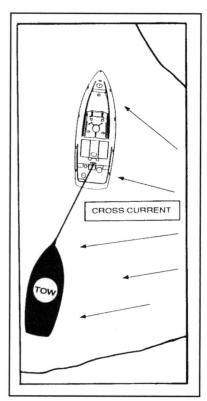

Figure 17-16 Effects of Head Current

Figure 17-17 Effects of Tail (Following) Current

Figure 17-18 Effects of Cross Current

D.42. **TAIL CURRENT**

This is a current flowing in the same direction as the course steered. Stay aware of how the influence of a tail current affects both vessels. As with the head current, in general, speed through the water indicates appropriate handling procedures, not speed over the ground.

OPEN WATER In open water, a tail current usually helps the tow along. However, when opposing the wind or seas, the tail current causes steeper waves. The steeper waves may require slowing the towing speed. Account for the tail current when estimating the time of arrival. All course changes or shortening-up of the tow must be done earlier, or the current will carry the tow past the desired point. Then, considerable effort will be needed to go back against the (now) head current.

NOTE

Compensate for a tail current by taking early action.

NARROW WATERWAY As with a head current, a tail current in a narrow waterway also affects how the tow handles. A common situation develops when the towing vessel gets into an area of lesser current then the towed vessel. This often occurs near turns and bends where it appears that the shortest distance is on the inside of the bend. If there is a significant difference in the current, the tow sheers off along the axis of the current. This will possibly cause slack in the tow rig, loss of firm control, and will potentially overrun the towing vessel.

- Minimize the possibility of loss of control in a tail current by staying in the same velocity of current as the tow. As with a head current, one way to do this is by shortening scope of the towline.

- If a tail current looks as if it will become unmanageable, it may be necessary to change course and steer more into the current.

D.43. **CROSS CURRENT**

This is a current that is flowing from either side, across the intended track. This current will require the towing vessel to adjust heading for set and drift for both vessels. At a towing speed of 7 knots, a 2-knot cross current will require a heading offset of over 15 degrees in order to follow the intended track. In open water, this may not pose a problem, if the towing vessel adjusts properly throughout the tow.

In restricted waters, suddenly encountering a cross-current, such as where an alongshore current crosses a harbor entrance channel, can initially cause the tow to appear to veer, even though the towing vessel is the one being affected. Then when the towed vessel encounters the flow, it will appear to veer the other way.

In restricted waters, the towing vessel must adjust accordingly for the amount the cross current offsets the towed vessel from the intended track. The cross current can push the towed vessel into danger.

- Minimize the possibility of a cross current pushing the towed vessel into danger through a combination of shortening tow and offsetting the towing vessel's intended track in an up-current direction.

As an example, if a cross-current moving from right to left is present near a channel entrance, shorten the tow before entering and line up the towing vessel to the right of the channel centerline. If unable to shorten tow, get well off to the up-current side of the channel centerline.

> **WARNING**
>
> While towing astern, if there is any cross-current in a channel marked by a navigational range, DO NOT steer the towing vessel exactly on the range. Doing so could stand the towed vessel into danger on the down-current side of the channel. If the towed vessel has any problems such as steering or stability, keep the towed vessel in good water (usually the center of the channel, marked by the range). Use the towed vessel's crew to inform you when on the range. Remember, when you take a vessel in tow, you become responsible for its safety.

D.44. COMBINATIONS OF CURRENTS

Seldom will the current be dead on the bow, from directly astern, or exactly on the beam. If it happens to be that way at the moment, it may not be for very long. The marine environment is constantly changing, including the motion of currents. Combine the general principles and specific procedures discussed above to effectively compensate for combinations of currents.

Closely watch the surface of the water for evidence of current changes. A "tide line" usually appears at the leading edge of a current change or marks the difference between two different flows. A river's color changes because of flow from another river. "Tide-rips" or bar conditions vary with the amount of current.

NOTE

There is no substitute for experience and preparation. Learn your area of operations and be alert to hazards so you will not be taken by surprise.

Shortening the Tow

D.45. GENERAL

When approaching safe haven, it may be necessary to shorten the towline to safely enter an inlet, cross a bar, tow in a channel or turn into a basin. Shorten the tow to increase control in confined areas and in current. The towline must be slack to shorten tow. The coxswain controls the amount of slack and the direction the towline tends while the crew recovers the tow line. The crew and coxswain must communicate and coordinate their efforts and actions to make the task as easy as possible without fouling the tow vessel's propellers or rudders. Keep towline recovery on the beam or quarter to keep the slack towline from fouling the propellers.

D.46. BEFORE SHORTENING A TOW

- Determine a safe area considering wind, depth of water, size of vessel, area to maneuver, etc.
- Determine the new desired towline length.
- Brief the towed vessel's crew.
- Brief own crew and assign tasks.
- Reduce speed slowly and gradually to prevent the tow from closing too fast, and risking collision. Due to momentum, a vessel with greater displacement will keep way on longer than a light displacement vessel. A vessel with way on will stop more quickly when turned into the wind and seas.
- As towline gets slack, direct crew to remove turns from the tow bitt. The crew member at the bitt pulls slack so as to be ready to take a turn if necessary.

D.47. PROCEDURES

Following are procedures describing how to shorten the tow.

1. As pivot begins, the coxswain directs the bitt

person to break the bitt and a line handler must begin to pull in the towline. Recover towline and take it up on the tow reel (if equipped). Do not let bights of towline litter the deck or the crew working area.

2. The coxswain backs as necessary to slack the line, which allows the line handler to haul in the line more easily.

3. If the wind is any angle off the bow, ensure the towing vessel is blown away from the towline.

4. If the severity of the weather hampers control of the towing vessel, shorten the tow in segments. If an attempt to shorten must be aborted, the coxswain directs the bitt person to take a working turn and remove any slack. The crew must clear out between the bitt and the towed vessel before there is strain at the bitt. Make up the bitt if needed to hold the strain. The coxswain must then maneuver and restart the procedure.

CAUTION!

Do not back too quickly and cause a large bight in the towline that increases risk of fouling propellers or rudders. Backing too quickly may also create too much strain for the line handler if the towline bight leads too far forward.

Once a short tow is set, the "shock absorber" effect of catenary and scope is reduced. Use special care to counteract shock loading.

D.48. AT SEA OR IN OTHER ROUGH CONDITIONS

Turn into the weather with seas or wind (whichever is greatest influence on tow vessel motion) 30 to 40 degrees off the bow. If a lot of towline must be recovered, put the towing vessel's bow directly into the seas. Whatever angle to the sea is chosen, pivot the towing vessel bow directly into the seas or wind whenever backing down to recover towline. Crew communication and boat handling skills are paramount in this situation to avoid fouling the towline in the towing vessel's propellers

The greatest control occurs when the wind and seas are off the towing vessel's bow while on the beam of the tow. The wind and seas will drift the tow away from the towline.

TOWING SPEED Reduce speed to lessen the forces on the towed vessel, which in turn are transferred to the towing vessel.

- In heavy weather, constantly adjust towing speed to prevent a tow from surfing on a wave or broaching.

- If a large wave approaches the stern of a tow, increase tow vessel speed to keep ahead of the tow as it is pushed by the swell.

- As a tow reaches the crest of a swell, reduce speed. Keep the towline taut. The coxswain must constantly watch the seas astern and the towed vessel until in sheltered waters.

- Deploy the drogue.

NOTE

This technique is very demanding and must be learned through training and experience. Throttle response (acceleration and deceleration) must be matched to the towed vessel's speed. If this technique is impractical to counteract shock-loading, speed reduction and quartering the seas may be your best options.

CALM CONDITIONS In calm conditions, if not much towline was out to begin with, shortening a tow may not be necessary. It may be easier to go directly to an alongside tow.

D.49. DISCONNECT TOW OR TOW ALONGSIDE

At the safe haven, the towing vessel will either moor the towed vessel or disconnect the tow so the towed vessel can anchor or be assisted by other resources.

NOTE

If you decide to disconnect the tow, determine beforehand whether any other part of the rig will stay aboard the towed vessel. The weight of shackles or a wire-rope bridle will increase the difficulty of towline recovery, and could pose additional risk of fouling in propellers or rudders.

DISCONNECT THE TOWLINE The towline should be shortened up to some extent already. Turn the towed vessel into the prevailing conditions for better control. This procedure makes towline recovery easier and safer because there is less towline for the crew to recover and less towline in the water to foul propellers. It also allows the towing vessel to maintain control of a tow a little longer. Once shortened, and with the tow barely moving to allow the towline to slacken, the coxswain signals for the towed vessel crew to disconnect the rig and let it go into the water. The towing vessel crew then hauls it aboard.

Towing Alongside

D.50. GENERAL

When set up properly, an alongside tow allows two vessels to be maneuvered as one. This advantage is necessary when approaching a dock, mooring, or anchorage in sheltered waters, or when maneuvering in congested or restricted waters. Most of the pre-tow procedures used for towing astern described earlier in the chapter are applicable. However, some additional preparations are needed and the make-up of the tow rig and approach will be different. The tow rig configuration and approach will be more like that for mooring.

D.51. PREPARATION

These additional preparations apply for an alongside tow.

DETERMINE SIDE OF TOW AND APPROACH Determine on which side the tow will be rigged. Note the effect of the weather and physical conditions on both vessels, and use them to your advantage. Although similar to a mooring approach, you must decide whether you want the wind to set the

Towing alongside allows the two vessels to be maneuvered as one.

other vessel down on you, or vice-versa. Assess the other vessel's drift rate and aspect to plan the speed and angle of your approach.

- If a vessel smaller than the towing vessel is being rapidly set towards a lee shore or obstructions, consider approaching from leeward, if sea room allows.

> **WARNING**
>
> Do not place the towing vessel between a larger towed vessel and a lee shore or obstruction. The towing vessel may not be able to overcome the other vessel's momentum before losing all room to maneuver. As with any towing approach, leave an escape route.

DECIDE USE OF TOWLINE If the alongside tow occurs at the completion of a stern tow, decide if the towline will be disconnected from the stern tow, or hauled in while still connected and used as a bow line for the alongside rig. If the stern tow required a bridle, disconnecting part of or all of the rig may be the only option to provide a fair lead for the alongside bow line.

> **CAUTION!**
>
> Use of a towline as the bow line in an alongside tow puts more line lying on deck and may be a tripping or fouling hazard.

PREPARE LINES Ready the proper size and number of lines to rig alongside. Determine where the attachment points on the towed vessel will be for each line.

DETERMINE HULL MATCH Determine hull match. Assess how the two hulls will align alongside. In towing alongside, the tow vessel may be angled, slightly bow-in to the towed vessel, with the towing vessel propeller(s) and rudder(s) aft of the towed vessel's transom, rudder or outdrive(s).

RIG FENDERS Rig all available fenders, except one for hand tending as the tow approaches, in potential contact points. Secure all fenders in place before bringing a tow alongside. Secure fenders using clove hitches or slip clove hitches.

BRIEF TOWED VESSEL

- Advise which side to prepare.

- If already in stern tow, describe shortening-up and whether towline will be used as bow line or whether (and when, "on signal") to cast off.

- Describe your approach and intended position alongside.

- Direct the towed vessel to clear as many obstructions from the side as possible (rigging, lines, outriggers, etc.).

- Direct the towed vessel to place fenders at obvious areas, such as trawler doors or topside vents.

- Designate attachment points.

- Direct crew how to assist.

D.52. MAKE THE APPROACH

Two alternatives are presented.

- Use towline as bow line

- Free approach

USE TOWLINE AS BOW LINE The towed vessel is already in a stern tow.

- Use the same methods as shortening the tow to take all headway off the tow before backing down. If the towed vessel has available propulsion, it may be able to assist by briefly backing down. If necessary, use the towline to change the heading of the towed vessel.

- When the tow has stopped all forward movement, the coxswain directs the crew to "break the bitt." The towing vessel slowly backs and the towline is hauled in. Try to keep some space abeam until the towed vessel is in the proper fore and aft position. As the distance between the vessels decreases and as directed by the coxswain, the crew walks the towline forward to a suitable bow fitting, takes a working turn on the line and takes in slack. The coxswain then moors the towing vessel alongside the towed vessel.

NOTE

Show the towed vessel crew where to attach the alongside mooring lines. Perform all line handling at coxswain direction, just as in mooring. Always pass the eye of alongside lines to a towed vessel. Keep the working ends of the lines aboard the towing vessel to adjust or relocate as necessary.

FREE APPROACH Make this approach as if mooring to a pier, but the first line over will be the bow line. There will not be a spring line to check your forward motion with respect to the towed vessel. The coxswain directs the crew to pass the bow line when alongside.

> **WARNING**
>
> **Do not fend off boat with your feet or hands.**

D.53. RIG ADDITIONAL LINES ALONGSIDE

Once alongside, with the bow line connected, position the tow so that the towing vessel's propeller(s) and rudder(s) are well aft of the towed vessel's stern. This affords best control for maneuvering in confined areas. Check fender placement and make adjustments so they provide maximum protection at contact points.

CALM CONDITIONS If there is little or no movement from wind, seas or current, rig lines in the following order:

- Second line: Rig a stern line from the towed vessel's towing bitt or post. This line holds the stern in while setting up the "spring lines."

- Third line: Rig a "tow strap" (forward spring line) from the towing vessel bow or forward mooring fitting to a point outboard and aft on the towed vessel.

- Fourth line: Rig a backing line (after spring line) from a quarter location on the towing vessel to a location forward on the towed vessel.

NOTE

For maximum control of a tow, all alongside lines should be as tight as possible. Spring lines are tightened by crew members taking up slack obtained when the coxswain throttles forward and reverse on the inside engine, pulling first against the tow strap then backing down against the backing line.

IN WIND, SEAS, OR CURRENT If conditions are setting the vessels into danger, i.e., toward shoals or breakwaters, and time is critical, follow this order:

- Second line: Rig a tow strap so that, once secured, the towing vessel can put headway on and move clear of any dangers.

- Third line: With headway still on, rig a backing line. You will need this to slow the towed vessel.

- Fourth line: The stern line.

D.54. MANEUVERING

Maneuvering with an alongside tow is a challenging boat-handling technique. To do it well and do it safely requires practice and experience. An accomplished coxswain will observe how winds, seas and current affect the combined tow and use these forces to the best advantage, often making the maneuver look easier than it really was.

APPROACH FOR MOORING To moor an alongside tow safely and skillfully:

- Anticipate well ahead of time and decrease speed gradually.

- Place the larger vessel against the dock or mooring.

- Making an approach into the wind and current if possible.

- Moor on the protected (leeward) side of a dock or pier.

Place a crew member in good position as a lookout aboard a towed vessel on approach. This extends a coxswain's vision for clearances and obstructions. Rig fenders and mooring lines from the tow if it is going to be placed against a dock or mooring.

Sinking Tows

D.55. GENERAL

When it becomes evident that a tow is about to sink, very quickly assess the situation. Quick decisive action to minimize loss of life is the first priority. Once abandon ship procedures are initiated, radio communications will likely be lost. The primary action is to rescue the people, either from the deck of the towed vessel or from the water.

A sinking tow can pull the stern of the towing vessel under unless all crew members pay close attention to the immediate situation. There will probably not be enough time to disconnect the towline from the towed vessel once it begins to sink.

If a tow begins to sink, stop all towing vessel headway. The force exerted through the towline increases the danger of the towed vessel yawing and capsizing.

D.56. MINIMIZE THE DANGER

Perform the following procedures:

- When it becomes obvious that sinking cannot be avoided, e.g., the tow has rolled on one side and is not righting itself or the tow's decks are submerging, cut the towline or slip the towline by breaking the bitt.

- Note the vessel's position by GPS, Loran or radar fix and request assistance. Once free of the tow, make preparations to rescue people who were on board.

WARNING

Do not attempt breaking the bitt if there is a strain on the towline. Instead, cut the towline using a knife. Cut towline directly behind the tow bitt.

CAUTION!

Be aware that the boat could become fouled in rigging or debris while attempting to rescue survivors.

D.57. MARK THE WRECK

If there were no people on board the tow, the water is shallow (depth less than towline length), and safety permits, pay out the towline until the tow reaches bottom. Tie a fender, life jacket or floatable object to the towline so it is visible on the surface, then cut the towline. The floating object will mark the location of the sunken vessel for salvage later.

Towing Precautions

Maintain communications between coxswain and crew.

Have all people on board a distressed boat don PFDs. If there are not enough PFDs, provide them.

Remove all people from a distressed boat when necessary, safe, or practical.

CAUTION!

Do not allow a distressed boat to become endangered while waiting for people to don PFDs. Take immediate action to remove the people or boat from danger.

Cast heaving lines well over a boat's center mass so they drop over the deck. Tell people on board what is going to occur. Call out "HEADS UP" just before casting a heaving line.

Establish and maintain clear communications with a towed vessel, including a backup means of communicating. Provide a portable radio if necessary. At a minimum, contact a tow every 30 minutes and more frequently if conditions warrant. Initially, get the following information from the operator of the towed boat:

- condition of towline, chafing gear, towline attachment point, and fair lead hardware
- level of water on board/rate of flooding (if taking on water)
- physical condition of people on board

When underway, keep personnel on board both boats clear of the tow rig.

Keep the tow rig attachment point as low and close to the centerline as possible.

Do not connect a tow rig to lifelines, stanchions, grab rails or ladders.

Do not connect the tow rig to cleats or bitts that are attached to the distressed boat's deck only with screws.

Avoid using lines provided by the distressed boat for any part of the tow rig.

Avoid using knots to join towlines.

Tend a towline by hand until secured to a distressed boat. Then, secure it to a bitt or cleat on the coxswain's command. Use two people, if possible, assigned as line handlers to tend the towline and a crew member to work the bitt.

Do not secure a towline to a bitt or cleat with half hitches. They cause jamming and fusing.

A crew member working the bitt or cleat must avoid crossing arms when securing the line to the bitt or cleat. Change hands to avoid becoming fouled in the turns.

Ensure the breaking strength of all shackles used in the tow rig is equal to or greater than the breaking strength of the towline.

Keep the towline clear of propellers, shafts and rudders.

Use chafing gear to minimize damage to a tow rig.

Avoid towing boats which exceed weight and length limits established for a Coast Guard boat.

Tow at a safe speed for the prevailing conditions. Prevent shock loading the tow rig.

Do not exceed the hull design speed of the boat. Sailboats have a low hull speed design.

Avoid sudden maneuvers and sharp turns.

Use a drogue to reduce or prevent yawing (as necessary).

Have someone at the helm of the towed vessel, if possible. Direct that person to steer the boat directly on the stern of the towing boat. If all people have been removed from a distressed boat, secure the rudder amidships. If a tow has an outboard or inboard/outboard engine, direct the operator to lower the outdrive(s) or motor(s) to normal operating position.

- Keep a towed boat in trim. Consider the following for trim:

    condition of a boat (structural damage, taking on water, etc.)

    structural design of a boat (low transom, low freeboard, etc.)

    cargo (fish holds, gear stowage, etc.) and how free surface effect (dynamics of free moving water in the bilge of a boat) influence ride

    number and location of people on board

WARNING

Overload astern, or along either side of a vessel's centerline, may swamp or capsize a vessel in tow.

Maintain a diligent towing watch and frequently account for all people on board the towed boat either visually or by radio.

NOTE

A towing watch has a critical responsibility. In addition to the crew member assigned, it is a collateral duty for all other members of a crew.

Ensure the breaking strengths of bridles in a tow rig are equal to or greater than the breaking strength of a towline or appropriately matched to the requirements of the tow and prevailing conditions.

If possible, load Loran or GPS positions and do all chart work at the dock. It is very difficult to do all of this while underway and being tossed about.

If the possibility exists that a drogue or pump will be required while under tow, pass the equipment before the tow rig is hooked up.

After a tow rig is set up, but before it is connected to a tow, a coxswain should inspect the entire tow rig and hookup points

When approaching a distressed boat, a coxswain should establish an imaginary danger zone around the craft based on prevailing conditions.

Firefighting, Rescue, and Assistance

Editor's Note: *How and when would you fight a fire on board your boat, or, for that matter, approach a burning boat to remove victims? If your boat were taking on water and a Coast Guard helicopter lowered a pump to your deck, would you know how to use it? Suppose you came across a semi-submerged runabout. Would you know how to right it and dewater it so you could tow it to safe harbor? This chapter holds the answers. Note that the chapter begins with a discussion of assessing the situation at hand. Risk assessment is essential to handling any emergency. For example, using the wrong extinguishing agent can spread a fire rather than extinguish it. Sometimes it's better to abandon the boat rather than attempt to fight a fire. On occasion, it may be appropriate to dewater a flooding boat. On the other hand, a boat becomes unstable as it floods and it may be best in some situations to remove the occupants and stand off. The point is that the ability to assess the situation is a necessary skill for a competent skipper and this chapter is a solid introduction to the topic.*

Overview

Introduction

As members of the U.S. Coast Guard and the Auxiliary, the boat crews have an important responsibility in maintaining their vessel and assisting those in distress. A primary responsibility of a boat crew is to save **lives**, not **property**. However, when and where possible, a boat crew will attempt to save property. Boat crew members may be called upon to react to a fire on their own boat, dewater vessels, and right vessels. This chapter discusses:

- safety and prevention measures to take when on a boat or assisting a distressed vessel;

- how to assess emergency situations;

- how to prevent, identify, and extinguish boat fires;

- how to dewater vessels; and

- several methods of righting overturned vessels.

It is very important to keep in mind that any vessel can fall victim to tragedy when proper prevention measures or rescue procedures are not followed correctly and precisely.

In this chapter

Section	Title	See Page(s)
A	Safety and Damage Control	371–72
B	Boat Fire Prevention and Susceptible Areas	372–74
C	Fire Theory, Classifications, and Fuel Sources	375–76
D	Extinguishing Agents	376
E	Applying Extinguishing Agents	376–80
F	Firefighting Equipment	380–88
G	Firefighting Procedures	388–91
H	Extinguishing Fires	391–94
I	Dewatering	394–98
J	Righting Powerboats and Sailboats	398–402
K	Flood Control	402

Safety and Damage Control

Overview

Introduction

Safety is paramount during all emergencies evolutions that you will be involved in as a member of a boat crew. Mishaps resulting in death or injury have occurred when boat crews responded to vessels in distress. Nearly every mishap that resulted in serious injuries had a common denominator. Serious injuries happen when common sense and a continuing regard for safety give way to reckless urgency.

As a boat crew member, your primary responsibility in emergency assistance is saving lives, not property. Boat crews must be aware of their limited roles in emergency assistance, particularly when responding to fire emergencies. Safety begins with assessing your primary responsibilities and capabilities for the variety of emergency situations you will encounter.

In this section

Topic	See Page(s)
Coast Guard Firefighting Activities Policy	371
Safety Assessment and Management Guidelines	371–72

Coast Guard Firefighting Activities Policy

A.1. COAST GUARD FIREFIGHTING ACTIVITIES POLICY

Among the provisions of the Ports and Waterways Safety Act of 1972 (PWSA) (33 U.S.C. 1221 *et seq.*) is an acknowledgment that increased supervision of port operations is necessary to prevent damage to structures in, on, or adjacent to the navigable waters of the United States, and to reduce the possibility of vessel or cargo loss, damage to life, property, and the marine environment. This statute, along with the traditional functions and powers of the Coast Guard to render aid and save property (14 U.S.C. 88(b)), is the basis for Coast Guard firefighting activities.

The Coast Guard has traditionally provided firefighting equipment and training to protect the lives of Coast Guard personnel, its vessels, and property. Coast Guard and Auxiliary units are also called upon to assist in fighting major fires on board other vessels and at waterfront facilities. Although the Coast Guard will help fight fires involving vessels or waterfront facilities, it is not a primary response capability. Local authorities are responsible for maintaining adequate firefighting capabilities in U.S. ports and harbors. The Coast Guard renders assistance as time and resources are available, based on the level of personnel training and adequacy of equipment available for a specific situation at hand.

Safety Assessment and Management Guidelines

A.2. SAFETY ASSESSMENT AND MANAGEMENT GUIDELINES

Emergency situations can cause people to panic or act before thinking despite the best of training and preparation. Therefore, boat crews must work together as a team to minimize any potential or immediate jeopardy for both civilian casualties and themselves. **Never** enter an emergency situation without first assessing the risk involved for the boat crew members and civilian victims **(Risk Assessment)**, always be aware of the dynamics of the emergency situation **(Situational Awareness)**, and implement a control plan that fits each unique **emergency (Damage Control Risk Management)**.

RISK ASSESSMENT AND MANAGEMENT Risk Assessment starts with realizing why mishaps occur. The responsibility for identifying and managing risk lies with every member of a boat crew. Realistic training based on standard techniques, critical analysis, and debriefing missions will help every person in a boat crew to contribute to developing and implementing a **Risk Management Plan**. A Risk Management Plan identifies and controls risk according to a set of preconceived parameters. Refer to Chapter 4 of this manual for a complete discussion of Risk Assessment and Risk Management Plans.

SITUATIONAL AWARENESS Situational Awareness is an important skill for you to develop as part of learning risk assessment. **Situational Awareness** is the **accurate** perception of factors and conditions affecting the boat crew at any given time during any evolution. More simply, situational awareness is knowing what is going on around you at all times.

Any time you identify an indication that situational awareness is about to be lost, you must make a decision whether or not to continue with the rescue attempt. Everyone in the crew owns some responsibility for making these important decisions. These decisions take the form of action/reaction and communication.

NOTE

Crews who have a high level of SITUATIONAL AWARENESS perform in a safe manner.

DAMAGE CONTROL RISK MANAGEMENT The precautions listed below include many of the considerations that can form a basis for a general **Damage Control Risk Management Plan**. Keep in mind that each emergency situation will be unique, therefore the plan must only be used as a **general** guideline. The experience and knowledge of each boat crew should be merged into a Risk Management Plan and used to fine-tune this list.

- Attempt to account for all persons.
- Attempt to have all lines, rigging, etc. removed from the water to avoid fouling your propellers.
- Maintain communications between the coxswain and crew members.
- Have all required equipment tested and ready.
- Approach distressed vessel with your fenders rigged and lines at the ready.
- Approach a vessel on fire from the windward side.
- Remove survivors first, then back off, and evaluate the fire.
- If the risk of explosion is not known (you cannot determine what cargo is on board), back off and do not attempt to fight the fire.
- When necessary, dewater distressed vessel while keeping all equipment aboard your vessel
- Always keep your operational commander or parent unit informed.

NOTE

See District policy on boarding a boat that is on fire.

Boat Fire Prevention and Susceptible Areas

Overview

Introduction

Fire is the greatest single potential for disaster on a boat. The possibility of fire can never be completely eliminated and is always a threat to watch for and guard against.

Boat crew members must be especially alert for fire, its possible causes, and areas on a boat that are very susceptible to fire. There are some causes of fire that are more frequently encountered on boats and you must learn to be especially watchful for them.

In this section

Topic	See Page(s)
Preventive Actions	372
Susceptible Areas	373–74

Preventive Actions

B.1. PREVENTIVE ACTIONS

In dealing with fire on your boat, the single most important consideration is prevention. During boat and equipment checks, all systems must be inspected including the fuel, oil system, and wiring. Check for abrasions, cracked wiring, or pinholes in oil and fuel lines. Any discrepancy must be corrected at the time it is discovered. The following are also good fire prevention measures for you to practice:

- Keep oil and grease out of bilges.
- Clean up any spilled fuel or lube oil immediately and properly dispose of it ashore.
- Stow cleaning materials off the boat.
- Keep all areas free of waste material.
- Use proper containers for flammable liquids.
- Be alert for suspicious odors and fumes, and vent all spaces thoroughly before starting engine(s).

Routine system inspections and safe operating procedures are essential for fire prevention on boats.

Susceptible Areas

B.2. SPONTANEOUS IGNITION

This source of fire is often overlooked as a cause of fire aboard a boat. Many common materials are subject to this dangerous "chemical reaction." A spontaneous ignition can easily occur aboard a boat when an oil or paint soaked rag is discarded in the corner of a compartment or engine room.

OXIDATION When an area is warm and there is no ventilation, oil on a rag begins to oxidize (to react chemically with the oxygen in the warm air around it). Oxidization is a natural process that produces heat. Heat produced by oxidization causes any remaining oil to oxidize even faster and produce still more heat.

VENTILATION Since heat is not drawn away by ventilation, it builds up around a rag and causes it to get hot enough to burst into flames, after which it can ignite any nearby flammable substance and start a major fire. All of this occurs without any additional or outside source of heat. In this case, fire prevention is a matter of good housekeeping. Cleaning rags and waste should be stored in closed or sealed metal containers and discarded as soon as possible.

B.3. ENGINE ROOM FIRES

Engine rooms are particularly vulnerable to electrical, fuel, and oil fires. There are several ways that engine room fires can readily start. Water spraying from ruptured seawater lines can cause severe short-circuiting and arcing in electric motors (alternators), electrical panels, and other ex-posed electrical equipment. This, in turn, can ignite insulation and nearby combustible materials. Even more serious than leaking seawater lines are ruptured fuel and oil lines near electrical equipment. **All** crew members must constantly monitor these lines for leaks.

ELECTRICAL SYSTEM The electrical system can short and cause a fire. These fires are typically small and easily controlled with either Carbon Dioxide (CO_2) or dry chemical (PKP) extinguishers.

FUEL LINE If fittings leak, fuel can drip onto a hot manifold and ignite. This situation could continue unnoticed for some time, allowing a major fire to develop when a manifold finally gets hot enough to ignite all leaked fuel.

LUBE OIL LINE This line, if leaking or ruptured, will allow lube oil to spill onto a hot engine. As the burning lube oil collects on and around an engine, the engine's fuel supply can burn through. This provides a fire with a continuous fuel supply, even after engines have been shut down. As fuel continues to spill into the bilges, spreading fire and blocking access to the engine compartment, a major fire can develop.

BILGE AREAS Fire occurs in bilge areas because of fuel or oil accumulation. Most often, oil or gas leaks into bilges from an undetected break in a fuel or lube oil line. The oil vaporizes, and flammable vapors build up in and around bilge areas. Once these vapors are mixed with air in the right proportions, a spark can ignite them and cause a fire or explosion. Bilge fires can move very quickly around machinery and piping and are not easily controlled. They are more difficult to extinguish than most other types of engine room fires. Bilge areas should be watched closely. Oil in a bilge nearly always indicates a leak and all fuel and lube oil lines should be checked until the leak is found.

> ## CAUTION!
> An explosion is a common accident for boats when bilges are not properly ventilated before starting up. A spark from "turning the key" can instantly ignite the trapped gas creating a potentially deadly explosion.

B.4. ELECTRICAL CIRCUITS AND EQUIPMENT

With properly insulated and wired equipment, electricity is a safe and convenient source of power. However, when electrical equipment exceeds its useful life, is misused, or is poorly wired, it can convert electrical energy to heat. Equipment then becomes a source of ignition and a "fire hazard." For this reason, electrical equipment must be installed, maintained, tested, and repaired in strict accordance with published regulations.

NOTE

All work on electrical equipment and circuits must be completed only by qualified personnel.

REPLACEMENT PARTS AND EQUIPMENT Standard residential or industrial electrical equipment does not last very long at sea. The salt air causes "corrosion," the boat's vibration breaks down the equipment, and a steel hull can cause erratic operation or a shorted circuit. As a result, equipment or its wiring may overheat or arc, causing a fire when flammable materials are located nearby. For this reason, **only** approved replacement parts and equipment should be installed aboard small boats. Given proper maintenance, these parts and equipment are designed to withstand the strenuous conditions encountered at sea.

WIRING AND FUSES Insulation on electrical wiring will not last forever. With age and use, it can become brittle and crack. It may be rubbed (chafed) through or broken by abuse or by the vibration of a boat. Once insulation is broken, bare wires are dangerous. A single exposed wire can arc to any metal object. If both wires are exposed, they can touch each other and cause a short circuit. Either condition could produce enough heat to ignite insulation on wiring or some other flammable material nearby. This type of fire can be prevented by replacing wires that have faulty or worn insulation. Install only fuses and circuit breakers of the proper size for their circuits.

WARNING

When a fuse or circuit breaker in a particular circuit is too large, a circuit will not "break" when overloaded. Instead, increased current will continue, a circuit will overheat, and eventually insulation will burn and may ignite other combustible material in the vicinity.

TEMPORARY AND UNAUTHORIZED REPAIRS AND PATCHES "Jury-rigging" of electrical panels to serve additional equipment is a dangerous practice. Wiring in every electrical circuit is designed to carry a specified maximum load. When circuit wiring is overloaded with too many pieces of operating equipment, it can overheat and burn its insulation. Hot wiring can also ignite flammable materials in surrounding areas.

ELECTRIC MOTORS (ALTERNATORS) Faulty electric motors are major causes of fire. Problems may result when a motor is not properly maintained or when it exceeds its useful life. A motor requires regular inspection, testing, lubrication, and cleaning. Sparks and arcing can result if a winding becomes short-circuited or grounded or if the brushes do not operate smoothly. If a spark or an arc is strong enough, it can ignite nearby combustible material. Lack of lubrication may cause the motor bearings to overheat, with the same result.

CHARGING BATTERIES When batteries are charging, they emit hydrogen, a highly flammable gas that is potentially explosive. Hydrogen is lighter than air and will rise as it is produced. If sufficient ventilation is not available at the highest point above where a battery is being charged, hydrogen will collect at the overhead. Then, any source of ignition will cause an explosion and fire.

CAUTION!

Battery gases are highly explosive. Never smoke around a battery and never disconnect a battery until the surrounding space has been thoroughly ventilated.

Fire Theory, Classifications, and Fuel Sources

Overview

Introduction

As a boat crew member, you will need to understand the theory of fire, the different classifications of fire, and the types of fuels that perpetuate fires. This knowledge will enable boat crew members to identify the type of precautions, equipment, and extinguishing agents required to successfully fight fires.

In this section

Fire Theory

C.1. GENERAL

Fire is a chemical reaction known as combustion. It is defined as rapid oxidation of combustible material accompanied by a release of energy in the form of heat and light.

C.2. FIRE TRIANGLE

For years, a three-sided figure called the **fire triangle** has been used to describe the combustion and extinguishing theory. This theory states that proper proportions of oxygen, heat, and fuel are required for a fire. If any one of the 3 elements is removed, a fire will cease to exist (see Figure 18-1).

C.3. FIRE TETRAHEDRON

A new theory has been developed to further explain fire combustion and extinguishment. This theory can be represented by a four-sided geometric figure, a tetrahedron. The base of this figure represents a chemical reaction. The three standing sides of the figure represent heat, oxygen, and fuel. Removing one or more of the 4 sides will make a tetrahedron incomplete and cause a fire to be extinguished (see Figure 18-2).

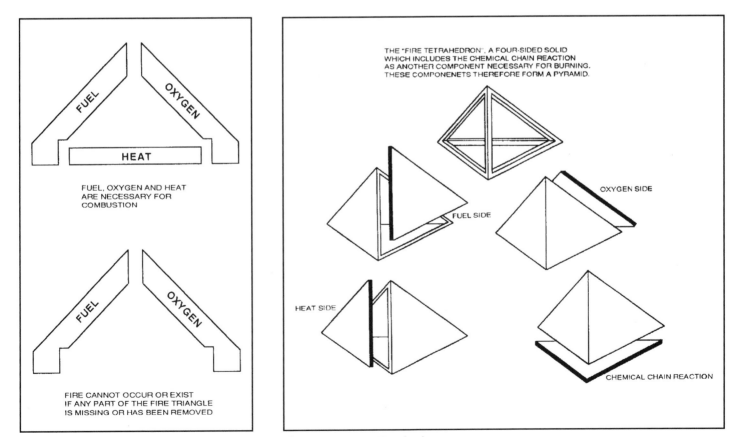

Figure 18-1 Fire Triangle

Figure 18-2 Fire Tetrahedron

Classifications of Fires and Fuel Sources

C.4. CLASS A

This class of fire involves common combustible materials. Fuel sources within this class include wood and wood-based materials, cloth, paper, rubber, and certain plastics.

C.5. CLASS B

This class of fire involves flammable or combustible liquids, flammable gases, greases, and similar products. Fuel sources within this class include petroleum products.

C.6. CLASS C

This class of fire involves energized electrical equipment, conductors, or appliances.

C.7. CLASS D

This class of fire involves combustible metals. Fuel sources within this class include sodium, potassium, magnesium, and titanium.

Extinguishing Agents

D.1. GENERAL

Extinguishing agents are defined as anything that eliminates one or more "sides" of a fire tetrahedron. When any one is removed, fire can no longer exist.

D.2. HOW IT WORKS

Extinguishing agents put out fires by breaking one or more of the four elements of a fire tetrahedron. They work by cooling, smothering, chain breaking, or by a process called oxygen dilution.

- **Cooling** reduces the temperature of a fuel source below the fuel's ignition point.

- **Smothering** separates a fuel source from its oxygen supply.

- **Chain Breaking** disrupts the chemical process necessary to sustain a fire. The element of a chain that is broken depends upon the class of fire and the type of extinguishing agent used.

- **Oxygen Dilution** is a smothering process that reduces the amount of oxygen available

to a level below that required to sustain combustion.

The different fire classes, the fuel source for each class, the type of extinguishing agent for each class, and the primary effect of each agent are described in the table at right.

Applying Extinguishing Agents

Overview

Introduction

Extinguishing agents can be applied in more than one way. Selecting the most appropriate method for applying extinguishing agents depends on the situation. Below are some general guidelines for applying different agents. Later we will address the equipment that must be used to apply these extinguishing agents.

In this section

Topic	See Page(s)
Applying Water	376–78
Applying Aqueous Film-Forming Foam (AFFF)	378
Applying Chemical Agents	378–79
Applying Halon	379–80
Applying FE-241	380

Applying Water

E.1. APPLYING WATER

On board Coast Guard vessels, water for firefighting comes from a built-in fire pump through the fire main and hose system. You apply water to a fire using one of three ways:

- Straight (solid) stream
- High-velocity fog
- Low-velocity fog

STRAIGHT (SOLID) STREAM A straight solid stream of water is used when long reach and penetrating power are critical. On Class A fires, its primary purpose is to break up burning material and to

Class	Fuel Sources	Primary Extinguishing Agent	Primary Effect
A	Common combustible materials such as wood and wood based materials, cloth, paper, rubber, and certain plastics.	• Water • ABC Dry Chemical	Removes the heat element.
B	Involves flammable or combustible liquids, flammable gasses, greases, petroleum products, and similar products.	• Foam AFFF (Aqueous Film Forming Foam) • CO_2 • PKP (dry chemical)	Removes the oxygen element.
C	Involves energized electrical equipment, conductors, or appliances.	• CO_2 (Carbon Dioxide) • PKP (dry chemical)	Removes the oxygen element, and temporarily removes elements of oxygen and heat.
D	Involves combustible metals, such as sodium, potassium, magnesium, and titanium.	• Water (high velocity fog) • Sand (placed underneath the metal)	Removes the heat and oxygen elements.

penetrate the base of a flame. Therefore, you must direct a solid stream at the base of flames in a Class A fire.

A solid stream of water is **not effective for extinguishing Class B fires**. It can cause a violent fire reaction if a water stream atomizes fuel into the air causing an increased surface area.

A straight solid stream can also be used on Class D fires for cooling and to wash burning materials over the side.

A straight solid stream of water should **not** be used on a Class C fire because it is a conductor of electricity and, therefore, could be hazardous to a firefighting team.

HIGH-VELOCITY FOG High-velocity fog is more useful than a solid stream on Class A fires. One reason is that high-velocity fog can cool a much wider surface than a steady stream and consequently, it can absorb more heat. Additionally, as fog comes into contact with any surface heated by fire, it becomes steam. Steam provides a secondary smothering effect which further aids in extinguishing the fire.

Because of the cooling qualities of finely divided water particles, you can use high-velocity fog successfully on Class B fires. You should use high-velocity fog on flammable liquids only when Aqueous Film-Forming Foam (see Section F.2) is not available.

When water is broken into small particles (nozzle fog patterns), there is little danger of it carrying electric current making high- or low-velocity fog safe to use on Class C fires. However, you should operate the nozzles at least four feet from a fire source.

NOTE

Nozzles can pose an electrical shock hazard to firefighters. If a nozzle or solid stream accidentally contacts electrical equipment or circuits, an electrical charge may be conducted back to the nozzle operator and cause injury.

Water is the recommended agent for Class D fires when applied in quantity as fog patterns. When water is applied to burning Class D materials, there may be small explosions. The fire fighter should apply water from a safe distance or from behind suitable shelter.

Class D materials will continue burning until the material is completely consumed but cooling streams of water can control the burn. However, your efforts should be directed at jettisoning or washing the materials over the side to avoid accumulating fire fighting water inside the vessel. Water fog can also be used to protect fire fighters from both convective and radiant heat.

LOW-VELOCITY FOG Low-velocity fog is applied with a vari-nozzle. Low-velocity fog is a less powerful pressurized spray than high-velocity fog. Because low-velocity fog covers more area than high-velocity fog, it may be used most effectively when you can get right up next to the fire.

Low-velocity water fog can also provide a heat shield by forming a screen of water droplets between a fire fighter and the fire. When firefighters are properly clothed and hose lines have vari-nozzles it is not necessary to use low-velocity water for personnel protection.

CAUTION!

Do not wet down the lead attack nozzleman. The combination of moisture and high temperature can cause steam burns.

Fog streams used improperly can injure personnel. The fog screen from high-velocity fog can obscure an attack nozzleman's visibility. This is extremely important to remember when no opening exists in the compartment or passageway other than the opening through which the nozzle is being advanced. In spaces with only one opening, heat and smoke can blow back or burst through or around a fog curtain. When circumstances require that you enter a compartment or passageway which has only one opening, direct short bursts of solid stream or fog toward the overhead to knock down the flames.

Using water as an extinguishing agent adds water and weight to a vessel. This can cause the vessel to become unstable. Normally, the water will be removed (dewatered) after the fire has been extinguished. However, to maintain stability and decrease the threat to your crew, dewater the vessel as soon as possible.

E.2. EFFECTIVENESS

Water can be effective on all classes of fire, when properly applied for the situation. However, it is most effective for Class A fires. It is recommended for use in Class D (combustible metals) fires for its cooling effect and ability to wash the material away.

Applying Aqueous Film-Forming Foam (AFFF)

E.3. APPLYING AQUEOUS FILM-FORMING FOAM (AFFF)

Foam is essentially a blanket of bubbles that extinguishes a fire mainly by smothering. The bubbles are formed by mixing water, air, and a foam-making agent called foam concentrate. The mixture of water, air, and foam concentrate becomes foam solution.

When using foam, you must coat the entire surface of a flame or uncovered areas will continue to burn. One gallon of liquid foam solution will produce about 133 gallons of mechanical foam. The contents of one 5-gallon can of liquid foam will last about 1½ minutes and will produce about 660 gallons of mechanical foam.

Foam may be used against Class C fires in an emergency and as a last resort. AFFF concentrate separates at temperatures below 35°F. This does not affect its usefulness provided you shake the can to re-mix components before use.

E.4. EFFECTIVENESS

Foam is effective against Class B fires. Foam solution is lighter than the lightest of flammable liquids. When applied to burning liquids, it floats on the surface and prevents oxygen from reaching the fuel source. In addition, the water content of foam provides a cooling effect on the fire.

Applying Chemical Agents

E.5. GENERAL

Chemical agents can be very effective firefighting tools. However, they can be ineffective and sometimes dangerous if they are not used properly. You must learn the proper use of each chemical agent, including its advantages and disadvantages, before using it to fight a fire. Two chemical agents are discussed below:

- Carbon Dioxide (CO_2)
- Potassium Bicarbonate (PKP)—most likely not found on Auxiliary facilities

E.6. CARBON DIOXIDE (CO_2)

CO_2 is a colorless gas about 50 percent heavier than air. When released from its container, the gas expands to 450 times its stored volume and smothers a fire by denying it oxygen. Because it is a non-conductor of electricity, **CO_2 is the primary agent used against electrical fires.** It can also be used effectively against an engine room fire. Additionally, CO_2 does not have to be cleaned up after use as does foam.

EFFECTIVENESS OF CO_2. CO_2 is effective on small class "A," "B," and "C" fires. It has a very limited cooling capacity and does not remove oxygen from a fuel source. Therefore, **CO_2 is only effective in knocking down flames.** Unless CO_2 is used continuously until all flames are extinguished, the fire could re-ignite (reflash). In fact, the likelihood of a reflash is greater when CO_2 is used against a fire than any other type of agent.

A continuous discharge of CO_2 from a fully charged 5 lb. extinguisher will last approximately 10 to 15 seconds. The effective range for the portable CO_2 extinguisher is approximately 5 feet. A distance of more than five feet may cause the CO_2 to mix with the air and become ineffective.

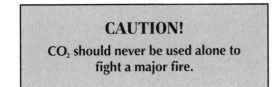

CAUTION!

CO_2 should never be used alone to fight a major fire.

DISCHARGING CO$_2$ CO_2 gas is not a conductor of electricity. However, when discharging the CO_2, static electricity may build up in the horn. This could be quite dangerous when extinguishing a fire where explosive gasses are present. CO_2 is most effective in closed spaces away from the effects of strong winds. The following are the operating procedures for the CO_2 extinguisher.

1. Remove the locking pin from the valve.

2. Carry the extinguisher in an upright position, approaching the fire as close as safety permits.

3. For the 5 lb. size, swing the horn up to a horizontal position.

4. Grasp the insulated horn handle and squeeze the release lever to start the extinguisher.

5. Direct the flow of CO_2 toward the *base* of the flame and attack the flame with a sweeping movement of the nozzle.

WARNING

CO_2 is extremely cold when discharged, and can "burn" or raise blisters. Keep hands on the insulated horn handle when using the CO_2 extinguisher.

E.7. POTASSIUM BICARBONATE (PKP)

PKP is also known as Purple K Powder. The ingredients used in PKP are non-toxic. When PKP is applied, a dense cloud is formed in the combustion area which limits the amount of heat that can be radiated back to the heart of the fire. Fewer fuel va-

pors are produced due to the reduced radiant heat. The dry chemical PKP extinguishes flames by breaking the combustion chain. PKP was developed to be used with AFFF.

EFFECTIVENESS OF PKP PKP does not have cooling capability. PKP may be effective as a temporary measure for extinguishing a flame, but it dissipates rapidly. Therefore, make certain all hot spots are cooled to prevent re-ignition. It is effective to some degree on all types of fires, but is particularly effective when used against burning liquids. Most extinguishers have an effective range of 10 to 12 feet and will last between 8–20 seconds in continuous use.

CAUTION!

PKP, like CO_2, should never be used against a major fire for it presents the same hazard of a reflash as CO_2.

DISCHARGING DRY CHEMICALS The dry chemical or powder contained in these portable containers is expelled by either a gas cartridge or by stored-pressure within the container. Following is the procedure for using this type of extinguisher.

1. Operate the dry chemical extinguisher by following the instructions printed on the extinguisher.

2. Control the discharge of the dry chemical by the nozzle shut-off valve for both cartridge-operated and pressurized dry chemical extinguishers.

3. Approach the fire as close as safety will allow.

4. Direct the discharge at the *base* of the flame and attack with a sweeping movement.

Applying Halon

E.8. GENERAL

Halon, a liquefied compressed gas, is odorless, colorless, and electrically nonconductive. Halon differs from the other extinguishing agents in the way it extinguishes fires. It has some of water's cooling effect and some of CO_2's smothering power, but Halon actually reacts chemically with the fire to interrupt the chain reaction that causes fire to spread. This process is known as "chain breaking," which was discussed in Section D of this chapter.

Halon flooding systems are typically used to extinguish fires in machinery spaces where Class C fires occur.

E.9. STORAGE AND SAFETY

All Halon is stored in liquid form in steel storage cylinders. Inside the cylinders, liquid Halon is pressurized using super-pressurized nitrogen. When activated, Halon is expelled as a gas. A Halon flooding system rapidly distributes a 5- to 7-percent concentration evenly throughout any space.

After a Halon system has been discharged in a confined space, the ventilation system must be run on high for a minimum of 15 minutes before personnel re-enter that space without a breathing devices. On vessels that have no mechanical ventilation, the space must be thoroughly ventilated using natural ventilation.

> **CAUTION!**
>
> **Personnel should not remain in a space where Halon has been released unless an oxygen breathing apparatus (OBA) is worn.**

E.10. EFFECTIVENESS

The mechanism by which Halon extinguishes a fire is not thoroughly understood. Halon acts by removing active chemical spaces involved in a flame chain reaction. Halon complements a total firefighting system as a final line of defense after other alternatives such as portable extinguishers have been used.

Applying FE-241

E.11. APPLYING FE-241

Like Halon, FE-241 is a liquefied compressed gas. It is classified as "clean agent," meaning it leaves no residue when used to extinguish fires. Its chemical name is Chlorotetrafluoroethane. Like Halon, it extinguishes fire by interfering *chemically* with the combustion process. However, FE-241 is an environmentally safe U.S. Coast Guard approved and EPA-accepted Halon alternate extinguishing agent. This means that FE-241 can be used in place of Halon to extinguish Class C fires.

Firefighting Equipment

Overview

Introduction

Specialized equipment is used to apply extinguishing agents. In this section, you will learn the "basics" of how to operate the most common kinds of firefighting equipment found on Coast Guard boats.

In this section

Fire Hose

F.1. GENERAL

Fire hoses are a basic firefighting tool. Although taken for granted, hoses are highly developed tools that must be used and cared for properly.

F.2. DESCRIPTION

A standard fire hose is a double-jacketed, cotton or nylon-impregnated, rubber-lined hose (orange in color). It comes in 2 common diameters: 1½-inch or 2½-inch and is produced in standard lengths of 50 feet. A length of fire hose on Coast Guard boats must be shorter than a standard length because of limited space. The 1½-inch hoses are available in 25 and 50-foot lengths and 2½-inch hoses come in 30-foot lengths.

F.3. SAFETY PRECAUTIONS

Before using a fire hose, you must perform several safety checks. These checks may seem needlessly time consuming at a fire scene. Nonetheless, they must be performed to prevent a malfunction in a hose system which could cause you to lose even more time. The following checks should be performed:

- Make certain all hose connections are tight and a hose is free of kinks and twists.

- Ensure the bail on a nozzle is closed before a hose is charged.

- Never lay a hose on an excessively hot deck.

- Be sure there are enough people available to control a fire hose before charging it. Never leave a charged hose unattended.

CAUTION!
A charged hose has considerable force and can swing out of control.

F.4. OPERATING PROCEDURES

A minimum of 2 people are recommended to control a 1½-inch hose.

F.5. COUPLING

A fire hose has brass or metal fittings, known as male and female couplings at its ends. This allows one hose to be attached to another or to a fitting. A female coupling connects to a boat's fire main. A male coupling connects to a nozzle or to a female coupling on another length of hose. To connect lengths of fire hose, take half a turn to the left on the female coupling to set the threads. Then turn to the right until the connection is tight. Fittings should be hand tight (see Figure 18-3).

F.6. MAINTENANCE

Remove dirt, grease, abrasives, and other foreign matter from the outer coverings of hoses. Clean fire hoses with a mild soap and water solution (inside and out). Do not use abrasives to clean hoses. After use, hoses must be stowed. To properly stow a fire hose, perform the following:

- Check a hose to make sure it is completely drained.

- Ensure that a proper gasket is in place inside the female coupling and that it is not cracked or damaged.

- Roll hoses so the male coupling is lying between hose layers to prevent damage to a coupling's threads. This also allows the female coupling to be connected, and hose rolled out without twisting.

Spanner Wrench

F.7. GENERAL

Spanner wrenches are very important when working with fire hoses. They are necessary to properly couple hoses together, to attach other equipment to hoses, or to attach hoses to water sources.

F.8. DESCRIPTION

A spanner wrench is adjustable so that is can be used with all standard sizes of fire hoses. A range of adjustment is indicated on the handle of a wrench. A curved tip on the working end of a wrench is made to fit all notches in a coupling.

F.9. SAFETY PRECAUTIONS

As with using any wrench, be careful not to get fingers or other objects caught between the wrench and the coupling. Ensure the working end of the wrench is in the notch before applying heavy pressure.

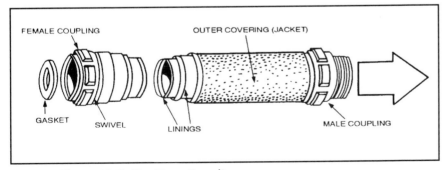

Figure 18-3 Fire Hose Coupling

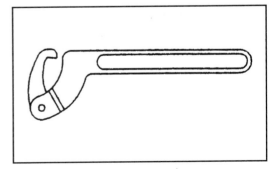

Figure 18-4 Spanner Wrench

F.10. OPERATING PROCEDURES

On properly maintained hoses, connections may be effectively tightened by hand. However, if there is water leakage at a connection, a spanner wrench may be used. Once a wrench is adjusted, just insert the tip of a wrench into the notch and pull the wrench handle to the right (see Figure 18-4).

F.11. MAINTENANCE

Spanner wrenches must be de-rusted and greased or oiled periodically.

Wye-Gate

F.12. GENERAL

Wye-gates are important firefighting tools. They allow a single stream of fire fighting water to be divided into 2 streams.

F.13. DESCRIPTION

The wye-gate is a Y-shaped fitting used to reduce fire hose line size and allow use of two separate hoses. It has one female 2½-inch inlet opening and two 1½-inch male outlet openings. A female end attaches to a fire main or between fire hose lengths (the 2½-inch being reduced to 1½-inch fire hoses). Male openings receive two 1½-inch fire hoses.

F.14. OPERATING PROCEDURES

A wye-gate makes it possible to fight fire with 2 hoses. A flow of water through each of the 1½-inch openings may be regulated or secured with the valves or gates. The two gates are independent of each other, so one can be closed while the other is open. A gate is opened or closed with a quarter turn. Figure 18-5 shows a wye-gate with one open and one closed gate. Note the gate position for each (see Figure 18-5).

F.15. MAINTENANCE

Wye-gates must be cleaned periodically of corrosion and greased or oiled.

Tri-Gate

F.16. TRI-GATE

Tri-gates, like wye-gates, divide a single stream of fire fighting water. However, they divide a single stream into three separate streams instead of only two streams.

F.17. DESCRIPTION

A tri-gate is another fitting to which fire hoses are frequently connected. A tri-gate has two 2½-inch openings and two 1½-inch openings. A tri-gate, like a wye-gate, is used when you must fight a fire with multiple fire hoses (see Figure 18-6).

F.18. SAFETY PRECAUTIONS

While both wye-gates and tri-gates allow additional fire hoses to be directed against a fire, their use may result in a large water pressure drop at the nozzle.

F.19. OPERATING PROCEDURES

The gates or valves on a tri-gate control the flow of water in the same fashion as regulating gates on a wye-gate. To use the tri-gate use the following procedures:

1. Break out the tri-gate
2. Connect the tri-gate to the fire main.

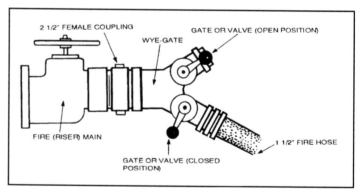

Figure 18-5 Wye-Gate Attached to Fire Main

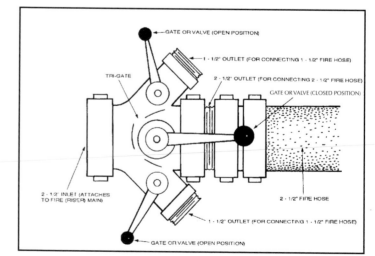

Figure 18-6 Tri-Gate

3. Connect a length of 2½" fire hose to the tri-gate.

4. Connect a length of 1½" fire hose to the tri-gate.

5. Place the gate regulating handle of the 2½" and 1½" hose outlets of the tri-gate of which the hoses are connect in the "OPEN" position.

6. Ensure the regulating gate of the second 1½" outlet is in the "CLOSED" position.

7. Charge the fire hoses (assisted by other crew members).

8. Check the tri-gate, valves, and hose connections for water leakage; tighten with a spanner wrench, if necessary.

F.20. MAINTENANCE

Tri-gates periodically must be cleaned of corrosion and greased or oiled.

Vari-Nozzle

F.21. GENERAL

This type of nozzle can be used for fighting all classes of fires and for personnel protection.

F.22. DESCRIPTION

A Navy vari-nozzle is fitted with a pistol grip handle on the underside of the nozzle. A bail handle opens and closes the nozzle. A 90° pattern is achieved at the wide angle setting. A vari-nozzle is a variable stream fog nozzle that is adjustable from straight stream to wide angle fog as well as intermediate patterns between these extremes.

F.23. OPERATING PROCEDURES

This nozzle is used with AFFF for extinguishing Class B fires (see Figure 18-7).

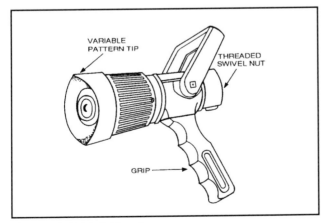

Figure 18-7 Vari-Nozzle

F.24. MAINTENANCE

Clean a nozzle with a mild solution of soap and water. Do not use abrasives to clean nozzles. After use, stow the nozzle. You should always stow a vari-nozzle with the bail handle in closed position with the nozzle set to a narrow angle (30° pattern) fog.

Fire Monitor

F.25. GENERAL

A fire monitor allows boats to stay away a safe distance while fighting large dock-side or shipboard fires (see Figure 18-8).

F.26. DESCRIPTION

A fire monitor mounts on top of the forward bitt of a Coast Guard 41-foot UTB. It is capable of projecting a solid stream of water over 130 feet to support major firefighting efforts.

Water is provided to the monitor by a fire pump installed on board the vessel. The pump is driven by a power take-off from the starboard main engine. When the fire pump is engaged, use of the starboard engine is limited and this, in turn, may restrict the capability and maneuverability of a vessel.

F.27. SAFETY PRECAUTIONS

A fire monitor is heavy to lift and awkward to handle. Do not attempt to mount it with a boat operating at more than idle speed or when a boat is rolling heavily, as the fire monitor may fall and seriously injure a crew member or it may be lost overboard.

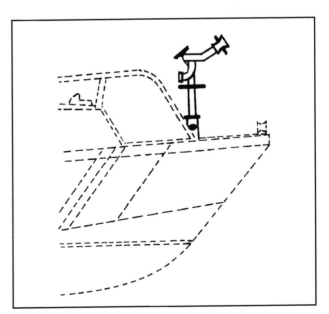

Figure 18-8 Fire Monitor

F.28. OPERATING PROCEDURES

Crew members designated by a coxswain should follow these steps to mount and operate a fire monitor on a 41-foot UTB.

1. Remove the forward bitt cover and place a mounting bracket for a fire monitor in the hole provided. Turn the mounting bracket until it locks into position.

2. Put the fire monitor on a stanchion and tighten the two hand screws to secure it into position.

3. Connect a tri-gate to the vessel's fire main.

4. Connect a 30-foot length of 2½-inch fire hose to the tri-gate and lead it forward alongside the pilot house.

5. Connect the other end of this 2½-inch hose to the fire monitor and tighten all connections with a spanner wrench.

6. Connect a 25-foot length of 1½-inch fire hose to the tri-gate and tighten all connections. This additional length of hose will serve as a backup hose to assist and protect an operator of a fire monitor.

7. At this point, other members of a boat crew will engage the fire pump and bring water pressure up to 100 PSI.

8. A fire monitor operator should now be in position and ready to operate the monitor. Other crew members should now assume control of the 1½-inch backup hose before continuing.

9. Charge the fire main and open tri-gate valves to charge the monitor and a backup hose.

10. Direct the fire monitor's stream at an appropriate area of a fire and adjust the water stream by turning a wheel atop the monitor.

11. Turn the control handle on the fire monitor nozzle to adjust a water stream from full fog to straight stream.

NOTE

If a fire monitor has been mounted for some time while a vessel has been underway, vibration may have loosened some connections. Check and re-tighten mounting stanchion and hose connections before charging hoses with water pressure.

In-Line Proportioner

F.29. GENERAL

An in-line proportioner is a device that mixes water and AFFF in proper proportions to create effective foam for firefighting. This is the same function performed by a mechanical foam nozzle. **However, an in-line proportioner may be placed between hoses away from the actual fire** while a mechanical foam nozzle mixes water, air, and AFFF at the nozzle. This difference avoids restricting the mobility of a nozzle operator as does a mechanical foam nozzle.

F.30. DESCRIPTION

Foam is applied by using an in-line proportioner with a mechanical foam nozzle or vari-nozzle. An in-line proportioner is inserted in a fire hose line, between the fire main and a nozzle, and supplies mechanical foam to a nozzle. It may be placed at convenient distances from a fire (see Figure 18-9).

F.31. OPERATING PROCEDURES

Procedures for operating an in-line proportioner are described below:

1. Attach the proportioner to a fire main.

2. Attach the male end of a fire hose (water supply) to the female end of the proportioner.

3. Attach a mechanical foam nozzle or vari-nozzle.

4. Remove the cap from a container of foam concentrate.

5. Insert the metal end of a pickup tube (crow's foot) into a container of foam concentrate.

6. Staff a fire hose and turn on the water.

Mechanical Foam Nozzle

F.32. MECHANICAL FOAM NOZZLE

A mechanical foam nozzle is a device that mixes water, air, and AFFF in proper proportions to produce effective fire fighting foam.

F.33. DESCRIPTION

A mechanical foam nozzle is attached to a standard fire hose running from the fire main system. It draws air in through air ports located in the water inlet end of a foam nozzle. When air and foam concentrate mix in a nozzle, foam is discharged toward a fire (see Figure 18-10).

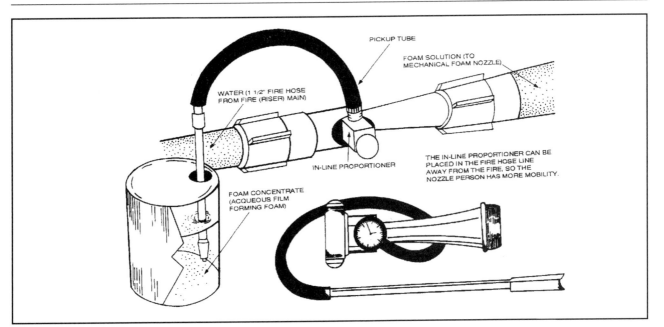

Figure 18-9 In-Line Proportioner

F.34. SAFETY PRECAUTIONS

A person operating a mechanical foam nozzle must be aware that the range of mobility is limited by the length of the pickup hose leading to a container of foam concentrate. If a nozzle operator moves too far, the pickup tube will lose suction and the nozzle will begin to discharge only water, not foam. Depending on the type of fire being fought, this may be very dangerous.

F.35. OPERATING PROCEDURES

The following steps describe a prescribed operating procedure for a mechanical foam nozzle.

1. Remove any other nozzle from the end of a fire hose.

2. Attach a 1½-inch mechanical foam nozzle to the fire hose.

3. Remove the plug from the butt end of the nozzle.

4. Screw the hose end of a pickup tube into the butt end of the nozzle.

5. Crew members must now take control of this hose and nozzle assembly, then charge it with water pressure.

6. Remove the cap from a container of foam concentrate.

7. Insert the metal end of a pickup tube (a crow's foot) firmly into a container of foam concentrate.

8. Direct a stream of foam at the appropriate part of a fire.

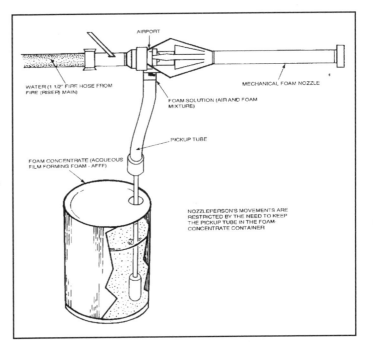

Figure 18-10 Mechanical Foam Nozzle

Drop Pump and AFFF

F.36. GENERAL

Use of a drop pump allows AFFF concentrate to be proportioned with water, adequately agitated, and delivered at a relatively high rate. A drop pump is designed to pump a large volume of water at low pressure.

F.37. DESCRIPTION

A P1 or P5 drop pump is designed to pump a large volume of water at low pressure. The drop pump is not intended for firefighting and therefore is not equipped with fire hose connections.

F.38. SAFETY PRECAUTIONS

AFFF must be mixed with water. Do not apply it to a fire directly from its container or when it has been mixed with water manually, i.e., without using a mechanical foam nozzle or a drop pump.

There are drawbacks to using a drop pump in place of a mechanical foam nozzle. Once a canister is empty, foam application must be halted so it can be refilled. In addition, the quality and density of foam is not optimum.

F.39. OPERATING PROCEDURES

It is not possible to apply mechanical foam with a drop pump in the conventional way by using an in-line proportioner and/or a mechanical foam nozzle. However, a drop pump can still be used for foam delivery by following the procedure below:

1. Break a pump out from its storage container and set it up to take suction.

2. Fill the storage container with water using the pump discharge hose. It will hold about 38 gallons of water.

3. Pour about 2 gallons of AFFF (about one-third of a standard AFFF container) into the pump's storage container.

4. After the storage container is full of water/AFFF mixture, transfer the pump's suction hose from over the side to the storage container (suction is taken from there). A discharge hose is about 15 feet in length. Use it as if it were a mechanical foam nozzle to fight fire in a conventional manner. This method allows a high volume of foam (AFFF) to be delivered in a short period of time.

Fire Axe

F.40. GENERAL

Coast Guard boats are equipped with a type of fire axe referred to as a "pike head axe."

F.41. DESCRIPTION

A pike head axe has a wooden handle securely attached to an axe head. The axe head has 2 different ends. One is a typical broad head blade, well sharpened along the leading edge. The other end of the head, the pike, is pointed and is also well sharpened.

F.42. SAFETY PRECAUTIONS

Crew members must always wear gloves, goggles, and other protective clothing when using axes to force a door or break glass.

F.43. OPERATING PROCEDURES

The pike, or pointed end of an axe, is used to break through light metal like that found in metal fire doors, to make quick openings that can be used to check for smoke and intensity of a fire. It may also be used for tearing apart mattresses or for shattering glass. The broad or blade end of an axe can be used to pry doors open, to pry other objects apart, to remove paneling, or to chop doors open.

F.44. MAINTENANCE

Both blade and pike should be kept sharp and oiled. The handle must always be tightly fitted into the head of an axe. It must be free of splits and splinters and should never be painted (see Figure 18-11).

Carbon Dioxide (CO$_2$) Extinguishers

F.45. CARBON DIOXIDE (CO$_2$) EXTINGUISHERS

Portable CO$_2$ extinguishers are used primarily for putting out electrical fires but they are effective on any small fire including burning oil, gasoline, paint, and trash cans.

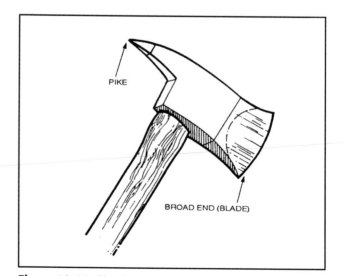

PIKE

BROAD END (BLADE)

Figure 18-11 Fire Axe

F.46. DESCRIPTION

A 10-pound cylinder is the standard CO_2 extinguisher used on Coast Guard small boats. The effective range of this extinguisher is approximately 5 feet from the outer edge of the horn. Once activated, the extinguisher will provide from 40 to 45 seconds of continuous use.

F.47. SAFETY PRECAUTIONS

When CO_2 is released from a container, it expands rapidly to 450 times its stored volume. This rapid expansion causes the gas temperature to drop to near 110°F below zero and form CO_2 "snow." Do not permit snow to come in contact with your skin because it will cause painful blisters (see Figure 18-12).

> **WARNING**
>
> CO_2 is extremely cold and can burn or raise blisters. Keep your hands on the insulated horn handle when using a cylinder.

F.48. OPERATING PROCEDURES

Procedures for using the CO_2 fire extinguisher are as follows:

1. Remove a locking pin from the valve.

2. Carry an extinguisher in an upright position and approach a fire until you are as close as possible.

3. Grasp the insulated horn handle and squeeze the release lever to activate an extinguisher. **Keep a cylinder grounded by touching it to a deck.**

4. Direct a flow of CO_2 at the base of flames.

Dry Chemical Extinguishers (PKP)

F.49. DRY CHEMICAL EXTINGUISHERS (PKP)

PKP extinguishers are primarily used for Class B fires.

F.50. DESCRIPTION

PKP is nontoxic and is four times as effective as CO_2 for extinguishing fuel fires. A PKP extinguisher

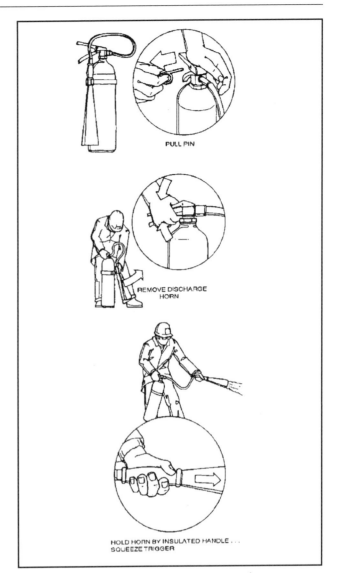

PULL PIN

REMOVE DISCHARGE HORN

HOLD HORN BY INSULATED HANDLE . . . SQUEEZE TRIGGER

Figure 18-12 Operating the CO_2 Extinguisher

has an effective range of about 20 feet from the end of its nozzle and will provide from 18 to 20 seconds continuous use (see Figure 18-13).

F.51. SAFETY PRECAUTIONS

PKP is effective on Class C fires, but it should not be used if CO_2 is available. PKP leaves behind a messy residue which can be avoided by using CO_2. Also, long discharges of PKP reduce visibility and may cause breathing difficulties and induce coughing. In confined spaces, PKP should **always** be used sparingly.

PKP is an excellent firefighting agent, but its effects are temporary. It has no cooling effect and provides no protection against reflash of a fire. Therefore, its use should always be immediately followed by an application of foam. A PKP extinguisher should not be pressurized until it is to be used.

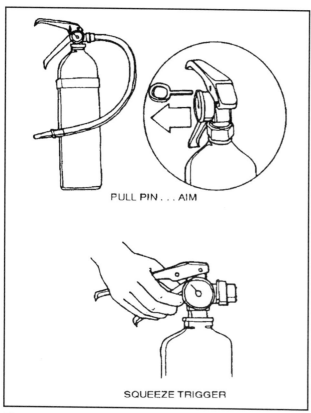

PULL PIN . . . AIM

SQUEEZE TRIGGER

Figure 18-13 Dry Chemical Extinguisher

F.52. OPERATING PROCEDURES

Procedures for using this extinguisher are explained below:

1. Check an extinguisher to ensure that its fill cap is tight.

2. Pull a locking pin from the cutter assembly.

3. Stand to one side of the bottle and push down on the puncture lever (marked push) to cut a seal on the CO_2 cartridge.

4. Approach a fire from the windward side and always remain at least 8 feet away from flames.

5. Discharge the chemical in short bursts by squeezing the nozzle grip. Direct chemical at the base of flames and sweep it rapidly from side to side. If a fire's heat is intense, a short burst of powder into the air will provide a heat shield.

Firefighting Procedures

Overview

Introduction

In the previous paragraphs you learned how to classify fires and use the classification system to select an appropriate extinguishing agent. You also learned how to use available boat firefighting equipment to apply extinguishing agents. The following paragraphs will explain some safety precautions you must observe when fighting fire as well as some tactical procedures to follow.

In this section

Topic	See Page(s)
Coast Guard's Firefighting Duty	**388**
Safety Precautions	**388–89**
Operations	**389–90**
Action	**390–91**

Coast Guard's Firefighting Duty

G.1. GENERAL

Boat crew members must always remember that boat crews are **not** firefighting professionals. According to the Coast Guard Firefighting Activities Policy, boat crews are to support firefighting professionals if necessary. However, if a boat crew were to be first on the scene of a boat fire or be the victims of a boat fire, their primary responsibility is to save **lives**, not property. Evacuate all people from a burning vessel, and then follow a Risk Assessment Plan if capable.

Refer to Section A of this chapter to view the Coast Guard Firefighting Activities Policy, and to Chapter 4 for discussion of a Risk Management Plan.

Safety Precautions

G.2. GENERAL

Firefighting can be very hazardous to anyone involved. Coast Guard personnel must always be alert and aware of their actions and decisions to avoid being injured or incapacitated performing firefighting duties that are not their responsibility.

Firefighting at sea is extremely dangerous and is often best left to professionals.

Losing the services of any Coast Guard person may keep a boat crew from preventing other injuries, loss of life, or loss of property. Refer to Chapter 4 of this manual for a discussion of risk assessment and risk management.

G.3. SALVORS AND MARINE CHEMISTS

Shipboard and waterfront fires frequently involve toxic or chemical hazards for firefighters. These hazards may be a source of fire or may be produced as a by-product of fire. Therefore, caution must be exercised and properly trained assistance **requested before becoming involved in fighting a fire**.

Many salvage companies operate over a wide geographic area. Thus, these companies can respond more quickly to these situations. In addition, they employ marine chemists who can obtain temperature readings, check for the presence and concentrations of gases, and can provide information to firefighting forces about chemical hazards they may encounter during response activities.

G.4. SMOKE PLUMES

Coxswains must always stay well clear of smoke plumes rising from a fire because they greatly reduce visibility and can pose a health hazard. Smoke is a visible product of fire and carries water vapor, acids, and other chemicals produced by fire and can be irritating or toxic when inhaled. A smoke plume is made of suspended particles of carbon and other unburned substances. These products of combustion are released into the atmosphere and travel downwind.

STAY UPWIND As a plume expands downwind and outward from a fire, toxic products will be less concentrated. The more toxic a product is, the larger the unsafe area will be, both downwind and to the sides of a plume. The decision to set a perimeter upwind of a toxic smoke or fire plume must be considered and executed when prudent. Individuals who remain a safe distance upwind should not be affected by unseen dangers of a smoke plume.

NOTE

Generally speaking, remaining upwind of the fire provides a safe area away from toxic hazards that are released in a fire plume.

SAFE DISTANCE Other decisions such as determining a safe distance from a plume of smoke should be made and constantly reevaluated as an incident develops. Any change in weather conditions could dictate a need to increase the initial size of a perimeter. If you can see a smoke plume and feel radiant heat, you are considered to be within a danger zone.

GASES AND VAPORS Smoke plumes also have other factors that must be considered such as the behavior of gases or vapors that extend beyond a perimeter of visible smoke and fire. Burning plastics and rubber products produce gases, heat, flame, and smoke. These by-products may contain elements of a toxic or lethal nature.

There are many other products of combustion which are dangerous and can be lethal under certain conditions.

Operations

G.5. GENERAL

A boat crew is faced with several responsibilities and decisions when a vessel or waterfront fire occurs. Decisions made may affect lives, millions of dollars in property, and free flow of maritime commerce. When determining a unit's assistance posture, consider the following:

- Level of the threat of fire
- Jurisdictions involved
- Capabilities of local fire departments
- Availability of Coast Guard equipment

- Level of Coast Guard training

Generally, Coast Guard personnel shall not engage in independent firefighting operations except to save a life or in the early stages of a fire, where they may avert a significant threat without undue risk. Coast Guard personnel shall not engage in firefighting (on other than Coast Guard units) except in support of a regular firefighting organization and under the supervision of a qualified fire officer.

NOTE

A qualified fire officer is a person who has been trained and certified, under National Fire Protection Association guidelines, to take command of firefighting operations.

G.6. PERSONNEL TRAINING

Coast Guard personnel engaged in firefighting operations must be properly trained and equipped for the task they are assigned. Therefore, the level of Coast Guard involvement is dependent available leadership, experience, training, and equipment.

Coast Guard planning and training efforts must be integrated with those of other responsible agencies, particularly local fire departments and port authorities. This is especially important for fires on large vessels and shore structures. Captains of the Port (COTPs) work closely with municipal fire departments, vessel and facility owners and operators, mutual aid groups, and other interested organizations. COTPs have developed a firefighting contingency plan which addresses firefighting in each port in the COTP zone.

Action

G.7. GENERAL

When a Coast Guard boat crew becomes involved in firefighting operations the situation will typically be one that fosters a great sense of urgency to extinguish a fire as rapidly as possible. All members of a boat crew must remember that haste and lack of a coordinated effort by boat crew members can recklessly endanger a boat and all crew members.

G.8. CREW BRIEF

A boat coxswain must brief crew members before arriving at the scene of a fire. This briefing details each crew member's assignments and emphasizes safety. Crew members are responsible for all duties assigned and must request clarification from the coxswain if they do not clearly understand the tasks assigned. Break out all necessary gear. All personnel must don *battle dress* before arriving on scene. *Battle dress* means that everyone will button their collars, wear gloves, don PFDs, and tuck trouser legs into their socks. The coxswain is responsible for inspecting all other crew members and making certain that battle dress has been donned.

G.9. INITIAL ACTION

Approach the boat from upwind. Immediately upon arriving on scene, all crew members should check the surrounding vicinity for persons in the water. Recover and evacuate all survivors to the Coast Guard vessel. Evaluate their physical conditions and render first aid if necessary. However, if the extent of injury requires more than minor first aid, evacuate survivors to another rescue vessel to immediately transport them for professional medical assistance. Inform operational command or Emergency Medical Service (EMS) of the situation. These steps are to be taken **before** attacking the fire. Remember, **life comes before property**. If there are no survivors or those recovered are in good physical condition and have been evacuated to a safe place, the next step is to stop and evaluate the fire.

G.10. SITUATION EVALUATION

As coxswain and crew you must evaluate the following elements of the situation:

- Location and extent of a fire
- Class of fire
- Class and extent of all cargo involved
- Possibility of explosion
- Possibility of any vessel involved sinking/capsizing within a navigable channel
- Hazard to your crew
- Maneuverability of your vessel
- Weather forecast
- Risk of a serious pollution incident

WARNING

If you are not certain what the risk of explosion is, back off a safe distance and establish a safety zone. Do not attempt to fight the fire.

If a fire can be put out with no danger to your crew or your vessel, proceed. If not, back off and maintain a safety zone so that no other vessel comes

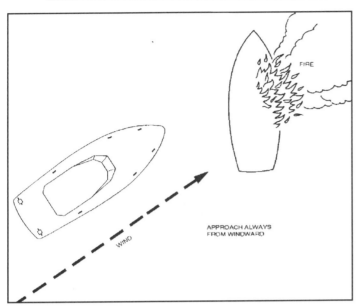

Figure 18-14 Approaching a Boat on Fire

too close to the fire scene. After completing your initial evaluation, you need to reevaluate a fire scene/situation frequently. A small fire can rage out of control in minutes and threaten more property and cargo. If you must approach a fire at any time, remember to always approach from windward (see Figure 18-14).

> **CAUTION!**
> Your decision regarding your
> role in the overall situation must
> be constantly reexamined.

If it becomes necessary to tie up alongside a burning vessel to fight a fire or to remove survivors, attach only one line to it and keep a sharp knife accessible for a quick break away.

G.11. OVERHAULING

Danger will still exist after a fire is believed to be extinguished. The process of overhauling the fire is done to avoid fire reflash. When a fire is out, check for hot spots and set a reflash watch. When danger of reflash is no longer a concern, dewater the distressed vessel.

Extinguishing Fires

Overview

Introduction

A fire discovered early and quickly fought can usually be extinguished easily. Portable fire extinguishers are used for a fast attack that will knock down flames. However, they contain a limited supply of extinguishing agent. Crew members with limited training in using of these extinguishers often waste extinguishing agent by using them improperly. Periodic training, including practice with actual types of extinguishers carried on board boats, will ensure proficient use of this equipment. Extinguishers that are due to be discharged and inspected should be used for training.

In this section

Safety Rules

H.1. GENERAL

The following safety rules should be observed when using portable fire extinguishers:

- **Immediately** upon discovering a fire, sound an alarm and summon help.

- Never pass a fire to get to an extinguisher.

- If you must enter a compartment to combat a fire, keep an escape path open. Never let a fire get between you and a door, hatch, or scuttle. Stay low.

- If you enter a compartment and fail to extinguish a fire with a portable fire extinguisher,

get out. Then close the door, hatch, or scuttle to confine the fire.

Fire Combat

H.2. GENERAL

An attack should be started immediately to gain control and to prevent extension of a fire to other areas of a boat. An attack will be either **direct** or **indirect**, depending on the fire situation. Both methods are efficient when properly employed.

H3. DIRECT ATTACK

In a direct attack, crew members advance to the immediate area of a fire and apply extinguishing agent directly on a fire, if a fire is small and has not gained headway. Once a fire has gained headway, an indirect attack should be used.

H.4. INDIRECT ATTACK

An indirect attack is best when it is impossible for crew members to reach a fire. Generally, this is in the lower portions of a boat, such as the engine room and bilge areas. The success of an indirect attack depends on completely containing a fire. **Every possible avenue a fire may travel must be cut off by closing doors, hatches, and scuttles and by securing all ventilation systems.**

Firefighting Procedures on Coast Guard Boats

H.5. PROCEDURES

Every fire will quickly spread to new sources of fuel or oxygen if they are available. However, the path through which a particular fire extends will depend on the location of a fire and the construction of surrounding spaces. These factors must be considered when fighting a fire. In addition, fuel and all products of its combustion will affect fire fighting operations. For these reasons, no fire can be fought routinely, and all fires must be fought systematically. The procedures described below should be part of every firefighting operation.

1. Sound an alarm. Any crew member who discovers a fire or any indication of fire must sound an alarm and give a location, e.g., "FIRE, FIRE, FIRE IN THE BILGES."

2. Evaluate a fire.
   * Determine the air supply to the fire.
   * Determine the class of fire (combustible material).

* Determine the fuel source to the fire.
* Select proper extinguishing agent.
* Determine method for fighting a fire (direct or indirect).
* Determine how to prevent spread of a fire.
* Determine required equipment and crew member assignments.

3. Determine the need to secure:
   * Electrical and electronic power panels.
   * Power to individual electrical and electronic equipment (alternator, radar, inverters).
   * Engine and fuel supply.
   * Air intakes (ventilation system, doors, hatches and scuttles).

4. Place all equipment necessary to combat a fire in an open deck area. This includes:
   * Portable fire extinguishers
   * Fire axe
   * Fire hoses
   * AFFF
   * Drop pump
   * First aid kit

5. Combat a fire with appropriate extinguishing agent(s).

6. Notify your parent unit at the earliest opportunity. Keep them fully advised of your situation.
   * Give position
   * Nature of fire
   * Number of persons on board
   * Your intentions
   * Keep them advised of changing situation and status of personnel

7. Overhaul a fire.
   * Inspect all overhead spaces, decks, and bulkheads.
   * Check where wiring and piping penetrate through bulkheads and decks.
   * Expose areas that are charred, blistered, or discolored by heat until a clean area is found.
   * Pull apart and examine any materials that might have been involved with the fire for hidden fire and hot embers. Jettison (throw overboard) all such material if necessary.
   * Set a reflash watch. One crew member must be assigned to do nothing but check for re-ignition and to sound an alarm if it occurs.

8. Restow all firefighting equipment.

- Recharge or replace portable fire extinguishers, even if only partially used, immediately upon arrival back at your unit.
- Replace used fire hoses with dry hoses. Drain, clean, dry, and roll up used hoses for storage.

9. Conduct a damage control check. Start any necessary dewatering operations.

> ## CAUTION!
> **Never fight a fire, however small it may seem, until an alarm has been sounded. Once a fire gains intensity, it spreads swiftly.**

> ## CAUTION!
> **Water can impair the stability of a boat. Make every effort to limit accumulation of water in compartments. Give preference to fog sprays over solid streams of water. Use only as much water as is absolutely necessary.**

Firefighting Procedures on Auxiliary Boats

H.6. PROCEDURES

Use the following procedures when battling a fire on an Auxiliary boat. When a crew member becomes aware of an engine compartment fire:

1. Shut off all engines, generators, and ventilation systems.

2. If boat is equipped with an automatic extinguishing system, ensure it is discharging. If the system is manually operated, energize it and check to ensure it is discharging.

3. Initiate a MAYDAY call to alert boats in the area of the situation.

4. Have all crew members don PFDs and everyone move to a smoke-free and flame-free area of the boat.

5. If a life raft or dinghy is available, put it over the side and inflate it, if necessary.

6. • If boat has a built-in CO_2 system, after fire is out, allow time for concentrations of CO_2 to ventilate to the atmosphere before entering the compartment.

- On boats fitted with a Halon system, the danger of toxic gases is not as great when entering the compartment, but always enter with caution.

H.7. OPENING A HATCH

If someone must open a hatch to discharge a portable extinguisher, expect the possibility of burned hands and/or a singed face. As the fresh air enters the compartment, it will feed the fire, and cause it to "blow up." The best method of opening a hatch is to stand to the hinged side of the hatch. Then while wearing gloves or using something other than bare hands, pull the hatch open. If the boat has a closed engine compartment and no fixed system, it is a good idea to make a small hole with a pivoted cover into the space. A portable extinguisher may be discharged through this hole. (See Figure 18-15.)

Fires Aboard Other Boats

H.8. PROCEDURES

Use the following procedures when battling a fire aboard other boats.

1. Brief crew members on appropriate procedures.

2. Assign each crew member specific duties.

3. While en route to the scene, establish communications with the distressed boat.

4. Approach the boat from upwind. Do not tie any lines to the distressed boat.

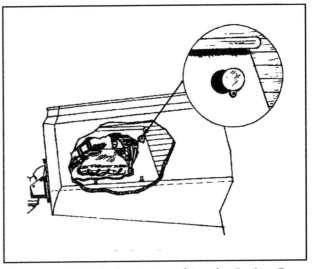

Figure 18-15 Hole for Extinguishing the Engine Compartment

5. If no one onboard, circle the boat (at a safe distance) searching for person in the water.

6. Advise all persons aboard the boat to move to a flame and smoke-free area, topside.

7. Attempt to determine the extent and source of the fire. If it is not obvious, ask the personnel aboard the distressed boat where the fire is located.

8. If the fire is beyond the crew members' fire fighting capabilities, evacuate the persons from the distressed boat and call for assistance.

9. If the fire is small and within the crew members capabilities, transfer the victims to the rescue boat.

10. Fight the fire in the same manner as a fire on an Auxiliary boat.

Fire Under Control

H.9. GENERAL

Under the following circumstances, you may consider a fire to be under control.

- Extinguishing agent is being applied to a fire and has effectively begun to cool it down.
- The main body of a fire (base) has been darkened. At this point, a fire cannot generate enough heat to involve nearby combustible materials.
- All possible routes of fire extension have been examined and found safe or protected (surrounding).

Fire Extinguished

H.10. GENERAL

Before a fire can be declared completely out, a coxswain must ensure the following actions have taken place.

- A thorough examination of the immediate fire area has been conducted.
- A complete overhaul of all burned material has been accomplished.
- A reflash watch has been set.
- All firefighting equipment has been restowed.
- A damage control check has been performed.
- All crew members have been accounted for.

Abandoning a Boat

H.11. ABANDONING A BOAT

Do not panic and hastily abandon a boat even when a fire is severe. Vigorous and proficient fire-fighting is normally a preferred alternative to abandoning a boat. However, do not hesitate to abandon the boat if you are becoming trapped by the flames, if you no longer have the equipment to fight the fire, if an explosion is likely (flames by the fuel tanks), or if similar life threatening situations are apparent. If able, inform OPCON of location and any other pertinent information. Make sure that:

- Distress call has been initiated
- All personnel are wearing life jackets
- Put over life raft or dinghy, if available
- Take portable radio
- Take extra signaling gear

Dewatering

Overview

Introduction

Dewatering a vessel is a consideration that is normally secondary to getting a fire put out. That is not to say, however, that dewatering is not important. Indeed, you may be able to use dewatering equipment to keep the boat from capsizing. You must not only know what equipment is available for dewatering, but how to use it.

In this section

Action Before Dewatering

I.1. GENERAL

Action taken before beginning to dewater a disabled vessel varies depending upon the nature of flooding. Regardless, a coxswain should always brief crew members on what procedures to follow while emphasizing safety. If crew members have just put out a fire on a boat, someone must then board the vessel and check for flooding, but only when safety permits. A coxswain will direct crew members how to safely accomplish this inspection for flooding.

When responding to a distress call of a disabled vessel taking on water, your initial action on the scene will be to search the immediate area for people in the water. After all survivors are recovered and all persons on board the sinking craft are accounted for and have been evacuated to a safe place, check the sinking craft for hull damage or other sources of flooding. Once a source of flooding is determined, crew members may take steps to reduce water flow into the boat. **Safety of the crew is the first priority.** The distressed vessel should not be boarded if it seems unstable and could possibly capsize. Once onboard, the crew members should wear PFDs and not go below decks if there is any threat of capsizing or sinking. When flooding has been controlled, or at least reduced to a minimum, dewatering can begin. How you dewater a vessel depends on the conditions that exist at the scene.

NOTE

Swimmers will not dive under or enter a capsized vessel. For more information refer to the *National Search and Rescue Manual Addendum*, chapters 4.I and 6.C.

NOTE

This manual does not cover technical information and use of commercial gasoline powered pumps, high capacity, manual, or electrical bailing pumps. See and follow the manufacturing instructions for usage while dewatering.

Dewatering with an Eductor

I.2. GENERAL

Dewatering with an eductor can be performed only when weather conditions permit your boat to safely come alongside a disabled vessel and remain close to it.

An eductor is used in conjunction with the fire pump on your boat. A 1½-inch fire hose attached to one of the 1½-inch outlets of the fire main is connected to the pressure supply inlet of the eductor. A 2½-inch fire hose is connected to the discharge outlet. The eductor itself is submerged, either vertically or horizontally, in the flooded area to be dewatered. Suction is obtained in either position because of uneven edges of the suction end of an eductor. All eductors operate in fundamentally the same manner. Water from a boat's fire pump is forced through a

fire main and out through the discharge hose. As pressure of this rapidly moving water passes over the suction opening, it creates a vacuum. The vacuum, or suction, pulls water up through a suction hose, out through the discharge hose, and over the side of your boat. You must always make certain that a discharge hose leads over the side and a suction hose is placed in flooded areas of a disabled boat. If you inadvertently reverse them, you will quickly fill a disabled vessel with water pumped aboard through the discharge line instead of dewatering it with a suction line (see Figure 18-16).

CAUTION!

Make certain there are no kinks or obstructions in a discharge line. Their presence will cause an eductor to pump water into a flooded boat through the suction line.

Dewatering Using a Drop Pump

I.3. GENERAL

Most Coast Guard boats carry a portable, gasoline-powered drop pump (see Figure 18-17). Dewatering with a drop pump is done with the pump placed on the disabled boat. A drop pump can pump 150 gallons of water per minute (GPM).

WARNING

Do not use a drop pump to dewater a boat with fuel contamination in its bilges.

I.4. PASSING A DROP PUMP

When secured in its watertight container, a drop pump can be easily passed from one boat to another. There are two methods for passing a pump.

DIRECTLY PASSING A DROP PUMP You should use the following procedures to directly pass a drop pump.

1. Determine your rate of drift.

2. Secure a 2-inch mooring line to a bridle attached to a pump container or pump container handles (see Figure 18-18).

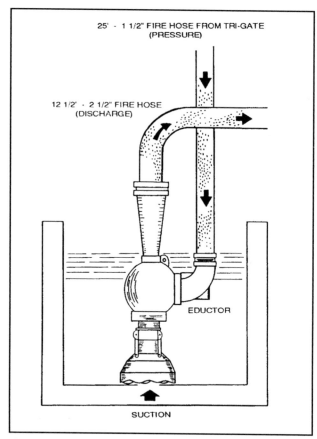

Figure 18-16 Aluminum Eductor Rigged for Dewatering

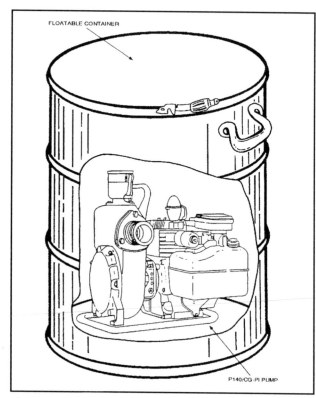

Figure 18-17 CG-P1 or CG-P5 Drop Pump

3. Secure a heaving line to the 2-inch mooring line.

4. Rig a tending line from the pump to your boat to enable you to control the pump's movement once it is in the water and to haul it back in the event of an emergency (see Figure 18-19).

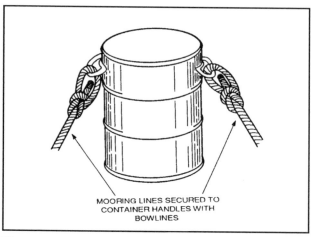

Figure 18-18 Securing Lines to Drop Pump Container

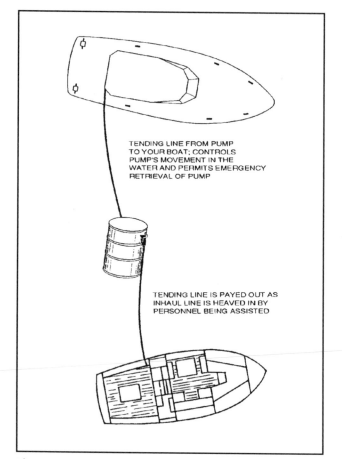

Figure 18-19 Directly Passing a Drop Pump Using Tending Lines.

5. Cast the heaving line, and direct people aboard the disabled boat to haul it in.

6. Lower the drop pump overboard and direct people aboard the disabled boat to haul in on the line. Pay out the tending end of the line as it is being hauled in.

PASSING A DROP PUMP INTO A BOAT IN TOW
You should use the following procedure for passing a drop pump to a boat in tow astern.

1. Rig a bridle to both handles of a pump storage bracket, if a permanent bridle has not already been attached.

2. Estimate the distance from the bow of the vessel back to the lowest point along the side of its hull. Make up a length of mooring line approximately equal to this distance. Secure the mooring line to the bridle rigged in step 1, with a shackle.

3. Make a bowline in the other end of the mooring line, around the tow line, so that the tow line passes through the eye of the bowline. A shackle may be substituted for a bowline. Regardless of the device used, bowline or shackle, the opening must be large enough for the mooring line to run freely down the tow line (see Figure 18-20).

4. Lower the pump over the side and allow it to float back to the boat in tow (see Figure 18-21).

5. Maintain only enough headway for steerage to keep the pump from submerging.

6. Instruct the vessel in tow to turn their rudder so as to head into the wind or current. This allows the pump to drift away from the towed vessel's bow and down its side unobstructed.

I.5. COMING ALONGSIDE A DISABLED BOAT

The procedure described above for directly passing a pump assumes that you cannot come alongside a disabled boat. If you can come alongside, the

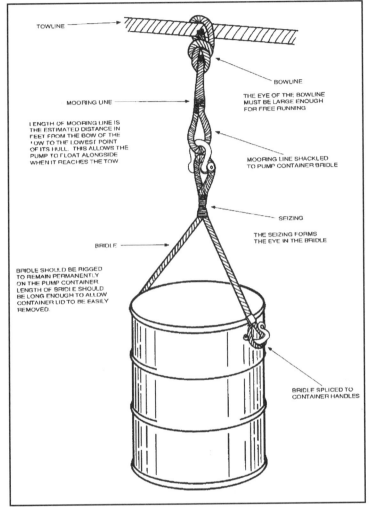

Figure 18-20 Drop Pump on the Towline

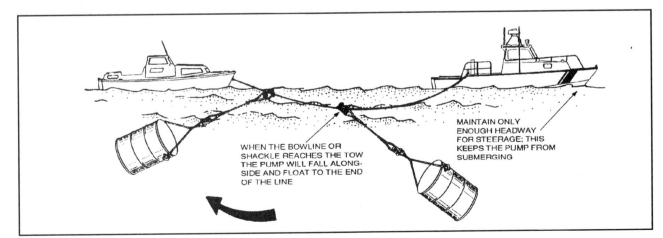

Figure 18-21 Passing a Drop Pump on the Towline

procedure is much simpler. All you need to do is pass the pump by hand from your boat across to the other boat. At least two people are always required to move a pump, because it is heavy and awkward to carry.

I.6. PUMP OPERATION

Follow the procedures below to operate a drop pump.

1. Pull the handle to release a tension ring on the storage container.

2. Lift the lid and open the plastic bag. Lift out the drop pump, hoses, and fuel.

3. Check the engine oil level. (Oil must be visible.)

4. Check the fuel tank and connection to the engine. Fill if needed. (Do not add oil to the fuel.)

5. Mount and connect fuel tank (P-1) only.

6. Connect a discharge hose and lay it out on deck so there are no kinks or twists. (Discharge hose must be manned or secured by tying off.)

7. Place the discharge valve on the pump in the closed position.

8. Place suction hose and strainer in water.

9. Actuate the hand priming pump. Grasp the handle, then raise and lower it until the pump is primed.

10. Place the choke lever on the engine in the "choke" position.

11. Pull the recoil starter.

12. Place the engine choke lever in the "run" position. Pull the recoil starter again.

13. After the engine starts, prime the pump again. A pump can run dry for up to one minute, but it was designed to be started only after suction has been taken.

14. Open the discharge valve slowly.

15. Post a watch on the pump. The engine will run approximately 2–3 hours on one tank of fuel, depending on conditions. A Pump Watch must be alert for debris around the strainer and must ensure the strainer remains submerged. Watch for fuel leaks.

16. Stop a pump and check the engine oil level after 5 hours of operation.

NOTE

If the pull cord on the recoil starter breaks, remove the thumb screws and start it manually using the extra pull cord supplied. For manual

starting, wrap the pull cord clockwise around the starter pulley. Grasp the pump handle to secure it and pull the cord.

CAUTION!

Breathing exhaust fumes can be dangerous. Do not attempt to start or operate a pump while it is in a container. Once a pump is started, ensure sufficient ventilation is present to allow exhaust gasses to dissipate into the atmosphere.

I.7. SECURING A PUMP

There are separate procedures for securing a drop pump depending on whether it is being secured because of an emergency or to be stowed.

EMERGENCY Push the stop lever against the spark plug. This allows a pump to stop for refueling, checking the oil, or standby.

SECURING FOR STORAGE Follow the procedures below when securing the pump for storage.

1. Disconnect the fuel line. The pump will run for approximately one minute and stop.

2. Remove the suction and discharge hose.

3. Drain both hoses and any water in the pump.

4. Flush pump and hoses with fresh water.

5. Place in a dry, protected area for drying.

6. After drying, restow all gear in a container.

SECTION J

Righting Powerboats and Sailboats

Overview

Introduction

Any attempt you make to right a capsized vessel must be carefully thought through before beginning. You must make absolutely certain that all crew members from a distressed vessel are accounted for before beginning any procedure to right the vessel. Survivors may be trapped inside the overturned hull.

When an inboard boat capsizes, dewatering cannot begin until the craft has been righted. There are several methods for righting vessels of this type. You will have to select the best one after evaluating the conditions on scene. Regardless of the method used, always get an accurate count of the persons aboard the capsized boat. Give them PFDs if necessary, and bring them aboard your boat before beginning the righting operation. Approach a disabled craft cautiously, watching for debris that may damage your boat or foul its propellers.

In this section

Topic	See Page(s)
Righting Powerboats	399–401
Righting Small Saiboats	401–2
Righting Large Sailboats	402

Righting Powerboats

J.1. GENERAL

The means you select for attaching lines determines the method of righting. Procedures for each method are outlined below.

J.2. RIGHTING BOATS BY PARBUCKLING

Follow these procedures when righting power boats by parbuckling (see Figure 18-22).

1. Approach a capsized boat cautiously. Keep clear of all lines and debris in the water.

2. Account for all personnel from the capsized boat.

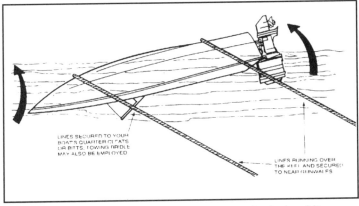

Figure 18-22 Righting Power Boats By Parbuckling

3. Recover all personnel from the water and provide PFDs to them as necessary.

4. Select a crew member to enter the water to prepare the boat for righting.

5. Direct a crew member to secure your towing bridle or mooring lines to the nearest gunwale of the capsized boat.

6. Then a person in the water leads bridle lines or mooring lines over the keel and down under the boat. Ensure that these lines are outboard of all handrails, lifelines, and stanchions. Then run the bridle back to your tow line, or run the mooring lines to your boat's rear quarter cleats or bitts.

7. Recover the tethered swimmer from the water.

8. Pay out enough tow line to prevent the boat from hitting your stern during righting and towing. Then, secure the tow line.

9. Gradually add power to your boat and increase speed. The boat should right itself.

10. Bring the righted boat alongside your boat and dewater using the most appropriate method.

11. Take in tow astern or alongside.

J.3. RIGHTING USING BOW AND TRANSOM EYEBOLT

Follow procedures below for righting a vessel using the bow and transom eyebolt.

1. Approach a capsized boat cautiously—from downwind, down current, or both—keeping clear of all lines and debris in the water.

2. Account for all personnel from the capsized boat.

3. Recover all personnel from the water and provide them PFDs as necessary.

4. Bring the capsized boat alongside the working area of your boat.

5. Use a shackle to secure your tow line to the trailer eyebolt of the capsized boat.

6. Secure a piece of mooring line to the capsized boat's outboard transom eyebolt (see Figure 18-23).

7. Pay out both a tow line and a scrap/mooring line and walk the capsized boat to a position astern of and athwartships to (from side to side) your boat.

8. Secure the scrap/mooring line to your boat's rear quarter cleat or bitt.

9. Pay out enough tow line to permit the boat to

remain clear of your stern when righting and towing commences. Secure the towline.

10. Gradually add power to your boat and increase speed. When the righting motion begins, cut or slip the scrap/mooring line. The boat should right itself. Tow the righted boat until you observe water being forced over the transom of the disabled boat.

11. When water ceases to flow over the towed boat's transom, reduce speed gradually, ensuring that enough water has been forced out of the boat during towing to allow it to float on its own.

12. Bring the righted boat alongside your boat and dewater it using the most appropriate method.

13. Take in tow astern or alongside.

J.4. RIGHTING USING TOWLINE FORE AND AFT OF BOAT'S KEEL

Follow the procedures below for righting a boat using a towline fore and aft of the boat's keel:

1. Approach the capsized boat cautiously—from downwind, down current, or both—keeping clear of all lines and debris in the water.

2. Account for all personnel from the capsized boat.

3. Recover all personnel from the water and provide PFDs to them as necessary.

4. If the operator is willing, one person wearing a PFD may be left in the water to assist in righting the boat.

5. If no one aboard the boat is able to assist, direct a crew member to enter the water to prepare the boat for righting.

6. Direct the person in the water or a crew member to run your towline fore and aft alongside the capsized boat's keel.

7. The person in the water will then secure your towline to the capsized boat's trailer eyebolt with a shackle.

8. Ensure the disabled boat is positioned fore and aft, directly astern of your boat (capsized boat's stern toward your boat's stern), and that the towline is running fore and aft along the capsized vessel's keel (see Figure 18-24).

9. Pay out enough slack in the towline to permit the boat to clear your stern when righting commences. Secure the towline.

10. Gradually add power to your boat and increase speed, pulling on the bow of the capsized boat. This pull will be countered by the aft portion of

the disabled boat, which is the heaviest part of the craft. As a result of these two forces, the boat will be righted.

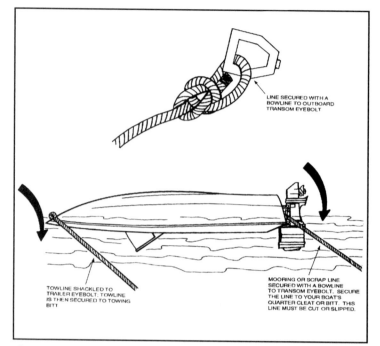

Figure 18-23 Righting Capsized Boats Using Bow and Transom Eyebolts

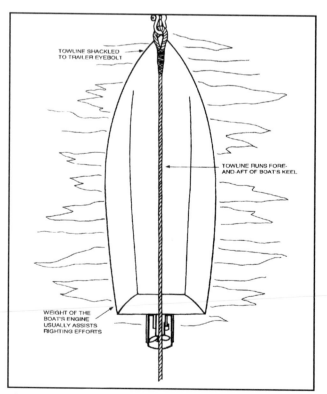

Figure 18-24 Righting Capsized Boats Using Towline Fore and Aft of Boat's Keel

11. Tow the righted boat until you observe water being forced over the transom of the disabled boat.

12. When water ceases to flow over the towed boat's transom, reduce speed gradually, ensuring that enough water has been forced out of the boat during the towing to allow it to float on its own.

13. Bring the righted boat alongside your boat and dewater it using the most appropriate method.

14. Take in tow astern or alongside.

J.5. REFLOATING SWAMPED BOATS ASTERN USING TRAILER EYEBOLT

This procedure is used for righting a boat that has been swamped from astern (see Figure 18-25).

1. Approach a swamped boat cautiously—from downwind, down current, or both—keeping clear of all lines and debris in the water.

2. Account for all personnel from the swamped boat.

3. Recover all personnel from the water and provide them PFDs if necessary.

4. Bring the swamped boat alongside the working area of your boat.

5. Secure your tow line to the trailer eyebolt of the swamped boat with a shackle.

6. Pay out your tow line and walk the swamped boat directly astern of your boat.

7. Pay out enough tow line to permit the swamped boat to remain clear of your stern when towing commences. Secure the towline.

8. Gradually add power to your boat and increase speed taking the swamped boat in tow. Tow the boat until you observe water being forced over the transom of the disabled boat.

9. When water ceases to flow over the towed boat's transom, reduce speed gradually, ensuring that enough water has been forced out of the boat during towing to allow it to float on its own.

10. Bring the boat alongside your boat and dewater it using the most appropriate method.

11. Take in tow astern or alongside.

Righting Small Sailboats

J.6. GENERAL

Approach the capsized sailboat from upwind, up current, or both, remaining clear of lines and debris. Account for all personnel from the sailboat and recover them as necessary. At least one person will be needed in the water from the capsized boat, to help in righting the boat. Do not attempt righting if the weather presents a hazard to the rescue boat or personnel.

J.7. PROCEDURES

The following procedures are for righting a small sailboat.

1. The person in the water unships or removes the sails.

2. The sails, if removed, should be put aboard the rescue boat or secured to the disabled boat.

3. The person in the water then stands on the keel or centerboard and leans back while holding on the gunwale. The boat should slowly begin to come back over.

4. Once the sailboat is righted, recover the swimmer and begin dewatering.

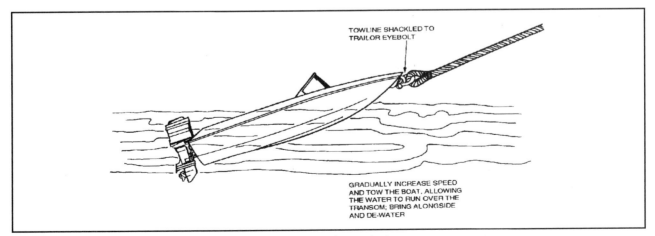

Figure 18-25 Refloating Boats Swamped Astern Using Trailer Eyebolt

NOTE

Sails still hoisted create severe drag and force against righting attempts. They may even cause the boat to capsize again once it is successfully righted.

Righting Large Sailboats

J.8. GENERAL

A procedure called parbuckling may be used to right capsized powerboats or sailboats over 25 feet in length. Also, parbuckling should be used for righting small sailboats that cannot be righted by the method previously described.

J.9. PROCEDURE

A person from the overturned boat or a crew member from the rescue boat must enter the water to prepare the boat for righting. The following is the procedure for righting a sailboat using parbuckling.

> ## CAUTION!
>
> **If the weather presents a danger to the person in the water or the boats involved, do not attempt righting.**

A Coast Guard Auxiliarist helps to right a capsized catamaran.

J.10. PROCEDURES

The following procedures are for righting a small sailboat.

1. Unship or remove the sails.

2. Have the person in the water run a bridle or towline to the capsized boat.

3. Ensure that the lines rigged for righting, are outboard of all stays, shrouds, lifelines and stanchions.

4. Secure lines to available deck fittings.

5. Connect the other end of the bridle to the towline. Pay out enough line to prevent the distressed boat's mast (if so equipped) from striking the rescue boat should the distressed boat continue to roll in that direction.

6. Recover the person in the water

7. Commence righting by going ahead *slowly* on the engines.

8. Once a sailboat is righted, crew members should board it from the stern (because of the boat's instability) and secure all loose lines.

9. Secure the boom to stop it from swinging and possibly capsizing the boat again.

10. Begin dewatering.

> ## WARNING
>
> **Do not secure any lines to the masts of sailboats. The force exerted during the righting may cause them to fracture.**

SECTION K

Flood Control

Overview

Introduction

Boats sometimes become damaged in groundings, collisions, or from striking submerged objects. These mishaps may result in a holed, cracked, or weakened hull. If the hull has been damaged to the extent that water is entering the interior of the boat, it must be plugged or patched to keep the boat afloat.

In this section

Plugging Holes

K.1. PLUGS

The simplest method of stopping a small hole in wooden or metal hulls is to insert a plug or plugs. Plugs are usually made of a soft wood such as pine or fir. Use plugs individually if they fit the hole, or use them in combination with other materials, to make a better fit.

K.2. PREPARE PLUG

Wrapping cloth around each plug before insert in them in the hole will help to keep the plug in place. It also fills the gaps between plugs.

K.3. INSERTING PLUGS

When plugging holes, it is usually easiest to insert the plugs from the inside. However, sometimes the rough edges protruding inward may make this method impossible. If it is necessary to insert the plugs from the outside, the inboard end(s) of the plug(s) should be fitted with screw eyes. Attach a line to each screw eye and fasten the line to a structure inside the boat. It will hold the plug in place (see Figure 18-26).

K.4. LARGE HOLES

Large holes are generally too difficult to plug. Use a patch to reduce the flow of water through a large hole, if an attempt is made.

K.5. FIBERGLASS HULLS

Fiberglass may be the most difficult of all hull materials to plug. Wooden conical plugs driven into the hole may do nothing more than cause further splitting and cracking and add to an already difficult situation. The best method of plugging a hole in fiberglass is to shove some pliable type of material into it such as a rag, shirt, or piece of canvas. A PFD or a blanket may also work well.

Patching Holes

K.6. HOLES BELOW THE WATERLINE

Patching holes below the waterline is usually a difficult task because of the pressure exerted by the water and the inaccessibility to the holed area. Patch small holes from the inside. Place some type of material over the hole and hold it in place with another object. For example, if the boat were holed in the bottom, place a PFD or seat cushion over the hole and hold it in place with a gas can, cooler, or tool box.

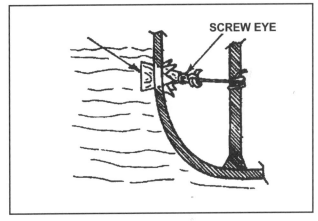

Figure 18-26 Screw Eye

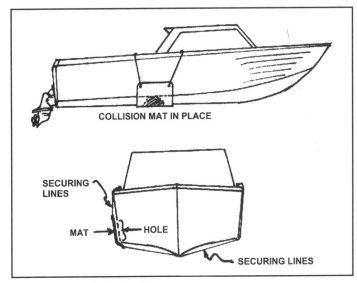

Figure 18-27 Collision Mat

K.7. LARGE HOLES BELOW THE WATERLINE

Large holes below the waterline are extremely difficult to patch. The pressure of the water flowing through the hole will not usually allow a patch to be installed from the inside.

COLLISION MAT If a collision mat (a large piece of canvas or vinyl) is available, use it to patch a large hole. Follow the procedures below while placing the patch over the hole (see Figure 18-27).

1. Tie four lines to the corners of the patch.

2. Position the patch by dripping the patch over the bow.

3. Have someone walk down each side of the boat, two of the lines for each person.

4. Slide the patch along the bottom of the boat.

5. Once the patch covers the hole, secure the four lines topside. The pressure of the water against the patch will also help to hold it in place.

BOX PATCH Box patches are effective, even on holes that have jagged edges protruding inward. The box patch is usually a prefabricated box, which is held in place with screws, nails, or it may be wedged in place with anything available. Put a gasket (anything available) between the box and the hull to make a good seal and to prevent the box from shifting (see Figure 18-28).

K.8. HOLES ABOVE THE WATERLINE

Holes above the waterline may be more dangerous than they appear. As the boat rolls, they admit water into the boat above the center of gravity. This water reduces the stability of the boat. Use plugs or patches on the inside or outside the hull to cover these type of holes. The following procedure is an effective method for patching holes above the waterline.

1. Use a pillow or cushion that has a small hole punched in the center.

2. Place the cushion over the holed area from the outside and back it with a board of the same approximate size. The board should also have a small hole through the center.

3. Pass a line through the board and cushion and knot the end of the line outside the board.

4. Secure the entire patch by attaching the other end of the line to something firm inside the boat (see Figure 18-29).

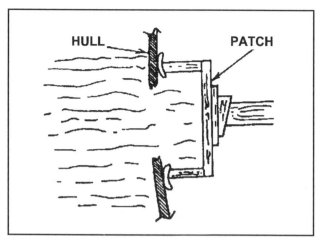

Figure 18-28 Box Patch

Figure 18-29 Patching Hole Above Waterline

Patching Cracks

K.9. CRACKS IN HULLS

To patch a crack in the hull, use the following procedures.

1. Stuff the crack with something pliable such as a rag or line.

2. Place a piece of canvas or rubber over the crack to serve as a gasket.

3. Back the patch with a solid object such as a piece of plywood, panel door, or similar material.

4. Use nails, screws, or wedges to hold the patch in place.

To prevent the crack from traveling, especially in fiberglass, drill holes at each end of the crack. These holes will relieve the pressure at the ends of the crack, Permitting the hull to flex without extending the crack.

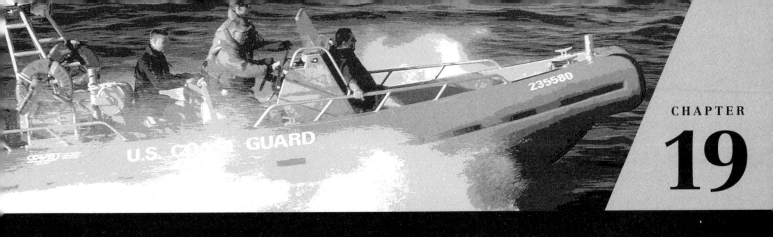

Air Operations

CHAPTER

19

Editor's Note: *Every year we see news footage of Coast Guard helicopter crews plucking victims from the decks of and waters surrounding distressed vessels. This chapter will tell you what to expect if you have to call the Coasties for an aerial ride home. You'll notice that preparation is essential. Clearing the decks of debris that could be hurled around by the helicopter's downwash is essential for safety—so too is knowing how to ground the static charge built up by the whirling helicopter blades and how to strap the victim (or yourself) into the pickup basket. Here's where you'll learn those techniques. You'll also find a discussion here on helping a crew of a downed helicopter—a dangerous undertaking under any circumstances.*

Overview

Introduction

Coordinated operation between boats and aircraft creates a valuable team for Coast Guard missions. While an aircraft can generally search an area faster or may arrive on-scene sooner, a vessel can investigate more thoroughly and usually provide more direct assistance. Whether a pollution incident or a SAR case, boats and aircraft may be called upon to work as a team.

Boat operations with aircraft usually involve transfer of a person or equipment between a helicopter (rotary-wing) and a boat. Sometimes, a boat must coordinate with a fixed-wing aircraft. The *Coast Guard Addendum to the National Search and Rescue Manual*, COMDTINST M16130.2 (series), has a list of capabilities and deliverable search and rescue (SAR) equipment for each type of Coast Guard aircraft. Auxiliary facilities include fixed-wing general aviation aircraft. Boat crews need to be aware that easily recognized Coast Guard aircraft and some privately owned small aircraft or Auxiliary air facility may try to contact and operate with them.

In this chapter

SECTION A

Helicopters and Equipment

Overview

Introduction

Excellent multi-mission capabilities are available in the Short-Range Recovery (SRR) helicopter HH-65A and the Medium-Range and Recovery (MRR) helicopter HH-60J. Helicopter maneuverability and outstanding crew visible scanning capabilities enable the crew to closely inspect sightings and search shorelines. They are flexible rescue platforms, capable of recovering people from a wide variety of distress situations on land or water. Both helicopters can:

- Hover
- Deploy rescue swimmers/emergency medical technicians (EMTs)
- Perform hoists using rescue basket, Stokes litter, or rescue strop
- Deliver equipment; e.g., dewatering pump and fire suppression kits, when available
- Deploy datum marker buoys
- Search with radar
- Provide night illumination
- Direction find
- Perform multi-mission patrols
- Conduct supply/replenishment operations

NOTE

The HH-60J has night vision goggles and forward-looking infrared capabilities.

In this section

HH-65A Dolphin

A.1. DESCRIPTION

The **HH-65A** "**Dolphin**," has two turbine engines that will produce a maximum airspeed of 165 knots (see Figures 19-1 and 19-2). The HH-65A cannot hover, hoist, or maneuver on just one engine. The normal crew is one or two pilots and a flight mechanic. For rescue missions, a rescue swimmer is normally carried in addition to the three crew members. The pilot in command sits in the right seat of the cockpit. Other general information includes:

- Maximum endurance with a crew of two pilots and one crew member is approximately three hours.
- Maximum of four passengers or survivors besides the three crew can be carried.
- Hoist capacity is 600 lbs. and the external cargo sling limit is 2,000 lbs.
- It will not land on the water except in an emergency. It will float if it is not badly damaged and the flotation bags are deployed.

Figure 19-2 depicts the front, top, and side views of the HH-65A. The **fan in tail** (Fenestron) rotor configuration is evident and is the easy way to visually identify the HH-65A. This Fenestron also gives it a distinct, high-pitched sound.

HH-60J Jayhawk

A.2. DESCRIPTION

The **HH-60J** "**Jayhawk**," has 2 turbine engines that, depending upon the gross weight of the helicopter, will produce a maximum airspeed of 180 knots (see Figure 19-3). Although equipped with two engines, the HH-60J can normally maintain flight with one engine. Losing one engine is an emergency situation. The normal crew is two pilots and two crew members. For rescue missions, a rescue swimmer is normally carried in addition to four crew members. Other general information includes:

- Maximum endurance of the aircraft with maximum fuel and crew is approximately six hours.
- Hoist capacity is 600 lbs. and the external cargo sling limit is 6,000 lbs.
- It will not land on the water except in an emergency. Even with flotation bags, it will stay afloat only long enough for the crew to exit. The HH-60J is *not* amphibious.

A.3. HELICOPTER EQUIPMENT

Hoists by Coast Guard helicopters will normally be done with the following rescue devices and equipment.

RESCUE BASKET The multi-jointed (M/J) rescue basket is the primary device for hoisting survivors from land or sea during helicopter rescue operations. It provides protection for the individual being hoisted from dangers, such as striking vessel rigging. It has the capability to float. Hinged at all four corners, it folds inward. (See Figure 19-5.) The basket is employed for personnel transfer in any weather condition.

STOKES LITTER The **Stokes litter** (see Figure 19-6) is a stretcher with a flotation collar and chest pad for buoyancy. A 5-lb. ballast weight provides stability. A permanently mounted hoisting sling attaches the litter to the helicopter hoist cable. For restraining patients, a minimum of four securing straps, including chest pad, are supplied. Additional information is in the *Coast Guard Rescue and Survival Systems Manual*, COMDTINST M10470.10 (series).

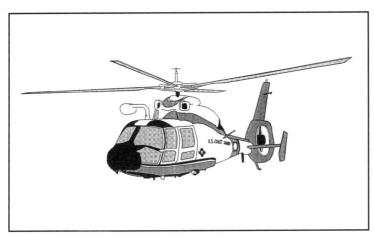

Figure 19-1 HH-65A (Dolphin) Helicopter Left Front View

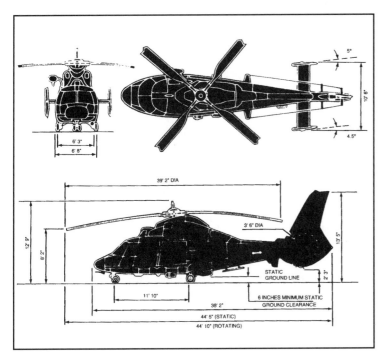

Figure 19-2 Front, Top, and Side Views of the HH-65A Helicopter

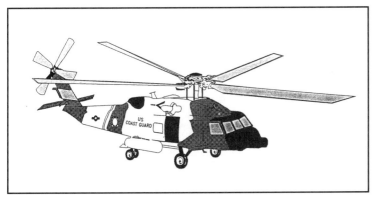

Figure 19-3 HH-60J (Jayhawk) Helicopter

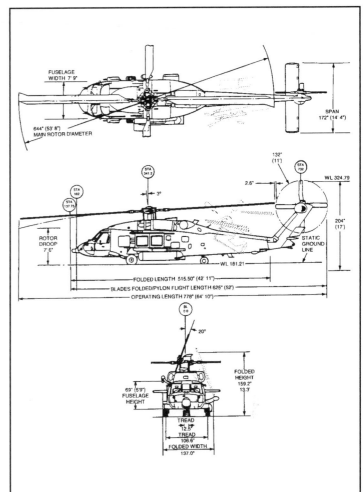

Figure 19-4 Top, Side, and Front Views of the HH-60J Helicopter

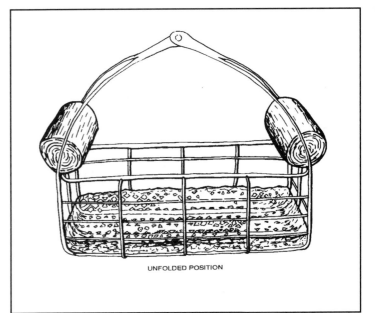

Figure 19-5 The M/J Rescue Basket

The Stokes litter is used to transfer an injured or unconscious person in any weather condition. It is generally used when the patient's condition prevents use of the basket. When the patient is placed in a litter a crew member must tighten all straps to keep the person securely bound to it. There are four straps, as shown in Figure 19-6.

RESCUE STROP The **rescue strop** (see Figure 19-7) is used only to rescue persons familiar with its proper use, for example, a military aviator. It can handle one survivor wearing the usual flight gear and PFD.

NOTE

Use of chest retainer strap is mandatory during use of the rescue strop, except when hoisting rescue swimmers.

Other Helicopter Equipment

A.4. TRAIL LINE

Use of a **trail line** minimizes the time a pilot must maintain a precise stable hover without a reference point. The trail line consists of 105 feet of orange polypropylene line with a weak link and snap link at one end, and a snap hook at the other. The weak link (see Figure 19-8) is a safety device between the trail line and hoist hook, which protects the helicopter by not allowing more than 300 lbs. of force to be applied to the hoist. If more force is applied, the weak link will part. A 5 lb. bag is attached to the trail line snap hook for ease in delivery of the trail line. When used, the trail line will:

- Stabilize a rescue device to prevent sailing, swinging, and possibly becoming fouled
- Reduce the time a pilot must maintain a precise hover
- Reduce time on-scene

A.5. DEWATERING PUMP KITS

Dewatering pumps provide emergency dewatering for boats in danger of sinking. Under a load, the pump will run 1.5 to 2.5 hours on one gallon of gasoline. The pumps are designed to fit into a standard round aluminum container.

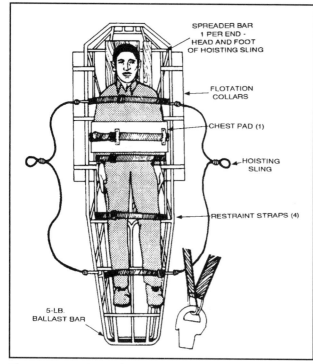

Figure 19-6 The Stokes Litter

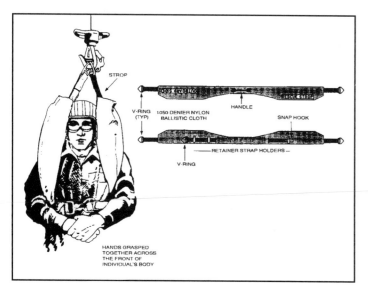

Figure 19-7 Rescue Strop

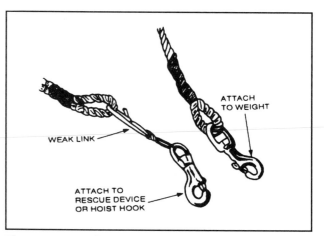

Figure 19-8 Trail Line's Weak Link

A United States Coast Guard HH-60 Jayhawk helicopter lowers its rescue basket during a search and rescue demonstration.

SECTION B

Helicopter Rescue Operations

Overview

Introduction

This section discusses the procedures and necessary safety precautions involved in a helicopter rescue operation.

In this section

Rescue Swimmer

B.1. GENERAL

The rescue swimmer (RS) is a properly trained and conditioned certified Emergency Medical Technician (EMT). The RS is trained to deploy from a helicopter to recover an incapacitated victim from the maritime environment, day or night. Since a helicopter has weight and space limitations, a boat may be requested to recover an RS. The RS is equipped with a strobe light and signal flares.

Helicopter Hoisting Operations

B.2. GENERAL

Helicopter hoisting operations off of a vessel can pose great hazard to the aircrew, boat crew, and to whatever is being hoisted. The safety and efficiency of helicopter hoist operations is greatly improved if the crew of the vessel is briefed in advance on what is required. Appendix 19-A has the internationally approved "Sample Briefing to Pass to Vessel Prior to Helicopter Hoisting." This briefing is particularly useful in case you conduct a boat-helicopter hoist or if you are asked to brief the distressed vessel as the helicopter is en route. The *Coast Guard Addendum to the National Search and Rescue Manual*, COMDTINST M16130.2 (series) has a similar version.

Boat-helicopter operations require team effort, alertness, and cooperation among crew members aboard both the boat and helicopter. Since the noise level may hinder communications, the coxswain and pilot usually plan the operation before the helicopter is overhead. Once the helicopter is in position, the aircrew member serving as hoist operator gives the pilot maneuvering instructions for guiding the rescue device to the boat deck below. The safety briefing discussed earlier in this section and provided in Appendix 19-A provides general guidelines. Specific guidelines for the boat crew are discussed below.

NOTE

The Coast Guard uses the term "hoist" while the international community uses the term "winch."

The international version in Appendix 19-A has the term winch replaced by hoist.

B.3. BOAT CREW PREPARATIONS FOR HOISTING

Before the helicopter arrives, the coxswain will complete action on the following general categories of preparation.

If radio communications are lost and an emergency breakaway is required, use the boat's blue emergency light or other emergency signal to signal the breakaway to the helicopter.

NAVIGATION Check charts for hazard that would prevent the boat from maintaining course and speed until the hoist is complete.

COMMUNICATIONS Establish communications with the helicopter as early as possible to exchange information and instructions. This includes:

- Use of primary and secondary working frequencies
- On-scene weather
- Exact position
- Condition of persons, if any, requiring medical attention
- Any information to aid the pilot in selecting the rescue device
- Total number of crew and other persons on board your boat, and total number on board the helicopter
- Conduct hoist briefing with the helicopter pilot

PROTECTIVE GEAR Ensure all **protective gear** is properly worn, including:

- Head (helmet), eye, hearing, and hand (gloves) protection
- PFDs, antiexposure coveralls, and dry suits (depending on weather conditions)

LOOSE GEAR Stow or secure all **loose gear** on deck (e.g., hats, cushions, loose paper, etc.).

RIGGING Lower and secure all antennas, booms, **rigging**, and flag staff, if possible.

HAND SIGNALS Designate one boat crew member to give **hand signals** to the hoist operator.

BRIEF CREW Brief the crew and person(s) to

be hoisted regarding the type of hoist to be expected (e.g., basket, litter, or strop).

B.4. BOAT CREW SAFETY PRECAUTIONS

During the hoisting evolution, **safety** is paramount. All boat crew members will observe the following safety precautions.

> **WARNING**
>
> The downwash of a helicopter is very powerful. It can blow a person overboard. It can also blow loose gear over the side. Loose objects such as articles of clothing can be caught in the air currents produced by the rotor blades and sucked into the engines.

- ALWAYS allow the rescue device to contact (ground to) the boat, water, or a "Deadman's Stick" (static discharge wand), BEFORE YOU TOUCH IT. A helicopter in flight builds up static electricity.
- ALWAYS TEND BY HAND any trail lines, basket slings, or hoisting cable. DO NOT ATTACH them to the boat.
- ALWAYS wait for slack in the hoist cable before attempting to hook onto the device to be hoisted. This precaution allows for relative motion between helicopter and boat.
- ALWAYS keep the trail line and hoisting cable clear of the boat's rigging.
- ALWAYS unhook the rescue device before moving it inside the boat.

> **WARNING**
>
> Never attach, tie, or secure anything to the boat that is also attached to the helicopter.

Helicopter Boat Positioning

B.5. GENERAL

When working with a helicopter at night, NEVER shine a light towards or take flash pictures of the helicopter. The sudden light may temporarily blind or disorient the pilot.

NEVER use pyrotechnics or illuminating signals without contacting the pilot.

B.6. COURSE AND SPEED

Hoists from standard boats are normally made from the stern. The pilot normally will direct the coxswain to assume a certain course and speed with a relative wind speed of 15 to 30 knots and 35–45 degrees off the port bow (see Figure 19-9). Sometimes, sea conditions may require departure from this rule, especially to minimize boat rolling. The boat must maintain a steady course and speed.

B.7. NONSTANDARD BOATS

Hoists from nonstandard boats (e.g., RIBs, UTLs,

Figure 19-9 Helicopter-Boat Positioning

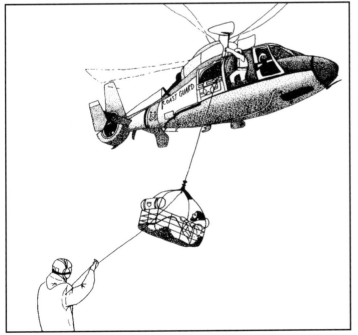

Figure 19-10 Trail Line Delivery of the M/J Rescue Basket

or Auxiliary craft) may require a different technique. The helicopter will hover and lower the rescue device to a stationary position near the surface. The boat should approach and maneuver under the hoist for delivery.

B.8. HELICOPTER-BOAT CONFIGURATION

The rescue device will be lowered from the right side of the aircraft. The helicopter will approach the boat from astern (downwind) and hover off the port side, aft of amidships. This method of approach allows the pilot and hoist operator (located on the right side of the aircraft) a full view of the boat during the evolution (see Figure 19-10).

B.9. DEAD IN THE WATER

When a boat is dead in the water (DIW), the helicopter may approach the boat's bow on the starboard side. Due to the downwash, the boat will almost always turn clockwise and the aircraft will maintain visual contact by turning in the same direction during the hoist.

Delivery of Rescue Device

B.10. GENERAL

Delivery of a rescue device from the helicopter to a vessel in distress or for training will be accomplished by one of three methods:

- Direct Delivery
- Trail Line Delivery
- Indirect Delivery

After the rescue device is delivered (and if previously agreed to in the aircraft brief), a boat crew member will disconnect the hook before moving away from the delivery/hoisting location. NEVER ATTACH THE HOOK TO ANY PART OF THE BOAT. Re-attach the cable to the device at a time agreed upon with the helicopter pilot.

B.11. DIRECT DELIVERY

The rescue device is lowered directly to the deck of the vessel.

B.12. TRAIL LINE DELIVERY

A 5-lb. weight bag is attached to the trail line and lowered from the helicopter to the vessel. The helicopter will then back off to a safe hoisting distance while paying out the trail line. The non-weighted end of the trail line is attached to the rescue device (weak link first) and lowered to the vessel (see Figures 19-11 and 19-10). Boat crew members will tend the trail line by hand-over-hand method, exerting enough strain to guide the rescue device to the delivery point on deck. A second crew member should back up and coil the line.

B.13. INDIRECT DELIVERY

This type of delivery is designed for delivery of the CG-P1B dewatering pump. The trail line, weighted bag attached to the weak link first, is delivered from the helicopter to the vessel. The helicopter will pay out the trail line as the helicopter backs off and establishes a low hover with the rotor blades and downwash clear of all rigging (see Figure 19-12). The hoist operator will then attach the end of the trail line to the pump container and deploy it to the water (see Figure 19-13). The boat crew member will than pull the pump aboard.

Hoisting

B.14. BASKET HOIST

Every person transferred must wear a PFD and head protection, if available. The person must be positioned in the basket with hands placed palms up under the thighs. This position will keep the arms tucked in close to the body and inside the basket. The crew member assisting the person into position must ensure that no part of the person's body is outside of the basket and that the basket does not hang up on equipment attached to the boat. When the individual to be hoisted is in the proper position, the boat crew member will give the "thumbs up" to the hoist operator, who will commence the hoist (see Figure 19-14). If a trail line is used, tend it over the side. Do not throw the end.

B.15. STOKES LITTER HOIST

The litter will be provided by the helicopter. When a boat has a hoistable litter (as outlined in the *Coast Guard Rescue and Survival Systems Manual*, COMDTINST M10470.10 (series)), the air-

> **CAUTION!**
> Helicopter rescue baskets are collapsible. When connecting and disconnecting the hoist cable, support both ends of the basket to avoid injury to the person in the basket.

Figure 19-11 M/J Rescue Basket Going Down

Figure 19-12 Indirect Delivery of Pump

Figure 19-13 Pump In the Water

Figure 19-14 M/J Rescue Basket With Person Properly Positioned and Ready For Hoist

craft commander will determine if it will be used. When the victim is placed in the litter, a boat crew member must tighten all restraining straps around the person. There are four straps and one chest pad. The crew member tending the litter must make certain it does not get hung up on boat equipment. When the person is to be hoisted, the boat crew member will give a "thumbs up" to the hoist operator, who will commence the hoist.

B.16. RESCUE STROP HOIST

The strop WILL ONLY BE USED to transfer trained, uninjured military personnel in fair weather. The strop is basically a collar which has one end attached to the hoist cable. When the person to be hoisted positions the collar under the armpits, a boat crew member must ensure the safety straps are fastened. The end of the collar opposite the hoist cable has a V-ring which attaches to the hook. Figure 19-7 shows how the strop looks when properly connected. This device is not likely to hang up on attached equipment as easily as the other rescue devices.

B.17. HOISTING OF EQUIPMENT

Secure and monitor all attachment points and the equipment, to keep it from hanging up.

B.18. COMMENCE HOIST

When a person or equipment is secured in the rescue device, the designated boat crew member will give the hoist operator a "thumbs up" hand signal. The hoist operator will then commence lifting the rescue device. During this procedure, the boat crew must ensure the rescue device is not caught on anything attached to the boat.

B.19. CAST OFF

When a trail line is employed, a boat crew member shall tend it until it reaches the weighted end. Then toss it over the side of the boat on which the hoist was conducted (normally the port side), but not upward toward the rotors.

B.20. POST HOIST

Once the trail line is cast off, the coxswain will maneuver to starboard and away from the helicopter.

B.21. EMERGENCY BREAKAWAY PROCEDURE

Safety during helicopter operations cannot be overemphasized. Crew members must stay alert and report any danger signs. If either the coxswain or pilot feels the operation is unsafe, then a breakaway should be conducted. Procedures for the coxswain to conduct a breakaway are:

- Direct the crew to push the loose cable, rescue device, and trail line over the side (toward the helicopter),
- Transmit the word "BREAKAWAY" to the pilot,
- Turn away from the helicopter, and
- Energize the blue emergency light or identification light, if practical or applicable.

SECTION C

Helicopter Ditching

C.1. GENERAL

There is always the possibility a helicopter may have to **ditch** in the water. Coast Guard air crews receive extensive training in escape procedures for such emergencies. However, they may be disoriented due to personal injuries, aircraft attitude, damage, and/or environmental factors. For this reason, boat crew members must be familiar with emergency exits and entrances. You may have to open emergency exits to pull trapped air crew members to safety. The HH-60J has five emergency openings and the HH-65A has four. (See Figures 19-15 through 19-18.)

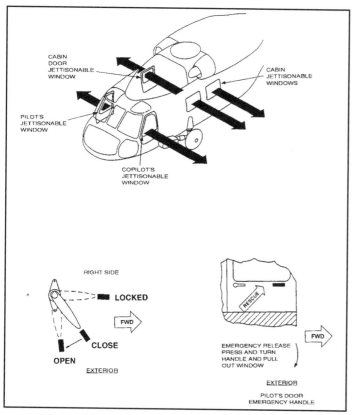

Figure 19-15 HH-60J Emergency Entrances

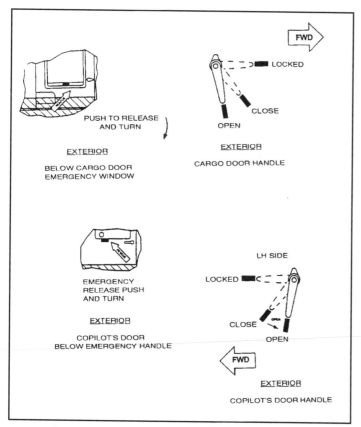

Figure 19-16 HH-60J Emergency Entrances (cont.)

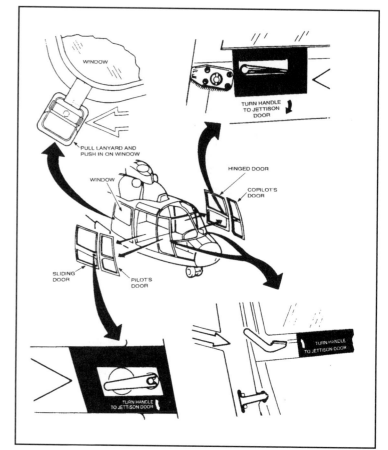

Figure 19-17 HH-65A Emergency Entrances

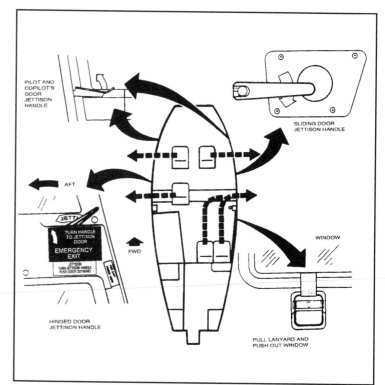

Figure 19-18 HH-65A Emergency Entrances (cont.)

C.2. ASSISTING A DOWNED HELICOPTER

If a helicopter goes down near your boat during a hoist operation or you are called to assist a downed helicopter, do the following.

- Ensure the operational commander is advised of the ditching.
- Approach bow on from the leeward side of the helicopter.
- Make minimal wake so the vertical stability is not disrupted (when the helicopter is in an upright position).
- Be alert to the position of the rotor blades when recovering air crew.
- If a boat crew member must enter the aircraft, that crew member must wear a surface swimmer's harness tended from the boat.

CAUTION!

Boat crew members will not enter an inverted aircraft! Only a qualified diver may enter a helicopter after it has inverted (turned upside-down).

SECTION D

Helicopter Salvage and Towing

D.1. GENERAL

After a helicopter ditches and the crew has been rescued, every effort should be made to salvage the airframe before it sinks. A Coast Guard helicopter can survive a ditching in limited wind and sea conditions, if its bottom integrity remains intact and flotation bags are deployed. If the helicopter becomes inverted (turned upside-down), it will have more severe damage and a greater risk of sinking.

D.2. INITIAL ACTIONS

When a helicopter ditches, the parent air station will assign a Salvage Officer and activate their Mishap Plan. Until the salvage officer arrives on scene, the senior aviator at the scene will act as the salvage officer. Boat handling, maneuvering, and the safety of the boat crew and survivors remain the coxswain's primary responsibility. If the aircraft is upright, the first boat on scene shall:

- If conditions permit, add flotation (e.g., flotation collars, inflatable life rafts, and boat fenders) to the helicopter to keep the helicopter from sinking. Once positive buoyancy is ensured, the salvage operation can proceed.
- Establish a security watch.

NOTE

The primary concern during salvage is preventing the aircraft from inverting from an upright attitude.

WARNING

Pyrotechnics become unstable when wet.

D.3. GENERAL TOWING PROCEDURES

Towing a helicopter is not an exact science! On-scene conditions may make it necessary to change from standard procedures. However, safety of people shall NEVER be compromised. When towing a Coast Guard helicopter, use the following procedures:

- Tow only when the aircraft cannot be hoisted onto a vessel in a timely manner.
- Remove the rotor blades (improves stability).
- Rig a light on the helicopter when towing between sunset and sunrise, or in restricted visibility.
- Tow only in calm seas.
- Remove all personnel from the aircraft.
- Use a drogue, if available, to minimize yawing.
- Tow at the slowest possible speed (do not exceed 5 knots).
- Place initial strain on the towing hawser at bare steerageway.
- Avoid towing the helicopter parallel to the wave trough to minimize risk of capsizing.
- Make all turns slow and wide to minimize risk of capsizing.
- Continuously monitor water depth to allow for the greater draft, when towing an inverted helicopter.
- Tow an inverted helicopter only after additional flotation is attached to it.

- Establish a tow watch

D.4. TOW WATCH

If ANY of the following conditions are seen, the tow SHALL be stopped:

- Change in attitude that would indicate compartment flooding.
- Deflation or loss of any flotation bags or buoyant devices attached to the aircraft.
- Aircraft roll increases to a point where vertical stability may be lost.

D.5. TOWING HELICOPTER FORWARD

Attach the towing bridle to both sides of the **14 degree frame**, the vertical frame only on the HH-65A, to which the pilot and co-pilot door is hinged (see Figure 19-19).

NOTE

Tow the helicopter forward whenever possible.

D.6. TOWING HELICOPTER BACKWARD

Attach the towing bridle to the left and right side of the horizontal stabilizer (see Figure 19-20).

NOTE

If the tail cone has flooded, backwards towing will not be possible because the horizontal stabilizer will cause the tail to dive.

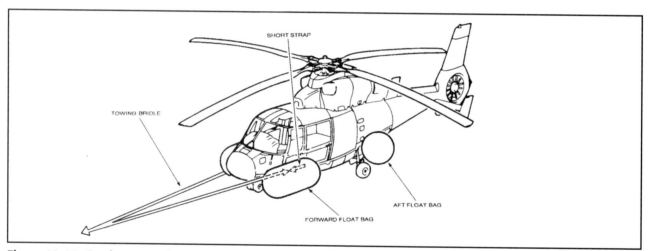

Figure 19-19 Configuration for Towing the HH-65A Helicopter Forward

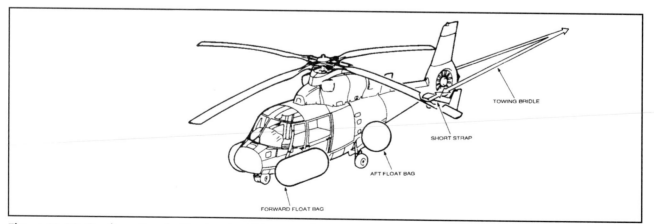

Figure 19-20 Configuration for Towing the HH-65A Helicopter Backward

D.7. HH-60J HELICOPTER SALVAGE AND TOWING

The HH-60J is configured with two flotation bags. When deployed, the bags will provide the air crew with a minimum of two minutes to effectively exit the helicopter. The HH-60J may not remain afloat long enough to be salvaged.

D.8. MULTI-UNIT (BOAT-HELICOPTER) SAR OPERATIONS

As a boat crew member, you will have many opportunities to work with helicopters on Coast Guard missions. Take every opportunity to familiarize yourself with the operations of the nearest local Coast Guard air station or other agency (e.g., Navy, Army, Air Force, National Guard, or state). Become acquainted with the different types of aircraft and their capabilities in your local operating area. General information about helicopters includes:

- Helicopters navigate in magnetic direction, similar to boats. They are equipped with superior navigation equipment. Their capabilities often exceed that of the average boat. In coastal operations, they can provide excellent navigation assistance.

- The helicopter's "Night Sun" search light is most effective as a search tool only on a clear, dry night. Moisture in the atmosphere refracts/scatters the light, making it less effective.

- When working with a helicopter at night, NEVER launch pyrotechnics/illumination signals (such as the MK-79/80 or M127A1) without first notifying the aircraft.

- When a helicopter hovers over surf or heavy seas, rotor downwash tends to blow the tops off breakers. This spray fills the air and greatly reduces visibility.

Fixed-Wing Aircraft

Introduction

Boat operations with fixed-wing aircraft are not frequently done. However, this type of aircraft can provide extended search of an area and increased communication range while the boat does the detailed search and the actual inspection or assistance. Coast Guard aircraft will have their distinctive painting design and carry a VHF-FM radio for contacting maritime vessels. Also, Coast Guard Auxiliary fixed-wing aircraft may be available to help.

E.1. AUXILIARY AIRCRAFT

Auxiliary aircraft are commonly known as "general aviation" aircraft. They are mostly single engine land planes, either high wing or low wing. There may be some twin engine aircraft, seaplanes, or helicopters. Auxiliary aircraft have no special painting design, but all are required to have their Federal Aviation Administration registration numbers on the fuselage or tail. The Coast Guard logo and lettering are not permitted; however, the facility decal is required The aircraft may also carry the Auxiliary logo decal aft of the wings and/or the word RESCUE on the bottom of the wing or fuselage in 12-inch letters (visible from low altitudes). From the surface, an Auxiliary aircraft looks like any other civilian airplane.

E.2. COMMUNICATIONS WITH AIRCRAFT

Communication between a boat and an aircraft can be done by voice radio or a variety of visual signals. Aircraft are equipped with VHF-AM aeronautical radios. In addition, those performing Coast Guard missions carry VHF-FM radios. The normal method for aircraft-boat contact is by means of the VHF-FM radio, calling on Channel 16 and then shifting over to a working frequency. Air-to-surface and surface-to-air visual signals may be used when a radio is not available.

AIR-TO-SURFACE VISUAL SIGNALS Figure 19-21 shows air-to-surface signals that an aircraft may send to a boat. An aircraft may use the following signals to direct a boat to a place:

1. Circle the vessel at least once.

2. Cross the vessel's projected course close ahead at a low altitude while rocking the wings (open-

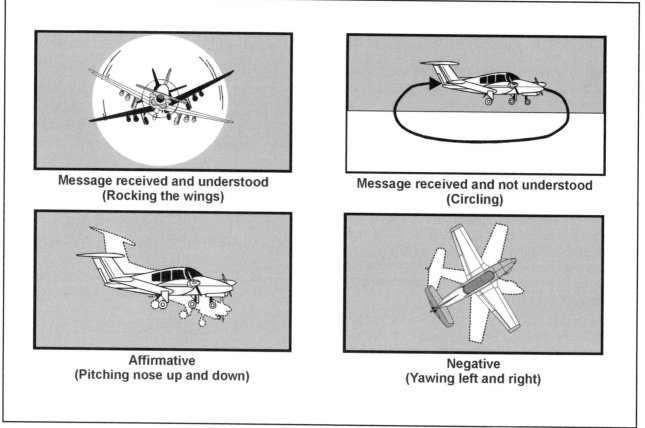

Figure 19-21 Air-to-Surface Visual Signals

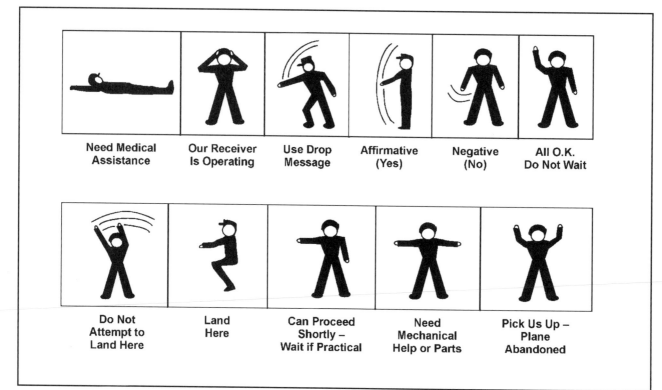

Figure 19-22 Surface-to-Air Visual Signals

ing and closing the throttle or changing the propeller pitch may be used instead of rocking the wings).

3. Head in the direction in which the vessel is to be directed.

An aircraft may show that assistance of the vessel is no longer required by crossing the vessel's wake close astern at low altitude while rocking the wings (opening and closing the throttle or changing the propeller pitch may be used instead of rocking the wings).

SURFACE-TO-AIR VISUAL SIGNALS Figure 19-22 shows surface-to-air visual signals that a boat crew member may send to an aircraft. Also, when an aircraft can not specifically identify the boat it is in contact with, the boat may make a tight turn. This distinctive, circular wake should stand out among the other boats.

E.3. TOWING FIXED-WING AIRCRAFT

Some fixed-wing aircraft are equipped with floats for short periods of travel on the surface of the water. Aircraft are fragile and can be easily damaged by a boat coming into contact. Always check with the aircraft crew to determine if a tow is desired and for advice on towing procedures. General guidance includes:

APPROACHING THE AIRCRAFT

- Ensure the propeller(s) is stopped.
- Extinguish all open flames and smoking material (aircraft fuel is highly flammable).
- Approach from upwind (the aircraft will likely have a faster drift rate than the boat).
- Steer the boat into the wind and back down to the aircraft but do not come in contact.
- Use minimum power to maneuver and fend off by hand (do not use a boat hook).
- Allow swells from passing boats to subside before getting close.

PICKING UP THE TOW

- Pass the towline to an aircraft crew member. If such a person is not available, carefully approach and attach the line to the appropriate fitting on the float(s).
- Single-float aircraft: secure the towline to the towing ring and pass it through the fairlead on the bow of the float, then to the towing boat.

- Twin-float aircraft: A bridle may be necessary. Connect a tow only to the special fittings provided. Damage could result if any other towing point is used.

TOWING THE AIRCRAFT

- Tow at low speed.
- Avoid towing in adverse conditions, if possible.
- Use a short towline.
- IF directional stability is of concern, consider use of "wing lines" tied to the wing struts or wing tips. Wing lines go from the boat's port quarter to the left wing, and the boat's starboard quarter to the right wing. Do not place any towing strain on the wing lines.
- The tow watch must watch closely so that the aircraft does not overtake the boat.

APPENDIX 19-A

Sample Briefing to Pass to Vessel Prior to Helicopter Hoisting

"A helicopter is proceeding to your position and should arrive at approximately _____. Maintain a radio watch on _____ MHz/kHz/Channel _____ VHF-FM. The helicopter will attempt to contact you. Provide a clear area for hoisting, preferably on the port stern. Lower all masts and booms that can be lowered. Secure all loose gear. Keep all unnecessary people clear of the hoisting area. Just before the helicopter arrives, secure the vessel's radar or put it in standby mode. Do not direct lights towards the helicopter as it will adversely affect the pilot's vision. Direct available lighting to illuminate the hoisting area. When the helicopter arrives, change course to place the wind 30 degrees on the port bow and maintain a steady course and steerageway. As the helicopter approaches, strong winds may be produced by the rotors, making it difficult to steer. The helicopter will provide all the equipment for the hoisting. A line will probably be trailed from the helicopter for your crew to guide the rescue device as it is lowered. Before touching the rescue device, allow it to touch your vessel. This will discharge static electricity. If you have to move the rescue device from the hoisting area to load the patient, unhook the cable from the rescue device and lay the loose hook on the deck so it can be retrieved by the helicopter. Do not attach the loose hook or the cable to your vessel. The helicopter may move to the side while the patient is being loaded. Have the patient wear a personal flotation device, and attach any important records, along with a record of medications that have been administered. When the patient is securely loaded, signal the helicopter to move into position and lower the hook. After allowing the hook to ground on the vessel, re-attach it to the rescue device. Signal the hoist operator with a "thumbs up" when you are ready for the hoisting to begin. As the rescue device is being retrieved, tend the trail line to prevent the device from swinging. When you reach the end of the trail line, gently toss it over the side."

NOTE: The briefing can be used for your own hoisting operations or you may be requested to pass this guidance on to the distressed vessel as the helicopter is en route to it. Also, some vessels or aircraft may use the term "winch" to mean the same thing as "hoist."

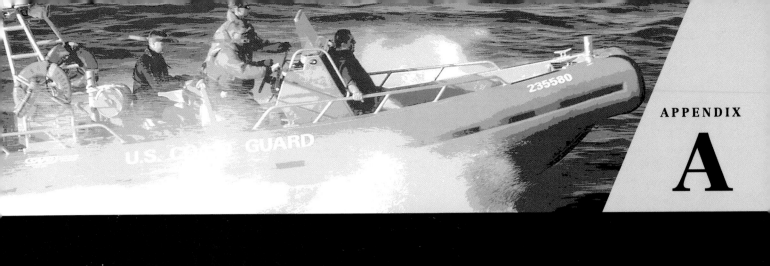

Fictitious Nautical Chart

(How the Visual Guide Would Appear on a Nautical Chart)

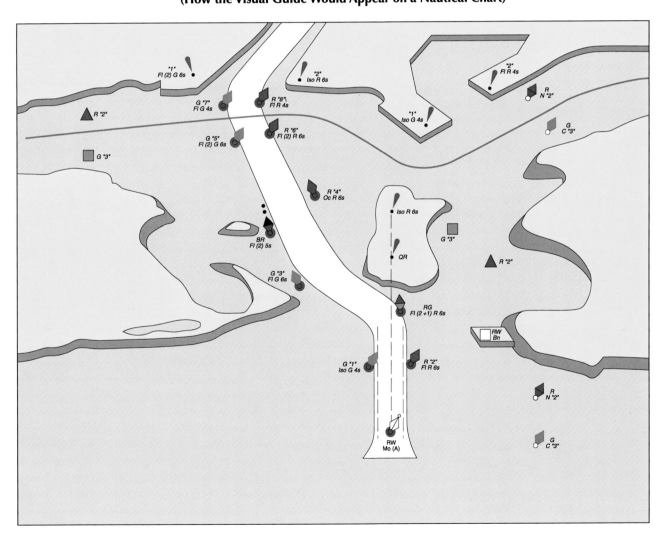

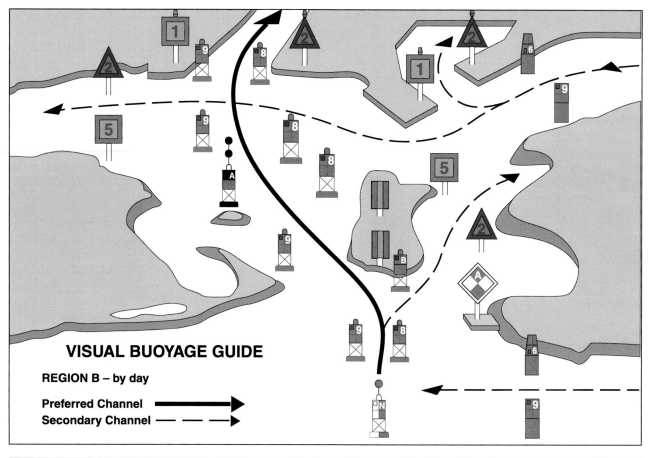

VISUAL BUOYAGE GUIDE

REGION B – by day

Preferred Channel ➤

Secondary Channel ➤

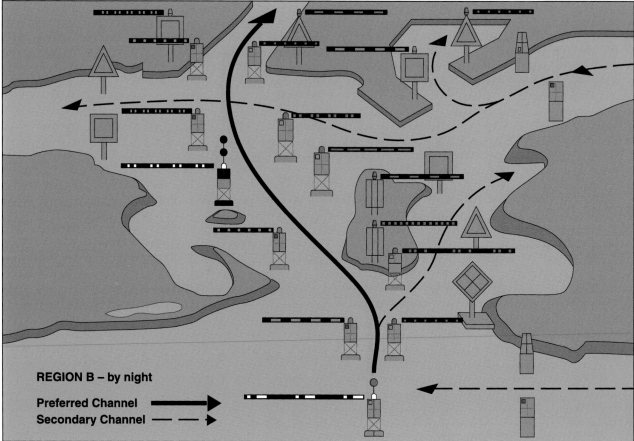

REGION B – by night

Preferred Channel ➤

Secondary Channel ➤

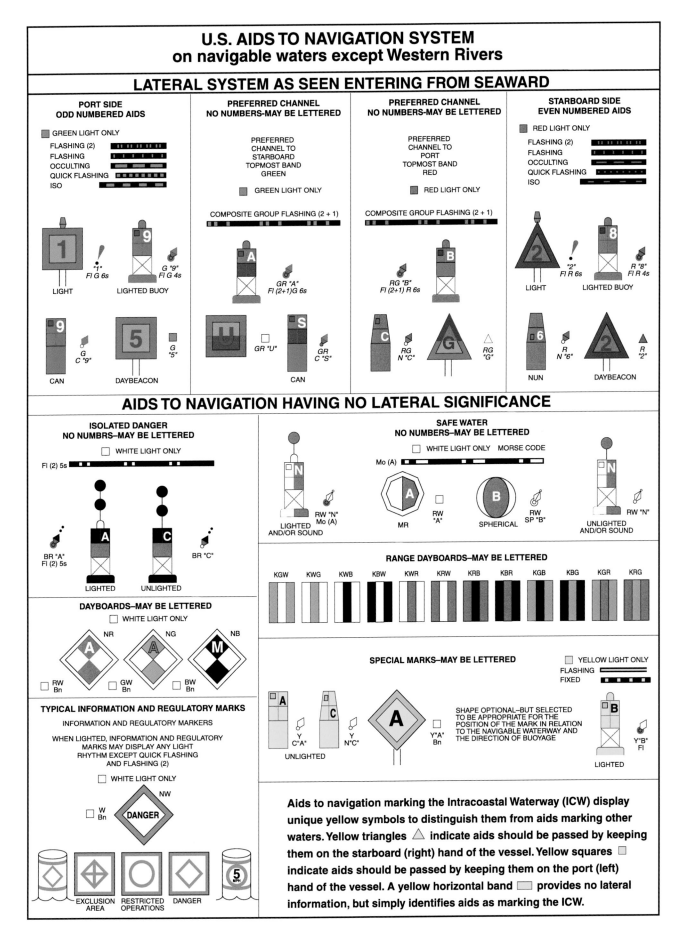

U.S. AIDS TO NAVIGATION SYSTEM
on navigable waters except Western Rivers

LATERAL SYSTEM AS SEEN ENTERING FROM SEAWARD

PORT SIDE
ODD NUMBERED AIDS

GREEN LIGHT ONLY

FLASHING (2)
FLASHING
OCCULTING
QUICK FLASHING
ISO

LIGHT — "1" Fl G 6s
LIGHTED BUOY — G "9" Fl G 4s
CAN — G C "9"
DAYBEACON — G "5"

PREFERRED CHANNEL
NO NUMBERS-MAY BE LETTERED

PREFERRED CHANNEL TO STARBOARD TOPMOST BAND GREEN

GREEN LIGHT ONLY

COMPOSITE GROUP FLASHING (2 + 1)

GR "A" Fl (2+1)G 6s
CAN — GR "U" / GR C "S"

PREFERRED CHANNEL
NO NUMBERS-MAY BE LETTERED

PREFERRED CHANNEL TO PORT TOPMOST BAND RED

RED LIGHT ONLY

COMPOSITE GROUP FLASHING (2 + 1)

RG "B" Fl (2+1) R 6s
RG N "C" / RG "G"

STARBOARD SIDE
EVEN NUMBERED AIDS

RED LIGHT ONLY

FLASHING (2)
FLASHING
OCCULTING
QUICK FLASHING
ISO

LIGHT — "2" Fl R 6s
LIGHTED BUOY — R "8" Fl R 4s
NUN — R N "6"
DAYBEACON — R "2"

AIDS TO NAVIGATION HAVING NO LATERAL SIGNIFICANCE

ISOLATED DANGER
NO NUMBRS–MAY BE LETTERED

WHITE LIGHT ONLY

Fl (2) 5s

BR "A" Fl (2) 5s — LIGHTED (A)
BR "C" — UNLIGHTED (C)

SAFE WATER
NO NUMBERS–MAY BE LETTERED

WHITE LIGHT ONLY   MORSE CODE

Mo (A)

RW "N" Mo (A) — LIGHTED AND/OR SOUND
RW "A" — MR
RW SP "B" — SPHERICAL
RW "N" — UNLIGHTED AND/OR SOUND

RANGE DAYBOARDS–MAY BE LETTERED

KGW KWG KWB KBW KWR KRW KRB KBR KGB KBG KGR KRG

DAYBOARDS–MAY BE LETTERED

WHITE LIGHT ONLY

NR — A / RW Bn
NG — A / GW Bn
NB — M / BW Bn

SPECIAL MARKS–MAY BE LETTERED

YELLOW LIGHT ONLY
FLASHING
FIXED

A / Y C"A"
C / Y N"C"
UNLIGHTED

A / Y"A" Bn

SHAPE OPTIONAL–BUT SELECTED TO BE APPROPRIATE FOR THE POSITION OF THE MARK IN RELATION TO THE NAVIGABLE WATERWAY AND THE DIRECTION OF BUOYAGE

B / Y"B" Fl
LIGHTED

TYPICAL INFORMATION AND REGULATORY MARKS

INFORMATION AND REGULATORY MARKERS

WHEN LIGHTED, INFORMATION AND REGULATORY MARKS MAY DISPLAY ANY LIGHT RHYTHM EXCEPT QUICK FLASHING AND FLASHING (2)

WHITE LIGHT ONLY

W Bn — DANGER NW

EXCLUSION AREA   RESTRICTED OPERATIONS   DANGER   5 MPH

Aids to navigation marking the Intracoastal Waterway (ICW) display unique yellow symbols to distinguish them from aids marking other waters. Yellow triangles △ indicate aids should be passed by keeping them on the starboard (right) hand of the vessel. Yellow squares □ indicate aids should be passed by keeping them on the port (left) hand of the vessel. A yellow horizontal band ▭ provides no lateral information, but simply identifies aids as marking the ICW.

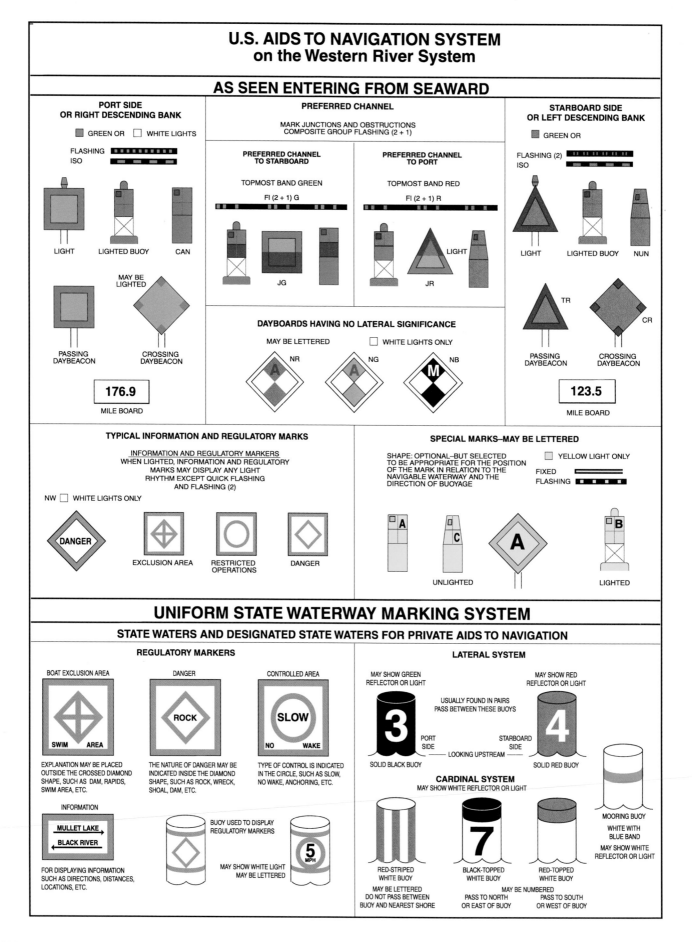

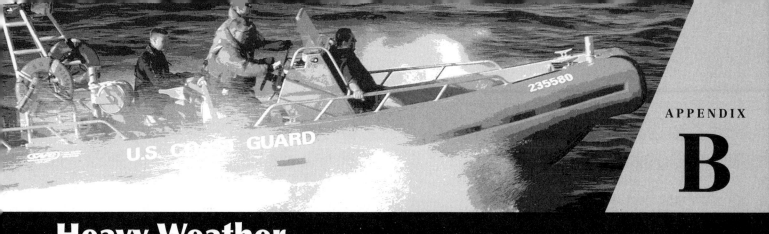

Heavy Weather Addendum

Editor's Note: *Sooner or later you'll find yourself operating your boat in heavy weather—at least heavy relative to the size and handling characteristics of your boat. This chapter presents the Coast Guard's best thinking on dealing with that situation. It's important to understand, however, that it is not the intention of this chapter to urge you into heavy weather. To the contrary, you should learn to handle your boat one step at a time, moving from the most benign conditions to more demanding situations, always leaving a large margin for safety. You'll notice that the Coast Guard prohibits its people from operating in surf conditions unless they've received appropriate training and are in boats designed for surf operations. Nevertheless, some of the techniques discussed here may help you survive should you find yourself operating in the surf or in heavy breaking seas—in an inlet, for example. As is the case in other chapters, the Coasties begin this subject with the statement that "proper risk assessment is essential."*

Overview

Introduction

This Addendum provides a general overview of boat operations in heavy weather. Heavy weather poses a particular threat to the boat and the safety of its crew. Boats are not to be operated beyond their operating limits and crews should not undertake operations beyond their capabilities. Proper risk management is essential. All boats can be expected to encounter heavy weather, but that does not mean specific operational evolutions must be undertaken. The boat crew must heed the guidance and warnings contained within this addendum. Surf operations are conducted only by surf-capable boats and specially trained crew.

In this addendum

SECTION A

Heavy Weather Wave and Surf Characteristics

Introduction

A thorough understanding of surf and wave action is essential for a boat crew to safely operate in a heavy weather/surf environment. Crews of Coast Guard motor lifeboats (MLB) and surf rescue boats (SRB) received special training for heavy weather operations. The other Coast Guard boats have operating limits that do not allow operations in surf. While theory and formulas may be of little use when you are faced with a series of 12- to 14-foot breakers, knowledge of how waves are formed and behave at sea, over shoals and in the surf zone will equip a coxswain to make the best possible decisions and minimize danger to the crew and boat. There are no such things as "sneaker" waves, only waves for which we have not prepared.

The combination of wave and surf factors can cause interference with an infinite number of possibilities, and coupled with the effects of currents, wind, and geographic factors can create situations in which no vessel or crew can operate safely. In heavy weather, awareness is the key to running the safest operations possible.

General wave and surf characteristics can be found in Chapter 12—Weather and Oceanography. This section covers only heavy weather wave and surf characteristics.

In this section

Waves in Heavy Weather

A.1. FORMATION OF OCEAN WAVES

There are several forces which create waves at sea, the most significant of which is wind. The factors which determine the characteristics of wind waves are:

- wind speed,
- wind duration, and
- fetch (the distance over open water which the wind has blown).

As the wind begins to blow, it creates seas, which are typically steep and choppy and have little pattern. As the wind continues, the seas begin to become more defined. In heavy weather, observing and measuring waves is important. You and your crew can operate appropriately if you can get a general sense of the waves in which you are working.

A.2. EFFECTS OF WIND

Strong winds usually have the same effects as strong currents on wave behavior, but because of the infinite variables of wind speed, direction and interaction with currents, it is often difficult to predict what effect the wind will have on waves.

Observing and Measuring Waves

A.3. GENERAL

The ability to recognize wave patterns and characteristics is essential to safe operation in surf and heavy weather. A coxswain operating in these conditions must be able to estimate wave heights accurately and to determine the timing of lulls and series.

A.4. TIMING

The lull period in a wave system is the safest time to transit a bar, an inlet, or a shoal area in heavy seas/surf. By timing the duration of the lull, you can be prepared to make a transit while the waves are smaller and you will also have some idea of how much time is available before the next big set rolls through. The basic technique is to use a stopwatch. After the last big wave of a series has passed, the timer is started. When the first big waves of the next set arrive the timer is stopped. The displayed time is the duration of the lull, which may range from less than a minute to several minutes. This pattern should be observed for as long as possible until you arrive at a useful consistent time. You may also find it useful to time the duration of the series and number of waves in the set. There may be circumstances in which the time is not consistent or the mission does not allow time to wait. In these circumstances, you may have to simply identify the beginning of the lull and make your move with the knowledge that another set could arrive at any time.

Heavy surf conditions require special training for boat operators.

A.5. ESTIMATING WAVE HEIGHT

An accurate estimate of wave height is subjective and sometimes difficult to accomplish, but there are a number of methods that, with practice, will give good results.

HEIGHT OF EYE OR FREEBOARD With the boat in the trough and on a level and even keel, any wave that obscures the horizon is greater than your height of eye. Your eye height while seated at the helm or standing flat in the deck house of a 44' MLB is about nine feet. You can also compare a wave to the deck edge or a structure such as the handrail. Observe the wave face while you are bow into it and in the trough on an even keel. This is also generally the best method for judging surf.

COMPARISON WITH FLOATING STRUCTURES OR VESSELS This technique is most useful when observing from land, but may be applied while underway. If you know that the freeboard of a buoy is 13 feet, you can use that information to determine the height of the waves passing it. A buoy can also be used to determine the wave period. You can observe a vessel underway and by estimating the freeboard of the vessel and observing its motions on the water, you can gain a fair estimate of the seas in which it is operating

COMPARISON WITH FIXED STRUCTURE Observation of waves as they pass a fixed structure, such as a breakwall, jetty, or pier can be very accurate and can also provide wave period.

DEPTH SOUNDER This method can be very accurate. A "flasher" type depth sounder works best, but a digital finder with a fast update speed will also work. By comparing the depth in the trough on even keel with the depth at the crest on even keel, you can arrive at an accurate measurement.

All of these methods can be useful and reasonably accurate, but they require practice and experience. By comparing a local Weather Service buoy report with your observations, you can fine-tune your sense of wave height. With enough practice, you should be able to judge wave heights simply by looking at the waves themselves.

Surf Zone

A.6. TYPES OF SURF

There are three basic types of breaking waves:

- plunging,
- spilling, and
- surging,

Each of which is discussed in Chapter 12—Weather and Oceanography. Each type of breaking waves brings its own hazards, such as suction currents, dropping huge quantities of water, and exerting a great deal of force. It is important to remember when operating in heavy weather that these hazards are often magnified beyond those encountered in calm water operations.

A.7. SURF ZONE CHARACTERISTICS

In normal operations and especially in heavy weather, there are a number of conditions created in the surf zone and in individual waves of which the coxswain must be aware. These are described in the following paragraphs.

WINDOWS A window is an area in which waves have momentarily stopped breaking, opening up a safer area of operation for your boat. Windows often form in the area of aerated water where a large set of waves has just finished breaking. A window may remain for a long time or may begin breaking again almost immediately. It is preferable to operate the boat in a windows whenever possible.

HIGH/LOW SIDE OF A WAVE The "high side" is defined as the section of a wave which carries the most potential energy. It may be the part that is still building towards breaking point, or it may be the part which has already broken. The "low side" is where the least potential energy exists and represents the safest direction to turn while running stern-to. These high and low sides often change rapidly, and the ability to quickly navigate the high and low sides is a critical skill for surf operations.

WAVE SADDLES The "saddle" is the lowest part of a wave, bordered on both sides by higher ones. Often it is a small, unbroken section of a wave that is breaking. It is preferable to drive a boat in the saddles if possible, thus avoiding the whitewater. While saddles are very useful, they must be watched carefully, because they easily turn into "close-outs."

CLOSEOUTS "Closeouts" occur when a wave breaks from the ends toward the middle, or two waves break towards each other. The middle may look like a good saddle, but can quickly turn into whitewater. Closeouts should be avoided because they can create more energy than a single break.

WAVE SHOULDER The "shoulder" is the edge of a wave. It may be the very edge of the whitewater on a breaker, or the edge of a high peaking wave that is about to break. The shoulder is usually lower in height than the middle of the wave. Driving on the shoulders can be particularly useful in a narrow surf zone because it allows you to drive very close to a break in relative safety.

RIP CURRENTS Rips are created along a long beach or reef surf zone. The water from waves hitting the beach travels out to the sides and parallel to the shore line, creating a "longshore current" that eventually returns to sea. This seaward flow creates deep channels in the sand offshore that can shift from day to day. In the case of a reef, the channels are permanent parts of the reef, but otherwise behave the same. In these channels, the waves or surf are usually smaller because of refraction over the deeper water. Because of this, a rip channel often represents a safer route into or out of a surf zone. A rip current may also carry a person in the water or a disabled vessel clear of the surf zone. If using a rip current, take great care to stay in the channel by watching the depth sounder. Be alert for debris, which tends to concentrate in these areas.

SECTION B

Heavy Weather Boat Handling

Introduction

In calm weather, there is no difference between handling a boat under power at sea or anywhere else, except that there is a lot more room to maneuver at sea. If there are waves of any size, you must understand the effects they will have on your boat and crew.

The discomfort that can be experienced when underway on boats in heavy seas is hard to describe to those who have not experienced them before. It can drain a person of all their energy and willpower at the times when they are needed most. Heavy weather pounding can hamper the capacity of a person to make a rational and prudent decisions in tough situations.

In this section

Title	See Page(s)
Motions	428–29
Control of Effects	429–30
Experience	430
Boat Handling	430–31

Motions

B.1. GENERAL

There are three basic motions that a boat experiences while operating in a seaway—rolling, pitching, and yawing. Each motion creates its own problems.

B.2. WAVE GENERATION

Before we can discuss the effects weather has on boats, you must understand that waves are generated by winds. As the wind is never regular, neither are the waves. A normal seaway may consist of different trains of waves, running in slightly different directions and heights. When waves coincide with each other, they can produce one wave as high as the sum of all their heights. Also, when troughs coincide, they can produce a trough with combined depths of all of them, or a trough combining with a wave producing a flat patch. Most of the time, waves vary a bit in height and direction, but now and then a big wave comes along, or a flat patch, or a deep hole in the water. All of these factors, alone or combined, play a part in how a boat reacts and moves in the water.

ROLLING Rolling of the vessel is caused by a wave lifting up one side of the boat, rolling under the boat and dropping that side, then lifting the other side and dropping it in turn. The next wave then approaches the boat and goes through the same sequence. Rolling occurs when a boat runs beam to the swell. The moment the boat starts rolling, it automatically rolls back and forth in accordance with the time of its natural roll period. This will cause the boat to roll against the next wave sometimes and with it at others. Usually the boat roll is altogether out of step with the arrival of the waves.

PITCHING Pitching occurs when the boat is running bow into the waves. Each wave first lifts up the bow, passes underneath and drops the bow, then lifts up the stern, passes underneath and drops it. Although not as dangerous as rolling, violent pitching in close steep seas puts great stress on both your boat and your crew. In suitable conditions, synchronous pitching can occur in the same manner as synchronous rolling, and the result is an increasingly violent and regular motion.

YAWING Yawing is caused when the boat is operating in a following sea. The wave approaches the stern of the boat, lifts it up, drops it, and travels forward, lifting the bow and dropping it in turn. In theory, this action is similar to pitching, but in reverse and usually much gentler because the boat is motoring away from, instead of into, the waves. As the wave lifts up the stern, the bow of the boat begins to be pushed forward through the water, causing a resistance against the boat's hull. With the combination of resistance and the speed of the wave, the stern tries to overtake the bow, causing it to broach. Once the wave clears the stern, it lifts the bow of the boat and the stern begins to slide down the backside of the wave, pulling the bow back around and causing the boat to straighten back out.

Control of Effects

B.3. GENERAL

Now that you have an understanding of what effects swells have on your boat, you need to know what corrective measures can be taken to decrease the effects.

B.4. ALTERING COURSE AND SPEED

Dangerous rolling is proceeded by discomfort, or at least a small period of concern. As explained before, rolling is caused when running beam to the seas or slightly quartered off the seas. To correct, alter your course. This interrupts the frequency of the period of contact with the beam seas. If you just slow down in this situation, there will be no difference in the motion of your boat because the speed has no bearing on the frequency of beam seas. When quartering the seas, you may also experience the rolling motion. If you are experiencing a great deal of rolling while quartering, your best course of action is to slow down, again interrupting frequency period. With the combination of altering course and speed, you and your crew should have a more comfortable ride.

B.5. PITCHING

Severe pitching will fatigue or injure your crew long before it damages your boat, and is the least dangerous in heavy weather. Violent pitching can be corrected in the same manner as correcting rolling: alter course and/or speed, interrupting frequency of

period of wave encounter. In heavy weather, watch for the possibility of very deep troughs so that the boat can be immediately slowed to reduce the impact as the boat falls into it.

B.6. YAWING

Running stern-to in heavy seas requires intense concentration, as steering corrections must be made the instant you feel the stern of the boat being lifted by the oncoming swell. If you are traveling too fast and not paying attention, the wave will lift up the stern and broach the boat one direction or the other. You may not be able to correct if the wave gets a hold of the boat and begins to surf it. Once the wave has control of your boat, it may roll, pitchpole, or strike another floating object. You will have no control in this situation; therefore, pay attention so you can apply corrective measures early enough to prevent disaster. To prevent yawing, watch for waves approaching your stern. If the approaching wave is large and steep, the possibility of surfing is great. Slow down before the wave gets to you, and allow it to pass underneath your boat. After the wave passes underneath the boat, increase power to the original RPM. If you are operating in fairly regular seas, steer the boat as you would normally. Turn in the direction toward which the stern tends to slip. No increase or decrease in power will be necessary as long as the swells are not big enough to cause your boat to surf. If you find yourself being lifted up and surfed, increase your power. As the bow begins to dig into the trough and veer to one direction, keep power on and turn the helm hard in that direction. This action will cause your boat to dig itself out of the wave and climb up over the top. Another method is to do an "S" turn. The "S" turn is a very effective and safe maneuver as long as it is done in time and done correctly. It the maneuver used most often to maintain control in steep stern seas.

B.7. WIND

Wind effects the boat AND the swell. Wind demands as much attention and concern as the sea state. No matter what operational function you are conducting, e.g., man overboard, towing, or just swimming, you need to be aware of the wind. As wind increases, so do the seas. As both wind and seas increase, the boat will be more and more difficult to handle. The slower the boat travels, the more effect the wind has, and the harder it is to maneuver. If the boat is dead in the water (DIW), the wind will push against any sail area causing the boat to turn in the direction in which the wind is blowing. The harder the wind is blowing, the faster the boat turns and the harder the helmsman has to work to control the turning moment. This situation becomes especially difficult when you're operating in close quarters, making a towing approach, or trying simply attempting to keep station.

COUNTERACT THE WIND To counteract the wind and/or seas, pivot the boat in against the wind. Don't be afraid to use the power; sometimes all it takes is very small amounts of asymmetric throttle to compensate for crosswind. Other times it might take massive amounts of power using both throttles together to counteract the wind. There no single technique for all wind situations. The appropriate technique depends on the amount of wind blowing against you. The boat will travel slower for a given power in a headwind; the greater the sail area, the greater the wind resistance. There is no real corrective action for this, but coxswains must be aware of the phenomenon. Similarly, if you are running with the wind on your stern your speed will increase depending on amount of sail area. In either case you'll have plenty of time for corrective action so long as you and your crew stay alert to environmental conditions.

Experience

B.8. GENERAL

As a coxswain in the Coast Guard, you have been entrusted with the safe operation of the boat and the safety of the crew. To accomplish this, you must have a complete grasp of boat handling in different situations and environments. This chapter will give you a basic understanding, but by no means will it give you a complete knowledge of how boats handle in different conditions. That knowledge will come with experience.

B.9. BOAT REACTION

Handling a boat in heavy weather is *similar* to handling a vessel in calm weather. Although the techniques are the same, the coxswain and crew will need higher levels of concentration and alertness. Often, helm and power movements must be larger and quicker.

B.10. PREPARATIONS

A number of items must be checked before the boat gets underway. They include:

- Check your boat to ensure that all the equipment is on board, in good condition and fully operational.
- Ensure that all electronics have been tested and are completely functional.

- Check throttles and steering to ensure that they are fully operational.
- Inspect your crew to ensure that they are qualified and certified and that they have all of their survival equipment. Check the weather and bar conditions.
- Most important, know what your mission is.

Boat Handling

B.11. GENERAL

A coxswain must be very familiar and confident in conducting these fundamental maneuvers.

B.12. STATION KEEPING

Station keeping is one of the hardest and most often used fundamentals used in boat operations. The maneuver is used for hooking up a tow, recovering a person in the water (PIW), transferring personnel and gear, and operating in surf conditions. Before you can station keep, you must be familiar with prevailing conditions. For example:

- How hard is the wind blowing, and from what directions?
- What is the swell direction?
- What direction are the seas and currents from?

It is important that you consider all of these factors; each will have a separate but important effect on the boat. The objective of station keeping is to be able to hold your bow squarely into the most predominant force—current or wind—while keeping your boat in one position. Normally the swell will be the predominant force, though the wind and sea may be more predominant in some situations. For the purpose of this chapter, swell will be considered the predominant force. If the wind and seas are not from the same direction as the swell, they will push against the sail areas of the boat, forcing the bow to fall off the swell to either port or starboard side. The coxswain needs to be aware that this is happening and begin corrective measures. The power of the natural forces working against the boat must be counteracted with the same amount of force from the boat. The coxswain will need to use both the rudders and throttles in conjunction with each other. Again, sometimes it takes only a small amount of power, and other times it may take a lot of power. Use whatever force is necessary to keep your bow from falling off the swell and keep your boat in one position. If the wind is pushing you on the port side, push back by pivoting the boat port. Turn your wheel to port while applying enough power to accomplish the results you want. Drive the boat, don't let the boat drive you!

B.13. BACKING

The ability to back your boat in a straight line is very important and can be very difficult. Most coxswains cannot back the boat any distance without allowing the bow to fall off the swell. Backing is used in the same situations as station keeping and all boat drivers need to be proficient in it. Before you can start backing, get your bow square to the swell, engage both throttles in reverse, put your helm amidships and start applying small amount of power and gradually increase the power. As the boat begins to back, the bow will start to fall off to one direction or the other depending on wind. As the bow slips to one side or the other, begin to counter with more throttle control and rudder. *For example:* if the bow slips to port, counter by shifting your rudder to port, increase starboard reverse power and decrease port reverse power. While doing this, you will observe the bow begin to straighten up to starboard. As it does, correct your rudder back to amidships and bring your throttles back to an even RPM. Repeat this technique throughout the entire evolution. Continue countering with rudder and throttles until you have backed to desired position. If your bow falls off too far before you begin to counter, you will not be able to correct by backing without subjecting your boat and crew to a very uncomfortable ride. If not corrected soon enough, the boat will fall completely to beam seas. When this happens, your best corrective action is to use what ever power is necessary to get your bow back square into the swell, then begin backing again. You should never back on the face of a large swell; if done incorrectly, the swell may take complete control of your boat. The swell action will amplify the amount bow falls off thus making correction difficult if not entirely impossible.

If you keep your bow square to the swell or most predominant force and use proper amounts of power for different situations, the boat can be handled without effectively. It takes many hours of training and practice to become proficient in these maneuvers.

NOTE

If you leave your rudder locked over in one direction while backing and pull your power off, the boat's rudders will take over and you will swing in that direction very dramatically. Rudders need constant propeller force in order to prevent this from happening. When the backing maneuver is complete, immediately shift your rudder amidships and apply forward propulsion.

Heavy Weather Piloting

Introduction

The distinction between "piloting" and "navigation" is outlined in many respected publications including Dutton's *Navigation and Piloting* and Bowditch's *Practical Navigator*. This chapter is designed to offer techniques that are unique to operations in heavy weather situations.

The importance of sound piloting is well described in Dutton's:

"Piloting requires the greatest experience and nicest judgment of any form of navigation. Constant vigilance, unfailing mental alertness, and a thorough knowledge of the principles involved are essential . . . In pilot waters there is little or no opportunity to correct errors. Even a slight blunder may result in disaster, perhaps involving the loss of life."

Some might consider this statement melodramatic, yet in essence it is true. Any stressful or confusing situation will be aggravated by heavy weather. The loss of life may not involve your crew, but if you are unable to pilot a vessel to persons in distress, it most certainly will involve the lives of mariners who entrust their lives to the abilities of boat operators to come to their assistance.

In this section

Title	See Page(s)
Preparation	**431–33**
Equipment Condition	**433**
Specific Techniques	**433–34**

Preparation

C.1. GENERAL

Being prepared is not limited to having the proper or sufficient equipment aboard. Preparation for a heavy weather case involving piloting (which all must if you leave the dock) can begin months before the mission. The primary tool to ensure success in any piloting evolution is local knowledge. The ability to quickly match objects seen visually or on radar with charted objects will increase a coxswain's capabilities. Naturally, calm weather affords the best situation to study your area underway, but observing your AOR during heavy weather from land or sea will enable you to identify areas that become particularly hazardous in inclement weather. Of course, none of the navigation tools or boat handling techniques are useful if you are not well versed in their use. No amount of studying or classroom instruction can substitute for underway training. You should take every opportunity to pilot, no matter what the conditions may be. The wise coxswain "overnavigates" the boat during fair weather so that he or she can acquire the skills to navigate in poor weather without fear or nervous strain.

C.2. PILOTING EQUIPMENT

Piloting in heavy weather can be enough of a challenge without the additional burden of substandard equipment. There are a few items that are absolutely necessary, and others that are helpful in easing the stress of any piloting evolution. They are listed below.

C.3. CHARTS

Often the most neglected but critically important piece of piloting equipment is the chart. Naturally, an up-to-date chart in good condition is required. The techniques of effective heavy weather piloting are based on the assumption that the coxswain is topside, near the radar, and standing up so that he or she can see all around the vessel and maintain strong lines of communication with the crew. Anyone who has ever tried to lay down a trackline or obtain a fix and plot it while underway knows how awkward the process can be. Prepare charts in advance to ease this problem. Using plastic-covered or laminated chartlets can help. Lay down the routes that you routinely take in your AOR, add some DRs for usual speeds traveled, some radar ranges and distances between fixed objects, and you will gain valuable time underway. It is unrealistic to have tracklines laid down for every position in the area, but you will have information to get you to a point where you can "jump off" from a preset trackline and pilot to datum. The initial time you will save will enable you to think about the next stage in your response to a distress

C.4. CHARTS AND EQUIPMENT PREPARATION

The following are some tried and tested methods of chart and equipment preparation—and some common mistakes to avoid.

PERSONAL PILOTING KIT Take the time to de-velop your personal piloting kit. Coast Guard standard boats are required to have all the necessary equipment in the chart box as per the type manual, but think of this as backup gear. Build your navigation kit to be user friendly. If space permits, carry duplicates of items that you use most. If you prefer the Weems plotter, carry an extra one. When the one you are using slides off the radar shelf and disappears under the coxswain grating, you will have a ready replacement. Any type of carrier that you are comfortable with will suffice. Briefcases, helmet bags, and large container-type clipboards are commonly used.

CHART PREPARATION Have the right chart for every mission. All too often, coxswains try to cover their entire operating area with one chart. Piloting in the harbor or river with a small-scale coastal chart is inaccurate and unsafe. Prepare your charts in advance with as much information as possible without cluttering them to the point of illegibility. More than likely, the courses from your dock to your entrance are consistently the same. One occasion where this might not be the case is during heavy weather where the entrance breaks and some alternate course is needed to compensate for unfavorable seas and wind. Draw out tracklines from the point of departure to a position where you would normally station keep before crossing the bar or inlet. Lay out DR positions along the trackline to aid in determining speed over ground and position. Be realistic about DRs on boats. If you have a three-mile trackline on a constant course with good water on either side, three minute DRs may be excessive and detract from your ability to monitor what is happening around you.

CHART LABELING Label your chart with all pertinent information. The chart should be labeled using common terminology. Labels should be neat and easily read. A good rule of thumb is that anyone should be able to pick up your chart and use it to pilot the area safely. Write course directions and their reciprocals specifying true or magnetic. Distances on all radar ranges and between aids or fixed objects along the track will also help in computing speed. Do not use a red pen or pencil as it will not-show up under a red light. Using a highlighter pen for some information on your chart will help in readily identifying important information.

RADAR RANGES One of the most underused methods in piloting is the use of radar ranges. Having a beam radar range at your DR positions takes a great deal of the guesswork out of navigation. If you have predetermined ranges laid out, you will be able to see at a glance how far you are left or right of track well before you reach the DR position. Having these ranges will also allow you to make constant minor changes to your course instead of major corrections at each DR position. To further simplify matters, lay out distances fore and aft as well. Often circumstance does not provide a fixed object directly ahead or astern, but even an object 10 to 30° off the bow or stern will give you an approximation of your progress along your trackline. These fore and aft ranges also are critical in computing speed over ground using the three-minute rule and its variations. If you are tasked with piloting to datum, lay out ranges to datum from known points of land or from charted floating aids to navigation. Attempt to use ranges as close to directly ahead or astern and directly abeam as possible. Then it will be easy to determine if you are right or left of track or too far up or down track.

CHART STOWAGE Learn to fold your chart properly. Hopefully, you will have taken the time to make chartlets or laminate charts of a workable size with the most common routes and positions already marked. But a chart cannot be prepared for every possible situation and it is very likely that you will have to plot a position on a chart, lay out a trackline and go. If the urgency of the case puts you on a boat heading to sea in heavy weather, take the time to fold your chart so that it is usable. You will be unable to unfold the chart every time you need the distance scale or compass rose. If possible, datum and ranges to datum should be on the same side of the folded chart. Do as much of the chart work as possible before you leave the dock. Everyone has felt the urgency of getting underway immediately, but remember, you are ultimately responsible for the safe navigation of your boat and no level of urgency will be an excuse for running aground or colliding with another vessel.

Equipment Condition

C.5. STRAIGHT EDGE

Although fairly self-explanatory, it is not uncommon to see coxswains using a set of parallel rules with chips along the edges or screws so loose that the legs move freely while they attempt to draw a line. The Weems plotter is underused. It can be very helpful in getting quick, reasonably accurate ranges and bearings, especially on a folded chart or chartlet.

C.6. DIVIDERS

This drafting instrument is an integral part of a successful piloting job. A "sloppy" pair of dividers is not only difficult to work with, but poses a hazard if it supplies you with inaccurate information There are numerous types of dividers available today that ensure a reasonable amount of friction to hold the legs in place. Specifically, the dividers that are adjusted with a center wheel are well suited for heavy weather piloting.

C.7. COMPASS

The compass (or *drawing compass* to distinguish it from the magnetic compass) is similar to dividers, but has a pencil lead inserted in one leg and is used for drawing arcs or circles. Always ensure that sharp, spare lead tips are available.

C.8. NAUTICAL SLIDE RULE

The nautical slide rule is a quick, efficient tool for determining speed, distance and time. The tool is accurate and easy to use, but also lends itself to decreasing a coxswain's ability to make mental calculations. A firm grasp of the three-minute rule and its variations is crucial for making quick, hands-off calculations of speed over ground.

C.9. RED LENS FLASHLIGHT

There is no substitute for a user-friendly red light for night operations. It is often difficult to hold a standard "C" or "D" cell flashlight and work additional navigation equipment simultaneously. Smaller lights, some adjustable with beams, have been modified for attachment to clothing and clipboards, freeing navigator's hands.

C.10. TIME KEEPING INSTRUMENTS

It is impossible to pilot a boat without a reliable method of keeping time. There should be two stopwatches on every boat—one at the chart table and one on the navigation receiver. One should always be used as a backup for the other in case they are inadvertently turned off. Remember, you can always compute your speed over ground by backtracking to the time you departed a known point. Always write down your departure time at a fixed aid or landmark for permanent record. It is prudent seamanship for every member of the boat crew to have a watch.

Specific Techniques

C.11. GENERAL

There are some practices that relate strictly to boats in heavy weather. First, a realistic approach must be taken. A boat is not designed to be handled in the same way as a cutter. The size of the crew and the motion of the boat in heavy weather make it very difficult to navigate. If a crew member is not below plotting and relaying information to the coxswain, then the coxswain is either below where he cannot monitor the crew, or he is working the radar and cannot check the plots. The coxswain should brief the crew on the scenario and assign duties. If possible, the coxswain should delegate tasks to other crew members as much as possible. For instance, have your helmsman monitor the depth sounder and give you periodic reports, ensuring that water depth does not drop below a specified amount. Unlike a larger cutter, the boat is a highly maneuverable, shallow-draft vessel that can stop fast and make sharp turns. A common-sense approach using standard navigation practices with the knowledge that the boat never was, is not, and will never be intended to be operated as a cutter will allow you to pilot safely and accurately within the guidelines set forth by higher authority.

Heavy Weather Person in the Water Recovery

Introduction

Recovering a person from the water in heavy weather requires special precautions beyond the routine described in Chapter 16 on person in the water (PIW) recovery procedures. It may be considered a given that a man overboard/PIW evolution will bring the coxswain and crew to a higher sense of awareness. However, due to the increased risk inherent in heavy weather operations, special considerations must be given to the level of experience and skill of the boat crew and the capabilities of the boat. It is up to the coxswain, in most cases, to act as he or she sees fit.

NOTE

Do not attempt a rescue in conditions that exceed the operational limitations of the boat and/or experience/skill level of the crew. Use common sense!

In this section

Title	See Page(s)
Man Overboard	434–36
Recovery of a PIW	436
Use of a Surface Swimmer	436
Multiple PIWs	436

Man Overboard

D.1. GENERAL

The general man overboard procedure is put in effect as soon as the alarm is sounded, but the nature of heavy weather adds complications.

D.2. DOWN SWELL RUN

If needed, the turn to run down swell and approach will be planned differently in heavy weather. The coxswain may not be able to turn the boat immediately after the alarm is given. Doing so may expose the bow of the boat to the swell enough that regaining control and getting the bow back into the seas might be very difficult.

The coxswain will push ahead a safe distance from the man overboard and station keep until the opportunity to turn presents itself. The turn is not made until the coxswain can do so without exposing the beam of the boat to the breaks or excessive swells. This is avoided by timing the turn to correspond with the lull in the breaks. Doing so allows the coxswain to take advantage of any window that may develop. Once the window has been identified, the coxswain turns, either port or starboard, using the techniques described in the Heavy Weather Boat Handling section. If the water depth allows, continue down swell past the man overboard. As you pass at a safe distance, make an assessment as to the condition of the man overboard (i.e., conscious and face-up, unconscious and face-down); this will help you decide how best to prepare for your final approach. Also, consider deploying another ring buoy if the first one is out of the victim's reach.

D.3. THE APPROACH

Once the run down swell is completed, the boat must be turned to make the approach. The turn should be made so as to simultaneously put the bow into the surf/swell and have the man overboard directly in front of the boat, keeping in mind the turning radius of the boat and the effect strong winds may have, make adjustments as necessary. This may require some lateral movement down-swell of the man overboard. The pointer must be able to communicate with the coxswain at all times. Positioning the pointer by the coxswain flat/cabin is recommended.

Once down swell, turn quickly and avoid getting caught broadside to the surf/swell. A break taken on the beam may roll the boat.

WARNING

Do not allow any crew to go forward at any time during this evolution. It puts them in great danger and decreases the crew's ability to communicate.

After completing the turn into the swell or breaks, stop forward momentum and, if practical, station keep by using references on the beach, jetty, and/or adjacent structures. Doing this will give you time to consider the following:

- Your position relative to the man overboard.
- Set and drift of your boat and the man overboard.
- Wind direction.
- Formation of a window/lull near the man overboard.
- Reestablishing crew responsibilities (if necessary).
- Sending a crewman to the man-overboard recovery area.

NOTE

On a CG standard boat, the crew must stay out of the recovery area until the turn is completed, the bow is back into the swell, and the coxswain gives the command.

D.4. THE RECOVERY

When making the final approach, the coxswain must adjust speed to avoid launching the boat off the back side of a wave. Use the bow bitt or other stationary object on the bow as a sight and aim the boat at the man overboard. Begin slowing to bare steerageway as you near the man overboard. This approach is made so that the man overboard is not in danger of being struck by the boat. Timing is essential! If the coxswain is able, wait for a lull to make the approach.

The crew must keep the coxswain informed of the man overboard's relationship to the boat at all times.

This can be done by using reference points on the boat and calling distance off the hull.

WARNING

A breaking wave or steep swell can surf a man overboard into the side of the boat or move him astern of it!

RECOVERY OF A CONSCIOUS MAN OVERBOARD Ideally, the boat should be stopped with the man overboard at arm's length from the recovery area. This allows a crewman there to reach out and pull in the man overboard for recovery. In the event the man overboard is too far away to reach by hand, he or she may be able to swim to a rescue heaving line and be pulled to the recovery area. Examine all of your options. Keep in mind that a person suffering from hypothermia and/or exhaustion may not be able to assist when being hoisted from the water. Also, remember that using a rescue heaving line in the surf is very risky. The crewman tending the line must remain alert to keep the line under control at all times, and must advise the coxswain when the line is in the water.

RECOVERY OF AN UNCONSCIOUS MAN OVERBOARD Recovery of an unconscious victim from the surf presents an even greater challenge. Because the man overboard is unable to swim to or hold on to the rescue heaving line, the coxswain must maneuver the boat so that the man overboard is taken alongside. Again, crew communication is critical. The coxswain steers the boat straight for the man overboard and as he or she begins to disappear under the bow flair, turns slightly to port or starboard (depending on which side is best for recovery) and windward of the man overboard if possible. At this point, the coxswain will lose sight of the man overboard under the bow flair. It is now the pointer's responsibility to inform the coxswain of the location of the man overboard, the distance off the hull, and how far the man overboard is passing down the hull. When the pointer reports that the man overboard is approaching the pilot house, the coxswain should begin glancing down at the water, watching for the man overboard to appear. When the man overboard is in sight, the coxswain may need to make a final speed adjustment. Foam or bubbles passing down the hull can help determine the boat's speed. Having all way off when the man overboard is approaching the recovery area is important for two reasons:

- First, it is very difficult to maintain a handhold on a person when the boat is still moving ahead.

- Second, having to back down with the man overboard near the recovery area is dangerous, and the discharge from backing down may push the man overboard farther away from the boat. Again, slow down well before the man overboard is at the recovery area.

To do this, the coxswain may back down on both engines or on the engine opposite the man overboard. Backing down on the opposite engine will kick the recovery area toward the man overboard. However, do not allow the bow to fall off the swell. Backing down must be done before the man overboard gets to the recovery area so that the boat has no way on during recovery. Also, do not rule out the use of the boat hook if the man overboard is too far away to retrieve by hand. It is better to use a boat hook and recover on the first approach than to back down or run stern to the surf/swell to make another approach. You may only get one chance to make the rescue. Make it good!

Recovery of a PIW

D.5. GENERAL

The technique for recovery of a PIW (from a capsized pleasure craft, for example) is much the same as for a man overboard. However, the coxswain may be required to enter the surf/swell by running laterally to it, backing in to a beach, or running stern-to the swell using techniques discussed in the Heavy Weather Boat Handling section. The coxswain will position the boat down swell of the PIW and make the approach as previously discussed.

Use of a Surface Swimmer

D.6. GENERAL

Using a surface swimmer in heavy weather or surf is extremely dangerous and should only be attempted as a last resort. Having a member of the crew enter the water presents problems including:

- Reducing crew size of an already minimal crew making it more difficult to retrieve the PIW.

- Increasing the likelihood of the tending line becoming fouled in the propeller.

Multiple PIWs

D.7. DECISION MAKING

For multiple survivors, the question becomes "which victim is to be recoverd first?" This is a hard question to answer and requires the coxswain's best judgment. Once on scene, an accurate assessment will dictate the coxswain's response. Consideration should be given to the following:

- Are one or more survivors injured?

- Which survivors are wearing PFDs and which are not?

- How close are the survivors to a beach or jetty?

- How old are they and what is their physical condition?

Using the above criteria may aid the coxswain in making this often difficult decision.

SECTION E

Surf Operations

Introduction

Crews for Coast Guard MLBs and SRBs receive special training for surf operations. The other Coast Guard boats have operating limits that do not allow operations in surf. Safe operation in these conditions requires excellent boat-handling skills, risk assessment, quick reactions and constant attention from the operator and crew. An understanding of surf behavior and characteristics also is critical. Before entering a surf zone, a coxswain must weigh carefully the capabilities of the boat and crew against the desired outcome.

Because of the substantial differences in handling characteristics found in the various types of surf boats, much of the information here is of a general nature. Many basic procedures and techniques can be applied to all boats but some techniques are type-specific. Additional guidance on boat type characteristics can be found in the applicable type-manual. The reader must also be aware that every area of operation has it's own distinctive characteristics and some of the techniques described may not be applicable in all cases. A strong understanding of these characteristics and intimate local knowledge are vital for safe operation.

In this section

Risk Management and Safety Considerations

E.1. SURF HEIGHT AND ZONE CHARACTERISTICS

Maximum operating conditions are set forth in the boat's type manual. Maximum operational and training conditions are set forth in the applicable District SOP. These limits have been established based on the capabilities of the boat and a realistic balance of risk versus benefits. They should not be exceeded.

The characteristics of the surf zone in question must also be considered carefully. Conditions such as very short wavelength, extreme reflection, refraction, shallow water or other factors may make an area too hazardous for operations even though the surf height is within limits.

E.2. SURVIVAL EQUIPMENT

Any crew operating in the surf must be properly equipped.

- Required hypothermia protective clothing, helmet, boat crew safety belt and signal kit are mandatory.

- Appropriate underclothing, waterproof footwear and gloves also should be worn.

- Goggles may be necessary for visibility, particularly for persons wearing glasses and will also protect against glass shards should a window be broken.

- Boat crew safety belt must be worn and adjusted correctly.

- Helmet straps must be secured and adjusted properly.

The coxswain is responsible for ensuring that all required equipment is worn, and worn correctly.

E.3. CREW PROCEDURES

The crew must be placed where they can use the safety belt padeyes, and where they will be protected from the force of oncoming waves. A large breaker striking the windshield may shatter it, and the crew should not look at the windows if breakage is possible.

The motions encountered in the surf can be extreme, and crew members must take care to brace properly to reduce body stresses. A shoulder-width stance with the knees flexed will provide the most safety and comfort. Try to anticipate boat motions and work with the motion of the boat rather than against it.

E.4. OTHER FACTORS

In addition to surf conditions, several other factors will determine whether you should enter the surf. These include but are not limited to:

- Your boat's seaworthiness, capabilities and limitations.

- Weather conditions and forecast.

- Depth of water in the surf zone.

- Severity of the case and potential benefits to be derived. Do not allow the urgency of the mission to cause you to hazard your vessel and crew unnecessarily.

- Availability of backup resources.

E.5. PRE-SURF CHECKS

Prior to entering the surf a complete round must be made of the boat.

- Stow all equipment, particularly large deck items. Unsecured gear will become a dangerous missile hazard in the surf.

- Make a final check of the engine room and engine parameters, and set watertight integrity.

- Test run the engines at full power.

- Check for proper throttle and reduction gear response in both forward and reverse.

- Check steering for proper effort and full travel from hard-left to hard-right and back.

- Ensure all required survival equipment is donned by all crew members.

> **WARNING**
>
> Do not enter the surf if a vital system is not functioning properly. Surf operations require constant attention from both boat and crew; any deficiencies can lead to mishap.

Forces Affecting Boat Handling in Surf

E.6. AERATED WATER

Aerated water in the surf zone is caused by breaking waves. As the wave breaks, water combines with air creating "whitewater" on the face of the breaker. As the breaker moves through the surf zone it leaves a trail of pale or white aerated water behind it which takes some time to dissipate. This air-water mix can create changes in a boat's handling that must be taken into account while maneuvering.

EFFECT ON PROPELLER A boat's propeller(s) will not create as much thrust when operating in heavily aerated water. The boat's response may be greatly slowed. This effect can be recognized by:

- Poor acceleration and/or apparently slow throttle response.
- Cavitation and/or excessive engine RPM for a given throttle setting.
- Poor turning performance, particularly on a twin propeller boat.

EFFECT ON RUDDER A boat's rudder(s) will not direct the propeller force as effectively in aerated water, nor will it have as much steering effect while moving through aerated water. This effect can be recognized by:

- Poor turning response;
- Reduced steering effort or "light rudders."

E.7. SHALLOW WATER

Operation in very shallow water can be complicated by serious effect on a boat's maneuverability. This effect is caused by resistance to the bow wave as it contacts the bottom, and drag due to the closeness of the bottom to the boat's hull, propellers and rudders. The situation can be recognized by:

- Reduced speed over ground.
- Reduced engine RPM for a given throttle position.
- Sluggish response to throttle and steering inputs, leading to poor acceleration and poor turning ability.
- Larger wake then normal.
- Change in trim caused by the bow riding up on its pressure wave and stern-squat caused by propeller suction. This change in trim can lead to grounding of the stern if the water is shallow enough.

NOTE

The effects of operating in aerated or shallow water are similar to the symptoms of serious engine, reduction gear or steering problems. Any indication of system trouble must be investigated as soon as possible once safely clear of the surf zone.

E.8. CHANGES IN CENTER OF GRAVITY AND TRIM

Changes in center of gravity or trim can lead to dramatic effects on the stability and handling of a boat in the surf. These changes are caused by external or internal forces, and can vary widely depending on condition, type of boat and other factors.

E.9. EXTERNAL FORCES

The primary external force for surf operations is the surf itself. A boat's position, speed and heading relative to a wave will dictate the effects on stability and handling. These effects are numerous and will not be covered entirely, but a description here of the most significant effects is provided.

RUNNING STERN-TO As an approaching wave reaches the stern, the stern will rise and the center of gravity and the pivot point are shifted forward. As this process develops, the trim of the boat changes and may reach a point where the propellers and rudders are no longer deep enough to be effective. This can cause a severe reduction in maneuverability or complete loss of control as the stern picks up and falls to either side in a broach.

This effect is most common on very steep swells or breakers, and can be greatly amplified if the operator reduces power, which causes an even greater shift in the center of gravity.

BROACHING, OR RUNNING BEAM-TO As the approaching wave reaches the boat, it will cause it to heel over and shift the center of gravity to the low side of the boat. This may lead to a reduction in effectiveness of the propeller and rudder on the high side, which will cause reduced maneuverability.

BOW INTO SEAS As the approaching wave picks up the bow, the center of gravity and pivot point will shift aft. If the boat does not have enough way on and the bow is not sufficiently square to the wave, the bow may fall to one side or the other as the force of the wave pushes it around the new pivot point.

E.10. INTERNAL FORCES

There are numerous internal forces—many of them permanent aspects of the boat's design—that affect its stability and handling. It is the responsibility of the operator to be familiar with the characteristics of the boat. The following is a description of those factors which are subject to change or under the direct control of the operator.

FREE SURFACE EFFECT The shifting of fuel or water inside a boat can have a great effect on stability and handling.

UNSECURED OR IMPROPERLY STOWED EQUIPMENT Loose equipment can be tossed to one side and affect stability by placing weight off center.

CHANGES IN THROTTLE OR HELM INPUT Generally, a rapid reduction in power will result in a forward shift of the center of gravity, while an increase in power will have the opposite effect. Large steering inputs will cause a boat to heel over, shifting the center to the low side.

E.11. ROLLOVER CAUSES

Rollovers have occurred in a wide variety of situations, and each rollover is unique. A rollover or knockdown (near roll) is never routine. A roll will generally occur when a boat is placed beam-to or broaches in a breaker the same height as the beam of the boat. The operator's actions at this point can determine whether or not the boat is spared. Some rollovers have occurred in smaller seas and some cases of open ocean rolls have been documented. The steepness of the wave has an effect as well as its height. Any situation which places the center of gravity over the center of buoyancy can result in a roll. A surf boat operator must be constantly aware of the conditions and take action to avoid being caught beam-to or broaching. A rollover is to be avoided at all costs.

E.12. PITCHPOLE OR BOW-ON CAUSES

A pitchpole or bow-on occurs when a boat is inverted end-over-end. This can occur when a boat is traveling stern-to a very steep breaker or large wave. As the stern is picked up, the boat begins to surf down the face and the center of gravity shifts forward. If the stern rises high enough, the bow will begin to dig deeply into the trough of the wave, and the resistance created will cause the boat to trip over itself tumbling end-over-end. A reverse pitchpole is also possible if a boat is surfed backwards while bow-to a large breaker.

Pitchpoles are rare, but are possible, particularly for a relatively small boat. More often, an impending pitchpole will turn into a broach and rollover. The operator must avoid situations which could lead to a pitchpole since they are violently destructive to the boat and its crew.

Basic Surf Operations

E.13. GENERAL

The scope of this Addendum does not allow a detailed discussion of boat type-specific handling characteristics or techniques, but general techniques and procedures can be covered. Because of various local conditions and requirements, there is absolutely no substitute for underway training. Frequent formal training should be conducted by certified personnel in a variety of surf conditions in the local area. Operators should be allowed to acquire the experience necessary to read the waves and get a solid feel for the capabilities and limitations of their boat. Published training limits should not be exceeded for good reason—the majority of surf mishaps have occurred during training rather than actual operations.

E.14. CONSTANT ACTION

Operations in surf or heavy seas requires constant action by the operator. Waves can travel at up to 35 knots, and few boats can outrun a fast wave or maintain a position on its backside.

Maintaining a 360 degree watch for approaching waves is important. The surf zone is a constantly changing, dynamic environment, and the fifth or sixth wave back is often as important as the one that you are immediately faced with. Crew members must be alert and familiar with surf characteristics, and a constant high level of communication is vital. The operator must concentrate on positioning the boat to avoid being caught under a breaker, or taking it at the wrong angle. Maneuvering to avoid the

---

WARNING

Never allow the boat to be caught below a breaking wave. Either allow it to break before it reaches you, or get to the top of the wave before it falls on you. One cubic yard of seawater weighs almost a ton. A 20-foot breaker can drop 1,500 tons of water on the boat and exert a force of up to 6,000 PSI.

---

breaks is preferable, but if one can not be avoided, it should be taken bow-on if possible.

E.15. TECHNIQUES

The following description of techniques has been organized to follow the sequences of an actual operational situation, such as entering a beach surf zone to recover persons in the water, or crossing a bar or inlet.

E.16. ENTERING A BEACH ZONE OR INBOUND TRANSIT OF BAR/INLET WITH SURF ON STERN

General steps are outlined below.

PREPARATIONS
1. Advise station and backup resources of intentions.

2. Acquire bar/inlet or surf zone conditions from all available sources, such as beach/tower personnel or other vessels in the vicinity. It is very difficult to evaluate actual conditions from seaward.

3. Brief the crew and assign duties.

4. Conduct a full pre-surf check of engine room and engine parameters. Check the entire boat for secure stowage. Set watertight integrity, and check boat crew protective clothing.

5. Test engine and steering system controls.

6. Identify any useful natural ranges and landmarks.

7. Identify safe operating areas and hazards. Evaluate surf conditions and possible safer routes, such as bar/reef openings or rip channels.

8. Stand off and observe wave trains. Attempt to identify any patterns such as lulls or series that may be present.

EXECUTION It is preferable to transit the surf during a lull period. Wait until the last big wave in a series has passed and proceed in closely behind it, at maximum comfortable speed. This reduces the relative speed at which the waves approach, and gives the operator more time to react, as well as getting you through the zone as quickly as possible. It may also provide the best maneuverability for some boats. The operator should attempt to work through the surf zone by driving through windows and wave saddles, thus avoiding the majority of the breakers. Some boats may be fast enough to avoid breakers by maintaining position in a trough or on the backside

of a swell while others will eventually be overtaken by every wave as it approaches.

If operating in an area of limiting maneuverability, such as a narrow inlet or bar, the operator may have to rely strictly on timing the waves and make the transit during lull periods. Also, it may be prudent to wait at sea until conditions improve if there is no discernible lull.

> ### WARNING
> Reducing speed after the wave has already picked up the boat will likely result in a loss of control and/or broach. Speed must be reduced before the wave arrives.

A number of techniques are available with which to deal with an overtaking breaker or peaking swell. They vary in success and safety based on conditions and boat type. Only experience will give the operator an understanding of the effectiveness and safety of a given technique.

These techniques are listed in descending order of preference and safety:

1. Maneuver left or right (lateral) to avoid the breaker completely by using windows and saddles.

2. Come about in sufficient time to meet the breaker bow-on.

3. Reduce speed before a steep, peaking (not breaking) swell reaches the boat allowing the swell to pass and break ahead of you. Then increase speed immediately to follow it in.

4. As a wave approaches, begin backing square into it. You should gain sternway and climb the wave before it breaks. Never allow the boat to be caught under a breaker. If it is necessary to back through the whitewater of a breaker, you must gain sternway before the whitewater reaches the propellers and rudders. Move smoothly into the wave as it lifts the stern, using only enough power to maintain sternway. The momentum of the boat will push it through the wave. Once the stern breaks through, ease off the throttles and prepare to resume your course ahead.

5. If you are overtaken by the white water of a breaker, your last resort is to try to get off the wave by applying full throttle, and steering for the "low side" of the wave, hopefully coming out the backside. Do not attempt to ride it out by

maintaining course. You must do something. Never forget to drive the boat.

6. A final option may be to back into the surf zone or across the bar, keeping the bow into the seas. This will be very difficult and time consuming. Excellent backing skills are mandatory. Strong opposing currents in the area may make backing impractical. Also, great care must be taken in shallow water, as the propellers and rudders will hit first if the boat strikes bottom.

WARNING

"Backing through" a breaker is an advanced emergency procedure which can easily result in personnel injuries or boat damage. It is a last-resort maneuver for experienced operators.

E.17. TRANSITING WITH SURF ON BEAM (LATERAL TRANSIT OF SURF ZONE)

General steps are outlined below.

PREPARATIONS

1. Brief crew and assign duties.

2. Identify safe operating areas and hazards. Evaluate surf conditions and possible safer routes, such as longshore channels where the surf may be smaller.

3. Advise station and backup resources.

EXECUTION It is preferable to make a beam transit during a lull, when the seas may be smaller. Wait for the last big series of waves to pass and commence the run. In the absence of lulls, great care and patience must be exercised, because you will be dealing with nearly constant beam surf and the boat is very vulnerable in this position. The operator should use maximum comfortable speed to minimize exposure to beam seas. Speed may be reduced to allow waves to pass ahead of the boat, or speed may be increased to avoid a breaker. Good timing and ability to read several waves back are critical. Any significant waves which cannot be avoided must be taken bow-on.

There are several techniques to deal with breaking seas on the beam. The suitability of a technique is dependent on the boat type and present conditions. The operator must have an understanding of the boat's capabilities, as some maneuvers may not be safe or effective in all cases. The following techniques are listed in descending order of preference and safety:

1. When it is apparent that the boat is about to be overtaken by a breaker, retain or increase speed and turn to meet it squarely with the bow. Once square to the wave, the helm must then be returned to amidships and throttles decreased to avoid launching through the crest. Station-keep if necessary and prepare to return to original course.

2. If a breaker is approaching from ahead of the boat, decrease speed to allow it to pass ahead. Time the maneuver to reach the back shoulder of the wave just as it passes in front. This timing will allow you to quickly get behind the wave and continue the transit, and hopefully avoid the next wave altogether. The crew must be alert for other waves building off the beam.

3. If a wave is some distance off the beam, you may be able to outrun it by increasing speed. If there is any chance that you will not beat the wave, you must turn to meet it or run away from it if space and time permit.

4. In some instances, there may be time and room available to find a window by running away from a breaker and placing it on the stern or quarter. This technique carries all the risks associated with running stern-to, and will also set you off the original track line or range as well as being time consuming. It is not the most efficient means of transiting, but may be a valuable safety maneuver depending on the circumstances.

5. When transiting very small surf relative to the size of the boat, it may be possible to maintain or slightly reduce speed and simply turn towards a small breaker at about a 45 degree angle, resuming course behind it after crossing the crest. **WARNING:** This maneuver is only safe in small conditions and must not be attempted if the operator has any doubts. Wave avoidance is still the preferred technique.

WARNING

Do not be surprised by a breaker on the beam while watching the one ahead, as there is a good chance of a rollover if you are hit on the beam at slow speed.

E.18. STATION KEEPING (BOW INTO SURF)

Station keeping is maintaining a given position in the surf. Station keeping is necessary to hold position while waiting for a window or lull, or holding position prior to and during recovery of a person in the water. Environmental factors such as the surf, wind or currents can make station keeping difficult, and good backing skill and proper application of power are essential. The following are guidelines for station keeping:

- Use only enough power to maintain position and counteract the force of the oncoming wave. On smaller waves, keeping the bow square with neutral throttles may be all that is needed. Larger waves may require a great deal of power to counteract. Using too much power will set you out of position and/or launch the boat. Too little power will set you backwards or broach the boat.

- Keep the bow as square to the seas as possible.

- If you are being set towards the seas by current or wind; it may be necessary to back down frequently to hold position, only applying forward power to meet oncoming waves. Wait until a wave crest passes and back down once on the backside. Do not back down on the face of a wave.

- By adjusting power, it may be possible to safely allow a wave to set you back to regain position. This technique requires practice, and the operator must maintain control of the maneuver at all times.

- It is possible to move laterally while station keeping by allowing the bow to fall slightly to the desired side and then using the throttles and helm to straighten out as the wave pushes the bow.

For example, to crab sideways to port, allow the bow to fall slightly to port and as the wave pushes the bow, apply power and steer to starboard finishing the maneuver with the bow once again square to the seas. This maneuver must not be attempted on large waves, and it is important not to allow the bow to fall off so far that the safety and control of the boat are compromised.

E.19. OUTBOUND TRANSIT OF BAR/INLET OR SURF ZONE (BOW INTO SURF)

An outbound transit of the surf may be necessary in crossing a bar/inlet or departing a surf zone. The operator should practice wave avoidance by picking a course through the windows and saddles, if available, minimizing risk to the boat and crew. The transit should be made at maximum comfortable speed, adjusting to avoid launching over the waves or avoiding them altogether when possible. The following guidelines apply to an outbound transit:

WARNING

Do not allow a wave to break over the boat while transiting outbound. If it appears that this may happen, you must either reach the top before it breaks, or slow down/stop, letting it break in front of you and then regaining headway in time to meet the whitewater.

- Choose a course through windows as much as possible, zigzagging as necessary to avoid breakers. Stay close to the shoulders of the waves, to take advantage of any window which may open up behind the wave as it passes.

- If a breaker cannot be avoided, try to go through the wave at the saddle, where it may not be breaking yet or its force may be less. If both ends of the wave are breaking towards the saddle, you may be caught in a closeout. Get through the saddle before it closes, or slow down to let it closeout well in front of you.

- Any breakers that cannot be avoided should be taken bow-on. Slow down and allow your momentum to carry you through. Do not meet breakers at high speed or you may plow into the face or launch off the back risking injuries or boat damage.

E.20. EMERGENCY PROCEDURES: ROLLOVER OR INVOLUNTARY BEACHING

A rollover or beaching is never routine, but always possible. These unpleasant events must be considered and planned for. Training and experience will give you the edge, but it can still happen to you simply because of the severe environment you are operating in. The following risk management practices should be followed:

- All crew members must be properly outfitted, and equipment must be worn properly.

- All surf boat crew members should be familiar with the causes of rollover and pitchpoling as well as how to recognize an impending rollover event, and what to expect when it happens.

- All crew members should be well trained in the procedure to be followed during a rollover or involuntary beaching. Crew members must be familiar with procedures for emergency anchoring and drogue deployment as well as the location of necessary equipment. If possible, the crew should be briefed on these procedures prior to entering a surf zone.

- Crew members should be capable of taking control of the boat in order to prevent further rolls should the operator. The ability to recover the operator is also highly desirable.

- A backup surf-capable resource or aircraft should be standing by whenever possible, and it should be positioned where it can observe the boat working in the surf.

- Backup communications (handheld VHF) should be aboard the boat in case the antennas are lost, or main radio damaged.

- Always assess the risks you take versus the potential benefits. Do not let a sense of urgency cloud your judgment or get you into a losing situation.

PROCEDURES

1. A rollover is usually the result of a severe broach. If your lower gunwale is under water, be prepared to roll. Experience and familiarity with the boat's normal motions may warn you of an abnormal situation.

2. If time allows, advise the crew to hold their breath. Hold on firmly to whatever you can. While upside down, you will be completely disoriented and unable to see. You may hear the engines.

3. Immediately upon re-righting, assess the situation, as you are still in the surf and must take quick action to meet the next wave correctly or you may roll again.

4. Check the crew to ensure that no one was lost overboard or seriously injured.

5. Check the deck and surrounding water for lines or equipment which could disable the boat.

6. If the engines are still working, move to safe water.

7. Once in safe water, the engineer should go below to check for damage. Secure non-vital electrical circuits. The engine room may be coated with water and oil, presenting a fire hazard. If there is no fire, the engineer should dewater the engine room, and check the oil in the engine(s).

8. Check the condition of the boat. Fuel may have spilled from the exterior vents, covering the weatherdeck and crew. The superstructure may be damaged, windows may be broken, and large fixtures such as the mast, anchor, pump can, towline reel, or helm chair may be damaged or missing. Installed electronics will likely be inoperative.

WARNING

Do not unfasten your safety belt or consider swimming to the surface. It is likely that the propellers will still be turning and the boat is designed to right itself in a few seconds.

CONTINUING OR RETURNING After damage and injuries have been assessed, you must determine whether to continue with the mission or return to the unit. The following factors should be considered:

- Condition of crew members.

- Overall material and operating condition of engines and boat structure.

- Condition of electronics, particularly communications.

- Urgency of mission and availability of backup resources.

Upon returning to the station, post-rollover procedures must be taken in accordance with the boat's type manual.

PROCEDURES FOR INVOLUNTARY BEACHING

If your boat is disabled in or near the surf, it will be driven into the shore. Notify the station or backup resource immediately. The chances of rollover or crew injuries can be reduced by taking these actions:

1. Try to set the anchor with as much scope as possible. If more line is needed, bend the towline to the anchor line.

2. If unable to anchor, attempt to set a drogue astern. This will minimize the chance of rolling, and hopefully cause the boat to beach bow first.

3. All crew should go below and secure the hatches. Strap yourselves in with the seat belts.

4. Stay with the boat and ride it out. You may capsize several times on your trip to the beach.

5. Once the boat is beached, stay put. The waves push the boat farther up the beach. Do not be in a hurry to leave the boat.

WARNING

Do not expose crew members to the likelihood of serious injury or loss overboard by sending them to the bow in heavy surf. It may be safer to sustain a roll while waiting for a lull. This is a judgment call.

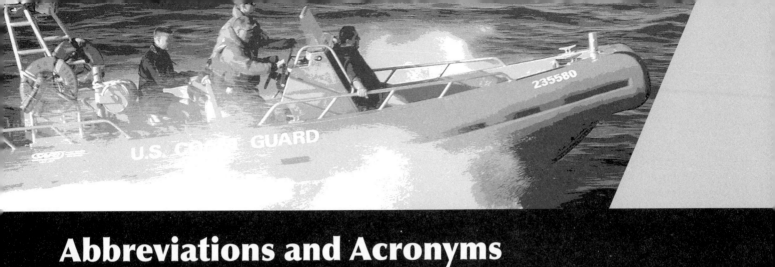

Abbreviations and Acronyms

A/C   Aircraft

AM   Amplitude Modulation

AMVER   Automated Mutual-assistance Vessel Rescue

AOR   Area of Responsibility

ATC   Air Traffic Control

ATON   Aids To Navigation

C   Course

C   Coverage Factor

C/C   Cabin Cruiser

CO   Commanding Officer

COLREGS   International Regulations for Prevention of Collisions at Sea.

CS   Call Sign

CS   Creeping Line Search

CSC   Creeping Line Search—Coordinated

CSP   Commence Search Point

DF   Direction Finding

DGPS   Differential Global Positioning System

DIW   Dead In The Water

DMB   Datum Marker Buoy

DR   Dead Reckoning

DSC   Digital Selective Calling

ELT   Emergency Locator Transmitter

EMT   Emergency Medical Technician

EPIRB   Emergency Position-Indicating Radio Beacon

ETA   Estimated Time of Arrival

ETD   Estimated Time of Departure

F/V   Fishing Vessel

FM   Frequency Modulation

GMDSS   Global Maritime Distress and Safety System

GPM   Gallons Per Minute

GPS   Global Positioning System

HF   High Frequency

I/B   Inboard

I/O   Inboard/Outdrive

ICS   Incident Command System

ICW   Intracoastal Waterway

IMO   International Maritime Organization

INMARSAT   International Monitoring Satellite Organization

KHz   Kilohertz

Kn or Kt   Knot (Nautical Mile Per Hour)

Lat   Latitude

LKP   Last Known Position

LNB   Large Navigation Buoy

Lon or Long   Longitude

LOP   Line of Position

m   Meter

M   Magnetic Course

M/V   Merchant Vessel

MEDEVAC   Medical Evacuation

MF   Medium Frequency

MHz   Megahertz

MLB   Motor Lifeboat

NM   Nautical Mile

NOS   National Ocean Service

NVG   Night Vision Goggles

O/B   Outboard

OIC   Officer-In-Charge; also OinC

OOD   Officer of the Deck (Day)

OPAREA   Operating Area

OSC   On-Scene Commander

P/C   Pleasure Craft

PFD   Personal Flotation Device

PIW   Person In Water

PML   Personnel Marker Light

POB   Persons On Board

POD   Probability of detection

POS   Probability of success

PS   Parallel Sweep Search

PSI   Pounds per Square Inch

RACON   Radar Beacon

RCC   Rescue Coordination Center

RHIB Rigid Hull Inflatable Boat
RPM Revolution Per Minute
RSC Rescue Sub-Center
S/S Steam Ship
S/V Sailing Vessel
SAR Search and Rescue
SARSAT Search and Rescue Satellite-Aided
  Tracking
SITREP Situation Report
SMC Search And Rescue
  Mission Coordinator
SOA Speed of Advance
SRB Surf Rescue Boat (Coast Guard)

SRU Search and Rescue Unit
SS Expanding Square Search
T True Course
TS Track Line Search or Track Spacing
UHF Ultra High Frequency
UMIB Urgent Marine Information Broadcast
USWMS Uniform State Waterway Marking System
UTB Utility Boat (Coast Guard)
UTC Universal Time Coordinated
VHF Very High Frequency
VS Sector Search
W Sweep Width

Glossary

abaft Behind, toward the stern of a vessel.

abeam To one side of a vessel, at a right angle to the fore-and-aft center line.

advection fog A type of fog that occurs when warm air moves over colder land or water surfaces; the greater the difference between the air temperature and the underlying surface temperature, the denser the fog, which is hardly affected by sunlight.

aft Near or toward the stern.

aground With the keel or bottom of a vessel fast on the sea floor.

Aids to Navigation (ATON) Lighthouses, lights, buoys, sound signals, racon, radiobeacons, electronic aids, and other markers on land or sea established to help navigators determine position or safe course, dangers, or obstructions to navigation.

allision The running of one vessel into or against another, as distinguished from a collision, i.e., the running of two vessel against each other. But this distinciton is not very carefully observed. Also used to refer to a vessel striking a fixed structure (i.e. bridge, pier, moored vessel, etc.) per marine inspection.

amidships In or towards center portion of the vessel, sometimes referred to as "midships."

anchorage area A customary, suitable, and generally designated area in which vessels may anchor.

astern The direction toward or beyond the back of a vessel.

athwartships Crosswise of a ship; bisecting the fore-and-aft line above the keel.

attitude A vessel's position relative to the wind, sea, hazard, or other vessel.

back and fill A technique where one relies on the tendency of a vessel to back to port, then uses the rudder to direct thrust when powering ahead. Also known as casting.

backing plate A reinforcement plate below a deck or behind a bulkhead used to back a deck fitting. It is usually made of wood or steel and distributes stress on a fitting over a larger area and prevents bolts from pulling through the deck.

backing spring (line) Line used when towing a vessel along side which may be secured near the towing vessel's stern and the towed vessel's bow.

ballast Weight placed in a vessel to maintain its stability.

beacon Any fixed aid to navigation placed ashore or on marine sites. If lighted, they are referred to as minor lights.

beam The widest point of a vessel on a line perpendicular to the keel, the fore-an-aft centerline.

Beaufort Wind Scale A scale whose numbers define a particular state of wind and wave, allowing mariners to estimate the wind speed based on the sea state.

bell buoy A floating aid to navigation with a short tower in which there are several clappers that strike the bell as it rocks with the motion of the sea.

below The space or spaces that are below a vessel's main deck.

bilge The lowest point of a vessel's inner hull, which is underwater.

bilge alarm system Alarm for warning of excessive water or liquid in the bilge.

bilge drain A drain used for removing water or liquid from the bilge.

bilge pump Pump used to clear water or liquid from the bilge.

bitt A strong post of wood or metal, on deck in the bow or stern, to which anchor, mooring, or towing lines may be fastened.

boat hook   A hook on a pole with a pushing surface at the end used to retrieve or pick up objects, or for pushing objects away.

bollard   A single strong vertical fitting, usually iron, on a deck, pier, or wharf, to which mooring lines or a hawser may be fastened.

bolo line   A nylon line with a padded or wrapped weight thrown from vessel to vessel or between vessels and shore which is used for passing a larger line (see heaving line).

boom   Spar used to spread a fore-and-aft sail, especially its foot; without a sail and with a suitable lift attached, it can be used as a lifting device or derrick.

boundary layer   A layer of water carried along the hull of a vessel varying in thickness from the bow to stern.

bow   Forward end of vessel.

bow line   A line secured from the bow of a vessel. In an alongside towing operation, the bow line is secured on both the towing and the towed vessel at or near the bow and may act as breast line of each.

bowline   A classic knot that forms an eye that will not slip come loose or jam, and is not difficult to untie after it has been under strain.

breakaway   Command given by coxswain, conning officer, or pilot when a helicopter hoisting operation, towing, or alongside evolution has to be terminated due to unsafe conditions.

breaker   A wave cresting with the top breaking down over its face.

breaker line   The outer limit of the surf.

breaking strength (BS)   Refers to the force needed to break or part a line. BS is measured in pounds, more specifically, it is the number of pounds of stress a line can hold before it parts.

breast line   Mooring or dock line extended laterally from a vessel to a pier or float as distinguished from a spring line.

bridge markings   Lights or signs which provide mariners information for safely passing a bridge over a waterway.

bridle   A device attached to a vessel or aircraft (in the water) in order for another vessel to tow it. Its use can reduce the effects of yawing, stress on towed vessel fittings, and generally gives the towing vessel greater control over the tow.

broach   To be thrown broadside to surf or heavy sea.

broadcast notice to mariners   A radio broadcast that provides important marine information.

broadside to the sea   Refers to a vessel being positioned so that the sea is hitting either the starboard or port side of the vessel.

bulkhead   Walls or partitions within a vessel with structural functions such as providing strength or watertightness. Light partitions are sometimes called partition bulkheads.

bullnose   A round opening at the forwardmost part of the bow through which a towline, mooring line or anchor line passes.

buoy   A floating aid to navigation anchored to the bottom that conveys information to navigators by their shape or color, by their visible or audible signals, or both.

buoy moorings   Chain or synthetic rope used to attach buoys to sinkers.

buoy station   Established (charted) location of a buoy.

buoyage   A system of buoys with assigned shapes, colors, or numbers.

buoyancy   The tendency or capacity of a vessel to remain afloat.

can buoy (cylindrical)   A cylindrical buoy, generally green, marking the left side of a channel or safe passage as seen entering from seaward, or from the north or east proceeding south or west.

capsize   To turn a vessel bottom side up.

cardinal marks   Indicate the location of navigable waters by reference to the cardinal directions (N,E,S,W) on a compass.

casting   See Back and Fill.

catenary   The sag in a length of chain, cable, or line because of its own weight and which provides a spring or elastic effect in towing, anchoring, or securing to a buoy.

cavitation   The formation of a partial vacuum around the propeller blades of a vessel.

center of gravity   Point in a ship where the sum of all moments of weight is zero. With the ship at rest the center of gravity and the center of buoyancy are always in a direct vertical line. For surface ships center of buoyancy is usually below center of gravity, and the ship is prevented from capsizing by the additional displacement on the low side during a roll. Thus the point at which the deck edge enters the water is critical because from here onward increased roll will not produce corresponding increased righting force.

center point method, circular area   In SAR, one of several methods to define a search area.

center point method, rectangular area   In SAR, one of several methods to define a search area.

center point method, rectangular area, bearing and distance In SAR, one of several methods to define a search area.

centerline An imaginary line down the middle of a vessel from bow to stern.

chafe To wear away by friction.

chaffing gear Material used to prevent chafing or wearing of a line or other surface.

characteristic The audible, visual, or electronic signal displayed by an aid to navigation to assist in the identification of an aid to navigation. Characteristic refers to lights, sound signals, racons, radiobeacons, and daybeacons.

chart A printed or electronic geographic representation generally showing depths of water, aids to navigation, dangers, and adjacent land features useful to mariners (see Nautical Chart).

chine The intersection of the bottom and the sides of a flat bottom or "V" hull boat.

chock Metal fitting through which hawsers and lines are passed. May be open or closed. Blocks used to prevent aircraft or vehicles from rolling. Also, blocks used to support a boat under repair.

chop Short steep waves usually generated by local winds and/or tidal changes. Change of operational control. The date and time at which the responsibility for operational control of a ship or convoy passes from one operational control authority to another.

cleat An anvil-shaped deck fitting for securing or belaying lines. Wedge cleats are used in yachting to hold sheets ready for instant release.

closeout Occurs when a wave breaks from the ends toward the middle, or two waves break towards each other; should be avoided because they can create more energy than a single break.

closing The act of one vessel reducing the distance between itself and another vessel, structure, or object.

clove hitch A hitch often used for fastening a line to a spar, ring, stanchion, or other larger lines or cables.

Coast Guard-approved Label denoting compliance with Coast Guard specifications and regulations relating to performance, construction, and materials.

coastal At or near a coast.

coil down To lay out a line in a circle with coils loosely on top on one anther (see Fake Down, Flemish Down).

comber A wave at the point of breaking.

combination buoy Buoy that combines the characteristics of both sound and light.

combustion Rapid oxidation of combustible material accompanied by a release of energy in the form of heat and light.

compartment A room or space on board ship. Usually lettered and numbered according to location and use.

compass Instrument for determining direction: magnetic, depending on the earth's magnetic field for its force; gyroscopic, depending on the tendency of a free-spinning body to seek to align its axis with that of the earth.

conventional direction of buoyage The general direction taken by the mariner when approaching a harbor, river, estuary, or other waterway from seaward, or proceeding upstream or in the direction of the main stream of flood tide, or in the direction indicated in appropriate nautical documents (normally, following a clockwise direction around land masses).

corner method In SAR, one of several methods to define a search area. Latitude and longitude or geographic features of corners of search area are identified.

Cospas-Sarsat system A satellite system designed to detect distress beacons transmitting on the frequencies 121.5 MHz and 406 MHz.

course (C) The horizontal direction in which a vessel is steered or intended to be steered, expressed as angular distance from north, usually from 000 degrees at north, clockwise through 360 degrees.

coverage factor (C) In SAR, a measure of search effectiveness; ration of sweep width to track spacing: C = W/S.

coxswain Person in charge of a boat, pronounced "COX-un."

crab To move sidewise through the water.

craft Any air or sea-surface vehicle, or submersible of any kind or size.

crash stop Immediately going from full speed ahead to full reverse throttle; this is an emergency maneuver. It is extremely harsh on the drive train and may cause engine stall.

crest The top of a wave, breaker, or swell.

crucifix Type of deck or boat fitting that resembles a cross, used to secure a line to. Ex.: Samson post

current (ocean) Continuous movement of the sea, sometimes caused by prevailing winds, as well as large constant forces, such as the rotation of the earth, or the apparent rotation of the sun and moon. Example is the Gulf Stream.

damage control Measures necessary to preserve and reestablish shipboard watertight integrity, stability, and maneuverability; to control list and trim; to make rapid repairs of material. Inspection of damage caused by fire, flooding, and/or collision and the subsequent control and corrective measures.

datum In SAR, refers to the probable location of a distressed vessel, downed aircraft or PIW, which is corrected for drift at any moment in time. Depending on the information received this may be represented as a point, a line or an area.

day mark The daytime identifier of an aid to navigation (see Daybeacon, Dayboard).

daybeacon An unlighted fixed structure which is equipped with a highly visible dayboard for daytime identification.

dayboard The daytime identifier of an aid to navigation presenting one of several standard shapes (square, triangle, rectangle) and colors (red, green, white, orange, yellow or black).

de-watering The act of removing water from inside compartments of a vessel. Water located high in the vessel, or sufficiently off-center should be removed first to restore the vessel's stability. Used to prevent sinking, capsizing or listing.

Dead in the Water (DIW) A vessel that has no means to maneuver, normally due to engine casualty. A vessel that is adrift or no means of propulsion.

Dead Reckoning (DR) Determination of estimated position of a craft by adding to the last fix the craft's course and speed for a given time.

deadman's stick See Static Discharge Wand.

deck The horizontal plating or planking on a ship or boat.

deck fitting Term for permanently installed fittings on the deck of a vessel which you can attach machinery or equipment.

deck scuttle Small, quick-closing access hole located on the deck of a vessel.

deep "V" hull A hull design generally used for faster seagoing types of boats.

desmoking The natural or forced ventilation of a vessel's compartment to remove smoke.

destroyer turn Used during person overboard situations. The boat is turned in the direction the individual fell overboard, to get the stern of the boat (and the screws) away from the person overboard.

Digital Selective Calling (DSC) A technique using digital codes which enables a radio station to establish contact with, and transfer information to, another station or group of stations.

Direction of current Direction toward which a current is flowing (see Set).

direction of waves, swells, or seas Direction to which the waves, swells, or seas are moving.

direction of wind Direction from which the wind is blowing.

displacement hull A hull that achieves its buoyancy or flotation capability by displacing a volume of water equal in weight to the hull and its load.

distress As used in the Coast Guard, when a craft or person is threatened by grave or imminent danger requiring immediate assistance.

ditching The forced landing of an aircraft on water.

dolphin A structure consisting of a number of piles driven into the seabed or river bed in a circular pattern and drawn together with wire rope. May be used as part of a dock structure or a minor aid to navigation. Commonly used when a single pile would not provide the desired strength.

downwash The resulting force of the movement of air in a downward motion from a helicopter in flight or hovering.

draft Measured from the waterline, it is the point on a vessel's underwater body that reaches the greatest depth.

drag Forces opposing direction of motion due to friction, profile and other components. The amount that a ship is down by the stern.

drift The rate/speed at which a vessel moves due to the effects of wind, wave, current, or the accumulative effects of each. Usually expressed in knots.

drogue Device used to slow rate of movement. Commonly rigged off the stern of a boat while under tow to reduce the effects of following seas. May prevent yawing and/or broaching (see Sea Anchor).

drop pump A portable, gasoline-powered pump that is transported in a water tight container. Used for de-watering a vessel.

dry suit A coverall type garment made of waterproof material having a rubber or neoprene seal around the neck and wrist cuffs. Allows the wearer to work in the water or in a marine environment without getting wet.

dynamic forces Forces associated with the changing environment e.g., the wind, current, weather.

ebb A tidal effect caused by the loss of water in a river, bay, or estuary resulting in discharge currents immediately followed by a low tidal condition.

ebb current The horizontal motion away from the land caused by a falling tide.

ebb direction The approximate true direction toward which the ebbing current flows; generally close to the reciprocal of the flood direction.

eddy A circular current.

eductor Siphon device that contains no moving parts. It moves water from one place to another by forcing the pumped liquid into a rapidly flowing stream. This is know as the venturi effect. Dewatering equipment used to remove fire-fighting and flooding water from a compartment in a vessel.

Emergency Locator Transmitter (ELT) Aeronautical radio distress beacon for alerting and transmitting homing signals.

Emergency Position-Indicating Radio Beacon (EPIRB) A device, usually carried aboard a maritime craft, that transmits a signal that alerts search and rescue authorities and enables rescue units to locate the scene of the distress.

emergency signal mirror Used to attract attention of passing aircraft or boats by reflecting light at them. Such reflected light may be seen up to five miles or more from the point of origin.

environmental forces Forces that affect the horizontal motion of a vessel; they include wind, seas and current.

eye The permanently fixed loop at the end of a line.

eye splice The splice needed to make a permanently fixed loop at the end of a line.

fairlead A point, usually a specialized fitting, such as a block, chock, or roller used to change the direction and increase effectiveness of a line or cable. It will, in most cases, reduce the effects of chaffing.

fairways (mid-channel) A channel that is marked by safemarks that indicate that the water is safe to travel around either side of the red and white vertically striped buoy.

fake down To lay out a line in long flat bights, that will pay out freely without bights or kinks. A coiled or flemished line cannot do this unless the coil of the line is able to turn, as on a reel. Other-

wise a twist results in the line which will produce a kink or jam (see Coil Down and Flemish Down).

fatigue Physical or mental weariness due to exertion. Exhausting effort or activity. Weakness in material, such as metal or wood, resulting from prolonged stress.

fender A device of canvas, wood, line, cork, rubber, wicker, or plastic slung over the side of a boat/ship in position to absorb the shock of contact between vessels or between a vessel and pier.

fender board A board that is hung outboard of your vessel's fenders. Used to protect the side of a vessel.

ferry To transport a boat, people or goods across a body of water.

fetch The unobstructed distance over which the wind blows across the surface of the water.

fitting Generic term for any part or piece of machinery or installed equipment.

fix A geographical position determined by visual reference to the surface, referencing to one or more radio navigation aids, celestial plotting, or other navigation device.

fixed light A light showing continuously and steadily, as opposed to a rhythmic light.

flash A relatively brief appearance of light, in comparison with the longest interval of darkness in the same character.

flashing light A light in which the total duration of light in each period is clearly shorter than the total duration of darkness and in which the flashes of light are all of equal duration. (Commonly used for a single-flashing light which exhibits only single flashes which are repeated at regular intervals.)

flemish (down) To coil down a line on deck in a flat, circular, tight arrangement. Useful for appearance only, since unless the twists in the line are removed it will kink when taken up or used (see Fake Down and Coil Down).

floating aid to navigation A buoy.

flood A tidal effect caused by the rise in water level in a river, bay, or estuary immediately followed by a high tidal condition.

flood current The horizontal motion of water toward the land caused by a rising tide.

flood direction The approximate true direction toward which the flooding current flows; generally close to the reciprocal of the ebb direction.

foam crest   Top of the foaming water that speeds toward the beach after the wave has broken; also known as white water.

fore   Something situated at or near the front. The front part, at, toward, or near the front; as in the forward part of a vessel.

forward   Towards the bow of a vessel.

foul   To entangle, confuse, or obstruct. Jammed or entangled; not clear for running. Covered with barnacles, as foul bottom.

frames   Any of the members of the skeletal structure of a vessel to which the exterior planking or plating is secured.

free communication with the sea   Movement of water in and out of a vessel through an opening in the hull.

freeboard   Distance from the weather deck to the waterline on a vessel.

furl   To make up in a bundle, as in furl the sail.

Global Positioning System (GPS)   A satellite-based radio navigation system that provides precise, continuous, worldwide, all-weather three-dimensional navigation for land, sea and air applications.

gong buoy   A wave actuated sound signal on buoys which uses a group of saucer-shaped bells to produce different tones. Found inside harbors and on inland waterways. Sound range about one mile.

grabline   A line hung along a vessels side near the waterline used for the recovery of persons in the water or to assist in the boarding of the vessel.

grommet   A round attaching point, of metal or plastic, normally found on fenders, tarps, etc.

ground fog   See Radiation Fog.

group-flashing light   A flashing light in which a group of flashes, specified in number, is regularly repeated.

group-occulting light   An occulting light in which a group of eclipses, specified in number, is regularly repeated.

gunwale   Upper edge of a boat's side. Pronounced "gun-ul."

half hitch   A hitch used for securing a line to a post; usually seen as two half hitches.

harbor   Anchorage and protection for ships. A shelter or refuge.

hatch   The covering, often watertight, placed over an opening on the horizontal surface of a boat/ship.

hawsepipe   A through deck fitting normally found above a line locker/hold which allows for the re-moval of line without accessing the compartment from below deck. Normally only slightly larger in diameter than the line itself.

head up (heads up)   A warning given before throwing a messenger, heaving, or towline to alert people to be ready for receipt of line and to avoid being hit by the object being thrown. Potential danger warning.

heading   The direction in which a ship or aircraft is pointed.

heaving line   Light, weighted line thrown across to a ship or pier when coming along side to act as a messenger for a mooring line. The weight is called a monkey fist.

heavy weather   Heavy weather is determined to exist when seas exceed 8 feet and/or winds are greater than 30 knots.

heel   Temporary leaning of a vessel to port or starboard caused by the wind and sea or by a high speed turn.

helm   The apparatus by which a vessel is steered; usually a steering wheel or tiller.

high seas   That body of water extending seaward of a country's territorial sea to the territorial sea of another country.

hoist   To lift. Display of signal flags at yardarm. The vertical portion of a flag alongside its staff.

hoisting cable   The cable used to perform a boat/helo hoisting evolution.

holed   Refers to a hole or opening in the hull of a damaged vessel.

hull   The body or shell of a ship or seaplane.

hull integrity   Refers to the hull's soundness.

hypothermia   A lowering of the core body temperature due to exposure of cold (water or air) resulting in a subnormal body temperature that can be dangerous or fatal. The word literally means "underheated."

impeller   A propulsion device that draws water in and forces it out through a nozzle.

in step (position)   Refers to the towing boat keeping the proper position with the towed boat. For example; the proper distance in relation to sea/swell patterns so that both boats ride over the seas in the same relative position wave crest to wave crest.

inboard   Toward the center of a ship or a group of ships, as opposed to outboard.

Inboard/Outdrive (I/O)   An inboard engine attached through the transom to the outdrive.

Incident Command System (ICS)   Management system for responding to major emergency events involving multiple jurisdictions and agencies. Coast Guard facilities may conduct simultaneous operations along with other types of responders under ICS management.

information marks   Aids to navigation that inform the mariner of dangers, restriction, or other information. Also referred to as regulatory marks.

inlet   A recess, as a bay or cove, along a coastline. A stream or bay leading inland, as from the ocean. A narrow passage of water, as between two islands.

isolated danger mark   A mark erected on, or moored above or very near, an isolated danger which has navigable water all around it.

junction   The point where a channel divides when proceeding seaward. The place where a branch of a river departs from the main stream.

junction aid (obstruction aid)   Horizontally striped aids that Indicate the preferred channel with the top color on the aid. They may also mark an obstruction.

kapok   A silky fiber obtained from the fruit of the silk-cotton tree and used for buoyancy, insulation and as padding in seat cushions and life preservers.

keel   Central, longitudinal beam or timber of a ship from which the frames and hull plating rise.

kicker hook   See Skiff Hook.

knot (kn or kt)   A unit of speed equivalent to one nautical mile (6,080 feet) per hour. A measurement of a ship's speed through water. A collective term for hitches and bends.

landmark boundaries method   In SAR, one of several methods to define a search area.

Lateral marks   Buoys or beacons that indicate port and starboard sides of a route and are used in conjunction with a "Conventional direction of buoyage."

lateral system   A system of aids to navigation in which characteristics of buoys and beacons indicate the sides of the channel or route relative to a conventional direction of buoyage (usually upstream).

Lateral System of Buoyage   See Lateral System.

latitude   The measure of angular distance in degrees, minutes, and seconds of arc from 0 degrees to 90 degrees north or south of the equator.

lazarette   Compartment in the extreme after part of the boat generally used for storage.

leeward   The side or direction away from the wind, the lee side.

leeway   Drift of an object with the wind, on the surface of the sea. The sideward motion of a ship because of wind and current, the difference between her heading (course steered) and her track (course made good). Sometimes called drift. In SAR, movement of search object through water caused by local winds blowing against that object.

life jacket   See Personal Flotation Device.

life ring (ring buoy)   Buoyant device, usually fitted with a light and smoke marker, for throwing to a person in the water.

lifeline   Line secured along the deck to lay hold of in heavy weather; any line used to assist personnel; knotted line secured to the span of lifeboat davits(manropes or monkey lines) for the use of the crew when hoisting and lowering. The lines between stanchions along the outboard edges of a ship's weather decks are all loosely referred to as lifelines, but specifically the top line is the lifeline, middle is the housing line, and bottom is the footline. Any line attached to a lifeboat or life raft to assist people in the water. Also called a grab rope.

light   The signal emitted by a lighted aid to navigation. The illuminating apparatus used to emit the light signal. A lighted aid to navigation on a fixed structure.

light buoy   Floating framework aid to navigation, supporting a light, usually powered by battery.

light list   A United States Coast Guard publication (multiple volumes) that gives detailed information on aids to navigation.

light rhythms   Different patterns of lights, and flashing combinations that indicate to the mariner the purpose of the aid to navigation on which it is installed.

light sector   The arc over which a light is visible, described in degrees true, as observed from seaward towards the light. May be used to define distinctive color difference of two adjoining sectors, or an obscured sector.

lighthouse   A lighted beacon of major importance. Fixed structures ranging in size from the typical major seacoast lighthouse to much smaller, single pile structures. Placed on shore or on marine sites and most often do not show lateral aid to navigation markings. They assist the mariner in determining his position or safe course, or warn of obstructions or dangers to navigation. Lighthouses with no lateral significance usually exhibit a white light, but can use sectored lights to mark shoals or warn mariners of other dangers.

list Permanent leaning of a vessel to port or starboard.

local notice to mariners A written document issued by each U.S. Coast Guard district to disseminate important information affecting aids to navigation, dredging, marine construction, special marine activities, and bridge construction on the waterways with that district.

log Device for measuring a ship's speed and distance traveled through the water. To record something is to log it. Short for logbook.

logbook Any chronological record of events, as an engineering watch log.

longitude A measure of angular distance in degrees, minutes, and seconds east or west of the Prime Meridian at Greenwich.

longitudinal A structural member laid parallel to the keel upon which the plating or planking is secured. Longitudinals usually intersect frames to complete the skeletal framework of a vessel.

longshore current Currents that run parallel to the shore and inside the breakers as a result of the water transported to the beach by the waves.

lookout A person stationed as a visual watch.

LORAN-C An acronym for LOng RAnge Navigation; an electronic aid to navigation consisting of shore-based radio transmitters.

loud hailer A loud speaker; public address system.

magnetic compass A compass using the earth's magnetic field to align the compass card (see Compass).

magnetic course (M) Course relative to magnetic north; compass course corrected for deviation.

MARB Marine Assistance Radio Broadcast

maritime Located on or close to the sea; of or concerned with shipping or navigation.

mark A visual aid to navigation. Often called navigation mark, includes floating marks (buoys) and fixed marks (beacons).

marline Small stuff (cord) tarred. Used for mousing, etc.

mast A spar located above the keel and rising above the main deck to which may be attached sails, navigation lights, and/or various electronic hardware. The mast will vary in height depending on vessel type or use.

MAYDAY Spoken international distress signal, repeated three times. Derived from the French m'aider (help me).

MEDEVAC "Medical Evacuation." Evacuation of a person for medical reasons.

messenger Light line used to carry across a larger line or hawser. Person who carries messages for OOD or other officers of the watch.

mid-channel Center of a navigable channel. May be marked by safemarks.

Modified U.S. Aid System Used on the Intracoastal waterway, these aids are also equipped with special yellow strips, triangles, or squares. When used on the western rivers (Mississippi River System), these aids are not numbered (Mississippi River System above Baton Rouge and Alabama Rivers).

mooring Chain or synthetic line that attaches a floating object to a stationary object. (e.g., dock, sinker).

mooring buoy White buoy with a blue stripe, used for a vessel to tie up to, also designates an anchorage area.

Motor Lifeboat (MLB) Coast Guard boat designed to perform SAR missions, including surf and bar operations, in adverse weather and sea conditions. They are self-righting and self-bailing.

mousing The use of small stuff or wire to hold together components that would otherwise work loose due to friction (i.e., mousing the screw pin of a shackle into place).

N-Dura hose Double synthetic jacketed and impregnated rubber lined hose, orange in color, used in the Coast Guard for firefighting.

nautical chart Printed or electronic geographic representation of waterways showing positions of aids to navigation and other fixed points and references to guide the mariner.

nautical mile (NM) 2000 yards; Length of one minute of arc of the great circle of the earth; 6,076 feet compared to 5,280 feet per a statute (land) mile.

nautical slide rule An instrument used to solve time, speed, and distance problems.

navigable channel A channel that has sufficient depth to be safely navigated by a vessel.

navigable waters Coastal waters, including bays, sounds, rivers, and lakes, that are navigable from the sea.

navigation The art and science of locating the position and plotting the course of a ship or aircraft

night sun A helicopter's light that is an effective search tool at night in a clear atmosphere with no moisture in the air.

noise The result of the propeller blade at the top of the arc transfering energy to the hull.

normal endurance The average length of time, i.e., the average length of time to expect a boat crew to remain on a mission.

nun buoy (conical) Buoy that is cylindrical at the water line, tapering to a blunt point at the top. Lateral mark that is red, even numbered, and usually marks the port hand side proceeding to seaward.

obstruction aid See Junction Aid.

occulting light A light in which the total duration of light in each period is clearly longer than the total duration of darkness and in which the intervals of darkness are all of equal duration. (Commonly used for single-occulting light which exhibits only single occulations that are repeated at regular intervals.) Officer of the Deck (day) (OOD) An officer in charge of the ship representing the commanding officer. Officer of the day at shore activities. offshore The region seaward of a specified depth. Opposite is inshore or near-shore. on scene The search area or the actual distress site. On Scene Commander (OSC) A person designated to coordinate search and rescue operations within a specified area associated with a distress incident. opening Refers to the increasing of distance between two vessels. out of step Refers to the position of two boats (i.e., towing operations) where one boat is on the top of the crest of a wave and the other is in the trough between the waves. outboard In the direction away from the center line of the ship. Opposite is inboard. outdrive A vessel's drive unit. overdue Term used when a vessel or person has not arrived at the time and place expected. overhauling the fire The general procedures done after a fire has been extinguished. They include breaking up combustible material with a fire ax or a fire rake and cooling the fire area with water or fog. overload Exceeding the designed load limits of a vessel; exceeding the recommended work load of line or wire rope.

pacing Refers to two vessels matching speed and course.

pad eye A metal ring welded to the deck or bulkhead.

painter line (painter) A line at the bow or stern of a boat which is used for making fast; a single line used to take a vessel in tow alongside, commonly used with ships and their boats when placing the boat into use over the side.

parallel approach Arc approach used where one vessel is approached parallel to another.

parallel track pattern In SAR, one of several types of search patterns. There are two parallel track patterns; they are (1) single unit (PS) (2) and multi-unit (PM).

passenger space A space aboard a vessel that is designated for passengers.

Persons On Board (POB) The number of people aboard a craft.

personal flotation device (PFD) A general name for various types of devices designed to keep a person afloat in water (e.g., life preserver, vest, cushion, ring, and other throwable items).

personnel marker light (PML) Device that uses either a battery or chemical action to provide light for the wearer to be seen during darkness.

piling A long, heavy timber driven into the seabed or river bed to serve as a support for an aid to navigation or dock.

pitch The vertical motion of a ship's bow or stern in a seaway about the athwartships axis. Of a propeller, the axial advance during one revolution (see Roll, Yaw, Heaving, Sway, Surge).

pitchpole Term that refers to a vessel going end-over-end, caused by large waves or heavy surf. The bow buries itself in the wave and the stern pitches over the bow, capsizing the vessel.

planing hull A boat design that allows the vessel to ride with the majority of it's hull out of the water once it's cruising speed is reached (e.g., 8 meter RHI).

polyethylene float line A line that floats, used with rescue devices, life rings.

port Left side of vessel looking forward toward the bow.

port hole An opening in the hull, door, or superstructure of a boat/ship often covered with a watertight closure made of metal or wood.

port light A port hole closure or covering having a glass lens through which light may pass.

preferred channel mark A lateral mark indicating a channel junction, or a wreck or other obstruction which, after consulting a chart, may be passed on either side.

preventer line (preventer) Any line used for additional safety or security or to keep something from falling or running free.

primary aid to navigation An aid to navigation established for the purpose of making landfalls and coastwise passages from headland to headland.

probability of detection (POD) The probability of the search object being detected, assuming it was in the areas searched.

probability of success (POS) The probability of finding the search object with a particular search.

proceeding from seaward Following the Atlantic coast in a southerly direction, northerly and westerly along the Gulf coast and in a northerly direction on the Pacific coast. On the Great Lakes proceeding from seaward means following a generally westerly and northerly direction, except on Lake Michigan where the direction is southerly. On the Mississippi and Ohio Rivers and their tributaries, proceeding from seaward means from the Gulf of Mexico toward the headwaters of the rivers (upstream).

prop wash The result of the propeller blade at the top of the arc transfering energy to the water surface.

propeller A device consisting of a central hub with radiating blades forming a helical pattern and when turned in the water creates a discharge that drives a boat.

pyrotechnics Ammunition, flares, or fireworks used for signaling, illuminating, or marking targets.

quarantine anchorage buoy A yellow special purpose buoy indicating a vessel is under quarantine.

quarter One side or the other of the stern of a ship. To be broad on the quarter means to be 45 degrees away from dead astern, starboard or port quarter is used to indicate a specific side.

RACON See Radar Beacon.

RADAR Radio Detecting And Ranging. An electronic system designed to transmit radio signals and receive reflected images of those signals from a "target" in order to determine the bearing and distance to the "target."

radar beacon (RACON) A radar beacon that produces a coded response, or radar paint, when triggered by a radar signal.

radar reflector A special fixture fitted to or incorporated into the design of certain aids to navigation to enhance their ability to reflect radar energy. In general, these fixtures will materially improve the aid to navigation for use by vessels with radar. They help radar equipped vessels to detect buoys and beacons. They do not positively identify a radar target as an aid to navigation. Also used on small craft with low RADAR profiles.

radiation fog A type of fog that occurs mainly at night with the cooling of the earth's surface and the air, which is then cooled below its dew point as it touches the ground; most common in middle and high latitudes, near the inland lakes and rivers; burns off with sunlight.

radio watch Person assigned to stand by and monitor the radios. Responsible for routine communication and logging, as well as properly handling responses to emergency radio communications.

radiobeacon Electronic apparatus which transmits a radio signal for use in providing a mariner a line of position. First electronic system of navigation. Provided offshore coverage and became the first all-weather electronic aid to navigation.

range A measurement of distance usually given in yards. Also, a line formed by the extension of a line connecting two charted points.

range lights Two lights associated to form a range which often, but not necessarily, indicates a channel centerline. The front range light is the lower of the two, and nearer to the mariner using the range. The rear range light is higher and further from the mariner.

range line The lining up of range lights and markers to determine the safe and correct line of travel, the specific course to steer to remain in the center of the channel.

range marker High visibility markers that have no lights (see Range Lights).

re-flash watch A watch established to prevent a possible re-flash or rekindle of a fire after a fire has been put out.

re-float The act of ungrounding a boat.

red, right, returning Saying to remember which aids you should be seeing off vessel's starboard side when returning from seaward.

regulatory marks A white and orange aid to navigation with no lateral significance. Used to indicate a special meaning to the mariner, such as danger, restricted operations, or exclusion area.

rescue basket Device for lifting an injured or exhausted person out of the water.

rescue swimmer In the Coast Guard, a specially trained individual that is deployed from a helicopters, boats, or cutters to recover an incapacitated victim from the water, day or night.

retroreflective material Material that reflects light. Can be found on equipment such as PFDs or hypothermia protective clothing.

rig   To devise, set up, arrange. An arrangement or contrivance. General description of a ship's upper works; to set up spars or to fit out. A distinctive arrangement of sails (rigging), as in a schooner rig. An arrangement of equipment and machinery, as an oil rig.

rigging   The ropes, lines, wires, turnbuckles, and other gear supporting and attached to stacks, masts and topside structures. Standing rigging more or less permanently fixed. Running rigging is adjustable, e.g., cargo handling gear.

rip current   Currents created along a long beach or reef surf zone due to water from waves hitting the beach and traveling out to the sides and parallel to the shore line, creating a longshore current that eventually returns to sea.

riprap   Stone or broken rock thrown together without order to form a protective wall around a navigation aid.

river current   Flow of water in a river.

roll   Vessel motion caused by a wave lifting up one side of the vessel, rolling under the vessel and dropping that side, then lifting the other side and dropping it in turn.

roller   A long usually non-breaking wave generated by distant winds and a source of big surf, which is a hazard to boats.

rooster tail   A pronounced aerated-water discharge astern of a craft; an indicator of waterjet propulsion.

rough bar   Rough bar is determined to exist when breaking seas exceed 8 feet and/or when, in the judgment of the Commanding Officer/Officer in Charge, rough bar/surf conditions exist, and/or whenever there is doubt in the judgment of the coxswain as to the present conditions.

RTV   Silicone rubber used for plugging holes and seams. Sticks to wet surfaces and will set up under water. Used in damage control for temporary repairs.

rubrail   A permanent fixture, often running the length of a boat, made of rubber that provides protection much as a fender would.

rudder   A flat surface rigged vertically astern used to steer a ship, boat, or aircraft.

safe water marks (fairways, mid-channels)   Used to mark fairways, mid-channels, and offshore approach points, and have unobstructed water on all sides. They may have a red spherical shape, or a red spherical topmark, are red and white vertically striped, and if lighted, display a white light with Morse code "A" (short-long flash).

sail area   On a vessel, the amount of surface upon which the wind acts.

Samson post   Vertical timber or metal post on the forward deck of a boat used in towing and securing. Sometimes used as synonym for King Post.

SAR emergency phases   Refers to 3 phases of SAR levels and responses. These are: (1) Uncertainty (key word: "doubt"); (2) Alert (key word: "apprehension"); and (3) Distress (key words: "grave and imminent danger" requiring "immediate assistance").

SAR incident folder/form   A form to record essential elements of a case. Information needed is outlined with blanks left to fill in necessary information as case progresses.

SAR Mission Coordinator (SMC)   The official temporarily assigned to coordinate response to an actual or apparent distress situation.

SARSAT   See Cospas-Sarsat System. Search and Rescue Satellite Aided Tracking.

scope   Length of anchor line or chain. Number of fathoms of chain out to anchor or mooring buoy. If to anchor, scope is increased in strong winds for more holding power. Also, the length of towline or distance from the stern of the towing vessel to the bow of the tow.

scouring   A method to refloat a stranded boat using the current from the assisting boat's screw to "scour" or create a channel for the grounded boat, in the sand, mud or gravel bottom when the water depth allows the assisting boat access.

screw   A vessel's propeller.

scupper   An opening in the gunwale or deck of a boat which allows water taken over the side to exit. Common to most self-bailing boats.

scuttle   Small, quick-closing access hole; to sink a ship deliberately.

sea anchor   Device, usually of wood and/or canvas, streamed by a vessel in heavy weather to hold the bow up to the sea. It's effect is similar to a drogue in that it slows the vessels rate of drift. However, it is usually made off to the bow opposed to the stern as in the use of a drogue.

sea chest   Intake between ship's side and sea valve or seacock. Sailor's trunk. A through hull fitting used in the vessels engine cooling systems. It allows the vessel to take on sea water through a closed piping system.

sea chest gate valve   A gate valve used in between the sea chest and the fire pump or engine cooling system.

sea cock Valve in the ship's hull through which sea water may pass.

sea current Movement of water in the open sea.

sea drogue See Sea Anchor.

seabed Ocean floor.

Search and Rescue Unit (SRU) A unit composed of trained personnel and provided with equipment suitable for the expeditious conduct of search and rescue operations.

search pattern A track line or procedure assigned to an SRU for searching a specified area.

seaward Toward the main body of water, ocean. On the Intracoastal Waterway, returning from seaward is from north to south on the eastern U.S. coast, east to west across the Gulf of Mexico, and south to north along the western seacoast.

seaworthy Refers to a vessel capable of putting to sea and meeting any usual sea condition. A seagoing ship may for some reason not be seaworthy, such as when damaged.

set (of a current) The direction toward which the water is flowing. A ship is set by the current. A southerly current and a north wind are going in the same direction. Measured in degrees (usually True).

shackle U-shaped metal fitting, closed at the open end with a pin, used to connect wire, chain, or line.

shaft A cylindrical bar that transmits energy from the engine to the propeller.

ship Any vessel of considerable size navigating deep water, especially one powered by engines and larger than a boat. Also, to set up, to secure in place. To take something aboard.

shock load Resistance forces caused by intermittent and varying forces of waves or sea conditions encounter by a towing boat on its towing lines and equipment.

short range aids to navigation Aids to navigation limited in visibility to the mariner (e.g., lighthouses, sector lights, ranges, LNBs, buoys, daymarks, etc.).

Signal Kit/MK-79 Used to signal aircraft and vessels. Each cartridge flare burns red, has a minimum duration of 4.5 seconds, and reaches a height of 250' to 600'.

sinkers Concrete anchors in various sizes and shapes on the seabed that buoy bodies are attached to by chain or synthetic rope moorings.

siren A sound signal which uses electricity or compressed air to actuate either a disc or a cup-shaped rotor.

Situation Report (SITREP) Reports to interested agencies to keep them informed of on-scene conditions and mission progress.

skeg Continuation of the keel aft under the propeller; in some cases, supports the rudder post.

skiff hook (kicker hook) Consists of a ladder hook or a stainless steel safety hook to which a six inch length of stainless steel round stock has been welded. A hook that is used in attaching a tow line to a small trailerable boat, using the trailer eyebolt on the boat.

slack water The period that occurs while the current is changing direction and has no horizontal motion.

sling A type of rescue device used by a helicopter to hoist uninjured personnel; a lifting device for hoisting cargo.

slip clove hitch Hitch used when it may be necessary to release a piece of equipment quickly (i.e., fenders or fender board).

smoke and illumination signal Signal used to attract vessels and aircraft. It has a night end and a day end. The night end produces a red flame, the day end has an orange smoke.

sound buoys Buoys that warn of danger; they are distinguished by their tone and phase characteristics.

sound signal A device that transmits sound, intended to provide information to mariners during periods of restricted visibility and foul weather; a signal used to communicate a maneuver between vessels in sight of each other.

special purpose buoys Also called Special Marks, they are yellow and are not intended to assist in navigation, but to alert the mariner to a special feature or area.

spring line A mooring line that makes an acute angle with the ship and the pier to which moored, as opposed to a breast line, which is perpendicular, or nearly so, to the pier face; a line used in towing alongside that enables the towing vessel to move the tow forward and/or back the tow (i.e., tow spring and backing spring).

square daymarks Seen entering from seaward or from north or east proceeding south or west on port hand side of channel (lateral system of buoyage). Green, odd numbered.

stanchion Vertical metal or wood post aboard a vessel.

standard navy preserver (vest type with collar) A Navy PFD vest used by the Coast Guard onboard cutters. Allows user to relax, save energy, increase survival time and will keep users head out of water, even if user is unconscious. Not found as part of a boat outfit.

starboard   Right side of the vessel looking forward toward the bow.

starboard hand mark   A buoy or beacon which is left to the starboard hand when proceeding in the "conventional direction of buoyage." Lateral marks positioned on the right side of the channel returning from seaward. Nun buoys are red, day beacons are red, bordered with dark red and triangular shaped.

static discharge wand   A pole like device used to discharge the static electricity during helicopter hoisting/rescue operations. Also known as a Deadman's Stick.

static electricity   A quantity of electricity that builds up in an object and does not discharge until provided a path of flow.

static forces   Constant or internal forces.

station buoy   An unlighted buoy set near a Large Navigation Buoy or an important buoy as a reference point should the primary aid to navigation be moved from its assigned position.

station keeping   The art of keeping a boat in position, relative to another boat, aid, or object with regard to current, sea, and/or weather conditions.

steerage   The act or practice of steering. A ship's steering mechanism.

steerageway   The lowest speed at which a vessel can be steered.

stem   The principal timber at the bow of a wooden ship, to which the bow planks are rabbeted. Its lower end is scarfed to the keel, and the bowsprit rests on the upper end. The cutwater, or false stem (analogous to false keel), is attached to the fore part of the stem and may be carved or otherwise embellished, especially in the vicinity of the figurehead, which usually rests upon it. In steel ships, the stem is the foremost vertical or near-vertical strength member, around which or to which the plating of the bow is welded or riveted. Compare sternpost (see Chapter 8).

stem pad eye (trailer eye bolt)   An attaching point available on most trailerized small boats.

stem the forces   To keep the current or wind directly on the bow or stern and hold position by setting boat speed to equally oppose the speed of drift.

stern   The extreme after end of a vessel.

Stokes litter   A rescue device generally used to transport non-ambulatory persons or persons who have injuries that might be aggravated by other means of transportation.

strobe light   Device that emits a high intensity flashing light visible for great distances. Used to attract the attention of aircraft, ships, or ground parties, it flashes white light at 50 plus or minus 10 times per minute.

strut   An external support for the propeller shaft integral to the hull/under water body.

superstructure   Any raised portion of a vessel's hull above a continuous deck (e.g., pilot house).

surf   In the Coast Guard, surf is determined to exist when breaking seas exceed 8 feet and/or when, in the judgment of the Commanding Officer/Officer in Charge, rough bar/surf conditions exist, and/or whenever there is doubt in the mind of the coxswain as to the present conditions.

surf line   The outermost line of waves that break near shore, over a reef, or shoal. Generally refers to the outermost line of consistent surf.

Surf Rescue Boat (SRB)   Coast Guard boat used to perform SAR missions, including surf and bar operations in adverse weather and sea conditions. They are self-righting and self-bailing. Fast response for rescuing people, and delivering damage control equipment or emergency medical services. They are an alternative, not a primary resource, and are used to arrive on scene quickly and stabilize a situation until a more capable unit arrives.

surf zone   The area near shore in which breaking occurs continuously in various intensities.

surface swimmer   In the Coast Guard, a specially trained individual that is deployed from floating units, piers, or the shore to help people in the water.

survival kit   Kit designed to aid a person in the water to survive. Consists of a belt attached around the waist. A personal signal kit is also attached. Boat crews are provided with a vest containing the items found in the signal kit as prescribed in the Rescue and Survival Systems Manual.

sweep width (W)   A measure of the detection capability, or distance on both sides of the SRU, based on target characteristics, weather, and other factors.

swell   Wind-generated waves which have advanced into a calmer area and are decreased in height and gaining a more rounded form. The heave of the sea (see Roller).

swimmer's harness A harness used to tether and retrieve surface swimmers during rescue/recovery operations.

tactical diameter The distance made to the right or left of the original course when a turn of 180 degrees has been completed with the rudder at a constant angle.

taffrail A rail around a vessel's stern over which a towline is passed. Used to reduce the effects of chaffing on the towline.

tag line (trail line) Line used to steady a load being swung in or out.

tandem An arrangement of two or more persons, vessels or objects placed one behind the other.

thimble Metal ring grooved to fit inside a grommet or eye splice.

through bolt A bolt that is used to fasten a fitting to the deck. It goes through the deck and backing plate (located below deck).

thumbs up Signal given by the designated crewmember to indicate hoisting operation is to begin.

tidal current Horizontal motion of water caused by the vertical rise and fall of the tide.

tide Periodic vertical rise and fall of the water resulting from the gravitational interactions between the sun, moon, and earth.

tie down Fittings that can be used to secure lines on a deck or dock.

toed ("toed in") In a side by side towing operation, "toed" refers to the bow of the towed boat slightly angled toward the bow of the towing boat.

topmarks One or more relatively small objects of characteristic shape and color placed on an aid to identify its purpose. (i.e., pillar buoys surmounted with colored shapes).

topside Area above the main deck on a vessel; weather deck.

towline A line, cable, or chain used in towing a vessel.

tow strap When towing along side the tow strap is secured near the towing vessel's bow and the towed vessel's stern (see Spring Line).

towing bridle See Bridle.

towing hardware Hardware used in towing. (i.e., towing bitt, various cleats, bitts, deck fittings, or trailer eyebolts)

towing watch A crewmember who monitors the safety of a towing operation. Responsible to the coxswain.

track spacing (S) The distance between adjacent parallel search tracks (legs).

trail line (tag line) A weighted line that is lowered from a helo before the rescue device. Its purpose is to allow the personnel below to guide and control the rescue device as it is lowered.

transom Planking across the stern of a vessel.

triage The process of assessing survivors according to medical condition and assigning them priorities for emergency care, treatment, and evacuation.

triangular daymark Seen entering rom seaward, or from the north or east proceeding south or west on starboard hand side of channel (lateral system of buoyage). Red, even numbered.

trim The fore-and-aft inclination of a ship, down by the head or down by the stern. Sometimes used to include list. Also means shipshape, neat.

trim control A control that adjusts the propeller axis angle with horizontal.

tripping line Small line attached to the small end of a drogue, so the device can be turned around to be retrieved.

trough The valley between waves.

U.S. Aids to Navigation System System encompasses buoys and beacons conforming to (or being converted to) the IALA (International Association of Lighthouse Authorities), buoyage guidelines and other short range aids to navigation not covered by these guidelines. These other aids to navigation are lighthouses, sector lights, ranges, and large navigation buoys (LNBs).

Uniform State Waterway Marking System (USWMS) Designed for use on lakes and other inland waterways that are not portrayed on nautical charts. Authorized for use on other waters as well. Supplemented the existing federal marking system and is generally compatible with it.

Utility Boat (UTB) 41' UTB, Coast Guard Utility boat is light weight and possesses a deep "V" planing hull constructed of aluminum. It is fast, powerful, maneuverable and designed to operate in moderate weather and sea conditions. It normally carries a crew of three, a coxswain, boat engineer, and crewmember.

vari-nozzle A fire-fighting nozzle having a fully adjustable spray head that allows the operator to deliver a wide range of spray patterns (from stream to low velocity fog).

venturi effect To move a water from one place to another by entraining the pumped liquid in a rapidly flowing stream. It is the principle used by the eductor in dewatering a vessel.

vessel By U.S. statutes, includes every description of craft, ship or other contrivance used as a means of transportation on water. "Any vehicle in which man or goods are carried on water" (see Ship).

waist and/or tag line Lines used to secure the hull or cabin bridles in position for towing.

wake The disturbed water astern of a moving vessel.

watch circle The circle in which an anchored buoy or object moves on the surface in relationship to tides, currents and wind.

watertight integrity The closing down of openings to prevent entrance of water into vessel.

wave Waves are periodic disturbances of the sea surface, caused by wind (and sometimes by earthquakes).

wave frequency The number of crests passing a fixed point in a given time.

wave height The height from the bottom of a wave's trough to the top of its crest; measured in the vertical, not diagonal.

wave interference Caused by waves, refracted or reflected, interacting with other waves, often increasing or decreasing wave height.

wave length The distance from one wave crest to the next in the same wave group or series.

wave period The time, in seconds, it takes for two successive crests to pass a fixed point.

wave reflection The tendency of a wave to move back towards the incoming waves in response to interaction with any obstacle.

wave refraction The tendency of a wave to bend in response to interaction with the bottom and slows in shoal areas. Refraction also occurs when a wave passes around a point of land, jetty, or an island.

wave saddle The lowest part of a wave, bordered on both sides by higher ones; often small, unbroken section of a wave that is breaking.

wave series A group of waves that seem to travel together, at the same speed.

wave shoulder The edge of a wave. It may be the very edge of the whitewater on a breaker, or the edge of a high peaking wave that is about to break.

wedge Used as temporary repair in event of damage aboard vessel. Made of soft wood they are forced into holes or damaged areas to stop leaking, or to plug damaged structures or to reinforce shoving. Part of a damage control kit.

well deck Part of the weather deck having some sort of superstructure both forward and aft of it. A vertically recessed area in the main deck that allows the crewmember to work low to the water.

wet suit A tight-fitting rubber suit worn by a skin diver in order to retain body heat. Designed to protect wearer from exposure to cold, wind, and spray. Constructed of foam neoprene, a durable and elastic material with excellent flotation characteristics. These buoyancy characteristics, which affect your entire body, will cause you to float horizontally, either face up or face down.

whistle A piece of survival equipment used to produce a shrill sound by blowing on or through it. To summon, signal or direct by whistling. A device for making whistling sounds by means of forced air or steam. A whistling sound used to summon or command. It is attached to some PFDs and is an optional item for the personal signal kit. It has proven very useful in locating survivors in inclement weather and can be heard up to 1,000 yards.

whistle buoy A wave actuated sound signal on buoys which produces sound by emitting compressed air through a circumferential slot into a cylindrical bell chamber. Found outside harbors. Sound range greater than 1 mile.

white water See Foam Crest.

Williamson turn Used if an individual or object falls overboard during periods of darkness or restricted visibility and the exact time of the incident is unknown. Done by turning 60 degrees to port or starboard from the original course, then shifting rudder until vessel comes about on a reverse course. May be of little value to boats having a small turning radius.

wind-chill factor An estimated measurement of the cooling effect of a combination of air temperature and wind speed in relation to the loss of body heat from exposed skin.

wind direction The true heading from which the wind blows.

wind driven current The effect of wind pushing water in the direction of the wind.

window An area where the waves have momentarily stopped breaking, opening up a safer area of operation for a vessel.

wind shadow When an object blocks the wind, creating an area of no wind.

windward Towards the wind.

yaw Rotary oscillation about a ship's vertical axis in a seaway. Sheering off alternately to port and starboard.

Index

Numbers in **bold** refer to pages with illustrations

A

adaptability and flexibility standards, 40
aids to navigation (ATON), 234–35
  beacons, 237–39, **242**–44
  IALA buoy systems, 235–36
  identification and significance, 236–**41**, **421**–23
  Intracoastal Waterway, 244–45, **423**
  Light List, 248–**49**
  patrols, 21
  radar beacon (RACON), 246
  radiobeacons, 246
  radionavigation systems, 247–48, 293–95, **294**
  Uniform State Waterway Marking System (USWMS), 236, 245–**46**, **424**
  Western Rivers, 245, **424**
aircraft, fixed-wing, 417–19, **418**
air emboli, 53
air-to-surface visual signs, 417–19, **418**
American Practical Navigator (Bowditch), 250, 431
anaphylactic shock, 51
anchor bend knot, **112**
anchoring, 199, 201–**4**
anchors, **200–201**, 204
anchor watch, 9–10
Anderson Turn, **327**
antiexposure coveralls, 78, **79**
Antimotion Sickness Medications (USCG), 28
artificial respiration, 52

assertiveness standards, 41–42
assistance policy, 306–7
Auxiliary Boat Crew Training and Qualifications Guide–Crewman and Coxswain (USCG), 2
Auxiliary Operations Policy Manual (USCG), 1, 2, 82, 307

B

back and fill maneuver, 178–79
back splice, **113**–14
bandages, 54–55, **58**
bank cushion, 170, 173, 196–**97**
bank suction, 170, 173, **197**
beaching, 443–44
beacons, 237–39, **242**–44
beam, 132, 138
beam sea, 193
Beaufort Wind Scale, 220, 221
bends (scuba incident), 53–54
bites and stings, 68, 69
bitt, **118**
bleeding, 55–58
boat crew, 1–2
boat crew briefing and debriefing, 45–46
boat crew duties
  cruising checklist, 11
  first aid, 47–49
  on life raft, 89
  by position, 2–5
  pre-underway checklist, 10–11, 12
  watchstanding responsibilities, 5–10
boat crew performance
  alcohol, 30
  caffeine, 30

carbon monoxide (CO) poisoning, 28–29, 68–69
clothing recommendations, 32–33, 35–36
dehydration, 33–34, 36
drugs, 30
fatigue, 26–27, 29, 31, 36
fever, 36
frostbite, 32
heat injuries, 33–36, 63–64
hypothermia, 31–32, 65–67
motion sickness, 27–28
physical fitness standards, 24–26
sun burns, 33
tobacco, 30
Boat Crew Signal Kit, 81–**85**
Boat Crew Training Manual (USCG), 2
boat engineer duties, 3
boat handling, 159
  controls training, 167–**68**
  currents and, **161**, 231
  in heavy weather, 428–31
  propulsion and steering, 161–67, **162**, **163**, **164**, **165**, 172–**73**
  speed and safety, 169–**70**
  in surf, 436–44
  wind and, **160**–61
boat maneuvers
  backing, 175–76, 431
  beaching, 443–44
  docking, 182, **183**
  forward movement, 168–74, **169**
  going alongside, 186–88
  in harbors and inlets, 193–95, 440–42
  in rivers, 196–99, **197**, **198**
  rollover, 439, 442–43
  in rough conditions, 188–96, 430–31, 439–40